Sara Benson
sa Dunford
n McCarthy

ZION & BRYCE CANYON NATIONAL PARKS

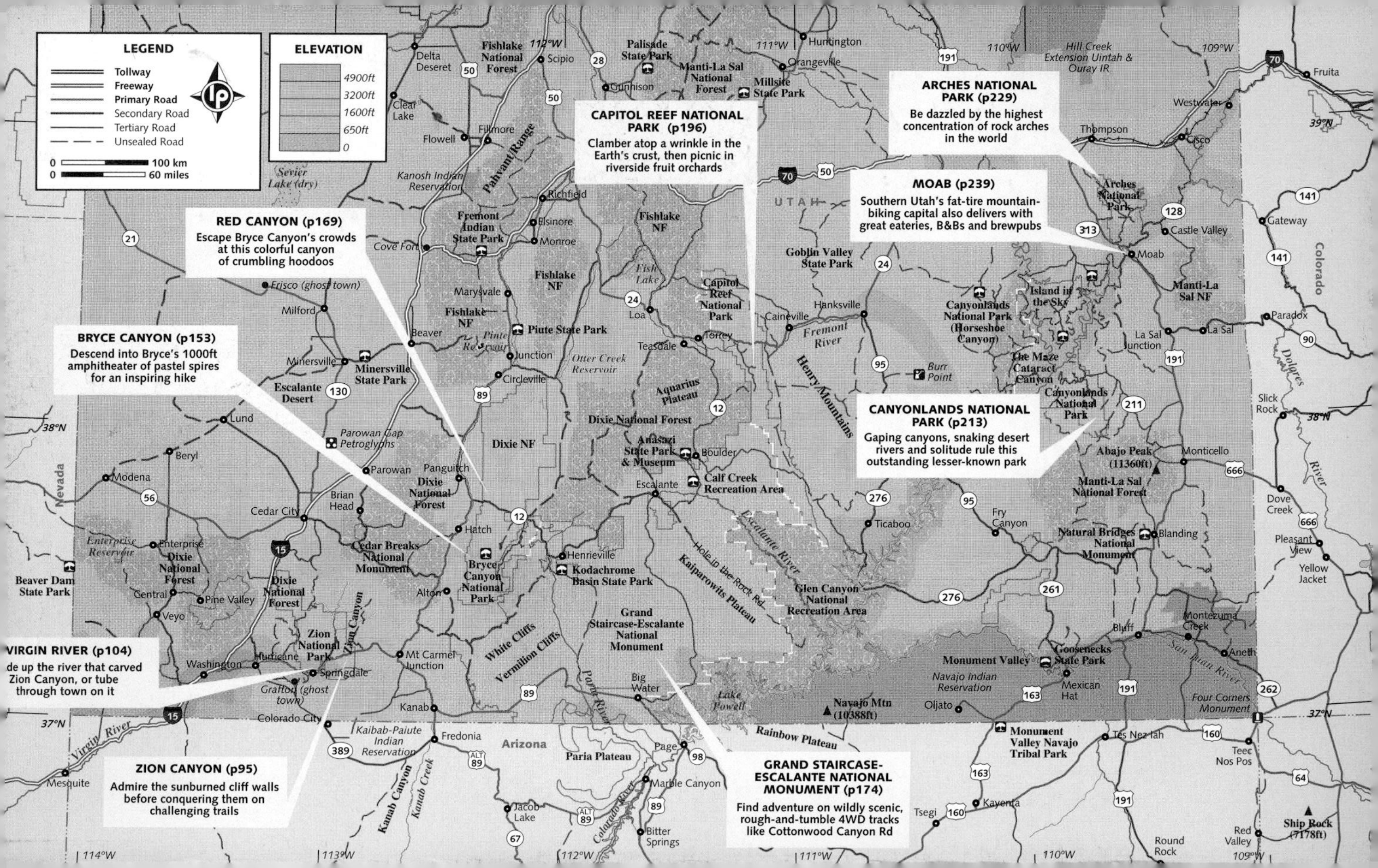
LEGEND
Tollway
Freeway
Primary Road
Secondary Road
Tertiary Road
Unsealed Road
0 100 km
0 60 miles
ELEVATION
4900ft
3200ft
1600ft
650ft
0
CAPITOL REEF NATIONAL PARK (p196)
Clamber atop a wrinkle in the Earth's crust, then picnic in riverside fruit orchards
ARCHES NATIONAL PARK (p229)
Be dazzled by the highest concentration of rock arches in the world
MOAB (p239)
Southern Utah's fat-tire mountain-biking capital also delivers with great eateries, B&Bs and brewpubs
RED CANYON (p169)
Escape Bryce Canyon's crowds at this colorful canyon of crumbling hoodoos
BRYCE CANYON (p153)
Descend into Bryce's 1000ft amphitheater of pastel spires for an inspiring hike
CANYONLANDS NATIONAL PARK (p213)
Gaping canyons, snaking desert rivers and solitude rule this outstanding lesser-known park
VIRGIN RIVER (p104)
de up the river that carved Zion Canyon, or tube through town on it
ZION CANYON (p95)
Admire the sunburned cliff walls before conquering them on challenging trails
GRAND STAIRCASE-ESCALANTE NATIONAL MONUMENT (p174)
Find adventure on wildly scenic, rough-and-tumble 4WD tracks like Cottonwood Canyon Rd
UTAH
Colorado
Nevada
Arizona
Delta
Deseret
Fishlake National Forest
Scipio
Palisade State Park
Huntington
Orangeville
Gunnison
Manti-La Sal National Forest
Millsite State Park
Hill Creek Extension Uintah & Ouray IR
Fruita
Clear Lake
Fillmore
Flowell
Pahvant Range
Kanosh Indian Reservation
Sevier Lake (dry)
Thompson
Westwater
Cisco
Richfield
Elsinore
Monroe
Fremont Indian State Park
Cove Fort
Fishlake NF
Arches National Park
Castle Valley
Gateway
Moab
Goblin Valley State Park
Erisco (ghost town)
Milford
Marysvale
Fish Lake
Loa
Capitol Reef National Park
Island in the Sky
Manti-La Sal NF
Caineville
Hanksville
Fremont River
Canyonlands National Park (Horseshoe Canyon)
Paradox
La Sal Junction
La Sal
Beaver
Piute State Park
Piute Reservoir
Teasdale
Torrey
Junction
Otter Creek Reservoir
Minersville
Minersville State Park
Circleville
The Maze
Cataract Canyon
Burr Point
Henry Mountains
Escalante Desert
Aquarius Plateau
Canyonlands National Park
Slick Rock
Dolores River
Lund
Dixie National Forest
Dixie NF
Parowan Gap Petroglyphs
Anasazi State Park & Museum
Boulder
Abajo Peak (11360ft)
Monticello
Beryl
Parowan
Panguitch
Modena
Calf Creek Recreation Area
Escalante
Manti-La Sal National Forest
Brian Head
Cedar City
Hatch
Ticaboo
Fry Canyon
Dove Creek
Enterprise Reservoir
Enterprise
Cedar Breaks National Monument
Bryce Canyon National Park
Henrieville
Kodachrome Basin State Park
Escalante River
Natural Bridges National Monument
Blanding
Pleasant View
Yellow Jacket
Beaver Dam State Park
Central
Pine Valley
Veyo
Alton
Hole in the Rock Rd
Kaiparowits Plateau
Glen Canyon National Recreation Area
Grand Staircase-Escalante National Monument
Zion National Park
Zion Canyon
White Cliffs
Vermilion Cliffs
Bluff
Montezuma Creek
Aneth
Washington
Hurricane
Springdale
Mt Carmel Junction
Monument Valley
Navajo Indian Reservation
Goosenecks State Park
Mexican Hat
San Juan River
Grafton (ghost town)
Big Water
Paria River
Lake Powell
Navajo Mtn (10388ft)
Oljato
Four Corners Monument
Kanab
Colorado City
Virgin River
Mesquite
Kaibab-Paiute Indian Reservation
Fredonia
Paria Plateau
Page
Rainbow Plateau
Monument Valley Navajo Tribal Park
Tes Nez Iah
Teec Nos Pos
Kanab Canyon
Kanab Creek
Marble Canyon
Colorado River
Jacob Lake
Bitter Springs
Tsegi
Kayenta
Round Rock
Red Valley
Ship Rock (7178ft)
114°W
113°W
112°W
111°W
110°W
109°W
39°N
38°N
37°N

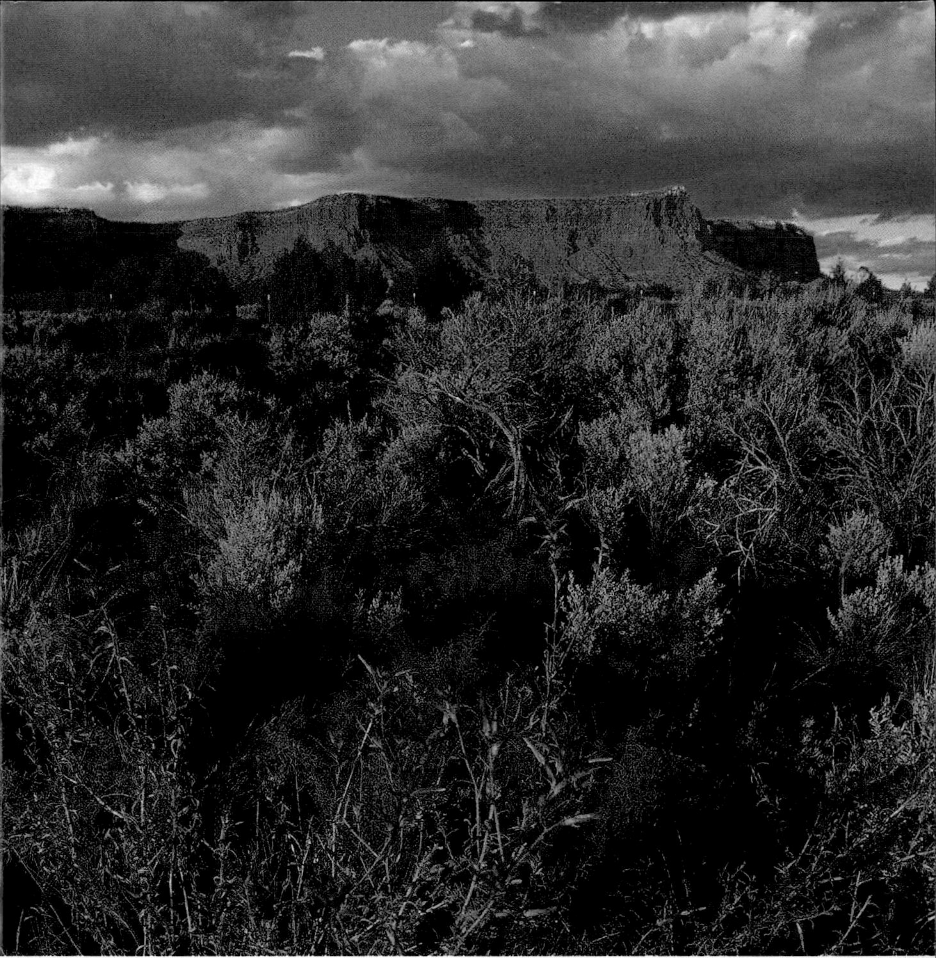

ZION & BRYCE CANYON NATIONAL PARKS

Southern Utah's national parks are wild, vast and rugged, almost beyond our ability to comprehend them, much less describe them. This remains the most remote and desolate corner of the continent, appearing much the same as when Western explorers first laid eyes upon it. It's shocking, and beautiful. It's half the Earth's life span laid bare. It's delicate wildflowers and crumbling mesas. It's how, with enough time, rivers become like rusty knives, cleaving gashes in the desert's body. There are cityscapes of candy-striped hoodoos, stone bridges and delicate arches, and acres of slickrock. If you think you've seen every possible hue of sandstone, the rising or setting sun will show you otherwise. Just open your eyes wider and take a look.

RICHARD CUMMINS

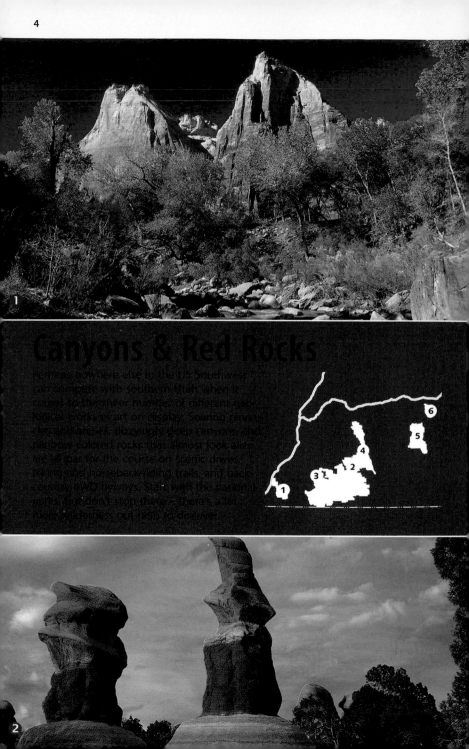

Canyons & Red Rocks

Perhaps nowhere else in the US Southwest can compete with southern Utah when it comes to the sheer number of different geological works of art on display. Soaring pinnacles and arches, dizzyingly deep canyons, and rainbow-colored rocks that almost look alien are all par for the course on scenic drives, hiking and horseback-riding trails, and backcountry 4WD byways. Start with the national parks, but don't stop there – there's a lot more wilderness out here to discover.

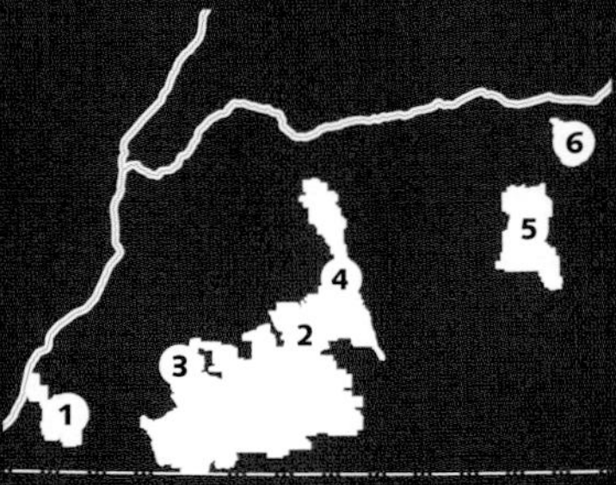

Author Tip

Early morning and evening, when the light isn't as harsh, are the best times to take photos in this stark desert landscape. Capturing southern Utah's warm palette of sunset colors and iconic red rocks takes a few special camera techniques and tricks. For helpful expert photography tips, see p49.

❶ Zion Canyon

Gaze in awe at the Court of the Patriarchs, the grand Organ and the Great White Throne, all soaring above the Virgin River along the park's scenic drive (p95).

❷ Grand Staircase-Escalante National Monument

Squeeze through twisting slot canyons along Coyote Gulch (p182), meditate in the Devils Garden (p179) and get an eyeful of red-rock paradise along the backcountry Burr Trail (p177).

❸ Bryce Canyon

On the geological staircase ascending from the Grand Canyon's North Rim, Bryce Canyon inspires with fantastically carved spires jutting up out of red rocks (p150).

❹ Capitol Reef National Park

Trace a wrinkle in the Earth's crust – the spectacular Waterpocket Fold, capped by domes of Navajo sandstone – and marvel at the freestanding pinnacles of mysterious-looking Cathedral Valley (p201).

❺ Canyonlands National Park

Get giddy by peering down into a maze of canyons carved by the Colorado River, especially impressive from Island in the Sky (p216), with its sculpted sandstone buttes.

❻ Arches National Park

Eroded over millions of years, the park's namesake formations elegantly defy gravity and struggle against the passage of time. Step inside the Fiery Furnace (p234), if you dare.

Outdoor Adventures

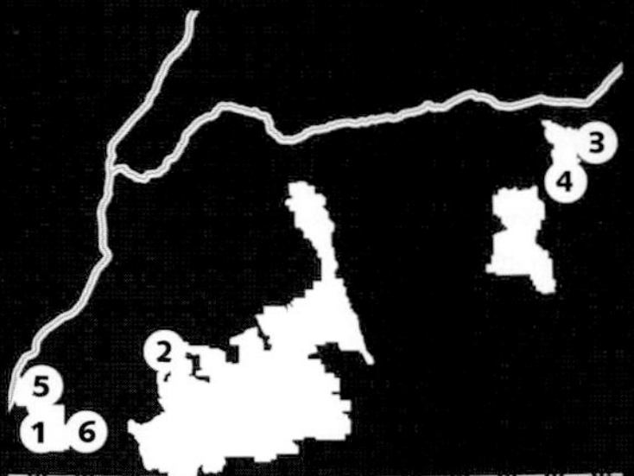

Author Tip

Southern Utah can be a deceptively beautiful place, but don't let yourself get lured into doing more than you can physically handle. For helpful desert travel tips, including how to stay healthy and safe while hiking and biking, turn to p283 and p286. If you've got kids in tow, or if you're traveling with four-legged family members (eg dogs, horses), we've got some smart suggestions to help you out (see p53).

❶ Hiking Zion Canyon

Brace yourself: it's a wet, wild walk through the Narrows (p115) of the Virgin River; or stay dry instead and ascend cables into the sky to Angels Landing (p105).

❷ Horseback Riding

Find where outlaw Butch Cassidy once hid out in red rocks near Bryce Canyon (p169) or wind down into the Grand Canyon (p192). Either way, it's time to giddyap, pardner!

❸ River Running

Get a taste for white water on the Colorado and Green Rivers outside Moab (p249), or just float along and paddle a canoe or kayak past vertical canyon walls.

❹ Mountain Biking Moab

Think all of southern Utah's scenery is just for hikers? Guess again in Moab (p246), the region's epicenter of mountain biking, from slickrock trails and 4WD roads to mountainous single-track.

❺ Canyoneering

Zion's Subway (p113) is a rite of passage, but there are plenty more spots in southern Utah (p47) to rappel, twist and splash your way through the Earth's inner workings.

❻ Watching Wildlife

Spot bighorn sheep and peregrine falcons in Zion Canyon (p120), watch California condors soar over the Vermilion Cliffs (p68) or drop by a prairie-dog town in Bryce Canyon (p163).

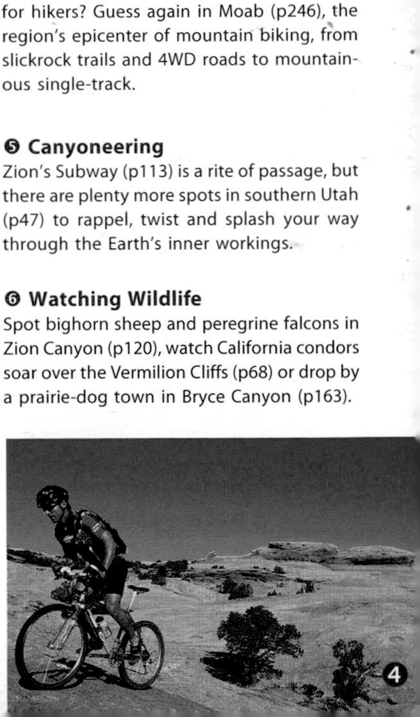

1

Scenic Drives & Lookouts

Though southern Utah's majestic parklands are hardly drive-by attractions, scenic roads abound. In fact, they're an essential part of your journey here in canyon country, whether you're driving, cycling, riding the free park shuttles in Zion and Bryce Canyons, or negotiating a bone-rattling, nerve-wracking 4WD road in the rugged backcountry of Grand Staircase-Escalante National Monument or Canyonlands. Wilderness can be as close as your windshield here, so make sure you slow down and enjoy the views.

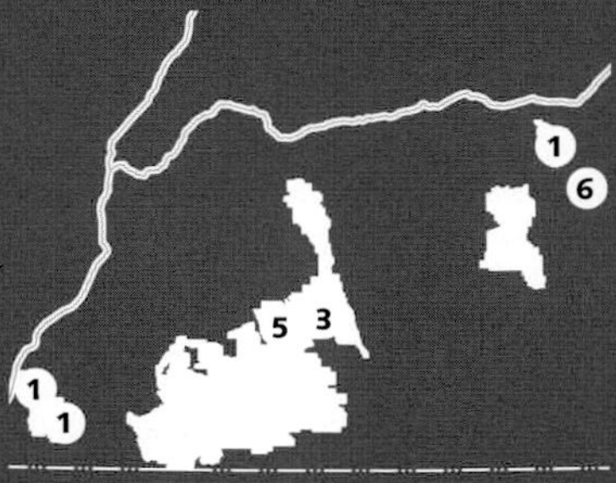

2

Author Tip

Southern Utah has dirt roads aplenty, and a 4WD vehicle is useful on all of them (especially if you've got high clearance). Luckily, when conditions allow, some backcountry roads are passable in a standard 2WD vehicle, as long as you take it slow and go easy on narrow, twisting switchbacks and rutted washboard sections. Ask at visitor centers about the latest road conditions – and the weather forecast! – before heading out.

❶ Arches Scenic Drive

Switchbacking heart-stoppingly up into the heart of Arches National Park, this paved scenic drive (p232) will have you stopping every five minutes to truly take in the awesome panoramas.

❷ Highway 12

Southern Utah's most popular scenic drive (p185) passes Red Canyon (p169), Bryce Canyon (p146), Capitol Reef (p196) and a jumble of small towns and wilderness areas, all ready for exploration.

❸ Burr Trail

The 'Burly Trail' might be a better name for this backcountry byway (p177), which starts off as a paved road, then drops down dramatic gravel switchbacks into Capitol Reef.

❹ Kolob Canyons Road

Not too many folks make it up to Zion's most remote corner (p99). Short and sweet, this scenic drive reaches grand overlooks, as does equally high-elevation Kolob Terrace Rd (p99).

❺ Highway 89

This meandering byway (p190) passes old Western movie locations, colorful cliffs and Glen Canyon's reservoirs, with an unmissable detour to the Grand Canyon's North Rim (p192).

❻ La Sal Mountain Loop Road

When you're finally parched from so much sun-baked desert, head up into the mountains outside Moab (p243), where cool woodlands and quaking aspens, which turn gold in autumn, await.

1

3
6
5
2
4
1

2

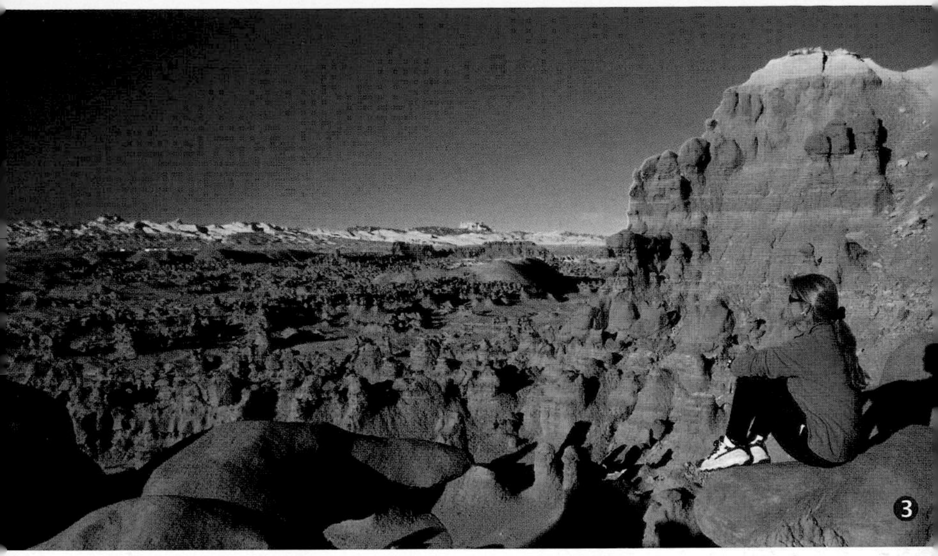

Author Tip

Maybe the single best reason for exploring beyond the national parks is to camp. All of southern Utah's national park campgrounds regularly fill up, both those that take reservations and those that are first-come, first-served. But state park, US Forest Service (USFS) and Bureau of Land Management (BLM) campgrounds might have space when the national parks hang out their 'Campground Full' signs. For more tips on choosing campsites and cabins, see p261.

❶ Monument Valley

Made famous by Wild West movies, these sandstone buttes (p243) will make you feel that you've really arrived in the Southwest of your dreams. It's worth the detour, promise.

❷ Cedar Breaks National Monument

Arguably the most beautiful viewpoint in southern Utah (and that's saying something!), Cedar Breaks (p135) remains off the beaten path. You can lose the crowds – and maybe yourself, too – here.

❸ Goblin Valley State Park

Way out in the middle of nowhere, this isolated, rocky wilderness desert preserve (p212) is famous for its mushroom-shaped sandstone knobs that look like a whimsical fairy-tale landscape.

❹ Dinosaur Discovery Site

At Johnson's Farm (p128) in St George, walk around one of the world's richest digs of dinosaur track fossils, now on display. It's a great rainy-day stop for families.

❺ Hell's Backbone Grill

Let's be honest: southern Utah is not a foodie place, unlike more modern metro areas of the Southwest. But this soulful, organic restaurant (p190) is heavenly, a don't-miss stop in Boulder.

❻ Moab

Southeastern Utah's outdoor-activities nerve center, Moab's (p239) main streets are always buzzing with coffee shops, brewpubs, art galleries and more. Come on, join the parade.

MARK NEWMAN
Moon over Bryce Canyon National Park

Contents

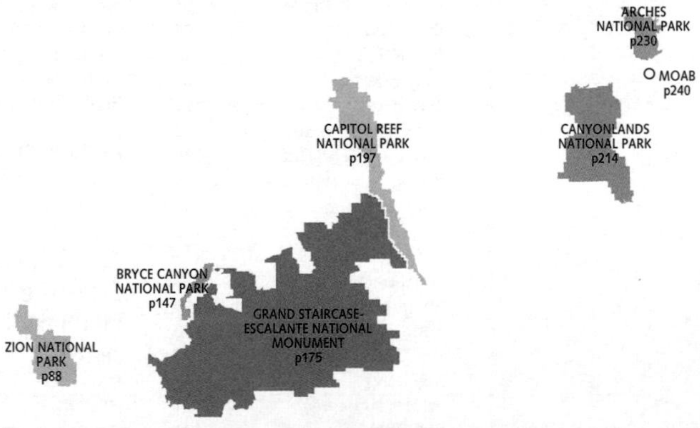
ARCHES NATIONAL PARK p230
MOAB p240
CANYONLANDS NATIONAL PARK p214
CAPITOL REEF NATIONAL PARK p197
BRYCE CANYON NATIONAL PARK p147
GRAND STAIRCASE-ESCALANTE NATIONAL MONUMENT p175
ZION NATIONAL PARK p88

The Authors

SARA BENSON

Coordinating Author, Las Vegas, Capitol Reef National Park

First awestruck by southern Utah's towering red rocks during a cross-country road trip after college, Sara has returned dozens of times to explore the Southwest's deserts and tribal lands. In between stints as a globe-trotting journalist and teacher, she has worked as a national park ranger in southern Utah and California. In her free time, she's an adventurous backpacker and all-seasons outdoor-sports enthusiast. Her writing features on popular travel websites and in magazines and newspapers from coast to coast, including the *Las Vegas Review-Journal* and *Salt Lake City Tribune*. The author of over 40 travel and nonfiction books, Sara also wrote Lonely Planet's *Las Vegas Encounter* and contributed to Lonely Planet's *Southwest USA* and *Arizona, New Mexico & the Grand Canyon Trips* books. Keep up with her latest adventures on her blog, The Indie Traveler (www.indietraveler.blogspot.com), or by following her on Twitter (@indie_traveler).

My Southern Utah Parks

Every time I escape the neon lights of Las Vegas (p137), I can feel my soul unwind as I drive out into the desert. I never tire of searching for hidden hanging gardens in Zion Canyon (p87), walking around the multicolored hoodoos of Bryce Canyon (p153) or standing atop head-spinning viewpoints on the Grand Canyon's North Rim (p192). It's also the smaller places hidden along southern Utah's rural highways that keep me bewitched, especially in Grand Staircase-Escalante National Monument (p174) and Capitol Reef (p196), where the world is cracked open for anyone to see. Moab (p239) is where I kick back and refuel before heading out into the inspiring landscapes of Arches (p229) or the serpentine backcountry of Canyonlands (p213).

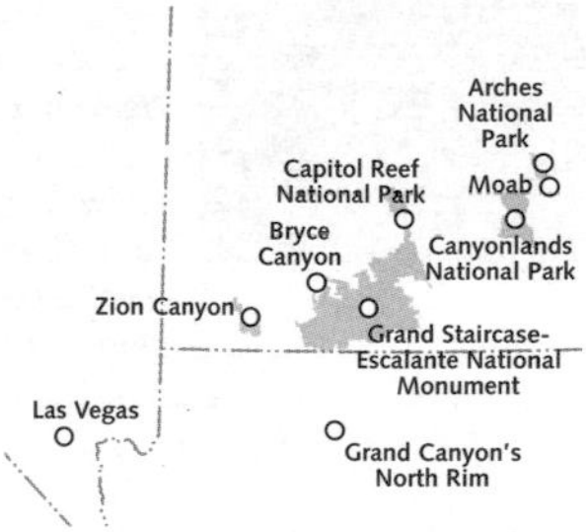

LONELY PLANET AUTHORS

Why is our travel information the best in the world? It's simple: our authors are passionate, dedicated travelers. They don't take freebies in exchange for positive coverage so you can be sure the advice you're given is impartial. They travel widely to all the popular spots, and off the beaten track. They don't research using just the internet or phone. They discover new places not included in any other guidebook. They personally visit thousands of hotels, restaurants, palaces, trails, galleries, temples and more. They speak with dozens of locals every day to make sure you get the kind of insider knowledge only a local could tell you. They take pride in getting all the details right, and in telling it how it is. Think you can do it? Find out how at lonelyplanet.com.

LISA DUNFORD

Zion National Park, Grand Staircase-Escalante National Monument

As one of the many great, great, great granddaughters of Brigham Young, it was ancestry that first drew Lisa to Utah. But it's the incredible parks of southern Utah that have kept her coming back. Slot canyons and slick-rock, ancient American ruins and rock art; here the earth seems at its most elemental. And she loves exploring every bit of the remote and rugged landscape, both on foot and by 4WD. Before becoming a freelance travel author and photographer 10 years ago, Lisa was a newspaper editor and writer in South Texas. Lisa is also the author of the Utah chapter of Lonely Planet's *Southwest USA* guide.

CAROLYN MCCARTHY

Bryce Canyon, Canyonlands and Arches National Parks; Moab

Author Carolyn McCarthy first reached Dead Horse Point one spring break in a vintage Volkswagen bus that barely made the trip. Before becoming a travel writer, she paddled a season as a river guide in Colorado and led trekking trips in southern Chile. Dozens of Vibram soles later, the Utah desert remains one of her favorite destinations. Her work for Lonely Planet includes *Yellowstone & Grand Teton National Parks* and *Trekking in the Patagonian Andes*, as well as *Chile & Easter Island*, *Panama* and *Central America on a Shoestring* guidebooks. Carolyn has also written for *National Geographic*, the *Boston Globe*, *Lonely Planet Magazine* and other publications. You can follow her Americas blog at www.carolynswildblueyonder.blogspot.com.

Destination Zion & Bryce Canyon National Parks

On first impression, southern Utah is a biblically forbidding landscape. Standing atop wind-whipped Angels Landing in Zion Canyon, or staring at ancient eroded hoodoos in the Silent City of the vast amphitheater of Bryce Canyon, what are we to make of what surrounds us? This is no gilded temple, no heavenly garden, but instead a sere, broken and primitive-looking land that extends as far as our disbelieving eyes can see. This place is clearly indifferent, even hostile, to human needs, threatening outsiders with black ravens, rattlesnakes, hungry vultures, a lack of water and even the risk of death. Yet for millennia people have found a way to survive and even thrive here.

Frankly, it's a wonder that any outsiders ever came here at all. That they still do, and at times in droves, is a testament to the sheer joy and amazement that this red-rock desert inspires. Become like a child again, running everywhere and nowhere all at once in your excitement. The erosion of this canyon country is so intricate and extensive, there's no single spot to aim for, no one iconic view where you can roll up to a canyon's rim, snap a dozen pictures and call it a day. Southern Utah's national parks don't lack for famous vistas and rock formations, but they're just never enough. The land here contains not one epiphany, but hundreds, thousands.

'The land here contains not one epiphany, but hundreds, thousands.'

The isolation and wide-open spaces of southern Utah's canyon country, pocketed with hidden springs, watering holes and rivers, is what originally drew the first emigrant Mormon settlers in the mid-19th century. Calling themselves Latter-Day Saints, they quickly displaced Native American tribal peoples who had long made their homes on the Colorado Plateau, notably the Southern Paiute.

Today, members of the Church of Latter-Day Saints make up over half of the state's population. Small rural towns in southern Utah tend to be politically conservative, but the land's rugged beauty attracts free-thinking artists and outdoors types who support a more tolerant live-and-let-live attitude. You're as likely to see a vintage 1970s VW van with mountain bikes roped up on the back and a peace-sign decal on the rear window as you are a church-bound minivan with a gaggle of Mormon children in their Sunday best.

Despite espousing wildly varying lifestyles and philosophical viewpoints, most locals in southern Utah agree on the vital importance of land. In coffee shops, printed newspapers and online, just listen to the passionate debates over who has the right to do what exactly where. Off-road drivers, hunters and conservationists may not agree on much, but many will dedicate their time, energy and money to fighting for what they believe are their rights and to ensure that their particular vision of how public lands should be managed and used is considered by state and federal agencies. Adding to this community mix is southern Utah's gaggle of visitors, from snowbird RVers who hail from colder climes and spend their winters here in the desert, to year-round tourists from across the USA and abroad.

Most of Zion National Park's nearly three million annual visitors stream through during summer, although late spring and early fall, when cooler temperatures make the desert more hospitable, are also busy times. On a hot July day, expect that Zion Canyon's Riverside Walk will feel as crowded as a sidewalk in NYC. The same goes for Bryce Canyon, which welcomes well over a million people each year. During summer vacation, Bryce's scenic rim-top drive can be jammed bumper-to-bumper. But even on a typical fast-view, drive-through visit to either (or better yet, both) of these iconic parks, escaping the crowds can be as easy as taking a hike or merely tramping 100 yards from a scenic overlook parking lot. The more time you spend, the more these canyons will reveal their subtle beauty and grandeur.

Mitigating the impact of tourist traffic to protect these parks and ensure their enjoyment by future generations is a top priority for the National Park Service (NPS). Shuttles serving Zion Canyon and that park's gateway town of Springdale, as well as part of Bryce Canyon's scenic drive, encourage visitors to get out of their cars and reduce traffic, and air and noise pollution. Zion Canyon's visitor center is a model of green architecture, using evaporative cooling, solar panels and other energy-saving measures. All of southern Utah's parks also have extensive recycling programs and free ranger-led activities that promote visitor awareness of climate change and the importance of wilderness conservation on our ever-more-crowded planet.

'it's a compelling constellation of wild lands'

In addition to Zion and Bryce Canyon, southern Utah's most popular national parks, this guide also covers Capitol Reef, Arches and Canyonlands National Parks, as well as Grand Staircase-Escalante National Monument. It also includes many other public recreation lands, along with detours to the Grand Canyon's North Rim and Monument Valley. Tourist bureaus call this the Grand Circle, and it's a compelling constellation of wild lands. With a few weeks at your disposal and unlimited mileage on your rental car, you can bag six national parks, three national monuments, two wilderness areas, at least eight state parks, a national scenic byway and much more. Nowhere else in the US can you string together so much officially sanctioned scenery so easily.

The desire to see and do it all can be intense. Adventure in southern Utah means hiking 2ft ledges along 1000ft drop-offs. It means canyoneering slot canyons so tortured the sun almost never hits bottom, and rock climbing some of the country's most famous big walls. It means river rafting, mountain biking, four-wheel driving and enough primitive backpacking to sate the most grizzled mountaineer. For adrenaline junkies, this is paradise. You can thank your air-conditioned stars that so much of this red-rock wilderness has been preserved nearly as it was when indigenous peoples first appeared on the scene. Southern Utah remains a spiritual experience of the highest order in nature's temple.

Planning Your Trip

They don't call it the Grand Circle for nothing. There's a lot to see in southern Utah, and few people have the time or stamina to do it all in one trip.

We've designed our Itineraries chapter (p25) to help you figure out the 'What can I do in just a day or a week?' quandary. When you're going will have a tremendous impact on what activities are possible (or enjoyable), what roads are open and how crowded it will be. For your trip to be a success, you'll need to do some advance planning, especially if you aim to stay at a national park lodge, get a popular backcountry permit or take a river-rafting trip.

See Climate Charts (p263) for more weather information.

Lodging reservations are recommended for busy weekends, throughout the summer and around holidays. However, southern Utah is rarely so crowded that you can't find a bed or a campsite somewhere (though it may be 15 or 50 miles down the road), and there's so much to explore, you'll never lack for unforgettable experiences.

If you can, allow for some flexibility. One of the best things about the region is constantly stumbling across the unexpected, and you should feel free to pursue every intriguing side canyon. We guarantee they'll be the ones you remember most.

DID YOU KNOW?

The hottest temperature ever recorded in Utah was 117°F in the city of St George on July 5, 1985.

WHEN TO GO

Southern Utah's national parks are open year-round, and great trips are possible in any season. High season varies a bit from place to place, but extends roughly from the start of April to the end of October at lower elevations, and from Memorial Day to Labor Day at higher elevations. By contrast, winter visitation drops so low that many businesses around the parks curtail their hours or close altogether, though that's no reason to stay away. What you miss out on in winter is more than outweighed by the peace you gain.

In spring and fall, crowds are typically limited to weekends. Spring weather is unpredictable, bringing both rain and sun. At higher elevations, snow can linger in quantity into May or June. Spring wildflowers begin to bloom in April at lower elevations, continuing into July at high-elevation spots like Cedar Breaks. By June, the average daytime temperature in Zion Canyon already tops 90°F. Everywhere, July and August are 'monsoon' season, when sudden, short thunderstorms may appear (often in the afternoon), interrupting the plans of canyoneers and making dirt roads impassable.

The National Weather Service (www.wrh.noaa.gov/slc) is your best source of weather forecasts for southern Utah's towns and parks, including Zion, Bryce Canyon and Grand Staircase-Escalante.

Many say fall is the best season in southern Utah's desert. September is still hot, but the days are usually clear, water in rivers and canyons remains warm, and foliage at high elevations begins to change color. This spectacular display continues through October below, while snow starts to close mountain roads and passes. At lower elevations, winter is mild. On clear days, temperatures can reach into the 60s and be quite lovely. However, storms can bring snow and ice, making driving hazardous just about anywhere. At higher elevations, winter storms are more serious deterrents to travel.

You should expect southern Utah's parks to be exceptionally busy on major holidays (p265). Otherwise, as a general rule, crowds are as localized as summer thunderstorms. National park scenic drives are the most crowded stretches, followed by easy walking trails just off these roads,

FESTIVALS & EVENTS

Aka 'Festival City USA,' Cedar City (p132) is southwest Utah's special-events epicenter. Befitting its nickname, the town hosts major festivals year-round, including a **Paiute tribal powwow**, the **Utah Summer Games**, the **Groovefest American Music Festival** and a **Western rodeo**. Beginning in late June, its main attraction is the three-months-plus **Shakespearean Festival**, which brings Tony Award–winning theater to the region, as does the summer **Neil Simon Festival**. The nearby ski resort of Brian Head hosts the **Utah Winter Games**. For more special events happening around Cedar City, browse the online calendar at www.scenicsouthernutah.com.

Active St George (p128) boasts its own **rodeo** in September; the **World Senior Games** and the **St George Marathon**, which descends from the neighboring Pine Valley Mountains, in October; and an **Ironman triathlon** in May. Even winter is a festive time in St George, with a Dickensian **Christmas celebration** in early December and a **winter bird festival** in January. The nearby town of Washington City hosts a traditional all-American **county fair** in August and the Mormon pioneer–themed **Cotton Days Celebration** in May. Visit www.stgeorgechamber.com for more regional festivals.

Giving Cedar City and St George a run for their money is Moab (p244), which is packed with events from spring to fall, many of which celebrate the outdoor activities that have made the town famous. March or April ushers in its huge **Jeep Safari**, September brings a **music festival**, October welcomes the **Fat Tire Bike Festival** and November sees an ecoconscious **folk festival**. In between are **bike races**, an **arts festival**, a **rodeo** and more. For more information, click to www.discovermoab.com.

If you're westward-bound to celebrate all things cowboy, don't miss Kanab's **Western Legends Roundup** (p190) in late August. If it's the stars you're aiming for, show up for Bryce Canyon's **Astronomy Festival** (p150) in early summer. Nearby Ruby's Inn (p150) hosts family-friendly events year-round, including the snow-sports **Winter Festival** in February and summer **rodeo shows**. Even little ol' Torrey (p210), Capitol Reef's gateway town, puts on a **music festival**, old-fashioned **Torrey Apple Days**, a kooky B-movie **film festival** and the '**fastest parade in America**,' all in July.

then by less-traveled moderate to difficult hikes. Finding solitude in peak season is often simply a matter of getting away from the main roads. Alternatively, another strategy for driving a popular scenic road is to do so very early or late in the day (which also provides the prettiest light for photographs). Or ride a bicycle, which, ecobenefits aside, prevents parking headaches.

HOW MUCH?

Shuttle ride in national parks free

National park campsite $10-20

Annual national parks pass $80

One-day canyoneering class $100-175

National park lodge double room $150-200

COSTS & MONEY

The cost of a trip in southern Utah varies considerably depending on how and when you travel, but it's usually not as cheap as people think.

The area is ill-served by public transportation, so renting a car (p273) is usually a necessity. Rentals can start at $25 per day (excluding insurance, taxes and fees) for the cheapest, no-frills compact model. Rates between different car-rental locations and airports can vary by at least that much per day, so call around. Then there's gas, and given the distances between southern Utah's sights, you'll burn a lot; plan on around $20 a day, depending on your itinerary.

Accommodations and food are the biggest expenses under your control. If you make your own meals and take advantage of free dispersed camping on public lands, you could scratch by on $15 a day. A more reasonable budget is $30 a day, which allows camping at established campgrounds in and around the national parks. The minute you start eating at diners and buying espresso, add at least $15 to your daily ration. If you're eating all your meals out, it will cost a minimum of $30 a day, not counting any steak dinners.

Decent motels cost at least $50 a night, some with steady year-round rates, though such places are rarely near the parks (eg Moab offers few, St George has plenty). During high season in towns closest to the parks, even the cheapest beds rise to $75 or more a night. Midrange motels run to $100 or more, while better hotels and upscale B&Bs command up to $150, and park lodges and ranch resorts rise even higher. Discounts are typically offered in early spring and late fall, while winter (outside of holidays) sees the best deals. Expect top-end rates to fall the furthest, some by as much as half.

Finally, factor in park fees, the cost of any necessary backcountry permits, rental equipment, shuttles, guided tours or outdoor activity lessons. Hiking is free, but invariably the more involved and active you want to be, the more you'll spend. Except for Grand Staircase-Escalante National Monument, every national park in this guide charges an entry fee ($5 to $25), usually valid for seven days. If you're only visiting the national parks and monuments near Moab, an annual 'local passport' costs $25. For details about annual and lifetime 'America the Beautiful' passes, which allow free entry to all national parks and federal recreation lands, see p264.

DID YOU KNOW

Even when national park campgrounds are full, free dispersed camping may be available on nearby USFS and BLM land. For more camping tips, see p261.

BOOKS

Southern Utah provides rich soil for writers. Any list of suggested reading can only skim the surface of the great books that tackle this complex land. For specialist outdoor activity guides, peruse the Activities chapter (p36); for field guides to geology, flora and fauna, check out the Environment chapter (p59); and for more biographies and true-life accounts, read the History chapter (p76).

Provocative, passionate about wilderness and hilariously cranky to boot, Edward Abbey wrote the classic must-read *Desert Solitaire* (1968) about his experiences as a ranger at Arches. See also the boxed text on p233.

Much is made of Everett Ruess, a writer, artist and wandered who dreamily loved the desert and mysteriously vanished into it in 1934 at

QUICK TRIP PLANNER

If you want to...	Then visit in...	And don't forget to...
Explore southern Utah in summer	Jul-Aug	Avoid midday heat and afternoon thunder storms by getting up early
Avoid the crowds in Zion Canyon	Apr & Oct	Pack layers of warm clothing
Through-hike the Narrows	late Jun–Sep	Check the weather report before heading out
See Bryce Canyon's highlights	May-Sep	Take a free guided shuttle-bus tour
Visit the Grand Canyon's North Rim	mid-May–mid-Sep	Make lodge and campground reservations far in advance
Explore Grand Staircase-Escalante National Monument's backcountry	Apr, May, Sep & Oct	Bring or rent a high-clearance 4WD vehicle
Track down ancient ruins and rock art	year-round	Hire a local guide or tour outfitter to lead you
Pick fruit in Capitol Reef's orchards	Jun-Oct	Follow signposted instructions on unlocked gates; don't climb trees
See wildflowers bloom in Canyonlands	Apr-May	Choose hiking trails with streams or meadows
Hike into Arches' Fiery Furnace	Mar, Apr, Sep & Oct	Make reservations at least four days in advance
Get a national park campsite without reservations	year-round	Show up between 8am and noon, especially on weekends

age 20. *Everett Ruess: A Vagabond for Beauty* (1983) by WL Rusho is one take on his story.

Coyote's Canyon, written by Terry Tempest Williams with photographs by John Melford, is a love letter to southern Utah – and an inspiring primer for first-time travelers to this stark desert land.

Craig Childs' *The Way Out: A True Story of Ruin and Survival* (2006) is a grittier, but just as personal, narrative of getting lost in southern Utah's labyrinthine, undeniably hostile and yet spellbindingly beautiful canyon country.

Jon Krakauer's *Under the Banner of Heaven* (2003) is perhaps the most high-profile book ever written on Utah. It's a compelling exposé of extremist polygamist groups and a provocative look at the state's oft-troubled history.

A Mormon, naturalist and environmentalist, Terry Tempest Williams evokes a desert sensibility and connects the personal with the political in our relationship to the land in *Red: Passion & Patience in the Desert* (2001).

For an easily readable general introduction to the region and some of the people who have made their name writing about its natural and cultural wonders, pick up the Travelers' Tales anthology *American Southwest* (2001).

Edited by Stephen Trimble and Terry Tempest Williams, *Testimony: Writers of the West Speak on Behalf of Utah's Wilderness* (1996) is a powerful collection of essays by citizen-writers and naturalists that successfully swayed public policy during the Clinton era.

The Redrock Chronicles: Saving Wild Utah (2000) is a compelling narrative that spans southern Utah's geologic beginnings to its present-day realities. Author TH Watkins doesn't let his love for the desert glaze his sharp observer's eye.

MAPS

If you're driving or taking the shuttle and hiking on frontcountry trails, the glossy fold-out, full-color map and seasonal park newspaper available at national park entrance stations and visitor centers is usually enough to get around. **Bureau of Land Management** (BLM; www.blm.gov) and **United States Forest Service** (USFS; www.fs.fed.us) offices give away or sell maps that cover lands under their jurisdiction. They may not be great maps for general use, but they're indispensable for exploring outside the national parks, where public recreation lands can be a patchwork of different agencies' jurisdictions and private landholdings.

Utah State Parks offers a free iPhone/iPod/iPad Touch app that's a handy mobile field guide, including maps, photo galleries and video – download it from www.apple.com/itunes.

The **United States Geological Survey** (USGS; ☎ 888-275-8747; www.usgs.gov) publishes the standard 1:24,000 (7.5-minute) topographical quadrangle maps, available as free downloads online in PDF format. The level of detail is more than most visitors will need, unless you're planning a backcountry trip. Keep in mind that some USGS map survey information may be outdated, and buying these maps can quickly become expensive if your route extends across multiple quads. You can order print copies ($8 per quad) directly from the website or look for them at southern Utah's national park bookstores, outdoor outfitters and public lands information offices (see the USGS website for a complete list of local retailers).

National Geographic (☎ 800-437-5521; http://shop.nationalgeographic.com) publishes the *Trails Illustrated* series of waterproof, tear-resistant topographic maps (scale varies from 1:35,000 to 1:70,000) that collectively cover all of southern Utah's national parks, as well as other wilderness areas, including around Moab. Based on USGS maps, but often helpfully marked up with more details for outdoor recreation, these foldable maps ($10 to $12 each) are widely available at national park visitor centers, bookstores and elsewhere. If you're traveling with a hand-held GPS, or want to customize trail maps to print out yourself at home, National Geographic's TOPO! mapping software is a good investment; the Utah state series costs $50.

For driving maps, the *Utah* state highway map is perfectly adequate. It's available free from many tourist information offices. In addition to more detailed regional driving maps, the American Automobile Association (p273) also publishes an *Indian Country Guide Map* ($5) that covers southern Utah, northern Arizona and the Four Corners area. AAA maps are free for auto-club members. For a handy driving and motorcycling road atlas, Benchmark Press' *Utah Road & Recreation Atlas* ($23) shows every road in the state, along with land and water features, outdoor recreation areas, campgrounds, trailheads and hundreds more points of interest.

Wondering if you'll get vertigo in southern Utah? Check out the 360-degree digital panoramas of Canyonlands National Park's famous viewpoints at www.nps.gov/cany/photosmultimedia/virtualtour.htm.

INTERNET RESOURCES

More information on Utah's national parks and monuments is available on the **National Park Service website** (www.nps.gov/state/UT/). The lone exception is Grand Staircase-Escalante National Monument, which is administered by the **BLM** (www.ut.blm.gov).

In addition to the useful organizations listed below, the following websites will also help you plan a southern Utah parks sojourn:

Discover Moab (www.discovermoab.com) Extensive sightseeing, outdoor recreation, lodging, restaurant and visitor information for southeastern Utah.

Great Outdoor Recreation Pages (www.gorp.com) All-round outdoor-activity resource with links to tour guides and outfitters, plus thumbnail guides to Utah's parks.

Lonely Planet (www.lonelyplanet.com) Destination tips, hotel and hostel bookings, Thorn Tree travelers' forums and much more.

My Zion Park (www.myzionpark.com) Free trip-planning and outdoor-activity info, scenic-drive and road-trip guides, videos, news, a blog and more.

Public Lands Information Center (www.publiclands.org) Information about all types of public land in Utah, with scores of useful links.

Utah Travel Council (www.utah.com) State-sponsored tourism website offering loads of free info, including festivals and special events, to help plan your trip.

USEFUL ORGANIZATIONS

Sometimes the best way to get up-to-date travel information about southern Utah's national and state parks is to go straight to the source:

Arches National Park (☎ 435-719-2299; www.nps.gov/arch)
Bryce Canyon National Park (☎ 435-834-5322; www.nps.gov/brca)
Canyonlands National Park (☎ 435-719-2313; www.nps.gov/cany)
Capitol Reef National Park (☎ 435-425-3791; www.nps.gov/care)
Cedar Breaks National Monument (☎ 435-586-9451; www.nps.gov/cebr)
Grand Staircase-Escalante National Monument (☎ 435-826-5499; www.ut.blm.gov/monument)
Pipe Spring National Monument (☎ 928-643-7105; www.nps.gov/pisp)
Utah State Parks (☎ 801-538-7220, 877-887-2757; www.stateparks.utah.gov)
Zion National Park (☎ 435-772-3256; www.nps.gov/zion)

Eager to see Bryce Canyon before you get there? Take a virtual tour of the park's scenic drive from your couch – just click to www.nps.gov/brca/photosmultimedia/etours.htm.

All of southern Utah's national parks have supporting natural history associations that also provide limited information, sell books and maps, and sometimes sponsor special events, field trips and classes (see also p263).

Bryce Canyon Natural History Association (☎ 435-834-4782; www.brycecanyon.org)
Canyonlands Natural History Association (☎ 435-259-6003, 800-840-8978; www.cnha.org) Also covers Arches National Park.
Capitol Reef Natural History Association (☎ 435-425-3791; www.capitolreefnha.org)
Zion Natural History Association (☎ 435-772-3265, 800-635-3959; www.zionpark.org)

Also try these nonprofit, outdoors-oriented organizations:

National Audubon Society, Red Cliffs Chapter (☎ 435-673-0996; www.redcliffsaudubon.org) Based out of St George.

Sierra Club (☎ 801-467-9297; http://utah.sierraclub.org) Based out of Salt Lake, with a southeastern Utah group around Glen Canyon.

Southern Utah Wilderness Alliance (☎ 801-486-3161; www.suwa.org) Based out of Salt Lake.

County and other regional travel bureaus are also helpful; see p268.

Itineraries

SOUTHERN UTAH'S PARKLANDS **Two Weeks**

- Start off your trip with a bang in **Las Vegas**, aka Sin City (p137).
- Swing through riverside **Zion National Park** and **Springdale**, following our three-day itinerary (p27).
- Detour for panoramic overlooks and cool, forested walks at the **Grand Canyon's North Rim** (p192).
- Say hello to hoodoos in **Bryce Canyon National Park** (p146) and **Red Canyon** (p169).
- Squeeze through slot canyons and follow 4WD tracks in **Grand Staircase-Escalante National Monument** (p174).
- Crack the geologists' code and go fruit-picking in the orchards of **Capitol Reef National Park** (p196).
- Drive to **Moab** (p239), heading to iconic, cinematic **Monument Valley** (p243) first, if you've got time.
- Explore even more epic scenery in **Arches National Park** (p229) and wilder **Canyonlands National Park** (p213).

Make the most of your sojourn in southern Utah with our ambitious two-week plan (which could easily take a month), covering almost 1000 miles, depending on which detours you choose.

A DAY IN ZION CANYON

One Day

Even if you only have a morning or an afternoon to spare, don't miss Zion Canyon, a desert oasis. You can leave your car behind on this 20-mile shuttle-bus route.

- Drop by the park's **visitor center** to get oriented and browse the bookstore (p91).
- Hop on the free shuttle, stopping off at Zion's **Human History Museum** (p96).
- Ride the shuttle all the way up canyon to the **Temple of Sinawava** (p97).
- Follow the **Riverside Walk**, splashing into the Virgin River at trail's end (p101).
- Catch the shuttle heading back down canyon, getting off to see **Weeping Rock** (p102).
- Have a picnic lunch beneath the giant cottonwood tree outside **Zion Lodge** (p122).
- Hike the **Emerald Pools Trail** in combination with the quieter **Kayenta Trail** (p103).
- Hop back on the shuttle, stopping at the **Court of the Patriarchs** (p97).
- Hop off at Canyon Junction and stroll the **Pa'rus Trail**, ideally around sunset (p101).
- Alternatively, follow the peaceful hilltop **Watchman Trail** (p102), which starts near the visitor center.
- Head back to **Springdale** for a hearty dinner and art-gallery hopping (p126).

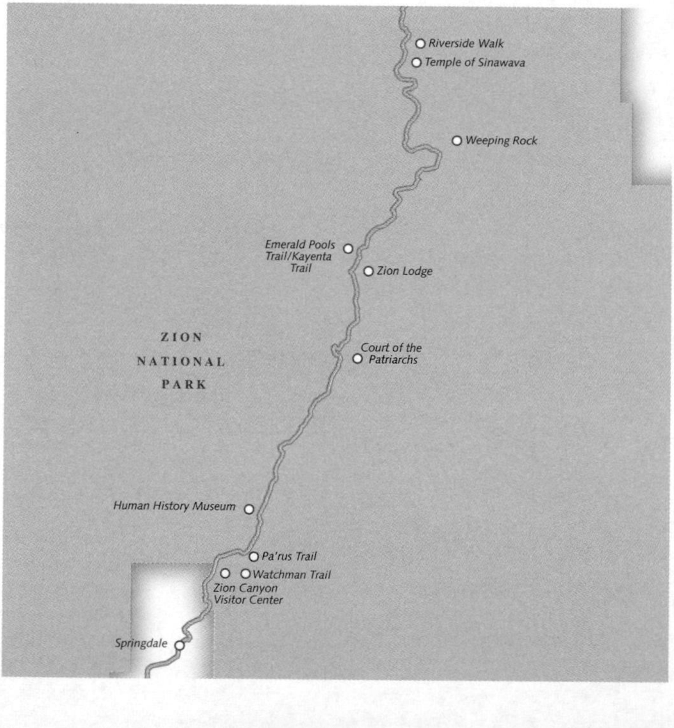

A LONG WEEKEND IN ZION NATIONAL PARK **Three Days**

- On your first day, follow our one-day itinerary and explore **Zion Canyon** (opposite).
- On your second day, hike the **Narrows** (p104) or to **Angels Landing** (p105).
- Not feeling quite so adventurous? The **Observation Point** trail is another rewarding workout (p106).
- If hiking doesn't appeal, take a **horseback ride** (p119) or an **inner-tube float** (p119).
- Drive **Hwy 9** through the **Zion–Mt Carmel Tunnel** to Checkerboard Mesa (p97).
- Before backtracking west to Zion Canyon, hike the slickrock **Canyon Overlook** trail (p109).
- In the afternoon, drive **Kolob Terrace Rd** to panoramic **Lava Point** (p99).
- Catch the sunset while driving back, perhaps stopping to hike the **Northgate Peaks Trail** (p108).
- Another great sunset-watching spot is atop the **Watchman Trail**, near the visitor center (p102).
- For a scenic afternoon drive further afield, head to remote **Kolob Canyons Rd** (p99).
- Have dinner and drinks, then kick back at your hotel in **Springdale** (p122).

See Zion Canyon from top to bottom, then head through the famous Zion–Mt Carmel Tunnel, wind up to Lava Point and climb through Kolob Canyons on this 180-mile jaunt.

A DAY IN BRYCE CANYON

One Day

Walk up, down and all around this high-elevation canyon, where cool pine forests and eerily eroded hoodoos await. The drive is about 40 miles long, with seasonal shuttles available partway.

- See the free film and pick up information at the **visitor center** (p148).
- Drive Bryce Canyon Scenic Drive all the way out to **Rainbow Point** (p150).
- Hike the short **Bristlecone Loop Trail**, with its awesome vistas and ancient trees (p154).
- Return along the **Scenic Drive**, stopping at the major sights along the way (p150).
- Grab lunch at **Bryce Canyon Lodge** (p168) or snacks at the **general store** (p168).
- Head to **Sunset Point** to glimpse the towering eroded hoodoos of Bryce Amphitheater (p153).
- Descend into the canyon on the **Navajo Loop** (p154) and/or **Queen's Garden Trail** (p155).
- Head down to **Bryce Point** (p152) and **Inspiration Point** (p153) by car or shuttle.
- Stroll along the **Rim Trail** and watch the light play on the hoodoos (p157).
- Alternatively, drive to **Paria View** to watch the sunset (p152).
- To really escape the crowds, detour out to serene, largely untrammeled **Fairyland Point** (p153).

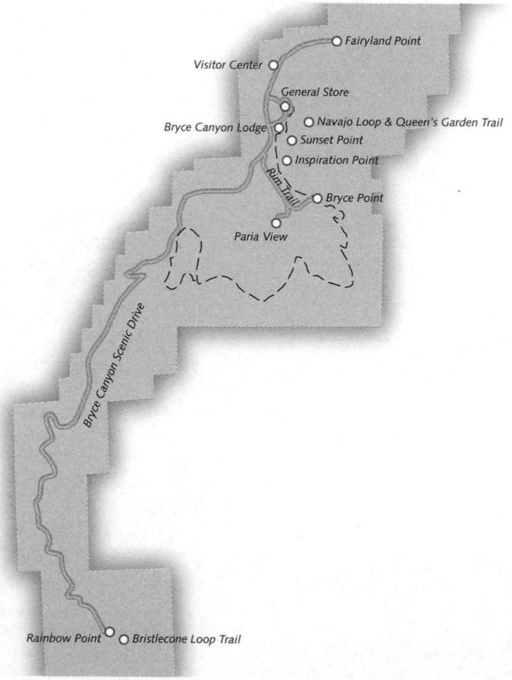

TWO DAYS IN BRYCE CANYON

Two Days

- Start exploring the park with our one-day itinerary (opposite).
- Once you've acclimated to the altitude, consider hiking the **Fairyland Loop** (p158).
- If you're in top shape, try tackling the **Riggs Spring Loop Trail** (p160).
- Or just hike as much of the **Rim Trail** as you want (p157).
- For a family-friendly nature walk, drive east to the **Mossy Cave** trailhead (p153).
- Or, give your feet a rest and take a half-day **horseback ride** instead (p163).
- If you feel like renting a bike, head over to nearby **Red Canyon** (p169).
- At the visitor center, check the schedule of **ranger-guided programs**, including campfire talks (p163).
- All ages can have fun completing the park's self-guided **junior ranger program** (p164).
- In summer, catch a **rodeo show** at Ruby's Inn outside the park (p166).
- Return to the park after dark for amazing stargazing from **Inspiration Point** (p153).

Take more time to examine this multicolored step of the Grand Staircase, visiting Bryce Canyon's more peaceful corners and going on multisport adventures. You'll drive under 100 miles.

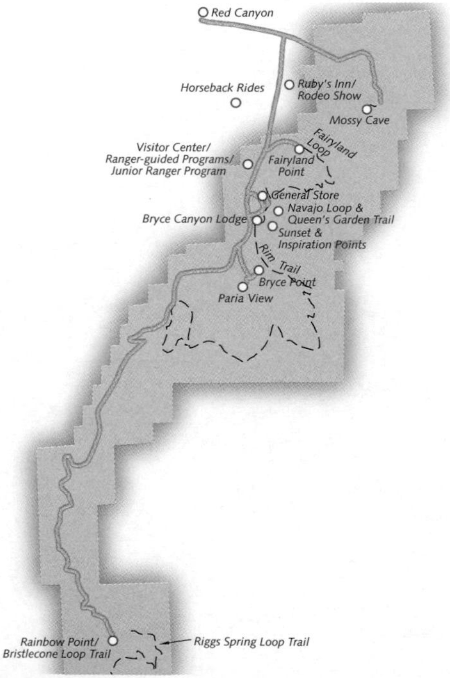

AROUND ZION & BRYCE CANYON WITH KIDS

One Week

Wanna keep the entire extended family happy on vacation? Then don't pack too much into your trip, and don't rush. This 275-mile trip is a fun-filled, all-ages outdoor adventure.

- On your first day, explore **Zion Canyon** (p95) and its **junior ranger program** (p119).
- On day two, go **horseback riding** (p119), **inner-tubing** (p119) or, with teens, **canyoneering** (p117).
- Take a side trip to **Grafton ghost town**, best visited at sunset (p95).
- On day three, take a break from hiking at St George's **Dinosaur Discovery Site** (p128).
- Go swimming at **Sand Hollow Aquatic Center** in the afternoon (p130).
- Around sunset, drive up **Kolob Canyons Rd** just for the views (p99).
- On day five, enjoy more vistas and easy hikes along **Hwy 14** (p135).
- In summer, escape to cooler climes at high-altitude **Cedar Breaks National Monument** (p135).
- If there's time, stretch your legs in **Red Canyon** before overnighting near Bryce (p169).
- Spend day six along the **Bryce Canyon Scenic Drive** (p150), making time for a **moonlight hike** (p164).
- On your last day, drive through the **Zion–Mt Carmel Tunnel** (p97) to Springdale.

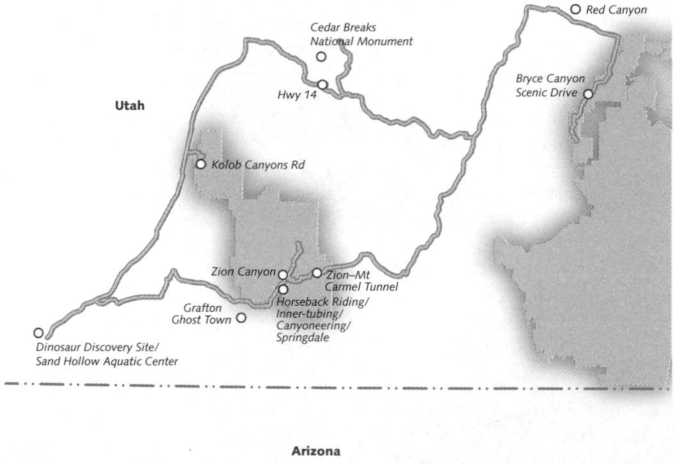

A WEEK IN GRAND STAIRCASE-ESCALANTE NATIONAL MONUMENT

One Week

- Drive from Las Vegas to the jaw-dropping **Grand Canyon North Rim** (p192).
- Stop at historic **Pipe Spring National Monument** along the way (p192).
- Visit Old West–flavored **Kanab** (p190), detouring east to **Paria Movie Set** (p193).
- Tackle **Cottonwood Canyon Rd** (p178) inside Grand Staircase-Escalante National Monument.
- Pass **Grosvenor Arch** (p178) before stopping at equally photogenic **Kodachrome Basin State Park** (p185).
- Drive east on **Hwy 12** (p185) to the helpful **Escalante Interagency Visitor Center** (p186).
- Look for **slot canyons** (p182) along bumpy **Hole-in-the-Rock Rd** (p178).
- Hike to **Escalante River Natural Bridge** (p180) or a waterfall in **Calf Creek Recreation Area** (p180).
- Mosey over to **Boulder** (p188) for a scenic drive along the **Burr Trail** (p177).
- Check out the re-created Ancestral Puebloan village at **Anasazi State Park Museum** (p189).
- Catch dinner on the open-air patio at **Hell's Backbone Grill**; reservations recommended (p190).

One week and over 650 miles of driving will only scratch the surface of southern Utah's most untamed wilderness, where 4WD roads, slot canyons and backcountry wonders call to adventurers.

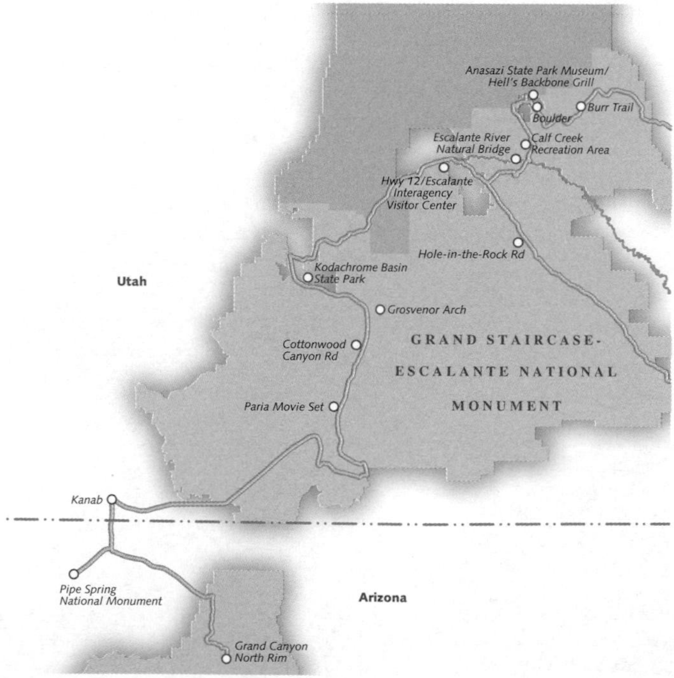

ITINERARIES

A DAY IN CAPITOL REEF NATIONAL PARK

One Day

You'll want to stay longer, but a day is just enough for a taste of Capitol Reef's geological marvels on this 45-mile drive, also traveled by fit, enthusiastic cyclists.

- Cruise **Hwy 24** east of Torrey, stopping for petroglyphs and pioneer historical sites (p199).
- Hike to **Hickman Bridge**, maybe splashing around in the Fremont River afterward (p203).
- Backtrack to the park's **visitor center** to watch the movie and browse books (p198).
- Have a picnic lunch in **Fruita** and go seasonal fruit-picking in the orchards (p198).
- Drop by the historic **Gifford Homestead** for homemade bread, jam and fruit pies (p199).
- Take a self-guided geology tour along Capitol Reef's mostly paved **Scenic Drive** (p200).
- See the sheer canyon walls of the Narrows on the **Grand Wash** trail (p202).
- Hike into **Capitol Gorge** (p202) or find a **swimming hole** (p208).
- Backtrack to the steep, hidden **Cohab Canyon** trail for bird's-eye viewpoints over Fruita (p204).
- Stop at **Goosenecks Overlook** (p199) and **Sunset Point** (p200) as you return west via Hwy 24.
- Grab a steak dinner or sample Southwestern cooking, then bed down in **Torrey** (p210).

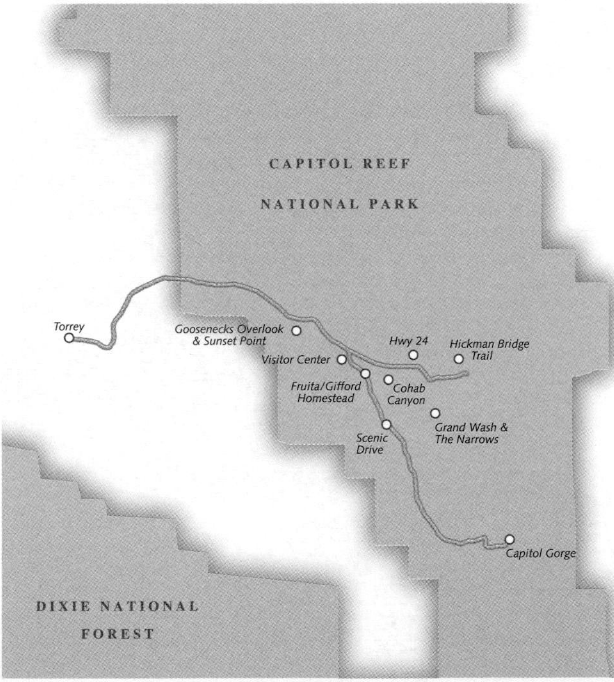

ITINERARIES

A DAY IN ARCHES NATIONAL PARK

One Day

- Get up early to beat the heat and stop at the **visitor center** (p231).
- Take the park's **Scenic Drive**, which passes all the major sights (p232).
- Walk among sandstone monoliths on the **Park Avenue** trail, best in the morning (p235).
- Don't miss the viewpoint turnout where you can spy on the **Three Gossips** (p235).
- Gawk at **Balanced Rock** (p234), then stroll beneath natural arches off **Windows Rd** (p233).
- Pause for 360-degree views and a geology lesson at **Panorama Point** (p233).
- Visit famous **Delicate Arch** at road's end; have a tailgate picnic afterward (p237).
- With advance reservations, you can take a ranger-guided hike in the **Fiery Furnace** (p234).
- With more energy to burn, hike to more arches from the **Devils Garden** (p236).
- For solitude and sunsets, take Salt Valley Rd out to the **Klondike Bluffs** (p231).
- Spend the evening eating, drinking, shopping and wandering around outdoorsy downtown **Moab** (p239).

Though Edward Abbey would call the plan ludicrous, it really is possible to see Arches National Park in just a day, covering 75 miles by car (and more on foot).

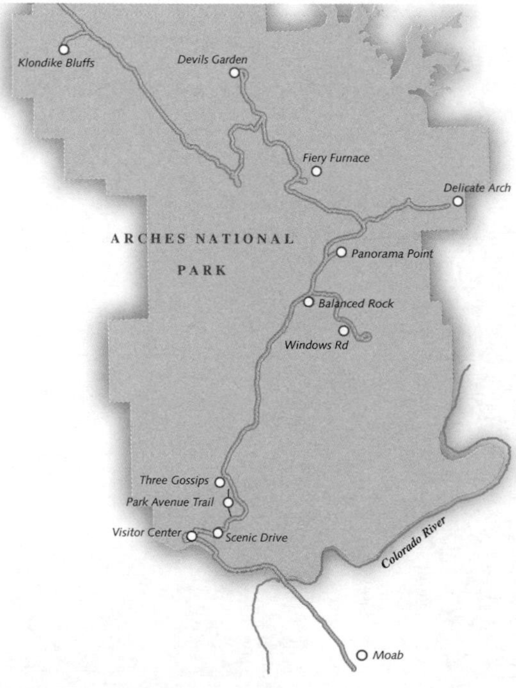

TWO DAYS IN CANYONLANDS NATIONAL PARK

Two Days

Although you could spend a week exploring 4WD roads and backcountry trails, this 275-mile drive gets you a good taste of the wild, rugged and remote terrain that defines Canyonlands.

- With limited time, it's a no-brainer: head directly to **Island in the Sky** (p216).
- Stop at the **visitor center** (p215), following the **Grand View Point Scenic Drive** (p217).
- Take your pick of several day hikes, but don't miss **Mesa Arch** (p218).
- Stop for a picnic lunch at the **White Rim Overlook** (p217).
- Head out to impressive **Grand View Point** for 100-mile views (p219).
- Backtrack, then follow the northwest fork of the scenic drive to **Upheaval Dome** (p218).
- Stop at **Dead Horse Point State Park** (p227) on your way back to Moab.
- Drive south to the **Needles** area of Canyonlands on your second day (p222).
- Stop at **Hole 'n the Rock** en route for kitschy roadside Americana (p242).
- Follow the **Big Spring Canyon Overlook** drive, doing all three easy hikes (p222).
- Take a side trip to **Canyon Rims Recreation Area** before returning to Moab (p245).

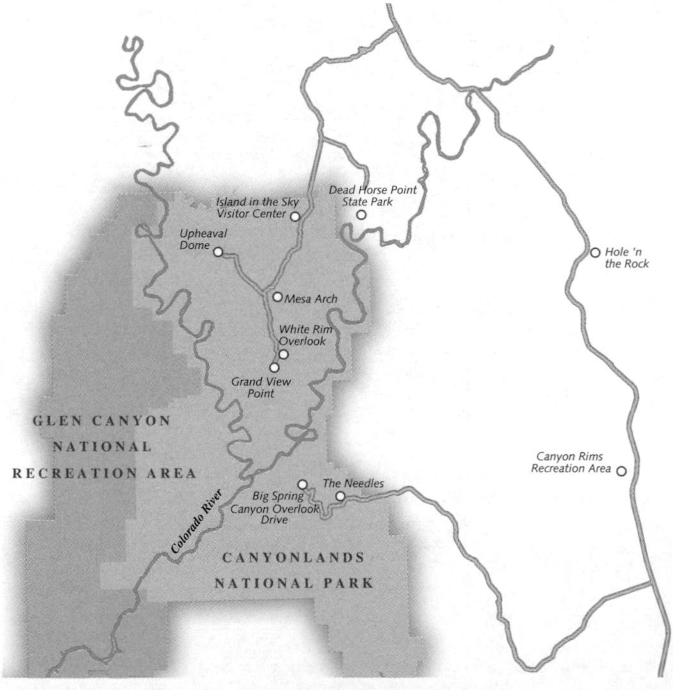

A LONG WEEKEND IN MOAB

Three Days

- Drop by the **Moab Museum of Film & Western Heritage** (p242) on Friday afternoon.
- Go dining, drinking, souvenir shopping or maybe just people-watching in downtown **Moab** (p239).
- Get up early to take a full-day **river trip**; reserve well in advance (p249).
- If you don't like navigating rapids, **canoe, kayak** or **float** along on flatwater (p249).
- In the afternoon, hit a **mountain biking trail** that matches your experience level (p246).
- Fuel up with shade-grown espresso the next morning at **Dave's Corner Market** (p258).
- Drive **La Sal Mountain Loop Rd** (p243) or take a **guided horseback ride** (p252).
- Alternatively, explore another of Moab's scenic byways, such as **Potash Rd** (p244).
- Go **rock climbing** or take a **canyoneering** class in the afternoon (p252).
- Hike the **Fisher Towers Trail** past sandstone monoliths at sunset; bring a flashlight (p245).
- Finish up with microbrews and tasty, standout pub grub at **Moab Brewery** (p258).

River running, mountain biking, rock climbing, canyoneering, hiking, 4WD roads – Moab is a multisport extravaganza. Do it all in just one weekend, covering around 150 miles by car.

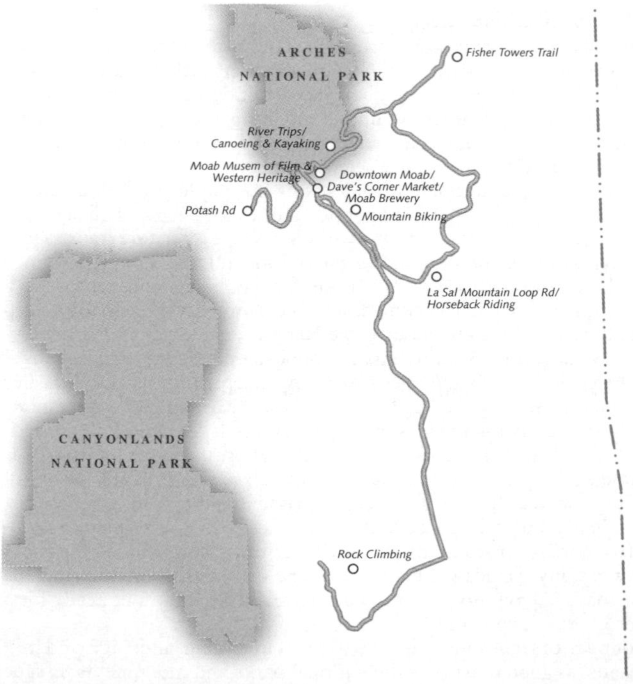

Activities

Utah's Incredible Backcountry Trails (2006) by David Day is an in-depth explorer's guide; about half of the wilderness trails he describes are in southern Utah.

For such a dry, brittle, barren place, there's a surprising sensuality to southern Utah's landscape. Water's signature is everywhere. Determined rivers have left behind majestic cliffs and slot canyons in their progress through ancient hardened seas whose layers can be ticked off like the colorful lines on a child's growth chart. To follow a wash through a narrow canyon and run your hands over the carved sandstone walls is to witness a river's hydraulics frozen in time. It's easy to become addicted, to want to explore deeper, further, higher – and you can.

It's possible to 'see' southern Utah only through the windows of a vehicle. There is certainly plenty of roadside scenery in the national parks and monuments. But more than most places in the world, this land should be experienced up close to fully appreciate it. It's not just a matter of beholding sights most others will never see. It's about leaving the literal and figurative safety of your car and the modern world behind. There's no place in the country quite like this, and you don't need cliff-hanging, death-defying determination to enter it. Just follow any trail. The desert will soon embrace you, revealing a vision of the earth so old and surreal it defies understanding. It doesn't matter whether you're rappeling through one of Zion's slot canyons, taking a moonlight hike or cross-country skiing at Bryce Canyon, riding horseback or four-wheel driving in the Grand Staircase-Escalante backcountry, or mountain biking atop slickrock or rafting outside Moab. You'll swear that southern Utah has it all.

Before you hit the trail, consider reading a general guide to desert hiking safety, such as *Desert Hiking Tips* (1999) by Bruce Grubbs.

HIKING & BACKPACKING

Hiking is the main and most accessible activity at all the national parks. It involves little more than walking, but with preparation and a purpose – and this is the thing to remember about hiking in southern Utah: be prepared. This wild desert is unlike anything most people have ever experienced, and designating certain parcels as 'national parks' has not tamed it. For hiking safety tips, see p283.

Throughout the destination chapters of this guide you'll find recommended hiking and backpacking opportunities for people of all ages and abilities. Every park offers one or two rewarding easy nature trails, plus a bewildering variety of more moderate to difficult trails. Zion (p100) may have the best overall selection of trails for day hikers and backpackers. Most trails in Zion Canyon either follow the Virgin River or climb its steep walls; the park's best-known trek, the Narrows, is literally *in* the river.

The book *50 Best Short Hikes in Utah's National Parks* (2001) by Ron Adkison also touches on trailside geology, flora and fauna.

Bryce Canyon (p153) presents the opposite configuration: easy hikes are along the rim, while longer hikes drop steeply into its amphitheater of hoodoos. Cedar Breaks (p135) is a cool escape in summer, where moderately strenuous forest trails wind past alpine lakes, wildflower meadows and ancient bristlecone pines. Grand Staircase-Escalante (p180) is a paradise for primitive backpackers, though it also provides plenty of easy to moderate trails – some very accessible, others along rough dirt roads. While Capitol Reef (p202) and Arches (p233) offer many easy to moderate trails off scenic drives, Arches is not recommended for backpacking. Canyonlands (p213) tends to the extremes: short trails off the main roads let you dip your toes, but to really get into it, be ready for a major backpacking trip.

Boundaries seem almost arbitrary in this unending landscape, and hiking is just as good outside of the national parks and monuments. Escape the crowds in the Pine Valley Mountains (p132) outside St George; the enormous Dixie National Forest, stretching from Cedar Breaks to Capitol Reef; or the La Sal Mountains (p246) near Moab. On the Utah–Arizona border, the Paria Canyon-Vermilion Cliffs Wilderness Area (p194) is among the most fantastical places on the planet, while state parks like Coral Pink Sand Dunes (p193), Goblin Valley (p212) and Dead Horse Point (p227) feature unusual spectacles with trails that are worth a detour.

Southern Utah's national and state parks and public lands information offices dispense free, basic maps and trail descriptions. They also sell more detailed topographic maps and hiking guides, which are stocked at local bookstores and outdoor outfitters' shops, too. All national parks offer free seasonal ranger-guided hikes, while cooperative nonprofit natural history associations (see p263) offer field trips and guided hikes for a fee. Also look for guided hikes and outings led by local chapters of the Sierra Club and the National Audubon Society (see p24). Private hiking guides and tours are recommended in the destination chapters.

Although some details are outdated (eg permit regulations, water sources), *Hiking Zion & Bryce National Parks* (2005) by Erik Molvar and Tamara Martin remains useful.

When to Hike

Though southern Utah is a year-round destination, variations by location and season are extreme. As the majority of parks, monuments and other hiking destinations are in the desert, spring and fall are often the best times to hike. Summer – the height of tourist season – can be the worst, as temperatures routinely top 100°F. One smart summertime strategy is to hike the big canyons only very early or late in the day, planning your hike for the side that will be in shade.

Elevation also plays a factor. At over 8000ft, Bryce Canyon's rim stays a bit cooler, as do other spots in the mountains. However, certain roads and trails at higher elevations may be closed to all but cross-country skiers and snowshoers until April, May or sometimes June (for example, at Cedar Breaks atop the Colorado Plateau). Some canyon hikes are not safe in spring, when runoff from snowmelt dangerously raises water levels. If you're planning on through-hiking the Narrows of the Virgin River in Zion Canyon, for example, you'll usually have to wait until late June.

Always check the weather forecast before you start hiking or backpacking. For local updates, go to www.wrh.noaa.gov/slc and click on the map for southern Utah.

Year-round, the weather in southern Utah is variable and often intense. When it rains, it rains hard and all at once. July and August are called 'monsoon season' because of sudden rainstorms that can send flash floods (see p285) coursing through canyons. Whatever the season, always hike with caution and awareness. Backcountry camping in summer can be dreadful if you don't find shade, while in spring and fall overnight temperatures can drop below freezing, even following days that are warm and sunny.

Hiking from Here to Wow: Utah Canyon Country (2008) by Kathy and Craig Copeland is a fun, opinionated guide, with descriptions of 90 hikes in southern Utah, from Arches to Zion and beyond.

Difficulty Levels

Hikes in this guide are rated by difficulty level, though such determinations are always subjective. Heat, elevation and trail grade are only a few of the variables you should consider when deciding how difficult a trail will be. When in doubt, assume trails will be harder and take longer than you think.

Easy: Generally level and easy to navigate, these trails are often paved, sometimes accessible to wheelchairs and usually suitable for young children.

Moderate: Trails involve some elevation gain and may be slightly rocky, rough and/or exposed, but can be hiked by anyone of average fitness.

Difficult: These are strenuous trails involving steep climbs, tricky route-finding and/or long distances.

All of the hikes included in this book, from day hikes to backcountry routes, follow marked, established trails. The distance listed for each is

HIKING IN ZION NATIONAL PARK

Name	Type	Start location	Distance R/T	Duration R/T	Difficulty	Elevation change
Angels Landing	Day Hike	Grotto	5.4 miles	4hr	Difficult	1488ft
Cable Mountain Trail	Day Hike	Zion Ponderosa Ranch	6.2 miles	3hr	Moderate	250ft
Canyon Overlook	Day Hike	East of Zion–Mt Carmel Tunnel	1 mile	45min	Easy-moderate	163ft
East Mesa Trail	Day Hike	Zion Ponderosa Ranch	6.4 miles	3hr	Moderate	500ft
Emerald Pools & Kayenta Trails	Day Hikes	Zion Lodge	3 miles	2½hr	Moderate	400ft
Grotto Trail	Easy Hike	Zion Lodge	0.5 miles	15min	Easy	Negligible
Hidden Canyon Trail	Day Hike	Weeping Rock	2.4 miles	2½hr	Moderate-difficult	850ft
La Verkin Creek Trail to Kolob Arch	Backcountry	Lee Pass	14 miles	8hr-2 days	Difficult	800ft
Narrows: From the Bottom	Day Hike	Riverside Walk	up to 10 miles	up to 8hr	Moderate-difficult	400ft
Narrows: From the Top	Backcountry	Chamberlain Ranch	16 miles one way	2 days	Difficult	1220ft
Northgate Peaks Trail	Day Hike	Wildcat Canyon trailhead	4.4 miles	2hr	Easy-moderate	110ft
Observation Point	Day Hike	Weeping Rock	8 miles	5hr	Difficult	2150ft
Pa'rus Trail	Easy Hike	Zion Canyon Visitor Center	3.5 miles	1½hr	Easy	Negligible
Riverside Walk	Easy Hike	Temple of Sinawava	2 miles	1hr	Easy	100ft
The Subway	Backcountry Hike	Wildcat Canyon trailhead	9.5 miles one way	7hr	Difficult	1850ft
Taylor Creek Middle Fork	Day Hike	Kolob Canyons Rd	5 miles	3hr	Moderate	450ft
Timber Creek Overlook	Day Hike	End of Kolob Canyons Rd	1 mile	30min	Easy-moderate	100ft
Trans-Park Connector	Backcountry	Lee Pass	15.5 miles one way	4 days	Difficult	4000ft
Watchman Trail	Day Hike	Zion Canyon Visitor Center	2.7 miles	1½-2hr	Easy-moderate	400ft
Weeping Rock Trail	Day Hike	Weeping Rock	0.5 miles	30min	Easy-moderate	100ft
West Rim Trail	Backcountry	Lava Point trailhead	14.5 miles one way	2 days	Difficult	3600ft

Views *Great for Families* *Rock Climbing* *Waterfalls* *Bicycles* *Restrooms* *Drinking Water*

round-trip, unless otherwise noted. The actual time spent hiking will vary with your ability. Hike descriptions in this guide detail sights and viewpoints en route.

EASY HIKES

The walks listed in the 'easy hikes' sections of this guide are less than 2 miles in length and cover fairly even, possibly paved terrain with no significant elevation gain or loss.

Features	Facilities	Description	Page
		Ascends switchbacks before reaching a rock fin with precipitous drop-offs and chain-assisted scrambles	105
		A mesa-top jaunt that ends at a historic cable works overlooking Zion Canyon	110
		A quick, elevated hike through canyon alcoves, past a giant proto-arch, to panoramic vistas	109
		Wanders through upcountry woods and then descends the 'sneaky way' to incredible Observation Point views	110
		Popular series of trails leads up to three pools, desert-varnished cliffs and trickling waterfalls	103
		Shady, even trail that connects Zion Lodge with the Grotto picnic grounds	101
		Hikes up exposed switchbacks to short sections of cliff-clinging ledges with assistance chains	104
		High-country, foothill hike along a desert river to views of a giant, but distant, arch	112
		The Virgin River is the trail, and you walk, wade or swim up it	104
		An in-the-river experience, swimming and hiking down through the park's most famous slot canyon	115
		Easy backcountry access on a pine-and-meadow trail to a lava outcrop overlooking the namesake peaks	108
		Strenuous hike climbs steeply, traversing a hanging chasm before reaching a rewarding Angels Landing overlook	106
		A paved, wheelchair- and bike-friendly path meandering along the river in the lower Zion Canyon	101
		An end-of-the-canyon trail follows the Virgin River past hanging gardens, weeping seeps and waterfalls	101
		To reach a surreal, tunnel-like rock, this challenging canyoneering route requires five rappels, plus swims	113
		Creekside trail passes historic cabins en route to the natural amphitheater of Double Arch Alcove	108
		A short, unimproved trail to 270-degree views of Kolob's finger canyons and mountains beyond	107
		Linking strenuous and varied trails allows backpackers to span Zion, northwest to southeast	113
		A short ascent leads to a loop with fine park formation views; great at sunset	102
		Falls that sometimes seep, sometimes weep lay at the end of a short-but-staircase-like hike	102
		Backcountry trail affords primo views while descending from Zion's high country to canyon floor	114

Public Transport · *Wheelchair Access* · *Ranger Station* · *Backcountry Campsite* · *Picnic Sites* · *Swimming*

DAY HIKES

The majority of hikes described in this guide are day hikes, taking anywhere from 20 minutes to eight hours. Durations do not account for breaks. On steep trails that lead from canyon floors to rims, or vice versa, a general guide is that it takes twice as long to ascend as to descend. For people who want to test themselves, or who don't have time for a full hike, it's always possible to tackle just the first few miles of a day or backcountry hike.

HIKING IN BRYCE CANYON NATIONAL PARK

Name	Type	Start location	Distance R/T	Duration R/T	Difficulty	Elevation change
Bristlecone Loop Trail	Easy Hike	Rainbow Point Lot	1 mile	30min-1hr	Easy	100ft
Fairyland Loop Trail	Day Hike	Fairyland Point	8 miles	4-5hr	Difficult	900ft
Mossy Cave Trail	Easy Hike	Mossy Cave trailhead, Hwy 12	0.8 miles	30min-1hr	Easy-moderate	150ft
Navajo Loop Trail	Day Hike	Sunset Point	1.3 miles	1-2hr	Moderate-difficult	521ft
Navajo Loop–Queen's Garden Combination	Day Hike	Sunrise Point	2.9 miles	2-3hr	Moderate	521ft
Peekaboo Loop Trail	Day Hike	Bryce Point	5.5 miles	3-5hr	Difficult	500-900ft
Queen's Garden Trail	Day Hike	Sunrise Point	1.8 miles	1-2hr	Moderate	320ft
Riggs Spring Loop Trail	Backcountry	Rainbow Point	8.8 miles	4-5hr	Difficult	1675ft
Rim Trail	Day Hike	Fairyland Point or any rim trailhead	5.5 miles one way	2-3hr	Easy-moderate	550ft
Under-the-Rim Trail	Backcountry Hike	Bryce Point	22.9 miles	3 days	Moderate-difficult	1315ft

Wildlife Watching · *Views* · *Great for Families* · *Waterfalls* · *Restrooms* · *Drinking Water* · *Backcountry Campsite*

Backpacker (www.backpacker.com/destinations) provides free downloadable hiking and backpacking online trail guides, with GPS waypoints and elevation profiles, for all of southern Utah's national parks and monuments.

BACKCOUNTRY HIKES

People can and do spend weeks hiking in the southern Utah desert, but it's something to build up to, once you get to know the place better. Backcountry hikes in this guide lean toward the easier ones, usually involving one to three nights out. When you're ready for more, park rangers and local outfitters can help you find new challenges. In general, Zion, Bryce Canyon and Capitol Reef offer a good selection of easy to moderate backpacking trips, while Canyonlands and Grand Staircase-Escalante are famous for their difficulty.

The most important consideration on any backcountry hike is water. Will there be any on your route, and of what quality and quantity? Southern Utah has been suffering drought for most of the last decade, so don't trust blue lines and circles on a topographic map. Always check with rangers or knowledgeable locals before trekking into the unknown.

Hiking Rules & Permits

Hiking and backcountry-use rules at the national parks and monuments are virtually the same. With minor exceptions, these are the guidelines for trail use:

- Day hikes on maintained trails do not require a permit.
- All overnight backcountry hikes require a permit; some permits are free, while others cost (typically $5 to $20).
- Pets are prohibited on all trails, whether day use or backcountry (Zion's Pa'rus Trail is the one exception). For more on hiking with pets, see p57.
- Bicycles are forbidden on all day-use or backcountry trails (again, Zion's Pa'rus Trail is the exception); however, bicycles are allowed on paved and dirt roads.

Features	Facilities	Description	Page
		Stroll the plateau's southernmost tip for views of the Grand Staircase	154
		Long hike away from crowds leads past castlelike formations, though not as spectacular as Bryce Amphitheater	158
		Hike beside running water to a waterfall and cave	153
		Short but spectacular, with hoodoo views, this sometimes steep hike packs a punch	154
		Most popular route in the park, a half-day that hits Bryce's signature features	155
		See the greatest variety of terrain and scenery in Bryce; horses allowed	156
		Gentlest descent into the canyon on eroding fins, passing myriad hoodoos	155
		This strenuous hike drops off the plateau's southern tip through three ecological zones	160
		Hike along canyon rim features stellar overlook of hoodoos	157
		Bryce's premier backcountry hike passes few hoodoos but promises wonderful solitude	160

- It's illegal to touch, disturb, take or deface any cultural sites or artifacts or to pick wildflowers or otherwise harm plants or animals. Never feed a wild animal either.

For backcountry camping and use, further rules apply:

- Group limits apply to backcountry use; these vary, so always ask.
- Certain other backcountry activities, like canyoneering in Zion and horseback riding or four-wheel driving in Canyonlands, require a day-use permit.
- Human waste must be carried out or buried in a 6in to 8in hole at least 100ft away from water sources, trails and campsites; consider using human-waste disposal bags.
- No dispersed camping is allowed within 200ft of streams or trails, nor within 0.25 miles of springs.
- No open fires are allowed in the backcountry; use a gas stove. The exceptions are Canyonlands and Grand Staircase-Escalante, which allow fires with restrictions.

Hiking the Southwest's Geology: Four Corners Region (2003) by Ralph Lee Hopkins includes nearly two dozen trails in southern Utah, from natural arches and bridges into the heart of canyon country, with great background reading for budding geologists.

ROCK CLIMBING

If Dr Seuss had designed a rock-climbing playground, it would look a lot like this: a surreal landscape filled with enormous blobs, spires, soaring cliffs and canyon walls in kaleidoscopic colors. Some of the country's best rock climbing lies in southern Utah, though many routes are for moderate to expert climbers. Zion (p118) is famous for big-wall climbs, while the St George area, particularly Snow Canyon State Park (p132), offers dozens of bolted and sport routes. You'll find great climbing in Arches (p238), Canyonlands (p216) and Capitol Reef (p209), although

HIKING IN GRAND STAIRCASE & CAPITOL REEF

Name	Type	Start location	Distance R/T	Duration R/T	Difficulty	Elevation change
Grand Staircase-Escalante National Monument						
Boulder Mail Trail	Backcountry Hike	Hell's Backbone Rd	16 miles one way	2-3 days	Difficult	1800ft
Escalante River Natural Bridge	Day Hike	Hwy 12	4.4 miles	3hr	Easy-moderate	200ft
Lower Calf Creek Falls	Day Hike	Calf Creek Recreation Area	6 miles	4hr	Moderate	250ft
Lower Hackberry Canyon	Day Hike	Cottonwood Canyon Rd	3-6 miles	2-3hr	Easy-moderate	100ft
Phipps Wash	Day Hike	Hwy 12	5 miles	4hr	Moderate	300ft
Slot Canyons of Dry Fork/Coyote Gulch	Day Hike	Hole-in-the-Rock Rd	4.5 miles	3hr	Moderate-difficult	600ft
Upper Calf Creek Falls	Day Hike	Hwy 12	2.2 miles	1½hr	Moderate	600ft
Willis Creek	Day Hike	Cottonwood Canyon Rd	up to 4.4 miles	up to 4hr	Easy-moderate	300ft
Capitol Reef National Park						
Capitol Gorge	Day Hike	Grand Wash trailhead	2.2 miles	1-2hr	Easy-moderate	125ft
Cohab Canyon	Day Hike	Cohab Canyon trailhead	1.7 miles one way	1-2hr	Moderate	400ft
Grand Wash	Day Hike	Grand Wash trailhead	2.25 miles one way	45min-1½hr	Easy	25ft
Hickman Bridge	Day Hike	Hickman Bridge trailhead	2 miles	1-2hr	Easy-moderate	400ft
Lower Muley Twist Canyon	Backcountry Hike	Lower Muley Twist Canyon trailhead	15 miles	1-2 days	Difficult	1000ft
Rim Overlook & Navajo Knobs	Day Hike	Hickman Bridge trailhead	9.5 miles	4-6hr	Difficult	1600ft
Upper Muley Twist Canyon	Backcountry Hike	Upper Muley Twist Canyon trailhead	15 miles	1-2 days	Difficult	1100ft

Wildlife Watching · *Views* · *Great for Families* · *Rock Climbing* · *Waterfalls* · *Restrooms* · *Backcountry Campsite*

Zion Climbing: Free and Clean (2009) by experienced local climber Bryan Bird is a comprehensive area climbing guide that tackles little boulder problems to epic wall and free climbs, including helpful maps and full-color photos.

restrictions apply. Several popular routes for all abilities await near Moab (p252). Although their focus may be on canyoneering, several outdoor outfitters (see the boxed text, p47) offer rock-climbing classes for beginners and sell climbing gear.

Climbing in summer can get exceptionally hot. When the air temperature reaches 100°F, the cliff face could top 115°F, and the rocks hold the heat all night. Spring and fall are better times to rock climb; if you do climb in summer, start early in the morning. Some parks enforce seasonal route closures to protect nesting or breeding wildlife. All parks prohibit power drills, discourage excess bolting and ask climbers to use subdued colors for hangers and slings. Ask at park visitor centers about the latest regulations and permits, which are usually required for overnight bivouacs. Even if you don't need a permit, stop by Zion's backcountry desk, where the rangers and volunteers are often climbers themselves, full of great local tips and advice.

Features	Facilities	Description	Page
		Hearty wilderness hike following the historic Boulder–Escalante mail route through Box-Death Hollow	183
		A flat, sandy trail crisscrosses the river numerous times before reaching a large natural bridge	180
		A sandy, creekside canyon walk past Native American sites to a 126ft-tall waterfall and pool	181
		A pleasant hike through a deep, narrow gorge that's cooled by a shallow stream	183
		Route-find your way through scrubby vegetation and along slickrock to reach two arches	181
		Drops steeply down slickrock to reach four sinuous slot canyons	182
		A short but strenuous trail down slickrock leads to falls and two sets of pools	180
		Accessible slot canyon that alternates between narrows and open sections along a seasonal creek	182
		Sheer-walled canyon wash features Indian petroglyphs, historical sites and secret watering holes	202
		In a hidden canyon high atop Capitol Reef, sidle past slickrock to head-spinning overlooks	204
		Flat trail passes between sheer 80-story-high canyon walls just 15ft apart	202
		Ascend over slickrock, past giant domes and a towering arch, ending with sweeping views	203
		Scramble through an 80-story-high red-rock canyon just 10ft wide, then loop back through a gulch	207
		Ascends from the Fremont River to an overlook, then climbs higher still for 360-degree panoramas	204
		Rugged backcountry loop features arches, sculpted sandstone narrows and long views of Waterpocket Fold	205

Swimming

MOUNTAIN BIKING & CYCLING

The fat-tire crowd already knows about Moab, a mountain-biking mecca for decades. The original **Slickrock Bike Trail** (p247) is there, among many others. If you're a novice rider, try the **Bar-M Loop** (p247). For slickrock virgins who have mountain-biking experience, the **Klondike Bluffs Trail** (p248) awaits. When the summer sun is baking the desert lowlands, riders can escape to the cool forests of the La Sal Mountains outside town, where the **Moonlight Meadow Trail** (p247) is a high-altitude downhill challenge, or the flat single-track of the **Intrepid Trail** (p228) at Dead Horse Point State Park. What mountain bikers might not know is that southwest Utah offers equally good slickrock trails in places outside **St George** (p130) and Zion, including at **Gooseberry Mesa** (p116) and **Brian Head** (p136), and on national forest land in **Red Canyon** (p169), west of Bryce Canyon. Even though mountain biking is prohibited on national park trails, it's permitted on dirt roads. In Canyonlands, Island in the Sky's

Visit www.trails.com to search for hiking, mountain biking, four-wheel driving, birding, cross-country skiing and other multisport trails across southern Utah (trail overview summaries are free).

HIKING IN CANYONLANDS & ARCHES

Name	Type	Start location	Distance R/T	Duration R/T	Difficulty	Elevation change
Island in the Sky (Canyonlands National Park)						
Aztec Butte Trail	Day Hike	Aztec Butte trailhead	2 miles	1-1½hr	Moderate	225ft
Grand View Point Trail	Easy Hike	Grand View Point parking area	2 miles	1-1½hr	Easy	50ft
Lathrop Canyon	Day Hike	Island in the Sky	5-22 miles	2½hr-2 days	Moderate	2100ft
Mesa Arch	Easy Hike	Mesa Arch trailhead	0.5 miles	30min	Easy	100ft
Neck Spring	Day Hike	Shafer Canyon Overlook parking area	6 miles	2½hr	Moderate	300ft
Upheaval Dome Overlook Trail	Easy Hike	Upheaval Dome parking area	0.8-1.8 miles	1-1½hr	Easy-moderate	50-200ft
The Needles (Canyonlands National Park)						
Cave Spring Trail	Easy Hike	Cave Spring trailhead	0.6 miles	30-45min	Easy-moderate	50ft
Chesler Park Loop & Joint Trail	Backcountry Hike	Elephant Hill trailhead	11 miles	1-2 days	Moderate-difficult	520ft
Pothole Point Trail	Easy Hike	Pothole Point trailhead	0.6 miles	45min	Easy	20ft
Slickrock Trail	Day Hike	Slickrock trailhead	2.4 miles	1½-2hr	Easy-moderate	70ft
Arches National Park						
Balanced Rock	Easy Hike	Balanced Rock parking area	0.3 miles	15-20min	Easy	20ft
Delicate Arch	Day Hike	Wolfe Ranch	3 miles	2-3hr	Moderate-difficult	480ft
Landscape Arch	Day Hikes	Devils Garden trailhead	2.1 miles	30min-1hr	Easy-	50ft moderate
Park Avenue	Easy Hike	Park Avenue trailhead	1 mile one way	30-45min	Easy-moderate	320ft
Sand Dune & Broken Arches	Day Hike	Sand Dune Arch parking area	2.4 miles	2hr	Easy-moderate	140ft
The Windows	Easy Hike	The Windows trailhead	0.6 miles	30min-1hr	Easy	140ft

Wildlife Watching *Views* *Great for Families* *Restrooms* *Drinking Water* *Backcountry Campsite* *Picnic Sites*

White Rim Road (p221) and the labyrinth of 4WD roads in the **Maze** (p227) are awesome experiences, as is **Cathedral Valley Loop** (p201) in Capitol Reef and backcountry roads in **Grand Staircase-Escalante** (p184). All mountain bikers should follow the guidelines in the boxed text on p46, particularly the rules about staying on trail.

Road cycling the paved scenic drives in Zion (p95), Bryce Canyon (p150) and Capitol Reef (p200) is an excellent way to take in the parks' sights. The steeper, longer and more challenging paved roads in Arches (p232) and Canyonlands (p213) are best left for experienced cyclists in good shape. Recreational cycling paths are uncommon in southern Utah, with the notable exceptions of Zion's **Pa'rus Trail** (p101) and **Red**

Features	Facilities	Description	Page
		Skitter up slickrock to an ancient Native American granary	220
		No place in Canyonlands offers such a sweeping view; watch for passing condors	219
		Extensive canyon hike with stellar views; less trodden and perfect for solitude	220
		Island in the Sky's most famous arch is gorgeous at sunrise	218
		This solitary stream canyon attracts wildlife and fills with wildflowers in springtime; look for the remnants of pioneer ranching	220
		Marvel at Island in the Sky's geologic mystery	219
		Past an abandoned cowboy camp, this trail climbs ladders up slickrock	223
		Popular trek passes grasslands and pinnacles and threads through narrow fractures	224
		Stop by natural potholes to spot tiny swimming organisms	223
		Semiloop trail with views of the Needles and La Sal and Abajo Mountains	223
		A precariously poised boulder perched atop a narrow rock spire	234
		Arches' premier hike ascends slickrock to the iconic Delicate Arch	237
		Short walk to one of the world's longest spans, with side hikes to smaller arches	235
		Sheer sandstone monoliths call to mind New York City skyscrapers	235
		Varied route that passes the Fiery Furnace fins and grasslands, threads through an arch and crosses slickrock	236
		Gravel loop that goes beneath three massive arches that frame stunning views	234

Canyon (p169), on USFS land outside Bryce Canyon. For safe biking tips, see p286.

You'll find outdoor outfitters and bicycle shops offering rentals and guided trips outside all of the national parks. **Cycling Escapes** (☎ 714-267-4591; www.cyclingescapes.com) offers multi-day road-cycling tours of southern Utah, usually departing in spring and fall.

HORSEBACK RIDING & PACK TRIPS

What, come out West and not ride a horse? Well, saddle up, pardner!

Canyon Trail Rides (☎ 435-679-8665; www.canyonrides.com) runs horseback and mule rides at Zion (p119), Bryce Canyon (p163) and the Grand Canyon's

DESERT ETIQUETTE

The desert is an exceedingly fragile environment, easily damaged by feet, tires and fires, and slow to heal. Even relatively small environmental changes can have long-lasting ramifications, as the margin between life and death is so thin for desert plants and animals.

Visitors to southern Utah should consider themselves its caretakers. Enjoy the desert, but leave it at least as healthy as it was when you arrived by following these simple guidelines. For more information, contact **Leave No Trace** (www.lnt.org).

- Stay on the trail, whether hiking, biking or driving. If it's muddy, either don't go or be willing to get dirty – it's better than creating wider, braided trails.
- If there is no trail, stay on slickrock, gravel or sand; never step or ride on plants or cryptobiotic soil.
- Pack it in, pack it out: bring resealable plastic bags to contain used wrappers and toilet paper; consider using a human-waste containment bag if camping.
- If camping, place your tent on established sites or durable surfaces, like bare dirt or slickrock.
- Protect all water sources and riparian areas: camp 200ft from any water, never wash yourself or dishes in creeks or springs and use minimal or no soap.
- Backcountry fires are usually prohibited and should be avoided even when allowed; use a self-contained camp stove instead.
- Never touch, move or take any cultural or archaeological artifacts; do not enter ruins and do not make rubbings, trace, repaint or otherwise deface petroglyphs or pictographs (for more about protecting rock art, see p78).

DID YOU KNOW?

You can bring along your own horses, mules or burros on day or overnight rides in all of southern Utah's national parks; see p58.

North Rim (p192). One- and two-hour rides and half-day trips cost from $40 to $75 per person. Some rides are offered year-round, although Grand Canyon trips are only available from mid-May to mid-October. You'll need to make reservations in advance, especially for the popular half-day mule rides down into the Grand Canyon. Children must be at least seven years old, while half-day rides only allow those 10 and over. The weight limit is 220 pounds per rider fully dressed.

Several outfitters can get you on horseback for rides in Red Canyon (p170), a former Wild West hideout of Butch Cassidy in the Dixie National Forest west of Bryce Canyon, as well as around Capitol Reef (p207) and into Grand Staircase-Escalante starting from Boulder (p189) and Kanab (p191). Nor will Moab (p252) outfitters and ranches disappoint; they can take you into the desert and La Sal Mountains, and some run trips that combine horseback riding with river running – not at the same time, naturally.

Red Rock Ride (☎ 435-679-8665; www.redrockride.com) offers week-long all-inclusive guided horseback trips visiting Zion, Bryce Canyon and the Grand Canyon's North Rim, Red Canyon in the Dixie National Forest and Paria Canyon in Grand Staircase-Escalante National Monument. Trips usually depart in spring and fall.

Backcountry Adventures Utah: The Ultimate Guide to the Utah Backcountry for Anyone with a Sport Utility Vehicle (2006) by Peter Massey is a very good, detailed 4WD guide, with trip mileage markers and GPS coordinates.

FOUR-WHEEL DRIVING

Southern Utah boasts dirt roads aplenty, and a 4WD vehicle is useful on all of them. The region also has many dirt roads – some of which are legendary – that are *only* manageable via 4WD. Yet if there's one piece of equipment that can get the inexperienced into trouble faster than a static canyoneering rope, it's a 4WD vehicle. A rental 4WD (see p274) is not a magic bullet; sometimes it's just a means for getting as far away from help as possible.

Before heading into the desert, know the capabilities of your vehicle. If you don't have the winches and experience to free a stuck vehicle, don't take chances on unknown roads. And before heading out, get current road and weather conditions from visitor centers and public lands information offices. GPS is delightful, but it's useless in a muddy wash with a storm coming. Expect that 4WD roads may be muddy and inaccessible for at least a day or two after even light rains, so wait until the road thoroughly dries out to tackle it. In winter, many 4WD roads in southern Utah may be impassable, especially when snow shuts in higher elevations. If you've never driven back roads in Utah before, consider taking a guided tour first – it's a good reality check.

Almost all roads in Grand Staircase-Escalante qualify as 4WD roads. The main roads, parts of which may be passable by 2WD passenger cars during dry conditions, are good for beginners, as they're fairly straightforward and see a decent amount of traffic. From east of Bryce Canyon,

Zion: Canyoneering (2006) by Tom Jones is a great guide for do-it-yourself canyoneering, with dozens of accurate, helpful off-trail hiking and technical canyoneering descriptions, and plenty of safety warnings and tips for avoiding accidents.

CANYONEERING

While Europeans have been wild about canyoneering for years, it's just now starting to catch on seriously in the US. One reason canyoneering is so popular is that it's relatively easy to learn, at least compared to rock climbing. Nothing is more thrilling than roping up and making your first descent through a twisting, narrow slot canyon, then swimming in icy waters to get an up-close look at southern Utah's hidden geologic wonders. Simply put, it's a rush.

Bear in mind that the recent flood of inexperienced canyoneers has been largely responsible for an increase in the number of rescues at Zion and elsewhere. Rappelling, it turns out, is a particularly easy way to put yourself into situations you're not experienced enough to get out of. Canyoneers must also be especially mindful of flash floods. Being inside the cogs and wheels of Earth's geological machinery is very cool until they switch on.

Canyoneering in Zion

Zion and its environs are the sport's epicenter in southern Utah. Before attempting any of the park's canyoneering routes unaided, it's smart to take a basic skills class or, at minimum, hire a guide to accompany you. The most famous routes for first-timers are the **Subway** (p113), aka the North Fork of the Virgin River, and **Orderville Canyon** (p118), which dumps you out in the Narrows. Canyoneers with more experience and the necessary technical skills can tackle easy-access **Mystery Canyon** (p118), another route that drops dramatically into the Virgin River.

Southern Utah's Other Canyons

You'll also find fantastic slot canyons along the **Escalante River** and **Hole-in-the-Rock Road** (p178) in Grand Staircase-Escalante National Monument. Routes include canyons for all skill levels, but getting lost is fairly easy, so consider going with a guide. The **Paria Canyon-Vermilion Cliffs Wilderness Area** (p194) is another awesome place for experienced canyoneers to explore, whether you're looking for a one-day slot-canyon challenge or an epic five-day canyoneering adventure through Paria Canyon to Lees Ferry, Arizona (permit required). Ask outfitters in Moab (p252) about more slot canyons in that region, including the wonderland of the **San Rafael Swell**, northwest of Moab off I-70, just west of the town of Green River.

Canyoneering Guides & Outfitters

In addition to outfitters recommended in the destination chapters, the **American Canyoneering Association** (ACA; www.canyoneering.net) offers lots of information online, from technical forums and canyoneering primers to guide referrals. ACA also runs a multitude of canyoneering courses across southern Utah, including in Cedar City, Escalante and Moab. For more informal advice and regional overviews, browse **Tom's Utah Canyoneering Guide** (www.canyoneeringusa.com/utah) online.

Canyoneering 1, 2 and *3* by Steve Allen are three top-notch guidebooks that cover southern Utah, particularly Grand Staircase-Escalante National Monument and the San Rafael Swell. Michael Kelsey has written several canyoneering guides, both for technical and nontechnical enthusiasts alike.

Skutumpah Road (p179) leads past multihued cliffs, while **Johnson Canyon Road** (p179) passes by the famous Grosvenor Arch to Paria Canyon. **Hole-in-the-Rock Road** (p178) is a gob-stopping pioneer route that visits the Devils Garden of rocks and a few slot canyons. Dozens of rough spurs and tracks branch off these roads, but unless you're an expert who's been here before, avoid them.

Utah Byways: 65 of Utah's Best Backcountry Drives (2006) is an essential spiral-bound 4WD guide that covers Arches and Canyonlands National Parks, Grand Staircase-Escalante National Monument, Glen Canyon National Recreation Area, Moab's La Sal Mountains and more.

Near Bryce Canyon, the Dixie National Forest, north of Hwy 12, has some good, mountainous 4WD roads. Capitol Reef offers several great roads, including the **Cathedral Valley Loop** (p201) and the **Burr Trail** (p177), which starts off paved inside Grand Staircase-Escalante National Monument, eventually becoming dirt and dropping down dramatic switchbacks to connect with **Notom-Bullfrog Road** (p199), leading all the way to Bullfrog Marina inside Glen Canyon National Recreation Area. Many of the best-known 4WD roads in southern Utah are found around Moab and nearby Canyonlands National Park. At Canyonlands' Island in the Sky, the **White Rim Road** (p221) is an epic multiday adventure (permit required), while the Needles contains more than 50 miles of 4WD roads (overnight and some day permits required), including the technical **Elephant Hill** (p226). The **Maze** (p227) is unbelievable, but it's only for hard-core, experienced 4WD pros. Around Moab, check out **Hurrah Pass Road** (p244) and, if you dare, **Hell's Revenge** (p251), among others. Arches National Park also has a couple of 4WD roads, best for solitude and views.

DID YOU KNOW?

Several 4WD roads in southern Utah follow the routes originally traveled by 19th-century Mormon settlers, including Grand Staircase-Escalante's incredible Hole-in-the-Rock Rd (p178).

See the boxed text on p46 for essential Leave No Trace guidelines. Remember, nothing ruins the desert's fragile cryptobiotic soil – which holds the entire ecosystem together – faster than car tires, and a single off-road joyride leaves harmful scars that can last decades.

SWIMMING & TUBING

Shocking but true – swimming options are limited in southern Utah's desert. Though great for rafting, the Colorado and Green Rivers near Moab are lousy places to swim; even at their mellowest, the currents are dangerously strong for swimmers. Zion's **Virgin River** (p119) is better. While generally shallow and cold, it does offer lots of swimming holes and warms up just enough later in summer to enjoy a dip. Tubing is prohibited within the park, but outfitters in Springdale rent inner tubes for popular local floats. You'll find more summer swimming holes along creeks in **Capitol Reef** (p208), as well as at **Calf Creek Recreation Area** (p177), where families can splash around and take a break from Grand Staircase-Escalante's dusty 4WD tracks.

EXTREME SPORTS

Bored? Need a thrill? Experts can try these:

- Climb **Prodigal Son**, **Space Shot** or one of Zion's other big walls (p118)
- Canyoneer and through-hike the **Subway** (p113) in Zion Canyon
- Raft **Cataract Canyon** (p250) on the Colorado River
- Four-wheel drive **Elephant Hill** (p226) in Canyonlands' Needles district
- Mountain bike Moab's famous **Slickrock Bike Trail** (p247)
- Kayak the **Narrows** (p120) of the Virgin River
- Four-wheel drive the **Cathedral Valley Loop** (p201) in Capitol Reef
- Canyoneer and backpack **Paria Canyon** (p194) to Lees Ferry, Arizona
- Skydive out of an airplane in **Moab** (p253)
- Trek from rim to rim in the **Grand Canyon** (p192)

TIPS FOR SHUTTERBUGS

Nothing is more disappointing than coming home from the desert and uploading your digital photos or getting your rolls of film developed to find dozens, if not hundreds of washed-out horizons, with tiny friends and family squint-smiling in the distance.

You're not alone. Even the best photographers can't get the whole desert in their pictures. But you can improve the quality and composition of your photos, whether your camera is a top-shelf digital masterpiece or a disposable throwaway.

If you have a digital camera, bring extra batteries and a charger; the instant gratification of your LCD preview screen will run the battery down fast.

- For print film, use 100 ASA film for all but the lowest light situations; it's the slowest film, and will enhance resolution. Color slide film is the best, though it's more expensive.
- A zoom lens is extremely useful; most SLR cameras have one. Use it to isolate the central subject of your photos. A common composition mistake is to include too much landscape around the person, or feature that's your main focus. Sacrifice background for foreground, and your photos will be more dramatic and interesting.
- Morning and evening are the best times to shoot. The same sandstone bluff can turn four or five different hues throughout the day, and the warmest hues will be at sunset. Because of the way a camera reads color (as grays), underexposing the shot slightly (by a half-stop or more) can bring out richer details in red tones.
- When shooting red rocks, a warming filter added to an SLR lens can enhance the colors of the rocks and reduce the blues of overcast or flat-light days. You can achieve the same affect on any digital camera by adjusting the white balance to the automatic 'cloudy' setting (or by reducing the color temperature).
- As a rule, don't shoot into the sun or include it in the frame; shoot what the sunlight is hitting. This is especially important when photographing people, who will turn into blackened silhouettes with the sun behind them. On bright days, move your subjects into shade for close-up portraits.
- A tripod is useful for low-exposure dusk shots but is cumbersome on hikes.
- Some digital cameras have waterproof cases that are worth the investment for canyoneers and river runners.
- That endless horizon? Move people out of the way and shoot it at sunset's last gasp. Check the weather report for sunset times, as well as when the moon rises. If you're traveling during a full moon, it can be fairly easy to arrange yourself in front of an iconic arch at dusk for that million-dollar shot.

For an in-depth regional photography guide, *Photographing the Southwest, Volume 1: Southern Utah* by Laurent Martres will take you around the national parks and off the beaten path. For photography classes, see p263.

KAYAKING, CANOEING & RAFTING

Folks with desert river-running fantasies of bashing through rapids should head directly to Moab (p249). The main white-water rafting season runs from April to September (jet-boating season lasts longer), with peak water flow usually occurring in May and June. Whatever your skill level, outfitters in Moab stand ready to provide everything you might need, from rental equipment, permits and shuttles to guided tours and lessons.

Moab offers an almost overwhelming number of types of river trips, from family-friendly floats and mellow flat-water canoe trips to daredevil rapids-rafting and jet-boating tours. For the calmest trips, rent equipment and paddle the upper portion of the Green River through **Labyrinth** and **Stillwater Canyons** (p251), starting from the town of Green River; or the **Daily** (p250), aka Fisher Towers, a section of the Colorado River alongside Hwy 128. More adventurous trips through Canyonlands National Park require a permit, and the easiest way to get one is to join a guided trip. If you are serious about white-water rafting, try **Westwater Canyon** (p250) for a one-day trip. Multiday trips will take you down the Green or Colorado Rivers, past the Confluence and into **Cataract Canyon** (p250), the region's ultimate challenge when it comes to technical white water.

The Utah Travel Council (www.utah.com/raft) provides free online tips for paddling and rafting trips, including a clickable map of rivers and detailed descriptions of popular routes.

Zion's **Virgin River** is too shallow for watercraft, except for the few days each year when kayakers are permitted (see p120).

FISHING

Utah is an anglers' paradise, offering scads of mountain lakes and rivers and oodles of stocked reservoirs, but not too many options exist in southern Utah, and the national parks are awful for fishing. C'mon, what'd you expect? It's a desert.

The mountains surrounding Zion harbor several good reservoirs stocked mostly with trout, including **Kolob Reservoir** (p100), off Kolob Terrace Rd; **Navajo Lake** (p135) and **Duck Creek** (p135) on Hwy 14, between Cedar City and Bryce Canyon; the reservoir in the **Pine Valley Mountains** (p132), outside St George; and **Panguitch Lake**, between Panguitch and Cedar Breaks National Monument, in the Dixie National Forest. Off Hwy 12 north of Boulder, **Boulder Mountain** is a popular fly-fishing destination; you'll find outfitters in Torrey. Near Moab, the **La Sal Mountains** (p243) harbor a few good trout-fishing lakes, while fly fishers can cast lines into small Mill Creek, which runs out of the mountains.

Utah's Division of Wildlife Resources (DWR) website offers free weekly fishing reports, including specifically for southern Utah, online at http://wildlife.utah.gov/hotspots/reports_sr.php.

Wherever you fish, including in the national parks, you'll need a Utah fishing license. Be sure to familiarize yourself with each fishing spot's particular restrictions. These vary and can be strict, limiting the type of bait or lure and the catch, sometimes to only one fish. Seasonal restrictions may also apply. All park visitor centers and public lands information offices in southern Utah should have the fishing information you'll need, including local regulations.

Contact the **Utah Division of Wildlife Resources** (DWR; ☎ 800-221-0659; www.wildlife.utah.gov) for up-to-date fishing regulations, including the state's annual fishing guidebook, available online as a free downloadable PDF. A resident/nonresident Utah fishing license costs $8/12 for one day and $26/32 for seven days; discounts are available for seniors citizens

TOP 10 COOLEST PLACES IN SUMMER

It's the desert – you know it's gonna be hot. To forget about the heat, escape to the following:

- Swimming holes on the Virgin River (p119)
- The Narrows (p104) of Zion Canyon
- High-elevation Cedar Breaks National Monument (p135)
- Sand Hollow Aquatic Center (p130) in St George
- Pine Valley Mountains (p132) outside St George
- Calf Creek Recreation Area (p177), especially Lower or Upper Calf Creek Falls
- Creeks winding through Capitol Reef National Park (p208)
- The shady pioneer-planted orchards of Fruita (p198), in Capitol Reef National Park
- Moab's lofty La Sal Mountains (p243)
- Lazy float trips or paddling a canoe or kayak on the Colorado and Green Rivers (p249), near Moab

ACTIVITIES

WATCHING WILDLIFE

Southern Utah is home to some fabulous wildlife. Zion protects mountain lions, bighorn sheep and nesting peregrine falcons, while Bryce is known for its 'towns' of endangered Utah prairie dogs. Bighorn sheep have been reintroduced into Canyonlands, and California condors now soar over the Grand Canyon and southern Utah. Almost anywhere it's possible to see coyotes and eagles, rattlesnakes and bats – though you have to be very lucky. Most of those desert species are very secretive, extremely rare or both.

More common are tame mule deer, proud cawing ravens and begging squirrels and chipmunks. Refrain from feeding these animals; they can carry disease, and if they become dependent on handouts, they will not survive in the wild. Feeding wildlife, even innocent-looking squirrels, also encourages the animals to act aggressively toward humans. For example, a few park visitors have been bitten by aggro squirrels along Zion's Riverside Walk.

One of the most satisfying activities is bird-watching: Utah is perched on a major migratory flyway. Ask at park visitor centers for free birding checklists. Park bookstores also sell helpful field guides for amateur to expert birders. Based out of St George, the **National Audubon Society's Red Cliffs Chapter** (☎ 435-673-0996; www.redcliffsaudubon.org) offers online birding reports, photographs, festival information and field trips for members.

To learn more about southern Utah's wildlife, turn to p64. Don't forget to bring binoculars!

and youth. Children under the age of 12 do not need a fishing license, although they must still obey all regulations. Licenses may be bought online or over the phone directly from DWR, or from local businesses near busy fishing spots.

WINTER ACTIVITIES

Baby, when it's cold outside, don't worry: there's still plenty to do in southern Utah. Several spots offer cross-country skiing and snowshoeing. Among the most popular is **Bryce Canyon** (p164), which features 10 miles of cross-country trails atop the canyon's rim, plus 20 miles more in the surrounding Dixie National Forest. During winter, park rangers offer guided snowshoe hikes, with free snowshoes loaned to participants. Otherwise, you can rent showshoes and skis at **Ruby's Inn** (p164), which also offers winter sleigh and horseback rides and snowmobiling tours outside the park. For the most fun in the snow, show up for the **Bryce Canyon Winter Festival** (p150), held annually in mid-February, featuring outdoor sports clinics, tours, ski races and competitions, as well as snow sculptures and sledding.

If you have your own skis, cross-country skiing is popular in the mountains east of Cedar City along **Highway 14** (p135). Visitors can also ski or snowshoe on Zion's **Kolob Terrace** and **Canyons Roads** (p121) and the scenic amphitheater rim at **Cedar Breaks** (p135), where a volunteer-staffed seasonal yurt lets you warm up with a cup of hot cocoa. The **La Sal Mountains** (p253) outside Moab feature great snowshoeing and cross-country skiing and even a hut-to-hut system. Outdoor outfitters in Moab rent equipment, sell maps and cold-weather gear, and can arrange self-guided overnight trips.

The only downhill skiing in the region is at **Brian Head** (p136), near Cedar City – that said, it's pretty good, with 65 trails, four terrain parks and two lifts on Navajo Mountain and Giant Steps Mountain, which both summit over 10,000ft. The winter sports season usually runs from mid-November until mid-April, when it offers opportunities for skiing, snowboarding, tubing and more. Rental equipment, lessons, outdoor

DID YOU KNOW?

Skiing off the rim down into Bryce Canyon is illegal, but when snows are deep enough, cross-country skiers can reach the bottom of Bryce's amphitheater by starting outside Tropic.

RANGER PROGRAMS

Every national park sponsors free ranger talks, guided hikes and evening programs that cover topics of main interest to visitors – geology, wildlife, ecology, human history and more.

Zion (p119) and Bryce Canyon (p163) boast the widest range of talks and activities. Zion offers ranger-guided park shuttle tours (sign up in person the day before at the visitor center) while Bryce features popular stargazing programs and full-moon and showshoe hikes (for the latter, sign up in person at the visitor center). Night skies here are among the darkest in North America – don't miss the chance to admire them.

Arches (p238) offers a very popular ranger-led hike into the Fiery Furnace. It's a hair-raising trip across slickrock, along narrow ledges and over vertiginous cracks. Reservations are required, and you can make them online months in advance. In spring and fall, Canyonlands rangers lead guided hikes around Horseshoe Canyon (see p227), while summer brings guided walks, talks and evening campfire programs to Capitol Reef (p208).

You can check what's going on during your trip in the free newspaper brochures handed out at entrance fee stations, or by stopping by any park visitor center or information desk. You can also check schedules online via some parks' websites (see p23).

To find out all about the national parks' junior ranger programs (which truthfully can be fun for all ages!), see p56.

clothing and gear shops, dining and lodging are all available at the full-service resort.

Ski Utah (www.skiutah.com) has updated snow reports, detailed statistics and helpful travel info and deals for skiing statewide, including at Brian Head and around Bryce Canyon.

Kids & Pets

You've stuffed the bags and car with sunscreen, Frisbee, cooler, water sandals, hiking boots and hats. You've expounded eloquently to the kids about the age of dinosaurs and the geology of the Grand Staircase, and have read books about Mormons, miners, cowboys and cowgirls. You've watched John Ford movies and have patiently explained that, yes, roadrunners really do exist and, no, they don't say 'beep-beep.' You've got a plan, an itinerary, a schedule.

But now you've been in the car for hours, and the whining and bickering in the backseat is giving you a headache. You remember that person at the gas station talking about petroglyphs out here somewhere, so you turn down a road you think she mentioned, and soon the pavement ends. A creek runs along the dirt road, and cottonwoods shade your drive. You pull over, pile out, stretch. One kid digs out the fly rod, the dog cautiously approaches the shallow water. Hours pass, and you never do find those petroglyphs. In fact, you don't do much of anything. And it's amazingly fun.

No, you probably won't make it to that national park tomorrow and no, you definitely won't pull into a motel in time for dinner and a swim. You may not even have a chance to wipe the red dirt off everyone's noses before putting the kids to bed, maybe after carrying their exhausted bodies from the car. We can advise you about where to go and what to do with kids and pets in southern Utah, and there's plenty to recommend. But in the end, it's about the journey, not the destination. Take it slow, and enjoy it all.

For more on traveling with little ones, especially for families who are going on the road together for the first time, check out Lonely Planet's *Travel with Children*.

BRINGING THE KIDS

Southern Utah's national parks are kid-friendly destinations. Zion and Bryce Canyon are particularly accessible for families, offering park lodges, free shuttle buses, kid-centric activities and easy, accessible hikes for everyone. Capitol Reef offers pick-your-own-fruit orchards and free family activity backpacks to borrow, while Arches is terrific place for short walks to scenic lookouts the whole family will appreciate. Canyonlands and Grand Staircase-Escalante are better suited for 4WD and hiking adventures, great for teens with some outdoors experience.

GAMES & ACTIVITIES FOR THE CAR

- *52 Fun Things to Do in a Car* by Lynn Gordon – a deck of cards, each with a different game or activity
- *Best Travel Activity Book Ever* – coloring and pencil games book, published by Rand McNally
- *Kids' Road Atlas* – educational fun for older kids, also from Rand McNally
- *Kids Travel: A Backseat Survival Kit* – spiral-bound all-in-one activity guide, from the Klutz editors
- *Mad Libs* – classic fill-in-the-blank word game, now available as an iPhone app
- *Regal Travel Auto Bingo Game Card* – old-fashioned sliding-window bingo cards, just like when you were a kid
- *TravelMates: Fun Games Kids Can Play in the Car or on the Go – No Materials Needed* by Story Evans and Lise O'Haire – out of print, but worth tracking down, especially if you've got more than one child

DID YOU KNOW?

Many Las Vegas hotel pools have height restrictions and are only open seasonally, so ask when making reservations to avoid disappointing the kids later.

One important thing to remember is that children are particularly vulnerable to the heat; they dehydrate faster, and symptoms can turn severe more quickly. Make sure they drink plenty of water, whether they've been active or not. For more tips on staying safe and healthy, see p279.

Utah's local culture (influenced by Mormonism) is very family-oriented. Both parents and children will find lots of impromptu companionship from locals and fellow travelers. Most businesses welcome children. Restaurants usually have booster seats; some also have crayons and coloring pages, as well as a special kids' menu. If not, ask your server if the kitchen can make a simple kids' meal – most will do so without a fuss. Throughout southern Utah, you'll also find touristy chuckwagon dinners, featuring cowboy shoot-outs and entertainment, and Western rodeo events, including at Ruby's Inn (p150) near Bryce Canyon.

Accommodations may charge for an extra bed or roll-away cot to be brought into your room, even if they advertise 'kids sleep free.' A Pack 'n Play or child-sized inflatable mattress will fit into most motel and hotel rooms. If you need a babysitter or child-care services, ask at the front desk or call a local tourist information office for recommendations. Many B&Bs don't allow children, especially those under 12 years of age.

DID YOU KNOW?

Bathrooms are few and far between on southern Utah's byways. Prepare kids for the possibility of potty stops behind a cactus, and always bring toilet paper.

On the road, Utah state law requires children under eight years old to sit in a car seat or booster. The only exception is for children taller than 57in; they may use the car seat belt alone. If you're renting a car (p273), reserve a child safety seat well in advance; expect to pay around $10/50 per day/week.

When it comes to things to see and do, children and families often enjoy discounted admission at museums and other attractions outside the parks. Whether you pay each national park entry fee separately or buy an annual America the Beautiful pass (p264), it'll cover two adults and all children under 16. Wherever outdoor-activity equipment (eg bicycles or inner tubes) is rented, child-sized gear is typically available, too.

Keep in mind that most of southern Utah's park gateway towns do not have large supermarkets or chain stores. Plan ahead and stock up on supplies for babies and toddlers at the start of your trip in urban areas like St George, Las Vegas or Salt Lake City.

An outdoor-activity book and fun field guide for all ages, the colorful *Redrock Canyon Explorer*, written and illustrated by Irene Brady, takes kids on a 'virtual visit to an imaginary canyon' in the Southwest.

Fun Stuff for Families

To find family-oriented sights, activities, lodgings, restaurants and more, just look for the child-friendly icon (🚸) with listings throughout this guide. Online, check out the 'For Kids' section of each national park's website (see p23). For more ideas, browse the Activities chapter (p36), which highlights southern Utah's best outdoor opportunities, from hikes for the little 'uns to canyoneering challenges for teens.

Many ranger-led programs and activities are appropriate for all ages and don't usually require reservations. Otherwise, book well in advance for backcountry hiking and camping permits, guided activities and tours (especially canyoneering classes and river-rafting trips), as well as educational field trips and volunteer opportunities offered by the parks' nonprofit natural history associations (p263).

A final word of advice: try not to squeeze too much in. Endless hours in the car rushing from overlook to overlook, sight to sight, can result in grumpy, tired kids and frustrated parents. After a while, canyon views start to look alike, and the trip can become a blur. Stop often and stay flexible.

HIKING

All of southern Utah's' national parks feature easy nature trails leading to awesome viewpoints and bizarre geological formations that will rate high on most kids' interest meters. Refer to the 'Easy Hikes' and 'Day Hikes' sections of each destination chapter, where the best trails for kids are described. Parents should gauge their children's abilities and choose hikes that won't overwhelm them. Never let your children, whether toddlers or teens, run loose on exposed trails or near cliff edges. Even short falls can be deadly. Also remember that altitude and the harsh desert environment can take a toll on children more quickly than adults. If you're carrying wee ones, choose a baby backpack with built-in shade. For more hiking safety tips, see p283.

Ever more outdoor-activity books are geared toward families. *The Sierra Club Family Outdoors Guide* by Marlyn Doan, is comprehensive, and it's useful for parents who are new to the outdoors themselves.

CYCLING & MOUNTAIN BIKING

Families can rent bikes in some park gateway towns, or bring their own from home. In Zion Canyon, the **Pa'rus Trail** (p101) is a paved recreational path and is one of the few park trails open to bikes. Zion Canyon's scenic drive is also a fun bike ride in reverse (p116); whenever you get tired, just hop back on the free park shuttle (maximum two bicycles per bus). There's a paved recreational cycling path running west of Bryce Canyon to Red Canyon (p170) and bike paths in the town of Moab. For safe biking tips, see p286. For more about mountain biking in southern Utah, see p43.

Best Hikes with Children: Utah by Maureen Keilty offers thoughtful advice for getting your kids excited about hiking and keeping them safe on the trail, including in southern Utah's national parks.

HISTORICAL SITES

Southern Utah is filled with Old West ghost towns and petroglyph panels that will fascinate kids of all ages. Among the former are **Grafton** (p95), outside Zion; Silver Reef, off I-15 between St George and Cedar City; and **Pahreah** (p89), in Grand Staircase-Escalante National Monument. Also worth visiting with kids is Kanab's **Frontier Movie Town Museum & Trading Post** (p191), with its Western movie sets, costume shop and mock gunfights. To find Native American petroglyph panels, ask at park visitor centers; some of the most easily accessible are inside Zion (see the boxed text, p98) and Capitol Reef (p200).

HORSEBACK RIDING

Guided trail rides around Zion (p119), Bryce Canyon (p163), the Grand Canyon's North Rim (p192), Boulder (p189), Kanab (p191), Capitol Reef (p207) and Moab (p252) are winning activities for the whole family,

TOP 10 FAMILY-FRIENDLY HIKES

- Riverside Walk (Zion National Park; p101)
- Emerald Pools (Zion National Park; p103)
- Jenny's Canyon (Snow Canyon State Park; p132)
- Mossy Cave (Bryce Canyon National Park; p153)
- Queen's Garden (Bryce Canyon National Park; p155)
- Lower Calf Creek Falls (Grand Staircase-Escalante National Monument; p181)
- Hickman Bridge (Capitol Reef National Park; p203)
- Cave Spring Trail (Canyonlands National Park; p223)
- Sand Dune & Broken Arches (Arches National Park; p236)
- Moonflower Canyon (Moab; p246)

specially if you want to get in the Western spirit of things. Note that the minimum age for kids is usually seven or 10 years of age. For more about guided horseback rides and pack trips, see p45. If you're bringing your own horses, see p58.

101 Questions About Desert Life by Alice Jablonsky is an educational little Q&A book with colorful illustrations. It helps kids explore desert ecosystems, investigating everything from why coyotes howl to whether roadrunners fly.

JUNIOR RANGER PROGRAMS & NATURE CENTERS

All of southern Utah's national parks offer **junior ranger programs** (www.nps.gov/learn), which focus on do-it-yourself activity books (typically costing just a few dollars) that kids can complete to get a special certificate and junior ranger badge. Of course, there's no age limit, and even adults can learn something and have fun doing the activities with their kids. For younger children, an easier activity sheet may be available for free – just ask.

In summer, Zion offers a drop-off junior ranger program at the **Zion Nature Center** (p119), where children join instructor-led activities, hikes and games. Capitol Reef has its own **Ripple Rock Nature Center** (p208), which hosts ranger-led programs for kids; borrow a free activity backpack for families here or at the park's main visitor center. Canyonlands also lets families borrow activity-based 'Explorer Packs' (p226).

WATER SPORTS

Summers in southern Utah are really hot. You can let the kids splash around and cool off in Zion's Virgin River (p119) or Capitol Reef's Fremont River (p208), but only once the spring snowmelt has run off and water levels are safe again. Ask at park visitor centers about current conditions and the best swimming holes. Outside Zion in Springdale, kids will love inner-tubing (p119) on the Virgin River, while the city of St George offers the indoor **Sand Hollow Aquatic Center** (p130). Off Hwy 12, **Escalante Petrified Forest State Park** (p186) has a small reservoir for swimming. The Colorado and Green Rivers outside Moab are not OK for swimming, but families can paddle a canoe or kayak, take a gentle float trip or even go white-water rafting (p249).

WINTER SPORTS

In winter, Bryce Canyon (p164) is a magical place for families to go snowshoeing or cross-country skiing, with more trails nearby in Red

INDOOR FAMILY FUN

Let's face it: sometimes summer in southern Utah is just too darn hot. But you don't have to stay inside your hotel room just to keep cool. It's the perfect excuse to try some of those indoor activities and attractions you otherwise might have missed.

Inside the parks, the **Zion Nature Center** (p119) and Capitol Reef's **Ripple Rock Nature Center** (p208) offer great indoor activities for kids during summer, including special ranger-led programs. Or hide out for a while in the **Zion Lodge** (p122) or the **Bryce Canyon Lodge** (p165), which have cozy common areas where kids can curl up with a good book or the whole family can play cards or board games. Zion's **Human History Museum** (p96) has indoor exhibits and shows a short, family-friendly park orientation movie, as do most other national park visitor centers.

You'll find much more to do on rainy days in gateway towns outside the parks. In St George, the **Dinosaur Discovery Site** (p128) is a cool place for kids to see real fossils, including dinosaur tracks, while the indoor **Sand Hollow Aquatic Center** (p130) is a great place to while away a lazy afternoon. So is the **Bryce Museum** (p169), with its stuffed wildlife dioramas. **Moqui Cave** (p191) near Kanab and **Hole 'n the Rock** (p242) outside Moab are both shameless tourist traps, but fun nonetheless (not to mention cooler inside). You'll find movie theaters in St George, Moab, Springdale, Kanab and the tiny town of Bicknell, northwest of Capitol Reef.

Canyon; rental equipment is available from Ruby's Inn (p150). The La Sal Mountains (p253) outside Moab are also popular for snow sports. The only downhill (alpine) skiing in southern Utah is at Brian Head (p136), a family-friendly resort offering equipment rentals, lessons and a snow-tubing park.

Canyonlands' website (www.nps.gov/cany/forkids) has printable coloring pages, games and educational activities to fuel kids' excitement, while Bryce Canyon's website (www.nps.gov/brca/forkids) offers online games and quizzes.

BRINGING THE PETS

Pets are allowed in southern Utah's national parks, but under a lot of restrictions (exceptions are made for service animals; see p269). Pets aren't allowed on any national park trails (Zion's Pa'rus Trail is the lone exception), at scenic viewpoints or in the backcountry. Remember that these rules are in place to protect the park's flora and fauna, and also to keep your best friend from getting hurt.

Pets are not allowed on any park shuttles. They *are* allowed in national park campgrounds and outside of cars on main roads. Dogs must remain on a 6ft-long leash and be accompanied by a person at all times. If you leave your dog tied up unattended at a park campground, you'll be cited by rangers. Pets may be left alone inside RVs during the day (keep those windows open!), but they may not be left in cars. Given summer temperatures, which can quickly become lethal, this is best for your pet's health anyway.

Some of southern Utah's national parks are located near kennels, where dogs and cats can be boarded for a day or overnight, including in Springdale (p91), Bryce Canyon City (p168) and Moab (p256). Contact park visitor centers and tourist information offices for more referrals, including to local veterinarians. If you're spending a long day in the car, vets recommend stopping at least every two hours to let your dog pee, stretch its legs and have a long drink of water.

Some motels and hotels allow pets these days, though many in southern Utah still do not. Those that do may charge extra – anywhere from $10 to $50 – and they might make you put down a hefty credit-card deposit when checking in. Others have weight restrictions – 35lb maximum is standard – and/or do not accept what they call 'aggressive' breeds (eg pit bulls, rottweilers). To avoid any unpleasant surprises, call in advance to check a property's pet policies, especially at independently owned lodgings. **Best Western** (☎ 800-780-7234; www.bestwestern.com) is the most friendly of the chains toward dogs, often with no weight limits or extra fees. **Motel 6** (☎ 800-466-8356; www.motel6.com) is another pet-accepting chain, typically charging a $10 nightly fee.

The Humane Society website (www.humanesociety.org) has a searchable database of helpful articles for pet owners, including the basics of how to travel safely and happily on long road trips.

Dog-Friendly Areas

To find places that welcome pets, including lodgings and restaurants, look for the pet-friendly icon (🐾) throughout this guide. In Grand Staircase-Escalante National Monument, Utah's state parks, national forests and Bureau of Land Management (BLM) lands, dogs are usually allowed on hiking trails and in the backcountry, except in specially designated wilderness areas. That said, think twice before taking your pets on desert hikes in the summer – it's excruciatingly hot and sand can burn tender paws – and always bring a water bowl. If you're camping, you'll need extra blankets year-round, as desert nights can be cold even after scorching summer days.

Outside the parks, southern Utah can be a pet-friendly travel destination, as long as you pay attention to a couple of rules. Don't immediately tie your dog up outside the first restaurant or cafe that you see. Instead, ask about local laws, to avoid ending up with a ticket. Some shops do allow dogs (often they'll post a note on the door or window saying so), or they might have a water bowl for customers' four-legged friends waiting outside.

In southern Utah, Kanab is easily the most pet-friendly town. It's home to **Best Friends Animal Sanctuary** (p191), a no-kill rescue center that's become famous for rehabilitating Michael Vick's pit bulls and for being featured on the popular National Geographic TV show *DogTown*. Many hotels and even a few restaurants allow dogs, while **Willow Canyon Outdoor** (p191) sells outdoor gear for your four-legged friend. Moab is another pet-friendly town, with dog-friendly hiking trails like Corona Arch, Negro Bill Canyon and Fisher Towers (p245). Drop by **Moab Barkery** (☎ 435-259-8080; www.moabbarkery.com; 82 N Main St; open daily, seasonal hours vary) for toys, treats and basic outdoor gear, including cooling vests. Around St George, you'll find off-leash areas for dogs at **JC Snow Park** (900 S 400 East; dawn-dusk) and a complete pet-supply shop, **Petco** (☎ 435-986-9704; 765 W Telegraph St, Washington; 9am-9pm Mon-Sat, 10am-7pm Sun).

Find up-to-date listings of dog-friendly hotels, campgrounds, attractions and more at www.dogfriendly.com.

You won't see too many dogs in Las Vegas, but the city has dozens of doggy day-care, canine spa and boarding facilities; contact the city's tourist information office (p139) or your hotel concierge for referrals. Otherwise, you'll likely have the best luck getting your dog a bed at one of the budget chains – Motel 6 has multiple locations, including near the Strip.

Horse Trails & Equestrian Facilities

You can bring horses, mules and burros into most of southern Utah's national parks, including Zion (p119), Bryce Canyon (p163), Capitol Reef (p207) and Canyonlands. Usually private stock are limited to specially designated trails and/or dirt roads. Stock may not be allowed at all during spring thaws and other periods when they could cause excessive trail damage. In canyon areas, watch out for descents that are steep, rocky and treacherous. Stock must be fed certified weed-free hay for at least 48 hours prior to their trip. Day rides in the national parks usually don't require permits (except in Canyonlands; see p216), but overnight backcountry trips do. Maximum group size is usually six to 12 animals. Consult each national park's website or call their visitor center or backcountry desk directly for updated regulations regarding private stock.

Throughout much of southern Utah, the **Dixie National Forest** (☎ 435-676-2676; www.fs.fed.us/r4/dixie) offers excellent riding opportunities with some trails open to horses and miles of dirt roads, as well as specially designated horse camps. Only certified hay is allowed within the forest. Some guided-tour companies and pack-trip outfitters (see p45) allow customers to bring along their own stock – be sure to ask when making reservations.

Traveling with a horse? Check out www.horsetrip.com, which offers a state-by-state directory of horse-friendly motels, campgrounds, B&Bs, farms and ranches with overnight stables and corrals.

If you're traveling with a horse, only a few lodgings will accept your four-legged friend. These include **Sandcreek RV Park** (p210) and **Cowboy Homestead Cabins** (p211) in Torrey, outside Capitol Reef. Horse-boarding facilities in southern Utah include **Lit'l Bit Ranch** (p191) in Kanab and **Red Cliffs Adventure Lodge** (p257) in Moab.

Environment

Spanning the Four Corners region – where the states of Utah, Colorado, New Mexico and Arizona meet – the Colorado Plateau is a geologic anomaly. Home to one of the world's densest concentrations of spectacularly exposed rock formations, it's a prime destination for geologists and curious travelers alike. In every direction you'll find dramatic evidence of soft, colorful rocks carved by the awesome power of water.

Lyrical and evocative of a beautifully sere landscape, *The Secret Knowledge of Water: Discovering the Essence of the American Desert* (2001) by Craig Childs is required reading for anyone heading out into southern Utah's backcountry wilds.

With few exceptions, however, southern Utah's parks and monuments protect arid desert zones, defined by their absence of water. Only a few mesas and slopes rise high enough to support mountain plants and animals, creating 'sky islands' scattered far and wide in a normally dry sea of desert. This isolation promotes the evolution of unique species, as barriers formed by sheer canyons and rivers separate populations into small groups that cannot interbreed.

Southern Utah's unique and diverse flora and fauna are one of the top reasons for visiting at any time of year. Seasons on the Colorado Plateau are as complex as the rock story of the landscape itself. As desert lowlands erupt into full bloom, towering mesa tops may still be buried under many feet of snow. Even in the same park on the same day, you could encounter a variety of climatic extremes, almost guaranteeing that you'll spot a surprising assortment of wildlife.

THE LAND

Surrounded by land that has been torturously buckled and jumbled over millions of years by the extreme forces of the shifting earth, the Colorado Plateau floats like a raft. Evidence of its long-term stability is readily apparent in the horizontal layers of sediment that have changed little from the day they were laid down. But to the west, thinning and stretching of the Earth's crust has been so vigorous that mountain ranges have collapsed onto their sides and entire valleys have fallen thousands of feet. To the east, colliding forces have crumpled the land to form the Rocky Mountains.

One of the best views of the Grand Staircase lies along Hwy 89A between Kanab, Utah, and Jacob Lake, Arizona, where the steps rise dramatically.

Starting out as a shallow basin collecting sediment from nearby mountains, the entire Colorado Plateau was uplifted some 60 million years ago. At that time, the plateau split along deep cracks called faults. Over time these cracks have eroded to form stupendous cliffs that subdivide the Colorado Plateau into several smaller plateaus. Along the Colorado Plateau's western edge, for example, a line of high, forested plateaus tower 3000ft above desert lowlands and valleys. Nicknamed the High Plateaus by geologist Clarence Dutton in 1880, the term encompasses the flat-topped mesas of Zion and Bryce Canyon National Parks and also Cedar Breaks National Monument.

From an aerial perspective, these lofty plateaus and cliffs form a remarkable staircase that steps down from southern Utah into northern Arizona. Topping this so-called 'Grand Staircase' are the Pink Cliffs of the Claron Formation, so extravagantly exposed in Bryce Canyon. Below them jut the Gray Cliffs of various Cretaceous formations. Next in line are the White Cliffs of Navajo sandstone that make Zion Canyon justly famous. These are followed by the Vermilion Cliffs near Lees Ferry, Arizona, and finally come the Chocolate Cliffs abutting the Kaibab Plateau and Grand Canyon.

Another way of understanding the Grand Staircase is to visualize that the top layers of exposed rock at the Grand Canyon form Zion's basement, and that Zion's top layers in turn form the bottom layers of Bryce Canyon National Park. Geologically speaking, one can imagine the parks as being stacked on top of each other. Hypothetically, a river cutting a canyon at Bryce would eventually form another Zion Canyon, and then over time create another Grand Canyon.

Singing Stone: A Natural History of the Escalante Canyons (1999) by Thomas Fleischner brings the geology of Grand Staircase-Escalante National Monument into understandable, human terms as it examines the land controversies of the New West.

A Four-Act Play

Perhaps the simplest way to approach the geologic story of the Colorado Plateau is to think of it as a four-act play. The first act features sedimentation, followed by lithification, then uplift and, finally, erosion. While this is an oversimplification, and there's overlap between the scenes, it offers a framework for understanding the region's geologic history.

More than 250 million years ago, the Colorado Plateau country was a shallow sea off the west coast of the young North American continent (which at the time was merged with other continents into a giant supercontinent known as Pangea). This time period, known as the Paleozoic Era, marked the dramatic transition from primitive organisms to an explosion of complex life-forms that spread into every available niche – the beginning of life as we know it. Fossils, limestone and other sediments from this era now comprise nearly all exposed rocks in the Grand Canyon, and they form the foundation that underlies all of the Colorado Plateau.

At the close of the Paleozoic, the land rose somewhat and the sea mostly drained away, though it advanced and retreated numerous times during the Mesozoic Era (250 million to 65 million years ago). Sedimentation continued as eroding mountains created deltas and floodplains, and as shallow seas and tidal flats left other deposits. Meanwhile, the rise of an island mountain chain off the coast apparently blocked moisture-bearing storms, and a vast Sahara-like desert developed across the region, piling thousands of feet of sand atop older floodplain sediments. Zion's monumental Navajo sandstone cliffs and Arches' soaring spans of Entrada sandstone preserve evidence of mighty sand dunes.

Think the Grand Canyon is the USA's deepest? It's not. That record is held by Kings Canyon, carved out of California's Sierra Nevada Mountains.

Over millions of years the weight of the accumulated layers (more than 2 miles thick) compacted loosely settled materials into rocks cemented together with mineral deposits – a process called lithification. Sandstone, siltstone and mudstone are each cemented together with calcium carbonate. Variations in particle size and quantities of cement account for these layers' differing strengths – weakly bonded rocks crumble relatively easily in water, while more durable rocks form sheer cliffs and angular blocks.

About 60 million years ago North America began a dramatic separation from Europe, sliding west over another part of the earth's crust and leaving behind an ever-widening gulf in the Atlantic Ocean. This movement caused the continent's leading edge to uplift, forever transforming the face of the continent by raising the Colorado Plateau more than a mile. Though the plateau avoided the geologic turmoil that deformed much of western North America, the forces of uplift did shatter the plateau along fault lines into stair-step subplateaus. Furthermore, the creation of the Rocky Mountains provided headwaters for great rivers that would chisel the newly risen plateau in their rush to the sea.

Armchair explorers can take a virtual field trip to southern Utah, or learn where to find dinosaur tracks, on the Utah Geological Survey's website (http://geology.utah.gov).

In fact, nearly every aspect of the Colorado Plateau landscape is shaped by erosion. Several factors make the forces of erosion particularly dramatic in the Southwest. First are the region's colorful rock layers themselves. As these layers rose, gravity enabled watercourses to gain momentum and carve through stone, while sporadic rainfall and an arid climate ensured the soft layers would otherwise remain intact. These factors have remained consistent over millennia, enabling fragile hoodoos, fins and arches to develop.

Water is by far the most dramatic shaping force. Flash floods tear through soft rock with immense power, tumbling house-sized boulders down narrow slot canyons and scooping out crumbling sediments like pudding. Those who witness summer thunderstorms will notice how quickly desert waters turn rust-red with dissolving sedimentary rock. Zion's Virgin River has been described as 'a red ribbon of liquid sandpaper' due to its relentless downward gouging.

As the rocks' calcium-carbonate cement dissolves in rainwater, it releases sand particles and flows down rock faces, then hardens again as it dries, leaving drippings that look like candle wax – a common feature on rock faces in both Zion and Bryce Canyons. Over time this leaching away of the cement also widens cracks and creates isolated fins that further split and dissolve into hoodoos, windows, arches and other fantastic forms, as seen in all of southern Utah's parks.

In winter, storm erosion works in tandem with another equally powerful force. As rainfall seeps into cracks, it freezes and then expands with incredible pressure (sometimes over 20,000lb per square foot), pushing open crevices and prying loose blocks of stone. At higher elevations such as Bryce Canyon, this freeze-thaw cycle is repeated more than 200 times each year, exacting a tremendous but ultimately beautiful toll on the natural landscape.

Challenging *Basin & Range* (1981) by Pulitzer Prize–winning writer John McPhee is as much about the journey through as the geology of the Great Basin, which covers much of western Utah, Nevada and eastern California.

Reading the Parks

It's a complex geologic tableau that characterizes the national parks of southern Utah, from Arches to Zion. In a sense it's a remarkably homogenous region, but at the same time, the forces of erosion have carved an amazingly intricate and diverse landscape that's difficult to comprehend. Each park and national monument reveals an astonishing geologic story that goes far beyond the scope of this brief introduction.

Roadside Geology of Utah (1990) by Halka Chronic is an invaluable companion for geology buffs, aspiring and otherwise. By the end of your trip, you'll never confuse your Navajo and Entrada sandstones again!

ZION NATIONAL PARK

Part of southern Utah's High Plateaus district, Zion sits on the southwest corner of the Colorado Plateau, marking the transition from relatively stable plateau country to the more tectonically active Great Basin. Separating these distinct regions is a long line of cliffs along the Hurricane Fault.

In Zion Canyon, massive cliffs expose over 2000ft of Navajo sandstone, formed by ancient sand dunes. Nowhere else in the world do these rock

SOUTHERN UTAH'S WEIRDEST ROCKS

The competition is stiff, but for some of the strangest bits of stone you'll ever see, you can't miss the following:

- **Goblin Valley State Park** (p212)
- **Devils Garden** (p179), Grand Staircase-Escalante National Monument
- **Bryce Canyon Amphitheater** (p146)
- **Kodachrome Basin State Park** (p185)
- **The Needles** (p222), Canyonlands National Park
- **Arches National Park** (p229)

formations reach such grand heights. Meanwhile, in the park's Kolob Canyons area, sheer cliffs jut abruptly from the Hurricane Fault as if they rose out of the ground just yesterday. The reddish coloration of all of these cliffs is caused by iron oxides. In the more freshly exposed rocks of Kolob Canyons, the red is evenly distributed. More oxides have leached out of Zion Canyon's ancient weathered cliffs, however, leaving the uppermost layers whitish.

DID YOU KNOW?

Zion's soaring cliffs were once humongous sand dunes – look closely for fine diagonal lines of cross-bedding, the marks of ancient winds that once swept the dunes.

Bisecting the national park, the Virgin River continues its steady march – cutting downward about 1000ft every million years – so rapidly, in fact, that side tributaries can't keep up and are left as hanging valleys high on cliff faces. The dynamic interplay between Navajo sandstone and the underlying Kayenta Formation largely shapes Zion Canyon. Through the Narrows, for example, the Virgin River flows entirely between sandstone walls, but where it cuts deeply enough, the river readily erodes the softer shale underneath the sandstone cliffs and dramatically widens the canyon.

BRYCE CANYON NATIONAL PARK

Bryce is not a canyon at all, but a series of amphitheaters gouged from the gorgeous Pink Cliffs. The park's central Claron Formation results from soft siltstone and mudstone that settled to the bottom of a giant freshwater lake 60 million years ago. Traces of manganese and iron account for this layer's fetching pink and orange hues. About 15 million years ago, the lakebed lifted, cracking from the stress along countless parallel joints, while further east the Aquarius Plateau rose even higher. The significant valley between the plateau and Bryce was carved by the Paria River, which over the past million years has begun to nip at the park's cliffs.

Want to know how things are looking in Zion Canyon today? Click on the Temples and Towers of the Virgin webcam at www.nps.gov/zion/photosmultimedia/webcams.htm.

Bryce features dramatic formations at all stages of development, from newly emerging fins to old weathered hoodoos beaten down into colorful mounds. Runoff along joints on the canyon rim forms parallel gullies with narrow rock walls, or fins, which ultimately erode into the isolated columns known as hoodoos. The layers are so soft that in heavy rains they would quickly dissolve into muddy little mounds, except that siltstone layers alternating with resistant limestone bands give the layers strength as they erode into towering hoodoos. Many hoodoos end up with a cap of harder limestone at their apex, protecting the softer material beneath.

GRAND STAIRCASE-ESCALANTE NATIONAL MONUMENT

This vast, complex region contains examples of nearly every rock type and structural feature found in the Colorado Plateau country. Revealed

DESERT VARNISH

Though the dark shiny coating on countless rock surfaces has borne the name 'desert varnish' for many years, scientists have only recently determined its origins. They originally thought that this golden to blackish iridescent varnish resulted from minerals leached from cliff faces in rainstorms.

Careful analysis has revealed, however, that the likely source is airborne dust sticking to the rock. Bacteria in the dust collect minute amounts of manganese iron, which over very long periods of time are oxidized to coat the rock in a dark varnish. Petroglyphs etched into such varnish thousands of years ago by indigenous peoples still look as fresh as the day they were made – vivid proof of how slowly new varnish accumulates.

Similar dark streaks on some cliff faces are not desert varnish, but tannic acid from coniferous trees on overhanging cliffs, which spills down in runoff from cracks and hanging valleys.

here are more than 200 million years of geologic history and one of the world's most exceptional fossil records of early vertebrate evolution. The entire period that dinosaurs ruled the earth is preserved here in remarkable detail. Grand arches, waterfalls, slot canyons, sculpted sandstone cliffs and challenging terrain make this a memorable place to visit.

The monument encompasses its namesake feature, the Grand Staircase, on its western edge. Over a dozen different geologic layers document Mesozoic seas, sand dunes and slow-moving waters that once teemed with abundant ancient life. Examples are as varied as the lavender, rose, burgundy and peach colors of volcanic ash and petrified forests of the Chinle Formation to the ancient sand dunes preserved in the bluffs of Wingate sandstone at Circle Cliffs.

Few other features characterize this place like the celebrated slot canyons of the Escalante River, carved by fast-moving waters entrenched in resistant sandstone channels that cut downward rather than spreading outward. At their upper ends these canyons modestly wind through the slickrock like tiny veins before feeding into increasingly larger arteries that eventually empty into the Colorado River.

Among the piles of slick picture books, *Water, Rock & Time* (2005) by Robert L Eves stands out. It pairs colorful illustrations and photos with eloquent writing and clear descriptions of Zion's geology, accessible for everyone.

CAPITOL REEF NATIONAL PARK

We've described the Colorado Plateau as floating serenely while all the lands around it are crumpled by the forces of the shifting earth. Capitol Reef is the exception to that rule. Here, along a narrow, 100-mile stretch, the earth's surface is bent in a giant wrinkle, exposing multiple rock formations in tilted and upended strata. This type of step-up feature is known as a monocline, and the Waterpocket Fold is one of the longest contiguously exposed monoclines in the world. Incredibly, the rock layers on the west side have been upended more than 7000ft higher than those to the east. Dubbed a reef by early explorers, who found it a barrier to travel, the fold is capped with bare rounded domes of Navajo sandstone reminiscent of the US Capitol building – hence the name Capitol Reef.

While just a few major canyons cut across the Waterpocket Fold, a baffling maze of side canyons crisscrosses the park in myriad directions. All formed along clefts and other weak points in the rock, where moisture collects (natural pools of water atop the fold account for its name) and eventually scours out ever-expanding gullies. Another sandstone layer, the Wingate Formation, gives the Waterpocket Fold a line of distinctive sheer red cliffs on its west side. A third sandstone layer, Entrada sandstone, forms the freestanding pinnacles and walls of Cathedral Valley.

Other formations add so much color and structural diversity that this park is considered without equal in a region chock-full of geologically impressive parks.

A technical and colorful overview of the region's rocks is provided in *Geology of Utah's Parks & Monuments* (2003), published by the Utah Geological Association, and edited by Douglas Sprinkel and a team of specialists.

CANYONLANDS NATIONAL PARK

Like Grand Canyon National Park, Canyonlands is defined by the mighty Colorado River. Although the river has already carved through 300 million years of the Earth's history, only the oldest 125 million years' worth of rock layers remain – a staggering testament to the power of erosion. When you gaze into the canyon depths from Grand View Point, you're only looking at the middle slices of a giant geologic cake, with the top layers eaten away and the bottom layers still unseen.

Canyonlands is even more diverse than the Grand Canyon, possessing not just two converging river canyons, but intervening high mesas and a complex landscape of slickrock canyons, spires and arches. Cradled between the two rivers, the Island in the Sky Mesa is a tableland of Wingate

Capitol Reef has lots to interest amateur paleontologists, including North America's oldest pre-dinosaur megatrack site. Find out more at www.nps.gov/care/naturescience/naturalfeatures andecosystems.htm.

sandstone topped with scattered buttes and domes of Navajo sandstone. Below the mesa, slopes plunge 2000ft to the rivers past a shelf of White Rim sandstone partway down. The Colorado and Green Rivers twist and turn along meandering paths inherited from the Miocene epoch (about 10 million years ago), when the land was still a flat plain.

East of the rivers is the Needles, where colorful red and white bands showcase a complicated, 250-million-year-old history of retreating and advancing shallow seas. The red layers formed in river flooding after the sea's retreat, while white layers represent ancient beaches and coastal dunes. To the west lies the Maze, an almost incomprehensibly convoluted landscape explored by backcountry adventurers.

Arches National Park has 2000 known arches within its boundaries, ranging in size from just 3ft to over 300ft wide; the largest is Landscape Arch (p235).

ARCHES NATIONAL PARK

Compared to the other parks, Arches' geologic makeup is relatively easy to understand. Ancient rock layers rose atop an expanding salt dome, which later collapsed, fracturing layers along the dome's flanks. These cracks then eroded along roughly parallel lines, leaving fins of freestanding Entrada sandstone. In the last 10 million years, erosion has removed roughly a vertical mile of rock, carrying away all older materials save for the freestanding fins. This process continues today: even as brittle arches occasionally collapse, new ones are always in the making.

An arch formation is more a matter of happenstance than a predictable pattern, as people pay scant attention to the countless 'almost' arches that crumble into oblivion. But in a few lucky cases, rock slabs flake from the sides of fins in just the right way to create small openings that grow into arches as water seeps into cracks, freezes and dislodges more pieces.

National park visitor centers sell inexpensive, fold-out field-guide brochures so you can easily identify many of the local plants and animals you'll see.

At times the rock itself assists by releasing tremendous internal pressures stored within its layers, which causes more slabs to pop off. The uniform strength and hard upper surfaces of Entrada sandstone are the perfect combination for creating such beautiful arches, and today this park has the world's greatest concentration of natural stone arches.

WILDLIFE

The Colorado Plateau's harsh and arid landscape asks a lot of the plants and animals that make their homes here. Water is always a problem – either it wafts away in the scorching sun or it's frozen solid in winter. The few times it does come in plenty – delivered by afternoon thunderstorms in the late-summer monsoon season – it comes down so hard and fast and rushes off so quickly that few living things can take advantage of its fleeting presence. Elsewhere, slickrock canyons and sandy flats offer little in the way of usable habitat, and virtually nothing can carve out a living on the countless sheer cliffs. Many plants and animals have found remarkable ways to survive on the plateau, however, from blooming cacti and tiny snails to owls and peregrine falcons.

A Naturalist's Guide to Canyon Country (2000) by David Williams comes as close as possible to a complete beginner's compendium – covering geology, birds, mammals, insects, reptiles, trees, wildflowers and more – primarily focusing on southeastern Utah.

Animals

Wildlife in southern Utah's parklands ranges from nimble bighorn sheep and speedy raptors to scampering lizards and nosy ringtail cats, all scattered across a vast and wild region. Only rarely do animals congregate in large or conspicuous numbers, however. During the hottest days of summer, most animal activity takes place in the early evening or at night, when temperatures drop. Bird-watching is a particularly rewarding activity in southern Utah, especially if you spot a peregrine falcon or rare California condor, two species that nearly became extinct before captive breeding, release and species-monitoring programs began.

LARGE MAMMALS

Desert bighorn sheep stand guard on inaccessible cliff faces, mule deer and elk wander through mountain meadows, and mountain lions lurk in the forest, but your chances of seeing such large mammals are relatively slim. They may show up when you least expect them, so keep your eyes open!

Utah's Division of Wildlife Resources offers a free online field guide (http://dwrcdc.nr.utah.gov/ucdc/default.asp) to wildlife inhabiting the Beehive State, from big-eared bats to tiny lizards.

Mountain Lions

Even veteran wildlife biologists rarely see a mountain lion, though a fair number reside in canyon country. Like their favorite prey, mule deer, mountain lions mostly inhabit forested areas. Reaching up to 8ft in length and weighing as much as 175lb, these solitary animals are formidable predators that rarely bother humans. A few attacks have occurred in areas where human encroachment has pushed hungry lions to their limits, mainly around rapidly growing towns and cities. For advice on what to do if a mountain lion attacks, see p286.

Mule Deer

Forests and meadows are the favored haunts of mule deer, which typically graze in the early morning and evening. Uncommon when settlers first arrived, and soon hunted out, mule deer nearly vanished around the turn of the 20th century, then quickly rebounded as their predators were eliminated. Today mule deer frequent park campgrounds and developed areas, often moving upslope to avoid summer heat and returning downslope as winter approaches.

An affordable, all-in-one companion on your desert travels, the *National Audubon Society Field Guide to the Southwestern States* (1999) is practically encyclopedic, covering everything from geology to astronomy to ecology, with over 1000 species identified.

Bighorn Sheep

Like solemn statues, desert bighorn sheep often stand motionless on distant cliff faces or ridgelines, distinguished by their distinctive curled horns. During the late-fall and early-winter breeding season, males charge each other at 20mph and ram horns so loudly that the sound can be heard for miles. Thanks to reintroduction efforts throughout southern Utah, bighorns are making a slow recovery after hunting and diseases introduced by domestic sheep drove their populations to record lows. Bring binoculars to spot theses sure-footed, cliff-climbing animals. Close sightings are rare and typically brief.

SMALL MAMMALS

Small mammals are more abundant than their larger cousins, and many types of squirrels, chipmunks and small carnivores can be spotted around the parks' campgrounds and picnic areas and along hiking trails. For more about Bryce Canyon's **prairie dogs**, see p163.

Pronghorn antelope are North America's fastest land mammals, running at speeds of up to 60mph. Catch them – in a photo, that is – at Bryce Canyon.

Chipmunks & Squirrels

Several species of small, striped chipmunks and ground squirrels are ubiquitous in the parks. The white- and brown- or black-striped **Uinta chipmunk** is especially common along the canyon rim in Bryce and on Zion's forested plateaus. Though it resembles a chipmunk, the **golden-mantled ground squirrel** lacks facial stripes. Both species scamper through the forest, searching for nuts and seeds. They also beg for handouts, but resist the urge to feed them.

On open desert flats you're more likely to see the **white-tailed antelope squirrel**, one of the few mammals active during the daytime. Look for its white tail, which it carries over its back like a reflective umbrella, shielding it from the sun as it darts between shady patches. True to its name, the speckled gray **rock squirrel** nearly always inhabits rocky areas. This large, bold squirrel often visits campgrounds, where it inquisitively explores unattended gear and food or sidles up close to picnicking campers to beg. Feeding them makes them more aggressive, so please don't.

Eating Stone: Imagination and the Loss of the Wild (2006) by Ellen Meloy is as much a rumination on the politics of wilderness preservation as an admittedly anthropomorphic study of bighorn sheep, including in southern Utah.

Beavers

Some of the first Western explorers to wander across the Colorado Plateau came in search of prized beaver pelts. Limited to the few large rivers, beavers have never been common in southern Utah, but they are frequently sighted, because most visitors flock to the parks' rivers. In Zion their persistent nocturnal gnawing on large cottonwood trees presents something of a quandary. Wire mesh protects the base of some trees, but the park must still address the bigger question of how to restore the original balance of beavers, spring floods and cottonwoods that existed before humans forced the river into its current channel.

Porcupines

Looking much like an arboreal pincushion, the porcupine spends its days sleeping in caves or the hollows of trees in piñon-juniper woodlands. It's easy to overlook this strange creature, though on occasion you might encounter one waddling slowly through the forest. It's most active at night, when it gnaws on the soft inner wood of trees or pads around in search of flowers, fruits, nuts and berries.

To learn more about Bryce Canyon's prairie-dog community, download the ranger podcast from the park's official website at www.nps.gov/brca/photosmultimedia/podcasts.htm.

Ringtail Cats

One of southern Utah's most intriguing creatures is the nocturnal ringtail cat, which looks like a masked chihuahua with a raccoon tail. It preys on mice and squirrels, but will eat lizards, birds or fruit in a pinch. Fairly common in rocky desert areas, ringtails may appear around campsites at night, though they are generally timid and secretive.

Wood Rats

Although they bear a superficial resemblance to city rats, wood rats are extraordinary, gentle creatures. The Colorado Plateau's species all share a

SIZE DOESN'T MATTER

Due to the Colorado Plateau's virtually impassable canyons and rivers, many of the region's smallest residents, especially insects, have evolved into myriad colorful local forms.

Boasting more than 1000 distinct subspecies, the **darkling beetle** eventually catches the eye of nearly every visitor. This squat-bodied, long-legged beetle trundles across sandy areas in search of edible vegetation. When disturbed, this 'stink bug' lowers its head and lifts its rear end high into the air – if would-be intruders probe any closer, the beetle emits a squirt of noxious, though nonpoisonous, chemicals.

Observant hikers will spot the ubiquitous **ant lion** (aka doodlebug), which in its larval form makes perfectly conical pits in sandy soils. Lurking at the bottom of these pits, the larva waits for hapless insects to slide in, then grabs them with its fierce jaws and sucks them dry. These ugly little grubs metamorphose into gossamer-winged adults that look like large damselflies.

Dangerous in its allure, the fuzzy-bodied **velvet ant** is actually a wasp in disguise. Covered in orange or red hairs, this small insect is a common sight on sandy trails. Children and adults may be tempted to pick up the cuddly looking bug for closer inspection. Beware: it delivers a particularly painful sting.

A good example of a specially adapted species is the famous **Zion snail**, found nowhere else in the world except the hanging gardens of Zion Canyon, where it grazes on algae and plants amid the thin sheets of water that trickle from the Navajo sandstone. It takes a sharp eye to find these tiny dark snails on the wet walls of the Riverside Walk or the Weeping Rock Trail.

maddening propensity for stealing small shiny objects like watches or rings and leaving bones, seeds or other small objects in exchange – hence the animal's common nickname, the pack rat. Wood rats build massive stick nests (middens) that are used by countless generations. Upon dismantling these middens and examining their contents, biologists have been able to document more than 50,000 years of environmental prehistory in the region.

BIRDS

Whether you get a thrill from watching the high-speed dives of white-throated swifts and peregrine falcons from atop towering cliffs, or the bright songs of canyon wrens echoing across the plateau, there's no question that southern Utah's 300-plus bird species are among the region's top highlights.

Birds of Utah Field Guide (2003) by Stan Tekeila is great for beginning birders, with full-page photos and species descriptions helpfully organized by color and size.

Small Birds

The first birds many people encounter are **white-throated swifts**, which swoop and dive in great numbers along cliff faces and canyon walls. Designed like sleek bullets, these sporty 'tuxedoed' birds seem to delight in riding every wind current and chasing each other in noisy, playful pursuit. Flying alongside the swifts are slightly less agile **violet-green swallows**, a familiar sight around campgrounds and park buildings. Both species catch their food 'on the wing.'

One bird with a unique call is the **blue grouse**. This resident of mountain forests vocalizes from the ground and has such a deep call that you almost feel it in your bones. Most sightings occur when a startled grouse erupts from your feet into flight. On rare occasions you may spot a male as it puffs up its chest and drums to attract a female.

The stirring song of the **canyon wren** is, for many people, the most evocative sound on the plateau. So haunting is the song it hardly seems possible that this tiny rust-red rock-dweller could produce such music. Starting as a fast run of sweet tinkling notes, the song fades gracefully into a rhythmic cadence that may leave you full of longing.

In contrast, the garrulous call of the **Steller's jay** can grate on your nerves like a loud rusty gate. But this iridescent blue mountain bird makes up for it with wonderfully inquisitive and confiding mannerisms. It often seems to have no fear of humans and eagerly gathers around picnic tables and campsites, hoping for leftovers – keep these birds wild by not giving them handouts or any other encouragement to beg.

Another common forest dweller is **Clark's nutcracker**, a grey bird with black wings and tail. Its highly specialized diet consists almost entirely of pine nuts, which it pries out of thick pine cones using its downturned bill like a crowbar. These birds may deposit up to 1000 ground caches of nuts in a single year, making its feeding habits integral to the survival and propagation of mountainous pine forests.

Curious about how endangered California condors are doing in southern Utah and northern Arizona's canyon country? Visit www.nps.gov/grca/naturescience/california-condors.htm for updates.

Rafters and riverside hikers will almost certainly meet the brilliant **blue grosbeak**, with its loud, long musical warbles. This migratory bird scours dense thickets for tasty insects and grubs, and males often ascend to high perches to defend their territory. The **American dipper** is often seen bobbing its head to snap up underwater insects, especially in Zion's Virgin River. This medium-sized gray fellow is North America's only true aquatic songbird, ably swimming in rapidly rushing rivers (without webbed feet!) to feed.

Large Birds

Of the various owls that reside on the Colorado Plateau, none is as familiar as the common and highly vocal **great horned owl**, which regularly

COMEBACK CONDORS

When critically endangered California condors were released at Vermilion Cliffs in 1996, the experience of visiting the Colorado Plateau was profoundly altered. As was the case when wolves were reintroduced to Yellowstone National Park, many visitors are fascinated by the condors. With 9.5ft wingspans and horridly wrinkled, featherless pink heads, these birds are an unforgettable sight.

It's a miracle that condors are around at all, seeing as their world population declined to fewer than two dozen birds in 1987. Many assumed these gigantic prehistoric birds were on the brink of extinction. Following a massive captive-breeding effort, however, wild condors once again fly in the Southwest. While most reside in the Vermilion Cliffs and Grand Canyon, they wander far and wide in search of large animal carcasses and are observed with increasing frequency in southern Utah. You never know when one will soar overhead in Zion Canyon, for instance.

Condor populations are far from secure, despite having enough food and room to roam. The true test will be whether the species can successfully reproduce. Pairs in the Grand Canyon laid one egg in 2001 and two eggs in 2002. These efforts failed, but one nest was successful in 2003, marking the beginning of this majestic bird's return to the wild. As of 2010, there were at least seven wild-bred condors flying free in northern Arizona and southern Utah. Given that condors can live for up to 60 years in the wild, hopefully that will be enough time for these birds to naturally fledge more young and start thriving once again.

fills the echoing canyons with its booming 'hoo-hoo hooo hooo' calls. This is among the largest and most fearsome of all raptors, and when one moves into the neighborhood, other owls and hawks hurry on to more favorable hunting grounds or run the risk of being hunted down as prey themselves. This bird's glaring face and prominent 'horns' (actually erect tufts of feathers) may startle hikers as it peers down at them from a crevice or dark cavity.

> Once threatened by extinction – and still a species of special concern in Utah – some bald eagles spend their winters in Zion and Bryce's canyon country.

The threatened **Mexican spotted owl** has garnered considerable media coverage over the years. In California and the Pacific Northwest, this owl nests solely in old-growth forests that are being logged, but the subspecies that lives on the Colorado Plateau makes its home in Utah's rugged canyons and mountain forests. Sightings are rare but thrilling.

Commanding vast hunting territories of some 60 sq miles, powerful **golden eagles** are typically observed in passing as they travel widely in search of jackrabbits and other prey (up to the size of an adult deer). Watch for the characteristic golden tint on the eagle's shoulders and neck. Boasting a 7ft wingspan, it is among the area's largest birds, second in size only to reintroduced **California condors** (see the boxed text, above). California condors are often confused with common **turkey vultures**. You can tell these fellow scavengers apart by the coloration on the undersides of their wings. Turkey vultures (or 'TVs') have black wings, with white tips. California condors also have black wings, but with white triangular-shaped patches on their undersides.

> *A Field Guide to Desert Holes* (2002) by Pinau Merlin is a quirky look at underground critters most visitors usually won't notice in the desert, unless you know where and how to look for them.

Despite their endangered status in recent decades, **peregrine falcons** thrive throughout the region, especially in Zion Canyon. There they find plenty of secluded, cliffside nesting sites, as well as one of their favorite food items, white-throated swifts, which they seize in midair. Look for the falcon's long, slender wings and dark 'moustache.'

The most ubiquitous large bird is the **common raven**, a bird that seems to delight in making a noisy scene with its raucous calls and ceaseless play. This bird is an especially common sight along roadsides, where roadkill provides it with a steady supply of food.

Visitors may be surprised to see **wild turkey**. Formerly hunted out, this flashy game bird has been making a slow comeback in areas where it's protected, particularly in Zion Canyon. In the spring mating season, males fan out their impressive tails and strut around to impress females.

Scat and Tracks of the Desert Southwest (2000) by James Halfpenny is a fun, all-ages field guide that teaches you how to follow the evidence that southern Utah's more elusive creatures leave behind in the sand.

AMPHIBIANS & REPTILES

Amphibians and reptiles seldom garner the attention they deserve, but a surprising variety of beautiful and unique species call southern Utah home. Fast-moving lizards skitter and snakes slither throughout the region, while frogs and toads are commonly found around water sources. For more about endangered **desert tortoises**, see p120.

Amphibians

Bleating choruses of common **canyon tree frogs** float up from boulder-strewn canyon streams each night. Gray-brown and speckled like stone, these tiny frogs dwell in damp crevices by day, emerging at night (and sometimes late afternoon) to sing beside rocky pools. Occupying a similar habitat is the aptly named **red-spotted toad**, a small species with red-tipped warts covering its body. Its nighttime song around breeding pools is a high, persistent musical trill.

More secretive, and thus rarely encountered, is the **tiger salamander**, the region's only salamander. Spending the majority of its life in a burrow, this creature emerges when abundant water triggers its breeding cycle. In order to fully develop, a larval salamander requires a water source, although some larvae never change into the adult form and become sexually mature while still in the larval stage. Coloration varies by region, but most are blackish all over.

In *Desert Solitaire*, Edward Abbey recounts how a gopher snake that lived beneath his trailer in Arches National Park seemed to keep the rattlesnakes away.

Lizards

Perhaps the region's most abundant and widespread reptile is the **eastern fence lizard**, a small creature you'll likely see perched atop rocks and logs or scampering across the trail. During breeding season, males bob enthusiastically while conspicuously displaying their shiny blue throats and bellies. Females have dark, wavy crossbars on their backs and only a pale bluish wash underneath.

Bold in comparison is the greenish **collared lizard**, a large-headed species with striking black bands around its neck. This fearsome lizard eats just

POTHOLES

A miracle of life unfolds wherever desert rains accumulate in what seem like lifeless, dusty bowls among the rocks. Hiding in the dust are the spores and eggs of creatures uniquely evolved to take advantage of ephemeral water. Within hours of rainfall, crustaceans, insects, protozoa and countless other organisms hatch and start swimming in this brew of life. Though most are microscopic or very small, there are also oddly shaped, 1in to 2in tadpole shrimp that resemble prehistoric trilobites.

Toads and frogs arrive the night after a rain and lay eggs that hatch quickly. Unlike amphibians in other areas, which can take months or years to develop, these tadpoles are champion athletes that emerge from the water in two to three weeks. No matter how productive a pothole may seem, however, its lifespan is limited by evaporation. All too soon, water levels drop, and everything turns to dust again. By then all the organisms have retreated into dormancy to wait for the next drenching rainstorm, which may be years or even decades away.

Because each pool is a fragile ecosystem, hikers should exercise special care when they find a pothole. If necessary, remove only a little water, and don't jump or swim in the water, because body oils, sunscreens and insect repellents can harm resident life. These creatures have nowhere else to go! Even when dry, these pools need our attention because the 'lifeless' dust is actually full of eggs and spores waiting to spring into life again.

about every small animal it can overpower. Because it has little to fear, it often perches conspicuously atop large boulders, scanning for movement in all directions. Like most of southern Utah's lizards, it's inactive during the coldest winter months.

You may also encounter the curiously flattened **horned lizard**, which looks like a spiny little pancake. This lizard's shape is an adaptation to its exclusive diet of ants. In order to survive on this nutrient-poor diet, the horned lizard must eat lots of ants and consequently has an extremely large stomach that lends it its short, round appearance. Its shape also makes it harder for predators to grasp its body.

For safety tips on encountering snakes, including what to do if you happen to get bitten (unlikely, but possible), see p282.

Snakes

The Colorado Plateau is excellent habitat for snakes, though visitors seldom encounter more than a few resident species. Most common is the **gopher snake**, easily mistaken for a rattlesnake because it hisses and vibrates its tail in dry leaves when threatened. Sporting a tan body with dark brown saddles, this 6ft to 8ft constrictor preys upon rodents, small birds, lizards and even the offspring of other snakes.

Nothing compares to the jolt of terror and adrenaline prompted by the angry behavior of a **rattlesnake**. Both humans and wild animals react with instinctive fear, even though rattlesnakes rarely strike unless provoked. These mild-mannered creatures would rather slide away unharmed than provoke a confrontation. A few species reside in the region, but only rarely does a visitor get close enough to tell them apart.

Another snake that keeps its distance is the **striped whipsnake**. This extremely slender 3ft to 6ft snake moves like lightning when alarmed and can climb into trees and bushes so quickly it seems like it's falling away from you. The snake uses this speed to capture lizards and rodents.

FISH

The Colorado River and its tributaries were once home to at least 14 native fish species, nearly all of them unique to these waters and highly adapted to extreme conditions. After the introduction of grazing, dams and other artificial changes to the landscape, dozens of introduced species are now outcompeting these native fish.

One representative native species is the threatened **Colorado pikeminnow**, North America's largest minnow, which can weigh up to 25lb and reach over 3ft in length. Once so abundant that it was pitchforked out of irrigation canals, the pikeminnow is in drastic decline, as many artificial dams block its 200-mile migration route. Three other endangered fish, the **humpback chub**, **bonytail** and **razorback sucker**, suffer similar fates. It's unclear whether they will survive the changes being made to the rivers.

Scientists have documented 16 native species of bats in Canyonlands National Park, accounting for nearly 90% of all bat species found in the entire state.

Plants

The Colorado Plateau's complex landscape supports an equally diverse mix of plant species. Many are specific to the plateau, while others are drawn from adjacent biological zones such as the Great Basin, Mojave Desert and Rocky Mountains. Each park and monument boasts a list of hundreds of species, and no two places are alike.

Most species are adapted in some way to the Southwest's arid environment, either laying dormant until rains arrive or toughing it out through dry spells. If you arrive in wet season or after a drenching rain, you may be lucky enough to witness the region at its full splendor, when flowers carpet the landscape in all directions.

What you'll witness more often, however, is the plodding life of plants that struggle to conserve every molecule of precious liquid. Many plants sport hairy or waxy leaves to prevent evaporation, while others bear tiny leaves. At least one common plant, Mormon tea, has done away with water-wasting leaves altogether and relies on its greenish, wiry stems for photosynthesis. Most species have long taproots to penetrate the soil in search of water.

The rapid rate of erosion on the Colorado Plateau also has a profound effect on the area's ecosystems. Unlike other regions, where eroded materials accumulate and cover vast areas with homogenous soils, erosion on the plateau carries sediments away. Plants have nowhere to live except on freshly exposed bedrock, and because each rock layer has its own distinctive composition and chemistry, this profoundly limits the species that can grow there.

TREES

Piñon pines are well known for their highly nutritious and flavorful seeds. These same seeds have long been a staple for Native Americans, and many animals also feast on the seeds when they ripen in the fall. Piñons bear stout rounded cones and short single needles. Together with **Utah junipers**, piñon pines form a distinctive plant community that

LIFE ZONES

Dominating southern Utah's parks, **desert scrub** is the hot, dry zone below 4000ft where scraggly shrubs cling to life on sandy flats. The most common are low-growing blackbrush, shadscale, Mormon tea and sagebrush. Annual precipitation is likely to average less than 8in, a number that includes winter snows as well, so it isn't very much rain, and most of it ends up running over bare rocks and washing away before plants can even use it.

Another widespread habitat is the open woodland of piñon pine and Utah juniper. **Piñon-juniper woodland** ('P-J' for short) grows mostly between 4000ft and 7000ft. Due to competition for water, trees are spaced widely here, though they still provide shade for many understory plants, as well as food and shelter for many animals. In some areas the trees grow in distinct lines, following cracks in the rock where water gathers after rain.

Growing in a narrow band between 7000ft and 8500ft, **ponderosa pine forest** indicates the presence of increased rainfall at higher elevations. In Zion, however, ponderosa pines grow at lower elevations, because porous Navajo sandstone is full of water, demonstrating once again how water dictates where plants can grow in this region. Ponderosa pines thrive in Zion and Bryce Canyon (with a few stands in Grand Staircase-Escalante) but are absent in lower-elevation Capitol Reef, Canyonlands and Arches.

Boreal forest above 8500ft has much in common with Rocky Mountain forests, even supporting many of the same plants and animals. This is a zone of cool, moist woodland and rainfall that exceeds 20in a year, conditions that favor trees like spruce, Douglas fir and quaking aspen. This forest populates a few high mesas in Zion, but the best examples are found at higher elevations in Bryce Canyon, particularly at road's end near Rainbow Point, where stands of ancient bristlecone pines survive.

Due to intensive grazing, the **grassland** that once covered much of this region has been largely replaced by desert scrub and alien weeds. Early Western explorers' journals describe a lush grassy landscape, though you'd hardly know it today. In areas of deeper sand and soil, where shrubs don't grow well, it's still possible to find pockets of galleta and Indian ricegrass.

Readily available water supports another set of unique habitats, ranging from **hanging gardens** clustered around cliffside seeps to **riparian woodland** lining perennial creeks and rivers. The presence of water attracts many plants and animals to these habitats. Monkeyflowers, columbines and ferns mark spots where springs flow from sandstone cliffs. Riverbanks that were once home to majestic cottonwood and willow stands are more likely today to harbor highly invasive tamarisk.

covers millions of acres of Southwestern desert. Blue, berrylike cones and diminutive scalelike needles distinguish junipers.

Mingling with piñons and junipers in some canyons is the beautiful little **Gambel oak**, with its dark green leaves turning shades of yellow and red in autumn and adding to the palette of color, particularly in Zion Canyon. Often growing in dense thickets, oaks produce copious quantities of nutritious, tasty acorns long favored by Native Americans and used to make ground meal, breads, cakes and soups.

To identify the stately **ponderosa pine**, look for large spiny cones, needles in clusters of three, and yellowish bark that smells like butterscotch or vanilla. Between 20,000 and 12,000 years ago, the **Douglas fir** was one of the region's dominant species, though today they are restricted to isolated mountaintops and north-facing slopes. This relict of an earlier time dramatically demonstrates how the region's vegetation has changed since the ice age. It's identified by its single needles and cones with three-pronged bracts on each seed.

Found amid damp mountain meadows, **quaking aspen** is immediately recognizable by its smooth, white bark and circular leaves. Every gust of wind sets these leaves quivering on their flattened stems, an adaptation for shaking off late snowfalls that would otherwise damage fragile leaves. Aspen groves comprise genetically identical trunks sprouting from a common root system that may grow to more than a hundred acres in size. By budding repeatedly from these root systems, aspens have what has been called 'theoretical immortality' – some aspen roots are thought to be more than a million years old.

Rivers and watercourses in this harsh desert landscape are lined with thin ribbons of water-loving plants that can't survive anywhere else. Towering prominently over all others is the showy **Fremont cottonwood**, whose large, vaguely heart-shaped leaves rustle wildly in any wind. Hikers in the canyons' scorching depths find welcome respite in the shade of this tree. In spring, cottonwoods produce vast quantities of cottony seed packets that fill the air and collect in every crack and crevice. **Box elder** is another common streamside plant. It issues winged, maplelike seeds and bears trifoliate leaves that resemble those of poison ivy.

Ancient bristlecone pines may be slow growing, but they're believed to be the oldest living single organisms on Earth, with some possibly 5000 years old.

Since 1920 the aggressive weedy **tamarisk** (salt cedar) has largely replaced native streamside plant communities. Though this delicately leaved plant from Eurasia and Africa sports a handsome coat of soft pink and white flowers through the summer, its charm ends there, for it robs water from the soil and completely overwhelms such native species as cottonwood and willow. Producing a billion seeds per plant and spreading quickly, this species now dominates virtually every source of water in the Southwest deserts, including the Colorado River (see p251).

SHRUBS

Blackbrush covers large tracts of Southwestern deserts. This dark shrub reaches great ages and is only rarely replaced by young seedlings. With wiry stems, shrunken leaves and yellowish-red petal-less flowers blooming only after heavy spring rains, it may look more dead than alive.

Also triggered by spring rains, the common **cliff rose** (or desert bitterbrush) paints rocky slopes with its white blossoms surrounding yellow stamens. You're likely to 'hear' this plant before you see it, as bees and insects swarm to its acrid-smelling flowers. Though its resinous, leathery leaves taste bitter, deer still munch on the plant in winter.

Narrowleaf yucca is a stout succulent related to agave and century plants. Yuccas favor sandy sites, while blackbrush predominates on thin gravelly soils. Growing in a dense rosette of thick leaves, this plant sends up a 5ft stalk of creamy flowers. A night-flying moth pollinates these flowers; in exchange, the caterpillars eat some seeds. Native Americans used yucca fibers to weave baskets and sandals.

Ripening in summer, the juicy black **canyon grape** is a tart favorite food of many different kinds of mammals and nearly 100 species of birds. Its vines snake over bushes and rocks in damp canyons, particularly in Zion Canyon, where its maplelike leaves turn yellow, orange and red in the fall.

Another distinctive shrub is **greenleaf manzanita**, which flourishes in ponderosa pine forests along the rim of Bryce Canyon. It bears reddish-brown bark and equally smooth, quarter-sized leaves. Bees alight on its pale pinkish flowers, while mammals and birds feed on its dark-red fruit.

The common desert shrub nicknamed Mormon tea is a species of Ephedra plant, which Native Americans also used for medicinal purposes, including as a stimulating brew.

WILDFLOWERS

A surprisingly large variety of wildflowers thrive in the Colorado Plateau's arid, rocky landscapes. While late-winter precipitation and spring snowmelt trigger some plants to flower, many others bloom following midsummer thunderstorms or when temperatures cool in early autumn.

Seeps, springs and stream banks host some of the most dramatic flower displays. The brilliant flash of **monkeyflowers** amid greenery comes as something of a shock for hikers who've trudged across miles of searing baked rock. These red, yellow and purple flowers with widely flared 'lips' are very tempting to hummingbirds.

Columbines are also common at the seeps and springs, though some species range up into forested areas as well. The **golden columbine** and crimson-colored **Western columbine** are most common in wet, shaded canyon recesses. **Rock columbine** grows amid Bryce Canyon's hoodoos, where its vivid blue flowers stand out against red-rock cliffs. The flowers of both species hold pockets of nectar that attract large numbers of butterflies and hummingbirds.

Wildflowers of Zion National Park (1999) by Stanley Welsh is an excellent pocket-sized guide that covers the most common wildflowers that hikers and visitors will encounter along the park's trails, blooming from spring through autumn.

The showy **prince's-plume** boldly marks selenium-rich desert soils with a 2ft to 3ft stalk of dainty yellow flowers. By using selenium in place of sulfur to manufacture its amino acids, this plant renders itself poisonous to herbivores and grows in soils that other plants can't tolerate. Prospectors once thought of this plant as an indicator of places to dig for uranium, as selenium deposits may naturally occur nearby. Other wildflowers that do well on dry, gravelly slopes include stalky **penstemon** and **paintbrush** varieties, all with bright, showy tubular flowers in a rainbow of colors.

In peak years **evening primroses** are so abundant that it looks like someone scattered white tissues over the sandy desert. Turning from white to rosy pink, the small flowers open at sunset and close by morning, thus avoiding the day's heat and conserving water. At night large sphinx moths dart from flower to flower, collecting nectar and laying eggs.

Blooming in late spring and early summer, the three-petaled **sego lily** is another white flowering plant that is also Utah's state flower. Native Americans and early Mormon settlers once harvested the plant's walnut-sized bulbs for food. Don't confuse its small, delicate blooms with the large, showy white flowers of **sacred datura**, which blooms from spring through fall. This poisonous plant was traditionally used by some indigenous tribes during religious rituals as a potent hallucinogenic, but it can be deadly.

OTHER PLANTS

Among the most common cacti in southern Utah are those belonging to the prickly pear group, familiar for their paddle-shaped pads. Both the pads and fruit of the **beavertail cactus** were traditionally eaten by Native Americans after proper preparation. Be aware that the barbed, bristlelike hairs (glochidia) detach easily on contact and are highly irritating. **Claret cup cacti** shine like jewels in the dusty desert landscape, where they are the first to bloom in spring. Their deep scarlet flowers burst forth from up to dozens of stems per clump, blooming simultaneously for several days.

Maidenhair fern deserves special mention because it adds bright green coloring to countless desert oases. Lacy and delicate, this fern requires a continuous supply of water. You'll recognize it by its leaves, arranged like an open hand from a central wiry black stem.

Wondering what flower you just saw? Use Arches National Park's online flower database, searchable by month, color and name, or download free plant-finder keys from www.nps.gov/arch/naturescience/flowerguide.htm.

A close examination of juniper tree branches reveals an extremely abundant but easily overlooked plant – yellowish-green **juniper mistletoe**. Partially parasitic, but not harming its host trees, mistletoe produces tiny fruits that some birds prefer to feed on. Carried in the birds' digestive tracts, the seeds adhere to new tree branches once excreted.

Formerly widespread across vast tracts of the desert, grasses like **Indian ricegrass** and **galleta** now survive only in relict patches. Along with this loss, an entire food chain of animals that relied on grasslands has also declined, evidenced by local extinctions of bears and wolves, for example. Bearing large nutritious seeds, ricegrass was also an important staple for Native Americans.

Take a sneak peek at Zion's comprehensive plant library – a virtual botanical treasure chest for researchers and park rangers – online at www.nps.gov/zion/naturescience.

ENVIRONMENTAL ISSUES & SUSTAINABILITY

With the highest concentration of protected lands in the continental US, plus protective management by a variety of governmental agencies, it seems that most of the damage to this landscape is a thing of the past. Unfortunately, grazing, mining and military exercises still create scars around southern Utah's parks and monuments. The worst damage may now come from the huge influx of recreationists and visitors who are in danger of loving the land to death.

In a region where life hangs by a fragile thread, the heavy trampling of human feet and off-road vehicles leaves lasting impressions. Desert

CRYPTOBIOTIC CRUSTS

One of the desert's most fascinating features is also one of its least visible and most fragile. Only in recent decades have cryptobiotic crusts begun to attract attention and concern. These living crusts cover and protect desert soils, gluing sand particles together so they don't blow away.

Cyanobacteria, among Earth's oldest living forms, start the process by extending mucous-covered filaments that wind through the dry soil. Over time these filaments and the sand particles adhering to them form a thin crust that is colonized by microscopic algae, lichens, fungi, and mosses. This crust absorbs huge amounts of rainwater, reducing runoff and minimizing erosion.

Unfortunately, this thin crust is instantly fragmented under the heavy impact of human footsteps, not to mention bicycle, motorcycle and car tires. Once broken, the crust can take up to 50 years to repair itself. In its absence, the wind and rains erode desert soils, and much of the water that would otherwise nourish desert plants is lost. Many of these soils formed during the wet climates of the Pleistocene and may be irreplaceable in today's arid conditions. Tragically, as soon as the crust is broken and soil is lost, grasses will be permanently replaced by shrubs, whose roots fare better in the thinner soils.

Visitors to the Southwest bear a special responsibility to protect cryptobiotic crusts by staying on established trails. Look closely before you walk anywhere – intact crusts form a rough glaze atop the soil, while fragmented crusts have sharp edges. At all costs, avoid walking or camping on these ancient soils.

For more conservation tips, see the Desert Etiquette boxed text (p46).

crusts, wet meadows and riverside campsites are slow to recover from such use, and repeated visits can cause permanent damage. The effects may accumulate so gradually they almost go unnoticed. Scientists at Bryce Canyon estimate that 3% of the vegetation disappears each year from people wandering off trail among the hoodoos – just tiny little bites that build up over time. Cryptobiotic crusts (see the boxed text, opposite) are of particular concern, and all the parks have 'Don't Bust the Crust' programs to educate visitors about their impact on desert soils.

Desert vegetation grows so slowly that even impacts left by early Western prospectors, ranchers and explorers may look fresh. Even protected parklands remain damaged by long-ago visitors. Cows have had such a devastating impact on the desert that it no longer functions as the same ecosystem. Only on a few inaccessible mesa tops do fragments of ancestral plant communities survive. Today's dry, brushy desert hardly resembles the landscape that existed even half a century ago, and it's not likely to recover for centuries to come.

Cadillac Desert: The American West and its Disappearing Water (1993) by Marc Reisner is an exhaustively researched, compelling account of the West's most critical issue: balancing development with its most precious resource.

Plants that adapt best seem to be invasive weeds, which have quickly overtaken areas damaged by cows and human activities. Introduced plants such as Russian thistle (tumbleweed) and cheatgrass pose a serious problem, as they can force out native plants and animals, creating extensive monocultures. Cheatgrass even alters the chemistry of the soil, possibly rendering it unusable to other plants. And many invasive plants are nearly impossible to remove once they gain a foothold.

Construction of dams and reservoirs throughout the Southwest has radically changed the delicate balance that has sustained life here for millennia. In place of floodplains that once richly nourished riparian and aquatic food chains, dams now release cold water in steady flows that favor introduced fish species and invasive weeds. In populated areas, the draining of underground aquifers is shrinking the water table and drying up desert springs and wetlands that animals have long depended on during the dry season.

With a mission to preserve public lands across the Colorado Plateau, the Southern Utah Wilderness Alliance (www.suwa.org) is a grassroots political voice for Utah's red-rock country.

Harder to quantify is the pall of air pollution that often hovers over the region. Emanating from distant cities, cars and factories, this hazy smog severely compromises the remarkable beauty of southern Utah's landscape and serves as a grim reminder of modern life. Local conservation groups continue to fight on behalf of these and other issues, but the outcome of political debates really depends on the waves of newcomers who will vote to shape the region's future.

The fact that nearly five million people a year visit this fragile desert landscape means that tourism development has a major and lasting impact. Nearly every park visitor arrives in a private car needing fresh drinking water, plus lodging and showers if they are staying overnight. The parks are acutely aware of this and actively try to mitigate visitor impacts wherever possible. Both Zion and Bryce Canyon have developed free public-transit systems and a growing network of pedestrian and bicycle trails as a way of reducing traffic congestion and air pollution. All of southern Utah's parks and concessionaire businesses now encourage and facilitate recycling. Zion's visitor center is a model of smart, sustainable ecobuilding practices that hopefully more national and state parks will imitate in future, as much as their operating budgets allow.

Edward Abbey's *The Monkey Wrench Gang* (1975) is a mostly fictionalized, raucous tale of 'ecowarriors' and their plan to blow up Glen Canyon Dam before it is built, flooding the canyon entirely.

History

The history of southern Utah is almost literally written in stone, and it lies jumbled on the desert's skin like a pile of dried bones. From the uplifted, eroded sandstone of the Colorado Plateau to the fossilized tracks of dinosaurs, to the carved etchings of ancestral tribes of indigenous inhabitants, to the farms and fruit orchards planted by early Mormon settlers, to the modern-day scars left by mining, grazing and an army of wheels and feet, the desert's story remains sun-baked and exposed under a clear-blue sky for anyone to read.

The University of Utah Press (www.uofupress.com) and the national parks' cooperative natural history associations (see p23) are your best sources of new history books, covering eras from indigenous tribes to Spanish explorers and Mormon settlers.

FIRST PEOPLES

It's not definitively known when humans first arrived in the Southwest. Most likely, nomadic peoples migrated from Asia across a land bridge between Siberia and Alaska, making their way south between 23,000 and 10,000 years ago. We know that they arrived by 10,000 BC, as archaeologists have dated spearheads found among the remains of woolly mammoths and other ice-age mammals. However, Native American creation stories say that the people have always been here, or that they descended from the spirit world.

However they arrived, these early groups were primarily skilled hunters. By 8500 BC, most large prehistoric mammals were extinct – some possibly hunted to that fate, though many were unable to adapt to the drying glacial climate. This led to what scholars call the Desert Archaic period, which lasted roughly from 6500 BC to AD 200. The term 'Desert Archaic' refers as much to the period's hunter-gatherer lifestyle as it does to an ecosystem or block of time.

Stephen Trimble's hefty tome *The People: Indians of the American Southwest* (1993) stitches together tribal histories and modern realities by letting Native Americans, including Utah's Southern Paiutes and Colorado River tribes, speak for themselves.

As a survival method, hunting and gathering proved remarkably adaptive and resilient in the Southwest. Early Desert Archaic peoples lived nomadically in small, unconcentrated groups, following the food supply of seasonal wild plants and such small animals as rabbits. Shelters were temporary, and caves were often used. These people became skilled at basketry, a functional craft for groups on the move.

Eventually, late Desert Archaic peoples established semiregular settlement patterns and started to cultivate crops such as primitive corn, beans and squash. By AD 200 several distinct cultures had emerged. Ancestral Puebloans dominated the Colorado Plateau, which encompasses south-

TIMELINE

250 million BC

Southern Utah's plateau country is a shallow sea off the western edge of the Earth's giant supercontinent known as Pangea.

60 million years ago

Seismic activity and the movement of continental plates uplifts the entire Colorado Plateau, creating the Grand Staircase and Rocky Mountains.

23,000 BC–10,000 BC

Made up of nomadic hunters and gatherers, groups of indigenous peoples migrate from Asia over the Bering Strait land bridge to North America.

6500 BC–AD 200

Desert Archaic cultures occupy southern Utah. These nomadic hunter-gatherers become adept at catching small game and adapting desert plants to new uses, including basketry.

200 BC–AD 1200

Ancestral Puebloans develop a vibrant culture, with pueblos, cliff dwellings and ceremonial centers spread across the Colorado Plateau; distinct Fremont Culture arises contemporaneously.

ern Utah, southwest Colorado and northern portions of Arizona and New Mexico. They were once called the Anasazi – a Navajo word meaning 'ancient enemy' – by archaeologists, but Ancestral Puebloans is now the preferred term, since contemporary tribes believe they are descended from these ancient peoples.

Ancestral Puebloans dominated the Colorado Plateau from around 200 BC to AD 1500, though in southern Utah they left a few centuries earlier, around AD 1200. There's no consensus over why Ancestral Puebloans abandoned the area when they did. It was likely a combination of drought, soil erosion, disease and conflict with other groups over dwindling resources.

Ancestral Puebloans adopted irrigated agriculture, became highly accomplished basket-makers and potters, and believed in a complex cosmology. They are best known for their cliff dwellings, pueblo villages and kivas (ceremonial underground chambers). While southern Utah contains far fewer of these ancient structures than surrounding states, it does boast abundant Ancestral Puebloan rock art.

Living in southern Utah concurrently were the Fremont people, who migrated from the north and continued a seminomadic existence, preferring hunting and gathering to farming and villages. They abandoned the area around the same time as the Ancestral Puebloans, and their distinctive rock art is also widespread.

Traces of Fremont: Society and Rock Art in Ancient Utah (2010), written by Steven R Simms with beautiful photographs by François Gohier, heralds an often-overlooked ancient indigenous people's legacy by examining evidence they left behind.

SOUTHERN PAIUTES & SPANIARDS

Southern Paiute tribes began emerging around AD 1100. Comprising a dozen or so distinct bands, Paiute territory extended from California's deserts east to Colorado, and from Utah's Great Basin south to Arizona's Painted Desert. The Kaibab Paiutes lived near what is now Zion National Park. Today, their tribal reservation surrounds Pipe Spring National Monument on the northern Arizona Strip.

Generally speaking, Southern Paiutes followed the same survival strategy as Desert Archaic peoples – migrating with the seasons, hunting small animals, gathering wild plants and tending a few modest crops. A staple of their diet was the piñon, or pine nut, and they continued the tradition of fine basketry. By contrast, their shelters and even their clothes often weren't made to last more than a season.

Southern Paiutes lived largely in peace for more than 500 years. No one coveted the unyielding land they called home, yet they found abundance in it. Deer were plentiful, the winters around present-day St George were

Guide to Rock Art of the Utah Region (2000) by Dennis Silfer is an authoritative overview of current scientific knowledge about prehistoric indigenous cultures, offering detailed, if somewhat dated descriptions and explanations of rock-art sites.

1100

Southern Paiute tribes emerge in the Colorado Plateau region, flourishing for the next 700 years until the arrival of Spanish explorers and Western settlers.

1776

In search of a shortcut from Santa Fe to California, the Domínguez-Escalante expedition brings the first non–Native Americans to explore the Colorado Plateau.

1839

After fleeing arrest in Missouri, Mormon founder Joseph Smith leads his followers to Nauvoo, Illinois, where a temple and town are built beside the Mississippi River.

1844

An armed mob of 200 men storms the jail in Carthage, Illinois, where Joseph Smith is imprisoned, shooting and killing the Mormon leader and self-confessed polygamist.

1847

Mormons fleeing religious persecution in the east start arriving in Salt Lake City; over the next two decades, more than 70,000 Mormons will migrate to Utah.

WRITTEN ON THE LAND

Anywhere in southern Utah you may encounter it: the pecked outlines of human figures and animals, painted handprints, squiggled lines etched into desert varnish. Rock art is mysterious and awesome and always leaves us wondering: who did this, and why? What were they trying to say?

Dating from at least 2000 BC to as late as the 19th century AD, rock art in Utah was once called 'a wilderness Louvre' by *National Geographic*. The rock art found in southern Utah has been attributed to every known ancestral and modern people, from ice-age hunters and Desert Archaic nomads to contemporary Native American tribes. One way archaeologists track the spread of ancestral cultures is by studying their distinctive rock-art styles, which tend to be either abstract or representational, both zoomorphic and anthropomorphic. Representational rock art is usually more recent, while abstract designs appear in all ages.

We can only speculate about why rock art was created and what it means. This symbolic writing becomes obscure the moment the cultural context for the symbols is lost. Much of the art was likely the work of shamans or tribal elders communicating with the divine. Some of the earliest, abstract designs may have been created in trance states or during religious rituals. Certain figures and motifs seem to reflect a heavenly pantheon, while other rock art may tell stories – real or mythical – of great hunts or battles.

mild, and in summer they fished mountain lakes. Ever-growing numbers of Europeans on the continent didn't know of them, and gold-hungry 16th-century Spanish conquistadors like Coronado never penetrated the Colorado Plateau's rugged territory.

Beneath These Red Cliffs: An Ethnohistory of the Utah Paiutes (2006) by Ronald L Holt, with a foreword by tribal chairwoman Lora Tom, is an unflinching tale of indigenous survival, from Western occupation to tribal restoration.

Then, in 1776, the same year the US declared its independence from Britain, the Domínguez-Escalante expedition encountered the Kaibab band of Southern Paiutes while skirting the western edge of the Colorado Plateau. In the first recorded European impressions of them, Silvestre Vélez de Escalante, a Franciscan friar and Spanish Catholic missionary, described 'a large number of people, all of pleasing appearance, very friendly and extremely timid.'

The Spanish expedition had two goals: to open a communication route from Santa Fe to California and to spread Christianity among indigenous peoples. But the Spanish never made it further west, nor did Spain fund the establishment of any Utah missions. Afterward, the Southern Paiutes were left mostly, but not entirely, alone. Some of the Spanish Trail trading route had been cut, and occasional trappers wandered through, as did strange diseases and even Ute and New Mexican slave traders, who often kidnapped Paiute children to sell for horses and goods elsewhere.

By the early 19th century the Southern Paiutes could weather the passing wagon trains, which trampled grasses and crops, but smallpox and

1848

The Mexican-American War ends with the 1848 Treaty of Guadalupe Hidalgo; Mexico cedes much of the present-day Southwest, including parts of Utah, to the USA.

1850

US federal government establishes the Territory of Utah after denying Latter-Day Saints leader Brigham Young's proposal for a more expansive State of Deseret (Mormon for 'honeybee').

1854

The Mormons send missionaries south to convert the Southern Paiutes; its success is largely due to Jacob Hamblin, dubbed the 'Mormon Leatherstocking.'

1857

Amid rising tensions with the US federal government, a Mormon militia group massacres 120 California-bound emigrant men, women and children at Mountain Meadows.

1858

Mormon missionary and scout Nephi Johnson becomes the first non–Native American to enter Zion Canyon; Isaac Behunin, the canyon's first Mormon settler, arrives five years later.

More prosaic explanations also exist. Some rock art may have marked tribal territory, and some may have been nothing more than idle doodling. But no matter what the meaning, each rock-art site – whether a petroglyph (inscribed or pecked into the stone) or pictograph (painted figure) – is irreplaceable, whether as a valuable part of the human archaeological record or the continuing religious traditions and cultural patrimony of contemporary tribes, including Utah's Southern Paiute.

Do what you can to preserve rock-art sites for other visitors and future generations by observing these rules of etiquette:

- Do not disturb or remove any artifacts or features of the site
- Do not trace, repaint, remove graffiti or otherwise touch or apply any materials to the rock art
- Stay back at least 10ft from all rock-art panels, using binoculars or a zoom lens for better views
- Do not climb the cliffs above rock-art sites, as that could let loose a rockslide that would damage the site
- Minimize the number of vehicles you bring to rock-art sites, and do not hike off-trail or build campfires nearby

measles were decimating them. By mid-century, before they'd ever had to fight or strike a deal with a Mormon missionary settler, some Southern Paiute populations had dwindled by two-thirds.

ARRIVAL OF THE MORMONS

In 1847, Brigham Young and party reached a point near Utah's Great Salt Lake. Fleeing persecution for their beliefs back east, the Mormons were charged by their prophet Joseph Smith to find a place out west where they could build a heavenly city on earth. They were looking, in other words, for what Southern Paiutes had long enjoyed – the solitude and freedom from interference this harsh land provided. As the story goes, Young sat upright out of his sickbed long enough to say, 'This is the right place. Drive on.'

The Mormons were not your average pioneers, and Young was not an average leader. The plan was to build an independent nation, a theocracy outside the boundaries of the USA. Within a year, however, the rapidly expanding country caught up with them. The 1848 Treaty of Guadalupe Hidalgo turned the Mexican territory into a US possession, and the concurrent discovery of gold in California attracted streams of passing miners, and with them, Manifest Destiny, the nationalistic belief that the US was ordained by God to stretch from 'sea to shining sea,' from the Atlantic to the Pacific Oceans. Utah would not remain isolated for long.

To learn more about the 1776 Domínguez-Escalante expedition and read excerpts from Escalante's own diary, track down *Pageant in the Wilderness* (1972) by Herbert Bolton; it's one of the first authoritative accounts.

HISTORY

1861

Nicknamed Utah's Dixie, the experimental farming community of St George is founded during the Mormon church's Cotton Mission days; scarce drinking water makes life difficult.

1861–65

US Civil War pits the Southern slave-holding Confederate States of America, led by plantation owner Jefferson Davis, against the mostly free states of the Union.

1863

Isaac Behunin and his sons are the first Mormons to settle Zion Canyon, building a cabin and clearing some farmland. Behunin is credited with naming Zion Canyon.

1865–67

Utah's Black Hawk War reaches its peak, with fighting between Mormon settlers and Ute, Paiute and Navajo tribespeople; Native American resistance does not end until 1872.

1869

First transcontinental railway line is completed north of Salt Lake City. John Wesley Powell successfully descends the Colorado River and begins a geologic survey of southern Utah.

LATTER-DAY SAINTS

Self-proclaimed prophet Joseph Smith was born in Vermont in 1805. The child of self-proclaimed mystics, Joseph came of age just as a widespread religious revival movement, called the Second Great Awakening, was feverishly beginning to take hold of the entire country. Religious revival camp meetings were a common sight, especially in rural towns and on the Western frontier.

Smith claimed to have received his first heavenly visit at age 18, when the angel Moroni revealed to him the location of golden tablets buried in the woods near his home in New York. This was three years after God told him in a vision that all churches currently in existence were false. The angel Moroni returned three more times, once a year. After the fourth visit, Smith was allowed to take the golden tablets home and, using 'stone spectacles' provided by the angel, read and transcribe the indecipherable word of God.

Three years later, in 1830, these revelations were published as the *Book of Mormon,* and the Church of Jesus Christ of Latter-Day Saints was established, with Smith as its charismatic leader. There's much more to the story of the Mormon faith – which thanks to globetrotting missionaries is one of the world's fastest-growing religions, with over 11 million members. If you're curious, just open the *Book of Mormon;* there's one in every hotel room in Utah.

In 1850 the Territory of Utah was established, with Young as territorial governor. If Young despaired over the political fate of his beloved State of Deseret, he didn't let on. Instead, he aspired to settle an empire larger than Texas as fast as he could. He sent Mormon pioneers in all directions to plow, irrigate and farm the desert into submission, which they did. The Mormons succeeded because they were zealously dedicated to their faith, tempered by their journey to Utah along the Mormon Trail, and organized. They attacked the land as a cohesive group, fired by visions of God, not gold.

With spare prose and uncommon insight, Western writer Wallace Stegner captures the early history of Utah and the Mormons in *The Gathering of Zion: The Story of the Mormon Trail* (1964) and *Mormon Country* (1942).

Everywhere they went in southern Utah, Mormons displaced Paiutes, appropriating water sources and the most desirable land. In an apparent contradiction, the Mormons also 'adopted' the Paiutes and gave them the only practical support they would receive, which they came to depend on. The *Book of Mormon* claims that Native Americans are one of Israel's lost tribes, so bringing them back into the fold was considered an important Mormon mission, even as racist attitudes toward indigenous peoples prevailed.

The end result for the Paiutes turned out to be much the same as for Native American tribes elsewhere in the Southwest – that is, cultural disenfranchisement, the loss of traditional hunting grounds and access to water sources, and a population decimated by foreign diseases and indentured servitude.

1870

Mormon pioneer Ebenezer Bryce and his family settle near Bryce Canyon, which he famously calls 'a hell of a place to lose a cow.'

1872

John Wesley Powell returns to southern Utah and explores Zion Canyon, calling it Mukuntuweap, which he believed was a Paiute word for 'straight canyon.'

1878

Mormons permanently settle in the Moab region. (Ute tribespeople violently thwarted a previous effort in the 1850s.) Agriculture and grazing quickly become the economic mainstays.

1883

Denver & Rio Grande Railroad reaches Grand Junction, Colorado, with a narrow-gauge connection to the transcontinental railroad at Salt Lake City; Moab is bypassed.

1889

Wild West outlaw Butch Cassidy, the son of Mormon immigrants, flees to southern Utah to hide out after robbing a bank in Telluride, Colorado.

A MASSACRE, A WAR & STATEHOOD

With their modern-day prophets, the practice of 'celestial marriage' (that is, polygamy) and theocratic territorial government, Mormons were perceived as a threat by federal authorities and everyday US citizens, whom the Mormons called Gentiles. In the 1850s, tensions ran high, and minor clashes were common. On September 11, 1857, in the mountains outside St George, building religious hysteria and fear of a federal invasion led a Mormon militia – possibly with the enlisted help of local Paiutes – to slaughter 120 innocent California-bound pioneers. Details of the Mountain Meadows Massacre are still debated today, but the incident confirmed the government's worst fears, prompting the US Army to surround and subdue Salt Lake City that same year.

No one was killed and hardly a shot fired in the so-called Mormon War, which had two main repercussions: it instituted a secular government in Utah, beneath which the religious hierarchy continued to operate for a decade or more; and it curtailed territorial ambitions, reducing the size of Utah. Through the Civil War and beyond, the territory petitioned for statehood, but it was continually denied, even as states around it were accepted. Animosity between Mormons and the federal government lingered, with polygamy as the sticking point. Finally, in 1890 the Mormon church officially repudiated polygamy and asked its followers to do the same. Six years later Utah won statehood.

A TALE OF TWO EXPLORERS

In their efforts to be self-sufficient, the Mormons established several missions in southern Utah in the 1850s and '60s: the Iron Mission, centered around Cedar City, mined ore and smelted iron for construction; while the Cotton Mission, centered around St George, grew cotton for Mormon use and export. Neither mission was ultimately successful. However, the Mormons also sent missionaries south to convert the Southern Paiutes, and its success was largely due to Jacob Hamblin, who arrived in 1854.

Dubbed the 'Mormon Leatherstocking,' Hamblin gained the respect and trust of some Native American tribes across the Southwest. He said he believed that if he always told the truth, listened and never shed Native American blood, he would be safe. Hamblin became a peacemaker who negotiated important treaties and, with Native American assistance, explored the Colorado Plateau as no non–Native American had before him, serving as an ambassador of the Mormon church, including to the Hopi mesas and the Navajo Nation.

In 1869, one-armed Civil War veteran and geologist John Wesley Powell became famous for being the first to descend the length of the

HBO's hit cable TV drama *Big Love* is a fictional depiction of fundamentalist Mormons and the contemporary practice of 'plural marriage' (ie polygamy) in Utah.

The inexpensive, spiral-bound *Pipe Spring Cookbook: Original Pioneer Recipes*, published by the Zion Natural History Association (www.zionpark.org), offers authentic tastes of early life on the frontier as experienced by 19th-century Mormon settlers.

Curious about early Mormon settlers' lives? Immerse yourself in the anthology *Pioneer Voices of Zion Canyon* (2006) by Eileen M Smith-Cavros, or *I Was Called to Dixie* (1979) by Andrew Karl Larson, a cotton missionary.

1890

Mormon president Wilford Woodruff signs a manifesto that officially ceases the practice of polygamy; plural marriage is still practiced today among fundamentalist groups in rural Utah.

1896

Utah is admitted to the Union as the 45th state after territorial politicians agree to explicitly ban the practice of polygamy in the new state constitution.

1916

President Woodrow Wilson signs the Organic Act, authorizing the establishment of the National Park Service (NPS); Methodist minister Frederick Vining Fisher visits Zion Canyon.

1919

Already national monuments, both Zion and the Grand Canyon officially become national parks; a dirt road to the Grand Canyon's North Rim is built from Kanab, Utah.

1923

Union Pacific Railroad is extended to Cedar City; building of Bryce Canyon Lodge, made of local timber and stone and designed by Gilbert Stanley Underwood, begins.

In *Massacre at Mountain Meadows* (2008), Ronald Walker and Richard Turley unflinchingly examine one of the darkest incidents in Mormon pioneer history. For another viewpoint, read journalist Jon Krakauer's *Under the Banner of Heaven* (2003).

To read about one-armed Civil War veteran and Western explorer John Wesley Powell's famous boat trip, pick up a modern reprint of Powell's very readable *Exploration of the Colorado River and its Canyons* (1875).

For more historical context on John Wesley Powell and his groundbreaking work, read Wallace Stegner's fascinating book *Beyond the Hundredth Meridian: John Wesley Powell and the Second Opening of the West* (1953).

Colorado River through the Grand Canyon. Unlike Hamblin, Powell's motivation was not religious, but to survey and explore the land and peoples of southern Utah for science. Thanks to his passion and rigor, Powell and his survey teams' geologic and ethnological work largely forms the basis of what we know about early southern Utah today. In 1870, Hamblin secured Powell's second expedition a welcome among Southern Paiutes. As Hamblin had done, Powell demonstrated respect and earned both safe passage and practical assistance from the Southern Paiutes.

TAMING ZION'S WILDERNESS

Earlier indigenous peoples undoubtedly knew and entered Zion Canyon, for they left evidence on the rocks, but to the Kaibab Paiutes it was a place to be avoided, particularly after sunset. Mysterious and foreboding, the canyon was seen as inhabited by trickster gods who were capricious, even willfully malicious. The first non–Native American to enter Zion Canyon was Nephi Johnson, a Mormon pioneer who came south with Jacob Hamblin on a mission. In 1858, at the behest of Brigham Young, Johnson explored the upper reaches of the Virgin River, looking for good places to settle. One can only imagine what he must have felt as he entered Zion Canyon alone, his Paiute guide waiting safely behind.

Mormons didn't settle in the canyon until 1863, when Isaac Behunin and his sons built the first cabin and cleared some farmland. Behunin is credited with naming Zion Canyon, saying that 'A man can worship god among these great cathedrals as well as in any man-made church.' When Brigham Young visited in 1870, he disagreed with the assessment. Whether due to the arduous journey or the forbidden tobacco Behunin was growing, Young proclaimed it 'Not Zion,' a name that stuck among Mormons for years.

After his first famous Colorado River expedition, John Wesley Powell returned to southern Utah and explored Zion Canyon in 1872. Powell called it Mukuntuweap, which he believed was a Paiute word for 'straight canyon.' But it was Clarence Dutton, a poet-geologist in Powell's employ, who captured its grandeur. Upon seeing the canyon in 1875, Dutton wrote: 'In coming time it will, I believe, take rank with a very small number of spectacles, each of which will, in its own way, be regarded as the most exquisite of its kind which the world discloses.'

In a 1908 official report, a government surveyor first suggested preserving Zion Canyon as a monument. President Taft signed the proclamation creating Mukuntuweap National Monument in 1909. Methodist minister Frederick Vining Fisher toured the canyon in the company of

1925

Designed by Gilbert Stanley Underwood, Zion Lodge opens to accommodate railway tourists following the 'Grand Circle' route around the Southwest.

1927

Laborious and often-dangerous construction starts on the Zion–Mt Carmel Hwy, which opens three years later, bringing more tourists to southern Utah.

1928

Named after Mormon settler Ebenezer Bryce, Bryce Canyon becomes Utah's second national park; over 25,000 tourists arrive that year, often en route to/from the Grand Canyon.

1931

Artist and writer Everett Reuss wanders in southern Utah's canyon country; three years later, the 20-year-old disappears into the wilderness nearly without a trace.

1933

During the Great Depression, President Roosevelt creates the Civilian Conservation Corps; in Utah, CCCs plant more than three million trees over the next decade.

a Latter-Day Saints bishop in 1916, giving names to many of the famous rock formations, including Angels Landing and the Great White Throne. In 1919 the monument's name and designation were officially changed by Congress, and thus Zion National Park was born.

Within a year, park visitation doubled to about 3700 people – hardly crowded, but still a lot considering road conditions and its remote location. To better facilitate tourism to southern Utah, a railroad spur was extended to Cedar City in 1923. Zion Lodge opened two years later, accommodating railway tourists following the 'Grand Circle' route around the Southwest. In 1930 the Zion–Mt Carmel Hwy and its tunnel were completed, offering a paved route into and through Zion, bringing in over 55,000 tourists that year.

Opening Zion: A Scrapbook of the Park's First Official Tourists (2010) by John and Melissa Clark depicts the real-life adventures of a group of young women who visited on the park's opening day in 1920.

A WAY STATION TO THE GRAND CANYON

Historically overlooked, Bryce Canyon nestles alongside the Paunsaugunt Plateau, the latter's name derived from a Paiute word meaning 'home of the beavers.' Fur trappers like Jedediah Smith who roamed the area in the early 19th century made no mention of Bryce's striking scenery, and neither did Spanish traders. During his 1869 survey, John Wesley Powell stuck to the rivers and passed right by. Captain Sutton, a member of Powell's survey, described the distant terrain as seeming 'traversable only by a creature with wings.'

Mormons scouts arrived at Bryce Canyon in the 1850s as they searched the entire Paunsaugunt Plateau for arable land. In the mid-1870s a small group settled in the adjacent valleys, which seemed well suited for grazing livestock. Among the latter was Ebenezer Bryce, who stayed in the area for five years, building an irrigation ditch and a road into the canyon. Bryce moved his family south to Arizona in 1880, but left behind in the canyon his name and the now famous epithet, 'It's a hell of a place to lose a cow.'

Like Zion Canyon, Bryce was popular among railway tourists and conservationists at the turn of the 20th century, though it was more difficult to reach. It wasn't until 1915, when JW Humphrey became the founding supervisor of Utah's Sevier National Forest that Bryce's fate would be sealed. In 1916 Humphrey brought in photographers to take the first pictures of the spectacular canyon for a promotional article that appeared in a Union Pacific Railroad publication. Word got out.

In 1919, the same year Zion became a national park, the state legislature recommended that Bryce also be protected. Four years later President Harding established Bryce Canyon National Monument. In 1928 Bryce became Utah's second national park. Throughout the 1920s,

The History of Southern Utah and its National Parks (1950) by AM Woodbury is as much a period piece as a source of reliable history written by a man who lived through the parks' founding.

1934

The Kaibab band of Paiutes achieve federal recognition as an indigenous Native American tribe; a tribal reservation is established near the Utah–Arizona border.

1936

After five years of back-breaking, sometimes life-taking construction work, Boulder (Hoover) Dam is finished on the Colorado River at the Nevada–Arizona state line near Las Vegas.

1941–45

During WWII Utah becomes an important state for defense operations, including military bases, mineral mining and arms manufacturing.

1950s

After getting a master's degree in philosophy, writer and political activist Edward Abbey works as a seasonal ranger at Arches National Monument.

1962

Utah's all-weather state Hwy 24 through the Fremont River canyon is finally finished and paved, opening up the Capitol Reef region to burgeoning tourism.

construction of Bryce Canyon Lodge, another Union Pacific Railroad 'Grand Circle' Southwest touring stop, was carried out using locally quarried stone and harvested timber.

A CAPITAL WONDERLAND

Those Who Came Before: Southwestern Archaeology in the National Park System (1993), by Robert and Florence Lister, puts Capitol Reef, Canyonlands and Arches in the greater context of the Colorado Plateau, with striking photographs.

Capitol Reef's European-American history dates back to 1872, when Mormon settlers first planted fruit trees along the banks of the Fremont River near the town of Junction. Once their trees flourished, the settlers renamed the town Fruita. Over the next decades, Torrey resident Ephraim Pectal sought to promote interest in 'Wayne Wonderland,' a nickname given to the Waterpocket Fold, which lies in Wayne County. Soon after being elected to the state legislature in 1933, Pectal lobbied President Franklin D Roosevelt to establish what he dubbed 'Wayne Wonderland National Monument.' In 1937 President Roosevelt signed a proclamation creating the mercifully renamed Capitol Reef National Monument.

Despite Depression-era improvements completed by the Civilian Conservation Corps, Capitol Reef National Monument was mostly neglected by the federal government for the next two decades. The first official park ranger didn't even arrive until 1958. But the nationwide 'Mission 66' national parks renewal project brought a host of new tourist facilities to serve over 145,000 annual visitors by 1967. In 1971 Congress finally made Capitol Reef a national park.

THE MAKING OF MOAB

Famous Western novelist Zane Grey used southern Utah as backdrop for many of his romanticized cowboy tales; *Riders of the Purple Sage* (1912) is his best-known story. It's a galloping read.

It wasn't until 1878 that Mormons permanently settled in the Moab region. (Ute tribespeople had violently thwarted a previous effort in the 1850s.) Agriculture and grazing quickly became the economic mainstays, although the new railroad that bypassed Moab in 1883 dealt a serious blow to this frontier community. Ranchers used much of the land in what is now Canyonlands National Park as winter pasture for grazing herds, a practice that continued through to 1975.

In the early 20th century, local residents, including the editor of Moab's first newspaper, touted southern Utah's geologic wonders, finally attracting the attention of the Rio Grande Western Railroad. Recognizing the potential of Arches as a tourist destination, the railroad lobbied the government for federal protection. In 1929 President Hoover established Arches as a national monument.

During the Cold War era of the 1950s, when the federal government subsidized uranium mining, Moab's population tripled in three years. By the early 1960s, Arches superintendent Bates Wilson started lobbying

1963
Controversial Glen Canyon Dam is finished and artificial Lake Powell begins to form, eventually covering up ancestral Native American sites and stunning rock formations.

1964
Canyonlands National Park is set aside by Congress, after a lobbying and public-opinion campaign jump-started by Arches National Monument superintendent Bates Wilson.

1966
Designed in the 1920s by famous park architect Gilbert Stanley Underwood, Zion Lodge burns to the ground, but is rebuilt in just 100 days.

1970
Interstate highway I-70 is dedicated; although construction is technically not finished for another 20 years, the new road makes southern Utah more accessible to tourists.

1971
After Congress passes a bill signed by President Richard Nixon, Arches and Capitol Reef become national parks.

for further protection of southeastern Utah's natural resources, calling for the establishment of a 'Grand View National Park.' In 1964 President Johnson established Canyonlands National Park. In 1971, Congress declared Arches a national park, too, and expanded the boundaries of Canyonlands to what they are today.

EXPLOITATION VS CONSERVATION

The amount of arable land in Utah is less than 5%, and in southern Utah that figure is less than 1%. What farmland there is and towns there are depend entirely on rivers. The rain that falls in the desert is hardly enough to work up a good spit. Twentieth-century development has been slow to recognize and adapt to these facts, however. Politicians have dammed countless rivers across the Southwest to try to control and divert their flow and create power: the Colorado River has been dammed twice, by Hoover Dam in 1936 and Glen Canyon Dam, among the world's largest, in 1963. Public works projects have repeatedly failed, often spectacularly and expensively, and yet the attempts continue. And still no Eden.

Throughout the busy Beehive State, mining has experienced various heydays – from the great silver mines of the 19th century to modern coal, oil and mineral mining, especially to support WWII military operations. In the 1950s the federal government subsidized uranium exploration, spurring more Cold War–era mining operations in southern Utah, especially around Moab. Though these efforts unearthed little of the radioactive element, mining roads further opened this once-remote landscape to recreational tourism and encouraged settlement. At the same time, all of this extraction has exacted a high toll on the slow-healing desert.

Today, southern Utah's desert settlements are well established, and politics demands they be supported, even as the economic and environmental costs keep growing. At the same time, many people – both outsiders and those who have made their homes in this seemingly inhospitable place – have long recognized the rare beauty of these lands and made efforts to preserve them. In fact, the first paintings of such Western landmarks as the Grand Canyon and Zion Canyon, by Albert Bierstadt and Thomas Moran, were instrumental in sparking the US conservation movement during the late 19th century, which in turn brought about the establishment of the National Park Service (NPS) in 1916.

Not everyone wants to see southern Utah's remaining wilderness protected. Established by President Clinton in 1996 and administered by the Bureau of Land Management (BLM), Grand Staircase-Escalante

Roadside History of Utah (1999) by Cynthia Larsen Bennett is an informative, thought-provoking if weighty companion for history buffs, covering both major interstates and rural highways throughout the state, including southern Utah's 'Forgotten Corridor.'

An expansive, well-researched history is *The Proper Edge of the Sky: High Plateau Country of Utah* (2002) by Edward Geary, who stitches together in telling detail the ongoing relationship of people and the land.

1979

The Grand Canyon is declared a Unesco World Heritage site, just one year after Mesa Verde National Park, also on the Colorado Plateau, is similarly recognized.

1987

World population of California condors plummets to less than two dozen wild birds; captive breeding efforts begin and the species is reintroduced to southern Utah in 1996.

1996

President Bill Clinton establishes Grand Staircase-Escalante National Monument, allowing for some land uses (eg hunting and grazing by permit) not allowed in national parks.

2000

Zion Canyon institutes a mandatory seasonal shuttle system to relieve car congestion and reduce air pollution, eliminating over 5 million pounds of carbon-dioxide emissions annually.

2002

The XIX Olympic Winter Games are held in Salt Lake City, bringing global attention and more tourism to Utah's outdoor recreational areas and parklands.

THE RED ROCK WILDERNESS ACT: A CITIZENS' PROPOSAL

Any attempt to conserve land in the Southwest stirs intense passions, and the Red Rock Wilderness Act is a doozy. If passed, it would set aside over 9 million acres of southern Utah desert as Congressionally designated wilderness areas, the most restrictive type of public lands. These prohibit motorized vehicles, resource extraction, road building and infrastructure development. Indeed, members of the public are only permitted to enter such areas on foot.

Nearly 80% of Utah's land already lies in public hands, 65% of which is owned by the federal government. The Red Rock Wilderness Act would change the status of about 15% of these existing federal lands. Opponents of the act frequently say that Utah has already done enough. Putting even more land off-limits to resource extraction and road building Is unfair. Why not, they say, focus conservation efforts on other Western states – they have plenty of land, right?

Land, yes. Wilderness, no. And there's the rub. Precious little land in the US remains pristine enough to qualify as wilderness. Southern Utah – the last US region to be settled by non-native peoples and mapped – has more than most. Much of Utah is already federally protected to some degree, but proponents say this amount and these protections aren't enough.

In 1985 the BLM itself identified more than 3 million acres for further possible wilderness designation in southern Utah, but a citizens' group did its own inventory and suggested that nearly 6 million acres could be added to that total. In 1989 it formalized its plan as a Congressional bill dubbed 'The Citizens' Proposal' – which was eventually renamed America's Red Rock Wilderness Act. The bill has since been reintroduced into every new session of Congress, before which it still sits – at least, for the time being.

To learn more or take action yourself, contact the **Southern Utah Wilderness Alliance** (SUWA; www.suwa.org).

Polygamy is still practiced in rural Utah. For a riveting real-life account, read *Escape!* (2008) by Carolyn Jessop, who broke free of a plural marriage forced upon her as a teenager by Mormon fundamentalists.

National Monument is southern Utah's most controversial federal land grab. Many of Utah's Republican majority believed the president was 'appeasing his Sierra Club constituents' by establishing a monument in a state that had not supported him in either election. Counties in southern Utah sued the federal government, claiming the executive branch lacked jurisdiction to declare a national monument. In 2004 a federal court ruled that the president had acted within his bounds under the authority of the 1906 Antiquities Act. Given ever-growing regional tourism, Grand Staircase-Escalante is likely not the last of southern Utah's vast wilderness to be set aside 'for the enjoyment, education, and inspiration of this and future generations,' as the NPS mission statement promises.

2007

Warren Jeffs, ex-president of the Fundamentalist Church of Latter-Day Saints (FLDS), is convicted as an accomplice to rape for arranging extralegal marriages between men and underage girls.

2008

One-time Mormon missionary, Senator Mitt Romney unsuccessfully campaigns for the Republican nomination in the US presidential election.

2009

Zion National Park celebrates its centennial, themed 'A Century of Sanctuary.' Over 2.7 million visitors arrive in the park that year.

2010

A Zion National Park commemorative coin journeys aboard the US space shuttle *Endeavor* and is returned, becoming part of the park's permanent museum collection.

2016

National Park Service (NPS) celebrates its 100th year of service, with special centennial birthday celebrations held at parks across the country, including in southern Utah.

Zion National Park

'I survived Angels Landing,' reads a popular T-shirt. And to be sure, conquering this iconic hike – with its 1400ft-plus elevation change, vertigo-inducing drop-offs and chain-assisted sections – is an essential part of the experience. But Zion National Park is so much more than extreme physical challenges and adrenaline. It's about feeling the majesty mid-canyon, appreciating a weeping grotto's delicate beauty and experiencing nature's power as you wade in the Virgin River.

The availability of water in a desert defines this park, in comparison to others in southern Utah. At lower elevations cottonwood and maple trees provide an interesting contrast to the massive rock formations, putting on a colorful show in autumn. Up country on the mesa tops, as high as 7000ft, ponderosa pine forests alternate with meadows.

Most of the 2.7 million annual visitors enter the park along Zion Canyon floor. Hiking and climbing up from there are indeed excellent adventures. The thrill of peering over a 2000ft sandstone cliff is indescribable; just don't expect to have the view to yourself from May through September. Though the canyon remains quiet because of a seasonal shuttle system, popular front-country hikes do get congested. It's easy enough to escape the crowds in the backcountry, where there's a lifetime worth of canyoneering routes to explore, or take an overlook drive in the much less trafficked Kolob Canyon area. Whatever section or season you visit, you'll be glad you've been there, done that – and bought the T-shirt.

HIGHLIGHTS

- Standing knee-deep In the Virgin River looking up at 1000ft walls in the **Narrows** (p104)
- Overlooking Angels Landing, 500ft below you, at **Observation Point** (p106)
- Watching the sun set on Watchman Mountain over the gourmet cuisine at **Parallel 88** (p127)
- Shuttling up then cycling down **Zion Canyon Scenic Drive** (p95)
- Rappelling down rockface for the first time on a guided **canyoneering trip** (p117)

- **Total Area** 229 sq miles
- **Elevation** 3940ft (at Zion Canyon Visitor Centre)
- **Average high/low temperature at Zion Canyon in July** 96°F/67°F

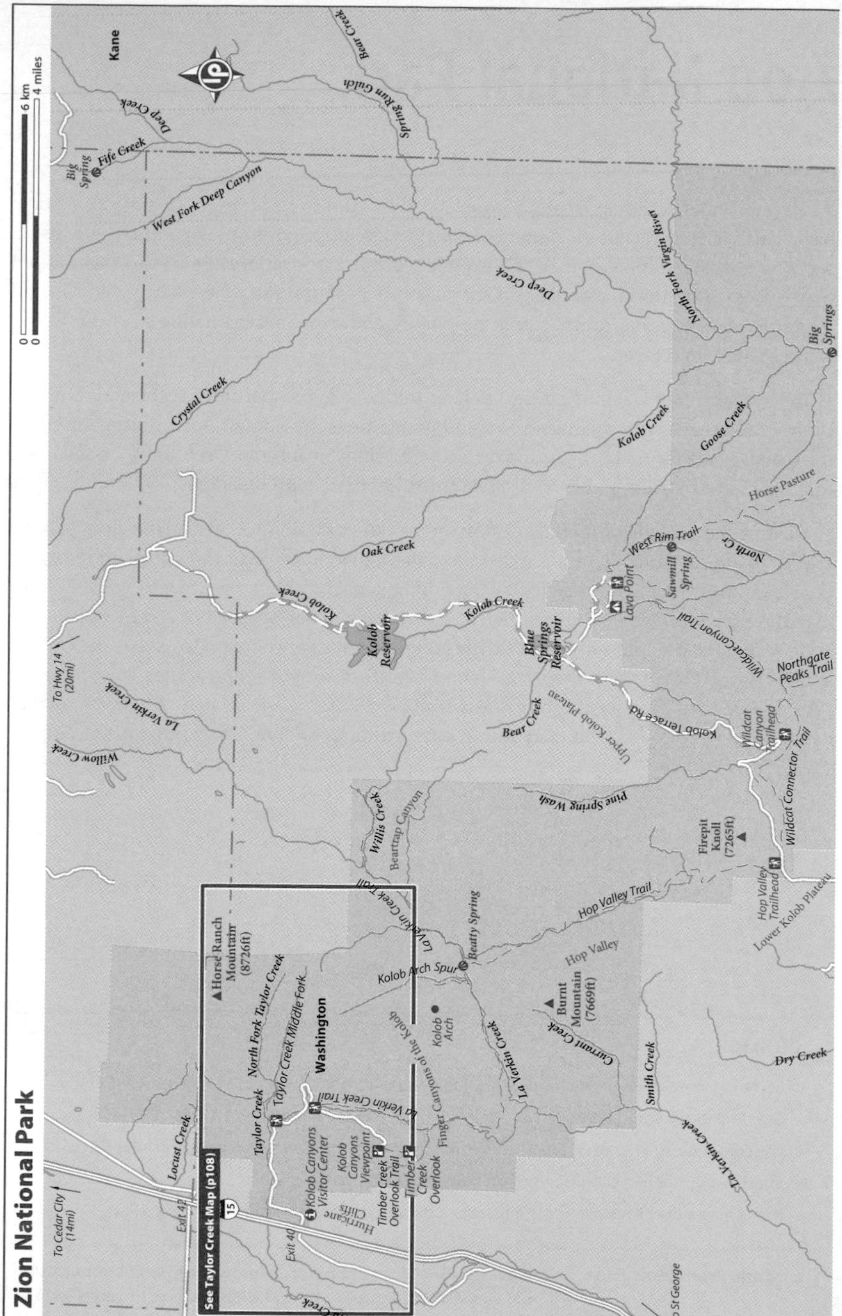

ZION NATIONAL PARK

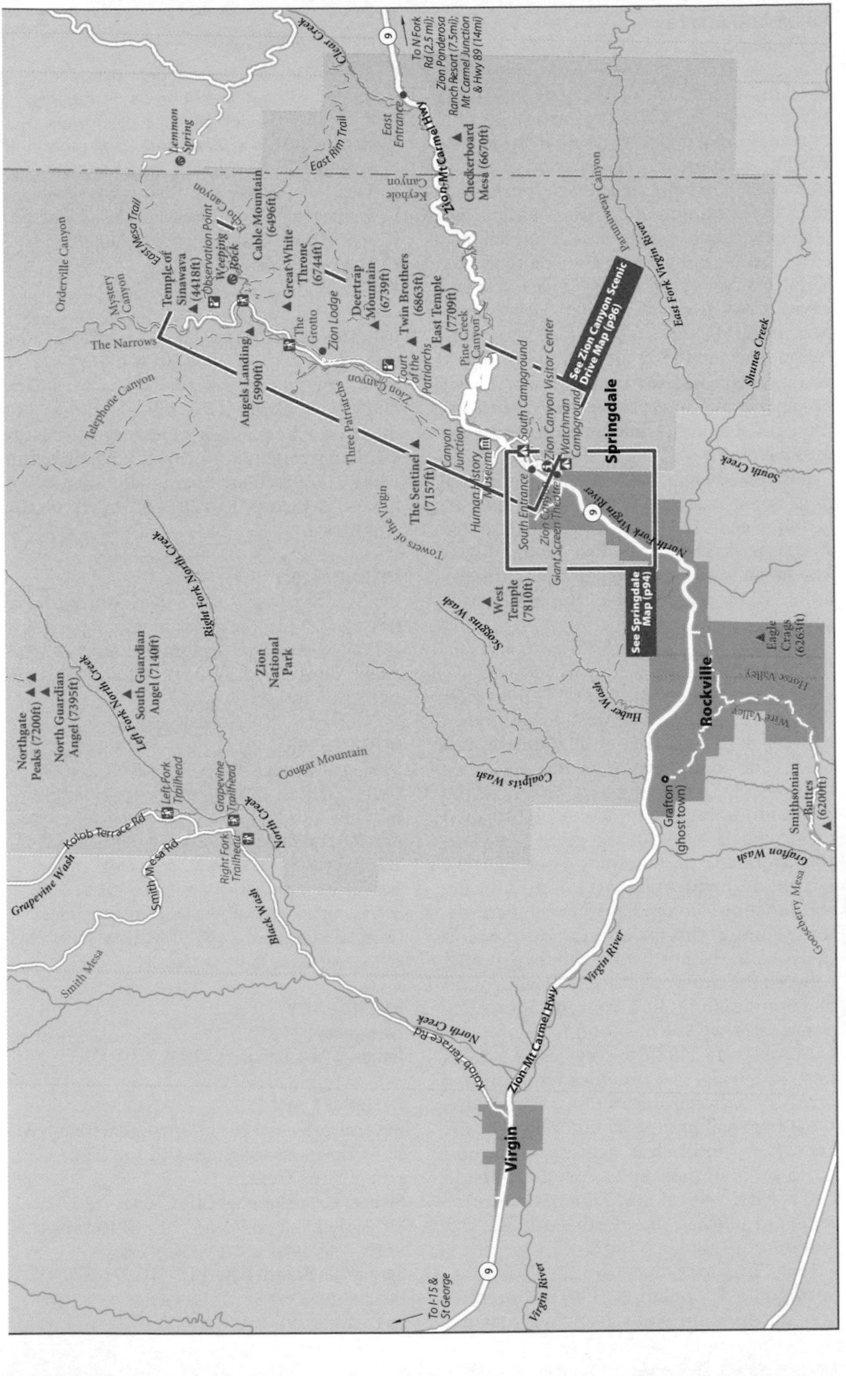

ZION NATIONAL PARK

When You Arrive

Zion National Park is open 24/7 year-round. Entrance fees are valid for seven days in all sections of the park and cost $25 per vehicle or $12 per pedestrian, bicycle or motorcycle. An annual Zion Pass is $50, and interagency and senior passes (see p264) are valid. All can be purchased at entrance stations and visitor centers. Remember to hold on to your receipt if you are traveling to both the Zion Canyon and Kolob Canyons sections, otherwise you will have to pay twice. Note that backcountry permits (p111) and RV tunnel escort fees (see boxed text, p92) are additional. Once you pay, you will receive a comprehensive newspaper and interpretive map describing the park. For more information, see www.nps.gov/zion.

National Geographic (www.natgeomaps.com) puts out a colorful, waterproof *Trails Illustrated* map (No 214) for Zion. The less snazzy park map from **Zion Natural History Association** (www.zionpark.org) also gets the job done. Both are available at park visitor centers.

KEEPING CLEAN

Remember that the national park campgrounds do not have showers. At the time of writing, the only place to pay for just a shower ($5) is at **Zion Rock & Mountain Guides** (☎ 435-772-3303; www.zionrockguides.com; 1458 Zion Park Blvd; 🕑 8am-8pm Mar-Oct, hours vary Nov-Feb). But you can always rent a space to camp at one of the campgrounds outside the park.

Orientation

Zion National Park occupies 147,000 acres that run roughly northwest to southeast between I-15 and Hwy 9 in southwestern Utah. The main section of the park, encompassing Zion Canyon, is closest to the South Entrance on Hwy 9 outside the town of Springdale. You can also get to 'the Canyon' from the East Entrance, which is 14 serpentine, uphill miles east toward Mt Carmel Junction. No roads within the park directly connect this main section with Kolob Canyons in the northwest. Unless you hike between the two, you'll have to drive around the 40 miles (an hour) from the South Entrance via Hwy 9, Rte 17 and I-15.

Kolob Terrace Rd (no services), 14 miles west of Springdale, provides backcountry access in between the sections. Park maps show the road ending at Kolob Reservoir, but when snows clear, you can continue north on it all the way to Hwy 14, outside Cedar City. Several East Zion backcountry trails are reached via North Fork Rd, 2.5 miles east of the East Entrance.

Just outside the South Entrance, Springdale (population 850) is an outdoorsy community of eclectic restaurants, galleries, motels and such that provide the majority of the services in the area. Other small towns line Hwy 9 farther west, including Rockville (3.5 miles), Virgin (14 miles), La Verkin (16 miles) and the largest, Hurricane (22 miles). If you can't find what you need in Springdale, your best bet is St George (p128), 41 miles to the southwest.

Information

Unless otherwise stated in the address, businesses outside the park are in Springdale (Map p94). Most lodgings listed in this chapter are completely nonsmoking; exceptions are noted below.

BOOKSTORES

Sundancer Books (☎ 435-772-3400; 975 Zion Park Blvd; 🕑 10:30am-8:30pm) Great selection of Southwestern writers.

Zion Natural History Association (ZNHA; ☎ 435-772-3265, 800-635-3959; www.zionpark.org; 🕑 8am-8pm Jun-Sep, 8am-5pm Nov-Apr, 8am-6pm May & Oct) Runs the excellent bookstore in the Zion Canyon Visitor Center, selling area and activity guides, histories, children's books, maps and more. Online sales, too.

EMERGENCY

Emergency (☎ 911)

National Park Rangers (☎ 435-772-3322)

INTERNET ACCESS

Several cafes (p126) in Springdale have wi-fi, as do most lodgings and the Zion Canyon Visitor Center.

Pioneer Lodge Internet Café (☎ 435-772-3233; 838 Zion Park Blvd; per 30min $3; 🕑 6:30am-9pm) A few terminals, OK coffee; next to the lodge lobby.

Springdale Branch Library (☎ 435-772-3676; 126 Lion Blvd; per 30min $1; 🕑 10am-6pm Mon-Fri, noon-5pm Sat) Internet access.

INTERNET RESOURCES

A to Zion (☎ 800-869-6635; www.atozion.com) St George tourism office–sponsored website covering the entire region. Look for the related brochure in St George (p128).

LAUNDRY

Zion Park Laundry (865 Zion Park Blvd; per load $2; ☎ 7am-9pm) Unstaffed laundromat on main street; soap available.

MEDICAL SERVICES

The nearest 24-hour emergency room is in St George (p128).

Zion Canyon Medical Clinic (☎ 435-772-3226; 120 Lion Blvd; 9am-5pm Tue-Sat Jun-Aug, Tue & Wed Sep-May) Walk-in clinic.

MONEY

Zions Bank (☎ 435-772-3274; 921 Zion Park Blvd; 9am-2pm Mon-Fri) Currency exchange and 24-hour ATM.

POST

Post Office (☎ 435-772-3950; 624 Zion Park Blvd; 7:30-11:30am & noon-3:30pm Mon-Fri, 10am-1pm Sat)

TELEPHONE

Cell-phone service is limited in Springdale. Verizon has the only local coverage. Even then, the signal will not reach far onto the park trails. Currently, coverage does not reach very far into the park beyond the visitor center and possibly around Zion Lodge. In Zion, pay phones are available at the visitor centers and behind the ranger station in Watchman campground.

TOURIST INFORMATION

Springdale has no tourist office, but the town produces a handy restaurant menu guide that's available at lodgings. For a travel planner, contact Zion Canyon Visitors Bureau.

Kolob Canyons Visitor Center (☎ 435-586-0895; Kolob Canyons Rd, off I-15; 8am-6pm late May-early Sep, 8am-5pm late Apr-late May & early Sep–mid-Oct, 8am-4:30pm mid-Oct–late Apr) Small, secondary visitor center in the northwest section of the park.

Zion Canyon Backcountry Desk (☎ 435-772-0170; www.nps.gov/zion/planyourvisit; Zion Canyon Visitor Center; 7am-8pm late May-early Sep, 7am-6pm late Apr-late May & early Sep–mid-Oct, 8am-4:30pm mid-Oct–late Apr) Issues backcountry trail and camping permits. Some permits available online.

Zion Canyon Visitor Center (☎ 435-772-3256; www.nps.gov/zion; 8am-8pm late May-early Sep, 8am-6pm late Apr-late May & early Sep–mid-Oct, 8am-5pm mid-Oct–late Apr) Several rangers are on hand to answer questions at the main visitor center; ask to see the picture binder of hikes to know what you're getting into.

Zion Canyon Visitors Bureau (☎ 888-518-7070; www.zionpark.com) No office. Provides great Springdale info online and detailed brochures by mail.

TRAVEL AGENCIES

Zion Travel Center (☎ 435-772-0559; ziontravelcenter@gmail.com; 198 Zion Park Blvd; 11am-6pm Mon-Sat) Books tours, lodging and dinner reservations.

Park Policies & Regulations

As at all national parks, you are not allowed to feed wildlife or to touch or deface any cultural artifact or site.

Pets are not permitted on park shuttles, in the backcountry, on trails or in park buildings. (For more see the Kids & Pets chapter, p53.) Bicycles and pets are allowed on one trail, the Pa'rus Trail (p101). Bicycles are welcome on park roads but may not be ridden through the Zion–Mt Carmel Tunnel.

Campfires are allowed only in fire grates in Watchman and South campgrounds.

IS ZION FIDO-FRIENDLY?

We can't say that Zion is the canine-friendliest of parks covered in this book. Dogs are only allowed on one trail, the Pa'rus, and perhaps because of that, few motels in the area allow pets. (Look for the symbol indicating those that do.) If you want to take your furry friend hiking, you can try the Bureau of Land Management (BLM) land south of Rockville, and Springdale River Park (p94) allows dogs. But honestly, you have many more hiking options in Grand Staircase-Escalante National Monument (p174), and lots of Kanab hotels put out the doggie welcome mat. So you might want to head that way.

About 4 miles west of Zion Canyon, **Doggy Dude Ranch** (☎ 435-772-3105; www.doggyduderanch.com; 800 E Main, Rockville; 8am-8pm Mon-Sat, 9am-5pm Sun) will keep your canine friend overnight. They provide large outdoor play areas with kiddie pools and they walk dogs big and small twice a day.

Wood gathering is not permitted in the park; buy all firewood in Springdale. When fire danger is high, all campfires may be banned. Fireworks are prohibited in the park.

People are not allowed in the Virgin River when it is flowing in excess of 120 cubic feet per second. Zion's hiking and backcountry-use regulations include those listed for all the parks in the Activities chapter (p40).

Getting Around

CAR, MOTORCYCLE & RV

How you get around Zion depends on the season. Between April and October, no passenger cars are allowed to tour Zion Canyon Scenic Drive; to access it you will have to take the Zion Park Shuttle (below). Personal vehicles are permitted between November and March, when the shuttle does not operate. Winter visitation is low enough that parking in Zion Canyon is almost never an issue. During shuttle season, it's still possible to drive through the southern section of Zion on Hwy 9, which connects Springdale with Mt Carmel Junction. The pretty drive offers several parking lots and turnouts. Zion–Mt Carmel Tunnel has vehicle size restrictions; if you're piloting an RV, see the boxed text, below.

Year-round you can drive on Kolob Canyons Scenic Drive. Kolob Terrace Rd becomes impassable when snows set in (roughly December into May).

SHUTTLE BUSES

From April 1 to October 31, two free, linked shuttle loops – one mandatory, one optional – operate quiet, propane-burning buses that are a boon both to the environment and to the peace of the park. For the most part, private vehicles are prohibited in Zion Canyon during the season; using the mandatory Zion Park Shuttle is the only way to get around. The shuttle makes nine stops along the scenic drive (p95), from the visitor center to the Temple of Sinawava (a 90-minute round-trip). The optional Springdale Town Shuttle makes six regular stops and three flag stops outside hotels and businesses along Hwy 9. The stop near Majestic View Lodge is the furthest from the park. The town shuttle terminates at Zion Canyon Giant Screen Theatre (p95). Passengers walk across a footbridge to a kiosk where rangers collect fees. The visitor center and the first Zion Canyon Shuttle stop lie just on the other side. It really couldn't be easier.

The wheelchair-accessible shuttle buses can accommodate large backpacks and carry up to two bicycles or one baby jogger. All shuttle stops feature a shaded wood bench with a posted route description.

Park shuttles operate late May through mid-September from 5:45am to 11pm; April to late May and mid-September through October from 6:45am to 10pm. Shuttles run every six to 10 minutes through the middle of the day and every 15 to 30 minutes early and late. An express town shuttle departs Majestic View Lodge at 5:30am in summer and 6:30am in spring and fall; otherwise, town buses start running around 7am.

There is a parking lot at the Zion Canyon Visitor Center, convenient if you plan on hitting the trail early. It fills up by 9am or 10am in season, so if you're sleeping in, you'll have to take the town shuttle. Most

SIZE MATTERS

Henry Ford's Model T was only 20 years old when engineers started blasting the Zion–Mt Carmel Tunnel, so forgive them for not anticipating today's internal-combustion behemoths.

Vehicles larger than 7ft, 10in wide or 11ft, 4in high cannot safely stay in their lane and must pay a $15 'escort fee' on top of park admission. Announce your need for an escort and pay the fee, good for two trips by the same vehicle in a seven-day period, at the east or south entrance stations. When you arrive at the tunnel, rangers will stop oncoming traffic, creating a one-way road. Oversize vehicles may only travel through the tunnel between 8am and 8pm May through August, 8am to 7pm in March, April and October, and 8am to 4:30pm November through March.

Vehicles prohibited at all times include those more than 13ft, 1in tall, single vehicles more than 40ft long and combined vehicles more than 50ft long, as well as semi-trucks, commercial trucks and trucks carrying hazardous materials. Bicycle and pedestrian traffic are also prohibited.

THE ART OF THE CANYON

With such incredible natural surrounds, it's no wonder that so many artists find inspiration in the canyon. You'll see the results hanging all over town – in restaurants, hotels and B&Bs. The big three photographers – David Petit, David West and Michael Fatali – all have galleries of their own. But a number of other galleries in town carry the work of various local photographers, painters and sculptors. Look for the three-dimensional oil paintings of Anna Weiler Brown, the multimedia works of Deb Durban and the creative ceramics of Ben Behunin (descendent of Isaac Behunin, credited with naming Zion). Note that gallery hours can be as mercurial as their owners. From north to south:

Fatali Gallery (☎ 435-772-2422; 105 Zion Park Blvd; 🕑 11am-7pm Mar-Nov, by appointment Dec-Feb) Otherworldly colors, sensation-causing national-park photography. Ask about photography courses and clinics.

Manzanita Trading Co (☎ 435-772-0123; 205 Zion Park Blvd; 🕑 10am-7pm Tue-Sun Mar-Oct, to 6pm Nov-Feb) Specializing in local art.

Worthington Gallery (☎ 435-772-0291; 789 Zion Park Blvd; 🕑 8am-7pm) Ceramics and works of famous landscape painter Jim Jones.

David J West Gallery (☎ 435-772-3510; 801 Zion Park Blvd; 🕑 10am-9pm Tue-Sun Mar-Oct, to 8pm Nov-Feb) Iconic local-landscape photography that is full of light, some photo gear.

David Petit Gallery (☎ 435-772-3206; 975 Zion Park Blvd; 🕑 10:30am-8pm Wed-Sat, 3-8pm Tue) Our favorite intrepid outdoorsman-photographer. His rock art and ruin photos are unlike any others.

De Zion Gallery (☎ 435-772-6888; 1051 Zion Park Blvd; 🕑 noon-6pm) Large studio, many Utah artists represented.

hotels are near shuttle stops, and you'll find tons of free shuttle parking along the town's main road (park inside the solid white line).

Note that guests of Zion Lodge may take their personal vehicles on Zion Canyon Scenic Drive as far as the hotel (no farther) – after they get their red pass upon check-in at the visitor center. Shuttle buses are wheelchair accessible; in rare cases where a disabled visitor requires vehicle-supported medical devices or conveyance that exceeds the shuttle size requirements, a special Zion Canyon driving permit may be issued at the visitor center. Like we said, these are rare, and they require medical documentation.

HIKER SHUTTLES

Outfitters offer hiker shuttles to one-way and hard-to-reach backcountry trailheads, including to the Narrows top hike on the east side of the park and Subway access in the west. For more on backcountry trails, see p111. Rates per person start around $30. Popular routes have daily scheduled departures May through October, but reservations are required for all shuttles.

Red Rock Shuttle & Tours (☎ 435-635-9104; www.redrockshuttle.com) Picks up from Zion Canyon Visitor Center

Zion Adventure Company (☎ 435-772-1001; www.zionadventures.com; 36 Lion Blvd)

Zion Rock & Mountain Guides (☎ 435-772-3303; www.zionrockguides.com; 1458 Zion Park Blvd)

TOURS

Reservations are essential. Private half- and full-day tours start from $100 per person.

Red Rock Shuttle & Tours (☎ 435-635-9104; www.redrockshuttle.com; pick up from Zion Canyon Visitor Center) Van tours of Zion.

Ride Along With A Ranger (☎ 435-772-3256; www.nps.gov/zion; Zion Canyon Visitor Center; tour free) Reserve ahead for an entertaining 90-minute, ranger-led Zion Canyon shuttle tour that makes stops not on the regular route. It's a great hiking alternative for those with limited mobility.

Southern Utah Scenic Tours (☎ 435 867-8690; www.utahscenictours.com) One-day Zion and two-day Zion and Bryce tours out of Vegas.

SIGHTS

All sights within Zion National Park, including the Human History Museum, are listed in the Hiking and Driving sections (p100 and p95). Listed below are a few minor diversions to occupy an afternoon in and around Springdale. If you're looking for shops, you'll have no trouble finding knick-knacky souvenirs and Zion NP hats at the stores along Zion Park Blvd, but the canyon also attracts more than its fair share

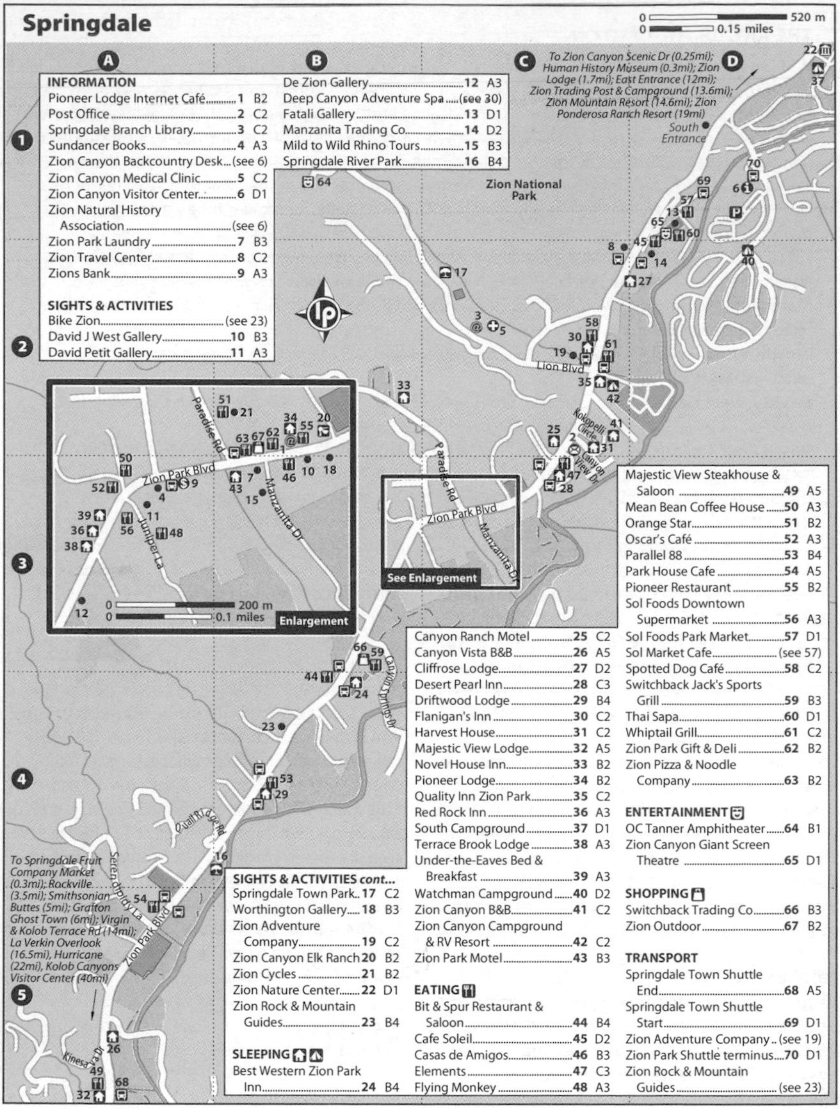

of excellent artists; for more on local galleries, see the boxed text, p93.

ZION CANYON ELK RANCH

You can't miss this **ranch** (☎ 435-619-2424; 792 Zion Park Blvd; feeding by donation; 🕑 dawn-dusk) right in the middle of town. It offers kids of all ages the chance to pet and feed the elk and buffalo. The property has been in the owner's family for more than 100 years.

PUBLIC PARKS

Springdale has two public parks; both are open dawn to dusk and feature nice lawns, shaded picnic tables, grills and bathrooms. **Springdale River Park**, about 2 miles from the

KEEPING KIDS ENTERTAINED

It's amazing how jaded a seven-year-old can be. Here are some entertaining alternatives to 'another dumb trail.'

- Feed the animals at **Zion Canyon Elk Ranch** (opposite)
- Explore the park on a kid-oriented guided hike with the **Junior Ranger program** (p119)
- Climb the playground jungle gym at **Springdale Town Park** (below)
- In Zion Canyon, kids seven and up can **ride a horse** (p119)
- Spend a sunny day on the Virgin River **tubing** (p119)

park entrance on Zion Park Blvd, includes a pretty riverside trail. **Springdale Town Park**, on Lion Blvd next to the town hall, boasts perhaps the most scenic playground in America, not to mention a baseball diamond, volleyball and tennis courts and a large gazebo.

THEATERS

Set beneath gorgeous red cliffs, the 2000-seat outdoor **OC Tanner Amphitheater** (☎ 435-652-7994; www.dixie.edu/tanner; 300 Lion Blvd; adult/under 18yr $10/5) hosts live concerts most Saturdays from May through August. The schedule includes the symphony, bluegrass, country, folk and cowboy music. Picnics, but no alcohol, allowed.

Catch the 40-minute film *Zion Canyon: Treasure of the Gods,* and other IMAX and Hollywood favorites, on the six-story screen at **Zion Canyon Giant Screen Theatre** (☎ 435-772-2400; www.zioncanyontheatre.com; 145 Zion Park Blvd; adult/under 12yr $10/7). Much of the history in *Treasure* is pure hokum, and some of the scenery is from other national parks, but it's stunningly dramatic nonetheless.

GRAFTON GHOST TOWN

The freely accessible Grafton ghost town, outside Rockville, achieved its 15 minutes of fame in 1969 as the setting for the bicycle scene in *Butch Cassidy & the Sundance Kid.* Originally settled in 1859, the town never amounted to much. Today, a restored 1886 meetinghouse, a well-maintained cemetery, the general store and some pioneer cabins remain. In Rockville, 3.5 miles west of Springdale, take Bridge Rd north; cross the bridge and turn right on Grafton Rd. After half a mile follow the main road, which bears left and becomes gravel. A mile further, bear right at the sign. After another 2 miles, you'll pass the cemetery on your left, then drive a quarter mile farther to the ghost town. Park at the red gate.

VIRGIN TRADING POST

Have your picture taken inside the 'Virgin Jail,' feed the donkey or buy fudge at the **Trading Post** (☎ 435-635-3455; 1000 W Hwy 9, Virgin; store free, set $2; ⏲ 10am-8pm). The cartoonish Wild West movie set out front is pure kitschy fun, as are the knick-knacks inside.

LA VERKIN OVERLOOK

West of Virgin on Hwy 9, before La Verkin, a 1.5-mile gravel-and-dirt road leads south to La Verkin Overlook. Stop for a fantastic 360-degree view of the surrounding 40 sq miles, from Zion to the Pine Valley Mountains. Trails lead along the ridge above the Virgin River. This is a great sunset perch.

DRIVING

Zion Canyon Scenic Drive, which pierces the heart of the canyon, is the prime destination for most visitors. If you have time for only one activity at Zion, touring this road is not a bad choice. Kolob Terrace Rd in the middle of the park, and Zion–Mt Carmel Hwy (Hwy 9), on the south side, also promise worthwhile drives. Branching off I-15, Kolob Canyons Rd is the sleeper of the bunch. The intense red Navajo sandstone and frequent overlooks make it a sure bet for those who want a lot of reward for little physical effort.

ZION CANYON SCENIC DRIVE

Duration 45 minutes–2 hours with stops
Distance 6.2 miles one way
Start/Finish Hwy 9
Nearest Town Springdale
Summary The premier drive in the park leads between towering cliffs of an incredible red-rock canyon and accesses all the major front-country trailheads. April through October, a shuttle bus is required.

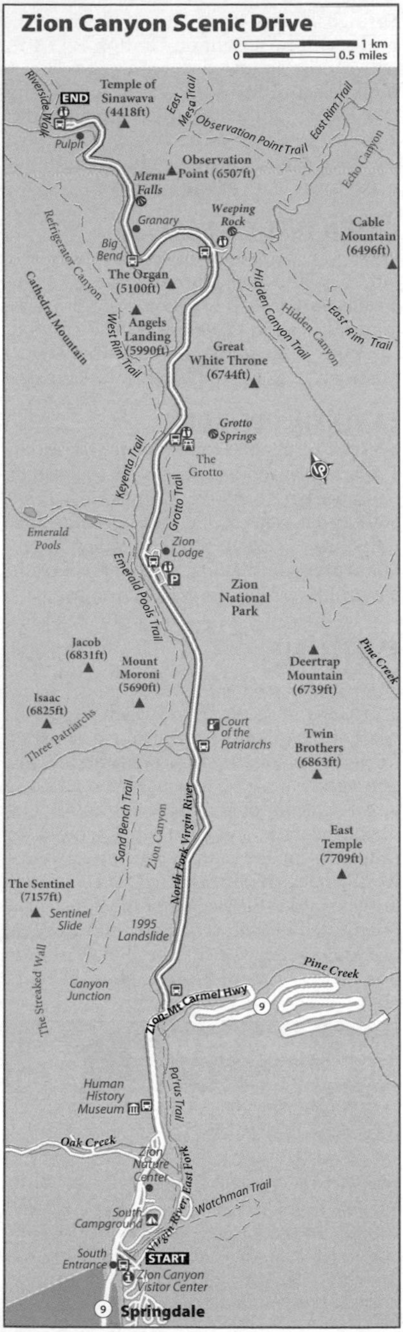

Zion Canyon Scenic Dr is closed to private vehicles April through October, when all visitors must ride the Zion Park Shuttle (p92). November through March, cars can drive freely up the spur road that leads just over 6 miles to the Temple of Sinawava. You have a limited field of view out shuttle windows, but you can hop on and hop off the bus without worrying about parking or distracted drivers. Expect a 90-minute round trip without stops by shuttle, 60 minutes if you drive your own car. This drive can also be done as an excellent bike ride (even better if you shuttle your bicycle up to the top and coast down). Note that the Ride Along with a Ranger (p93) tour provides more information than the standard Zion Park Shuttle loudspeaker recordings. Shuttle riders usually start at the visitor center, and so do we.

First stop is the **Human History Museum** (☎ 435-772-0168; admission free; 🕒 9am-7pm late May-early Sep, 10am-5pm early Mar-late May & early Sep-Nov, closed Dec-early Mar), an air-conditioned oasis. Well-done exhibits here cover the geology and human history of Zion Canyon, as well as its creation and management as a national park. The building itself is part of an original Mormon homestead settled by the Crawford family. Make sure to see the 22-minute film, screened every half-hour; it's a beautiful – and accurate – introduction to the park. Outside the museum, look for the interpretive signs that point out the park's tallest sandstone cliffs, including the **West Temple** (7810ft) and the **Towers of the Virgin**. Look for the natural arch near the peak of **Bridge Mountain** to the south.

Just past the museum on Hwy 9 are a few turnouts that overlook the **Streaked Wall**. In spring, with binoculars, scan the rim for nesting peregrine falcons. Officially, the scenic drive begins where you turn north, and cars are restricted, at **Canyon Junction**. This stop marks one end of the **Pa'rus Trail** (p101), which accesses wading spots along the Virgin River.

Continuing up the canyon, you'll pass the **Sentinel Slide** on the left. About, oh, 4000 years ago or so, a big chunk of the cliff face sloughed off and blocked the water flow, turning the canyon into a big lake. (That's why the up-canyon features you see are more rounded and sculptural than in a typical river-cut gorge like the Grand Canyon.) The water eventually carved its way through the blockage and carried on. The

TOP VISTAS & VANTAGE POINTS

- **Majestic View Lodge parking lot** (p124) The location lives up to its name, especially at sunset.
- **La Verkin Overlook** (p95) Seemingly endless, 360-degree views.
- **Smithsonian Buttes** (p120) Rough road, panoramic look back at Mt Kinesava and the Towers of the Virgins.
- **End of the Watchman Trail** (p102) The mountain sentinel is last to be lit by sunset.

slide became active again in 1995, when it covered the road and trapped tourists at the Zion Lodge for three days, and again in 1998 when the road washed away. It's all been properly reinforced now, but you'll notice that the rock looks a lot more loose and crumbly here than in other areas.

Next, the **Court of the Patriarchs** stop fronts the shortest trail in the park, a 50yd, staircaselike walk uphill to a view of the namesake peaks. Named by a Methodist minister in 1916, from left to right are Abraham, Isaac and Jacob, while crouching in front of Jacob is Mt Moroni (named for a Mormon angel). Though many people skip it, even the road-level view is nice, especially at sunset.

Ahead on your right, **Zion Lodge** (p122) houses the park's only cafe and restaurant. The lodge was first built in the 1920s, but burnt down in 1966. The rebuilt lodge is not as grand as those in other states. But the wide grassy front lawn – shaded by a giant cottonwood tree – is a favored place for a posthike ice cream and nap. Across the road from the lodge is the corral for **horseback rides** (p119) and the trailhead for the **Emerald Pools** (p103).

The **Grotto** (p101), barely a half-mile north, is a large, cottonwood-shaded picnic area with plenty of tables, restrooms and drinking water. From the picnic area, the Grotto Trail leads south to Zion Lodge. Across the road from the picnic area, the **West Rim Trail** (p114) leads north toward **Angels Landing** (p105). Those who'd rather admire Angels Landing than climb it should stroll the first flat quarter mile of the West Rim Trail to a stone bench for the perfect vantage.

Make sure you spend some time at **Weeping Rock**. There's a lot to see at this bend in the river, a great example of an 'incised meander.' Pause to admire **Angels Landing**, the **Organ**, **Cable Mountain**, the **Great White Throne** and looming **Observation Point**. A short detour up the bucolic **Weeping Rock Trail** (p102) to a sheltered alcove and hanging garden is a worthwhile driving diversion. Two other great trails are accessed from here: the chain-assist **Hidden Canyon Trail** (p104) and the Papa Bear of workouts, **Observation Point** (p106).

There are no trailheads at **Big Bend**, but rock climbers get out here on their way to some of Zion's famous walls. Others just soak up the view, which is a different vantage of the features seen from Weeping Rock. It's a good place to bring binoculars and scan the skies for California condors (see boxed text, p68).

If you're using the shuttle, the only way to the next two sights is to walk. As you continue north, on a ledge up to the right look for a reconstructed **granary**. Although ancient Native American in origin, it was rebuilt in the 1930s by the Boy Scouts. After about a half-mile, you get to **Menu Falls**, so-named because it was pictured on Zion Lodge's first menu cover. The multilevel deck with overlook is the most popular place to get married in the park. From there it's easier to backtrack to Big Bend shuttle than to hoof it all the way up to the last stop. The canyon narrows near the 4418ft cliff face that forms a natural amphitheater known as the **Temple of Sinawava**, at the road's end. Across the road the rock called the **Pulpit** does indeed look a bit like a giant lectern. From here you can take the popular **Riverside Walk** (p101) to the **Narrows** (p104). Interpretive signs explain how the seemingly soft and gentle Virgin River could have carved this 1500ft gash.

ZION–MT CARMEL HIGHWAY (HIGHWAY 9)

Duration 45 minutes–2 hours with stops
Distance 12 miles one way
Start South Entrance
Finish East Entrance
Nearest Town Springdale
Summary Accessible year round, a 12-mile stretch of Hwy 9 traverses Zion National Park, twisting and turning its way up to Zion–Mt Carmel Tunnel and on to the evocative slickrock covering the park's east side.

Hwy 9 is not just the most direct route between Springdale and Mt Carmel, it is also a beautifully scenic drive through the southern expanse of Zion National Park – one that's open to private vehicles year-round.

From the ranger-staffed **South Entrance** gate, where you pay your fees and get your maps, the turn-off to **Zion Canyon Visitor Center** (p91) is immediately on your right. In addition to being the font for all park information and shuttle central, the visitor center is a model of functional and attractive environmental architecture. Despite its lack of air-conditioning or heating units, the building remains pleasant year-round. Cooling towers harness summer winds to cool water and funnel colder, heavier air into the building, while passive solar walls are positioned to catch the winter sun. The **Pa'rus Trail** (p101), along the Virgin River, and the **Watchman Trail** (p102) also begin here.

A quarter-mile further is the signed turnoff for **South Campground** (p121) and the summer-only **Zion Nature Center** (p119), home to many of Zion's children's programs. The gymlike building with flora and fauna exhibits sits beside a grassy riverside picnic area that makes a great place to chill out during the midday heat.

Also just off the highway is the **Human History Museum** (p96). Past Canyon Junction, Hwy 9 climbs a 3.5-mile series of long, steep switchbacks. This scenic stretch offers windows full of red rock and amazing views of the **Great Arch**.

Make sure to stop at one of the several large turnouts before you get to the engineering marvel that is **Zion–Mt Carmel Tunnel** (see the boxed text, p92, for information on tunnel restrictions).

At the time of its completion, the 1.1-mile tunnel was the longest in the United States. Engineers had to construct an aerial tramway just to create a workers' base camp.

During the three years of construction (from 1927 to 1930), more than 146 tonnes of dynamite were used to move 72,000 cubic yards of stone. Much of it was thrown out of the six 'galleries' you see as you drive through; the remainder was used to fill in the roadway below.

At the tunnel's east entrance is a small parking lot with pit toilets and the trailhead for the **Canyon Overlook** (p109), an unchallenging cliff-hugging detour with an interesting perspective. From here the road passes vast undulating fields of pale beige and yellow slickrock (not red!). Here the fracture lines make the sandstone look liquid, and brittle slabs ooze right up to the road. Make use of scenic turnouts, as the highway is narrow and winding.

After about 3.5 miles, you get your first glimpse of **Checkerboard Mesa**, a huge sloping face of light slickrock etched, well, like a giant checkerboard.

It's another mile to the official Checkerboard Mesa viewpoint, your last must-see stop. About a quarter-mile further on is the **East Entrance**, beyond which is the park boundary.

SACRIFICE ROCK

Spend a week in Zion and you may not realize that ancient peoples had much of a presence here. The National Park Service does its best to protect and preserve the natural and cultural resources under its care. But when it comes to the rock art and ruins left by ancestral inhabitants, there's only so much they can do. The South Gate Petroglyphs, aka 'Sacrifice Rock' is a case in point. The handful of intriguing designs and animals are a few steps from the road near the South Entrance. What strikes one most, however, is not the petroglyphs themselves but the overwhelming amount of modern graffiti surrounding them. 'Jayrod' may indeed rock, but did he need to let everyone know right here, for all eternity?

So you'll understand if Zion rangers do not advertise rock-art locations, and ruins are strictly off-limits. Ask a general 'I've heard there are petroglyphs in the park?' and you'll get a purposely obtuse 'Yes, I've heard that too' in response. There is at least one other rock art site close to a road. If you do your research and ask a specific question, the rangers can answer. But please remember to regard all ancient sites as you would a museum. These locations are both priceless artifacts and spiritual sites for the modern-day tribes whose ancestors created them.

KOLOB CANYONS ROAD

Duration 30–90 minutes with stops
Distance 5 miles one way
Start/Finish Kolob Canyons Visitor Center
Nearest Town Cedar City (p132)
Summary The less-visited, higher-elevation alternative to Zion Canyon Scenic Drive. Sweeping vistas of cliffs, mountains and finger canyons dominate this short, overlook-rich, red-rock route.

The saying 'short but sweet' has never been more aptly applied than to the Kolob Canyons Rd scenic drive. It's only 5 miles long, but around every curve looms a stunning red-rock vista. One-tenth the number of visitors come here as compared to Zion Canyon. That's a shame, especially for drivers, since the overlooks pack such up-close, visual punch. Late May through June abundant upcountry wildflowers bloom; in winter, the road remains plowed, but may shut temporarily for snow. Forty miles from Springdale and 20 miles from Cedar City, just off I-15, pay your fee or show your receipt or pass at the tiny **Kolob Canyons Visitor Center** (p91). From there the road is wonderfully steep, ascending from a beginning elevation of 5350ft. (It's a great drive, but not a favorite cycling route.) All along the way there are pullouts and interesting interpretive signs; make sure to stop.

After 1.8 miles you'll reach the trailhead to the **Taylor Creek Middle Fork** (p108), along with your first good views of the **finger canyons** and Zion's highest point, **Horse Ranch Mountain** (8726ft). As the road affords a high vantage point, the rough-hewn cliffs appear shorter than those in Zion Canyon, but they are every bit as tall and have an equivalent flair for the dramatic.

At **Lee Pass**, you'll find the trailhead for the hardcore **La Verkin Creek Trail** (p112) to Kolob Arch. About a mile further is the end of the road, marked by a large parking area and pit toilets. To the west you can see the **Hurricane Cliffs** and the **Pine Valley Mountains**. You have to climb up the mile-long **Timber Creek Overlook** (p107) to see the finger canyons from here. About 100yd along the trail, a picnic area in the scrub forest provides a good spot for a rest or lunch.

KOLOB TERRACE ROAD

Duration 60–90 minutes with stops
Distance 33.5 miles one way
Start Hwy 9
Finish Lava Point
Nearest Town Springdale
Summary Rise above it all driving up to the high plateau that bisects the park's sections. En route you'll see cinder cones and sandstone cliffs, and be able to overlook Zion Canyon in the distance

Even in season you'll see relatively few other cars on this subtly scenic high-plateau road, where striking rock formation views alternate with pastoral rangeland. The road leaves and re-enters the park several times. It's free to drive Zion's narrow waist, but if you do stop to picnic or hike, be ready to show your park pass or entrance receipt to rangers. There are no services up here besides some pit toilets at trailheads. The upper reaches of the road close due to snow from November through May.

In the tiny burg of Virgin, just shy of 14 miles west of Zion's South Entrance, turn north off Hwy 9 onto Kolob Terrace Rd. Uninspiring residential development and farmland is the first thing that comes into view. Once inside the park there are two trailheads for canyoneering routes: at 6.8 miles, the **Right Fork trailhead**, and at 7.2 miles, the **Grapevine trailhead.**

A quarter-mile further is the turnoff for **Smith Mesa Rd**. This well-graded dirt road (passable to cars when dry, impassable to all when wet) leaves the park after a mile as it winds along the top of Smith Mesa. The first few miles are worth the detour for the views back toward **Tabernacle Dome**, **South Guardian Angel** and **Cougar Mountain.**

Past the Smith Mesa turnoff is the **Left Fork trailhead**, the jumping-off point for the popular canyoneering route called the Subway (p113).

From there you start ascending until you're 3000ft above where you started. The white and red Navajo sandstones you see at eye level up here are the same as those seen at the top of Zion Canyon. A series of turnouts offer splendid views of **Spendlove** and **Firepit Knolls**, cinder cones that are reminders of the volcanism that once dominated this

TIP

Time your return journey on Kolob Terrace Rd for sunset. The views are even better on the way back, so why not appreciate them in the best light?

region. About 13 miles from Hwy 9, the **Hop Valley trailhead** (see p113), takes off across sandy rangeland toward the park's Kolob Canyons section. This point in the road is also about as far as snowplows go in winter.

Three miles past Hop Valley is the **Wildcat Canyon trailhead**, the start of the Subway (p113) and the **Northgate Peaks Trail** (p108). Just past this turnoff is one of the largest scenic turnouts along the road, with benches.

Some 21 miles from Hwy 9, you reach the junction for the graded gravel road to **Lava Point**. Don't make this journey without visiting the point, 1.8 miles further on. At 7890ft, this one-time fire lookout (though the tower was removed in 2000) is one of Zion's highest and best vantage points. A virtual diorama of the park spreads before you, with views south to Arizona on clear days. There's also a six-site primitive campground (p121) here, and pit toilets. A half-mile further on you reach the trailhead for the **West Rim Trail** (p114).

Traveling north again on Kolob Terrace Rd, you exit the park boundaries and reach **Kolob Reservoir**, 33.5 miles north of Hwy 9. It's a popular spot among local anglers and also offers free dispersed camping. Visit in fall to appreciate the spectacular aspen stands. Our drive ends here. But beyond the reservoir, the road reverts to dirt and continues 20 miles farther to Hwy 14, outside Cedar City. Lingering snow and runoff make this stretch wet and hazardous through late June.

SMITHSONIAN BUTTE BACKCOUNTRY BYWAY

Duration 35 minutes
Distance 9 miles one way
Start Hwy 9
Finish Hwy 59, Big Plain Junction
Nearest Town Springdale
Summary A rough-and-tumble back way climbs up through the desert vegetation between two valleys for a panoramic look back at Zion and access to area mesas south of Rockville.

Stratified buttes, slickrock pinnacles and balancing rocks are all part of the attraction on this challenging backcountry drive. Though rated for regular passenger vehicles, the road is not well maintained – ruts can be giant and 4WD is never a bad idea. In Rockville turn south on Bridge Rd. The road will veer before you get to the left-hand turn for Smithsonian Butte Rd. (Follow signs to the right and you'll reach **Grafton Ghost Town**, p95.)

Start your trip counter here. Once you turn south, you'll be winding your way up with **Wire Valley** on your right and **Horse Valley** on the left. The raggedly eroded formation to the southeast (left) is **Eagle Crags**. Make sure to look around as you ascend. About a mile up the road the first panorama of Zion National Park formations unfolds; stop along the way to look at the other angles that follow. At 4.5 miles, the road to **Gooseberry Mesa**, a premier mountain-biking trail, branches off to the right. Shortly after, you're rounding **Smithsonian Butte** on BLM land to your left, in an area where petroglyphs have been found. The drive is almost as you descend onto a plain and into **Apple Valley**. From there Hwy 59 leads toward Hurricane in one direction, and Arizona in the other.

HIKING

Zion seems to have been cut and crafted with hikers in mind. Its wealth of experiences and scenery rivals that of any national park, and most of it is accessible on day hikes. Even backcountry routes like the West Rim and the Narrows trails are doable in a single (admittedly long and challenging) day.

Though each of Zion's areas offers hikes, Zion Canyon boasts the lion's share of trails, and they tend to be the most crowded. Most canyon trails are paved to some degree, even the steepest; route-finding is barely an issue. Every trailhead features a signboard with a map and all are near Zion Park Shuttle stops. Bus drivers usually announce the trails at each stop. Remember that off-season you will have to make round-trip hikes in order to get back to your car.

For more on ranger-led hikes and Zion Canyon Field Institute workshops that include hiking, see the boxed text, p119. Zion

Rock & Mountain Guides (p105) also offers interpretive hikes in the park. Falcon Guide's *Hiking Zion & Bryce Canyon National Parks* is the most thorough trekking manual. No matter how short your planned hike, bring water and appropriate footwear. For hiking safety tips, see p283. For desert hiking etiquette, see the boxed text, p46. For definitions of our hike difficulty ratings, see p37.

EASY HIKES

Note that we do not always agree with the park's definition of 'wheelchair accessible'; exceptions are noted below. In Zion Canyon several easy paths follow the river or floodplain, instead of climbing the steep canyon walls.

PA'RUS TRAIL

Duration 1½ hours
Distance 1.7 miles one way
Difficulty Easy
Start Zion Canyon Visitor Center
Finish Canyon Junction
Nearest Town Springdale
Transportation Zion Park Shuttle
Summary A paved, wheelchair-, pet- and bike-friendly trail that meanders along beside and across the Virgin River, passing the South Campground and the Human History Museum.

The Pa'rus (PAH-roos) is one of Zion's busiest thoroughfares. That's because this paved, wheelchair-accessible trail is the only trail in Zion open to bicycles and dogs, which must remain on a leash. It's also one of only two routes that start from near the visitor center (the other is the Watchman Trail). But don't come for convenience alone. With some distance between them, this is a pleasant mid-canyon stroll along the **Virgin River**. Here the widely spread canyon walls are stately and majestic rather than awesome and overpowering. The trail is the perfect place to contemplate the **Towers of the Virgin**, the **Streaked Wall**, **Bridge Mountain** and the **Watchman**. Four footbridges along the way crisscross the river, and numerous dirt paths lead down to the water where you can play. At trail's end, Canyon Junction, you can turn around or hop on a return shuttle.

RIVERSIDE WALK

Duration 1 hour
Distance 2 miles
Difficulty Easy
Start/Finish Temple of Sinawava
Nearest Town Springdale
Transportation Zion Park Shuttle
Summary A popular paved path follows the river at the end of the canyon, accessing seeps, hanging gardens and wading spots – a must on any visit to Zion.

Shadowed from the slanting sun by towering walls, this fun walk (a kids' favorite) parallels the slippery cobblestones of the **Virgin River** up-canyon. Interpretive signs explain the geology and ecology of the corridor, and various mini-spur trails lead to the river itself. The water is a great place to play from mid-June through August. Starting from the Temple of Sinawava at the end of Zion Canyon Rd, the crowded trail also serves as a feeder for the Narrows hike (p104).

Look up and around when you set off; the canyon walls around Temple of Sinawava are popular rock-climbing sites. From the start, the pavement undulates up and down over roots and in and around water-carved alcoves. Park literature describes the walk as 'wheelchair accessible with assistance'. We think someone pretty darn strong would have to be doing the pushing; strollers work fine though. The paved trail ends where the **Narrows** begin, at a raised cul-de-sac with benches. Steps leads down to a rocky fan at the river's edge. Wear shoes you don't mind getting wet; you may not be able to resist the river, which beckons all – even those not hiking further up-canyon.

GROTTO TRAIL

Duration 15 minutes
Distance 0.5 miles one way
Difficulty Easy
Start Zion Lodge
Finish Grotto picnic grounds
Nearest Town Springdale
Transportation Zion Park Shuttle
Summary A pleasant walk through the trees beneath the canyon wall en route from the lodge to a picnic table in a grove of leafy cottonwoods.

If you don't feel like picnicking with the masses on the lawn of Zion Park Lodge, grab your sandwich and take this easy-peasy stroll through the trees to the Grotto picnic area (a Zion Park Shuttle stop). A tiny old brick building there was the first Zion NP visitor center and is now an artist retreat. The short hike would also make a fine evening's stretch for lodge guests. For hearty hikers, it's mainly useful off-season as part of a loop connecting the Kayenta and the Emerald Pools trails (p103). Terrain is unpaved, and unsuitable for wheelchairs.

DAY HIKES

Zion Canyon

Many area trails are steep. Remember as far as you go up, you'll also have to come down. Our suggestion? Know your limitations and enjoy the trail, not just the destination.

WEEPING ROCK TRAIL

Duration 30 minutes
Distance 0.5 miles
Difficulty Easy–moderate
Start/Finish Weeping Rock
Nearest Town Springdale
Transportation Zion Park Shuttle
Summary Cool even in summer, a short-but-steep climb leads to an impressive alcove and hanging garden with water that sometimes seeps, sometimes weeps.

For a trail that's over almost before it's begun, this one is surprisingly memorable. The enormous, cool alcove at trail's end contains the park's largest hanging garden and an incredible amount of plant diversity. Interpretive signs explain much of the blooming foliage. The popular, mostly paved trek climbs 100ft (some stairs) to a romantically framed view of the **White Throne** and Zion Canyon. When the water is really running, it forms a veil from above; in all temperate seasons, expect to get a bit damp. In winter the weep can form giant icicles that may cause trail closure.

The Weeping Rock stop is also the trailhead for Observation Point and Hidden Canyon day hikes. For a map, see the Observation Point trail (Map p107).

WATCHMAN TRAIL

Duration 1½–2 hours
Distance 2.7 miles
Difficulty Easy–moderate
Start/Finish Zion Canyon Visitor Center
Nearest Town Springdale
Transportation Zion Park Shuttle
Summary The sunset trail of choice in Zion Canyon; ascend a mere 400ft to a short loop that provides fine views of the park's mountainlike formations

Don't be put off by the name; you're not climbing the monumental Watchman spire, but overlooking it. Wait until the midday heat has waned, then start off across the road from the visitor center on the same trailhead as Pa'rus (p101). At first a dusty path along the Virgin River, the trail gently ascends to a small canyon at the base of **Bridge Mountain**. Continue your ascent on several long switchbacks past moderate drop-offs to the top of a foothill, where the trail emerges to wide views. The pungent scent of sagebrush and spring blooms of prickly-pear cactus make this an enjoyable ramble.

At the end a 0.3-mile loop trail skirts the foothill, leading to several prime overlooks of the **Towers of the Virgin** and the town of

GEARING UP

Some of the more strenuous hikes in Zion are serious business. Be prepared with the right footwear and gear. (We personally love those water-bladder backpacks that allow you to suck from a straw.) Both outfitters in Springdale, **Zion Rock & Mountain Guides** (☎ 435-772-3303; www.zionrockguides.com; 1458 Zion Park Blvd; 🕑 8am-8pm Mar-Oct, hours vary Nov-Feb) and **Zion Adventure Company** (☎ 435-772-1001; www.zionadventures.com; 36 Lion Blvd; 🕑 8am-8pm Mar-Oct, 9am-noon & 4-7pm Nov-Feb) rent river footwear and wetsuits, plus camping equipment, and sell a variety of packs and gear.

For clothing and shoes especially, also try **Zion Outdoor** (☎ 435-772-0630; 868 Zion Park Blvd; 🕑 9am-8pm, closed Dec & Jan), which sells a mix of hiking gadgets and garments.

GETTING AWAY FROM IT ALL

Summer weekends when the Zion Park Shuttle is standing-room only, popular trails like Emerald Pools can be a great place to meet travelers from around the world. (Angels Landing gets so busy, there really should be traffic cops.) But you do have choices if you want to get away from them all.

Any hike not starting from a Zion Canyon Shuttle stop (think Kolob Terrace Rd, East Zion and Kolob Canyons) will by definition have fewer visitors. **Northgate Peaks** (p108) is an easy, upcountry option that also has the advantage of being about 3000ft higher, and at least 10 degrees cooler, than the canyon floor.

The more adventurous could seek out trails on BLM land south of Rockville that are favored by locals. **Eagle Crags** is a 6.2-mile round-trip, three-hour trek, up to and around the well-eroded pinnacles rising south of Springdale. The trail starts off Bridge Rd. Get a good map, and ask directions. A high-clearance vehicle is required, but you are allowed to hike with your dog.

Another option is to do some **slickrock hiking**. East of the Zion Canyon Scenic Drive, especially east of the Zion–Mt Carmel Tunnel, you can drop down into the drainages and explore to your heart's content – as long as you stay on slickrock or in the washes, and off the cryptobiotic soil (see p74). Look for places where there are cars parked, but no one around and no obvious overlooks. These are often good starting points.

Springdale. Rising alone to the south you'll see the ragged **Eagle Crags**. The angular **Watchman** is the last formation to catch the fading light of sunset; bring a flashlight, or one of those handy-dandy headlamps, for the return hike.

EMERALD POOLS & KAYENTA TRAILS

Duration 2½ hours
Distance 3 miles
Difficulty Moderate
Start/Finish Zion Lodge
Nearest Town Springdale
Transportation Zion Park Shuttle
Summary An extremely popular sequence of trails links to a series of bucolic ponds, stunning desert-varnished rocks and a surprisingly verdant oasis in a desert.

Water seeps from sandstone and colorful pools are rimmed with life; wildflowers spring up in May and autumn leaves turn in October. No wonder this interconnecting series of trails and four pools is extremely popular.

From Zion Lodge, cross the road and bridge to get to the trailhead. The **Middle Pools** path heads left (take it if you don't mind going up steeply at first and want to be traveling opposite the crowds).

The **Lower Pools** trail, to the right, leads to the same pools. Follow that gradually rising-and-falling paved path for less than a mile to get to the **Lower Pool**. Here waterfalls cascade down a multicolored, mineral-stained overhang in a long arc, misting the trail (and you) as you pass beneath. Those with physical limitations should turn around here and return the way they came.

Others follow the dirt trail up to the left as it ascends 150ft to the two, less dramatic, **Middle Pools** that feed the waterfalls below. (Be careful on the steps.)

From between the ponds, a steep, rocky half-mile one-way spur requires a little scrambling to get to the **Upper Pool**. This, the loveliest grotto of all, is surrounded by the sheer-walled skirts of **Lady Mountain**. If you're lucky, you'll get to watch the canyon wren at play. But, please stay out of the ecologically sensitive water.

One you've backtracked down, you could return to Zion Lodge on the Middle Pools trail. But why be like everyone else? We recommend continuing in the opposite direction, northwest on the **Kayenta Trail**. That way you can get a spectacular eye-to-falls overlook of the Lower Pool (and all the people) below. The 1-mile trail is natural and rugged; expect to be picking your way among rocks and vegetation before you descend to the **Grotto** picnic grounds.

Hop a shuttle here, or follow the easy **Grotto Trail** back to the lodge for the full 3-mile loop.

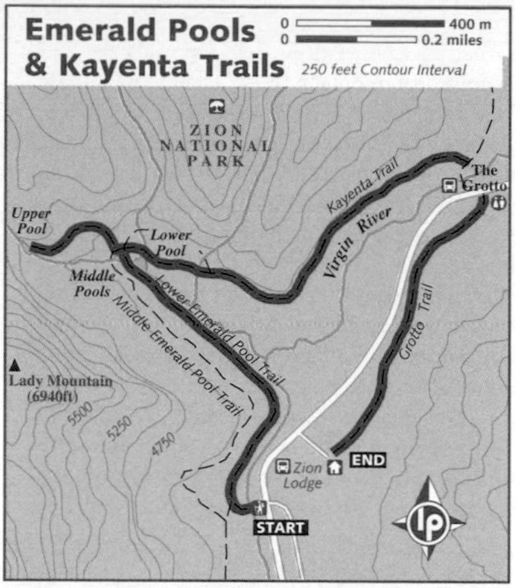

Onward, the trail skirts a slickrock ledge as it threads in and out of a draw. Chains are bolted into the rock at the most exposed points. Make use of them – from the thin ledges, it's nearly a thousand feet straight down. Fifty yards beyond the ledges, you'll reach the mouth of **Hidden Canyon**. There is no trail on the slickrock here; watch for cairns and steps cut into the rock.

You can extend the hike by entering the scenic narrow canyon, which is sandy, rocky and crowded with bigtooth maples. Its left wall is as sheer as a loaf of country bread cut in half. A quarter mile in on your right, you'll reach a **standing arch**. Farther on, the canyon narrows, and a series of increasingly large rock falls make hiking difficult, and then impossible; only those with climbing experience should continue past the arch.

HIDDEN CANYON TRAIL

Duration 2½ hours
Distance 2.4 miles
Difficulty Moderate–difficult
Start/Finish Weeping Rock
Nearest Town Springdale
Transportation Zion Park Shuttle
Summary Up you go, 850ft in little over a mile. Short chain-assist sections cling to a cliff edge, but this is actually quite moderate compared to some of the park's trails.

For fit hikers, this is the perfect warm-up to Zion's more challenging hikes; for beginners, it serves as a good test of your stamina and your comfort with heights. Either way, the only time to tackle the Hidden Canyon Trail is in the early morning, when the difficult initial ascent is in the shade. Otherwise it's searing desert sun all the way, baby. Hidden Canyon and Observation Point share a trailhead; for a hiking map, see p107.

From the Weeping Rock shuttle stop, the largely paved trail leads right, quickly ascending a series of long switchbacks that put your legs and lungs to work.

After half a mile, the trail to Observation Point (p106) branches to the left. Follow the Hidden Canyon sign and bear right up a series of even steeper zigzags to an unprotected point with vertiginous views.

NARROWS: FROM THE BOTTOM

Duration up to 8 hours
Distance up to 10 miles
Difficulty Moderate–difficult
Start/Finish Temple of Sinawava
Nearest Town Springdale
Transportation Zion Park Shuttle
Summary Sometimes a bit more of a swim than a hike, as the Virgin River *is* the trail. You'll be in the water the majority of the way upstream through this impressive slot canyon system.

Hiking through a rocky river in ankle- to chest-deep water, as the canyon walls seem to grow and press in on you: the Narrows is a quintessential Zion experience. Most people tackle it from the bottom rather than attempt the more adventurous backcountry trip from the top (p115). From the bottom, you don't need a permit and you can still reach the narrowest and most spectacular section. If you trek the entire 5 miles to Big Springs (as far as day hikers are allowed), you'll outpace most of the dabblers and running kids.

Preparation and timing are the keys to a successful Narrows adventure. Always, and we mean always, check conditions with a ranger before hiking. When the river is running more than 120 cubic feet per second (usually in April and May); the Narrows

The Narrows: From the Bottom

0 — 2 km
0 — 1 mile
500 feet Contour Interval

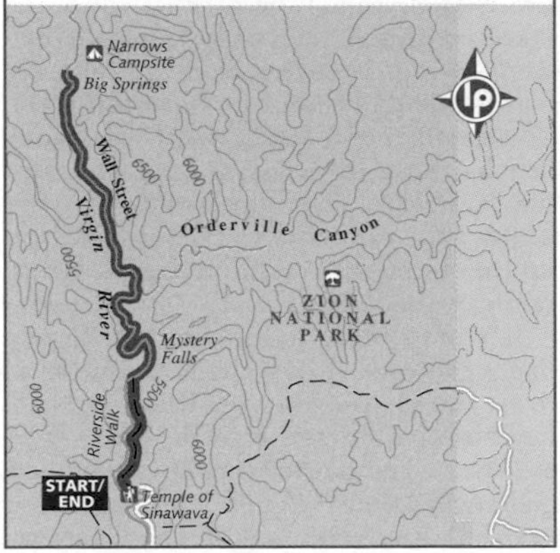

is closed. In winter, wet or dry suits are required, and specialized footwear (all for rent at local outfitters) is always recommended. Those wearing Tevas and clutching their Ozarka bottle won't make it far. For more information, see p115).

The 'trail' begins at the end of the **Riverside Walk** (p101), where you enter and start following the river. Around the first bend is **Mystery Falls**, the exit point for Mystery Canyon. You may catch canyoneers on their last rappel here. As you hike, each alcove, bowl, hollow, crack and arch seems its own secret place. Ravens glide low over the water, and you can sometimes hear waterfalls spilling down from inside the rock.

It's about 2.5 miles to the junction with **Orderville Canyon**, which is another popular canyoneering route. Beyond that, you'll enter **Wall Street**, where the sheerness, nearness and height of the cliffs shatter whatever remains of your perspective. After this section, the canyon opens slightly again, the water gets periodically deeper (usually requiring swimming), and your fellow hikers thin out.

After the 4-mile point, you'll negotiate a series of huge boulders, and the canyon, though gorgeous, becomes somewhat less otherworldly. At 5 miles you come to **Big Springs**, a fern-fringed rush of water much larger than anything so far. Here day hikers are required to turn around.

While it can take up to eight hours to do the full round-trip to Big Springs, set aside a minimum of five hours so you'll at least have time to reach memorable Wall Street. Don't forget you also have to hike the Riverside Trail back to the Temple of Sinawava shuttle or parking lot.

ANGELS LANDING

Duration 4 hours
Distance 5.4 miles
Difficulty Difficult
Start/Finish Grotto
Nearest Town Springdale
Transportation Zion Park Shuttle
Summary The most well known of Zion's canyon hikes ascends endlessly (OK, really about 1000ft) before getting to the main attraction – a narrow rock fin with precipitous drop-offs and a final 488ft elevation gain on the chain-assisted scramble to the top.

'How far did you get?' is the question asked every morning at coffee shops all over Springdale, as hikers compare notes on Angels Landing. This strenuous hike is not just a physical challenge, but a mental one for those with a fear of heights. By all means, start as early as possible. Not only to avoid the heat, but because the number of people on the trail by noon in season causes traffic

IT'S A BIRD, IT'S A PLANE, IT'S A CONDOR!

With a wingspan of up to 10ft, the endangered California condor is the largest feathered flyer in North America. In recent years, captive-bred birds released around the Grand Canyon have moved north. In Zion they seem to like to circle above Angels Landing and other tall park features. The Big Bend shuttle stop is a good vantage point from which to look for them, and they have also been spotted around Lava Point. Bring binoculars. Condors are basically big vultures, and they can be hard to differentiate from the common variety. To identify the real thing, look for all black wings with a triangle of white at the tip underneath, visible when they fly. For more on the plight of the condor, see the boxed text, p68.

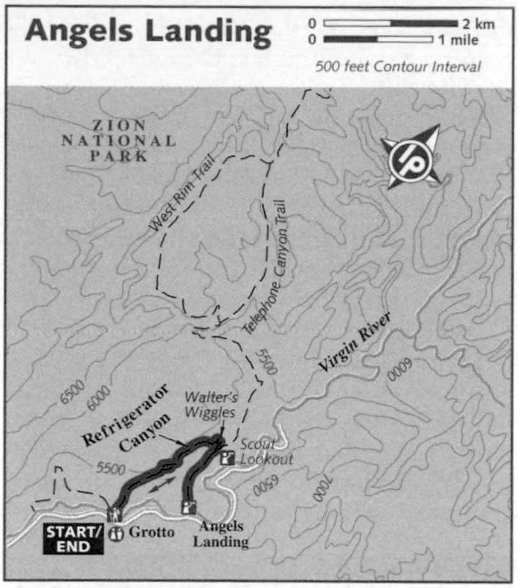

jams. At the narrowest, chain-assisted sections there is not room for two people to pass side by side. Not sure if you're willing to brave it? Check out the national park's virtual 'eHike' at www.nps.gov/zion/photosmultimedia/virtualtour.htm.

At the trailhead across the road from the Grotto picnic area, bear right. From here to just before Scout Lookout, you're tracing part of West Rim Trail (p114). At first the trail meanders along the desert floor then ascends gradually but relentlessly, becoming steeper as you begin long, paved switchbacks up the canyon wall. The last switchback crosses beneath a rock overhang. Beyond it, the trail levels out a little, and runs deep into narrow, slightly cooler **Refrigerator Canyon**.

THIS IS NOT DISNEYLAND

Sure you get an adrenaline rush conquering your fears while hiking up steep ascents past sheer drop-offs. But this is not Disneyland. The danger is real. Loose stones can be slippery, and every year people die from falls off cliffs. Even minor injuries can turn serious when difficult terrain means rescuers are hours away. Just be prepared and pay attention. We can't believe we have to say this, but flip-flops (thongs) are not appropriate hiking footwear for Angels Landing. And parents, please keep hold of young children. We want you, and your offspring, to be reading our books for years to come.

Once through the canyon, you'll ascend a few more switchbacks before reaching **Walter's Wiggles**, one of the park's engineering marvels. This set of 21 short, steep stonework zigzags is named after the early superintendent of Zion who imagined them. You emerge atop **Scout Lookout** at a sandy bench with a pit toilet and a turnoff for the West Rim. (Tip: those who don't like chains and narrow footways could continue up the strenuous West Rim Trail to panoramic overlooks.)

If you've made it this far, you should really continue at least the next 70ft or so to see the incredible views. To do so, you'll have to brave the first part of the scary stuff – a cliff-face climb using carved-out footfalls and anchor-bolted chains. Afterwards, you get your first good look at **Angels Landing**. Seeing the thin saddle you have to cross – at times 5ft wide and some 1000ft above the canyon floor on either side – stops many people in their tracks. Once across, the last 0.5 miles of the 'trail,' such as it is, gets much steeper and rockier. Chains are bolted into the rock for much of the way. Trail's end, a sloping 30ft-wide flat rock surface at the top, is abundantly clear. Sit and take in the stunning 360-degree view of nearly all of Zion Canyon. You've earned it.

OBSERVATION POINT

Duration 5 hours
Distance 8 miles
Difficulty Difficult
Start/Finish Weeping Rock
Nearest Town Springdale
Transportation Zion Park Shuttle
Summary An intensely rewarding, and strenuous, hike to some of the best views in the park. In the course of 4 miles, the trail climbs switchbacks and crosses a canyon to reach an Angels Landing overlook.

Yeah, we know, we know; you want to climb Angels Landing. That's great, but for our effort spent, Observation Point is a much better trail: fewer people, an incredible hanging-chasm slot canyon and the best views in the park at day's end. Be warned though, this is one of the most difficult day hikes in Zion, rising 2150ft in total. Bring plenty of water – and food. You have two

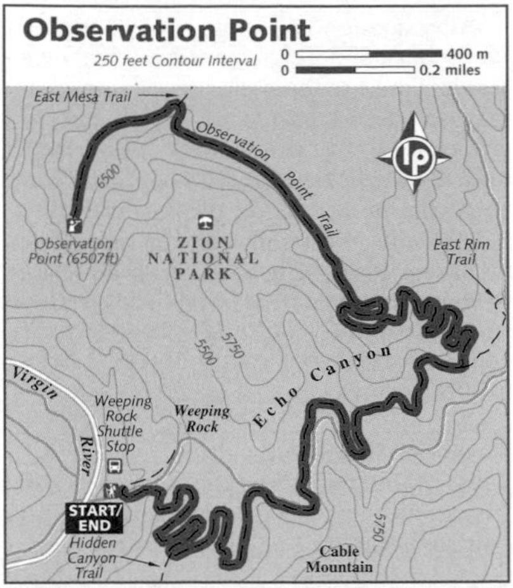

choices: start really early so that the initial challenging mile of switchbacks is sheltered from the sun, or make it a late-afternoon hike so that by then the steepest ascent, out of Echo Canyon, lies in blessed shade. The trail is paved all the way to the mesa top, where it becomes dirt, and later sand.

Starting from the Weeping Rock stop, the first half-mile of the trail is the same as that for Hidden Canyon (p104), ascending long, steep, leg-burning switchbacks. After you branch left at a signed junction, the switchbacks continue for another half-mile until you make a turn north and enter **Echo Canyon**, a beautiful hanging chasm. Here the trail levels out briefly, hugging the serpentine cliff as the water-eroded chasm yawns below. The sculptural walls close in to an almost-arms'-length slot. Towering above, the flat face of **Cable Mountain** is truly a sight to behold. After the canyon floor rises, you're trekking through a sandy wash that turns into a bowl and, before you realize it, you're climbing again. In spring, purple penstemon and crimson paintbrush flowers dot the slickrock crevices; lizards skitter about year-round.

At the 2-mile point, you reach a junction with the **East Rim Trail**, which also leads to Cable and Deertrap Mountains. After this, a long series of tough switchbacks draw you up the mountain. The trail is exposed to a long drop, but it's wide – no chains necessary. That plus having a mountain on one side makes it much less dizzying than the Angels Landing ascent. After about a mile, you'll reach the mesa top, and the trail is fairly level as it skirts the rim. Bear left at the signed junction with the **East Mesa Trail** (p110).

For the final half-mile, you'll traverse a sandy piñon-juniper forest to **Observation Point**. From this perch at 6508ft, you can peer 600ft *down* to the knife-edge of **Angels Landing** and 2150ft to the **Virgin River** – an incredible perspective on an infamous hike. The raven's-eye view down the canyon also includes a nice perspective of **Red Arch Mountain**. To the west, you're level with white **Cathedral Mountain** as the whole Zion world seems to spread out before you.

A SHORT-CUT OF SORTS

Observation Point has some great views, but climbing up from the canyon floor requires serious stamina. Those equipped for a backcountry adventure can actually make a *descent* to the Point from the **East Mesa Trail** (p110). According to one ranger, that's the 'sneaky' way.

Kolob Canyons

Zion's northwest section, about 40 miles from Springdale, includes only three maintained trails. Want a challenge? Also consider day hiking La Verkin Creek Trail (p112).

TIMBER CREEK OVERLOOK

Duration 30 minutes
Distance 1 mile
Difficulty Easy–moderate
Start/Finish End of Kolob Canyon's Rd
Nearest Town Cedar City (p132)
Transportation Private
Summary A short dirt trail to a promontory with 270-degree views of canyons and mountains. The track gets a bit steep and rocky, but unless elevation affects you, it isn't difficult.

The shortest of the Kolob Canyon hiking options provides a chance to stretch your legs at the end of the scenic drive, but it's not the best of the park's overlooks. Remember that you're above 6300ft here, so the elevation may wind you more than the 100ft ascent. Start at the end of Kolob Canyons Rd; about 100yd along the trail, you'll find picnic benches nestled beneath the Gambel oaks and junipers. The view at trail's end encompasses the ragged, finger-like **Kolob Canyons** to the east and the flat mesas of the **Lower Kolob Plateau** to the south. From here, **Zion Canyon** is a wispy haze, unrecognizable as the mighty trench and inspiration of majestic homilies that it is.

TAYLOR CREEK MIDDLE FORK

Duration 3 hours
Distance 5 miles
Difficulty Moderate
Start/Finish Kolob Canyons Rd
Nearest Town Cedar City (p132)
Transportation Private
Summary A refreshing trip that crisscrosses Taylor Creek, passing through juniper, sage and piñon to get to two historic cabins. The real payoff is at the end: views of Double Arch Alcove, a natural amphitheater.

From the start at a parking lot mid-scenic drive, the path quickly drops down stairs and sand to creek level; the overall elevation change is 450ft. From there trail and water interweave like a strand of DNA. Pay attention; in places, informal spurs obscure the main trail. Though the creek is small, expect to get a little wet and muddy, and maybe harassed by bugs.

After about a mile, you come to the 1930 **Larson Cabin** and a sign identifying the Taylor Creek Trail. As the trail enters a finger canyon between **Tucupit** and **Paria Points**, the walls narrow, and your steady ascent grows steeper still. A mile farther **Fife Cabin** appears. It, like its predecessor, is too fragile to enter; respect the chicken wire on the windows and doors.

The last half-mile leads to **Double Arch Alcove**, where the seep-stained red rock glows and echoes with dripping water and swirling wind. It's a cool, refreshing break before your return trip.

Kolob Terrace Road

Most of the trails along the scenic road that bisects the park are considered backcountry routes, but there's one notable exception.

NORTHGATE PEAKS TRAIL

Duration 2 hours
Distance 4.4 miles
Difficulty Easy–moderate
Start/Finish Wildcat Canyon trailhead, Kolob Terrace Rd
Nearest Town Springdale
Transportation Private
Summary An overlooked west-side gem: traipse through sage meadows and pine forest to reach a lava outcrop with a view of 7000ft-plus peaks.

Looking for a cool retreat on a hot summer day? Starting at 6500ft makes a big tem-

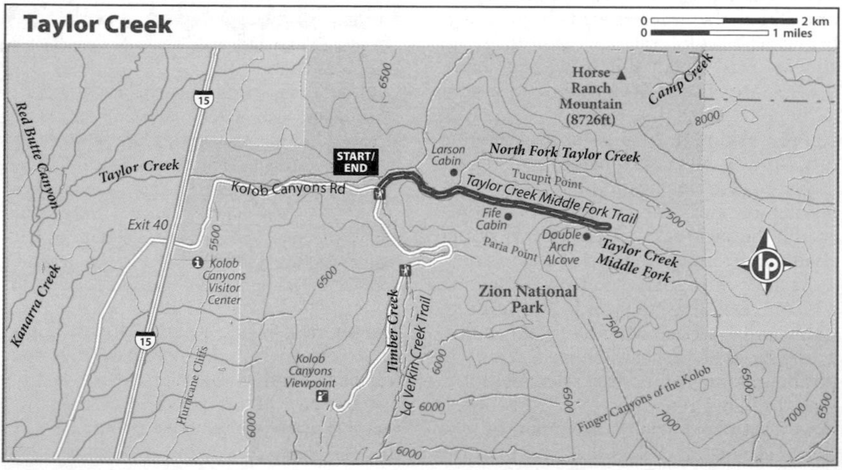

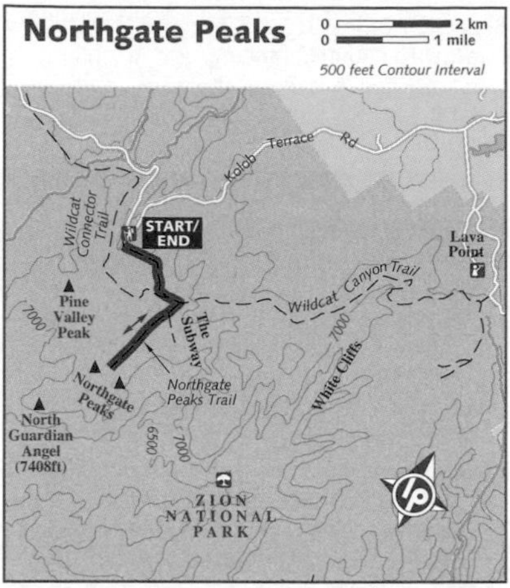

perature difference. And since this area sees so little traffic, this pleasant trail remains largely uncrowded. About 16 miles north of Hwy 9 on Kolob Terrace Rd, look for the sign to Wildcat Canyon trailhead. The dirt path starts at the end of the parking area.

For about a mile, you'll wander through an open meadow of sage and scrub. At the first junction, stay straight, following the sign for the **West Rim Trail**. (The **Wildcat Connector Trail** branches right and connects with the **Hop Valley Trail**). At 100yd further, look for the signed Northgate Peaks Trail junction and turn right. The ponderosa pines, manzanita and oodles of spring wildflowers (June through early July) are a welcome rest for rock-weary eyes. You soon crest a rise to a final Y junction. Here, the trailhead for the backcountry canyoneering route, the **Subway** (p113), branches left. Keep going straight.

The aptly named **White Cliffs** tower to the east as you gently ascend and descend to a lava-rock outcrop at trail's end – a good perch to admire the stunning terrain. On either side, seemingly close enough to touch, are the pale, crosshatched **Northgate Peaks**. Front and center is **North Guardian Angel**, with an arch so deep it's more of a cave. Framed amid these in the distance is the heart of **Zion Canyon**, including **East and West Temples** and **Deertrap Mountain**, on the East Rim.

East Zion

East-side trailheads are not on Zion Canyon Scenic Drive, and are therefore not served by shuttles. It will take more time (and sometimes 4WD or hiker transport) to get here; from Springdale to Zion Ponderosa Ranch Resort it's at least 35 minutes. But you may also have the advantage of driving up 2000ft to start, instead of climbing it.

CANYON OVERLOOK

Duration 45 minutes
Distance 1 mile
Difficulty Easy–moderate
Start/Finish East of Zion–Mt Carmel Tunnel
Nearest Town Springdale
Transportation Private
Summary A convenient stop off Hwy 9, Canyon Overlook is a relatively quick hike that rewards with intimate canyon experiences and ends in much-photographed panoramic vistas.

Get up close and personal with the wind- and water-carved features on a quick trip through a canyon. Though it starts with stairs, this uneven dirt trail has less than 200ft elevation change over all, and is enjoyable for a range of ages and fitness levels.

At the east end of the Zion–Mt Carmel Tunnel, park and cross the road to the trailhead near the tunnel ranger booth. (If the small lot is full, try parking areas just east up the road.)

After an initial staircase ascent, the trail clings to the cliff walls, passes beneath overhangs sheltering fern gardens and bridges over sheer drops.

Peer into the dark, narrow recesses as you cross **Pine Creek Canyon**, a favorite rappelling site.

You can observe geologic formation at work in the **Great Arch**, which is actually a proto-arch that won't fulfill its potential for thousands of years. After you cross the slickrock, you can have a good look at it from the final sweeping **Canyon Overlook**.

From here you also have fine views of lower Zion Canyon features, including the **East and West Temples**, the **Towers of the Virgin**, and the **Beehives** (large red-and-white, two-tone monoliths that are hard to miss).

The viewpoint is wide enough for visitors to spread out comfortably as they admire the views. Watch small children near the edge, which overlooks an adrenaline-boosting 700ft drop.

CABLE MOUNTAIN TRAIL

Duration 3 hours
Distance 6.2 miles
Difficulty Moderate
Start/Finish West Pine Rd, inside Zion Ponderosa Ranch Resort
Nearest Town Springdale
Transportation Private high-clearance vehicle or hiker shuttle
Summary An upcountry hike through ponderosa pines leads to your choice of Zion Canyon overlooks. Best of all, you'll encounter few fellow hikers on this trail, which is long but has little elevation change.

Seeking solitude? Any of the upcountry East Zion trails are tailor-made for you. The route to **Cable Mountain** is one of the easiest, and for those who want to make a long day of it, it can be combined with a hike to **Deertrap Mountain**. Even in season, you may not see a soul. Both are mainly plateau hikes that end at almost indescribable viewpoints over Zion Canyon.

To reach the trailhead, 2.5 miles east of the East Entrance turn up North Fork Rd and continue 5 miles to **Zion Ponderosa Ranch Resort** (p125), a lodge bordering the park that allows public access to trails. Enter the ranch and the road quickly becomes gravel and dirt. In half a mile, turn left at the signed junction for Cable Mountain onto Buck Rd. After 0.6 miles, turn left at an unsigned junction, and in 100yd turn right onto West Pine Rd. In half a mile, this road dead-ends at the fence for the national park. There is no parking area; try not to block the gate.

The clear dirt trail starts by threading through ponderosa pine forest, and in a quarter-mile, passes a signed junction with a trail to **Echo Canyon**. After ascending for a steady half-mile through scrub forest, you'll reach a signed junction with the **East Rim Trail**. A mile further bear northward at the signed turnoff for Cable Mountain (Deertrap Mountain is another 2 miles straight on from this point.)

The trail soon tops out and descends a final mile to the **historic cable works**, once used to haul down lumber. The wooden structure is rickety; don't climb on it. Instead, enjoy the panorama, overlooking the **Big Bend** of the Virgin River and the Oxbow containing **Angels Landing**. On a clear day you can see north to the pink cliffs and **Cedar Breaks** (p135).

EAST MESA TRAIL

Duration 3 hours
Distance 6.4 miles
Difficulty Moderate
Start/Finish Zion Ponderosa Ranch, Beaver Rd
Nearest Town Springdale
Transportation Private high-clearance 4WD or hiker shuttle
Summary The sneaky, backcountry approach to Observation Point. The trail starts off a 4WD road on the east side of Zion and traverses upcountry ecosystems before dropping down to the overlook.

It feels deliciously like cheating to wander through the woods and then descend (500ft elevation change overall) to Observation Point instead of hiking 2500ft uphill from Zion Canyon. Either way, you get some of the park's best perspectives.

Getting to the trailhead requires a 4WD for the last few miles, but Springdale outfitters (p93) and Zion Ponderosa Ranch Resort (p125) can provide hiker shuttles. Zion Ponderosa Ranch Resort is 2.5 miles east of the park's East Entrance, 5 miles north up North Fork Rd. Note that this is also the trailhead to the Mystery Canyon canyoneering route. At 6500ft, this trail may be closed to snow November through March.

The first 2 trail miles meander through open stands of tall ponderosa pines, which may show signs of the periodic park-prescribed burns. In May and June, keep an eye out for showy upcountry wildflowers. To the right you'll see canyon views open up in the distance before you get to the cairns marking **Mystery Canyon**. Take a short detour up the slickrock to the right to overlook the white, fingerlike canyons stretching out below.

From there the main trail turns southwest and starts gradually descending, with glimpses of **Echo Canyon** on your left and Zion Canyon on your right. Further descent down slickrock and lose stones, shaded by juniper and piñon, leads past some sandy

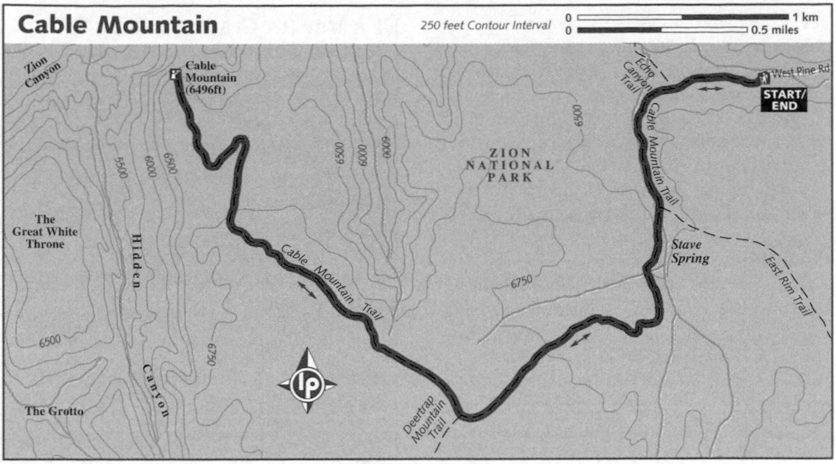

sites and to the **Observation Point** (p106) spur at 3 miles. Sharing the last 0.2 miles of the trail with so many other people can be jarring. But just think how much easier it was for you to get here.

BACKCOUNTRY HIKES

Despite its accessibility, Zion's backcountry sees relatively little use compared to other major national parks. Thus hikers can enjoy the park's ethereal and overwhelming beauty in near solitude, even on summer weekends when the Zion Park Shuttle is standing-room only.

One thing Zion doesn't have many of is multiday routes. The longest trip you can take within park borders is the four-day Trans-Park Connector journey. Most trails listed here need at most a single overnight to complete, but all require permits. For more on backcountry permits, regulations and camping, see p111.

PLANNING

One reason the Zion backcountry is so quiet is that it can be a hot, dry, extremely remote place – preparation is essential. The **Backcountry Desk** (☎ 435-772-0170; www.nps.gov/zion/planyourvisit; 🕑 8am-6pm Jun-Sep, 7am-8pm May & Oct, 8am-4:30pm Nov-Apr) in the Zion Canyon Visitor Center serves as your main information resource and permit vendor. Here you can peruse binders with exhaustive descriptions (and often photos) of every backcountry trail and campsite, climbing route and slot canyon. They also have up-to-the-minute weather reports, water-level and temperature reports for the Virgin River, and information on water availability at backcountry springs. An informal rideshare board is posted behind the desk.

You can also get backcountry information and permits at the Kolob Canyons Visitor Center (p91). Pick up a seasonal *Zion National Park Backcountry Planner* newspaper, with basic map, at either center.

Permits

Permits are required for all overnight trips (including rock climbs with bivouacs), all through-hikes of the Virgin River (including the Narrows top hike) and any canyoneering hikes requiring ropes for descent. Online permit reservations ($5 reservation fee) for many trips are available up until 5pm the preceding day. Two of the most sought-after routes are an exception: three months in advance an online-reservation lottery is held for the Subway and Mystery Canyon permits. Note that a reservation is not the permit itself, which you must pick up in person at either visitor center. If you're a frequent park visitor (at least once every three years), you can go through orientation at the Backcountry Desk and join Zion Express Permits, which allows you to purchase an actual permit online.

Twenty-five percent of available permits remain reserved for walk-in visitors the day before or day of a trip. Trying to get a next-day walk-in permit on a busy weekend is like trying to get tickets to a rock concert; lines form at the Backcountry Desk by 6am or earlier.

Use limits are in effect on some routes to protect the environment. Permit fees (which are in addition to the reservation fee) are $10 for one to two hikers, $15 for three to seven hikers, and $20 for eight to 12 hikers.

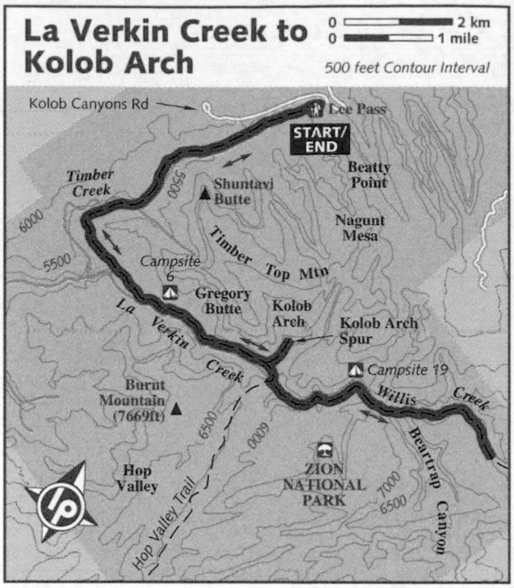

Camping

The map on the *Backcountry Planner* shows trails where camping is limited to designated sights, including the Narrows, West Rim, La Verkin Creek and Hop Valley on the park Trans-Park Connector trail. More detailed site maps are available at the visitor centers. While campsites can only be reserved for one night online (again, a $5 reservation fee), you can arrange multinight stays in person at the Backcountry Desk. Designated backcountry campsites are primitive, offering only a numbered marker and a cleared area.

In other areas, at-large camping is allowed – if you camp more than a mile from roads, out of sight of trails and at least a quarter-mile from any spring – but backcountry permits are still required.

Kolob Canyons

Cedar City, 20 miles north, is the closest town to the Kolob Canyons entrance; but hiker shuttles leave from Springdale (40 miles southeast).

LA VERKIN CREEK TRAIL TO KOLOB ARCH

Duration 8 hours–2 days
Distance 14 miles
Difficulty Difficult
Start/Finish Lee Pass on Kolob Canyons Rd
Nearest Town Cedar City (p132)
Transportation Private
Summary One of the world's largest freestanding arches rewards at the end of an intense day hike, or a less strenuous backpack. Trek through high-country foothills, following creeks and passing peaks along the way.

Hiking along Timber, La Verkin, and maybe Willis, creeks is lovely in spring (late April to May-ish) and fall (September and October). Early summer, biting goat flies can hound hikers and high-season temperatures are discouraging. It's a strenuous day hike due to length, sand and elevation changes (800ft overall); an overnight is both easier and allows time to explore the highly recommended Willis Creek area.

The trailhead is just south of the Lee Pass parking area on **Kolob Canyons Rd**. For the first 2 miles or so, you descend an open ridge with fine views of the **finger canyons**. Eventually, you'll skirt the spire of **Shuntavi Butte** and descend more steeply through piñon-juniper forest along **Timber Creek**.

The trail then turns east to the north bank of **La Verkin Creek**, a permanent, vigorous stream lined with the most convenient **campsites** (numbers 6 through 19). The trail is sandy and slowgoing here. Ponderosa pines provide shade, while orange butterfly weed makes a pretty diversion.

After about 6.25 miles, follow the signed **Kolob Arch Trail** turnoff. The half-mile spur is as far as day hikers should travel. Some scrambling and routefinding is required. When you reach a sign advising against further travel up-canyon, look high on the west wall for **Kolob Arch**. Though its 310ft opening may be the largest in the world, the distant arch is so dwarfed by massive walls that it at first seems strangely anticlimactic. Spend some time watching the sun cloak the rock in ever-shifting shadows, however, and it soon makes a satisfying destination after all.

Just beyond the spur lies the signed junction for the Hop Valley Trail, which you can use as part of the **Trans-Park Connector** (below). Past this, La Verkin Creek Trail continues for 4.5 miles, steadily narrowing, then turning up **Willis Creek**, a steep defile with towering sheer walls that open up near the park boundary. Don't leave the park limits, as private-property owners have been known to run off stray hikers.

TRANS-PARK CONNECTOR

Duration 4 days
Distance 15.5 miles one way
Difficulty Difficult
Start Lee Pass on Kolob Canyons Rd
Finish Grotto in Zion Canyon
Nearest Town Cedar City (p132), Springdale
Transportation Hiker shuttle
Summary Several Zion trails link to create a four-day backpack covering most of the park and its impressive features – high-country plateaus, sandy creeks, towering rocks, steep descents and ever-changing views of the stunning red canyon.

You may not be able to drive directly from one section of the park to the other, but you can hike between them. The most popular way to traverse Zion is to trek northwest to southeast over four days. Always check with rangers when planning, and get detailed directions and maps. There's very little water along this route. The only absolutely reliable source is La Verkin Creek; others are seasonal. Spring is your best bet for water, while fall brings spectacular colors. Summer is hot, and parts of the trail may be closed because of snow November through March. Note that you will likely need a hiker shuttle (p93).

Spend the first night on **La Verkin Creek Trail** (opposite), heading head south from there on the 6.7-mile **Hop Valley Trail**, which begins with amazing views then descends about 1000ft on long, hot, sandy stretches, emerging at **Kolob Terrace Rd**.

The 4-mile **Wildcat Connector Trail** links Hop Valley with the 4.7-mile **Wildcat Canyon Trail**. Together, the Wildcats comprise an uneven ascent of nearly 2000ft. Two sites offer dispersed camping there if you'd rather not press on to **Lava Point Campground** (p121) for the second night. From Lava Point trek on along the **West Rim Trail** (p114), where you'll spend your third night, descend past **Angels Landing** and emerge eventually at the **Grotto** picnic area in Zion Canyon.

Kolob Terrace Road

The scenic Kolob Terrace Rd takes off north from the tiny town of Virgin. Backcountry hikes from here are usually one way and require a hiker shuttle.

THE SUBWAY

Duration 7 hours
Distance 9.5 miles one way
Difficulty Difficult
Start Wildcat Canyon trailhead
Finish Left Fork trailhead
Nearest Town Springdale
Transportation Hiker shuttle
Summary An eerie tunnel-like rock on this canyoneering route make it the park's most photographed backcountry feature by far. The challenging, one-way trail requires up to five rappels and descends more than 1800ft, often in water.

Though the left fork of North Creek – better known as the **Subway** – is technically a canyoneering route, we've included a basic description here because of its incredible popularity. This is unquestionably the hardest backcountry permit to get. Only the descent from the top is recommended; day hiking from the bottom (permit also required) is a long slog in and out, with full sun, and you see fewer than half the features. While the route is easy by canyoneering standards – four or five short rappels of 20ft or less – you still need to know what you're doing. (For more on canyoneering, see p117.) Seek technical advice, get good maps and arrange a hiker shuttle (p93). The one-way trail starts at the Wildcat Canyon trailhead, about 16 miles north of Hwy 9 on Kolob Terrace Rd.

At first, the route follows the **Northgate Peaks Trail** (p108). Once you get to the signed spur to the Subway, the real adventure – and route-finding on slickrock – begins. You parallel, then cross the wooded **Russell Gulch** to an amazing bowl of sculpted rock.

After deep, downhill scrambles and clefts in the rockface you approach the **left fork drainage**. There you're alternating between rock and sand, short rappels and cold pools of increasingly clear water (some swimming involved). The last of these rappels is **Keyhole Falls**, the barrier to day hikers headed upstream.

The whole sculpted canyon is full of surprises, beauty and camera-worthy moments, including the curving walls that form the tunnel-like Subway formation and hard-to-find dinosaur tracks. Along the way, the creek tumbles scenically over low slickrock ledges, gives way to boulders and meanders in and out of the stream bed. After the signs for the **Left Fork trailhead**, the steep trail climbs sharply up before it reaches the plateau and meanders to the parking lot. The hike out takes about two hours.

WEST RIM TRAIL

Duration 2 days
Distance 14.5 miles one way
Difficulty Difficult
Start Lava Point trailhead
Finish Grotto picnic area
Nearest Town Springdale
Transportation Hiker shuttle
Summary An attractive upcountry trail that leads from one of Zion's highest points to one of its lowest, affording primo views during the course of a 3600ft descent.

Starting on a high plateau, climbing down past Angels Landing, this is Zion's most popular backcountry trail. That said, until you get to Scout Lookout, it's far from crowded. And the spectacular views, especially at sunset, will leave you breathless. Note that parts of the trail can be closed due to snow November through May.

Unless you have two cars and two drivers, arrange a hiker shuttle (p93) up to **Lava Point** trailhead, about 21 miles north of Virgin on Kolob Terrace Rd. There's a primitive campground here. After crossing **Horse Pasture Plateau**, the trail descends oh-so-gently for about 5 miles. In about a mile, you'll reach the spur trail to the semi-reliable **Sawmill Spring**. Abundant trailside wildflowers (late June through July) include

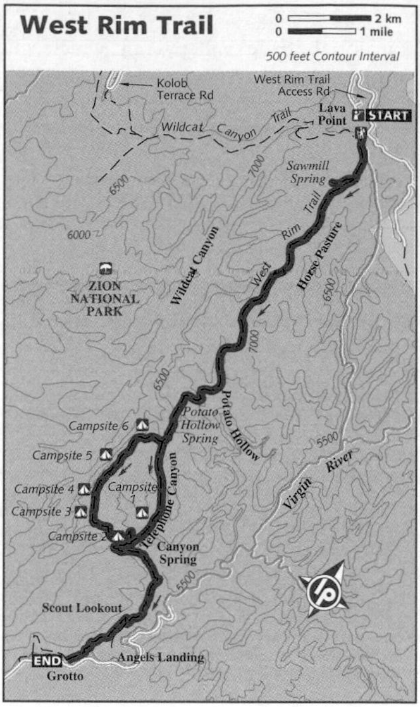

arrowleaf balsamroot, desert phlox, larkspur and Uinta groundsel.

The first big view west opens up at around 4 miles, stretching for what seems forever across the valley of the **left fork of North Creek**. A mile or so further you'll descend into the grassy meadows of **Potato Hollow**, where a spur leads to a good-sized spring. So long as it's running, this is the best place to get water and a perfect shady spot for lunch.

The hike up and out of the hollow is a bit of a workout, mitigated by the increasingly dramatic views west. After about 2 miles, you'll reach the junction with the **Telephone Canyon Trail**, a shorter route to Cabin Spring, but don't take it. The next 2-mile stretch is an incredible experience and is the primary reason for this trail's enduring popularity.

Campsites 3 through 6 are spread along this edge of the mesa; reserve one of these blessed perches if you can. (For more on backcountry camping, see p112). It can get windy, so bring rope for your tent, and never build a campfire.

Soon the trail descends steeply and, except for a half-mile stretch midway down, keeps descending sharply all the way to the Grotto. **Cabin Spring** is a major junction. From there, short spur trails lead to the spring itself (a trickle) and **campsite 2**. Telephone Canyon connects here, and **campsite 1** is not far along it. Though both campsites are very nice, the views don't quite compare.

About 12.5 miles from Lava Point, you get to **Scout Lookout** (where there's a nearby pit toilet) and the junction for **Angels Landing**. Those with the legs and stomach for it should at least climb out to the saddle for a look. Beyond the junction, it's a 2-mile drop to the canyon floor and your shuttle ride to the visitor center.

East Zion

Note that both the East Mesa and Cable/Deertrap Mountain day hikes (p110) can be turned into overnights. The hard core might also want to ask the Backcountry Desk about the challenging East Rim Trail, which climbs steeply up from near the East Entrance.

NARROWS: FROM THE TOP

Duration 2 days
Distance 16 miles one way
Difficulty Difficult
Start Chamberlain's Ranch
Finish Temple of Sinawava
Nearest Town Springdale
Transportation Hiker shuttle
Summary An incredible in-the-river experience hiking down more than 1200ft through the park's most famous slot canyon. Taking two days makes this route more enjoyable and less of an all-out fitness test.

If there's one route that's made Zion famous, it's the wade down the Virgin River through a 1000ft sheer gorge known as the **Narrows**. Soaring walls, sculpted alcoves – and hiking over slippery, submerged, bowling ball–like rocks – make it memorable. Overnight camping promises the best experience, though you can hike from the top in one very strenuous, long day (90 minutes driving from Springdale to Chamberlain's Ranch, up to 12 hours hiking). You can also day hike the Narrows from the bottom (p104), the only approach that doesn't require a permit.

The Narrows permits are some of the most sought-after in the park. They are not issued any time the river is flowing more than 120 cubic feet per second, so the Narrows may be closed between early March and early June. The optimum time to hike is late June through September. Flash floods are not uncommon in late summer, when, again, the park may close the route (for more on flash floods, see p283). The rest of the year, wet, or even dry suits are necessary, as hypothermia is a real danger. The Backcountry Desk carefully tracks weather, and Springdale outfitters (boxed text, p102) rent all the appropriate gear. A summer-season checklist includes two walking sticks, heavy-duty footwear and neoprene socks, nylon clothing, extra fleece layers and dry bags (you will fall in the water at least once). Overnight hikers are required to use human-waste disposal bags, which are given free to permit holders.

The trail begins at **Chamberlain's Ranch**, on the east side of the park, 90 minutes'

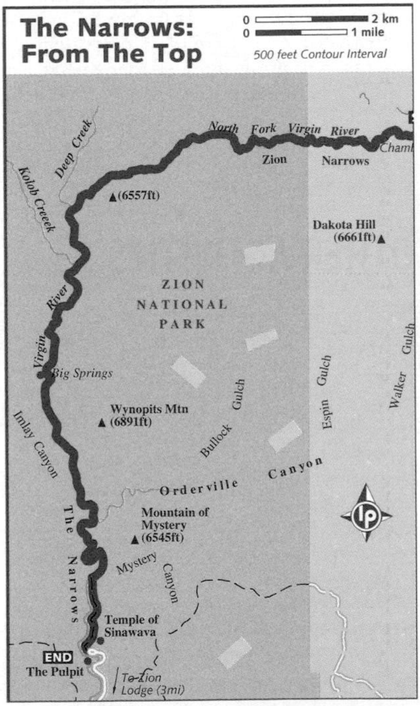

FLASH FLOODS

Before you hike any narrow canyon, check the weather carefully. Do not enter the canyon if storms threaten. Even if the weather seems good, you should watch for signs of a flash flood. A two-week drought is meaningless once a single rain cloud arrives. For telltale signs of danger and what to do to stay safe, see p285.

drive from the South Entrance. This is a one-way hike, so make reservations for a hiker shuttle (p93), unless you have two cars and drivers. Past the ranch gate, a dirt road leads to the river, where you'll find an NPS trailhead marker.

From here, the trail *is* the river. The first 9 miles are the quietest and easiest, the flowing water and undulating walls casting a mesmerizing spell. **Deep Creek** is the first major confluence, doubling the river's volume. In the subsequent 2-mile stretch, expect secretive side canyons and faster water, sometimes waist deep and involving swims. This area north of **Big Water** also contains most of the 12 campsites lining the river.

Below Big Water are the 5 miles open to day hikers; coming upon so many people is a little like being woken from a dream. In 2 miles you'll reach well-known **Wall Street**, and your company will steadily increase until you're just one of the crowd on the **Riverside Walk** (p101).

OTHER ACTIVITIES

Besides hiking, the two most popular activities in Zion are canyoneering its slot canyons and climbing its massive sandstone walls – both world-class experiences. There are also opportunities for biking, horseback riding, swimming and tubing, and though the Virgin River is not normally deep enough, for kayaking. It is *not* a successful spot for anglers.

Note that classes and ranger-led programs are available, too; for more see the boxed text, p119.

BIKING

In the park, cycling is allowed on roads and on the **Pa'rus Trail** (p101), both of which are very pleasant and popular. In fact, the lack of cars from April through October makes cycling a great way to see the canyon. We recommend that you shuttle your bike up to the Temple of Sinawava and follow our **Zion Canyon Scenic Drive** (p95) in reverse. It's all downhill from there. Being under your own steam allows you to stop at turnouts where the shuttle doesn't. Do note that the park requires that you pull over and let shuttles pass. In practice this is not really much of an inconvenience and it keeps the majority of park visitors on the road, so be courteous.

Enthusiasts can also ride quite comfortably along Hwy 9 through Springdale to the Zion Canyon drive. Speed limits are low and cars usually crawl along the super-flat stretch. Note that east of the Zion Canyon turnoff the road climbs precipitously, and bicycles are not allowed in the Zion–Mt Carmel Tunnel.

As at all national parks, mountain biking is prohibited, but nearby areas provide trails on a par with any in southern Utah – even Moab. Technical slickrock, with audacious obstacles, and genuine singletrack make **Gooseberry Mesa**, off Smithsonian Buttes Rd south of Rockville, one of the most popular trails. Occasional sweeping views of Zion's panorama make it all the more attractive. Also try **Hurricane Cliffs**, outside Kolob Canyons, and **Rockville Bench**, southwest of Zion Canyon. Springdale bike shops can provide directions and point you to all the trails. Just remember, summer is hot, hot, hot; spring and fall are the most enjoyable times for biking.

There are two full-service bike shops in town, associated with the two outfitters. Look for **Zion Cycles** (☎ 435-772-0400; www.zioncycles.com; 868 Zion Park Blvd; 🕑 9am-7pm) set back behind Zion Pizza & Noodle, next to Orange Frozen Yogurt. It offers half- and full-day bike tours outside the park in conjunction with Zion Adventure. **Bike Zion** (☎ 435-772-3303; www.bikingzion.com; 1458 Zion Park Blvd; 🕑 8am-8pm Mar-Oct, hours vary Nov-Feb) is in the same building as Zion Rock & Mountain Guides. In addition to day trips, it also offers multiday and multisport tours (hiking, biking, canyoneering and/or climbing).

Both shops rent road, mountain and hybrid bikes (from $35 per day), as well as trailers and car racks. If you want to get a superearly start, ask – you may be able to pick the bike up at closing time and return it at store opening for the one-hour rate (from $15), or by noon for four hours.

Options outside Springdale:

Mountain Bike Buddies (☎ 800-860-6460; www.mountainbikebuddies.com; 642 N Bandolier Ln, Washington) By reservation, arranges do-it-yourself bike tours that include hotel pick-up, bike rental and shuttle to and from trailheads around Zion, St George and Cedar City.

Over the Edge Sports (☎ 435-635-5455; http://otehurricane.com; 76 E 100 S, Hurricane; 9am-6pm daily Mar-Dec, closed Tue Jan & Feb) Bike rentals and tours.

CANYONEERING

If there's one sport that makes Zion special, it's canyoneering. Rappelling 100ft over the lip of a sandstone bowl, swimming icy pools, tracing a slot canyon's sculpted curves, staring up at a ragged gash of blue sky – canyoneering is beautiful, dangerous and sublime all at once. And it's not terribly hard to learn.

As such, canyoneering has become the fastest-growing activity at Zion. The park service sets day-use limits to protect many routes, and permits (p111) are required for all. None of the canyons should be taken lightly; classes are available from area outfitters. Even if you've never considered canyoneering before, a half-day guided trip (no experience required) can be the highlight of your visit to Zion.

Outfitters

Guided canyoneering is prohibited in the park, but two Springdale outfitters offer half-day to multiday training – and highly recommended half- and full-day guided trips – on the every-bit-as-beautiful public lands surrounding. (Rates start at $150 per person for a half-day.) You can also take a half-day course that includes preparation and equipment rental for a self-guided excursion on one of the easier park routes (permit required) later in the day. Both

LOCAL VOICE: GREG ISTOCK

A 'rock' star in more than one sense, musician Greg Istock was first drawn to Zion in 1999. He and his wife, Valerie, returned frequently until they relocated and Greg became a canyoneering and climbing guide in 2006.

How did you get here? We fell in love with the landscape. The color of it, the openness of it, the people that live here…

But it's not always easy to live in a desert. No. The Canyon has a say in it. The landscape accepts or rejects you. But if you love something, you go toward it.

What makes Zion so special for canyoneering? There's more here than in most places; within a few hours you can get to so many canyons. If you're really into the sport, there are dangerous, but downright fun, routes that you're going to want to seek out.

Do you have favorites? I'm asked that so often, but there are a lot of great, really technical ones. Heap's Canyon, Mystery Canyon, multiday sleepouts…

And for beginners? Trips like Orderville Canyon require an eight-hour commitment with a shuttle. Keyhole Canyon is a great introductory hike. Access is right from the road; within the first couple of hours you can be canyoneering. You drop through a 'keyhole' into a pool, so you have to be cold water–prepared. It's dark and it's creepy…it's awesome. Your senses are going to be tested, but that's the fun.

What about climbing? There are no beginner routes in the park, but there's great advanced rock climbing. To me climbing is about a personal physical challenge. Canyoneering is more of an adventure, a movie unfolding. There are obstacles to overcome, and there are consequences. Obstacles and beauty. It keeps you going.

Is there anything you'd like to add? We have this unique, pristine environment. For the most part, the canyons are still in really good shape. In the last season or two we've started seeing people writing their names… We need to have a respect for the nature of this environment; if not, access is going to be – and should be – shut down by the park.

Greg Istock is a backcountry guide with Zion Rock & Mountain Guides.

outfitters are one-stop shops for all your canyoneering needs. They sell ropes and maps, provide advice and suit you up with rental gear (harnesses, helmets, canyoneering shoes, dry suits, fleece layers, waterproof packs and more). The hiker shuttles they offer are especially handy for one-way slot-canyon routes. Both companies have excellent reputations and tons of experience around Zion.

If we had to identify a difference, we'd say that **Zion Rock & Mountain Guides** (☎ 435-772-3303; www.zionrockguides.com; 1458 Zion Park Blvd; 🕑 8am-8pm Mar-Oct, hour vary Nov-Feb) is a bit more down-to-business. Their super-knowledgeable guides are long-term area residents who want to show you rather than tell you what to do, so you have time to do more of it. All classes and trips are private, for your group alone. Zion Rock is the only place that rents static canyon ropes.

Zion Adventure Company (☎ 435-772-1001; www.zionadventures.com; 36 Lion Blvd; 🕑 8am-8pm Mar-Oct, 9am-noon & 4-7pm Nov-Feb) provides a bit more hand-holding, with introductory videos, life-size pictures of the rappels and a crack staff that will take their time with every detail before you go. You may get a rappel or two fewer in the same amount of time, but you'll have just as much fun. Those traveling alone have an advantage here; Zion Adventure allows you to join other groups, bringing the cost down. In general, we'd recommend the seriously sporty go with Zion Rocks and younger families head for Zion Adventure, but anyone could have an enjoyable trip with either – we have!

Routes

Zion National Park and surrounding lands contain dozens of slot canyons. All canyoneering routes in the park require permits. These canyons are the park's most sought-after backcountry experience, so it's best to reserve your dates as soon as possible.

On the west side of the park off Kolob Terrace Rd, the left fork of North Creek, better known as the **Subway** (p113) is perhaps the most well-known route, and is fairly easy in canyoneering terms. **Orderville Canyon**, off North Fork Rd on the park's east side, ends at the Narrows (p104) and is another basic route. In terms of equipment, these require only about 60ft of rope or webbing (basically flat rope), a submersible daypack, canyoneering shoes and, in every season but summer, a wet or dry suit. From June through August, water in the canyons is usually just warm enough to swim in shorts. Quick-drying nylon is best.

Keyhole Canyon, off Hwy 9 east of the Zion–Mt Carmel Tunnel, is a gem of a narrow slot that drops down two 20ft rappels and into a cold pool swim. It requires about 100ft of rope, and a wet suit even in summer.

For people who know how to use a harness (and who can ascend and belay others), **Pine Creek Canyon**, off Hwy 9 east of the South Entrance, and **Mystery Canyon**, off North Fork Rd on the east side of the park, are two gorgeous, very popular routes. They offer moderate challenges, with seven or eight rappels of 50ft to 100ft. Pine Creek features easy access, while Mystery Canyon lets you be a rock star – the last rappel drops you into the Virgin River in front of admiring crowds day-hiking the Narrows.

ROCK CLIMBING

Zion Canyon contains some of the most famous big-wall climbs in the country, including **Moonlight Buttress**, **Prodigal Son**, **Touchstone** and **Space Shot**. These are epic, aided climbs that draw the best of the best for their challenge and beauty. Though there are a number of mapped routes in the park, if you climb with a local, be prepared for many stops while he or she stares at an opposing cliff face, pondering a new route.

This is all well and good for experts and those ready to tackle their first big wall or bivouac, but Zion isn't for beginners. Those seeking sport climbs and bolted routes will find opportunities outside Zion, at such places as **Snow Canyon State Park** (p132) near St George.

While day climbs in Zion do not require a permit, all overnights and bivouacs do (for more on permits, see p111). Talk to Zion's Backcountry Desk; they keep an ever-growing binder of climber-written route descriptions. Note that some formations are off-limits from March through August to protect nesting peregrine falcons.

Both outfitters listed left offer recommended rock-climbing courses for beginners and intermediates, as well as guided day climbs outside the park limits. Zion

WHO KNEW LEARNING COULD BE SO MUCH FUN?

A Moenav-va-what formation? From fascinating geological forces to extreme desert flora and fauna, there's a lot to learn around Zion National Park. The wide variety of **ranger-led activities** are a great place to start. Daily talks (more frequent June through August) at the Human History Museum (p96) cover topics such as the survival of species in the desert and the culture of the area's ancients. Guided hikes explore topics like the power of water and indigenous plant life along some of the most popular trails, including Emerald Pools and Riverside Walk. Occasionally, evening programs are held at Watchman Campground and Zion Lodge, and Kolob Canyons hosts limited talks and walks of their own. Visitor centers post lists of each week's programs and a schedule is available online at www.nps.gov/zion.

Even more in-depth are the courses offered by **Zion Canyon Field Institute** (☎ 435-772-3264, 800-635-3959; www.zionpark.org) in conjunction with Zion Natural History Association. All involve accompanying an expert outdoors, and some are strenuous. This is your chance to hike the Narrows with a geologist, to learn to paint *en plen air* with an artist, or dig in the dirt with an archaeologist. Photography classes are quite popular; wildflower walks are some of our favorites. The majority of the excellent half-day to multiday seminars take place between April and October, but classes are offered year-round. Prices start at about $50 per person; class sizes are usually limited to 12 to 14 people.

Rock has a wider selection of climbing gear for sale, as well as route books that are as up-to-date as the park service's.

KIDS' ACTIVITIES

Late May through late August, Zion National Park offers a series of children's programs for various age groups. Many are based at **Zion Nature Center** (☎ 435-772-3256; South Campground, off Hwy 9; admission free; ⏰ noon-5pm late May-late Aug), but some take place at Zion Lodge or on trails. You might hunt for animal habitats along the Virgin River or hear stories about the life of the first pioneer settlers in the area. Plans are even underway for a geo-waypointing scavenger hunt aimed at teens. For schedules check online (www.nps.gov/zion) or in the summer park newspaper. The nature center itself has a variety of interactive flora- and fauna-focused exhibits. The littlest little ones love dressing up like rangers and using the animal puppets.

Year-round, children six to 12 can earn a patch and become a Junior Ranger by completing the activity-filled *Junior Ranger Handbook* ($1) available at both visitor centers and the Human History Museum. If you have a little one under five, pick up the free Junior Ranger Helper Activity Sheet so they can earn a pin. The bookstores also sell *Zion Canyon Adventure*, a fun and informative illustrated 'guidebook' to the park.

On rainy days, you could check out the education games and such on the park service's site, **Web Rangers** (www.nps.gov/webrangers).

HORSEBACK RIDING

Canyon Trail Rides (☎ 435-679-8665, 435-772-3810; www.canyonrides.com) is Zion's official horseback riding concessionaire, operating from a corral across the road from Zion Lodge. Every day from March through November, they offer four one-hour rides (from $40) and two half-day rides (from $75). Both follow the **Sand Bench Trail**, which runs along the Virgin River. The longer route passes the Court of the Patriarchs, the Sentinel Slide and the Beehives formations. Note that there's a 220lb weight limit, and children must be seven years and 10 years old, respectively, for the hour/half-day rides.

You can ride your own horse as well. In Zion Canyon, the only trail open to horses is the Sand Bench Trail; horses are allowed on most trails in the backcountry. Permits are not required for day trips; maximum group size is six animals. The only overnight stock camp is on the Hop Valley Trail, off Kolob Terrace Rd. For more about regulations and overnight permits, contact the Backcountry Desk (p111).

SWIMMING & TUBING

The Virgin River is fairly swift and shallow, generally no more than knee-deep. Though usually too cold for swimming, it warms to

SLOW: DESERT TORTOISE X-ING

One of the most endangered park residents is the tortoise, which inhabits the Mojave and Sonoran deserts. Though slow moving, a desert tortoise can live for up to 80 years, munching on wildflowers and grasses. With its canteen-like bladder, it can go up to a year without drinking. Using its strong hind legs, it burrows to escape the summer heat and freezing winter temperatures, and also to lay eggs. The sex of the hatchlings is determined by temperature: cooler for males, hotter for females.

Disease, predation and shrinking habitat have decimated the desert tortoise population. They like to rest in the shade, including under parked cars, so take a quick look around before driving away. They are often hit by high-speed and/or off-road drivers. If you see a tortoise in trouble, call a ranger. Do not pick it up, as a frightened tortoise may often pee on what it perceives to be an attacker, possibly leading to it dying of dehydration before the next rains come.

Sara Benson

between 55°F and 65°F from June through September. You can wade and play at numerous river access points both on the **Riverside Walk** (p101) and the **Pa'rus Trail** (p101). Off Hwy 9 on the east side of Zion–Mt Carmel Tunnel, **Pine Creek** has deeper swimming holes that are popular with locals.

Tubing is prohibited within Zion but is quite popular outside the park. From Memorial Day through Labor Day, **Zion Adventure Company** (☎ 435-772-1001; www.zionadventures.com; 36 Lion Blvd; 🕒 8am-8pm Mar-Oct, 9am-noon & 4-7pm Nov-Feb) offers a river-tubing package that includes drop-off, pick-up, tube and water-sock rental (one trip $15). The float stretches about 2.5 miles, and last from 90 minutes to two hours depending on water flow. Much faster, high-adventure packages (including safety gear) are available when the river is running from spring melt-off, late March through May. You can also just rent a tube (from $20 per day) and transport yourself. Good river play places include Springdale River Park (p94), and from the campground at Zion Canyon Campground & RV Resort. Note that any hotel, B&B or campgrounds near the river likely has easy water access.

FOUR-WHEEL DRIVING

Obviously, no vehicles are allowed off-road in the national park. But there are a number of backcountry and 4WD roads, off Kolob Terrace Rd and on surrounding public lands, that tour companies can use. Three-hour tours start from $60/40 for adult/under 12 years. Reservations are required.

Zion Outback Safaris (☎ 866-946-6494; www.zionjeeptours.com) offers backroad Smithsonian Buttes and Grafton ghost-town tours, plus sunset Kolob Terrace runs, in 'safari vehicles' (4WD pick-ups outfitted with open, caravan-style seating above the bed). **Zion Rock & Mountain Guides** (☎ 435-772-3303; www.zionrockguides.com; 1458 Zion Park Blvd) uses four-door jeeps for your private excursion on similar routes. They also offer some genuine off-roading on the east-side slot-canyon tour, and an extended trip all the way north to Brian Head. You'll be riding in an open-air Mercedes-Benz Unimog (a WWII-developed utility vehicle) if you take the backroad tour with **Zion Adventure Company** (☎ 435-772-1001; www.zionadventures.com; 36 Lion Blvd).

Drive it yourself with **Mild to Wild Rhino Tours** (☎ 435-216-8298, 866-964-7961; www.mildtowildrhinotours.com; 839 Lion Blvd). Guides teach you to use the four-seat, open-air Yamaha Rhino utility vehicle and then lead you around BLM lands like Gooseberry and Little Creek Mesa. The 'wild' option is if their experts drive while you ride.

WATCHING WILDLIFE

Desert wildlife tends to be secretive, so while Zion is home to mountain lions, bighorn sheep, ringtail cats, rattlesnakes and nesting peregrine falcons, few visitors ever see them. Keep your eyes peeled for the rare Mojave tortoise (boxed text, above). You might spy a California condor (boxed text, p105), and mule deer and wild turkeys are frequently seen near Zion Lodge. Then, of course, there are the lizards, which skitter seemingly at your every step. For more about area animals, see p64.

KAYAKING

Kayaking in Zion is mostly a sport of opportunity for experienced locals. There are no rentals available in the area, and only expert paddlers prepared to survive days without assistance should consider such a trip.

The Backcountry Desk (p111) issues permits for kayaking when the Virgin River runs more than 140 cubic feet per second and less than 600. This happens a few days a year, usually during the spring snowmelt between March and May. Some years, as few as 10 permits have been issued. The park rates a trip beginning at the Narrows (p115) as Class V, because of the difficult obstacles and few escape routes in this slot canyon. Miles-long portages may be necessary. Talk to the Backcountry Desk about this or any other launches you are considering.

WINTER ACTIVITIES

Snows set in along central Kolob Terrace Rd (p99) from November through May. Above 7000ft, there's often enough snowpack for cross-country skiing and snowshoeing on trails like the West Rim and Wildcat Canyon. Kolob Canyons also has routes. Snowshoe and crampon rentals (no skis) are available from canyoneering outfitter Zion Adventure Company (p118).

SLEEPING

Zion itself boasts just one lodge and a few basic campgrounds, which book up on weekends and in summer. Thankfully, lodging-rich Springdale is right outside the park's front door. That's not to say prices in high season (late May through September) are reasonable. If you're looking for budget digs beyond camping, you'll have to drive to Hurricane; Mt Carmel (p136), 27 slow miles east; or even St George (p128), 41 miles west.

ZION CANYON & KOLOB TERRACE ROAD

Just inside Zion's South Entrance are the park's two main campgrounds, Watchman and South. They are adjacent to each other and to the visitor center. Neither has showers, laundry facilities or a general store; these are available in Springdale. At both, there is a maximum stay of 14 days from March through October, 30 days the rest of the year. Two vehicles are allowed per site. Owners of an interagency or senior national park pass receive a 50% discount on camping fees. The allergy-prone should note that the campgrounds' cottonwoods pollinate can be thick as snow in May.

Watchman Campground (☎ 435-772-3256, for reservations 877-444-6777; www.recreation.gov; Zion Canyon Visitor Center, Hwy 9; tent & RV sites $; 🕑 year-round; ♿ 🐾) Towering cottonwoods provide fairly good shade for the 165 well-spaced sites at Watchman (95 have electricity). Facilities include restrooms (but no showers), drinking water, picnic tables, fire grates, a dump station and recycling bins. No generators are allowed. Sites are by reservation (six months in advance) from early March through late October; the rest of the year it's first-come, first-served. At the time of writing, some construction is scheduled; call to make sure there are no closures.Sites along the Virgin River are the most in-demand (and cost $2 extra, but include electricity). These are odd-number sites A1 through A15 and even-number sites B42 through B56. Note that the hotel that backs up to the other side of the river is quite close to Loop A. Our favorites sites are the semi-secluded, tent-only spots that back up to the red-rock cliff on Loop D (odd numbers D19 to D33, plus D20 and D36). Group sites available, too.

South Campground (☎ 435-772-3256; Zion Canyon Visitor Center, off Hwy 9; campsites $; 🕑 Mar-Oct; 🐾) In front of the visitor center instead of behind it, the South Campground has very similar scenery to Watchman. The main difference is that this ground sits beside the busy Pa'rus Trail, and so has a bit more company. South Campground has no electrical hookups; generator use is allowed from 8am to 10am and 6pm to 8pm. There is a dump station as well as the other facilities, which are similar to those at Watchman. South, however, is entirely first-come, first-served. On busy spring and fall weekends, and all summer, it's full by late morning. Official checkout is 11am, but the best strategy is to pick up a pay envelope at the self-service kiosk and start prowling by 9am. Someone has usually left by then. Note that the pretty Virgin River sites at South (numbers 58 to 82 inclusive) are also those closest to the trail. A few walk-in sites are available. No group sites.

Lava Point Campground (Lava Point Rd, off Kolob Terrace Rd; tent sites free; 🕑 Jun-Sep; 🐾) An attractive loop of six first-come, first-served

CAMPING IN & AROUND ZION NATIONAL PARK

Campground	Location	Number of sites	Elevation (ft)	Open	Reservations available?
Cedar Breaks National Monument Campground	Cedar Breaks	28	10,350	late Jun-Aug	no
Cedar City KOA	Cedar City	76	5900	year-round	yes
Duck Creek Campground	Hwy 14	87	8400	late May-early Sep	yes
Lava Point Campground	Kolob Terrace Rd	6	7900	Jun-Sep	no
Mosquito Cove	Rockville	unlimited	3230	no	year-round
Snow Canyon State Park Campground	St George area	30	3200	year-round	yes
South Campground	Zion Canyon	127	3940ft	Mar-Oct	no
Temple View RV Resort	St George	260	2800	year-round	yes
Watchman Campground	Zion Canyon	165	3940	year-round	yes
Zion Canyon Campground & RV Resort	Springdale	200	3898	year-round	yes
Zion Ponderosa Ranch Resort	East Zion	18	6500	May-Nov	yes
Zion River Resort	Virgin	122	3552	year-round	yes
Zion Trading Post & Campground	East Zion	50	5000	year-round	no

Drinking Water · *Flush Toilets* · *Ranger Station* · *Great for Families* · *Wheelchair Accessible* · *Dogs Allowed* · *Grocery Store Nearby*

park sites sits off Kolob Terrace Rd (p99) at 7900ft. There's a pit toilet, picnic tables and fire grates, but no water. The campground is rarely full, as it's an hour from the South Entrance and Springdale. If it is occupied, drive north to Kolob Reservoir for free dispersed camping.

Zion Lodge (lodge 435-772-7700, reservations 888-297-2757; www.zionlodge.com; Zion Canyon Scenic Dr; r & cabins $$$;) Stunning red-rock cliffs surround you on all sides and, for many, the location in the middle of Zion Canyon (and the red permit that allows you to drive to the lodge in shuttle season) is enough. We can't help but wish the accommodations rivaled the setting. 'Western cabins' (actually duplexes and four-plexes) do have gas fireplaces, wood floors and elaborate headboards, but they also come with paper-thin walls separating you from neighbors. Motel rooms are just that; the six suites are two motel rooms joined together. For the best views, request a 2nd-floor Building A room, overlooking the lawn and canyon. For a bit of quiet, ask for a rear Building B room, which faces the much closer cliff. There are no room TVs, but shared board games are available. There are two eateries and a big lawn for lounging outside. In the end your choice is all about location, and Springdale is awfully close…

SPRINGDALE & AROUND

Unless otherwise noted, all lodgings below are in Springdale (see Map p94), within walking distance of a Springdale Town Shuttle stop.

Camping

Zion Canyon Campground & RV Resort (435-772-3237; www.zioncamp.com; 479 Zion Park Blvd; tent & RV sites $; year-round;) Amenities are the attraction at this 200-site campground on the Virgin River. A heated pool, show-

Facilities	Description	Page
	High up above a multicolor rock amphitheater; short season. Water; no showers, no hookups.	136
	Outfitted for big-rigs (100ft pull-throughs) more than tent campers. Pool, showers, wi-fi, bicycle rental.	133
	Pine-shaded sites at a blissfully cool 8400ft, outside Cedar City. Water; no showers, no hookups.	135
	Tiny, primitive NPS ground high in the upcountry. Tents only, no water.	121
	Free camping on public BLM land. No services.	below
	Fabulous red-rock formations, little shade (avoid summer). Hot showers, water and electrical hookups.	132
	Alternative to Watchman Campground; near busy trail and river. No electricity, no showers.	121
	Attracts St George snowbirds who live here all winter. Far from park, lots of services.	130
	Immensely popular NPS campground between red rock and river (booked May-Aug). Some electric hookups, no showers.	121
	Crowded, friendly in-town ground with pool and river access. Full hookups, hot showers, wi-fi.	122
	Upcountry mesa-top camping at activity-oriented ranch. Wi-fi, great showers.	125
	Fancy RV-centric private ground with 70ft pull-throughs and river sites. Loads of amenities.	below
	Primitive east-side campground with no services and limited appeal besides shade; no hookups, no water.	125

Restaurant Nearby *Payphone* *Summertime Campfire Program* *RV Dump Station*

ers, a laundry, camp store, playground, river and tubing access are all here. Plus the associated Quality Inn has an internet terminal and restaurant. Sites are squeezed together, but there are both RV and tent spots riverfront; reserve ahead. Not all sites have shade.

Zion River Resort (☎ 435-635-8594, 888-822-8594; www.zionriverresort.com; Hwy 9, Virgin; tent & RV sites $, cabins $$; year-round;) The massive RV resort outside Virgin, 12 miles west of Springdale, caters to upscale big rigs with long pull-throughs and phone and cable hookups. There are only a handful of tent sites and camping cabins (no linens). Quality shower rooms, coin laundry, barbecue pavilion, guest kitchen, heated pool, and game and media room are tops

Mosquito Cove (www.blm.gov; off Hwy 9, Rockville; campsites free; year-round) This free dispersed camping area (no services) on BLM land along the Virgin River is a rowdy, crowded local hangout. At Mile 24 on Hwy 9 east of Rockville, look for an unsigned dirt road on the left (south).

Hotels & Motels

Remember that shoulder season (April and October) costs less, and in winter prices can drop by 20% to 50%. All Springdale rooms are nonsmoking.

Zion Park Motel (☎ 435-772-3251; www.zionparkmotel.com; 855 Zion Park Blvd; r $, ste $$;) It's a wonder what a coat of paint can do for old wood-paneled rooms. Microwaves and minifridges were also part of the renovation at this family-owned and supremely central budget option.

our pick **Canyon Ranch Motel** (☎ 435-772-3357, 866-946-6276; www.canyonranchmotel.com; 668 Zion Park Blvd; r $-$$, apt $$;) Cottagey buildings surround a shaded lawn with redwood swings, picnic tables and a small pool with hot tub at this original motor-court motel.

ROOMS WITH A VIEW

- **Driftwood Lodge** (p124) Watchman suite balconies and patios look across a pastoral field to the namesake mountain.
- **Zion Lodge** (p122) Building A has front-row seats for a Zion Canyon show.
- **Majestic View Lodge** (right) Rooms southeast across Hwy 9 provide an unobstructed panorama of Eagle Crags.
- **Zion Canyon Campground** (p122) Not a room, but a site; spaces R4-7 sit beside the scenic Virgin River.
- **Cliffrose Lodge** (below) 'Canyon' rooms are worth the extra money for garden and red-cliff views.

Inside, rooms are thoroughly modern; apartments have full kitchens. Pet fee ($25) first night only.

Pioneer Lodge (435-772-3233, 888-772-3233; www.pioneerlodge.com; 838 Zion Park Blvd; r $$;) This rustic lodging, historic restaurant and cafe always seems to be bustling in the center of town. Pine-log beds carry the Western theme along. Aim for the popular 2nd-floor 'Canyon view' rooms that share a massive deck.

Best Western Zion Park Inn (435-772-3200, 800-934-7275; www.zionparkinn.com; 1215 Zion Park Blvd; incl breakfast r $$, ste $$$;) Timber frames welcome you to the rambling, lodgelike complex that includes a great room, putting green, badminton court, two pools, two restaurants and a liquor store(!). Two pet rooms ($25 fee).

Cliffrose Lodge (435-772-3234, 800-243-8824; www.cliffroselodge.com; 281 Zion Park Blvd; r $$-$$$, ste $$$;) Kick back in a lounge chair or enjoy a picnic lunch on the 5 gorgeous acres of lawn and flower gardens surrounding the pool and leading down to the river. Rooms are not as stunning as the grounds, but they do have pillow-top mattresses. Just avoid the noisy streetfront ones.

Desert Pearl Inn (435-772-8888, 888-828-0898; www.desertpearl.com; 707 Zion Park Blvd; r & ste $$$;) What a naturally stylish inn: twig art decorates the walls, sculptural metal headboards resemble art and full granite showers surround you with luxury. Outside, terraces and expert landscaping eclipse the pool's near-road location. Opt for a spacious riverside king suite to get a waterfront patio.

Driftwood Lodge (435-772-3262, 888-801-8811; www.driftwoodlodge.net; 1515 Zion Park Blvd; r $$-$$$, ste $$$;) Having the top restaurant in town, Parallel 88, on-site is enough reason for some to stay in the upscale rooms here. Request a Watchman suite and you get pastoral sunset views of field, river and mountain beyond. Pet fee ($25).

Hurricane has several cheap, very basic, chain motels like the **Rodeway Inn** (435-635-4010, 800-304-3665; www.rodewayinn.com; 650 W State St; r $;), in the thick of town, and **Comfort Inn** (435-635-3500, 800-635-3577; www.comfortinnzion.com; 43 N 2600 W; r incl breakfast $;), on the quiet western edge. All have smoking rooms available. Don't expect much and you'll be happy.

Additional Springdale options:

Terrace Brook Lodge (435-772-3932, 800-342-6779; www.terracebrooklodge.com; 990 Zion Park Blvd; s & d $;) Bare-bones basic motel. The two-bed rooms are newer than the singles.

Quality Inn Zion Park (435-772-3237, 877-424-6423; www.zioncamp.com; 479 Zion Park Blvd; r incl breakfast $$;) Easy river-tubing access at adjacent campground.

Flanigan's Inn (435-772-3244, 800-765-7787; www.flanigans.com; 428 Zion Park Blvd; r $$-$$$, ste $$$;) Each suite is named for the local artist whose work graces its walls.

Majestic View Lodge (435-772-0665, 866-772-0665; www.majesticviewlodge.com; 2400 Zion Park Blvd; r & ste $$$;) Epitomizing the log-and-antler school of design at the end of the shuttle's road.

B&Bs

Since sizeable morning repasts are included, and because rates don't rise when town occupancy is extra high, B&Bs are often the best deals in the town.

Under-the-Eaves Bed & Breakfast (435-772-3457, 866-261-2655; www.under-the-eaves.com; 980 Zion Park Blvd; incl breakfast r $$, ste $$$;) From colorful tractor reflectors to angel art, the owners' collections enliven every corner of this 1930s bungalow. The fireplace suite 'under the eaves' is huge; otherwise rooms are snug. But there's plenty of space to hang out in the Craftsman living room or on Adirondack chairs in the gardens. Breakfast is at a local restaurant. Gay friendly; (loveable) dogs on-site.

Canyon Vista B&B (☎ 435-772-3801; www.canyonvistabandb.com; 2175 Zion Park Blvd; ste incl breakfast $$; wi-fi) All the homey touches of a B&B, plus the privacy of a hotel. Individual entrances lead out onto a wooden porch or a sprawling patio and lawn with river access. In the Pa'rus and Mukuntuweap rooms especially, modern comfort meets Old World style. All have kitchenettes. Breakfast coupons; hot tub on-site.

Novel House Inn (☎ 435-772-3650, 800-711-8400; www.novelhouse.com; 73 Paradise Rd; r $$-$$$; air-con) Incredible detail has gone into each of the 17 themed rooms, named and designed for favorite authors. Rudyard Kipling has animal prints and mosquito netting, a pillow in the Victorian Dickens room reads 'Bah Humbug'… Large common rooms and an outdoor hot tub add to this purpose-built inn's attraction.

Harvest House (☎ 435-772-3880, 800-719-7493; www.harvesthouse.net; 29 Canyon View Dr; r incl breakfast $$; air-con wi-fi) Casual contemporary rooms all either have seating areas or access to a private deck for lounging. In a residential area, a fenced yard screening the shared hot tub is a good thing. Full, hot breakfasts served.

Red Rock Inn (☎ 435-772-3139; www.redrockinn.com; 998 Zion Park Blvd; cottages incl breakfast $$-$$$; air-con wi-fi) The five romantic rooms here are all little B&B cottages, each with a whirlpool or hot tub. In the morning an egg and pastry breakfast basket arrives at your door, to be enjoyed on your small terrace or up the hill in a desert garden.

Zion Canyon B&B (☎ 435-772-9466; www.zioncanyonbandb.com; 101 Kokopelli Circle; r $$-$$$; air-con wi-fi internet) Everywhere you turn there's another gorgeous red-rock view framed perfectly in an oversized window. Deep canyon wall colors – magenta, eggplant, burnt sienna – compliment not only the scenery, but the rustic Southwestern decor. Think gourmet dishes, like German puff pancakes, for breakfast.

> **SOOTHING SORE MUSCLES**
>
> How fitting would a hot river-rock massage be after a long day hiking the Narrows? **Deep Canyon Adventure Spa** (☎ 435-772-3244, 800-765-7787; www.deepcanyonspa.com; Flanigan's Inn, 428 Zion Park Blvd; ⏲ 9am-7pm) has a full menu of pampering for when your hotel's hot tub is just not enough.

B&Bs in Rockville, about 3.5 miles west of Springdale, are removed from town and restaurants, but generally have lower prices:

Bunk House at Zion (☎ 435-772-3393; www.bunkhouseatzion.com; 149 E Main St; r incl breakfast $; air-con wi-fi) A thoroughly green two-bedroom B&B: organic breakfasts with ingredients from the on-site orchard, 100% renewable energy, even an antique wood-fired stove and push mowers are used here.

Amber Inn (☎ 435-772-9597, 866-370-1515; www.amber-inn.com; 244 W Main St; r incl breakfast $-$$; air-con wi-fi) Affordable rooms in a rambling house. Pay attention to the policies; two cats on-site.

Desert Thistle Bed & Breakfast (☎ 435-772-0251; www.thedesertthistle.com; 37 W Main St; r incl breakfast $$; air-con wi-fi pool) A big backyard pool, resort-quality rooms and breakfast on the terrace make this the top choice for summer.

EAST ZION

Zion Trading Post & Campground (☎ 435-648-3302-1039;Hwy 9, campsites $; ⏲ year round) This campground run out of a trading post and pizzeria is, at this writing, primitive. But showers are in the works. Associated with Zion Mountain Resort, it's a mile west of the resort.

Zion Ponderosa Ranch Resort (☎ 435-648-2700, 800-293-5444; www.zionponderosa.com; N Fork Rd, off Hwy 9; tent & RV sites $, cabins without bathroom $, ste $$; wi-fi pool family) Families love this activity-rich ranch occupying 4000 acres on Zion's eastern, upcountry side. Driving to Springdale and Zion Canyon takes about 35 minutes, but several East Zion trails (p115) lead directly from here into the park. You may never leave the property since you can hike, bike, canyoneer, climb, swim, play sports, ride four-wheelers and horses, and eat three meals a day here (packages available). Wi-fi–enabled camping sites and cabins (linens included), served by huge shower/bathrooms, are real bargains. The fancier cabin suites are the only lodging here with air-con, but it's less essential up here above 6000ft. North Fork Rd is about 2.5 miles from the park's East Entrance; continue 5 miles north of Hwy 9 from there.

Zion Mountain Resort (ZMR; ☎ 435-688-1039, 866-648-2555; http://zionmountainresort.com; Hwy 9; cabins $$, ste $$$; air-con internet wi-fi pool family) Buffalo roam (and appear on the dinner menu) at this 2700-acre resort along Hwy 9. The upscale accommodations are a bit more like log homes than rustic cabins, but most can see the road. Choose from a full slate of outdoor activities. In season they run a restaurant, too. Registration is 2.6 miles east of the East Entrance.

EATING & DRINKING

Zion Lodge is the only place within the park that serves or sells food, but the quality does not match the unparalleled surroundings. Thankfully, Springdale offers a handful of really good options – and some so-so ones that take advantage of the fact they will probably only ever see tourist patrons once.

ZION CANYON

Castle Dome Cafe (☎ 435-772-7700; Zion Park Lodge; mains $; ☽ 11am-5pm, ice cream until 6pm, closed Oct-Apr; ✤) The quick cafe serves sandwiches, burgers, pizza and salads. Most importantly, it sells ice cream, which you can enjoy under the lodge's giant cottonwood tree. Yum!

Red Rock Grill (☎ 435-772-7760; Zion Park Lodge; breakfast $$, lunch $-$$, dinner mains $$-$$$; ☽ breakfast, lunch & dinner) The lodge's restaurant is on the 2nd floor, and the best thing about it is the spacious deck, where you can soak up the magnificent red-cliff views. Breakfast is a basic buffet, and lunch choices are mainly sandwiches, burgers and wraps. Though the dinner menu touts its sustainable-cuisine stance for dishes like roast pork loin and flatiron steak, the results are decidedly hit-or-miss; reservations required. Full bar.

Red Rock Grill Lounge (☎ 435-772-7760; Zion Park Lodge; ☽ 11:30am-9pm) You could be excused if you missed the restaurant-attached 'lounge', a tiny alcove of view-less seats behind the hostess station. But you can get a hard drink and some light food here.

SPRINGDALE & AROUND
Grocery Stores

Sol Foods Park Market (☎ 435-772-0277; 95 Zion Park Blvd; ☽ 8am-10pm Apr-Oct, 10am-6pm Nov-Mar) The small market adjacent to the park is a convenient place to buy beverages or snacks for the trail. The attached cafe will even do the sandwich fixing for you.

Springdale Fruit Company Market (☎ 435-772-3222; 2491 Zion Park Blvd; ☽ 8am-8pm Apr-Oct, closed Nov-Mar; Ⓥ) The selection of high-quality organic, vegan and gluten-free foodstocks

here is great. On-site orchards produce peaches and apples for sale beginning in summer. The store also makes to order focaccia sandwiches and fruit smoothies, best enjoyed on the shady tables outside in the parklike surrounds.

Sol Foods Downtown Supermarket (☎ 435-772-3100; 995 Zion Park Blvd; ☽ 7am-11pm Apr-Oct, 9am-8pm Nov-Mar) The 'big' supermarket in Springdale has most everything you can think of, including butchered meat – albeit at prices noticeably higher than at city grocery stores. The $8 per lb take-out salad bar has a nice mix of vegetables, as well as rice and couscous concoctions.

The closest giant-size (ie normal) grocery stores are in Hurricane. If price and selection are your concerns, stock up at **Lin's** (☎ 435-635-4477; 1120 W State St, Hurricane; ☽ 6am-midnight) or the **Super Wal-Mart** (☎ 435-635-6945; 180 N 3400 W, Hurricane; ☽ 24hr).

May through September there's a **farmers market** (1212 Zion Park Blvd; ☽ 9-11:30am) in the Bit & Spur parking lot.

Cafes

Note that Springdale Fruit Company Market (left) also serves sandwiches. Both Cafe Soleil and Mean Bean are great places to pick up lunches and baked goods packed for a hike.

Mean Bean Coffee House (☎ 435-772-0654; 932 Zion Park Blvd; breakfast & sandwiches $; ☽ 7am-5pm Jun-Aug, 7am-2pm Sep-May; ☜) Probably the town's best brew. This great local hangout attracts outdoorsy types for their first cuppa organic java, soy latte or chai of the day. Take your breakfast burrito or panini up to the roof deck.

Cafe Soleil (☎ 435-772-0505; 205 Zion Park Blvd; breakfasts & sandwiches $; ☽ 7am-8pm; ☜) The food is every bit as good as the coffee at Cafe Soleil. Try the Mediterranean hummus wrap or giant vegetable frittata (breakfast served till noon). Pizza and salads, too.

Elements (☎ 435-722-8888; Desert Pearl Inn, 707 Zion Park Blvd; baked goods $; ☽ 7am-7pm; ☐ ☜) Enjoy the Starbucks coffee brewed here in esoteric gift store surrounds. Yummies like the cherry-lemon pound cake are baked on-site.

Park House Cafe (☎ 435-722-0100; 1880 Zion Park Blvd; breakfasts & sandwiches $-$$; ☽ 7am-4pm Mon-Fri) Wake up as late as you like, Park House Cafe serves their Asiago bagel with egg and avocado – along with other breakfast items – until 2pm. Burgers, sandwiches and salads are all made from the freshest ingredients. Great little walled patio, too.

Orange Star (☎ 435-772-0255; 868 Zion Park Blvd; sandwiches & smoothies $; 🕑 11am-8pm) Fresh fro-yo smoothies, shakes and homemade subs. The 'Angels Landing' mixes non-fat chocolate yogurt, Ghirardelli's chocolate and toffee chips – need we say more?

Also try:

Pioneer Lodge Internet Cafe (☎ 435-772-3233; 838 Zion Park Blvd; baked goods $; 🕑 6am-9pm; 💻 📶) Seattle's Best Coffee and goodies off the Pioneer Lodge lobby.

Sol Market Cafe (☎ 435-772-0277; 95 Zion Park Blvd; breakfast & sandwiches $; 🕑 8am-6pm) Self-service deli and ice-cream counter attached to the parkside market.

Zion Park Gift & Deli (☎ 435-772-3843; 866 Zion Park Blvd; sandwiches & ice cream $; 🕑 8:30am-10pm) Come for the 'caribou caramel' and 'brownies over the moon' ice creams.

Restaurants

Breakfast places listed below serve at least until 11am. Unless otherwise noted, restaurants offer only beer and wine.

Flying Monkey (☎ 435-772-3333; 975 Zion Park Blvd; mains $; 🕑 11am-9:30pm) Wood-fired goodness at great prices. Expect interesting ingredients like fennel and yellow squash on your roast veggie pizza or Italian sausage with the prosciutto on your oven-baked sandwich. Burgers, salads and pastas, too.

Pioneer Restaurant (☎ 435-772-3009; 828 Zion Park Blvd; mains $-$$; 🕑 7am-10pm) Carb load for a big hike with chicken-fried steak and eggs at breakfast or lasagna with meat sauce for dinner. This is country-diner food served with a smile. On weekends ask about the prime-rib special.

Switchback Jack's Sports Grill (☎ 435-772-3700; 1149 Zion Park Blvd; mains $-$$; 🕑 noon-10pm) One of the few full bars in town, Jack's serves hot and cold sandwiches, rice bowls and appetizers to go with your cocktails.

Whiptail Grill (☎ 435-772-0283; 445 Zion Park Blvd; mains $-$$; 🕑 11am-7pm Apr-Oct, closed Nov-Mar) The old gas-station building isn't much to look at, but man, you can't beat the fresh tastes here – pan-seared tilapia tacos, chipotle chicken enchiladas, organic beef Mexican pizza… Numerous vegetarian options as well.

our pick Oscar's Café (☎ 435-772-3232; 948 Zion Park Blvd; breakfast & sandwiches $, mains $$; 🕑 7:30am-10pm) From green chili–laden omelets to pork verde burritos, Oscar's has the Southwestern spice going on. But it also does smoky ribs, shrimp and garlic burgers well. Evenings, the living-room-like, Mexican-tiled patio with twinkly lights (and heaters) is a favorite hang-out.

Majestic View Steakhouse & Saloon (☎ 435-772-0665; 2400 Zion Park Blvd; burgers $, mains $$; 🕑 lunch & dinner) Antler chandeliers let you know meat (including elk and buffalo) is on this hotel restaurant's menu. On tap at the (usually empty) saloon: stacked burgers and Zion Canyon Brewing Co beer concocted in the basement here.

Bit & Spur Restaurant & Saloon (☎ 435-772-3498; 1212 Zion Park Blvd; mains $$-$$$; 🕑 dinner) Sweet-potato tamales and chile-rubbed rib-eyes are two of the classics at this local institution. Inside the walls are wild with local art; outside it's all about the red-rock sunset.

Spotted Dog Café (☎ 435-772-3244; 428 Zion Park Blvd; breakfast $, brunch $$, dinner mains $$-$$$; 🕑 breakfast & dinner daily, brunch 10am-2pm Sun) At the time of writing the Dog is having a bit of an identity crisis. But all-American fine dining is clearly still the aim. Full bar.

Parallel 88 (☎ 435-772-3588; Driftwood Lodge, 1515 Zion Park Blvd; breakfast $$, dinner mains $$$; 🕑 breakfast & dinner) Chef Jeff Crosland has mastered 'casually elegant' with a top-notch seasonal menu, gorgeous red-cliff views and friendly service. Most nights he can be seen chatting with guests on the patio as they nosh on impossibly tender green-apple pork loin or vegetable terrine.

BEST BURGERS

- To-die-for chipotle-and-garlic aioli tops the 'murder burger' at **Oscar's Café** (below)
- Dig into a burger as big as your face at **Pioneer Restaurant** (below)
- Let your bacon burger have the blues (cheese, that is) at **Park House Cafe** (opposite)
- Things could get spicy with the green chile burger at **Whiptail Grill** (below)
- Shaved prime rib on a burger? Yep, they pile it on at **Majestic View Steakhouse & Saloon** (below)

POLYGAMY PORTER & MORE

Local Zion Canyon Brewing Co beers are available at markets and restaurants around town, as are other Utah brews like Polygamy Porter. If you're looking for a bottle of something harder to bring back to your room, the only liquor store for miles is in **Switchback Trading Co** (☎ 435-772-3200; 1149 Zion Park Blvd; noon-9pm Mon-Sat), part of the Best Western complex.

Second choices:

Casas de Amigos (☎ 435-772-0422; 805 Zion Park Blvd; mains $-$$; 9am-1am May-Sep, hours vary Oct-Apr) At least it has a full bar with margaritas…

Thai Sapa (☎ 435-772-0510; 145 Zion Park Blvd; mains $-$$; noon-9:30pm Apr-Oct, hours vary Nov-Mar) The best we can say is that this mix of Thai, Chinese and Vietnamese cuisine is your only ethnic option in town.

Zion Pizza & Noodle Company (☎ 435-772-3815; 868 Zion Park Blvd; mains $-$$; 4-10pm) Central location, OK pizza and beer. Cash only.

Bars & Pubs

There are no stand-alone bars in Springdale, but a few area eateries have bar sections. For a laid-back local vibe try the beer and wine at the Bit & Spur. Switchback Jack's Sports Grille, with a full liquor menu, has super-comfy club chairs and a sports-bar feel to it. Even though Utah's alcohol laws (see boxed text, p265) have eased a little, you'll still have to buy at least chips and salsa to drink.

AROUND ZION

ST GEORGE

pop 71,200 / elevation 2880ft

Blessed with a mild climate and about 300 days of sunshine a year, Utah's southernmost city has long been attracting winter residents and retirees. Brigham Young, second president of the Mormon church, was one of the first snowbirds to arrive in the one-time farming community (growing cotton, fruit trees, and even silk worms). Today by some estimates, half the city qualifies for a senior discount. Outside the small historic center, strip malls, golf courses and RV parks flourish. Nightlife doesn't.

Traveling to or from Vegas, you're likely to pass through St George. Stopping over can be a good budget break; doing so also puts you within easy striking distance of Zion National Park's Kolob Canyons section and Snow Canyon State Park.

Orientation

St George is on I-15 just north of the Arizona border, 125 miles from Las Vegas, 41 miles from Zion's South Entrance, 35 miles from Kolob Canyons and 55 miles from Cedar City. The city's main commercial streets are St George Blvd and Bluff St, which form a business-laden triangle with I-15.

Information

More info is available online at www.sgcity.org, www.utahsdixie.com and www.atozion.com.

Chamber of Commerce (☎ 435-628-1658; www.stgeorgechamber.com; 97 E St George Blvd; 9am-5pm Mon-Fri) Visitor center catering mainly to relocating retirees; loads of city info.

Dixie Regional Medical Center (☎ 435-251-1000; http://intermountainhealthcare.org; 1380 E Medical Center Dr) Hospital.

Library (☎ 435-634-5737; 88 W 100 S; 10am-8pm Mon-Thu, to 6pm Fri & Sat) Internet access ($2 per hour).

Police (☎ 435-627-4301; 265 N 200 E)

Post Office (☎ 435-673-3312; 180 N Main St)

St George Field Office (☎ 435-688-3200; 345 E Riverside Dr; 7:45am-3:45pm Mon-Fri) Get interagency information on surrounding public lands: USFS, BLM and state parks. Topo maps and guides available.

Utah Welcome Center (☎ 435-673-4542; http://travel.utah.gov; Dixie Convention Center, I-15; 8:30am-5:30pm) Statewide information 2 miles south of St George. There's a wildlife museum (think taxidermy) on-site with same hours.

Zions Bank (☎ 435-626-2308; 40 E St George Blvd; 9am-5pm Mon-Fri) Currency exchange and 24-hour ATM.

Sights

History lovers will find plenty to see in town at pioneer and Mormon church (today called the Church of Jesus Christ of Latter Day Saints, or LDS) sights; anyone who digs dinosaurs is in for a rare treat.

DINOSAUR DISCOVERY SITE

In spring of 2000, 74-year-old alfalfa farmer Sheldon Johnson was leveling some 'useless' land when he turned over a sandstone slab and recognized three-toed dinosaur tracks. When slab after slab had incredibly clear markings, he wondered if someone might

INFORMATION
Chamber of Commerce.......1 B1
Library.......2 B1
Police Station.......3 B1
Post Office.......4 B1
St George Field Office.......5 B4
Zions Bank.......6 B1

SIGHTS & ACTIVITIES
Bicycles Unlimited.......7 B2
Daughters of Utah Pioneers Museum.......8 B1
Desert Rat Outdoor Store.......9 A1
Mormon Tabernacle.......10 B1
Mormon Temple.......11 B2
Red Rock Bicycle Company.......12 A1
Town Square.......13 B1

SLEEPING
Best Western Coral Hills.......14 B1
Dixie Palm Motel.......15 B1
Green Gate Village.......16 B1
Seven Wives Inn.......17 B1
Temple View RV Resort.......18 B4

EATING
Benja Thai & Sushi.......19 B1
Painted Pony.......(see 19)
Thomas Judd's General Store.......(see 16)
Twenty-five on Main.......20 B1

TRANSPORT
Greyhound Bus Stop.......21 B4
St George Shuttle.......22 A3

be playing a practical joke. It turned out to be no joke…the age, size and complexity of the tracks makes this one of the richest repositories on earth. Johnson donated the land to the city and today the 15,000-sq-ft **Dinosaur Discovery Site** (☎ 435-574-3766; www.dinotrax.com; 2200 E Riverside Dr; adult/under 12yr $6/3; 10am-6pm Mon-Sat) protects his find. Entry gets you an interpretive tour of the huge collection of tracks, beginning with an orientation video. From there you walk on catwalks above the early Jurassic (195- to

198-million-year-old) footprints, many belonging to small dinosaurs, and the rare tail swim tracks. Ask about spring and fall tours that include digging at a paleontological site (or 'bone bed') in the area.

HISTORIC MORMON SITES

Twenty-seven of the original town buildings stand in good stead downtown. Pick up a full-color, self-guided walking-tour brochure at the Chamber of Commerce. The 1877, red-brick **Mormon Temple** (☎ 435-673-5181; 440 S 300 E; ⏲ visitor center 9am-9pm) was Utah's first. The sanctuary itself is closed to non-members, but its extensive visitor center isn't. Ask here about the two LDS-run area pioneer homes you can tour. The pretty **Mormon Tabernacle** (☎ 435-628-4072; Tabernacle & Main St; admission free; ⏲ 9am-6pm) is also open to the public and hosts free music programs. Kids love splashing in the sidewalk fountain by the clocktower on the adjacent **Town Square**.

The two floors of the **Daughters of Utah Pioneers Museum** (☎ 435-628-7274; 145 N 100 E; ⏲ 10am-5pm Mon-Sat) are crammed with pioneer artifacts – furniture, photographs, quilts, guns and so on.

Activities

The town sponsors active events throughout the year, including the **St George Marathon** (www.stgeorgemarathon.com) in October and the **Ironman St George** (www.ironmanstgeorge.com) in April.

Desert Rat Outdoor Store (☎ 435-628-7277; www.thedesertrat.net; 468 West St; ⏲ 9am-7pm Mon-Fri, 9am-6pm Sat) will outfit you for any activity and provide area advice. Remember that Snow Canyon State Park (p132) is quite close.

A network of interconnected trails crisscross St George. Pick up maps at the Chamber of Commerce or log on to www.utahstgeorge.com/trails.html. The 6-mile **Green Valley Trail** (also called Bearclaw Poppy), off Sunbrook Rd, has first-rate, playground-like mountain biking on slickrock. So far the much more level **Virgin River Trail**, accessed along Riverside Dr, only goes to Washington; it will theoretically extend to Zion eventually.

Both **Red Rock Bicycle Company** (☎ 435-674-3185; www.redrockbicycle.com; 446 W 100 S; ⏲ 9am-7pm Mon-Sat, 9am-6pm Sat, 9am-3pm Sun) and **Bicycles Unlimited** (☎ 435-673-4492; www.bicyclesunlimited.com; 90 S 100 E; ⏲ 9am-6pm Mon-Sat) have full-day rentals (from $50) and sell trail books.

Book ahead for road or mountain-bike tours with **Paragon Adventures** (☎ 435-673-1709; www.paragonadventure.com). They also offer local rock-climbing lessons and tours, small-group canyoneering, interpretive hikes, zip-line courses – and babysitting. Trips from $55 per hour.

Looking for a cool diversion for kids? The spraying water and toys at the indoor **Sand Hollow Aquatic Center** (☎ 435-634-5938; 1144 N Lava Flow Dr; adult/under 17yr $6/5.50; ⏲ 1-5pm & 6:30-9pm Mon-Fri, noon-6pm Sat) are a big hit.

A handful of local golf courses are open to the public (many more are private). Reserve up to two weeks in advance online at www.sgcity.org/golf.

Sleeping

When events aren't going on, lodging is plentiful and affordable; when they are, prices skyrocket. Nearly every chain hotel known to man is represented somewhere in St George.

CAMPING

For tent camping, head to Snow Canyon State Park (p132) or Zion National Park (p121).

Temple View RV Resort (☎ 435-673-6400, 800-776-6410; www.templeviewrv.com; 975 S Main St; RV & tent sites $; 💻 📶 🏊) The 260 sites at this big resort mostly accommodate up to 45ft RVs, but there are a few not-so-shady tent spots. Amenities include a rec room, business center, swimming pool, gym, putting green, cable hookups and wi-fi.

HOTELS & MOTELS

Old budget motels abound on St George Blvd, but the prices are usually much more attractive than the scuffed-up rooms. Chains cluster near I-15 at Bluff St, and near Red Cliffs Mall.

America's Best Inn & Suites (☎ 435-652-3030, 800-718-0297; www.stgeorgeinnsuites.com; 245 N Red Cliffs Dr; r incl breakfast $-$$; 🐾 💻 📶 🏊) Well positioned for fast out-of-town access off I-15, this economic choice is also surprisingly quiet. Minifridges and microwaves come standard in the tidy rooms. Coin laundry on property.

Best Western Coral Hills (☎ 435-673-4844; www.coralhills.com; 125 E St George Blvd; r incl breakfast $-$$;

) You can't beat being a block or two from downtown restaurants and historic sights. Waterfalls and spiffed-up decor set this locally owned franchise apart.

Red Mountain Resort & Spa (435-673-4905, 877-246-4453; http://redmountainspa.com; 1275 E Red Mountain Circle; r $$$;) A Zen-chic sensibility pervades the low-profile adobe resort, right down to the copper silk pillows that echo the color of surrounding cliffs. Guided hikes, spa services, fitness classes and healthy meals can all be included.

Yet more options:

Dixie Palm Motel (435-673-3531, 866-651-3997; www.dixiepalmsmotel.com; 185 E St George Blvd; r $;) Older motel with regular maintenance and caring owners. Microwaves and minifridges.

Red Cliffs Inn (435-673-3537, 800-733-8338; http://redcliffsinn.com; 912 W Red Cliffs Dr; r incl breakfast $-$$;) Modern motel rooms with Serta Perfect mattresses; smoking available.

B&BS

Green Gate Village (435-628-6999, 800-350-6999; www.greengatevillageinn.com; 76 W Tabernacle St; r incl breakfast $$;) Book a room or a house among nine historic buildings brought together to make a B&B town of sorts. Antiques such as white iron beds and ornate carved vanities figure prominently in all the lodgings.

Seven Wives Inn (435-628-3737, 800-600-3737; www.sevenwivesinn.com; 217 N 100 West; r incl breakfast $$-$$$;) The stately gray-and-white facades of two homes surround a small pool and lovely gardens at this charming inn. And it's true, an ancestor of the innkeeper had seven wives and the original owner harbored fugitive polygamists in the 1800s.

Eating & Drinking

All the chains you'd expect, along with supermart grocery stores, line I-15.

Thomas Judd's General Store (435-628-2596; 76 Tabernacle St; ice cream $; 11am-9pm Mon-Sat) When walking around the old town, stop for a sweet scoop of ice cream or piece of nostalgic candy in Green Gate Village.

Twenty-five on Main (435-628-7110; 25 N Main St; mains $; 8am-9pm Mon-Thu, to 10pm Fri & Sat;) Homemade cupcakes are not all this bakery-cafe does well. We also like the breakfast panini, the warm salmon salad and the pasta primavera, overflowing with veggies.

Benja Thai & Sushi (435-628-9538; 2 W St George Blvd, Ancestor Sq; mains $$; 11:30am-10pm Mon-Sat, 5-9pm Sun) A pan-Asian menu is certainly more eclectic than most offerings in St George, but results are mixed. Steer away from the curries and try something from the extensive sushi-roll list.

Xetava Gardens Cafe (435-656-0165; 815 Coyote Gulch Ct, Ivins; breakfast $, mains $$-$$$; 8am-5pm Mon-Wed, 8am-9:30pm Thu-Sat; V) Creative cuisine in a stunning red-rock setting. It's well worth driving the 8 miles north of town for dishes like organic blue-corn waffles and chile-rubbed lamb.

More upmarket options:

Painted Pony (435-634-1700; 2 W St George Blvd, Ancestor Sq; lunch $$, dinner mains $$$; lunch & dinner Mon-Sat, dinner Sun) Upscale mains, like juniper-brined pork chop, served at dinner; at lunch it's gourmet comfort foods, like meatloaf with a port wine reduction.

Anasazi Steakhouse (435-674-0095; 1234 W Sunset Blvd; mains $$-$$$; dinner) Grill your steak (or shrimp or portobello mushroom…) yourself on a hot volcanic rock.

Entertainment

Outdoor **Tuacahn Amphitheater** (435-652-3300, 800-746-9882; www.tuacahn.org; 1100 Tuacahn Dr, Ivins; Mar-Oct), 8 miles northwest of town, hosts Broadway musicals and concerts.

Two Friday evenings a month the city screens kid-oriented movies on the **Town Square** (www.sgcity.org; admission free; May-Sep).

Getting There & Away

In early 2011, the new **SGU Municipal Airport** (435-673-3451; www.sgcity.org/airport; Southern Parkway & Airport Access Rd) opened 5 miles southeast of town. Skywest Airlines operates the daily **Delta** (800-221-1212; www.delta.com) flights to and from Salt Lake City. Look for services to expand in the future.

St George Shuttle (435-628-8320, 800-933-8320; www.stgshuttle.com; 790 S Bluff St; 6am-10pm) has a daily shared van service to Las Vegas Airport (two hours, $25) and Salt Lake City (4½ hours, $55). **Aztec Shuttle** (435-656-9040; www.aztecshuttle.com; 806 N Bluff St; 7am-9pm) runs a similar service to Salt Lake from its stop at Fabulous Freddy's Car Wash, plus it has charters to Vegas and southern Utah national parks.

Greyhound (435-673-2933, 800-231-2222; www.greyhound.com) buses leave from the McDonald's at 1235 S Bluff and connect to/from

Salt Lake City (from $50, six hours) once daily and Las Vegas (from $30, two hours) four times a day.

Getting Around

Chain rental-car outfits **Avis** (☎ 435-627-2002, 800-331-1212; www.avis.com), **Budget** (☎ 435-673-6825, 800-527-0700; www.budget.com) and others operate from the airport; **Enterprise** (☎ 435-634-1556, 800-736-8222; www.enterprise.com) will pick you up around town by arrangement.

SunTran (☎ 435-673-8726; www.sgcity.org/suntran; ride $1), St George's public-transport buses, run Monday through Saturday. The Greyhound stop is on the local Riverside route.

SNOW CANYON STATE PARK

In this beautiful canyon, red-and-white sandstone flows like lava, and lava lies broken like sheets of smashed marble. Small and accessible, **Snow Canyon** (☎ 435-628-2255; http://stateparks.utah.gov; 1002 Snow Canyon Dr, Ivins; per vehicle $6; day use 6am-10pm) is a human-scale version of all of southwest Utah, just 8 miles north of St George. Short easy trails lead to tiny slot canyons, cinder cones, lava tubes and vast fields of undulating slickrock. The only catch is that summer is blazing hot, so plan your activities for early morning, or come in another season. For the record, winter rarely sees any of the white stuff here. (The park is named after early Utah pioneers Lorenzo and Erastus Snow.)

Of the numerous hiking routes accessing the features in the 7400-acre desert park, **Jenny's Canyon** is the shortest; a quick quarter-mile leads to a little slot canyon. The mild ups and downs of the 2-mile round-trip **Johnson Canyon** hike lead past old lava flows, red-rock walls and a 200ft arch. A 1000ft stretch of vegetation-free **Sand Dunes** serves as a playground for the kiddies, near a picnic area.

> **DETOUR: PAROWAN GAP**
>
> Just under 16 miles north of Cedar City off Rte 130, detour to the freely accessible **Parowan Gap** (www.blm.gov) to see not only petroglyph panels, but dinosaur tracks. Pick up a color brochure at Cedar City & Brian Head Tourism Bureau (opposite).

With more than 150 traditional bolted and sport routes, plus top roping, the **rock climbing** is great here, particularly for beginners. Cycling is popular on the **Snow Canyon Loop**, which follows the main park road and creates a 17-mile round trip if you travel all the way from St George.

There's not much shade (again, avoid August), but the red sandstone provides a pretty backdrop for the **campground** (☎ reservations 800-322-3770; http://utahstateparks.reserveamerica.com; campsites $; year-round;). You can reserve the 30 sites (14 with electrical and water hookups) up to four months in advance. There's hot showers and a dump station.

PINE VALLEY MOUNTAIN WILDERNESS AREA

Utah's second-largest wilderness area (70 sq miles) is mountainous, forested and crisscrossed by rushing streams; quite a difference from the intense desert heat and barren sandstone sculptures below. The highest points in these sharply rising mountains (6535ft to 10,365ft) remain capped by snow until June. Midsummer, this wilderness area offers a crowd-free, temperate respite, 32 miles north of St George. Note that most hikes begin with strenuous climbs. A 6.5-mile trek up from Pine Valley to **Signal Peak** rewards the intrepid with incredible vistas. The St George Field Office (p128) can provide further information and free backcountry camping permits.

CEDAR CITY

pop 27,800 / elevation 5800ft

This sleepy college town comes to life every summer when the Shakespeare festival takes over. Associated events, plays and tours continue into fall. Year-round you can make one of the many B&Bs a quiet home base for exploring the Kolob Canyons section of Zion National Park or Cedar Breaks National Monument. At nearly 6000ft elevation, cooler temperatures prevail in Cedar City (even the occasional snow in May) compared to Springdale or St George.

Orientation & Information

Cedar City is on I-15, 55 miles from (and 3000ft higher than) St George, 180 miles from Las Vegas and 260 miles from Salt Lake City. Bryce Canyon is 80 miles east and Zion's South Entrance is 60 miles,

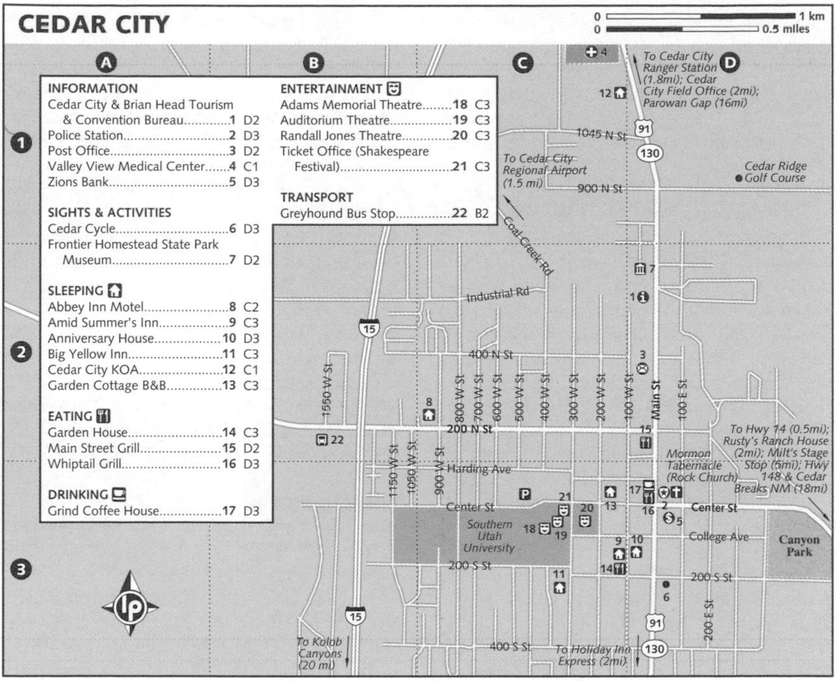

while the Kolob Canyons section lies just 20 miles south. Most Cedar City businesses front Main St.

Cedar City & Brian Head Tourism & Convention Bureau (☎ 435-586-5124, 800-354-4849; www.scenicsouthernutah.com; 581 N Main St; 8am-5pm Mon-Fri, 9am-1pm Sat) Info and free internet use.

Cedar City Field Office ☎ 435-586-2401; 176 E DL Sargent Dr; 7:45am-3:45pm Mon-Fri) BLM office that manages free public camping and land west of I-15, including Parowan Gap.

Cedar City Ranger Station (☎ 435-865-3700; www.fs.fed.us; 1789 N Wedgewood Ln; 8am-5pm Mon-Fri) Provides camping and other Dixie National Forest information.

Police (☎ 435-586-2956; 10 N Main St)

Post office (☎ 435-586-6701; 333 N Main St)

Valley View Medical Center (☎ 435-868-5000; http://intermountainhealthcare.org; 1303 N Main St) Hospital.

Zions Bank (☎ 435-586-2448; 3 S Main St; 9am-5pm Mon-Fri, 9am-1pm Sat) Currency exchange and ATM.

Sights & Activities

The Shakespeare festival (p134) and area B&Bs are the town's main draws.

You might also stop to see the cabins, brightly painted 19th-century buggies and garden full of rusting farm equipment at the **Frontier Homestead State Park Museum** (☎ 435-586-9290; http://stateparks.utah.gov; 635 N Main St; admission $3; 9am-5pm Mon-Sat). Living history demos take place June through August.

Hiking opportunities are to be found at Cedar Breaks (p135), in Kolob Canyons (p107) and off Hwy 14 (p135).

Cedar Cycle (☎ 435-586-5210; www.cedarcyle.com; 38 E 200 South; 9am-5pm Mon-Fri, 9am-2pm Sat) rents bikes (from $30 a day) and can point you to local trails.

Sleeping

To do Cedar City right, you should really stay in one of its B&Bs (for a full list, see www.scenicsouthernutah.com). Remember to reserve ahead if you're visiting June through August. Single travelers especially should call and ask about B&B specials off-season. For tent camping, try US Forest Service (USFS) grounds on Hwy 14 (p135).

Cedar City KOA (☎ 435-586-9872; 1121 N Main St; tent & RV sites $, cabins $;) Far from secluded, this in-town ground caters to long RVs. Bicycle rental available.

Anniversary House (☎ 435-865-1266; http://theanniversaryhouse.com; 133 S 100 W; r incl breakfast $-$$;) Rooms here are both refined and remarkably comfortable. Dig into freshly baked cake and complimentary beverages in the mission-style dining room or lounge around in the landscaped backyard, where there's an outdoor kennel for your dog.

Amid Summer's Inn (☎ 435-586-2600, 888-586-2601; www.amidsummersinn.com; 140 S 100 W; r incl breakfast $$;) Evening turn-down, dinner reservations and romance packages are just some of the pampering services offered by the innkeepers. Given the simple exterior, there's a certain wow factor when you first see the lavish guest quarters.

Garden Cottage B&B (☎ 435-586-4919, 866-586-4919; www.thegardencottagebnb.com; 16 N 200 W; r incl breakfast $$;) Romantic vines climb up the steep-roofed cottage walls, and in season a fantasia of blooms grow in the award-winning gardens. Even the five precious rooms are named for flowers. No room TVs.

Big Yellow Inn (☎ 435-586-0960; www.bigyellowinn.com; 234 S 300 W; r incl breakfast $$-$$$;) This purpose-built Georgian Revival–style inn has room to roam. Relax in the Victorian dining room, in the library or on the many porches. Upstairs rooms are elegantly ornate. Downstairs, the walk-out rooms are simpler, a bit more country – and closer to a cozy den with guest refrigerator. The owners also oversee several adjunct B&B properties and house rentals around town.

Most of the big-name budget chains are represented here. If you must stay at a motel, you could try these:

Abbey Inn Motel (☎ 435-586-9966, 800-325-5411; www.abbeyinncedar.com; 940 W 200 N; r incl breakfast $-$$;) Colonial-esque furnishings, upgraded mattresses and flat-screen TVs.

Holiday Inn Express ☎ 435-865-7799, 888-465-4329; www.hiexpress.com; 1555 S Old Hwy 91; r $$;) All the most modern comforts.

Eating & Drinking

Wouldn't it be nice if Cedar City offered fine dining to compliment its theater? Alas, poor Yorick, it doth not.

Grind Coffee House (☎ 435-867-5333; 19 N Main St; 7am-6pm Mon-Sat, 8am-2pm Sun;) The barista brews a mean espresso at this laid-back, local hangout. Special evenings feature local musicians.

Main Street Grill (☎ 435-586-8389; 155 N Main St; dishes $; 7am-3pm) Eavesdrop on town gossip over your flapjacks or grilled cheese.

Garden House (☎ 435-586-6110; 164 S 100 W; sandwiches $, mains $$; 11am-9:30pm Mon-Sat) Homemade soups, sandwiches, pastas and seafood dishes top the menu at this historic home-turned-restaurant. No alcohol served.

Whiptail Grill (☎ 435-867-9447; 5 N Main St; mains $$; 11am-9pm) Inventive Southwestern cuisine with intense flavors, like chipotle, make Whiptail a standout. Listen for live music some weekend evenings.

Along Hwy 14 are two popular and unpretentious Western steakhouses in red-rock settings: **Rusty's Ranch House** (☎ 435-586-3839; mains $$; dinner Mon-Sat) is 2 miles east of Cedar City, and **Milt's Stage Stop** (☎ 435-586-9344; mains $$; dinner) is 5 miles east.

Entertainment

The play's the thing at **Utah Shakespearean Festival** (☎ 435-586-7878, for tickets 800-752-9849; www.bard.org; tickets $25-75), Cedar City's main event held since 1962 at **Southern Utah University** (SUU; ☎ 435-586-7700; www.suu.edu; 351 W Center St). From late June into September, three of the bard's plays and three contemporary dramas take the stage. From mid-September into late October three more plays are presented – one Shakespearean, one dramatic and one musical. Productions are well regarded, but you also shouldn't miss the extras. 'Greenshows' with Elizabethan minstrels, literary seminars discussing the plays and costume classes are all free. Backstage and scene-changing tours cost extra. Children under six are not allowed at performances; free childcare is available.

The venues are the open-air **Adams Shakespearean Theatre**, an 819-seat reproduction of London's Globe Theater; the modern 769-seat **Randall L Jones Theatre**, where backstage tours are held; and the less noteworthy **Auditorium Theatre** used for matinees and rainy days. Make reservations at least a few weeks in advance. At 10am on the day of show, obscured-view gallery seats for the Adams performance go on sale at the walk-up **ticket office** (cnr 300 W & W Center Sts; 10am-7pm late Jun-Aug & mid-Sep–Oct).

Getting There & Away

Cedar City Regional Airport (☎ 435-867-9408; www.cedarcity.org/airport.html; Aviation Way, off Hwy 56) is

FESTIVAL CITY USA

Cedar City prides itself on celebrating – Neil Simon plays, amateur Olympics, hot-air balloons, American folk music. For a full event listing, log on to www.scenicsouthernutah.com.

2 miles northwest of town. **Delta** (☎ 435-586-3033, 800-221-1212; www.delta.com) flies to and from Salt Lake City at least once daily. **Enterprise** (☎ 435-865-1435, 800-261-7331; www.enterprise.com) rents cars from the airport.

Greyhound (☎ 800-231-2222; www.greyhound.com) buses leave from the Sinclair Gas Station at 1495 W 200 North en route to Las Vegas (from $40, three hours). A few stop at St George (from $20, 50 minutes).

HIGHWAY 14 EAST OF CEDAR CITY

As scenic drives go, Hwy 14 is one of the best. It leads 42 miles over the Markagunt Plateau, cresting at 10,000ft and offering unbelievable vistas of Zion National Park and Arizona to the south. Along the way you'll find several highly recommended hiking trails, fishing lakes, campgrounds and overlooks, most of which are part of **Dixie National Forest** (www.fs.fed.us/r4/dixie). Stop by the Cedar City Ranger Station (p133) for maps and information. Though Hwy 14 remains open all winter, snow tires or chains are required between November and April.

About 16 miles east of Cedar City, **Zion Overlook** is a hugely popular pull-out facing south to the national park. For less crowded views, continue 1 mile further to the paved area on the south side that serves as the parking lot for the **Bristlecone Trail**. An easy loop of less than a mile leads beneath spruce, fir and ancient bristlecone pines to a platform with views of the north fork of the Virgin River and the start of Zion Canyon in the distance.

About 18 miles east of Cedar City, Hwy 148 turns north to **Cedar Breaks National Monument** (right).

The signed turnoff at 24.5 miles leads to jumbled **lava beds**. At 25 miles, you reach **Navajo Lake**, where boating and fishing are the activities of choice. You can rent a motorboat or stay over in a historic 1920s cabin at **Navajo Lake Lodge** (☎ 702-646-4197; www.navajolakelodge.com; cabins $; ⏰ late May-Oct; 🐾). The rustic lodgings include fireplaces and bedding, but no refrigerators.

Five miles further east, the USFS **Duck Creek Visitor Center** (☎ 435-682-2432; Hwy 14; ⏰ 9am-4:30pm late May-early Sep) lies adjacent to a pretty pond and stream popular with anglers. Forest Service Rd 54 continues from here 3.6 miles southwest to **Cascade Falls Trail**, on the southern edge of Cow Lake. Another easy half-mile hike leads to a platform over the falls. From there you can also access the 32-mile **Virgin River Rim Trail**.

Across the street from the visitor center, the 87-site **Duck Creek Campground** (💻 877-444-6777; www.recreation.gov; Hwy 14; ⏰ late May-early Sep) has flush toilets and water, but no showers or hookups. Pine-shaded sites here at 8400ft are blissfully cool in summer. The ever-expanding log-cabin town at nearby **Duck Creek Village** (www.duckcreekvillage.com) has more services, including a couple of restaurants, realty offices, cabin rental outfits, a laundromat and an internet cafe. The village area is big with off-road enthusiasts – ATVs in summer and snowmobiles in winter. Set on 6 acres across the street, **Pinewood Resort** (☎ 435-682-2512; 800-848-2525; www.pinewoodsresort.com; 121 Duck Creek Ridge Rd; r $, cabins $$; 💻 📶) not only has motel rooms and cabins, it rents out off-road toys.

About 7 miles east of Duck Creek, a signed, passable dirt road leads the 10 miles to **Strawberry Point**, a scenic overlook of red-rock formations and forest lands. There's another Virgin River Rim Trail access point here.

CEDAR BREAKS NATIONAL MONUMENT

elevation 10,300ft

If southern Utah held a natural-beauty contest, Cedar Breaks would be a finalist among some amazing contenders. In its wildly eroded and striped natural amphitheater, sculpted cliffs and hoodoos glow like neon tie-dye – a kaleidoscope of magenta, salmon, plum, rust and ochre. Geologists refer to Cedar Breaks as the icing on the Grand Staircase cake – it contains the same geologic layers as Bryce but is more than 1000ft higher, rising to 10,450ft atop the Markagunt Plateau. But, for the record, there are no cedar trees here; early pioneers mislabeled the abundant evergreen junipers.

DETOUR: BRIAN HEAD

Did someone mention skiing in the desert? Advanced slope jockeys might grow impatient with the short trails (320ft vertical drop, base elevation 9600ft), but there's lots to love for beginners, intermediates and free-riders at the 500-acre **Brian Head Resort** (☎ 435-677-2035; www.brianhead.com; Hwy 143), 7 miles north of Cedar Breaks. Lines are usually short and it's the only resort in Utah within sight of red rock. In summer, the mountain morphs into a premier biking destination.

The compact park lies 22 miles east and north of Cedar City, off Hwy 14, about 60 miles from Bryce and 70 miles from Zion's East Entrance. Snow typically limits access to the park between October and at least late May, when plows may finally be able to clear Hwy 148. In season, rangers hold geology talks and star parties at the small **visitor center** (☎ 435-586-9451; www.nps.gov/cebr; 8am-6pm Jun–mid-Oct). Park entrance is $3 per person, and national-park passes are accepted. The pretty, first-come, first-served 28-site **campground** (sites $; late Jun-Aug) provides water and restrooms but no showers. It's rarely full. The weather has something to do with that: summer temperatures range from 40°F to 70°F, and brief storms can drop rain, hail and even snow.

Including **Point Supreme** at the visitor center, the five viewpoints off Hwy 148 are the park's must-sees. Just two hiking trails trace the rim; no park trails descend into the breaks. The best hikeable views are along the 4-mile round-trip **Ramparts Trail**, beginning at the visitor center. After a mile it reaches **Spectra Point**, and in another mile it ends at an unnamed promontory, dropping 400ft along the way. The wild-and-colorful rock formation vistas are indescribable. Due to the elevation, this should be considered moderately difficult; it's easy to get winded.

The less dramatic 2-mile **Alpine Pond Trail** traipses through forest and meadow on the upper loop, and past the scenic 'Breaks' on the lower one. The namesake pond provides a pleasant place to rest. Experienced hikers might consider tackling the strenuous and unmaintained 9-mile **Rattlesnake Creek Trail**, just outside the park's north entrance. It skirts the edge of the park in the adjacent national forest and drops 2500ft to the canyon floor.

In mid-July the park hosts an annual **Wildflower Festival** to celebrate the area's abundant blooms. October is another colorful time, when the autumn leaves turn. And once snow blankets the trails in November or December, the park is open to cross-country skiing and snowmobiles (which must follow the groomed trail above Hwy 148). Volunteers staff a heated **yurt** (Alpine Pond trailhead; 11am-3pm Sat & Sun Dec-Apr) where you can stop for hot chocolate and ski-trail information. Just watch out for the 20ft snow drifts.

GLENDALE & AROUND

Four tiny towns dot the 10 miles of Hwy 89 between the junction with Hwy 14 and Hwy 9: Glendale, Orderville, Mt Carmel and Mt Carmel Junction. Lack of crowds and lower prices are common; though these little towns are at a crossroads for the southeastern parks, few people ever stop. Glendale is 42 miles southeast of Cedar Breaks, 34 miles northeast of Zion Canyon Visitor Center, 53 miles southwest of Bryce Canyon and 27 miles north of Kanab. For more area info, check out www.eastziontourismcouncil.org.

The **Historic Smith Hotel** (☎ 435-648-2156, 800-528-3558; www.historicsmithhotel.com; 295 N Main St, Glendale; r $;) is as comfortable as a favorite old sweater. Don't let sagging floors and small, well-loved rooms turn you off. Proprietors are a great help in planning your day and the big breakfast tables are a perfect place to meet other intrepid travelers. Next door, **Buffalo Bistro** (☎ 435-648-2778; 305 N Main St, Glendale; burgers $, mains $$-$$$; 4-9:30pm Thu-Mon May-Sep, Thu-Sun Oct-Apr) conjures a laid-back Western spirit with a breezy porch and eclectic menu. Try buffalo steaks or wild boar ribs, rabbit or rattlesnake sausage and, yes, rocky-mountain oysters.

From town the rough-and-tumble **Glendale Bench Rd** takes off toward Johnson Canyon (paved) and Skutumpah (definitely not paved) roads in Grand Staircase-Escalante National Monument (p177). Turn onto 300 North from Hwy 89; a faded 'Glendale Bench' sign marks the intersection.

Continuing south down Hwy 89, rock hounds should definitely make a stop in **Orderville** where rock shops just about outnumber the residents.

In Mt Carmel, the **Thunderbird Foundation for the Arts** (☎ 435-648-2653; www.thunderbirdfoundation.com; Mile 84, Hwy 89, Mt Carmel) runs exhibits and artist retreats in adjacent spaces. The beautiful **Maynard Dixon Home & Studio** (self-guided tour $10; 10am-5pm May-Oct) is where Western artist Maynard Dixon (1875–45) lived and worked with his second wife, artist Edith Hamlin, from 1939 until his death in 1946. Three buildings house works by Dixon and Hamlin, plus photos by his first wife, Dorothea Lange, and his friend Ansel Adams. Tours begin next door at the **Bingham Gallery** (admission free; 10am-5pm May-Oct), which hosts shows of modern-day, area-related artists.

At the turnoff for Hwy 9, Mt Carmel Junction has two gas stations (one with a sandwich counter) and a couple of decent sleeping options just 12 slow and scenic miles from the East Entrance of Zion, 26 miles from Springdale. Expect possible delays for Zion–Mt Carmel Tunnel traffic during the busiest months, May through September. The Navajo look on the outside of the **Best Western East Zion Thunderbird Lodge** (☎ 435-648-2203, 800-780-7234; www.bestwesternutah.com; cnr Hwys 9 & 89, Mt Carmel Junction; r $;) is just a facade; the economical rooms within are standard Best Western. An on-site diner cooks surprisingly good prime rib, and there's a nine-hole golf course attached.

Cabins at **Arrowhead Country Inn** (☎ 435-648-2569, 888-821-1670; www.arrowheadbb.com; 2155 S State St, Mt Carmel Junction; r $-$$, cabins $$-$$$, both incl breakfast;) won't save you much money, but the quilt-covered four-poster beds sure are comfy. The east fork of the Virgin River meanders behind the inn and a trail leads from here to the base of the white cliffs.

LAS VEGAS

pop 607,900 / elevation 2030ft

This isn't your parents' Vegas, but a blazing oasis of glitz and fantasy aiming to please its over 36 million visitors per year. The city demands a suspension of disbelief, so don't take it too seriously. A Bible-toting Elvis kisses a giddy couple that just pledged eternity in a drive-thru wedding chapel. A blue-haired granny pumps dollar bills into a slot machine while millions are lost in no-limit Texas Hold'em poker rooms. A porn star saunters by a nightclub's velvet rope. Blink, and you'll miss it. Sleep? Fuhgeddaboutit.

Then again, park travelers using Las Vegas as a jumping-off point may be more interested in what many locals savor: proximity to the great outdoors. Red Rock Canyon is just a fat-tire hop away, and even the Grand Canyon's South Rim is a doable day trip from the Strip.

Orientation

Most visitors confine their carousing to the glittering north–south artery known as the Strip, a 4-mile stretch of Las Vegas Blvd S, parallel to I-15. South of Tropicana Ave, Mandalay Bay is the start of the Strip; the Strip's upper end is at the Stratosphere Tower, north of Sahara Ave.

North of the Strip, the Fremont Street Experience is a pedestrian mall that has breathed new life into old downtown. The wasteland along Las Vegas Blvd linking downtown with the Strip has little to offer. East of Las Vegas Blvd, Fremont St gets seedy.

Information

INTERNET ACCESS

At casino-hotels, you'll pay $10 or more for 24 hours of in-room internet access (wired or wireless). Cybercafes at the Strip's souvenir shops charge about 20¢ per minute. You can quickly check your email for free at the Fashion Show Mall's Apple Store. Free wi-fi hot spots include the Venetian and Palazzo casino-hotels and McCarran International Airport.

MEDICAL SERVICES

Harmon Medical Center (☎ 702-796-1116; 150 E Harmon Ave; 8am-5pm Mon-Fri) Urgent-care clinic near the Strip.

University Medical Center (☎ 702-383-2000; 1800 W Charleston Blvd; 24hr emergency room) Nevada's most advanced trauma center.

Walgreens (☎ 702-739-9645; 3765 Las Vegas Blvd S; store 24hr, pharmacy 8am-10pm, clinic 8am-7:30pm Mon-Fri, 9:30am-5pm Sat & Sun) Walk-in clinic for minor matters.

MONEY

Every casino hotel and bank, and most convenience stores, have ATMs. Fees imposed by casinos for ATM transactions or foreign-currency exchange are much higher than at banks.

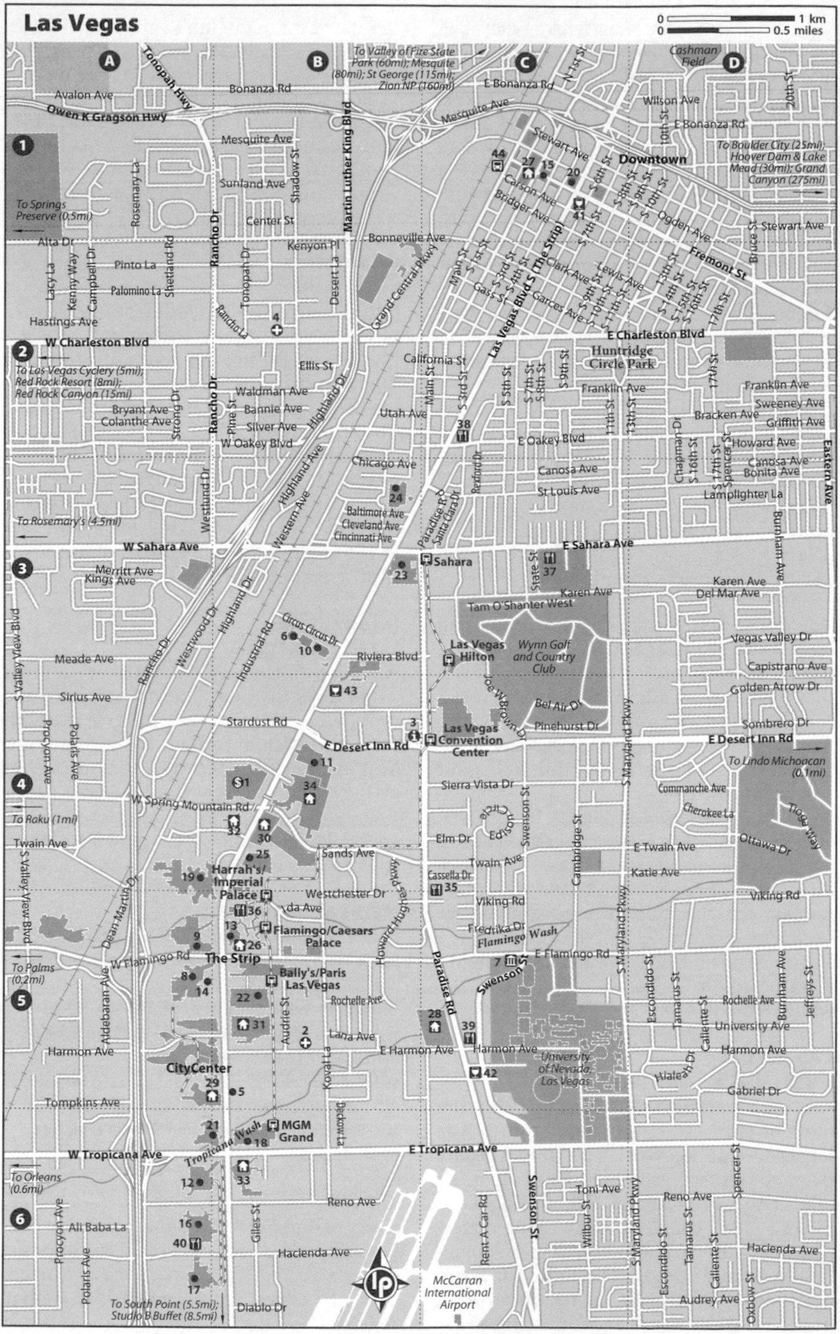
Las Vegas
0 1 km
0 0.5 miles
A
B
C
D
1
2
3
4
5
6
To Valley of Fire State Park (60mi); Mesquite (80mi); St George (115mi); Zion NP (160mi)
To Boulder City (25mi); Hoover Dam & Lake Mead (30mi); Grand Canyon (275mi)
To Springs Preserve (0.5mi)
To Las Vegas Cyclery (5mi); Red Rock Resort (8mi); Red Rock Canyon (15mi)
To Rosemary's (4.5mi)
To Raku (1mi)
To Palms (0.2mi)
To Orleans (0.6mi)
To South Point (5.5mi); Studio B Buffet (8.5mi)
To Lindo Michoacan (0.1mi)
Cashman Field
Downtown
Huntridge Circle Park
Wynn Golf and Country Club
Las Vegas Hilton
Las Vegas Convention Center
Sahara
Harrah's/Imperial Palace
Flamingo/Caesars Palace
Bally's/Paris Las Vegas
The Strip
CityCenter
MGM Grand
University of Nevada, Las Vegas
McCarran International Airport
Flamingo Wash
Tropicana Wash
Tonopah Hwy
Owen K Gragson Hwy
Avalon Ave
Bonanza Rd
E Bonanza Rd
Mesquite Ave
Sunland Ave
Center St
Alta Dr
Martin Luther King Blvd
Rancho Dr
Rosemary La
Shadow St
Kenyon Pl
Bonneville Ave
Grand Central Pkwy
Pinto La
Palomino La
Hastings Ave
Lacy La
Kenny Way
Campbell Dr
Shetland Rd
Tonopah Dr
Desert La
W Charleston Blvd
E Charleston Blvd
Ellis St
California St
Waldman Ave
Bannie Ave
Silver Ave
W Oakey Blvd
E Oakey Blvd
Bryant Ave
Colanthe Ave
Strong Dr
Pine St
Highland Dr
Highland Ave
Western Ave
Utah Ave
Chicago Ave
Baltimore Ave
Cleveland Ave
Cincinnati Ave
Westlund Dr
Main St
S 3rd St
Paradise Rd
Santa Clara Dr
Rexford Dr
Las Vegas Blvd S (The Strip)
Mesquite Ave
Stewart Ave
Carson Ave
Bridger Ave
Ogden Ave
Fremont St
Clark Ave
Lewis Ave
Garces Ave
Gass St
N 1st St
S 1st St
S 3rd St
S 4th St
S 5th St
S 6th St
S 7th St
S 8th St
S 9th St
S 10th St
S 11th St
11th St
13th St
10th St
13th St
S 14th St
S 15th St
S 16th St
17th St
20th St
Wilson Ave
Bruce St
Stewart Ave
Franklin Ave
Sweeney Ave
Bracken Ave
Griffith Ave
Howard Ave
Canosa Ave
Bonita Ave
St Louis Ave
Lamplighter La
Chapman Dr
S 17th St
Spencer St
Eastern Ave
W Sahara Ave
E Sahara Ave
Merritt Ave
Kings Ave
State St
Karen Ave
Del Mar Ave
Tam O'Shanter West
Westwood Dr
Industrial Rd
Circus Circus Dr
Riviera Blvd
Joe W Brown Dr
Bel Air Dr
Pinehurst Dr
Vegas Valley Dr
Capistrano Ave
Golden Arrow Dr
Sombrero Dr
Burnham Ave
S Valley View Blvd
Meade Ave
Sirius Ave
Stardust Rd
E Desert Inn Rd
Procyon Ave
Polaris Ave
S Maryland Pkwy
W Spring Mountain Rd
Sierra Vista Dr
Edison Circle
Swenson St
Cambridge St
Commanche Ave
Cherokee La
Tioga Way
Ottawa Dr
Twain Ave
E Twain Ave
Elm Dr
Sands Ave
Katie Ave
Cassella Dr
Westchester Dr
Viking Rd
Dean Martin Dr
Howard Hughes Pkwy
Fredrika Dr
W Flamingo Rd
E Flamingo Rd
Aldebaran Ave
Escondido St
Tamarus St
Caliente St
Jeffreys St
Rochelle Ave
University Ave
Audrie St
Lana Ave
Koval La
Harmon Ave
E Harmon Ave
Hialeah Dr
Gabriel Dr
Tompkins Ave
Dechow La
W Tropicana Ave
E Tropicana Ave
Toni Ave
Reno Ave
Wilbur St
Spencer St
Giles St
Rent A Car Rd
Ali Baba La
Hacienda Ave
Diablo Dr
Audrey Ave
Oxbow St
1
2
3
4
5
6
7
8
9
10
11
12
13
14
15
16
17
18
19
20
21
22
23
24
25
26
27
28
29
30
31
32
33
34
35
36
37
38
39
40
41
42
43
44

INFORMATION
American Express 1 B4
Apple Store .... (see 1)
Harmon Medical Center 2 B5
Las Vegas Convention & Visitors Authority 3 B4
University Medical Center 4 B2
Walgreens 5 B5

SIGHTS & ACTIVITIES
Adventuredome 6 B3
Atomic Testing Museum 7 C5
Bellagio 8 A5
Bellagio Conservatory .... (see 8)
Caesars Palace 9 A5
Circus Circus 10 B3
Eiffel Tower .... (see 22)
Encore 11 B4
Excalibur 12 A6
Flamingo 13 B5
Fountains of Bellagio 14 A5
Fremont Street Experience 15 C1
Las Vegas Cyber Speedway .... (see 23)
Lion Habitat .... (see 18)
Luxor 16 A6
Mandalay Bay 17 A6
MGM Grand 18 B6
Minus 5 Ice Lounge .... (see 17)
Mirage 19 A4
Mirage Volcano .... (see 19)
Neon Museum 20 C1
Neonopolis .... (see 20)
New York–New York 21 B6
Paris Las Vegas 22 B5
Roller Coaster .... (see 21)
Sahara 23 B3
Shark Reef .... (see 17)
Speed .... (see 23)
Stratosphere 24 B3
Stratosphere Tower .... (see 24)
Venetian 25 B4
Venetian Gondolas .... (see 25)
Wildlife Habitat .... (see 13)

SLEEPING
Bill's Gamblin' Hall & Saloon 26 B5
Caesars Palace .... (see 9)
Circus Circus .... (see 10)
Encore .... (see 11)
Golden Nugget 27 C1
Hard Rock 28 C5
Mandalay Bay .... (see 17)
MGM Grand .... (see 18)
Monte Carlo 29 B5
Palazzo 30 B4
Planet Hollywood 31 B5
TI (Treasure Island) 32 B4
Tropicana 33 B6
Venetian .... (see 25)
Wynn 34 B4

EATING
Bellagio Buffet .... (see 8)
BLT Burger .... (see 19)
Cut .... (see 30)
Firefly 35 C4
First Food & Bar .... (see 25)
Grotto .... (see 27)
Hash House a Go Go 36 B5
Le Village Buffet .... (see 22)
Lotus of Siam 37 C3
Luv-It Frozen Custard 38 C2
Mon Ami Gabi .... (see 22)
Origin India 39 C5
Payard Bistro .... (see 9)
Restaurant Guy Savoy .... (see 9)
RM Seafood 40 A6
Spice Market Buffet .... (see 31)
Village Eateries .... (see 21)
Wynn Buffet .... (see 34)

DRINKING
Beauty Bar 41 C1
Double Down Saloon 42 C5
Fireside Lounge 43 B4
Mix .... (see 17)
Revolution Lounge .... (see 19)
Tao .... (see 25)
Wet Republic .... (see 33)
XS .... (see 11)

ENTERTAINMENT
House of Blues .... (see 17)
Kà .... (see 18)
LOVE .... (see 19)
Mystère .... (see 32)
O .... (see 8)
Tix 4 Tonight .... (see 1)

TRANSPORT
Greyhound Bus Station 44 C1

American Express (702-739-8474; Fashion Show Mall, 3200 Las Vegas Blvd S; 10am-9pm Mon-Fri, 10am-8pm Sat, 11am-6pm Sun) Competitive currency-exchange rates.

TOURIST INFORMATION

Shops advertising 'tourist information' along the Strip are usually outlets selling helicopter tours, show tickets and so on.

Las Vegas Convention & Visitors Authority (LVCVA; 877-847-4858; www.visitlasvegas.com; 3150 Paradise Rd; office 8am-5pm, hotline 7am-7pm) City's only official tourist office.

Nevada Welcome Center (877-637-7848; I-15, exit 22, Mesquite; 8am-4:30pm) Handy coming from Utah.

Sights & Activities

Just because casino resorts now bring the bling doesn't mean the campy side of Las Vegas has changed all that much. Apart from the casino crawl, you'll find many other attractions on and off the Strip.

SOUTH STRIP

Hidden inside Mandalay Bay, the **Shark Reef** (702-632-4555; 3950 Las Vegas Blvd S; adult/child $7/11; 10am-8pm Sun-Thu, 10am-10pm Fri & Sat, last entry 1hr before closing;) is a gigantic walk-through aquarium that's home to over 2000 submarine beasties, including jellyfish, moray eels, stingrays and some of the world's last remaining golden crocodiles.

It's impossible to miss the 100,000lb bronze lion mascot surrounded by spritzing fountains outside the MGM Grand. Step inside to see real, live felines in the walk-through **lion habitat** (702-891-1111; 3799 Las Vegas Blvd S; admission free; 11am-7pm;). Opposite, the mini-megapolis of New York–New York features scaled-down replicas of the Big Apple's skyline, Statue of Liberty and Brooklyn Bridge, plus a bone-rattling **roller coaster** (702-740-6969; www.nynyhotelcasino.com; 3790 Las Vegas Blvd S; ride $14; 11am-11pm Sun-Thu, 10:30am-midnight Fri & Sat, weather permitting;).

MID-STRIP

Paris Las Vegas prides itself on a half-scale replica of the **Eiffel Tower** (702-946-7000; www.parislasvegas.com; 3655 Las Vegas Blvd S; adult/child $10/7, after 7:15pm $15; 9:30am-12:30pm, weather permitting), with an observation deck overlooking the Strip's neon lights and the **Fountains of Bellagio** (702-693-7111; www.bellagio.com; 3600 Las

Vegas Blvd S; every 15-30min 3pm-midnight Mon-Fri, noon-midnight Sat & Sun), which put on a hypnotizing show with music, lights and choreographed dancing plumes of water. The Bellagio's indoor **conservatory** (admission free; 24hr) flaunts ostentatious seasonal floral arrangements installed by crane through a 50ft-high glass ceiling.

Across from laughably kitschy Caesars Palace, the Mafia-built Flamingo casino hotel was once the talk of the town; when it opened in 1946, even the janitors wore tuxedos. Its walk-through **wildlife habitat** (702-733-3111; www.flamingolasvegas.com; 3555 Las Vegas Blvd S; admission free; 24hr;) sports real flamingos, penguins, exotic birds and ornamental koi.

The Polynesian-inspired Mirage, with its interior rainforest atrium and saltwater aquariums, has a fiery faux **volcano** (702-791-7111; www.mirage.com; 3400 Las Vegas Blvd S; hourly dusk-midnight) out front that erupts nightly. Or float away on the Italianate Venetian's canals, plied by **gondolas** (702-414-4300; www.venetian.com; 3355 Las Vegas Blvd S; per person $16, private 2-person ride $64; 10am-10:45pm Sun-Thu, 10am-11:45pm Fri & Sat) – same-day, in-person reservations required.

NORTH STRIP

Inside **Circus Circus** (702-734-0410; www.circuscircus.com; 2880 Las Vegas Blvd S; admission free; shows every 30min 11am-midnight;), aerialists, contortionists and magicians perform above the casino floor. The **Adventuredome** (702-794-3939; www.adventuredome.com; rides $4-7, all-day pass over/under 48in tall $25/15; hours vary;) is an indoor amusement park offering tame thrills for the pre-teen set.

Farther north at the vintage Moroccan-themed **Sahara** (702-737-2111; www.saharavegas.com; 2535 Las Vegas Blvd S), jump on the Strip's best roller coaster, **Speed** (noon-8pm Mon-Thu, noon-10pm Fri & Sat, weather permitting;), or virtually race a Formula One car at the indoor **Las Vegas Cyber Speedway** (noon-10pm); each ride costs $10, or get an all-day pass ($25).

Looming nearby, the iconic **Stratosphere Tower** (702-380-7777; www.stratospherehotel.com; 2000 Las Vegas Blvd S; elevator adult/child $16/10, incl 3 thrill rides $30, SkyJump $100;) has indoor/outdoor observation decks and some of the world's highest thrill rides, including SkyJump, a free-fall from 108 stories above the Strip.

FREMONT STREET EXPERIENCE

Electrifying Las Vegas' historic downtown gambling quarter, aka Glitter Gulch, this five-block **pedestrian mall** (702-678-5800; www.vegasexperience.com; Fremont St, btwn Main St & Las Vegas Blvd; free hourly shows dusk-midnight) boasts an arched steel canopy where cheesy animation shows play on a super-big Viva Vision screen enhanced by 12.5 million synchronized LEDs and 550,000 watts of concert-hall sound. Live cover bands rock the crowds in summer. You can easily stroll between a dozen smoky, old-school gambling joints nearby.

NEON MUSEUM

This alfresco assemblage of vintage neon, with its genie lamps, glowing martini glasses and 1940s motel marquees, brightens up downtown, especially on cul-de-sacs north of the Fremont Street Experience and in the Neonopolis' courtyard. While the permanent **museum** (702-387-6366; www.neonmuseum.org) is a work in progress, tours of the giant 'boneyard' of rescued signs are available by appointment.

ATOMIC TESTING MUSEUM

During the atomic heyday of the 1950s, gamblers and tourists alike watched as mushroom clouds rose on the desert horizon, and the city crowned a Miss Atomic Bomb. Learn more at this intriguing Smithsonian-associated **museum** (702-794-5161; www.atomictestingmuseum.org; 755 E Flamingo Rd; adult/concession $12/9; 10am-5pm Mon-Sat, noon-5pm Sun). Buy tickets at the replica Nevada Test Site guard station, then watch documentary footage inside the Ground Zero Theater, which mimics a concrete test bunker.

SPRINGS PRESERVE

A desert oasis in the middle of the city, this 180-acre **eco-complex** (702-822-7700; www.springspreserve.org; 333 S Valley View Blvd; adult/child $19/11; 10am-6pm;) is a family-friendly place to while away an afternoon. Nearly 2 miles of trails meander through botanical gardens to a *ciénega* (wetland). Browse cool, interactive indoor exhibits about Nevada's natural and cultural history in the Origen Experience, then swing by the LEED-certified green buildings of the Desert Living Center to learn about the secret life of garbage.

OUT OF TOWN

Red Rock Canyon

A 40-minute drive west of the Strip is this **national conservation area** (☎ 702-515-5350; www.nv.blm.gov/redrockcanyon; cyclist/car $3/7, campsite $15; visitor center 8am-4:30pm, scenic loop 6am-8pm Apr-Sep, 6am-7pm Oct, 6am-5pm Nov-Feb, 7am-7pm Mar). A 13-mile scenic loop takes drivers and cyclists past rock-climbing areas and hiking trails leading to petroglyph panels, riparian areas and lookouts.

From I-15, take I-215 or Blue Diamond Rd (Hwy 160) west to Hwy 159, leading to the scenic loop entrance. The BLM's basic, no-reservations (and no water!) campground is 2 miles east of the scenic drive entrance, off Hwy 159. For bike rentals and tours, see right.

Hoover Dam

Once the world's tallest, **Hoover Dam** (☎ 702-494-2517; www.usbr.gov/lc/hooverdam; tours adult/child from $11/9, parking garage $7; visitor center 9am-5pm, to 6pm summer, last ticket sold 45min before closing) is an engineering marvel, its imposing, graceful Art Deco concrete curve filling a dramatic canyon. The dam was built primarily to control floods on the lower Colorado River, which irrigates a million acres of land in the USA and half a million in Mexico.

Take a tour and ride the elevator over 50 stories below ground to see the massive power generators, then zoom back up to view the exhibit halls, outdoor spillways and Winged Figures of the Republic memorial. Arrive early or late in the day to avoid the longest lines. For kayaking tours, see right.

From the Strip, it's a 30-mile drive; take I-15 south to I-215, then I-515/US Hwys 93 & 95 past Boulder City. Nearby **Lake Mead National Recreation Area** (☎ 702-293-8990; www.nps.gov/lame; entry per vehicle $5, campsites $10; 24hr, visitor center 8:30am-4:30pm) offers first-come, first-serve campgrounds.

Valley of Fire

At this **state park** (☎ 702-397-2088; http://parks.nv.gov/vf.htm; entry per vehicle $10, campsites $20-30; 24hr, visitor center 8:30am-4:30pm) is a masterpiece of Southwestern desert scenery, where sandstone has been eroded into fantastical shapes. Follow the scenic drive out to White Domes, passing Rainbow Vista and the detour to Fire Canyon and Silica Dome. It's most photogenic – and significantly cooler – at dawn and dusk. Some first-come, first-served campsites have RV hookups. It's about an hour's drive northeast of Las Vegas, en route to/from Utah; take I-15 exit 75, then drive east on Hwy 169 toward Lake Mead.

Tours

Las Vegas is an especially popular gateway for visiting the Grand Canyon's South Rim.

Bootleg Canyon Flightlines (☎ 702-293-6885; www.bcflightlines.com; 1512 Industrial Rd, Boulder City; 2½hr tour $149) En route to Hoover Dam, this aerial adventure is like zip-lining, but with a paragliding harness.

Boulder City Outfitters (☎ 702-293-1190, 800-748-3702; www.bouldercityoutfitters.com; 111 Veterans Memorial Dr, Boulder City; tours $150, canoe or kayak rental $50-60, launch shuttle $30) Guided kayak tours (two-person minimum) start beneath Hoover Dam, stopping at hot springs and waterfalls.

Las Vegas Cyclery (☎ 702-596-2953; www.lasvegascyclery.com; 8221 W Charleston Blvd; tours $109-179, road or mountain-bike rentals $30-75; 10am-6pm Mon-Fri, 9am-6pm Sat, 10am-4pm Sun) Offers guided hiking and biking tours.

McGhie's Bike Outpost (☎ 702-865-4820; http://mcghies.com; 16 Cottonwood #B; tours $119-169, mountain-bike rentals $40-65; 7am-3pm Wed-Sun) Trail maps and guided mountain-biking tours.

Papillon (☎ 702-736-7243, 888-635-7272; www.papillon.com; tours $65-600) Top-flight outfit offers small-plane and helicopter tours of the Strip, Hoover Dam and the Grand Canyon (SkyWalk and river-rafting combos available).

Pink Jeep Tours (☎ 888-900-4480; www.pinkjeep.com; tours $90-350) Day trips include Red Rock Canyon, Valley of Fire, Death Valley and mining ghost towns.

Sleeping

Las Vegas room rates fluctuate wildly with demand. Prices midweek are often 50% less than weekend rates, but then triple during big conventions and major holidays like New Year's Eve. Whatever you do, don't arrive without a reservation! For discounted room rates, check casino website promotions and online booking agents like www.travelworm.com or www.tripres.com. Casino hotel rooms often lack basic motel amenities (eg coffee makers, mini-fridges).

For camping, drive outside town to Lake Mead, Valley of Fire or Red Rock Canyon (above). RVs are welcome at Circus Circus (p142).

THE STRIP

Many Strip casino hotels charge an additional daily resort fee ($5 to $25).

Circus Circus (☎ 702-691-5950, 800-634-3450; www.circuscircus.com; 2880 Las Vegas Blvd S; r $;) It's a circus here, literally, with acrobats flying overhead and clowns working the floor – making it the Strip's most kid-friendly casino hotel. There's a KOA RV park out back.

Tropicana (☎ 702-739-2222, 888-826-8767; www.troplv.com; 3801 Las Vegas Blvd S; r $;) The vintage 1950s Tropicana has gotten a snazzy facelift. Its tropical Miami-meets-Havana theme includes a palm-fringed pool area with a waterfall and swim-up blackjack. Paradise Tower rooms are your best bet.

Bill's Gamblin' Hall & Saloon (☎ 702-737-2100, 866-245-5745; www.billslasvegas.com; 3595 Las Vegas Blvd; r $;) Stained glass and dark polished wood evoke the spirit of a turn-of-the-20th-century Barbary Coast brothel. With its corner location and comfy rooms at civilized prices, it's a sweet deal for the Strip.

Monte Carlo (☎ 702-730-7777, 800-311-8999; www.montecarlo.com; 3770 Las Vegas Blvd S; r $$;) Literally the next best thing to CityCenter, this Euro-style hotel is much more than just a poor man's Bellagio. Plush rooms and a lazy river ride by the pool await.

Planet Hollywood (☎ 702-785-5555, 866-919-7472; www.planethollywoodresort.com; 3667 Las Vegas Blvd S; r $$;) With a rock 'n' roll soundtrack, the youthful PH offers oversized 'Hollywood Hip' rooms draped in contemporary cool. Miracle Mile shops and Paris' Eiffel Tower are next door.

MGM Grand (☎ 702-891-7777, 877-880-0880; www.mgmgrand.com; 3799 Las Vegas Blvd S; r $$;) It's the city's biggest casino hotel, so don't stay at this sprawling property if you don't like walking. Sexy, minimalist-mod West Wing rooms have walk-in showers built for two.

TI (Treasure Island) (☎ 702-894-7111, 800-288-7206; www.treasureisland.com; 3300 Las Vegas Blvd S; r $$;) Come to score some sexy pirate booty and for the hot-tub party atmosphere by the pool. Floor-to-ceiling windows make petite rooms with pillowtop beds seem larger than they are.

Mandalay Bay (☎ 702-632-7777, 877-632-7800; www.mandalaybay.com; 3950 Las Vegas Blvd S; r $$;) Elegant M-Bay's tropical pool complex is the Strip's best, with an artificial wave pool, lazy river ride and an artificial beach made of imported California sand.

Wynn (☎ 702-770-7000, 877-321-9966; www.wynnlasvegas.com; 3131 Las Vegas Blvd; r $$$;) Curved copper-toned towers signal luxury. Be refreshed by the profusion of greenery and natural light, a rarity on the Strip. Wynn's adjacent Encore hotel is equally gracious.

Venetian (☎ 702-414-1000; www.venetian.com; 3355 Las Vegas Blvd S; r $$$;) Suites at this nouveau-riche tribute to the romantic waterways and artistry of Venice are unapologetically sumptuous and spacious, just like at its sister resort next door, the Palazzo.

OFF-STRIP

Many off-Strip casino hotels offer free guest shuttles to/from the Strip. Cheapie chains near the airport and convention center are deadly dull.

South Point (☎ 702-796-7111, 866-791-7626; www.southpointcasino.com; 9777 Las Vegas Blvd S; r $;) With rooms this huge and beds this divine, who needs a suite? Popular for its equestrian events center, cineplex and bowling alley, it's a short drive south of the Strip.

Orleans (☎ 702-365-7111, 800-675-3267; www.orleanscasino.com; 4500 W Tropicana Ave; r $;) West of the Strip, the Orleans is decked out in festive Mardi Gras colors, with a 70-lane bowling alley and movie theater. Childcare center and small gym on-site.

Golden Nugget (☎ 702-385-7111, 800-846-5336; www.goldennugget.com; 129 E Fremont; r $$;) Understated elegance keeps the shine on the Nugget, which retains its old-school appeal. Incredibly, the outdoor pool's water slide twists through a shark tank. Standard rooms are good value; Rush Tower and Gold Club rooms are downtown's most posh.

Hard Rock (☎ 702-693-5000, 800-473-7625; www.hardrockhotel.com; 4455 Paradise Rd; r $$;) Hip rooms inhabit this vainglorious shrine to rock 'n' roll, which pulls in a sexy crowd from Southern California. French doors grace the stylish Euro-minimalist rooms. In summer, swim-up blackjack awaits at the celeb-happy beach club.

Palms (☎ 702-942-7777, 866-942-7770; www.palms.com; 4321 W Flamingo Rd; r $$;) The Palms caters to a younger, flashier crowd, with some of the hottest nightclubs in town. Themed luxury suites have extraordinary extras like bowling lanes and basketball half-courts. The next-door high-rise Palms Place rents out mod condos.

Red Rock Resort (☎ 702-797-7777, 866-767-7773; www.redrocklasvegas.com; 11011 W Charleston Blvd; r $$$;) If hiking Red Rock Canyon takes priority over strolling the Strip, consider staying here. With all the amenities of a Vegas casino and a tip-top spa, you're guaranteed easy access to outdoor adventures. It's about 8 miles northwest of the Strip.

Eating

With so many stellar (but also overhyped) restaurants in town, we've listed just a few reliable favorites here. You can have breakfast at noon or midnight in almost any 24-hour casino coffee shop.

THE STRIP

Cheaper casino hotels have fast-food options, too.

Village Eateries (☎ 702-740-6969; New York-New York, 3790 Las Vegas Blvd S; mains $$; daily, hours vary) The cobblestone streets of Greenwich Village are chock-a-block with just-OK, wallet-saving options, including Greenberg's Deli and Fulton's Original Fish Frye.

Hash House a Go Go (☎ 702-254-4646; Imperial Palace, 3535 Las Vegas Blvd S; mains $$; 7am-11pm Sun-Thu, 7am-2am Fri & Sat) This SoCal import's 'twisted farm food' has to be seen to be believed: pancakes as big as tractor tires, farm-egg scrambles and house-made hashes that could knock over a cow.

Payard Bistro (☎ 702-731-7292; Caesars Palace, 3570 Las Vegas Blvd S; snacks $, mains $$; bistro 6:30am-3pm, patisserie 6:30am-11pm) Third-generation chocolatier Françoise Payard offers exquisite French pastries and sweet concoctions with rich espresso, and perfectly executed bistro classics for breakfast and lunch.

BLT Burger (☎ 702-792-7888; Mirage, 3400 Las Vegas Blvd S; mains $$; 11am-2am Sun-Thu, 10am-4am Fri & Sat;) NYC chef Laurent Tourondel's kitchen grills up haute beef, lamb, turkey, chicken, pork and veggie burgers with all the trimmings, plus dreamy liqueur-spiked 'adult' milkshakes and peanut-buttery s'mores for dessert.

Mon Ami Gabi (☎ 702-944-4224; Paris Las Vegas, 3655 Las Vegas Blvd S; 7am-11pm Sun-Fri, 7am-midnight Sat) Think *trés* charming outdoor Champs Élysées bistro beneath Vegas' Eiffel Tower. Though the French fare is far from *magnifique*, they've got classic steak frites, vegetarian crepes, quiches and salads, and a respectable wine list.

First Food & Bar (☎ 702-607-3478; Shoppes at the Palazzo, 3327 Las Vegas Blvd S; 11am-1am Sun-Thu, 11am-4am Fri & Sat) At this industrial mod bar-and-grill with a seriously creative edge, order up Philly cheesesteak dumplings, Dr Pepper ribs with cheesy grits or a cotton candy–flavored cocktail. A clubby crowd takes over after dark.

RM Seafood (☎ 702-632-9300; Mandalay Place, 3930 Las Vegas Blvd S; mains $$$; cafe 11:30am-11pm daily, restaurant 5:30-10pm Tue-Sat) From eco-conscious chef Rick Moonen, modern American seafood dishes, such as Cajun popcorn shrimp and clam chowder, come with comfort-food sides (like gourmet mac 'n' cheese) and a raw shellfish and sushi bar.

Cut (☎ 702-607-6300; Palazzo, 3325 Las Vegas Blvd S; mains $$$; 5:30-10pm Sun-Thu, 5:30-11pm Fri & Sat) Peripatetic chef Wolfgang Puck is on fire – it's 1200°F in the broiler, to be exact. Puck's innovative steakhouse menu doesn't hesitate to infuse Indian spices into Kobe beef or match Nebraska corn-fed steaks with Argentinean chimichurri sauce.

Restaurant Guy Savoy (☎ 877-346-4642; Caesars Palace, 3570 Las Vegas Blvd S; mains $$$; 5:30-9:30pm Wed-Sun) If this three-star Michelin chef's

BELLY-BUSTING BUFFETS

When it comes to all-you-can-eat buffets, the old adage 'you get what you pay for' was never truer: classier casino hotels usually have better buffets. Expect to pay $7 to $15 for breakfast, $15 to $20 for lunch or $20 to $40 for dinner; all-day buffet passes cost from $30. Rave reviews go to:

Le Village Buffet (Paris Las Vegas; p139)
Spice Market Buffet (Planet Hollywood; p142)
Studio B (☎ 702-797-1000; M Resort, 12300 Las Vegas Blvd S, off I-15)
The Buffet (Bellagio; p139)
The Buffet (Wynn; p142)

high-flying modern French tasting menus would break the bank, just perch at the Bubble Bar for champagne by the glass and elegant appetizers, such as artichoke black-truffle soup. Dress to impress.

OFF-STRIP

Get off the Strip for more reasonable prices.

Luv-It Frozen Custard (☎ 702-384-6452; 505 E Oakey Blvd; mains $; 1-10pm Sun-Thu, 1-11pm Fri & Sat;) Open since 1973, Luv-It's handmade custard concoctions are creamier than ice cream. Try a chocolate-dipped 'Luv Stick' bar or Western sundae. Cash only.

Lindo Michoacan (☎ 702-735-6828; 2655 E Desert Inn Rd; mains $-$$; 10:30am-11pm Mon-Thu, 10:30am-midnight Fri & Sat, 9am-11pm Sun) Adobe walls hung with Mexican ceramics are colorful touches at this family-friendly, authentic Mexican kitchen, where the motto is 'Save water, drink margaritas.' Free Strip shuttle (reservations required).

Lotus of Siam (☎ 735-3033; Commercial Center, 953 E Sahara Ave; mains $-$$; 11:30am-2pm Mon-Fri, 5:30-9:30pm Sun-Thu, 5:30-10pm Fri-Sun; V) West of the Sahara, the strip-mall hole-in-the-wall kitchen may not look like much, but foodies flock here. Saipin Chutima's authentic northern Thai cooking has won almost as many awards as her wine cellar.

Firefly (☎ 702-369-3971; 3900 Paradise Rd; mains $$; 11:30am-2am) North of the Hard Rock, Firefly is always hopping. Shake hands with Spanish tapas traditions, as chorizo clams jostle alongside *patatas bravas*. The backlit bar pours fruit-infused mojitos and sangria. There's a downtown branch inside the Plaza casino on the Fremont Street Experience (p140).

Origin India (☎ 702-734-6342; 4480 Paradise Rd; mains $$; 11:30am-11:30pm; V) Opposite the Hard Rock, an imaginative Indian menu ranges across the subcontinent, dishing up centuries-old royal and Ayurvedic recipes alongside modern fusion tastes. The epic New World and European wine list is a bonus.

Grotto (☎ 702-385-7111; Golden Nugget, 129 E Fremont St; mains $$; 11:30am-10:30pm Sun-Thu, 11:30am-11:30pm Fri & Sat, pizza bar to midnight Sun-Thu, to 1am Fri & Sat;) Wood oven–fired pizzas and a 200-bottle list of Italian wines are the stars at this downtown Italian joint. Sunny patio seats spy on the Nugget's shark-tank water slide.

our pick **Raku** (☎ 702-367-3511; 5030 W Spring Mountain Rd; mains $$; 6pm-3am Mon-Sat) On the outskirts of Chinatown, this Japanese *robata*-style grill only has a handful of tables, so make reservations. Take flight on an imported sake sampler, then dig into creative hot and cold appetizers, salty yakitori skewers, steaming bowls of udon noodle soup or daily specials. Make reservations.

Rosemary's (☎ 702-869-2251; 8125 W Sahara Ave; mains $$, prix fixe $$$; dinner form 5:30pm daily) Words fail to describe the epicurean ecstasy you'll encounter here. Once you bite into Southern-influenced offerings like Texas BBQ shrimp with Maytag blue-cheese slaw, you'll forget all about the long drive northwest of the Strip. Superb wine and beer pairings. Reservations essential.

Drinking

Drinks are free while you're gambling in casinos; do tip your cocktail server.

Revolution Lounge (☎ 702-693-8300; Mirage, 3400 Las Vegas Blvd S; cover $5-20; 10pm-4am Wed-Mon) At Cirque du Soleil's psychedelic Beatles-themed ultra lounge, DJs spin everything, from house, hip-hop, Brit-pop and world music to mash-ups of classic rock and '80s new wave. The no-cover Abbey Road Bar opens at noon daily.

Mix (☎ 702-632-9500; 64th fl, THEhotel at Mandalay Bay, 3950 Las Vegas Blvd S; cover after 10pm $25; 5pm-2am Sun-Thu, 5pm-4am Fri & Sat) This is THE place to grab sunset cocktails. The glassed-in elevator alone has heady views, and that's before you glimpse the champagne bar and mod decor. Join the glitterati on the sky-high patio.

Fireside Lounge (☎ 702-735-4177; Peppermill, 2985 Las Vegas Blvd S; 24hr) The North Strip's most unlikely romantic hideaway is inside a retro coffee shop. Cooing couples flock here for the sunken fire pit, cozy blue-velvet nooks and candy-colored tropical cocktails.

Beauty Bar (☎ 702-598-1965; 517 E Fremont St; cover free-$10; usually 10pm-4am) At the salvaged innards of a 1950s New Jersey beauty salon, get down with DJs and indie bands. Nearby are the chilled-out Griffin bar and Downtown Cocktail Room, a speakeasy-style lounge.

Double Down Saloon (☎ 702-91-5775; 4640 Paradise Rd, enter off Swenson St; 24hr) You just gotta love a punk dive bar (cash only) where the tangy, blood-red house drink is named 'Ass Juice.' Expect lotsa attitude, lunatic-fringe bands and a legendary jukebox. Check out the owner's Frankie's Tiki Room, just west of I-15 on Charleston Blvd.

XS (☎ 702-770-0097; www.xslasvegas.com; Encore, 3111 Las Vegas Blvd S; cover $20-40; 🕑 10pm-4am Fri-Mon) Snake-skin banquettes, ultra-suede sofas, a glittering chandelier and arty gold facades adorn this deluxe club. Kick back with your entourage by the outdoor lagoon, where dancing divas make a splash.

Tao (☎ 702-388-8588; http://taolasvegas.com; Grand Canal Shoppes, Venetian, 3355 Las Vegas Blvd S; cover $20-40; 🕑 10pm-4am Thu-Sat) At this Asian-themed megaclub, nearly naked girls covered by strategically placed flowers splash in bathtubs. On the risque dance floor, Paris Hilton lookalikes forego enlightenment to bump-and-grind to hip-hop instead.

Wet Republic (☎ 702-891-3563; http://wetrepublic.com; MGM Grand, 3799 Las Vegas Blvd S; cover $10-50; 🕑 11am-dusk May-Sep) Why stop partying after sunrise? This adults-only 'ultra pool' brings out bathing beauties, DJs and celeb hosts and plenty of pitchers of frozen cocktails for VIP cabanas.

Entertainment

Pro fighters, pop stars and Broadway musicals all find audiences in Vegas, as do over-the-tosp stage spectaculars like Cirque du Soleil. Buy discounted same-day show tickets at **Tix4Tonight** (☎ 877-849-4868; www.tix4tonight.com; 🕑 from 10am daily), with multiple locations on and off the Strip.

Blues is the tip of the hog at **House of Blues** (☎ 702-632-7600; www.hob.com; Mandalay Bay, 3950 Las Vegas Blvd S; most tickets $25-100; 🕑 hours vary), a Mississippi Delta–themed juke joint where living legends to alt-rockers kick it. Touring bands and comedians also play the Hard Rock's The Joint and the Palms' The Pearl.

O (☎ 702-693-7722, 888-488-7111; www.cirquedusoleil.com; Bellagio, 3600 Las Vegas Blvd S; admission $95-150; 🕑 7:30pm & 10:30pm Wed-Sun) – or 'Eau' (French for water) – is Cirque du Soleil's original epic venture into aquatic theater. Also check out Cirque's LOVE, a Beatles-themed musical journey; Kà, with martial arts on moving platforms; and whimsical Mystère, featuring aerialists, acrobats and clowns.

Getting There & Around

AIR

Las Vegas is served by **McCarran International Airport** (☎ 702-261-5211; www.mccarran.com; 5757 Wayne Newton Blvd; 📶), one of the USA's 10 busiest airports. Taxis to Strip hotels average $15 to $20 (cash only, plus tip); superslow airport shuttle buses charge half as much. (For airport shuttles to/from St George, Utah, see p131.)

BUS

Long-distance **Greyhound** (☎ 800-231-2222; www.greyhound.com) buses arrive at the downtown **bus station** (☎ 702-383-9792; 200 S Main St), near the Fremont Street Experience.

Ace and double-decker Deuce public buses slowly operate 24 hours between the Strip and downtown (per ride/24-hour pass $3/7). The zero-emissions monorail ($5/12) connects some Strip casino hotels, operating from 7am to 2am (till 3am on Friday and Saturday).

CAR

Major car-rental agencies (p273) are based at the airport's rent-a-car center, accessible via a free shuttle from outside the main terminal. Free self-parking and valet (tip $3 to $5) are available at most casino hotels. From Las Vegas, it's about a three-hour drive to Zion National Park via I-15 north to Hwy 9 east.

TAXI

It's illegal to hail a cab on the street. Look for taxi stands at casinos, hotels and shopping malls, or call ☎ 702-873-2000. Fares are metered; a lift up or down the Strip averages $12 to $16, plus tip.

Bryce Canyon National Park

Sand-castle spires known as hoodoos, whittled arches and deep narrows have etched this ever-changing landscape into one that's utterly unique in the world. For most, the sight of Bryce Canyon falls nothing short of otherworldly. Not actually a canyon, Bryce comprises the eastern edge of an 18-mile plateau. Hiking and horse trails descend through these 1000ft amphitheaters of pastel daggers into a maze of fragrant juniper and hilly high-mountain desert. Though the smallest of southern Utah's national parks, Bryce Canyon is fast becoming among the most prized.

The park's Pink Cliffs mark the top step of the Grand Staircase, a giant geologic terrace whose reach stretches to the Grand Canyon. In the park, repeated freezes and thaws are the forces of erosion, shaping soft sandstone and limestone into windows, jutting fins and spindly towers. The high altitude means cooler summer temperatures than other Utah parks. Clean, dry air also means excellent visibility. Bryce is one of the best destinations to wish upon a star. On clear nights views reach all the way into the Andromeda galaxy 2.2 million miles away.

From May through September, the park's sole road and scenic overlooks can get pretty crowded. For solitude, hike off-hours or seek out less-traveled trails under the rim.

HIGHLIGHTS

- Seeing the hoodoos burst into color as the sun rises over **Bryce Amphitheater** (p152)
- **Horseback riding** (p163) beneath the soaring Wall of Windows on the Peekaboo Loop Trail
- Watching the sunset stripe the hoodoos from **Paria View** (p152)
- Dusting off and dining in high style at the **Bryce Canyon Lodge** (p168)
- Adventuring into a canyon of jagged shadows on a **moonlight hike** (p164)

| ■ **Total Area** 56 sq miles | ■ **Elevation** 7894ft (at the visitor center) | ■ **Average high/low temperature in July** 83°F/25°F |

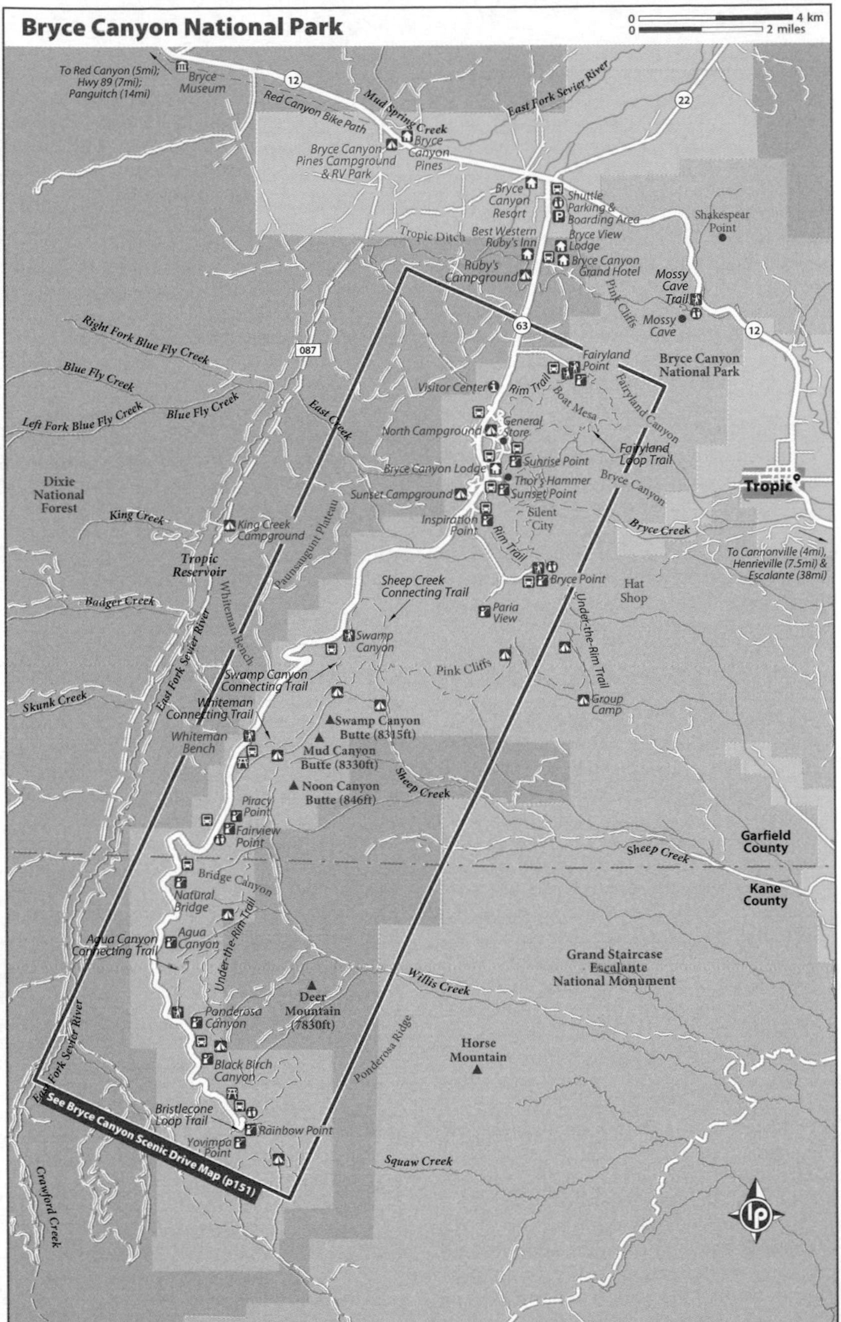
Bryce Canyon National Park
0 4 km
0 2 miles
To Red Canyon (5mi); Hwy 89 (7mi); Panguitch (14mi)
Bryce Museum
Red Canyon Bike Path
Mud Spring Creek
East Fork Sevier River
Bryce Canyon Pines Campground & RV Park
Bryce Canyon Pines
Bryce Canyon Resort
Shuttle Parking & Boarding Area
Shakespear Point
Tropic Ditch
Best Western Ruby's Inn
Bryce View Lodge
Bryce Canyon Grand Hotel
Ruby's Campground
Pink Cliffs
Mossy Cave Trail
Mossy Cave
Right Fork Blue Fly Creek
Blue Fly Creek
Left Fork Blue Fly Creek
Fairyland Point
Bryce Canyon National Park
Visitor Center
Rim Trail
Boat Mesa
Fairyland Canyon
East Creek
North Campground
General Store
Fairyland Loop Trail
Sunrise Point
Bryce Canyon Lodge
Thor's Hammer
Bryce Canyon
Tropic
Dixie National Forest
Sunset Campground
Sunset Point
King Creek
King Creek Campground
Paunsaugunt Plateau
Inspiration Point
Silent City
Bryce Creek
To Cannonville (4mi), Henrieville (7.5mi) & Escalante (38mi)
Tropic Reservoir
Bryce Point
Hat Shop
Sheep Creek Connecting Trail
Badger Creek
Whiteman Bench
Paria View
Under-the-Rim Trail
Swamp Canyon
Swamp Canyon Connecting Trail
Pink Cliffs
Group Camp
Skunk Creek
Whiteman Connecting Trail
Swamp Canyon Butte (8315ft)
Mud Canyon Butte (8330ft)
Noon Canyon Butte (846ft)
Sheep Creek
Piracy Point
Fairview Point
Garfield County
Kane County
Bridge Canyon
Natural Bridge
Agua Canyon Connecting Trail
Agua Canyon
Grand Staircase Escalante National Monument
Willis Creek
Deer Mountain (7830ft)
Ponderosa Canyon
Ponderosa Ridge
Horse Mountain
Black Birch Canyon
Bristlecone Loop Trail
Rainbow Point
Yovimpa Point
See Bryce Canyon Scenic Drive Map (p151)
Squaw Creek
Crawford Creek
12
22
63
087

When You Arrive

As you approach, tune your radio to AM 1590 for current general park information. Bryce Canyon is open 24 hours a day, 365 days a year. Admission, good for seven days, costs $25 per car or $12 per person arriving by motorcycle, bicycle or foot.

At the entrance kiosk you'll receive a park brochure that includes a good driving map, general information about facilities, and details about the park's geology and wildlife. You'll also get a copy of the park newspaper, the *Hoodoo,* which gives up-to-date information about opening hours, ranger-led activities, hiking trails, backpacking and shuttle information.

Orientation

Compared with the vast landscape that surrounds it, Bryce is small (only 56 sq miles), its jagged boundaries stretching 16 miles long and only 4 miles across at its widest point. Shaped somewhat like a seahorse, the long, narrow park is an extension of the sloping Paunsaugunt Plateau and runs north–south, rising from 6600ft on the canyon floor to 7894ft at the visitor center and 9115ft at Rainbow Point, the plateau's southernmost tip.

The park's sole vehicle entrance is 3 miles south of Utah Hwy 12, via Hwy 63. Though the park gate is always open, entrance kiosks are unmanned at night. The park's well-paved, 18-mile-long main road dead ends at the south end of the plateau. The route gets jammed on summer weekends, sometimes with more cars than available parking spots. To alleviate congestion between mid-May and late September, the park employs a system of voluntary shuttles, which you can board either inside the park or 2 miles north of the entrance station, at the south end of Bryce Canyon City. For shuttle information, see opposite.

The famed hoodoo amphitheaters line the eastern rim of the plateau. Sunrise, Sunset and Inspiration Points are 2 miles from the visitor center; Bryce Point is 4 miles. If you're tight on time, these are the sights to see, but also the most crowded.

Aside from lodging and dining at Bryce Canyon Lodge, and camping supplies and groceries at the general store (both near Sunrise Point), the park lacks commercial services. En route to the park, just north of the entrance gate along Hwy 63, you'll pass the privately owned Ruby's Inn, a giant, garish motel complex that encompasses, among other things, a campground, post office, grocery store, restaurants and gas stations. Because Ruby's is so big and so near the park, it's often referenced for shuttle stops and equipment rental.

Information

Upon arrival at the park, stop at the **visitor center** (☎ 435-834-5322; www.nps.gov/brca; Hwy 63; 8am-8pm May-Sep, to 6pm Oct & Apr, to 4:30pm Nov-Mar; wi-fi), immediately adjacent to the entrance station, to pick up maps and books, check weather and road conditions, inquire about campground availability, talk to rangers and watch an excellent 20-minute orientation video, *Bryce Canyon: Shadows of Time,* which describes the park layout, discusses the geologic history of the Colorado Plateau, explains how hoodoos form, shows the park in various seasons and highlights park wildlife and plant life.

Large digital information screens list everything from campground availability to atmospheric conditions (including sunrise and moonrise), schedules of ranger-led programs, hiking-trail descriptions, and a calendar of events. Interpretive exhibits show plant and animal life, as well as geologic displays that explain how Bryce connects with the Grand Canyon and Grand Staircase. If you want to buy maps or souvenirs, doing so here instead of outside the park will help support education in the park. Park headquarters is here, as are first aid, telephones and wi-fi in the lobby (if you need an internet cafe, go to the lobby of

DON'T MISS

- Best short hike into the canyon: Navajo Loop Trail (p154)
- Best colored rock: Bryce Amphitheater (p152) at sunrise
- Best long hike for solitude among the amphitheaters: Fairyland Loop Trail (p158)
- Most stunning hoodoos, viewed from the rim: Silent City from Inspiration Point (p152)
- Best Overlooked Sight: 1600-year-old trees on Bristlecone Loop Trail (p154)

Ruby's Inn, p166). If you have children, you can pick up Junior Ranger Activity Guides and learn more about kids' activities (p164).

The nonprofit **Bryce Canyon Natural History Association** (☎ 435-834-4782, 888-362-2642; www.brycecanyon.org) aids the park service with educational, scientific and interpretive activities at Bryce Canyon. The association operates the bookstore, and trained staff members are on duty to answer questions in the visitor center. It also runs an excellent online shop that sells books, maps, videos, music and trip-planning packets tailored to individual travelers' needs.

Due to Bryce's high elevation, some visitors may experience altitude sickness; see p281).

Park Policies & Regulations

It's particularly important not to feed wild animals. Pets must be kept on a leash and are only allowed on paved surfaces in the park (roads, parking lots, paved scenic overlooks and the section of Rim Trail between Sunset and Sunrise Points). They are not allowed on unpaved trails or in public buildings. For kennels, see the boxed text, p168.

See p40 for Bryce Canyon's hiking and backcountry-use regulations.

Getting Around

Most people arrive at Bryce in their own car. In summer take advantage of the park's free shuttle buses, which stop at all of the major sights and trailheads.

Unless you're on an organized tour, the only way to get around the park from fall through spring is in a private vehicle. The park's main road is easily navigable and well maintained, with turnouts and parking areas clearly marked in the brochure you receive upon paying your fee. Posted speed limits in the park range from 25mph to 45mph. Rangers do give traffic tickets, so avoid speeding.

The closest gas stations are 3 miles north, in Bryce Canyon City. If you're towing a trailer, you are not permitted to take it to Bryce Point or Paria View. You can park it at the trailer turnaround lot in summer or the visitor center parking lot in winter. (If camping, you can leave the trailer at your campsite.)

For information about car repairs and towing, see p277.

EVENTS: ALTERNATIVE BRYCE

Go beyond standard sightseeing at these top events:

- See stars loud and clear through telescopes at the Astronomy Festival (p150)
- Bound the lip of Bryce Canyon at the **Rim Run** (www.rubysinn.com/run.html), an annual 5-mile running race held in August
- Join rock jocks examining Bryce's amazing formations during the Geology Festival (p150)
- Watch broncos buck at the Bryce Canyon Country Rodeo, near Ruby's Inn at 7pm in summer
- Ditch your flashlight and join a ranger for summer's cool moonlight hikes (p164); reservation required

SHUTTLE BUS

If visiting during a peak period, such as a summer weekend, seriously consider riding the free shuttle bus into the park, as parking lots at the major overlooks and visitor center fill up fast. Leave your car in the large lot at the shuttle staging area, 2 miles north of the park's entrance station, at the south end of Bryce Canyon City. If you do pay your fee and drive into the park only to find that parking lots are full, you can easily turn around and drive the five minutes back to the shuttle staging area. Make sure to bring your admission receipt with you on the bus to avoid having to pay again. Tune your radio to AM 1610 as you approach the park to learn about current shuttle service and boarding instructions.

Currently service is available from May through September, about every 13 minutes from 8am to 8pm. Shuttle information may change, so check with rangers for current schedules. The *Hoodoo* newspaper has updated routes. Buses run from the shuttle staging area north of the park to the visitor center and the major Bryce Amphitheater overlooks as far south as Bryce Point. Depending on the park budget, there may be service to points south. If not, you'll have to take your own vehicle or join an organized tour. The free Rainbow Point bus tour hits the highlights daily at

FESTIVAL & EVENTS

Within the park, the annual **Astronomy Festival** celebrates the exceptional viewing of the night skies at Bryce. The four-day event is held in June or July, featuring a keynote speaker, night programs and guided walks. Forty telescopes are made available for stargazing by the visitor center. For kids, there's a wildly popular rocket-launching workshop. The **Geology Festival**, held at the end of July, also has talks, walks and kids programs. All events are free.

Just north of the park boundary, **Ruby's Inn** (☎ 435-834-5341, 866-866-6616; www.rubysinn.com) hosts several annual events not affiliated with the park. Often these are geared at the whole family.

In February, over President's Day weekend, the **Bryce Canyon Winter Festival** includes everything from cross-country skiing and snowmobiling to archery and snow sculpting. For more details, contact Ruby's Inn or the **Garfield County Office of Tourism** (☎ 435-676-1160, 800-444-6689; www.brycecanyoncountry.com).

9am and 1pm. Hikers can also take this bus to trailheads.

SIGHTS

Bryce Canyon's major sights are easily accessible along the park's scenic drive (below).

DRIVING

The maximum speed limit in the park is 45mph, with slower speeds posted in more congested areas; however, traffic may slow significantly on weekends in high season, when lumbering RVs clog lanes. Traffic generally eases the further you drive into the park, as most visitors stick to Bryce Amphitheater's main overlooks, which are concentrated near the visitor center.

Lightning strikes are very common at Bryce. If caught at an overlook during a sudden thunderstorm, immediately take shelter. The safest retreat is inside your vehicle.

BRYCE CANYON SCENIC DRIVE

Duration 2 hours
Distance 34 miles
Start/Finish Visitor center
Nearest Town Tropic
Summary Spanning the length of the park, this out-and-back route hits all the park highlights. Drive to the end point first to avoid left-hand turns into the lookouts.

The scenic drive winds south for 17 miles and roughly parallels the canyon rim, climbing from 7894ft at the visitor center to 9115ft at Rainbow Point, the plateau's southern tip at road's end. While park officials do their best to keep the road to Rainbow Point plowed in winter, severe snowstorms may close the road. Check at the visitor center for current road conditions.

As all viewpoints lie on the east side of the road (or left side as you drive south), you may want head directly to Rainbow Point (the drive from the visitor center takes about 35 minutes), then work your way back, stopping at the scenic overlooks and turnouts as you reach them. While ascending the plateau, note the change in plant life as you move from the ponderosa pine community to the fir-spruce community. The higher you go, the cooler the temperature and the greater the precipitation. In autumn stands of aspen turn a brilliant gold.

First visit **Rainbow Point**, reached on a short, paved, wheelchair-accessible path at the far end of the parking lot. From the overlook, you'll get your first jaw-dropping glimpse of canyon country. On a clear day you can see more than 100 miles. Giant sloping plateaus, tilted mesas and towering buttes jut above the vast landscape, and interpretive panels explain the sights. On the northeastern horizon look for the Aquarius Plateau – the very top step of the Grand Staircase – rising 2000ft higher than Bryce. You'll spot this vast, pink-edged plateau from many angles during your trip, especially if you also travel on Hwy 12 (p185).

When ready, stroll to the other end of the parking lot, where another short, paved, wheelchair-accessible trail leads to **Yovimpa Point**, one of the park's windiest spots. The southwest-facing view reveals more forested slopes and less eroding rock. Look for Molly's Nipple, an eroded sandstone dome often mistaken for a volcano – you'll also spot this dome from many angles during your visit. Dipping below the horizon is the Kaibab Plateau, marking the Arizona border and the Grand Canyon.

For a short, easy hike, the 1-mile **Bristlecone Loop Trail** (p154) starts and ends at Rainbow Point. Yovimpa Point also offers a great tree-shaded picnic area.

Just north of mile marker 16, at 8750ft, the small **Black Birch Canyon** overlook demonstrates just how precipitously the cliffs drop from the road. It also offers your first up-close look at hoodoos – though these are modest in comparison to those at Bryce Amphitheater. There are no trailheads here, only a small lookout, so if the parking lot is full, don't sweat having to skip this stop. More glorious views lie ahead.

Higher than the previous stop, **Ponderosa Canyon** offers long vistas like those at Rainbow Point. Below, note the namesake giant ponderosa pines, some as much as 150ft tall. If you're thinking of waiting in the car because the view doesn't look like much, don't be deceived: this small amphitheater

THE ORIGINAL BRYCE

Bryce Canyon borrows its moniker from an early pioneer who settled in the valley east of the park. In 1870 Ebenezer Bryce made the journey from Salt Lake City with other Mormon pioneers hoping to establish permanent settlements. During Ebenezer's five-year stint here, he surveyed the 10-mile-long Tropic Ditch, looking for a means to deliver water for crops and livestock. Today the ditch still provides water to the town of Tropic (you can stroll beside it on the Mossy Cave Trail, p154). The canyon behind Ebenezer's home was dubbed 'Bryce's Canyon.'

Forget romantic illusions. Bryce described his namesake canyon as 'a hell of a place to lose a cow.' Just gaze off the rim into a maze of hoodoos to understand exactly what he meant.

Bryce Canyon Scenic Drive

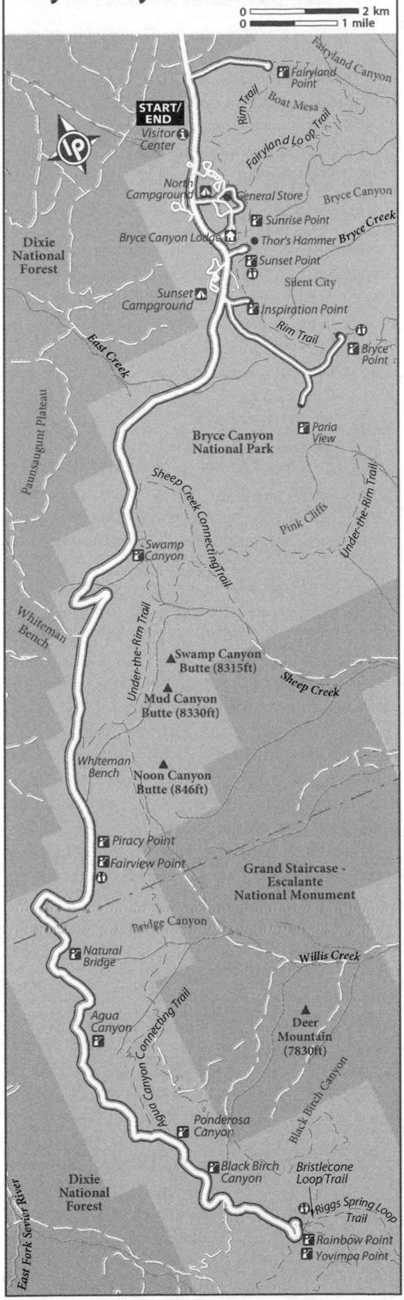

TOP FIVE UNTRODDEN TRAILS

Go wild – you'll see fewer crowds at these spots:

- **Fairyland Loop Trail** (p158)
- **Riggs Spring Loop Trail** (p160)
- **Sheep Creek Connecting Trail** (p162)
- **Agua Canyon Connecting Trail** (p152)
- **Under-the-Rim Trail** (p160)

of hoodoos and burnt-orange cliffs is breathtaking, especially in morning light. If you're feeling ambitious, descend a stretch of the moderately strenuous **Agua Canyon Connecting Trail**, a lightly traveled, steep trail that drops past woods into a brilliant amphitheater of hoodoos before joining the **Under-the-Rim Trail** (p160) after 1.6 miles.

One of the best stops at this end of the park, the **Agua Canyon** viewpoint overlooks two large formations of precariously balanced, top-heavy hoodoos that could – quite literally – fall at any time. That you can only see the tops of these giant spires, not their bases, ought to give you an idea of the precipitous drop-off at your feet. On the ridge above, note the distinct sedimentary lines between iron-rich red rock and white limestone. Clear days promise mesmerizing vistas of the purple and blue horizon.

The parking lot at **Natural Bridge** is the biggest since Rainbow Point, and with good reason: a stunning span of eroded, red-hued limestone juts from the edge of the overlook. Though called a bridge, it's technically an arch. A bridge forms when running water, such as a stream, causes the erosion. In this case, freezing and thawing of water inside cracks and crevices, combined with gravity, shattered rock to create the window. Even if you're tight on time, squeeze this stop onto your agenda.

As its name suggests, the stop at **Fairview Point** offers a grand view of the tree-studded rises and benches, giant plateaus, blue-hued mesas and buttes that extend from the skirts of Bryce into the Grand Staircase, as far as the eye can see. Navajo Mountain lies 80 miles away on the Arizona border, but even that's not the furthest visible point. On clear days you can see 160 miles to Arizona's Black Mesas. A short walk from here leads to another overlook at **Piracy Point**, and though it's not much different, the walk among the deep-green, vanilla-scented pines is a great chance to stretch your legs before getting back in the car. You'll also find toilets here, but no running water.

The overlook at **Swamp Canyon** sits in a forested dip between two ridgelines that extend into the canyon as fins, dropping to hoodoo formations. From the turnout you can take a short walk through the trees and descend slightly to towering pink-orange cliffs of crumbling limestone, one of the more intimate views along the drive. Trees extend from the rim into the canyon, as does red-barked greenleaf manzanita. Nature lovers like the variety of plant and animal life here; kids like the steep trail into the canyon. This is also the jumping-off point for the scenic **Swamp Canyon Connecting Trail**, which drops into the canyon and follows a series of switchbacks about a mile to the Under-the-Rim Trail (to do this hike, bear right at the fork in the trail below the parking area).

Three miles north of Swamp Canyon, turn right and follow signs to the **Paria View** viewpoint, 2 miles off the main road. If you're tired of RVs and buses, you'll be pleased to learn that this small overlook is for cars only – though it's reserved for cross-country skiers in winter, when the access road isn't plowed. This is *the* place to come for sunsets. Most of the hoodoo amphitheaters at Bryce face east, making them particularly beautiful at sunrise, but not sunset. The amphitheater here, small by comparison but beautiful nonetheless, faces west toward the Paria River watershed.

If you stop nowhere else along the scenic drive, be sure to catch the stunning views from **Bryce Point**. You can walk the rim above **Bryce Amphitheater** for awesome views of the **Silent City**, an assemblage of hoodoos so dense, gigantic and hypnotic that you'll surely begin to see shapes of figures frozen in the rock. Be sure to follow the path to the actual point, a fenced-in promontory that juts out over the forested canyon floor, 1000ft below. The extension allows a broad view of the hoodoos. This rivals any overlook in the park for splendor and eye-popping color. An interpretive panel tells the story of Ebenezer and Mary Bryce.

Bryce Point marks the beginning of the 5.5-mile **Rim Trail** (p157). The **Peekaboo Loop Trail** (p156) also begins here. There's also a chemical toilet.

At **Inspiration Point** a short ascent up a paved path takes you to another overlook into Bryce Amphitheater. Inspiration Point sits lower than Bryce Point and provides much the same view, though seen from here, the Silent City is more compelling than from any other rim-top viewpoint. The hoodoos feel closer here, and you can make out more details on the canyon floor below. To the left, follow the sweep of trees along the rim to spot the next stops along the drive. No trails lead into the canyon from here.

Inspiration Point is a great place to return for stargazing – Bryce Point sits up too high, in view of the too-bright lights further north at Bryce Canyon City, and east in the town of Tropic.

Views into Bryce Amphitheater at **Sunset Point** are as good as they get, but don't expect solitude. You're at the core of the park here, near campgrounds, the lodge and all visitor services. Aside from great views of the Silent City, this point is known for **Thor's Hammer**, a big square-capped rock balanced atop a spindly hoodoo. Just left of the point, it stands apart from the other hoodoos and makes a great picture. This is the starting point for the **Navajo Loop Trail** (p154), the park's most popular hike. You'll also find restrooms, drinking water and picnic tables. Don't be fooled by the name of this point. Because it faces east, sunrises are better here than sunsets.

Marking the north end of Bryce Amphitheater, the southeast-facing **Sunrise Point** offers great views of hoodoos, the Aquarius Plateau and the Sinking Ship, a sloping mesa that looks like a ship's stern rising out of the water. Keep your eyes peeled for the **Limber Pine**, a spindly pine tree whose roots have been exposed through erosion, but which remains anchored to the receding sand nonetheless. Within walking distance or a one-minute drive are the Bryce Canyon General Store, drinking water, restrooms, picnic tables and a snack bar; head north toward the campground on the loop road.

End your driving tour at the visitor center (p148) or, if you have time, head to **Fairyland Point**. To reach the point, drive a mile north of the entrance gate, then a mile east of the main road (the turnoff is marked only to northbound traffic – you won't see it on your way into the park). Fairyland is a less-visited spot with wooded views north toward the Aquarius Plateau. Here you can see hoodoos at all stages of evolution, from fin to crumbling tower, and start the **Fairyland Loop Trail** (p158).

HIKING

Though you can see much of Bryce's spectacular rock formations from turnouts along the scenic drive, the best way to appreciate hoodoos is from the canyon floor, as they tower above and around you.

Carry lots of water; don't expect to find any along trails. Though temperatures are often comfortable at Bryce, remember you're at 8000ft in a high desert. The sun is stronger at altitude and it's easy to get dehydrated. Until you're acclimated to the elevation, you may get winded quickly. Take it slow and pace yourself, especially ascending out of the canyon.

Loose rocks act like marbles under your feet; ankle injuries are extremely common and can ruin your trip. Always wear well-fitting hiking boots with ankle support, and lace boots all the way up.

Stay on trails at all times: high-mountain desert vegetation is easily damaged. If you must leave the trail, attempt to step on rocks instead of soil. Rangers lead seasonal hikes; ask at the visitor center for current schedules. Commercial outfitters do not offer guided hiking in Bryce Canyon.

In winter many of these trails are impassable due to snow; some are reserved for cross-country skiing and snowshoeing. Check with rangers at the visitor center.

EASY HIKES

Sometimes it's best to start slow. The following are ideal for families.

MOSSY CAVE TRAIL

Duration 30 minutes–1 hour
Distance 0.8 miles
Difficulty Easy–moderate
Start/Finish Mossy Cave trailhead, Hwy 12
Nearest Town Tropic
Transportation Private
Summary A streamside hike to a mossy overhang. It's relatively cool and interesting for those into plants or geology. Features gentle grades and minimal elevation changes.

If you're visiting Bryce in the heat of summer, you can cool off beside a year-round waterfall off Hwy 12 at the north end of the park and check out a small, damp cave with permanent moss, a rarity in this dry climate. If the trail is passable in winter, Mossy Cave is hung with icicles, a dramatic sight.

Though within the park, the trail lies outside the section requiring an entrance fee. From the Hwy 12/63 junction north of the park, turn east on Hwy 12 and drive just past mile marker 17 (about 3.5 miles) to a small parking area on the right. A placard at the trailhead shows the route. New restrooms flank the trailhead.

Skirting the **Tropic Ditch**, the main water channel for the town of Tropic, the route takes you across two wooden footbridges into small Water Canyon. Take the right fork to reach the **waterfall** or the left fork to reach **Mossy Cave**; both are 0.4 miles from the parking lot.

Don't attempt to climb down the small cliffs to the base of the falls. Instead, at the second footbridge, hop off the path and walk up the wash alongside the creek. Beware of flash floods following rainstorms. Above the falls you can cross the creek and scramble up a short, steep trail to the small arches and windows in the salmon-colored rock.

Mossy Cave may be a slight disappointment for spelunkers, since it's more overhang than cave. Stay behind the railing at the cave to avoid unsafe footing and prevent trampling the fragile mosses.

BRISTLECONE LOOP TRAIL

Duration 30 minutes–1 hour
Distance 1 mile
Difficulty Easy
Start/Finish Rainbow Point parking lot
Nearest Towns Tropic, Panguitch (p170)
Transportation Park shuttle
Summary This quick loop spans fir forests to high cliffs, revealing how Bryce Canyon – the top step of the Grand Staircase – fits into the surrounding landscape and larger Colorado Plateau.

If driving to Rainbow Point, this short hike is a must-do. Starting at 9115ft at the south tip of the Paunsaugunt Plateau, it's Bryce's highest trail. Though the trail isn't wheelchair accessible, the spur to adjacent **Yovimpa Point** is.

Along the way are places to rest and take in the marvelous vistas: on clear days you can see as far as 200 miles! Though you'll spot hoodoos rising from the forested canyon floor, first from the trailhead and again at the tip of the plateau, they are not the focus of this walk.

Park at the Rainbow Point lot, 17 miles from the visitor center. From the overlook kiosk, the well-marked trail ducks into the woods. Bear left at the beginning of the loop. You'll quickly descend below the rim, cross the Under-the-Rim Trail (p160) and enter pine stands. Interpretive panels along the route discuss forest ecology.

At the tip there's a gazebo to get out of the sun (or escape a summer thunderstorm). Enjoy the view before continuing west to see the ancient **bristlecone pines**. This is the breeziest spot in the park, so carry a windbreaker and hold on to your hat. A short ascent leads back to the parking lot, but bear left when you reach the paved path to **Yovimpa Point**, a fenced-in overlook at the edge of sheer drop-offs.

DAY HIKES

Bryce is a relatively small park and most trails are day hikes around and into Bryce Amphitheater, home to the highest concentration of hoodoos. Hikes range from easy walks on paved paths along the rim (with some stretches suitable for wheelchairs) to steep switchbacks up and down sometimes muddy, sometimes dusty, packed-earth trails. Further south or north on the plateau, you won't see as many hoodoos – or as many people.

NAVAJO LOOP TRAIL

Duration 1–2 hours
Distance 1.3 miles
Difficulty Moderate–difficult
Start/Finish Sunset Point
Nearest Town Tropic, Panguitch (p170)
Transportation Park shuttle
Summary This sometimes-steep hike is short but spectacular. From the trailhead at Sunset Point, you drop right into the canyon beneath towering hoodoos that dwarf onlookers.

This popular trail passes alongside Thor's Hammer, the park's most famous rock formation; beneath Two Bridges, a pair of small water-carved arches; and through Wall Street, a narrow canyon with steep rock walls that reveal only a sliver of sky above. It's a steep ascent and descent, but the trail is clearly marked and fairly wide. Those in reasonably good shape won't have a problem. Rangers strongly recommend hiking it clockwise to avoid a steep descent through Wall Street, a notorious ankle-buster. To lengthen your hike by 30 minutes to an hour, you could also start at Queen's Garden Trail; see below.

From the wide, fenced-in viewing area at Sunset Point, follow signs for the Navajo Loop. The trail drops immediately into a switchback, then forks about 100 yards ahead. Take the left fork, which leads past **Thor's Hammer** down a long slope to the canyon floor. Entering the canyon, you can follow the sign on your left to see Two Bridges.

At the canyon floor, turn right to continue the loop and ascend back to the rim. Sometimes closed due to rockfall (check ahead with rangers), **Wall Street** features 100ft walls which block much of the sunlight, keeping the canyon shady and cool. The giant Douglas fir trees towering between the walls are more than 750 years old!

To the left of the Wall Street trail, the **Silent City** looms large. If the spur trail through the tunnel on your left is open, take a quick jaunt to look down on these eerie pinnacles. The trail finishes with a steep ascent and some 30 switchbacks that lead to the rim.

QUEEN'S GARDEN TRAIL

Duration 1–2 hours
Distance 1.8 miles
Difficulty Moderate
Start/Finish Sunrise Point
Nearest Towns Tropic, Panguitch (p170)
Transportation Park shuttle
Summary Good for kids, the easiest trail into the canyon makes a gentle descent over sloping erosional fins. It passes elegant hoodoo formations but stops short of the canyon floor.

The hike to Queen's Garden is not a loop, but an in-and-out hike. You can also add the Queen's Garden Connecting Trail, part of the Navajo Loop–Queen's Garden Combination (right).

From Sunrise Point, follow signs to the trailhead off the Rim Trail. Views of the amphitheater as you descend are superb – a maze of colorful rock spires extends to Bryce Point, and deep-green pines dot the canyon floor beneath undulating slopes seemingly tie-dyed pink, orange and white. As you drop below the rim, watch for the stark and primitive **bristlecone pines**, which at Bryce are about 1600 years old (specimens in California are 5000 years old). These ancient trees' dense needles cluster like foxtails on the ends of the branches.

After a series of switchbacks, turn right and follow signs to Queen's Garden. The short spur from the main trail passes through a tunnel and emerges among exceptionally beautiful hoodoo castles in striking whites and oranges amid rich-green pines. After looping around a high wall and passing through two more tunnels, bear right and follow signs to **Queen Victoria**. The trail's namesake monarch peers down from a white-capped rock, perched atop her throne, lording over her kingdom.

Return to the rim or link up with the Navajo Loop via the Queen's Garden Connecting Trail, which drops to the canyon floor.

NAVAJO LOOP–QUEEN'S GARDEN COMBINATION

Duration 2–3 hours
Distance 2.9 miles
Difficulty Moderate
Start/Finish Sunrise Point
Nearest Towns Tropic, Panguitch (p170)
Transportation Park shuttle
Summary The most popular route in the park, and fairly gentle, it hits Bryce's signature features in a relatively short amount of time, despite the sometimes-steep grade.

Begin with Queen's Garden to avoid the steep descent through Wall Street (it does a number on ankles). Check ahead with rangers for trail-closure information, particularly after winter.

Start at Sunrise Point and follow the Queen's Garden Trail description (left). Follow signs for the Queen's Garden Connecting Trail, which descends to the garden of spires and follows the canyon floor. Another advantage of taking this trail is

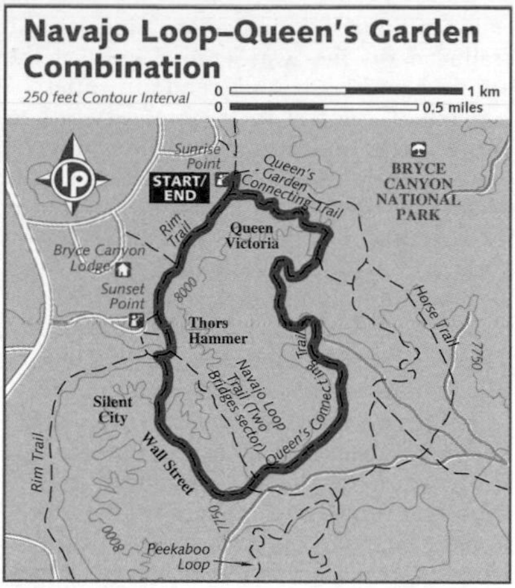

time spent on the canyon floor, where tall pines provide shade and offer perspective on oversized hoodoos. The final push, a steep ascent through **Wall Street** and past the **Silent City**, is the more visually stunning of the two trails. If Wall Street is closed due to rockfall, opt to ascend to the rim via the Two Bridges side of the Navajo Loop Trail (see p154).

Before you top out on the rim, detour right a short distance to see **Thor's Hammer**. Then stroll back to Sunrise Point along the Rim Trail, gazing into the canyon for yet another perspective on the hoodoos.

PEEKABOO LOOP TRAIL

Duration 3–5 hours
Distance 5.5 miles from Bryce Point
Difficulty Difficult
Start/Finish Bryce Point
Nearest Towns Tropic, Panguitch (p170)
Transportation Park shuttle
Summary An ideal day hike, Peekaboo Loop Trail sees the most variety of terrain and scenery in Bryce, with 1500ft to 1800ft of cumulative elevation changes.

Access to this circular trail is via either the Navajo Loop (p154) or the Queen's Garden Connecting Trail (p155). The following description starts from Bryce Point – if starting from Sunrise Point it's a 6.6-mile hike; from Sunset Point it's 5 miles.

The Peekaboo Loop Trail is also a horse trail, so expect to see occasional teams. They move slowly, so you'll have plenty of advance warning. Stock animals have right of way – step off the trail and let them pass undisturbed. If you don't want to navigate around horse droppings, consider another route. But views here are among the best in the park, particularly of the Wall of Windows, the Silent City and the Fairy Castle. You'll also find shady spots to rest, a picnic area and pit toilets (the latter are on the loop, just west of its intersection with the connecting trail to Bryce Point).

This trail rises and falls many times. Be prepared for a workout. If you're afraid of heights, be forewarned that in places you'll pass sheer drops, though the trail is wide enough for a horse, so don't worry.

From Bryce Point follow signs to the Peekaboo Connecting Trail, just east of the parking area. Bear left at the fork where you'll descend 1.1 miles down the connecting trail. You'll pass through mixed conifers, then swoop out along a gray-white limestone fin beneath the Bryce Point overlook. Further down the trail, hoodoo columns take on a bright-orange hue. After passing through a man-made tunnel, look for the **Alligator** in the white rock ahead. As you work your way down the switchbacks, watch for the **Wall of Windows**, which juts above bright-orange hoodoos atop a sheer vertical cliff face perpendicular to the canyon rim. The windows line the top of this wall.

At the loop trail junction, bear right. As you pass beneath healthy fir and spruce trees, you'll spot a few blackened snags – victims of electrical storms, not forest fires. The plateau's high elevation and isolated trees attract lightning. Also look for ancient bristlecone pines; an inch of these trees' trunks represents 100 years' growth.

Climbing a saddle, you'll rise to eye level with the hoodoo tops before dropping over the other side to the cluster of delicate red spires at **Fairy Castle**. Midway around, just past the turnoff for the Navajo Loop, the trail climbs again to spectacular views of the Silent City and passes beneath the **Cathedral**, a majestic wall of buttress-like hoodoos. The rolling trail skirts the Wall of Windows, threads through a tunnel and switchbacks down. Notice the rapidly changing views as you pass the huge Wall of

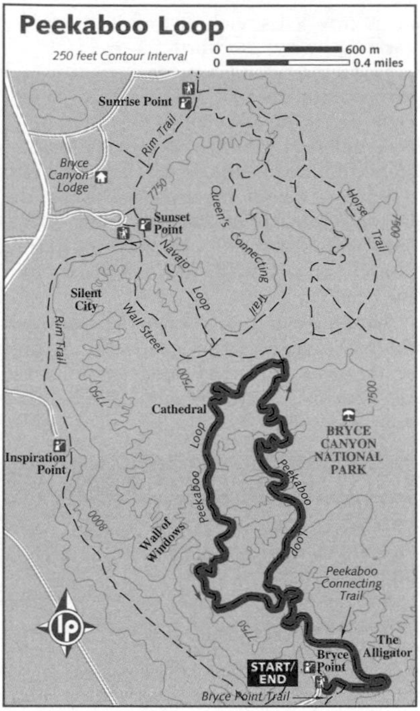

Windows. The trail turns west and climbs, then drops again amid more hoodoos. As you approach the Bryce Point trail, take the spur on your right to the lush green rest area near the horse corral for a cooldown or picnic before climbing out of the canyon.

RIM TRAIL

Duration 2–3 hours
Distance 5.5 miles one way
Difficulty Easy-moderate
Start Bryce Point
Finish Fairyland Point
Nearest Towns Tropic, Panguitch (p170)
Transportation Park shuttle
Summary With great views, this trail hugs the canyon rim, stretching from the south end of Bryce Amphitheater at Bryce Point all the way to Fairyland Point, near the northern park boundary.

Sections of this trail are level, particularly between Sunrise and Sunset Points, where the path is paved and wheelchair accessible. Log rail fences mark vertical drop-offs in many places. In other spots you'll ascend moderately steep, wooded rises to seek shade beneath the pines, watch wildlife or soak up vibrant displays of spring wildflowers. The colors in the rock pop out most when lit by the morning or afternoon sun.

You can join the trail anywhere along its 5.5-mile route – just keep in mind that unless the shuttle is running or you arrange to be picked up, you'll have to walk back. If you plan on taking the shuttle, note that buses don't stop at Fairyland.

You'll find restrooms and drinking water at Sunset Point, and the general store and snack bar (both open spring through fall) near Sunrise Point, the approximate midpoint of the hike. You can also duck into Bryce Canyon Lodge for lunch, restrooms and drinking water.

Remember that Bryce sits atop a sloping plateau. The north end of the Rim Trail is lower than the south end, so it's downhill to walk from Bryce Point to Fairyland Point, though the trail rises and falls in a few spots, particularly in its climb from Sunrise Point to North Campground.

During the walk, you'll leave behind Bryce Amphitheater and arrive above Campbell Canyon and Fairyland Amphitheater. You'll find fewer formations at this end of the park, but giant Boat Mesa and her high cliffs rise majestically to the north.

From Bryce Point to Inspiration Point the trail skirts the canyon rim atop white cliffs, revealing gorgeous formations, including the **Wall of Windows**. After passing briefly through trees, it continues along the ridgetop to the uppermost level of **Inspiration Point**, 1.3 miles from Bryce Point.

The leg to Sunset Point drops 200ft in 0.75 miles, winding its way along limestone-capped cliffs that yield to orange sandstone fins. Below the rim the **Silent City** rises in all its hoodoo glory; the lower you go, the higher the rock spires rise up beside you.

At **Sunset Point** you may wish to detour along the Navajo Loop Trail (p154) for a taste of the canyon; you can reemerge on the Rim Trail further ahead by adding the Queen's Garden Connecting Trail (p155). Otherwise, stay the course and look for **Thor's Hammer** as you continue the 0.5-mile stroll along a paved path to **Sunrise Point** – the

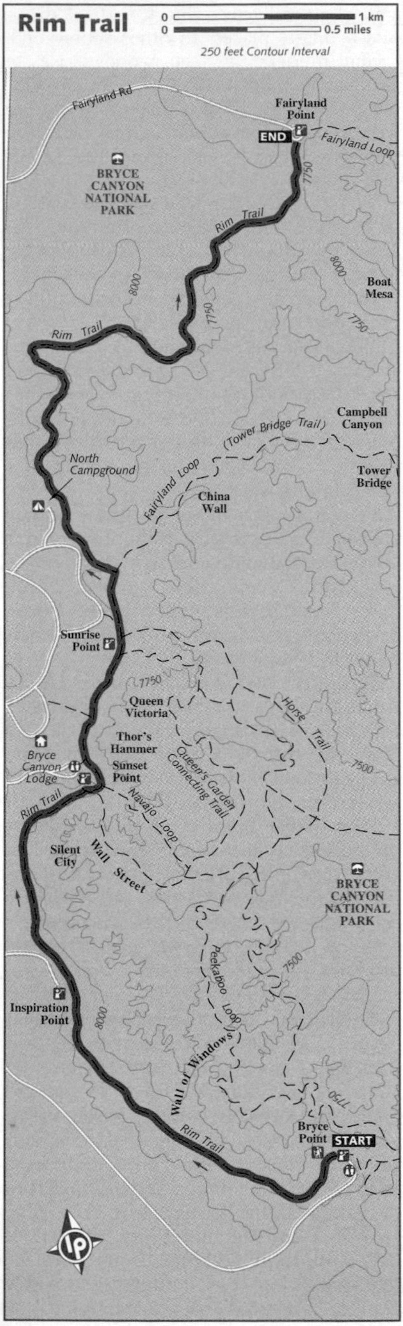

most crowded stretch of trail in the entire park. The views are worth it.

Past Sunset Point, crowds thin as the trail climbs 150ft toward North Campground. Fork left at the Fairyland Loop Trail junction, unless you'd like to follow the moderately difficult, 3-mile round-trip spur into the canyon (950ft elevation loss) to see the window-laced **China Wall** and **Tower Bridge**, twin arches between chunky rock spires. Otherwise, watch for these features from the Rim Trail.

Topping out near North Campground, the path ambles across gently rolling hills on the forested plateau before rejoining the canyon rim at **Fairyland Point**, 2.5 miles from Sunrise Point.

FAIRYLAND LOOP TRAIL

Duration 4–5 hours
Distance 8 miles
Difficulty Difficult
Start/Finish Fairyland Point
Nearest Towns Tropic, Panguitch (p170)
Transportation Private
Summary A great day hike and a good workout, with multiple elevation changes. Unlike Bryce Amphitheater, Fairyland is spared the crowds.

This trail begins at Fairyland Point and circles the majestic cliffs of flat-topped, 8076ft Boat Mesa, emerging on the rim near Sunrise Point. There are fewer hoodoos in this area. The last 2.5 miles of the loop follow the Rim Trail back to the trailhead. Note that the park shuttle doesn't stop at Fairyland.

This trail is difficult primarily because it meanders – in and out of the hoodoos, down into washes, up and over saddles etc. Carry plenty of water, and pace yourself.

From the point, the trail dips gradually below the rim – watch your footing on the narrow sections. To the south, Boat Mesa stands between you and views of the park. A short walk leads past ancient **bristlecone pines**, some clinging precariously to the ragged cliffs, their 1000-plus-year-old roots curled up like wizened fingers. Looping around hoodoos that rise like castle turrets and towers, the trail soon drops to the canyon floor and a seasonal wash. Much of the north-facing terrain here holds its snowpack until May, sometimes June.

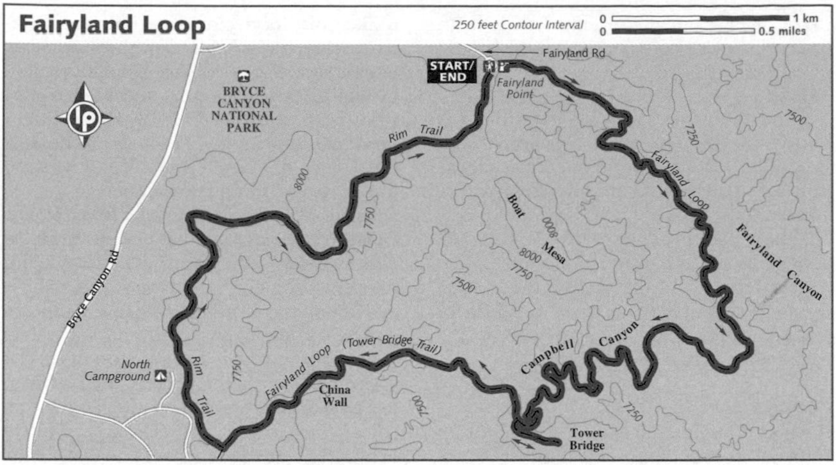

At **Fairyland Canyon**, 600ft below your starting point, towers of deep-orange stone rise like giant totem poles. The trail rises and falls before traversing a ridge toward **Campbell Canyon**. As you walk beneath Boat Mesa's great cliffs, notice how the formation comes to a point like the bow of a ship – you'll quickly understand how it got its name.

Zigzagging up and down, the trail eventually reaches a seasonal wash on the floor of Campbell Canyon. Keep an eye out for **Tower Bridge**, which connects three spires to two windows. To reach the base of the formation, take the clearly marked dead-end spur from the wash. From Tower Bridge it's a 950ft climb in 1.5 miles to the Rim Trail, some of it strenuous. En route, to your left, look for the long, white **China Wall** and its little windows. A look back at Boat Mesa shows the changing vistas of canyon country.

BACKCOUNTRY HIKES

Only 1% of park visitors venture into the backcountry, virtually guaranteeing those who do a peaceful hike. Unlike other parks, most of Bryce's stunning features are in the front country. The backcountry trails were originally made as boundary and fire-control routes, not for the landscape itself. If you come here, it's for the solitude. You won't encounter as many hoodoo formations as you would on day hikes through the major amphitheaters, but you will get a keen sense of the park's three distinct plant and animal communities as you pass through forest and meadow, with distant views of rock formations.

Most backcountry trails are covered with snow from late October to March or April; even in May, snowpack sometimes obscures sections of trail. June and September are ideal, while in July and August you'll have to contend with thunderstorms. Mosquitoes are rare, but cedar gnats are annoying in early summer. At any time of year, bring a fleece jacket for the cool nights.

Bryce features two backcountry trails: the Under-the-Rim Trail and the Riggs Spring Loop Trail. Due to its length and diverse terrain, the Under-the-Rim Trail is the premier overnight hike. This one-way trail, 500ft to 1000ft beneath the rim, roughly parallels the scenic drive. You'll neither hear nor see the road until you return to the rim.

The park's southernmost trail, the Riggs Spring Loop, can be done as a day hike from Rainbow or Yovimpa Points, offering an excellent backcountry sampler. Because of the trail's great elevation loss, however, most hikers make this an overnight hike. A slower trip also lets you enjoy the transition from spectacular Pink Cliffs to rolling green hills and canyons.

If you plan on hiking the Under-the-Rim Trail, Riggs Spring or any trails at the park's south end, pick up the medium-scale *National Geographic Trails Illustrated Map*

($12), which shows the entire park, with brief trail descriptions and topographic lines.

Safety

Beyond the usual safety preparations for hiking in the deserts of southern Utah (see p283), the primary concern is elevation (see p281). Take it slow until you're acclimated.

When you pick up your permit, ask about availability of water along your route, which depends on the season and annual drought cycles. Plan to carry a gallon of water per person, per day. All water in the backcountry must be purified.

Permits

A backcountry permit costs $5 to $15 for up to 14 days, depending on the number of hikers in your party. Permits are only available at the visitor center between 8am and one hour prior to the center's closing time. You cannot place an advance order by telephone or email, but you can make reservations in person up to 48 hours in advance. Processing permits takes time; plan to spend at least 30 minutes at the visitor center. In winter you must have an interview with the backcountry ranger to discuss hazards.

Backcountry Camping

Hikers may camp only at designated backcountry campsites. Bryce offers 10 individual campsites, each with a six-person capacity, and two group sites, each with a 15-person capacity.

You'll be assigned a campsite when you purchase your backcountry permit. You may only stay at a particular site for a maximum of three nights.

RIGGS SPRING LOOP TRAIL

Duration 4–5 hours (or overnight)
Distance 8.8 miles
Difficulty Difficult
Start/Finish Rainbow Point
Nearest Towns Tropic, Panguitch (p170)
Transportation Park shuttle
Summary This tough trail loops from the tip of the Paunsaugunt Plateau, descending beneath the spectacular Pink Cliffs through spruce, fir and aspen, then through ponderosa pines to a desert habitat of sagebrush and scrub oak.

Make this loop clockwise, not counterclockwise; it's a safer way through steep terrain. Extend the hike to an overnight outing to ease your pace and soak up the solitude. Starting at Rainbow Point, follow the Bristlecone Loop Trail to the turnoff for the Under-the-Rim Trail and follow signs to the Riggs Spring Loop Trail.

The trail descends the Pink Cliffs onto the **Promontory**, a ridgeline that juts out from the plateau in a sweeping arc south. Molly's Nipple rises to the southeast; Navajo Mountain is on the horizon 80 miles to the east-southeast.

After dropping off the Promontory along treed slopes, you'll double back north for grand views of the Pink Cliffs, then descend to **Coral Hollow campsite**. This site lies beneath oak and pine trees 3.6 miles from, and 1200ft below, Rainbow Point; there's no water here.

From Coral Hollow you'll loop below Yovimpa Point on a gradual descent through pines to **Mutton Hollow**. **Riggs Spring campsite** (7480ft) sits amid pines at the base of this hollow. Of the three camps on this loop, this one is most idyllic. You'll almost always find water at Riggs Spring, hemmed in by a log fence. This is the lowest point along the trail.

Onward, the increasingly steep trail climbs past towering ponderosa pines en route to **Yovimpa Pass**, which lies atop a plateau at 8360ft. The higher you get, the better the views of the approaching cliffs. Perched atop this plateau, the **Yovimpa Pass campsite** provides little shade but often has water.

The last 1.6 miles of the trail skirt the edge of the plateau through woods before rejoining the rim at **Yovimpa Point**. Breaks in the forest reveal views of the Grand Staircase and the hoodoos below Rainbow Point.

UNDER-THE-RIM TRAIL

Duration 3 days
Distance 22.9 miles one way
Difficulty Moderate–difficult
Start Bryce Point
Finish Rainbow Point
Nearest Towns Tropic, Panguitch (p170)
Transportation Park shuttle
Summary Ideal for getting away from it all, this multiday hike skirts beneath cliffs, through amphitheaters and amid pines and aspens. Originally fire trails, they lack some of the drama of backcountry hikes elsewhere.

Starting at Bryce Point and ending at Rainbow Point, the park's primary backcountry trail can be hiked in two days, though three are recommended. In either direction you'll face a hefty ascent the last 3 miles. By hiking north to south, you'll have the sun at your back in the afternoon and Rainbow Point as the grand finale.

Running nearly the length of the park, the trail rises from the piñon juniper community (6600ft to 7000ft), through the ponderosa pine community (7000ft to 8500ft) to the fir-spruce community (8500ft to 9100ft), touching the rim only at the trailheads.

Descending from the scenic drive, four connecting trails link up with the Under-the-Rim Trail, each near a backcountry campsite. These connecting trails allow hikers to approach any section as a day hike. Rangers can offer details on the connecting trails. You could also set up base camp at one of the sites and take day hikes in either direction. If you have the time, extend your trek south along the 8.8-mile Riggs Spring Loop Trail (p160).

This is a one-way hike, so consider leaving a car at one or both ends. Shuttle service (p149) to Rainbow Point may be available – inquire at the visitor center. Hitchhiking is prohibited in the park, but hikers can sometimes catch rides back to Bryce Point without much difficulty.

Day 1: Bryce Point to Right Fork Swamp Canyon Campsite

4–6 hours, 10.5 miles

From Bryce Point the trail descends steeply almost due east, then swings south. After 0.5 miles you'll wind down to a ridge, where the earth changes from gray to orange. Over the next 0.5 miles Rainbow Point comes into view above the ridge in the foreground.

As the trail traces a south-facing promontory, look north for a grand panorama of the Pink Cliffs. On the right (west) the Right Fork Yellow Creek forms a steep-sided drainage. Two miles in you'll pass the **Hat Shop**, its gray boulder caps perched atop spindly conglomerate stands.

At the base of this descent, 2.8 miles from Bryce Point, is the **Right Fork Yellow Creek campsite**, a good spot in a clearing beside the creek, which runs all year.

From the campsite, follow the left (east) bank of the creek for half a mile, then cross

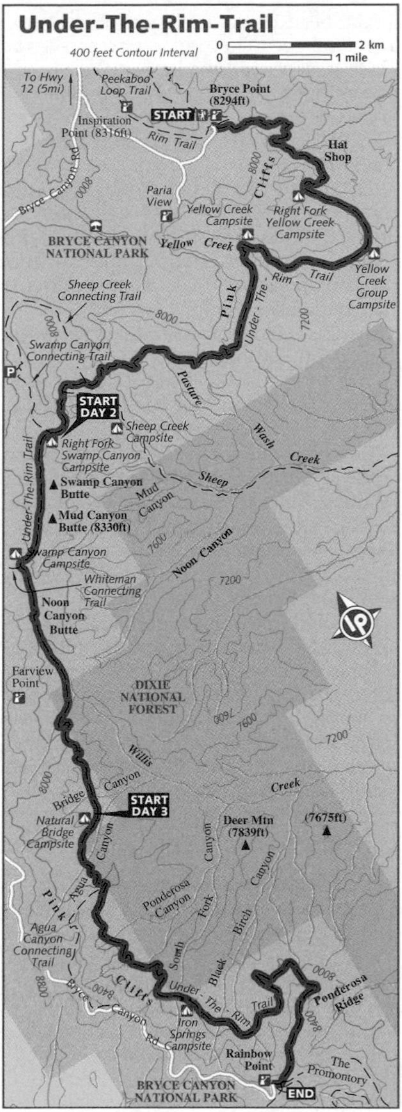

it and bear south. Here the landscape is a semidesert, with little shade and plenty of pungent sage growing in the sandy soil. As the trail turns west, you'll pass the **Yellow Creek group campsite** on the left.

A quarter-mile beyond the campsite, you'll reach **Yellow Creek**. The trail follows the creek and climbs toward the Pink Cliffs at the head of the creek and Paria View, 1000ft above. The trail soon crosses the creek; cairns point the way.

Another 0.25 miles brings you to the **Yellow Creek campsite**, in plenty of shade beside the creek. It's a great spot to watch the sunset.

From here you'll turn southwest up a short, steep hill. The trail undulates for about 2 miles, crossing a slope between two amphitheaters. After 1.5 miles the trail drops into Pasture Wash. Follow cairns to the south edge of the wash and look for a sharp uphill turn, where the trail visibly zigzags up and out of the wash. The view (north to south) of Swamp Canyon, Mud Canyon and Noon Canyon Buttes will reward your effort.

Descend into the valley to the junction with the **Sheep Creek Connecting Trail**, which climbs 2 miles to the scenic drive. A well-marked spur leads 0.5 miles south to the **Sheep Creek campsite**, its beauty second only to the Yellow Creek site; you can usually find water here.

From the junction, the trail climbs 150ft – crossing from the Sheep Creek amphitheater to the Swamp Canyon amphitheater – then descends into Swamp Canyon amid a stand of large quaking aspens. On the left (southeast), in a clearing among large ponderosa pines, is the **Right Fork Swamp Canyon campsite**; water is sometimes available in upper Swamp Canyon, 100yd north of the campsite.

Day 2: Right Fork Swamp Canyon Campsite to Natural Bridge Campsite

1½–2½ hours, 4.6 miles

Three hundred feet past the campsite is the junction with the mile-long Swamp Canyon Connecting Trail, which climbs north to the scenic drive. From the connecting trail junction, you'll climb steadily south, then turn west up switchbacks. Just beyond, at 8200ft, is the **Swamp Canyon campsite**. Although there's not much flat ground, and the site is near the trail, it's cool in summer. You'll sometimes find water 0.25 miles up the Whiteman Connecting Trail, which climbs 0.9 miles to the scenic drive.

Beyond camp the trail passes aspens and pines, then descends to the base of Farview Cliffs. From here you'll skirt **Willis Creek** for a mile until it turns southeast. You may find it difficult to distinguish the trail from other small creeks; bear south and west.

The trail ducks into Dixie National Forest for 0.25 miles, then curves sharply east to climb an eroded sandstone slope southwest of Willis Creek. At the top, the sandy trail snakes around the east edge of a promontory for gorgeous views of the Pink Cliffs.

Descend to a southern tributary of Willis Creek and continue 0.5 miles (you may need to cross several times if the water is running high) to the **Natural Bridge campsite**, which lacks water.

Day 3: Natural Bridge Campsite to Rainbow Point

3–5 hours, 7.8 miles

Half a mile out of camp, the trail traverses a sage meadow toward Agua Canyon. Crossing this canyon may prove tricky: on older topo maps, the trail turns slightly west and cuts straight across the canyon, but due to floods you now need to hike up canyon 0.75 miles, then switchback up the canyon's south ridge. When in doubt, follow the cairns. The switchbacks are snowed under until late spring. Atop this ridge, the Agua Canyon Connecting Trail climbs 1.6 miles to the scenic drive.

From the connecting trail junction, you'll skirt a pink promontory, descend into Ponderosa Canyon, then zigzag up and down to South Fork Canyon. Just past the head of the canyon, you'll reach the **Iron Spring campsite** on your right; the east-facing ridge leaves little room to spread out. Amid a grove of aspens 600ft up canyon (southwest) from the campsite, **Iron Spring** supplies year-round water. The turnoff for the spring lies 100yd north of the campsite.

The trail continues its undulating rhythm, dipping to cross both arms of Black Birch Canyon, where directional cairns are sometimes obscured by debris. After clambering over the lower slopes of a northwest-jutting promontory, you'll enter the southernmost amphitheater of Bryce Canyon's Pink Cliffs.

The trail traces the hammer-shaped ridge below Rainbow Point, climbing steadily and offering unsurpassed views. Ascend the final 1.5 miles up the back (south) side of the amphitheater to the rim. You'll cross the Riggs Spring Loop Trail just beneath the rim, 100yd east of the Rainbow Point parking lot. While the urge to peer over

PRAIRIE DOGS

Although prairie dogs once numbered in the billions across the West, a century of shooting and poisoning at the hands of ranchers drove the Utah prairie dog to near extinction by 1950. This cheeky, dynamic animal was as important as the grassland ecosystem it depended on, but decades passed before anyone realized how critical this loss was and tried to reverse it.

In 1974 scientists established a small prairie dog colony in the meadows at Bryce Canyon National Park and carefully monitored these small rodents (named 'dogs' by the Lewis and Clark expedition because the animals communicate with barks). Each March, as snows begin to melt, about 300 prairie dogs emerge from hibernation and begin a luxurious summer of calling, mating and fattening up on sweet grasses.

The meadows around the visitor center and campgrounds are now home to this rare animal, and park visitors often stop to watch their lively antics. When grasses dry out in July, prairie dogs return underground to begin their eight-month hibernation. The park asks that you stay out of the colonies and avoid the temptation to feed or pester the animals.

the rim is irresistible, use extreme caution, as the edges are unstable.

OTHER ACTIVITIES

When your feet grow tired of hiking, you can explore the amphitheaters on horseback, or perch beside a meadow to bird-watch. Rangers lead walks and talks, and at night the sky glows with the lights of a million stars. For courses offered in the park, see p264.

HORSEBACK RIDING

Horses are permitted in the park on specific trails, most notably the Peekaboo Loop Trail (p156). If you don't have the energy to hike this fantastic trail, or if you have little ones who can't walk that far, book a half-day trail ride. Alternatively, you can descend the canyon on a two-hour round-trip ride below the Queen's Garden Trail (p155). There are no overnight backcountry tours within the park.

Try the excellent **Canyon Trail Rides** (☎ 435-679-8665; www.canyonrides.com; PO Box 128, Tropic, UT 84776; 2hr/half-day ride $50/75), which operates out of Bryce Canyon Lodge. It uses both horses and mules (mules offer a smoother ride). There's also **Ruby's Red Canyon Horseback Rides** (☎ 435-834-5341, 800-468-8660; www.rubysinn.com; 1000 S Hwy 63; 90min/half-day/full-day ride $55/75/125), based at Ruby's Inn (p166). For rides into Dixie National Forest or BLM lands around Bryce, call **Scenic Rim Trail Rides** (☎ 435-679-8761, 800-679-5859; www.brycecanyonhorseback.com; Ruby's Inn, 1000 S Hwy 63); rates match those for the national park. All outfitters have a limit of 220 pounds for riders.

If you want to bring your own horse to Bryce, you must coordinate with Canyon Trail Rides. Contact the park for regulations. There are no backcountry campgrounds suitable for stock animals.

WATCHING WILDLIFE

Bryce Canyon is home to 59 mammal species, 11 reptile species, four amphibian species and more than 1000 insect species. As many as 175 bird species pass through annually, though large, highly adaptable ravens are among the few birds found year-round in the park. If you're lucky, you might also spot California condors (see p68) or a peregrine falcon. Keep an eye to the ground for the threatened Utah prairie dog (see the boxed text, above).

For more information, pick up books and wildlife charts at the visitor center, or visit www.nps.gov/brca/naturescience/animals.htm.

BIKING

Several companies lead bicycle tours in and around Bryce, including **Backroads** (☎ 510-527-1555, 800-462-2848; www.backroads.com; 801 Cedar St, Berkeley, CA 94710-1800), **Rim Tours** (☎ 435-259-5223, 800-626-7335; www.rimtours.com; 1233 S Hwy 191, Moab, UT 84532) and **Western Spirit Cycling** (☎ 435-259-8732, 800-845-2453; www.westernspirit.com; 478 Mill Creek Rd, Moab, UT 84532).

RANGER PROGRAMS

From early summer until fall, rangers lead rim walks, hikes amid the hoodoos, short geology lectures, evening programs, kids' ecology walks and astronomy talks, with

ESSENTIALS: SUDS & SCRUBS

In the park, the showers and coin-op laundry facilities for Sunset Campground (right) are actually found at **Bryce Canyon General Store** (☎ 435-834-5361; ⏰ 8am-8pm summer, to 6pm spring & fall, closed Nov-Mar). North of the park, **Ruby's Campground** (☎ 435-834-5301; 1000 S Hwy 63; ⏰ 7am-9pm) offers coin-operated laundry; buy soap next door at the general store. It also has showers.

telescopes. Check the *Hoodoo* newspaper or ask at the visitor center for current schedules, or visit the park website for general information. If you time your visit to coincide with the full moon (and clear skies), don't miss the **moonlight hike**, a two-hour stroll among the hoodoos; register at the visitor center on the day of the hike, but book early due to limited capacity.

KIDS' ACTIVITIES

When you arrive at the park, stop by the visitor center to pick up a **Junior Ranger Activity Guide**. Once kids complete certain activities, they can return to the visitor center to receive a badge from a ranger. The visitor center also sells coloring books specific to Bryce, as well as bookmark magnifying glasses and 3-D View-Master reels.

WINTER ACTIVITIES

In winter Bryce's rosy rock formations and pine forests wear a blanket of fresh powder. Though nighttime temperatures can drop below freezing for more than 200 consecutive nights, days are often mild and sunny, perfect for snowshoeing or cross-country skiing. Snowfall averages 100in per winter. Visitors become scarce, and the dry, light powder is perfect for snowshoeing and cross-country skiing. Ten miles of Bryce's dedicated ski trails (ungroomed) connect with 20 additional miles of groomed trails through Dixie National Forest. Trail use in the national forest is free, though snowmobiles are also granted access, so keep watch for traffic. Rent skis, snowshoes and snow boots (half-day $7, full day $10) at **Ruby's Inn** (p166); it also has trail maps. You can also ski from here.

When snow and staff are sufficient, rangers offer guided snowshoe hikes along the plateau top. Inquire at the visitor center.

Every Presidents Day weekend in February, the **Bryce Canyon Winter Festival** is hosted at Ruby's Inn. In addition to races, there are free ski and photography clinics, kids' races and snow sculptures.

SLEEPING

The park is home to two campgrounds and a lodge. However, most visitors stay at lodgings just north or west of the park, or 11 miles east, in the town of Tropic (p167). If nearby lodgings are full, consider staying in or around Panguitch (p171), 24 miles west of the park, or Kodachrome Basin State Park (p185), 19 miles east.

Dixie National Forest, which surrounds Bryce Canyon, offers several campgrounds within a short drive of the park. For a complete list, visit www.fs.fed.us/dxnf (the Powell and Escalante ranger districts are closest to Bryce). The ranger stations in Panguitch and Escalante can provide maps and information.

IN THE PARK

Camping

Bryce's two campgrounds are extremely popular. With recent renovations, they have updated bathroom facilities as well as recycling (at entrances).

North Campground (☎ reservations 877-444-6777; www.recreation.gov; sites $; ⏰ year-round) Just off the scenic drive near the visitor center, this popular campground is enormous, with 101 sites. It's divided into four loops. In summer Loops A and B are for RVs over 20ft only and provide many pull-through spots. Loops C and D accommodate vehicles less than 20ft. Loops A and B sit up high amid tall trees, while Loop C is closest to the canyon rim (sites 59 through 61 have canyon views, though little privacy). Loop D sits on a hill amid small to medium-sized trees. All sites include campfire rings, and a short walk from the campground takes you to showers, a coin laundry and a general store (open April through October). A fee-for-use sanitary dump station is available in summer months at the south end of North Campground. Reservations are accepted early May through late September.

Sunset Campground (sites $; ⏰ late spring-fall) Just south of Sunset Point, this 102-site campground offers more shade than North

Campground but has few amenities beyond flush toilets (for laundry, showers and groceries, see boxed text, opposite). Inquire about availability at the visitor center, and secure your site early. Loop A allows RVs, though it has few pull-through spots (generators are allowed 8am to 8pm). Loops B and C are reserved for vehicles under 20ft. Loop B offers less shade, while Loop C's sites vary widely in quality; for shade and privacy, try for sites on the outer ring. Twenty sites can be reserved May through September.

Hotels

Bryce Canyon Lodge (☎ 435-834-8700, 877-386-4383; www.brycecanyonforever.com; r $$-$$$; ⏲ Apr-Oct) Built in the 1920s, this lodge is the essence of old Western park grandeur. The only lodge still standing in its original form from the parks' railroad boom, it exudes rustic mountain charm. Flanked by hickory rocking chairs, a stone fireplace dominates the lobby, where orange-hued, wood-paneled walls and ceiling echo the color of canyon hoodoos. Ranging from modern hotel units to freestanding cabins, most rooms are in satellite buildings and decor is significantly dated, with dull browns and greens. Hotel rooms are in discrete, two-story wood-and-timber buildings and feature private balconies or porches and bathrooms tiled in attractive stone.

The cabins have their inherent charm, with peaked roofs with exposed raw-bark timbers, gas fireplaces, private baths and small porches. All are duplexes. Be warned: the walls prove thin if the neighbors decide to get noisy. Furnishings are dated, but the creaky porch and woodsy setting are pure romance.

All accommodations include two queen beds; none have air-conditioning or TV. In summer, evening programs are presented by rangers in the lodge auditorium, which boasts a 30ft cathedral ceiling and giant fireplace. You'll also find a gift shop but no bar. Wi-fi is slated to arrive soon. Pets are not allowed.

BRYCE CANYON CITY

The village of Bryce Canyon City is located just outside the park. Not an actual town, it is a growing tourist center with minimarts, outfitters, a gas station and hotels.

Camping

If you're unable to secure a reservation, and don't arrive early enough to get a site in the park, you could spend a night at a Bryce Canyon City campground and return early in the morning to grab a spot in the park.

Bryce Canyon Pines Campground & RV Park (☎ 435-834-5441, 800-892-7923; www.brycecanyonmotel.com; Hwy 12; sites $; ⏲ Apr-Oct) Across the street from the hotel, 4 miles west of the Hwy 12/63 junction, this campground sits behind a gas station and general store. The roadside location is convenient, but not exactly ambient. Showers are available for guests. Note that at 7700ft it can be windy and cold in spring.

Ruby's Campground (☎ 435-834-5301, 866-866-6616; www.brycecanyoncampgrounds.com; Hwy 63; sites $; ⏲ Apr-Oct; ♿) This crowded campground just outside Bryce, 3 miles north of the visitor center, boasts lots of amenities, including flush toilets, showers, drinking water, a coin laundry, electrical hookups, a dump station, restaurant, general store and a hot tub. Both cabins and tepees use shared camp bathroom facilities. Bring your own sleeping bag. While tepees require cots, the cabins have double bunks. Though over-the-top

REMINDERS OF RAILROAD DAYS

In the early 1920s, the Union Pacific Railroad saw vast profit potential in bringing tourists to the majestic but still-inaccessible canyons of southern Utah and northern Arizona. They funded and built great lodges laden with modern comforts at the Grand Canyon, Zion, Cedar Breaks and Bryce Canyon. Trains arrived at Cedar City, where guests were shuttled via motor coach on a loop the railroad dubbed the Grand Circle Tour.

Railroad brochures whet travelers' appetites for Bryce, 'probably the most astonishing blend of exquisite beauty and grotesque grandeur ever produced by the forces of erosion. It is not to be described, however imperfectly, except in the language of fancy.' Today Bryce Canyon Lodge, the last of the original lodges, is the final remnant of the long-lost era of luxury rail travel in America.

CAMPGROUNDS IN & AROUND BRYCE CANYON

Campground	Location	Number of sites	Elevation (ft)	Open	Reservations available?
In the Park					
North	Bryce Canyon	101	8000	year-round	early May-late Sep
Sunset	Bryce Canyon	102	8000	late spring-fall	May-Sep
Outside the Park					
Bryce Canyon Pines Campground & RV Park	Bryce Canyon City	24	7700	Apr-Oct	yes
King Creek	USFS Rd 287, near Tropic	37	8000	mid-May–Oct 1	no
KOA of Cannonville	Hwy 12, east of Tropic	80	6000	Mar-Dec	partial
Pine Lake	Clay Creek	33	8000	Jun-Sep	groups only
Red Canyon	Hwy 12, Red Canyon	37	7400	mid-May–Oct 1	no
Red Canyon RV Park	cnr Hwys 12 & 89	24	6500	Apr-Sep	partial
Ruby's Campground	Bryce Canyon City	200	8000	Apr-Oct	partial

Drinking Water · *Flush Toilets* · *Great for Families* · *Wheelchair Accessible* · *Dogs Allowed* · *Grocery Store Nearby* · *Restaurant Nearby*

commercial, it's nonetheless convenient. Online reservations and walk-ins accepted.

Hotels

Except for a few notable exceptions, lodgings at Bryce are nothing special. Expect motel rooms with fiberglass tub-shower combinations and plastic drinking cups by the sink. A coffeemaker is a luxury. For more character, book a B&B in nearby towns. Rates drop in the fall and spring; most properties close in winter.

Bryce Canyon Resort (435-834-5351, 800-834-0043; www.brycecanyonresort.com; cnr Hwys 12 & 63; r $-$$;) Four miles from the park, this is a great alternative to Ruby's Inn. Remodeled rooms include newer furnishings and extra amenities, while economy rooms are standard. Some units have kitchenettes. Cottages have kitchenettes and sleep up to six. Pets are $10 extra. There's also a small campground and restaurant (p169).

Bryce View Lodge (435-834-5180, 888-279-2304; www.bryceviewlodge.com; r $$) Geared to budget travelers, these 130 standard rooms are older and smaller than Ruby's Inn with fewer amenities, but joint ownership means there's free access to all the facilities across the street at Ruby's, including the pool and hot tub.

Bryce Canyon Grand Hotel (866-866-6634; www.brycecanyongrand.com; 30 N 100 East; r $$;) New in 2009, this Best Western hotel is the best digs in the area, with stylish, ample rooms, wi-fi in the rooms and a free breakfast bar. It's operated by the same family who owns Ruby's Inn, so all the amenities at Ruby's are available to guests of the Grand Hotel.

Bryce Canyon Pines (435-834-5441, 800-892-7923; www.brycecanyonmotel.com; Hwy 12; r $$; Apr-Oct;) If everything else is booked, check out these plain motel rooms, 4 miles west of the Hwy 12/63 junction. The complex is a bit dreary and rather outdated but the attached restaurant (p168) is a favorite of locals. There's also a small campground (p165).

Best Western Ruby's Inn (435-834-5341, 866-866-6616; www.rubysinn.com; 1000 S Hwy 63; r $$-$$$;) A gargantuan motel complex 1 mile north of the park entrance, Ruby's has 369 standard rooms with amenities like coffeemakers, hair dryers, ironing boards and irons. All rooms include two

Facilities	Description	Page
	Large, private and forested, recycling bins, good amenities and direct trail access.	164
	Shady, few amenities, best for last-minute availability in the park.	164
	Convenient behind gas station minimart but bare and lacking ambience.	165
	Woodsy and well-maintained, near river, popular with (loud) off-road vehicles (ORVs).	below
	Great for families, ample amenities include pool and roadside ambience.	below
	Pretty and forested with basic amenities, popular with ORVs.	below
	Lovely and private, trailside in pine forest with good amenities.	170
	Friendly roadside RV village, convenient but with little privacy.	170
	Packed with amenities, near the park entrance; little privacy.	165

Payphone Campfire Program RV Dump Station

beds, either queen- or king-size. The facilities are the major attraction. Open to nonguests, the sprawling property includes a grocery store (camping supplies, books, clothing and souvenirs), two gas stations, a post office, coin laundry, a pool and hot tub, showers, a foreign-currency exchange, gift shops, email kiosks, wi-fi, one-hour film processing and a liquor store (a rarity around here). The tour desk can book helicopter tours and horseback riding. Ruby's also rents bicycles and all-terrain vehicles (ATVs). In summer there's a nightly rodeo (except Sunday); it's best to make reservations in high season. Nonguests can use the internet cafe in the lobby.

TROPIC & AROUND
Camping
King Creek (☎ Powell Ranger District 435-676-8815, group reservations 877-444-6777; www.fs.fed.us/dxnf; sites $; ☉ mid-May–Oct 1) Near Bryce's western boundary, 3 miles west of the Hwy 12/63 junction then 7 miles south via unpaved USFS Rd 087, this woodsy, well-maintained, first-come, first-served 37-site campground is adjacent to Tropic Reservoir and the

Sevier River (bring bug spray). It's also popular with ATV riders (bring earplugs). Amenities include flush toilets, drinking water and a dump station.

KOA of Cannonville (☎ 435-679-8988; www.koa.com; Hwy 12; sites $; ☉ Mar-Dec; ☎ ☒) Particularly good for families, it provides lots of amenities (flush toilets, drinking water, dump station, electrical hookups etc, spotlessly clean bathrooms and showers). It's 5 miles east of Tropic, and has 80 sites and five cabins.

Pine Lake (☎ Escalante Ranger District 435-826-5400, group reservations 877-444-6777; www.fs.fed.us/dxnf; sites $; ☉ Jun-Sep) In a pretty pine forest near a reservoir, 11 miles north of the Hwy 12/63 junction then 6 miles east on unpaved Clay Creek. Powerboats aren't allowed, but expect ATVs. Only groups may reserve. There's no trash collection and amenities are limited to vault toilets and drinking water.

Hotels
Bryce Canyon Inn (☎ 435-679-8502, 800-592-1468; www.brycecanyoninn.com; 21 N Main St; r $; ☒ ☎) These immaculate pine-scented, roadside

DOG LODGING

Even picky pet owners laud **Pawz** (☎ 435-691-3696; www.pawzdogz.com), a down-home kennel located in rural sagebrush country. Features include indoor dog beds and yards with pools. It's 5 miles out of Panguitch but doggie pick ups are available in town with advance notice. There's both day camp and overnight options. Another acceptable option, **Canyon Park Animal Retreat** (☎ 435-679-8548),is in Tropic, 11 miles east of Bryce.

rooms feature quilted beds and free continental breakfast. Cabins are tightly spaced, but feature a refrigerator, coffeemaker and TV. There's also an on-site pizzeria (p169).

Bryce Valley Inn (☎ 435-679-8811, 800-442-1890; www.brycevalleyinn.com; 199 N Main St; r $; ☒) Standard rooms in a boxy setting; book online with a value club card for discounts.

Bryce Pioneer Village (☎ 435-679-8546, 800-222-0381; www.brycepioneervillage.com; 80 S Main St; cabins $; ☒) On the edge of town with 14 acres of land, these cabins are standard and a little cramped. There's also an RV campground featuring full electrical hookup and showers included in the camping fee.

our pick **Bryce Country Cabins** (☎ 435-679-8643, 888-679-8643; www.brycecountrycabins.com; 320 N Main St; cabins $-$$; ☒ ☎) Friendly and family-run, these well-designed pine cabins are centered around an outdoor fire pit perfect for stargazing around a bonfire. The only drawback is they're right on the main street. New deluxe cabins have cozy furniture and vaulted ceilings. Perks include TVs, coffeemakers, small porches and charm – it's among the best simple accommodations near Bryce.

Bullberry Inn (☎ 435-679-8820; www.bullberryinn. com; 412 S Hwy 12; r $-$$; ☒) Though the home dates only to 1998, this farmhouse-style inn serves up traditional Utah, down to the Bulberry jelly, a recipe that's been in the family for generations. The family gives a warm welcome and the country-cozy theme goes far – from ample log and bear themed rooms to a full country breakfast.

Bryce Trails B&B (☎ 435-679-8700, 866-215-5043; www.brycetrails.com; 1001 W Bryce Way; r $$-$$$; ☒) Reticent toward walk-ins, this tidy lodging nonetheless offers bright and slightly kitsch

Western theme rooms, some with deck or Jacuzzi. It's located 1 mile from Main St.

Stone Canyon Inn (☎ 435-679-8611, 866-489-4680; www.stonecanyoninn.com; 1220 Stone Canyon Lane; r $$-$$$; ☺ Feb-Nov; ☒) In a Wild West setting of scrub hills backed by technicolor sunsets, this stately stone-and-wood lodging offers adventure out the back door – you could stroll or bike until your heart's content. New cabins are spacious and luxuriantly private, though trumped by the charm of the main house, serving hot breakfasts with homemade pastries and breads. It's 1.3 miles from Main St.

EATING

Food around Bryce isn't nearly as good as the scenery. Service may be poky, coffee watered-down and vegetables possibly limited to the speck of garnish alongside your chicken-fried steak. Particularly for vegetarians, it's worth traveling with a cooler of fresh fruit and vegetables.

IN THE PARK

Bryce Canyon General Store & Snack Bar (☎ 435-834-5361; snacks $; ☺ 8am-8pm summer, to 6pm spring & fall, closed Nov-Mar) In addition to foodstuff and sundries, the general store near Sunrise Point sells hot dogs, cold drinks, packaged sandwiches, chili, soup and pizza.

our pick **Bryce Canyon Lodge** (☎ 435-834-8700; mains $-$$$; ☺ 6:30-10:30am, 11:30am-3pm & 5-10pm Apr-Oct) Refreshed with new management, this is the best restaurant in the region. Be warned, service may be slow but meals deliver, with excellent regional cuisine, ranging from fresh green salads to bison burgers, braised portobellos and steak. All food is made on site and the certified green menu offers only sustainable seafood. The wine list is decent and, best of all, the low-lit room is forgiving if you come covered in trail dust.

BRYCE CANYON CITY

Ruby's Inn General Store (☎ 435-834-5341; Best Western Ruby's Inn, 1000 S Hwy 63; ☺ 7am-10pm) Sells groceries with a considerable markup, plus sundries, clothing and camping supplies.

Bryce Canyon Pines (☎ 435-834-5441; Hwy 12; mains $-$$; ☺ 6:30am-9:30pm Apr-Oct) This super-cute diner is classic Utah, with wait staff that dotes, Naugahyde booths and even a crackling fire on cold days. Expect hearty plates of meat and potatoes, perfect BLTs and meal-size soups. While mains feel run-of-the-mill, locals come for towering wedges of home-made pie like banana blueberry creme.

Bryce Canyon Resort (☎ 435-834-5351; cnr Hwys 12 & 63; mains $-$$; 7am-9pm) If you're hungry even before you get to the park, this is a decent spot to grab a bite, serving classic American fare as well as new classic American fare: fajitas and burritos. Breakfast is also available and there's a small sports bar (beer and wine only; no margaritas).

Best Western Ruby's Inn (☎ 435-834-5341; 1000 S Hwy 63; mains $-$$$; 6:30am-9pm) Ruby's operates two restaurants: a full-service dining room and buffet off the lobby, and an economical diner that serves pizza, burgers and fried food. Both serve mediocre assembly-line cooking that's overpriced but convenient. For fresher food, order off the menu instead of the buffet. Expect a wait at dinner.

Ebenezer's Bar & Grill (☎ 800-468-8660; 1000 S Hwy 63; dinner show $$$; 7pm nightly May-Oct) A kitschy but good-natured evening of country-and-western music with a big BBQ dinner (drinks not included). Options include salmon, beef or chicken served with beans and cornbread. Since it's wildly popular, reservations are necessary. It's run by Ruby's and located across the street.

TROPIC

Bryce Canyon Inn & Pizza (☎ 435-679-8888; 21 N Main St; mains $-$$; noon-10pm) If you want to keep it simple, the pizzeria is a solid bet for steak and cheese sandwiches or taco pizza. It's a well-scrubbed family locale and the pulse of Tropic.

AROUND BRYCE CANYON

RED CANYON

If you're heading to Bryce Canyon from the west, Red Canyon provides your first arresting view of magnificent rock formations. Aptly named, the canyon's iron-rich limestone towers are saturated a deep red. Legend has it that outlaw Butch Cassidy once rode trails in this area, and one of the toughest hiking routes (Cassidy Trail) bears his name.

Orientation & Information

Red Canyon is on Hwy 12, 1.5 miles from the Hwy 89 junction south of Panguitch, and 15 miles from Bryce Canyon. The excellent **visitor center** (☎ 435-676-2676; Hwy 12; 9am-6pm summer, 10am-4pm spring & fall, closed Oct-Apr) provides regional maps, hiking information, historical displays, local crafts and hands-on children's displays. Red Canyon is in the **Dixie National Forest Powell ranger district** (☎ 435-676-9300; www.fs.fed.us/dxnf; 225 E Center St, Panguitch; 8am-4:30pm Mon-Fri).

Sights

The **Bryce Museum** (☎ 435-676-2500; www.brycewildlifeadventure.com; 1945 W Hwy 12; adult/child 6-12 $8/5; 9am-8pm May-Oct) displays dioramas of over 800 animals from around the world and live fallow deer, as well as Indian artifacts, and butterfly and giant-bug exhibits. It also rents bicycles and ATVs (see p170) and it's a good location to start the nearby bike path (p170).

THE BORN & BRED LOCAL

All of Tropic knows Charlie Francisco. Now 85, his first job was finding lost sheep in the hoodoos around Bryce Canyon. He's also been a hunter, horseback-riding guide and innkeeper.

How have you seen the area change? Bryce wasn't very popular until 10 years ago. Before Hwy 12, only two or three cars came in a year.

What was it like in your youth? The only work was shepherding. Rounding up horses at 4am was scary for a teenager! We roamed three counties herding sheep on horseback.

Tell us about your favorite experience. Having a bed and breakfast with my wife, I met people from everywhere. Some don't understand having strangers into the house. But we didn't have much. I figured if anybody needed something worse than us, why, they could just take it.

What surprises visitors? This is a town without a police officer. People can't believe that.

Charlie Francisco is a lifelong resident of Tropic.

Activities

Red Canyon has excellent recreation areas and less restrictions than the nearby national park. Hiking, mountain biking, horseback riding and ATV riding are the primary activities. Pick up a trail-map brochure, which details all the routes, at the visitor center.

Several moderately easy **hiking trails** begin near the visitor center: the 0.7-mile (30-minute) **Arches Trail** passes 15 arches as it winds through a canyon; and the 0.5-mile (30-minute) **Pink Ledges Trail** winds through red-rock formations. For a harder hike, try the 2.8-mile (two to four hours) **Golden Wall Trail**; you can extend it to a 5-mile round-trip by adding **Buckhorn Trail**. Check at the visitor center for current trail conditions.

If you like horseback riding, arrange a guided ride with **Scenic Rim Trail Rides** (☎ 435-679-8761, 800-679-5859; www.brycecanyonhorseback.com; Ruby's Inn, 1000 S Hwy 63), based at Best Western Ruby's Inn (p166). Rides are offered on Thunder Mountain ($85) and other Red Canyon locations.

Unlike much of the region around Bryce, mountain-biking trails abound at Red Canyon. The best is the **Thunder Mountain Trail**: 5 miles of this loop trail are paved and suit families; the other 7.8 are strenuous and involve sand and switchbacks (start the ride uphill toward Bryce to ride uphill on the pavement and downhill on the dirt).

SPLURGE: COTTONWOOD MEADOW

Dubbed 'Cowboy-liscious' by a wizened ranch hand, **Cottonwood Meadow** (☎ 435-676-8950; www.cottonwoodmeadowlodge.com; Hwy 89; cabins $$-$$$; 🕒 Apr-Oct; ⊠ 📶) delivers open-range dreams. Recycled from a Mormon saw town, this ultraprivate ranch, 2 miles south of Hwy 12, near Panguitch, occupies acres of tawny grass and tumbling sagebrush backed by mountains. Cabins range from a rustic-chic bunkhouse with wooden plank floors to a few stylish farmhouses with gleaming kitchens, blazing hearths and porch rockers. A trout pond stocked with browns and rainbows is in easy reach; otherwise there are miles of roads and open space for country walkers and mountain bikers. Lest they help themselves to the grass-raised beef on-site, pets are not allowed.

Be aware that horses share the trail; also, it isn't worth going after a rainy day because of the mud factor. Red Canyon also includes ATV trails.

The recently built **Red Canyon Bike Path** currently runs 8.6 miles along Hwy 12 from Thunder Mountain trailhead to East Fork Rd. It's paved and perfect for families. There are plans to eventually extend the path all the way to Bryce.

Mountain bike (half-/full day $20/35) and ATV rentals (per hour $40) are available from kiosks outside **Bryce Museum** (☎ 435-676-2500; www.brycewildlifeadventure.com; 1945 W Hwy 12) or from the Sinclair Station across the street from Ruby's Inn; helmets are included. Call ahead to see if kid-sized bikes are available. You can also rent a bike rack for your car.

Sleeping & Eating

It's a 20-minute drive from Red Canyon to Bryce, or 10 minutes to Panguitch.

Red Canyon campground (☎ Powell Ranger District 877-444-6777; www.sceniccanyons.com; Hwy 12; sites $; 🕒 mid-May–Oct 1) One of the best-maintained campgrounds in the national forest, Red Canyon has pretty hiking trails and doesn't allow ATVs. Amenities include showers, flush toilets, drinking water and a dump station. The 37 sites are first-come, first-served. It's 10 miles west of the Hwy 12/63 junction.

Red Canyon RV Park (☎ 435-676-2243; www.redcanyon.net/rc_rvpark; cnr Hwys 12 & 89; sites $; 🕒 Apr-Sep) If you can't secure a site at the campground, try this park which also operates a small store. Options include tent sites, RV hookups and cabins. Cabins are microsized, without private bathrooms.

Harold's Place (☎ 435-676-2350; www.haroldsplace.net; Hwy 12; r $; ⊠ 📶) Just east of the Hwy 89 junction, this family-run spot maintains 20 cozy, modern, pine-paneled log cabins and spotless inn rooms. Rooms at the inn have free wi-fi. Locals recommend the above-average restaurant (meals $ to $$; open 8am to 11am and 5pm to 8pm) for favorites like balsamic chicken and pecan-crusted trout.

PANGUITCH

pop 1623 / elevation 6666ft

Founded in 1864, Panguitch (*pang*-witch) was traditionally a center for the local ranching and lumber communities. In recent years tourism has taken over as

LITTLE BUTCH

In the wee town of **Circleville**, located 28 miles north of Panguitch, stands the boyhood home of the gun-slingin' bandit Butch Cassidy. The cabin, partially renovated but uninhabited, sits 2 miles south of town on the west side of Hwy 89. After the release of the film *Butch Cassidy and the Sundance Kid* (1969), reporters met the outlaw's sister, who claimed that Butch didn't die in South America in 1908, but circled back to visit.

For more of all things Butch, check out Red Canyon (p169), where one trail is named for the outlaw who rode the area.

the number-one industry. A hip influx of transplants from Las Vegas and California is slowly changing the old-fashioned feel. Nonetheless, taxidermy is still common restaurant decor, and you can see locals on ride-on lawnmowers headed to the minimart on Main St.

Popular with passing travelers, the town enjoys pleasant summer weather and is crisscrossed by scenic byways – Hwy 89 to the north and south, Hwy 143 to the west and Hwy 12 to the east. Panguitch is the Garfield County seat and has long been the gateway to Bryce Canyon (24 miles to the east).

Orientation & Information

The main drag through town, Hwy 89 comes in on Main St from the north, then turns east on Center St. South of Center, Main becomes Hwy 143 leading to Panguitch Lake.

Dixie National Forest Powell Ranger Station (☎ 435-676-8815; www.fs.fed.us/dxnf; 225 E Center St)

Garfield County Tourism Office (☎ 435-676-1160, 800-444-6689; www.brycecanyoncountry.com; 55 S Main St; 🕑 9am-5pm) Provides regional travel and event information.

Hospital (☎ 435-676-8811; 224 N 400 East)

Library (☎ 435-676-2431; 25 S 200 East; 🕑 1-5pm Mon-Fri) Get online or use wi-fi.

Police (☎ 435-676-8807; 45 S Main St)

Post office (☎ 435-676-8853; 65 N 100 West)

Sights

Panguitch once hosted a brick factory and boasts a number of beautiful **red-brick houses**. The information booth provides a self-guided tour pamphlet. Panguitch is also a short drive to the hometown of outlaw Butch Cassidy (see the boxed text, above).

Festivals take center stage in summer. Every June, the **Quilt Walk Festival** honors pioneer history (see the boxed text, p172). June also hosts **Panguitch Valley Balloon Rally** (www.panguitchvalleyballoonrally.com), a huge hot-air balloon festival. July's **Pioneer Days** include a rodeo. The **Garfield County Fair** takes place in August.

Sleeping

CAMPING

Most private campgrounds close in winter. **Panguitch KOA** (☎ 435-676-2225, 800-562-1625; www.koa.com; 555 S Main St; sites $; 📶 🏊) offers complete facilities, with tent and RV sites and cabins. Showers cost $5 for nonguests. Both **Hitch-n-Post** (☎ 435-676-2436; 420 N Main St; 📶 🐾) and **Paradise Campground** (☎ 435-676-8348; 2153 N Hwy 89; 📶 🐾), 2 miles north, provide tent and RV sites. Hitch-n-Post could use more shade; both campgrounds allow pets.

Showers are also available at Owen's Travel Center (below).

HOTELS

Panguitch and the area around the Hwy 89/12 junction (7 miles south) feature a good selection of budget and midrange accommodations that are uniformly clean and well kept (with a few exceptions). If you pull into town without a reservation, rates may be higher. Properties open in the off-season (November to March) reduce rates significantly. Motels that allow pets generally only keep a few pet-friendly rooms, best reserved in advance. Some will want to decide in person if Spot is well behaved.

The cheapest sleeps include **Owen's Travel Center** (☎ 435-676-8986; www.panguitchlakegeneralstore.com/owens_travel_center; 445 E Center St; r $; ❄), essentially a truck stop with saggy beds above the minimart, and the **Bryce Canyon Motel** (☎ 435-676-8441; 308 N Main St; r $; 🕑 Apr-Oct), where the otherwise-clean rooms need updating.

THE QUILT WALK FESTIVAL

In quaint homes around Panguitch, quilters are working as feverishly as Penelope at the loom. This subculture owes its origin to history, when the settlers nearly perished in their first winter. With food scarce during the brutal winter of 1884, seven men set out on a 40-mile journey in a wagon pulled by oxen to find provisions. Impeded by deep snow, they would have perished but found that the quilts that they used to pray on also served to compact the snow. Panguitch legend has it that they completed the journey by laying quilts across the snow and walking over them. They are now honored by the annual **Quilt Walk Festival** (www.quiltwalk.com), a week-long event that has banished local hunger with tall stacks of pancakes offered post–tractor pull. There are also races, parades, quilt shows and an art fair.

Color Country (☎ 435-676-2386, 800-225-6518; www.colorcountrymotel.com; 526 N Main St; r $;) An economical, standard motel with laminate furniture and floral bedcovers; upstairs rooms are newer. Perks include a pool and outdoor hot tub. Pets are $10 extra.

Marianna Inn Motel (☎ 435-676-8844, 800-598-9190; www.mariannainn.com; 699 N Main St; $;) Pull over at the pink-and-lavender motel with the shaded swing deck. Dollhouse rooms are decent but the newest additions – deluxe log-style rooms – are worth splurging on. Some rooms have refrigerators, dryers and microwaves. Pets are $10 extra.

Canyon Lodge (☎ 435-676-8292, 800-440-8292; www.colorcountry.net/~cache; 210 N Main St; r $; Mar-Oct;) A little frayed around the edges, this clean 10-room motel also offers a hot tub and massage. Pet charge is $10 extra.

Horizon Motel (☎ 435-676-2651, 800-776-2651; www.horizonmotel.net; 730 N Main St; r $; Mar-Nov;) An old-fashioned motel with quilted beds, refrigerators and microwaves. Seniors get a discount. Pet fee is $10 extra.

Purple Sage (☎ 435-676-2659, 800-241-6889; www.purplesagemotel.biz; 132 E Center St; r $; Mar-Oct;) Comfy, as motels go, and helpfully chatty too, this tidy motel slips in sweet extras like pillow-top mattresses, new furnishings and coffeemakers. Pets may be allowed, check first in person.

New Western Motel (☎ 435-676-8876; 200 E Center St; r $;) Charges more than similar competitors but is still recommended.

Grandma's Cottage (☎ 435-690-9495; www.aperfectplacetostay.net; 90 N 100 West; cottages $, houses $$-$$$; Mar-Nov;) An excellent option for groups and families, these renovated cottages and homes around central Panguitch have been lovingly put together by a semi-retired couple. But, except for the studio cottage, the interior decoration is nothing like grandma's. Think savvy and stylish. Themes vary – there's a 1960s hideout, a country cottage and a historic brick home put together with gorgeous touches. All accommodations have television and some have cooking facilities and washer/dryer.

our pick **Red Brick Inn** (☎ 435-676-2141, 866-732-2745; www.redbrickinnutah.com; 161 N 100 W; r $$; May-Oct;) Chill out swinging in a garden hammock or pedaling a loan bike. A warm California native, Peggy runs this 1919 charmer that once served as the town hospital. Stories abound, rooms are cozy and comfortable, and there's an outdoor hot tub. Has a two-night minimum; ask first about pets.

Eating & Drinking

Panguitch's dining scene doesn't have much variety.

The **C-Stop Pizza & Deli** (☎ 435-676-8366; 561 E Center St; mains $-$$; 10:30am-10pm, shorter winter hr) serves pizza and sandwiches.

The family-run **Foy's Country Corner Café** (☎ 435-676-8851; 80 N Main St; mains $-$$; 7am-9pm Mon-Sat) is at its best when 95-year-old grandma is cooking omelets. Similar is **Flying M Restaurant** (☎ 435-676-8008; 580 Main St; mains $-$$; 7am-10pm, t 9pm in winter), a run-of-the-mill family diner.

Sweet staff at **Cowboy's Smokehouse BBQ** (☎ 435-676-8030; 95 N Main St; mains $-$$$; 6:30am-10pm Mon-Sat Mar-Oct) serve steaks and brisket with house-made sauce, but the food quality can be erratic. Portions are generous.

For espresso, stop by **Bronco Bobbi's** (☎ 435-676-8899; 37 N Main St; coffee $; 9am-5pm Mon-Sat;) and browse the embroidered cowboy boots and funky gift-shop items while sipping.

Getting There & Away

Hwy 89 is the main route through town. There are no scheduled bus, air or train services to Panguitch.

Grand Staircase-Escalante National Monument

Nearly twice the size of Rhode Island, Grand Staircase-Escalante National Monument (GSENM) is by far the largest park in the Southwest. Yet its spectacular scenery is some of the least visited. Here, a 150-mile-long series of geological strata begins at the bottom of the Grand Canyon and rises, like a staircase, 3500ft to Bryce Canyon and the Escalante River canyons. Together the layers of rock reveal 260 million years of history in a riot of color. The formations may not be as in-your-face as those in the nearby national parks, but the variety is astounding – pink, white, chocolate and red cliffs, swirling wavelike slickrock, hardened sand dunes, coral sand and slot canyons galore. Best of all, you don't have to go far to experience this splendor in solitude; most of the monument is off the beaten path.

The monument was established in 1996 by President Bill Clinton. Some locals say it wasn't by accident that he dedicated it in Arizona – the move wasn't entirely popular here. Many ranchers and residents who used the land felt they were given little notice. Local legislators and businesses that had hoped to explore the area's mining potential were stymied. Overnight, environment activists appeared and bitter conflicts ensued. Years later there seems to be a broad, general recognition that the land needs some protection (if only from all the visitors the monument's creation attracted). Nevertheless, federal versus local control issues still come up. In 2010 Kane County sued the US government, and lost, in a case of road-ownership rights on these lands.

HIGHLIGHTS

- Driving one of the monument's rough and scenic roads, like **Cottonwood Canyon** (p178)
- Taking a sandy canyon stroll past ancient and pioneer sites to **Lower Calf Creek Falls** (p181)
- Getting a sense of old Hollywood's 'Wild West' in **Kanab** (p190)
- Slipping in and out of towering slot canyons with little effort at **Willis Creek** (p182)
- Eating creative, organic cuisine in the tiny mountain town of **Boulder** (p188)

Total Area 2969 sq miles	**Elevation** 4900ft (at Escalante)	**Average high/low temperature in July** 91°F/55°F

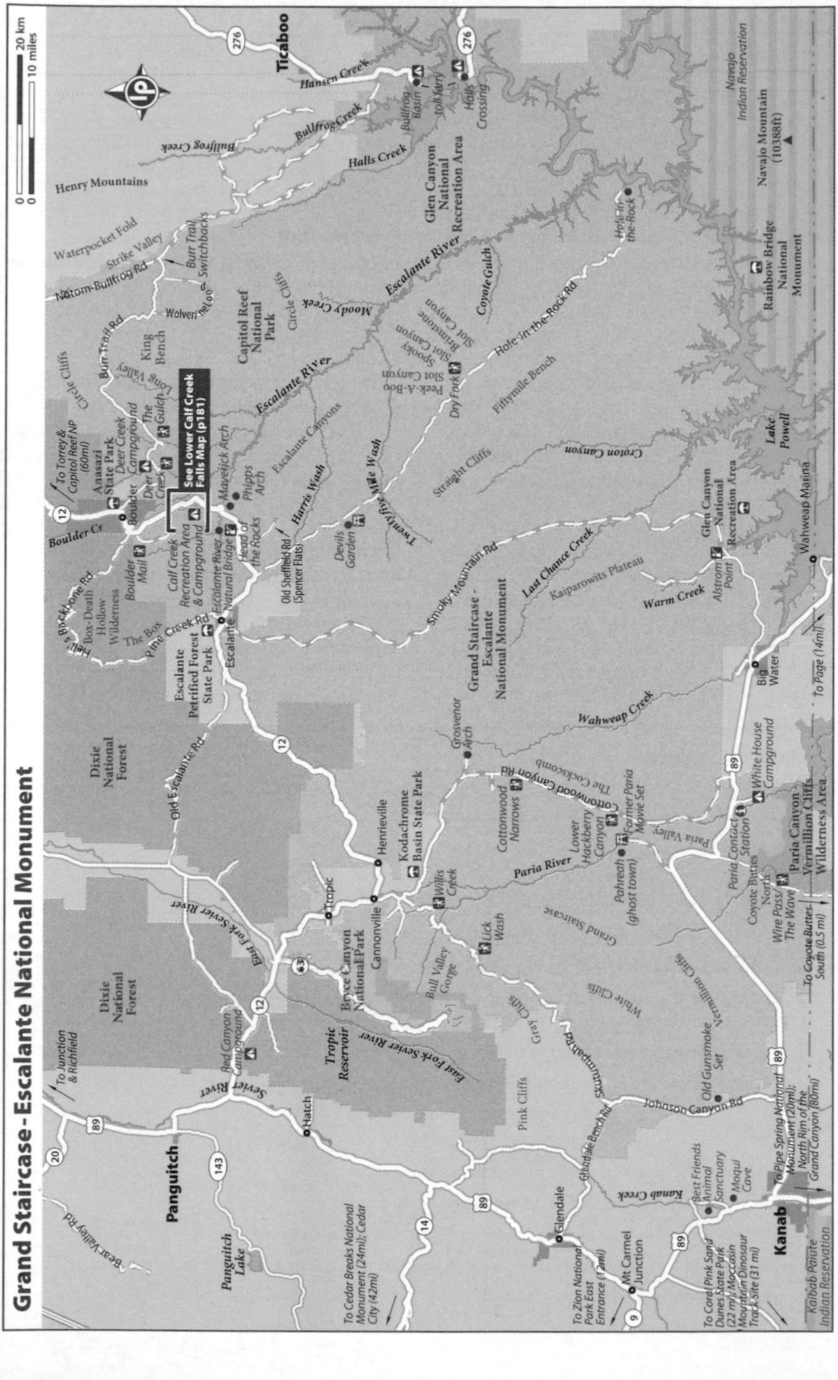
Grand Staircase-Escalante National Monument
0 20 km
0 10 miles
Henry Mountains
Waterpocket Fold
Strike Valley
Notom-Bullfrog Rd
Burr Trail Switchbacks
Bullfrog Creek
Hansen Creek
Ticaboo
276
Bullfrog Basin
Toll Ferry
Halls Crossing
Halls Creek
Glen Canyon National Recreation Area
Capitol Reef National Park
Circle Cliffs
Wolverine Loop
King Bench
Burr Trail Rd
Long Valley
The Gulch
Deer Creek Campground
Deer Creek
Anasazi State Park
To Torrey & Capitol Reef NP (60mi)
Boulder
Boulder Cr
12
See Lower Calf Creek Falls Map (p181)
Calf Creek Recreation Area & Campground
Escalante River & Natural Bridge
Head of the Rocks
Maverick Arch
Phipps Arch
Escalante River
Escalante Canyons
Moody Creek
Coyote Gulch
Brimstone Slot Canyon
Spooky Slot Canyon
Peek-A-Boo Slot Canyon
Dry Fork
Hole-in-the-Rock Rd
Hole-in-the-Rock
Fiftymile Bench
Harris Wash
Twentyfive Mile Wash
Devils Garden
Old Sheffield Rd (Spencer Flats)
Straight Cliffs
Croton Canyon
Navajo Indian Reservation
Navajo Mountain (10388ft)
Rainbow Bridge National Monument
Lake Powell
Glen Canyon National Recreation Area
Wahweap Marina
Hell's Backbone Rd
Box-Death Hollow Wilderness
Boulder Mail
The Box
Pine Creek Rd
Escalante
Escalante Petrified Forest State Park
Smoky Mountain Rd
Last Chance Creek
Kaiparowits Plateau
Warm Creek
Alstrom Point
Grand Staircase-Escalante National Monument
Big Water
To Page (14mi)
Wahweap Creek
Dixie National Forest
Old Escalante Rd
Grosvenor Arch
Cottonwood Canyon Rd
The Cockscomb
Cottonwood Narrows
Former Paria Movie Set
Lower Hackberry Canyon
Paria Valley
89
White House Campground
Paria Contact Station
Paria Canyon-Vermillion Cliffs Wilderness Area
Henrieville
Kodachrome Basin State Park
Cannonville
Tropic
Willis Creek
Paria River
Pahreah (ghost town)
Grand Staircase
Coyote Buttes North
Wire Pass/The Wave
To Coyote Buttes South (0.5 mi)
East Fork Sevier River
63
Bryce Canyon National Park
Bull Valley Gorge
Lick Wash
Gray Cliffs
White Cliffs
Vermillion Cliffs
Dixie National Forest
Red Canyon Campground
Tropic Reservoir
Skutumpah Rd
Old Gunsmoke Set
Johnson Canyon Rd
Pink Cliffs
Glendale Bench Rd
To Junction & Richfield
Sevier River
Hatch
20
Panguitch
143
Panguitch Lake
Bear Valley Rd
14
To Cedar Breaks National Monument (24mi); Cedar City (42mi)
Glendale
To Zion National Park East Entrance (12mi)
Mt Carmel Junction
9
To Coral Pink Sand Dunes State Park (22 mi); Moccasin Mountain Dinosaur Track Site (31 mi)
Best Friends Animal Sanctuary
Moqui Cave
Kanab Creek
Kanab
To Pipe Spring National Monument (20mi); North Rim of the Grand Canyon (80mi)
Kaibab Paiute Indian Reservation

When You Arrive

There are no entrance stations for Grand Staircase-Escalante National Monument, which is accessible 24/7. Nor are there generally fees for day use. A free park bulletin and map are available at the visitor centers. They also sell more detailed maps, like the USGS 7.5-quadrangles, which can be helpful in such a remote area. No shiny **National Geographic Trails Illustrated** (www.natgeomaps.com) map exists for the entire monument, but No 710, *Canyons of the Escalante,* covers the northeast corner.

Orientation

The monument encompasses three major geologic areas: the westernmost Grand Staircase, south of Bryce Canyon and west of Cottonwood Canyon Rd; central Kaiparowits Plateau, east of Cottonwood Canyon Rd and west of Hole-in-the-Rock Rd; and the eastern Escalante Canyons, southwest of the Burr Trail. In the north, scenic Hwy 12 skirts the boundary of GSENM, passing through the small towns of Escalante and Boulder. In the south, Hwy 89 arcs east from the larger town of Kanab. Three unpaved roads cross the park between the highways, roughly north to south: Skutumpah and Johnson Canyon Rds, Cottonwood Canyon Rd and Smoky Mountain Rd. Hole-in-the-Rock Rd, a dead end, leads southeast from Hwy 12 toward Glen Canyon National Recreation Area. Partly paved Burr Trail crosses the monument's northeast corner from Boulder into Capitol Reef.

For distances to other parks, see p274.

Information

Food, gas, lodging and other services are available in Boulder (p188), Escalante (p186) and Kanab (p190). Note that most of the lodgings in this chapter are entirely nonsmoking.

Interagency desks answer questions about all area public lands: National Park Service (NPS), US Forest Service (USFS) and Bureau of Land Management (BLM).

Anasazi State Park interagency desk (☎ 435-335-7308; 460 N Hwy 12, Boulder; 🕑 9am-5pm mid-Mar–mid-Nov)

Big Water visitor center (☎ 435-675-3200; 100 Upper Revolution Way, Big Water; 🕑 9am-6pm Apr-Oct, 8am-5pm Nov-Mar) Dinosaur interpretive exhibits; near Lake Powell, Arizona.

Cannonville visitor center (☎ 435-826-5640; 10 Center St, Cannonville; 🕑 8am-4:30pm Apr-Oct) Not far from Bryce Canyon, at the head of Cottonwood Rd.

ALWAYS... NEVER

Please remember that Grand Staircase-Escalante National Monument is a remote desert wilderness park with few services and flash-flood danger.

Always

- check with a ranger about weather and road conditions before driving or hiking
- keep your gas tank as full as possible; stations are few and far between
- carry extra water and food in case of a breakdown
- stop the car and wait for the storm to pass if it does start raining unexpectedly; roads dry quickly, sometimes within 30 minutes.
- let someone know where you're going and when you plan to return if you're traveling alone
- take sun protection and a gallon of water per day when hiking in the desert

Never

- attempt a 4WD road beyond your vehicle's capability
- park in a wash; like we said, flash floods come suddenly
- start a slot-canyon hike or long back-road drive when rain is imminent
- remove or defile Native American artifacts or sites; it's against the law
- walk on cryptobiotic crust (see p74)

Escalante interagency office (☎ 435-826-5499; 775 W Main St, Escalante; 🕑 7am-5:30pm mid-Mar–mid-Nov, 8am-4:30pm mid-Nov–mid-Mar) Ecology displays.
Grand Staircase-Escalante National Monument (☎ 435-826-5499; www.ut.blm.gov/monument; PO Box 225, Escalante, UT 84726) Write-ahead information available.
Kanab visitor center (☎ 435-644-4680; 745 E Hwy 89, Kanab; 🕑 8am-5pm) Exhibits focus on archaeology and geology.

Park Policies & Regulations

The monument is unique for an area managed by the BLM. While it does allow some uses that would be banned if this was a national park (such as grazing), it permits fewer uses than other BLM lands in order to maintain its wilderness status. If you plan to car-camp or backpack overnight, you'll need a free permit (from any visitor center, information kiosk or major trailhead). Only Calf Creek Recreation Area, carries a day-use fee.

Off-roading is forbidden. All vehicles must stay on designated roads, which are open to mountain bikes, cars, 4WDs, all-terrain vehicles (ATVs) and other off-highway vehicles.

Campfires in developed campgrounds are restricted to fire rings; elsewhere you're allowed to use a fire pan, unless otherwise posted. You may not light fires at archaeological sites or in rock shelters or alcoves.

Banned in Coyote Gulch, dogs are allowed elsewhere in the monument. They must be leashed at Deer Creek Campground, around Calf Creek Recreation Area and on trails.

Getting Around

The only way to get around the monument is in a private vehicle or on foot. Some unpaved roads require high-clearance 4WD. Note that most off-the-lot SUVs and light trucks are *not* high clearance.

Towns outside the park – Escalante, Boulder and Kanab – have all services, including gas stations and hiker shuttles. Escalante and Kanab have one 4WD Jeep rental place apiece. However, it's cheaper per day to rent upon arrival in Las Vegas (p137).

SIGHTS

Most sights are listed under Driving (right) and Hiking (p180). The starting point for the monument's only maintained hiking trail, **Calf Creek Recreation Area** (☎ 435-826-5499; www.ut.blm.gov/monument; Hwy 12; day use $2; 🕑 day use dawn-dusk), also has one of the few campgrounds. Make it a point to stop when driving between Escalante and Boulder; it's between mile markers 75 and 76. Wading through the cool creek waters in the shade of mature cottonwoods is a refreshing treat. Picnic tables available.

DRIVING

Driving in the monument – over hair-raising ridges, around crosshatched slickrock formations and past hardened sandstone dunes that look like emerging monsters – is a must-do experience. But it can also be dangerous. Check road conditions before entering the monument and note that high-clearance 4WD is recommended for some of the roads below.

The main northern artery, **Hwy 12** (p185), is a winding, scenic drive in itself.

BURR TRAIL

Duration 3 hours
Distance 60 miles
Start/Finish Hwy 12, Boulder (p188)
Summary This paved route provides an intro to all park formations – cliffs, canyons, buttes, mesas and monoliths – in colors from sandy white to deep coral red. Sweeping curves and steep up-and-downs add to the attraction.

The most immediately gratifying, dramatic drive in the area, the Burr Trail heads east from Boulder as a paved road, crosses GSENM's northeast corner and, after 30 miles, arrives at Capitol Reef National Park, where the road becomes loose gravel. This first section is quite a challenging road-bike ride, as well.

Once you enter the monument, it's not far to the two trailheads: the 7-mile-long **Deer Creek trail** and the 52-mile trek through **Grand Gulch**, popular with backpackers. Check with rangers for details on these spectacular hikes through riparian zones and red-rock desert. Deer Creek also has a tiny campground (p185).

Just past the creek, the road enters **Long Canyon** beneath towering vertical slabs of red rock. At 11 miles look for an unmarked pullout on the road's left side. You'll see the opening for a side **slot canyon** north across a scrubby wash. Poke about the narrowing red-rock slot as far as you like.

Driving out of Long Canyon, stop at the crest for views beyond of the sheer **Circle Cliffs**, which hang like curtains above the undulating valley floor. Still snowcapped in summer, the **Henry Mountains** rise above 11,000ft on the horizon. **Wolverine Loop** is a 25-mile, 4WD road that circles south through an area riddled with scrubland, canyons and nearby cliffs. Several hiking trails lead off from there, and the area is popular with mountain bikers. Continuing on Burr Trail, you cross the **White Canyon Flat** plateau before the pavement ends and the road meets the giant, angled buttes of 100-mile **Waterpocket Fold** in Capitol Reef, the feature that blocked 19th-century settlers' passage west. Trailhead access to **Muley Twist Canyon** (p205) is nearby. Just ahead, the **Burr Trail Switchbacks** follow an original wagon route through the fold. You can continue onto **Notom-Bullfrog Rd** (p199) and north to Hwy 24 or south to Glen Canyon. But if you plan to turn around and return to Boulder, first drive the switchbacks – the magnificence and scale of the landscape will blow your mind.

COTTONWOOD CANYON ROAD

Duration 3 hours
Distance 46 miles one way
Start Hwy 12, 34 miles west of Escalante
Finish Hwy 89, 45 miles east of Kanab
Nearest Towns Escalante (p186), Kanab (p190)
Summary Sculpted red sandstone monoliths, pale beige-and-yellow towering arches and charcoal-gray peaks: mile by mile, Cottonwood Canyon Rd unfolds as a striking geology lesson. Don't forget to get out and look around.

If you make only one of the three cross-monument drives, we suggest it be Cottonwood Canyon Rd, with its stunning geological sights, interesting hikes and ever-changing geography. The rough road is passable only when dry. Usually 2WD vehicles will do, but 4WD is never a bad idea.

The first 9 miles of road to **Kodachrome Basin State Park** (p185) are paved. Stop at the park to see a wonderland of red-rock spires, balancing rocks and mini-buttes. South from here, the road gets bumpy. After about 20 miles, and a short side detour, you'll reach the 90ft-high **Grosvenor Arch**. Follow the level sidewalk to stand beneath this rare yellow- and sand-colored stone double arch towering so far above. Definitely a Kodak moment. (Picnic tables and pit toilets available.)

The main road continues south, weaving in and among rock formations (look for the stark white pinnacles contrasting with red hoodoos, for example). You're traveling along the west side of the **Cockscomb**, a distinctive, long, narrow monocline caused by a fold in the Earth's crust. **Cottonwood Narrows** is a 1.5-mile hike through a sandstone slot canyon. Soon after, stands of cottonwoods appear in the wash on the right, and the rutted road rises along a narrow shelf.

Lower Hackberry Canyon (p183) is another good day hike, right before **Yellow Rock.** You can climb up on this tan-, mustard- and mango-swirled slickrock with elaborate cross-bedding and fracture lines, but it's tough.

From there, interesting features abound as the landscape morphs from jagged rock into coal-colored dirt hills before the road reaches the pastoral **Paria Valley** and Hwy 89 beyond.

HOLE-IN-THE-ROCK ROAD

Duration 8–9 hours
Distance 114 miles
Start/Finish Hwy 12, 5 miles east of Escalante
Nearest Town Escalante (p186)
Summary A much-traveled, washboard-rough road follows the route of a historic wagon trail, providing access to area attractions and trails. Expect to be sucking at least a little dust behind other cars.

The history is wilder than the scenery along this dust pit of a road. From 1879 to 1880, more than 200 pioneering Mormons followed this route on their way to settle southeast Utah. When the precipitous walls of Glen Canyon on the Colorado River blocked their path, they blasted and hammered through the cliff, creating a hole wide enough to lower their 80 wagons through –

a feat that is honored by the road's name today. The final part of their trail lies submerged beneath Lake Powell. History buffs should pick up Stewart Aitchison's *Hole-in-the-Rock Trail* for a detailed account.

The road is passable to ordinary passenger cars when dry, except for the last 7 miles, which always require 4WD. Even if you don't drive the entire route, at least visit the freely accessible **Devils Garden**, 12 miles in. Here rock fists, orbs, spires and fingers rise up to 40ft above the desert floor. It's a sandy but fairly short walk from the parking lot to the formations. Climbing on, over and under the giant sandstone slabs, nature becomes your playground.

About 26 miles in, **Dry Fork** (p182) has the most well-known slot-canyon day hikes on the road. While there are no facilities on the road, dispersed camping is permitted with a free backcountry permit.

The last 7 miles are so rugged, they can take almost as long to traverse as the first 50. The road stops short of the actual **Hole-in-the-Rock**. But hikers can trek out and scramble down past the 'hole' to **Lake Powell** in less than an hour. Sorry, no elevators for the climb back up.

SKUTUMPAH & JOHNSON CANYON ROADS

Duration 2½ hours
Distance 51 miles one way
Start Hwy 89, 9 miles east of Kanab
Finish Cannonville
Nearest Town Kanab (p190)
Summary A partially paved, partially dirt road crosses the monument beneath Bryce Canyon. En route it passes through the Vermillion, White, Gray and Pink Cliffs, the latter of which are particularly dramatic.

Together these two roads comprise the monument's westernmost route. Paved Johnson Canyon Rd trundles north for 16 miles to intersect Skutumpah (*scoot*-em-pah) Rd. This very rutted dirt route (4WD recommended, and sometimes required) continues for 35 miles to Cannonville on Hwy 12. Driving south–north provides the best perspective.

Start out in very scenic **Johnson Canyon**, which has distant views the of the coral

DETOUR: 4WD ADVENTURE

Looking for even more 4WD adventure than the cross-monument drives offer? You have alternatives.

- **Hell's Backbone Road** Loops a gravel-strewn 48 miles off Hwy 12 between Boulder and Escalante. The original mule-mail route, it crosses rugged Box-Death Wilderness area. The highlight is a single-lane track atop an impossibly narrow ridge.
- **Old Sheffield Road (or Spencer Flats)** Undulates for 3 sand-and-gravel miles through desert, slickrock formations and canyons. Some great backcountry camping is to be found out here too. The road leaves Hwy 12, 6 miles east of Escalante.

Vermillion Cliffs. About 6 miles along, you'll see the crumbling wooden buildings of the old **Gunsmoke set**, where the TV western was filmed. They are on private property, but easily visible from the road. Soon after, the landscape changes color as the **White Cliffs** appear to the east.

Those who don't have the time, or a proper vehicle, to tackle Skutumpah Rd could turn off at the junction onto the 15-mile **Glendale Bench Rd**, a much easier 2WD dirt track that leads east to Glendale (p136) on Hwy 89.

Once on Skutumpah Rd, there are numerous old side roads, so pay attention and keep to the main road. Here the **Gray Cliffs** rise to the north and you pass through pastureland before reaching the trailhead for **Lick Wash**. Ask at one of the visitor centers about the 8-mile trail that penetrates the cross-bedded sandstone to the south. Continuing on, the road gets steep and rocky before **Bull Valley Gorge**. Stop at the wide spot in the road and walk left along the gorge rim; after about 50ft look back at the debris beneath the 'bridge' you're about to drive across. If you have good eyesight, or binoculars, you might make out a wheel or a window of the **1950s truck** that fell off the road and now forms part of the bridge base. Exploring the gorge itself requires rock-climbing skills.

Soon after, on the road north, is the trailhead parking lot (and pit toilet) for **Willis**

Creek (p182), an easy slot-canyon hike. The dramatic **Pink Cliffs** are the last thing you see before the sharp decent to the valley intersection with **Cottonwood Canyon Rd** (p178), just south of Cannonville.

SMOKY MOUNTAIN ROAD

Duration 6 hours
Distance 78 miles one way
Start Escalante (p186)
Finish Big Water (p195)
Summary A rugged backcountry route that provides a 4WD experience, but not as many scenic thrills as the other roads that cross through the monument.

Few drivers brave this challenging, 78-mile dirt-and-gravel road, passable by 4WD vehicle only (preferably with high clearance). With few trailheads and no named sights, there's not much reason to. From Escalante in the north, the road crosses the rugged **Kaiparowits Plateau** and emerges at the Big Water visitor center on Hwy 89, just west of Glen Canyon National Recreation Area. The prime destination is **Alstrom Point**, 12.5 miles from Hwy 89, a plateau-top vantage with stunning views that include Lake Powell.

HIKING

The BLM puts out handy one-page summaries of all hikes (there are far too many to list here); pick up copies at any visitor center. Falcon Guide's *Hiking Grand Staircase-Escalante* is the most thorough area trekking handbook, but we like the more opinionated *Hiking From Here to Wow: Utah Canyon Country* – snazzy color pics, too.

No easy hikes exist in the monument. For brief forays into the park, see **Devils Garden** (p179) and **Grosvenor Arch** (p178). There's also a little side-slot diversion in **Long Canyon** (p177).

For definitions of our hike difficulty ratings, see p37.

DAY HIKES

Though most of the park's trails are not maintained, the majority of those we list below are well-trodden routes.

ESCALANTE RIVER NATURAL BRIDGE

Duration 3 hours
Distance 4.4 miles
Difficulty Easy–moderate
Start/Finish Hwy 12, 15 miles east of Escalante
Nearest Town Escalante (p186)
Transportation Private
Summary A fairly flat, but sometimes sandy, trail crisscrosses the river seven times before reaching a large natural bridge and arch beyond. Be prepared to get your feet wet.

If you want a level walk with dramatic scenery, you've found it. The Escalante River hike is not as demanding as Lower Calf Creek Falls and it allows (requires) you to play in the water. Park at the trailhead by the Hwy 12 bridge over the Escalante River, just west of the Calf Creek Recreation Area. Water sandals are best for the alternating sandy and wet conditions. Note that biting flies can be bothersome in early summer.

Descend and cross the **Escalante River**. Walk through cottonwoods then an exposed sagebrush and sand valley. Trees appear again when you get closer to the second river crossing, and the cliff walls close in before the third. After another full-sun stint, a **natural bridge** appears off to the left. The 130ft-high sandstone arch with a 100ft span is best viewed from the fourth crossing at 1.8 miles.

Continue on and look up and left for the rock alcove that has a small **granary ruin**. You'll ford the river three more times before you get to an **arch** up on the skyline to the southwest. Note that this is the end for the day hike, but you can continue on this trail for a total of 15 miles and end up at a trailhead back in Escalante town.

UPPER CALF CREEK FALLS

Duration 1½ hours
Distance 2.2 miles
Difficulty Moderate
Start/Finish Hwy 12
Nearest Town Boulder (p188)
Transportation Private
Summary A short, but steep and strenuous, trail down slickrock leads through a desert moonscape to an oasis. The two sets of pools and waterfalls at hike's end appear like a mirage.

Soaking your feet in a moss-covered pool while canyon wrens and mountain bluebirds dart about seems like an impossible dream when you first start your slickrock descent. The upper hike may not be as well-known or dramatic as Lower Calf Creek Falls (below), but stick with it and you're rewarded with unexpected beauty. The 0.25-mile unmarked dirt road to the trailhead is outside of Boulder, on the north side of Hwy 12 between mile markers 80 and 81.

Starting at the rim, you overlook all of **Calf Creek Canyon** and the **Straight Cliffs** beyond. From there the trail descends 550ft down steep white Navajo sandstone littered with dark volcanic boulders. Follow the cairns down until the incline levels off. The rock becomes more stratified and colorful just about the time you get a glimpse of treetops in the inner canyon to the west.

Shortly after you'll come to a fork. Follow cairns down to the left and you reach the **lower pool** of the Upper trail – a vegetation-covered oasis beneath an 86ft waterfall. Follow the path up to the right for the **upper pools**, where water cascades through shallow potholes and ponds before falling over the rim. Take the time to explore both pools: swim if it's warm, look over the canyon edge and appreciate the isolation.

LOWER CALF CREEK FALLS

Duration 4 hours
Distance 6 miles
Difficulty Moderate
Start/Finish Calf Creek Recreation Area, Hwy 12, 14 miles east of Escalante
Nearest Town Escalante (p186)
Transportation Private
Summary The sandy track eventually follows a year-round running creek through a spectacular canyon before arriving at a 126ft waterfall, a joy on a hot day.

Lower Calf Creek Falls' beauty is no secret; this is easily the most heavily traveled trail in the entire monument. Its accessibility – right off Hwy 12 between Escalante and Boulder – makes it a perfect stopover. Though it doesn't climb much, the trail has long sandy stretches that can take a lot out of you. Carry plenty of water (available at the trailhead); the creek is not safe for drinking.

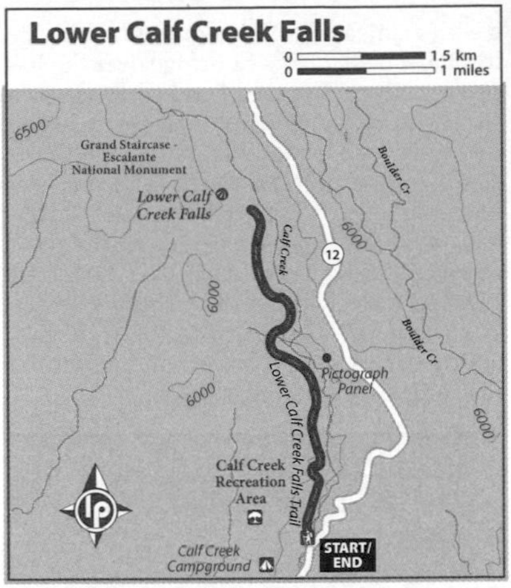

Park at the **Calf Creek Recreation Area** (day use $2) and campground, between mile markers 75 and 76 on Hwy 12. As you work your way toward the creek, you'll pass honeycombed rocks and Navajo sandstone domes, an 800-year-old Native American **granary**, a box canyon where calves were once herded (hence the name Calf Creek), **prehistoric pictographs** and lush green wetlands.

Past the last bend, the trail ends in amphitheater of rock with a 126ft-tall **waterfall** with a thin stream cascading into a large pool. The sandy shore and extended knee-deep wading area, before the deeper drop-off, make this a favorite with families. Remember, the sandy walk out is as strenuous as the walk in, so pace yourself.

PHIPPS WASH

Duration 4 hours
Distance 5 miles
Difficulty Moderate
Start/Finish Hwy 12, 15 miles east of Escalante
Nearest Town Escalante (p186)
Transportation Private
Summary Phipps Wash takes you through a riparian zone, beneath cottonwood trees and alongside a drainage to two formidable arches. In some seasons, you may get wet.

A lesser alternative to the nearby Escalante River Natural Bridge hike (p180). Expect to fight your way through riparian growth and to possibly get your feet wet;

basic orienteering skills a must. Start at the trailhead by the Hwy 12 bridge over the Escalante River. The trail heads downstream along the Escalante River on a well-marked route through private property, then cuts southwest into **Phipps Wash**. Take the first major drainage to the right to reach **Maverick Arch**, about 1.5 miles from the trailhead. Return to the main wash and continue south toward **Phipps Arch**, a chunky sweep of rock about 2 miles from the trailhead, which you can reach by scrambling up the east wall of the drainage.

SLOT CANYONS OF DRY FORK/ COYOTE GULCH

Duration 3 hours
Distance 4.5 miles
Difficulty Moderate–difficult
Start/Finish Dry Fork Rd, off Hole-in-the-Rock Rd
Nearest Town Escalante (p186)
Transportation Private
Summary A remote but popular Hole-in-the-Rock Rd hike leads to four different slot canyons, complete with serpentine walls, incredible narrows and bouldering obstacles.

GSENM is famous for its sculpted slot canyons, spillways of brightly colored, weathered rock; the four slots on this route are some of the most visited in the monument. Expect to encounter pools of water in some. From Hwy 12, drive 26 miles down Hole-in-the-Rock Rd (p178) to Dry Fork Rd (Rte 252), turn left, and drive 1.7 miles to the parking area, bearing left at all junctions.

From the parking area the route switchbacks steeply down the slickrock and you find yourself alternately sidestepping and pitching forward. An overabundance of willy-nilly rock cairns can lead you astray here. Look up and see where you're headed: toward the reddish-brown dirt hills with little vegetation to the north (leftish). You reach the bottom in **Coyote Gulch** wash. Follow it north, and when you emerge into an opening, **Dry Fork** slot canyon is immediately to the left (west). Dry Fork is often overlooked as not tight or physically challenging enough, but it's our favorite. You can walk for miles between undulating orange walls, with only a few small boulder step-ups.

Double back to Coyote Gulch and head downstream (east), keeping your eyes peeled

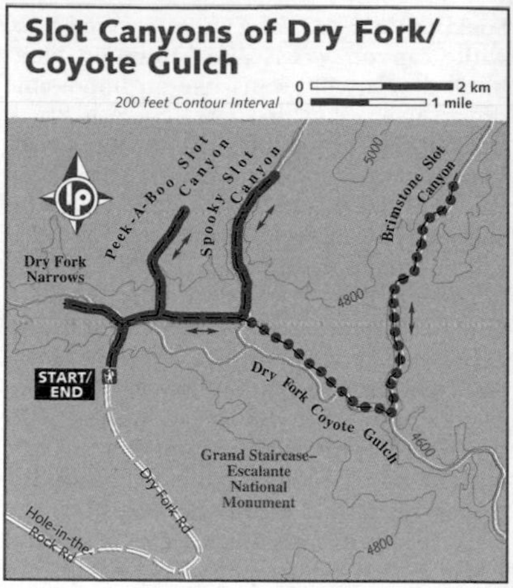

for the first slot on the left, **Peek-a-Boo**. Even to get into this dramatic canyon, you have to climb up a 12ft handhold-carved wall (much easier if you're tall or not alone). From there the hanging slot tightens dramatically and passes under several arches. You may have to navigate some water, and scrambling is definitely required, before the route becomes impassable 0.25 miles later.

A half-mile further downstream, veer left and hike through the sandy wash to **Spooky Gulch**, which is even narrower. The 0.3-mile slot is less technically challenging, but impassable for larger hikers. Return to the trailhead from here. We don't recommend you try to climb up and over Peek-a-Boo to sneak up behind Spooky; it's too easy to get lost.

If you really want to lengthen your hike, you could continue to **Brimstone Gulch**; it's 0.5 miles further, but not as interesting.

WILLIS CREEK

Duration up to 4 hours
Distance up to 4.4 miles
Difficulty Easy–moderate
Start/Finish Cottonwood Canyon Rd, 34 miles west of Escalante
Nearest Town Escalante (p186)
Transportation Private
Summary A great little slot-canyon hike, accessible to young and old. Actually it's more like four little slot canyons, as you alternate between open and narrow sections.

Unlike most of GSENM's slot canyons, the cliffs around Willis Creek are light beige, not red – an interesting contrast to the oftentimes orange mineral stream flowing through it. The trail starts 3 miles south of Cannonville on Cottonwood Canyon Rd (p178). Easy access and an almost-level canyon floor make this a great family route.

Across the road from the parking lot, follow the well-worn path down the hill and proceede left, down canyon. In less than five minutes the serpentine walls rise around you. There's no trail per se, you're just wandering from bank to bank following **Willis Creek**. The narrows open up after about 0.5 miles, and this is where many people turn around. But you shouldn't.

Once you hike around, not slide down, the 11ft **waterfall** (OK, it's called a pour off), the canyon deepens. At times cliffs tower 200ft above, only 6ft apart. Tight and narrow sections alternate until 2.2 miles along you reach the confluence with **Sheep Creek**, the end to this day hike.

LOWER HACKBERRY CANYON

Duration 2–3 hours
Distance 3–6 miles
Difficulty Easy–moderate
Start/Finish Cottonwood Canyon Rd, 14 miles north of Hwy 89
Nearest Town Kanab (p190)
Transportation Private
Summary A pleasant hike through a cool gorge that flows with a shallow stream. Walk as much or as little as you like – Lower Hackberry continues for 26 miles.

This narrow gorge hike provides a welcome stretch for drivers on Cottonwood Canyon Rd (p178). The marked trailhead takes about half an hour to reach from Hwy 89. From Cannonville and Hwy 12, the trailhead is 31 miles south.

Follow the dirt track to a typically dry wash. Past the corral you'll reach **Lower Hackberry Canyon**. Water often flows down the canyon, and many stream crossings are required, but it's not usually deep – normally a few inches. Wander as far as you like; the first few miles of the canyon are the most narrow and interesting. After a while, the canyon opens up; in early summer, clouds of gnats often choose this point to attack. Mostly only backpackers proceed from here.

BACKCOUNTRY HIKES

The monument is a mecca for hardcore backcountry adventurers, but significant route-finding skills are required – GPS skills don't count. Be sure to carry 7.5-minute USGS maps. Talk to rangers before heading out, and don't take unnecessary risks. In addition to the epic trail below, ask rangers about Coyote Gulch, off Hole-in-the-Rock Rd, and the Gulch, off Burr Trail Rd. Escalante River Natural Bridge day hike (p180) can also be stretched into a 15-mile trek.

A free permit is needed for overnight hikes, and can be picked up at any visitor center, information kiosk or trailhead register.

BOULDER MAIL TRAIL

Duration 2 days
Distance 16 miles one way
Difficulty Difficult
Start Boulder landing strip
Finish Upper Escalante River trailhead
Nearest Towns Boulder (p188), Escalante (p186)
Transportation Hiker shuttle
Summary A hearty wilderness hike follows the historic Boulder–Escalante mail route around rugged Box-Death Hollow. Detouring into the slickrock wilderness area provides an interesting extra day's adventure.

This historic trail was once the supply and mail route between Boulder and Escalante. Much of it is unmarked or follows cairns. Most people do the one-way trip in two days, but a third day allows you to do some cross-country wandering and further explore Phipps-Death Hollow, a world of gullies, grottoes, spires and other slickrock wonders perched on the east edge of your route.

There are still serious ups and downs along the trail, but we recommend beginning at the Boulder landing strip, off Hell's Backbone Rd outside of Boulder at 6800ft, and ending at the Upper Escalante River trailhead, less than a mile outside Escalante at 5800ft. Arrange a hiker shuttle (p187) to and from, or just back to your car from the endpoint. The following description is general and is not meant to be your sole

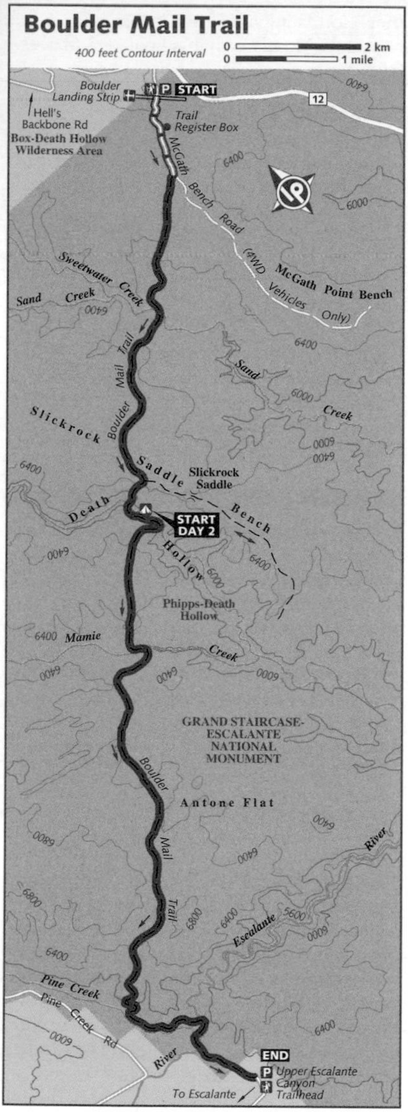

route guide; get detailed maps like the USGS Escalante, Calf Creek and Boulder Town quadrangles. Check with rangers for current conditions and descriptions.

The first leg takes you from the landing strip to **Phipps-Death Hollow** (four to five hours, 5.5 miles). Don't start late: you'll want plenty of light for the final descent. A mile-long 4WD road leads from the parking lot to the sign marking the start of the Boulder Mail Trail and the flats atop **New Home Bench**. From there it's 450ft down to the **Sand Creek** drainage, where cottonwoods offer shade and there's sometimes water. Then it's a 400ft trudge back up to the **Slickrock Saddle Bench** before making the precipitous 900ft drop into Death Hollow, a gorgeous, riparian canyon named for mules lost on the steep trip down. Several campsites lie within 0.25 miles of where the trail meets the creek here; some of the best are 300yd downstream.

A strenuous 800ft ascent out of Death Hollow kicks things off on day two. The trail then crosses to a slickrock plateau, descends to dry **Mamie Creek** and along and over a cracked sandstone formation resembling a giant cerebellum. At **Antone Flat** you come into open country, where a chalky-white slickrock draw may hold water in deep pockets.

After another 900ft slickrock decent, you climb down to **Pine Creek**. The creek's west bank is private, so follow its east bank to the **Escalante River**. To the west the canyon opens and the trail swings south through the brush, meeting a 4WD road and the Upper Escalante Canyon trailhead.

OTHER ACTIVITIES

Outfitters in Escalante, Boulder and Kanab offer half-, full- and multiday guided treks into the monument, often supported by pack animals – even llamas and goats! Horseback riding is available out of Boulder and Kanab; fly-fishing from Escalante.

Learn how to survive in this forbidding wilderness by studying with the **Boulder Outdoor Survival School** (☎ 303-444-9779; www.boss-inc.com). Based in Colorado, the school operates multiday courses in GSENM.

BIKING

Though the monument is laced with old ranching roads, like **Wolverine Loop** (p178), that could be used for mountain biking, the sport really hasn't caught on here. Escalante Outfitters (p187) does rent mountain bikes. For more on trails, look under 'Visitor Information', then 'Recreation Activities' on www.ut.blm.gov/monument. Road cyclists seem to enjoy the challenging hills of paved **Burr Trail** (p179). For more on cycling tours that cover several parks, GSENM included, see p45.

SLEEPING

Free dispersed backcountry camping – outside wilderness study areas – is widely available in the monument, but you need a permit. Pick one up at any visitor center, where you can discuss locations with rangers, or at major trailheads. For more on rules and regulations, see p177.

Outside the monument, campgrounds at Kodachrome Basin (p185), Escalante Petrified Forest (p186) and Coral Pink Sand Dunes (p193) State Parks have both running water and hot showers. Area towns are the only option for lodging with walls.

In the monument's two campgrounds you have to pack out trash, but leashed pets are allowed. Both are first-come, first-served.

Deer Creek Campground (Burr Trail Rd; tent & RV sites $; mid-May–mid-Sep;) This pretty camp sits beside a small creek beneath tall trees and red-rock formations, 6 miles southeast of Boulder. Amenities include fire pits, picnic tables and pit toilets. Seven sites, no water. Two sites fit small trailers; no hookups.

Calf Creek Campground (435-335-7382; Hwy 12; campsites $; year-round;) Surrounded by red-rock canyons, straddling a year-round creek at the Lower Calf Creek Falls trailhead, 15 miles east of Escalante, this campground is quite popular. Its 14 sites accommodate trailers up to 25ft long, and the campground has picnic tables, fire pits and toilets. Running water is on tap, but there are no showers.

AROUND GRAND STAIRCASE-ESCALANTE NATIONAL MONUMENT

Two main highways border GSENM: Hwy 12 in the north and Hwy 89 in the south. The towns with all the park services, along with other attractions, fall along these two routes.

HIGHWAY 12

Designated an All-American Road by the Federal Highway Administration, **Scenic Byway 12** (www.scenicbyway12.com) is spectacular. Stop at the numerous turnouts and viewpoints to see how quickly and dramatically the land changes from wooded plateau to red-rock canyon and from slickrock desert to alpine forest. The road's 125-mile course begins south of Panguitch at Hwy 89, heads east past Bryce Canyon and ends just west of Capitol Reef, in Torrey. This chapter deals only with the portion that skirts the northern boundaries of GSENM. The most noteworthy stretch winds its way up and down through moonscapelike slickrock between Escalante and Boulder. There has been talk of extending the bike trail that runs beside the road near Bryce Canyon all the way to Capitol Reef.

Kodachrome Basin State Park

Off Cottonwood Canyon Rd (p178), 9 miles south of Cannonville, you'll find one of the gems of the Utah State Park system, **Kodachrome** (435-679-8562; www.stateparks.utah.gov; admission $6; day use 6am-10pm). Petrified geysers and dozens of red, pink and white sandstone chimneys – some nearly 170ft tall – stand clustered together and resemble everything from a sphinx to a snowmobile. Visit in the early morning or late afternoon for the best light, when shadows play on the red rock. The moderately easy 3-mile **Panorama Trail** provides the best overview; be sure to take the side trails to **Indian Cave**, where you can check out the handprints on the wall (cowboys' or Indians'?), and to **Secret Passage**, a short narrow slot canyon. **Angel Palace Trail** (1-mile moderate loop) has great desert views from on high.

Red Stone Cabins (435-679-8536; www.redstonecabins.com; Kodachrome Basin State Park; cabin $$; Mar-Nov, by prearrangement Dec-Feb;) runs a little **camp store** (8am-6:30pm Sun-Thu, to 8pm Fri & Sat Apr-Oct) with all the essentials. Its four full-service cabins (linens, microwave, minifridge and coffee maker) are simple but cozy, with either a king bed or two queens.

The superclean, hot showers at the park-operated **campground** (801-322-3770, 800-322-3770; http://utahstateparks.reserveamerica.com; campsites $; year-round) are quite the treat in the desert. Sites are partially shaded and fairly well spaced, though numbers 12 through 14 are a little more removed, back by a canyon wall. Site 15 provides wheelchair access. No hookups; reservations advised.

CAMPGROUNDS IN & AROUND GSENM

Campground	Location	Number of sites	Elevation (ft)	Open	Reservations available?
Broken Bow RV Park	Escalante	28	5800	year-round	yes
Calf Creek	Hwy 12	14	5400	year-round	no
Coral Pink Sand Dunes State Park	Sand Dunes Rd	22	6000	year-round	yes
Deer Creek	Burr Trail Rd	7	5800	mid-May–mid-Sep	no
Escalante Petrified Forest State Park	Escalante Petrified Forest State Park	22	5900	year-round	yes
Hitch-N-Post	Kanab	16	4900	year-round	yes
Kanab RV Corral	Kanab	44	4900	year-round	yes
Kodachrome Basin State Park	Cottonwood Canyon Rd	24	5800	year-round	yes
White House	Paria Canyon-Vermillion Cliffs Wilderness Area	5	3000	year-round	no

Drinking Water · *Flush Toilets* · *Ranger Station* · *Great for Families* · *Wheelchair Accessible* · *Dogs Allowed* · *Grocery Store Nearby*

Escalante Petrified Forest State Park

Check out the small 'forest' of petrified wood and the 130-acre lake at this **state park** (☎ 435-826-4466; www.stateparks.utah.gov; day use $6; day use 8am-10pm), a little over a mile northwest of Escalante on Hwy 12. Visitor-center exhibits include 100-million-year-old dinosaur bones, and you can follow a short interpretive trail past examples of the mineralized wood. The 22-site, reserveable **campground** (☎ 800-322-3770; http://utahstateparks.reserveamerica.com; campsites $; year-round;) has hot showers, grills, fire pits, picnic tables and a dump station. Swimming is in the nearby reservoir, which, at the time of writing, was undergoing some dam reconstruction.

Escalante

pop 850 / elevation 5600ft

With a whopping population of 850, Escalante is the largest settlement on the north side of the monument. Folks here are an interesting mix of old-timers, artists, and post-monument-creation outdoors lovers. The town itself isn't much to speak of, but it does have lodgings and a handful of restaurants. Numerous outfitters make this their base for GSENM excursions, and you could too. Lying at the head of several park back roads, not far from the most popular hikes, the location is good.

ORIENTATION & INFORMATION

Escalante is 55 miles east of Bryce Canyon and 28 miles southwest of Boulder. Even in the center of the one-street town, cell-phone reception is spotty at best. For more local info, log on to www.escalante-cc.com. Note that November through March, owners may shorten business hours, depending on need.

Escalante Interagency visitor center (☎ 435-826-5499; www.ut.blm.gov/monument; 755 W Main St; 7:30am-5:30pm) Ask here about all public lands, trails, road conditions and camping.

Kazan Memorial Clinic (☎ 435-826-4374; 65 W Main St; 9am-5pm Mon, Wed & Fri) Limited medical care; the closest hospital is in Panguitch (p171).

Post office (☎ 435-826-4314; 230 W Main St; 7:15am-3:45pm Mon-Fri, 8:30am-noon Sat)

Wells Fargo ATM (250 W Main St; 24hr)

SIGHTS & ACTIVITIES

Gallery Escalante (☎ 435-826-4080; http://galleryescalante.com; 425 W Main St; 9am-5pm) is owned by Tracy and Jana Hasset; he does photography, she does the beadwork. They dis-

Facilities	Description	Page
	RV-oriented, in-town ground with open tent area, showers, laundry, full hookups and wi-fi.	188
	Popular canyon ground near year-round creek and the monument's only marked trail. Water, no showers.	185
	Near stunning pink dunes outside Kanab; can get windy, all-terrain-vehicle use noisy. Showers, no hookups.	193
	Primitive campground near Boulder: creek, trees and red rock. No water, no hookups.	185
	By a swimmable reservoir and forest outside Escalante, with showers, and electrical and water hookups. Interpretive trail.	186
	Shady little rustic campground in the center of Kanab. Full hookups, pull-through sites and wi-fi.	192
	Well-manicured RV ground with gardens, pool, showers, laundry and wi-fi. Big-rig access, full hookups.	193
	A rock formation–filled park not far from Bryce Canyon. Trailers to 45ft, no hookups, hot showers.	185
	Primitive campground at White House trailhead with pit toilets; no water, no trash collection. Tents only.	194

Restaurant Nearby *Pay-phone* *RV Dump Station*

play/sell other local artists' works as well as their own. Their multiday Photoshop workshops send students out into the field 'on assignment,' then bring them back into the studio to learn how to process the shots.

You'll find books, maps, camping and hiking supplies, USGS 7.5-quadrangle maps, wi-fi access, beer, and bicycle rental at **Escalante Outfitters** (☎ 435-826-4266; www.escalanteoutfitters.com; 310 W Main St; 8am-9pm Mar-Oct, 9am-6pm Tue-Sat Nov-Feb) store and cafe. A whiteboard in front lists guided treks with space available in the days ahead.

Hiking and driving in the monument are the main activities here. Reserve ahead to rent Jeep Wranglers from **Escalante Jeep Rental** (☎ 435-616-4144; www.escalantejeeprentals.com; 495 W Main St; 10am-5pm) and ATVs and 4WD utility vehicles at **High Adventure Rentals** (☎ 435-616-4640; www.highadventurerentals.com); both from $180 per day.

With local knowledge and 4WD or pack-animal support, outfitters can take you further than you can reach on your own. Rates start around $80 per person for a half-day. Tours operate May through October and reservations are required. Operators include the following:

Escalante Backroads (☎ 435-633-5637; www.escalantebackroads.com) Mountain-biker and hiker shuttles, 4WD back-road tours.

Escalante Outfitters (☎ 435-826-4266; www.escalanteoutfitters.com; 310 W Main St) Recommended naturalist walks and guided fly-fishing.

Escape Goats (☎ 435-826-4652; http://escapegoats.us) Hiker shuttles, great slot-canyon and ancient-site tours, plus multiday pack trips with goats. Yeah, really – goats.

Excursions of Escalante (☎ 800-839-7567; www.excursionsofescalante.com; Trailhead Cafe, 125 E Main St) The best for canyoneering, climbing and adventure hikes. Hiker shuttles and photo walks, too.

Grand Staircase Adventure Guides (☎ 435-826-4122; www.gsadventureguides.com) Backpacking specialist; day hikes and shuttles, too.

Utah Canyons (☎ 435-826-4967; www.utahcanyons.com; 325 W Main St) Guided day hikes, multiday supported treks and hiker shuttles.

SLEEPING

Escalante Outfitters Bunkhouse Cabins (☎ 435-826-4266; www.escalanteoutfitters.com; 310 W Main St; tent sites & cabins $; wi-fi) Pitch a tent or rent a rustic, but heated, teeny-tiny log cabin (linens included, shared bathroom, no air-conditioning) in a shady yard. Picnic tables and grills available.

Circle D Motel (435-826-4297; www.escalantecircledmotel.com; 475 W Main St; r $;) It's just an updated, older motel, but the friendly proprietor goes out of his way to accommodate guests. Room microwaves and minifridges included; pet fee $10.

Rainbow Country Bed & Breakfast (435-826-4567, 800-252-8824; www.bnbescalante.com; 586 E 300 S; r incl breakfast $;) You couldn't ask for better trail advice than you receive over big home-cooked breakfasts here. The ranch-like house on the edge of town is not flashy, just comfortable and homey – with a big TV lounge (no room TVs), guest refrigerator and outdoor hot tub.

Canyons Bed & Breakfast (435-826-4747, 866-526-9667; www.canyonsbnb.com; 120 E Main St; r incl breakfast $$;) Upscale, cabin-rooms with porches surround a shaded terrace and gardens where you can enjoy your gourmet breakfast each morning. Except for a small dining area, the wooden 1905 ranch house on site is for the owners.

Even more options:

Broken Bow RV Park & Cabins (435-826-4959, 888-241-8785; www.brokenbowrvpark.com; 495 W Main St; tent & RV sites $, cabins $; year-round;) Small campground with public (fee) showers and laundry.

Cowboy Country Inn (435-826-4250; www.cowboycountryinn.com; 95 W Main St; r $, ste $$;) Six theme rooms (Aztec, lonestar, blue etc) are more like a basic B&B than a tiny strip motel.

Slot Canyons Inn (435-826-4901, 866-889-8375; www.slotcanyonsinn.com; 3680 W Hwy 12; r incl breakfast $$$;) An architectural show piece on the edge of the desert; upscale all the way.

EATING

Griffin Grocery (435-826-4226; 30 W Main St; 8am-7pm Mon-Sat) Fruit and vegetables are delivered to the only grocery in town on Tuesday and Friday mornings. Get there early if you want some.

Trailhead Cafe (435-826-4714, 800-839-7567; 125 E Main St; 8am-8pm Wed-Mon May-Oct) In an 1880s building, this little cafe/outfitter headquarters serves ice cream and local-beef burgers.

Esca-Latte Cafe & Pizza (435-826-4266; 310 W Main St; breakfast $, pizza $$; 8am-9pm Mar-Oct;) For granola and eggs at breakfast, and tasty homemade pizza and beer for lunch and dinner, visit Escalante Outfitters' eatery.

Cowboy Blues (435-826-4577; 530 W Main St; sandwiches & mains $-$$; 11am-10pm) All-American cooking includes dishes such as meatloaf, steaks and seafood. The rustic dining room also serves liquor.

Georgie's Corner Cafe (435-826-4784; 190 W Main St; mains $-$$; dinner Mon-Sat) Fresh Mexican and Southwestern food tastes even better when served in an eclectic old house covered with artist murals. Be sure to try the made-to-order hot chips and salsa.

Head of the Rocks

At mile marker 69.8, about 8 miles east of Escalante, pull off the highway for one of the most arresting roadside views in Utah. The **Aquarius Plateau** lords over giant mesas, towering domes, deep canyons and undulating slickrock that unfurl in an explosion of color.

Further east, near mile marker 73, stop for coffee and take in canyon views at the must-see **Kiva Koffeehouse** (435-826-4550; www.kivakoffeehouse.com; Hwy 12; breakfast & sandwiches $; 8am-4:30pm Wed-Mon Apr-Oct;). Built to resemble a traditional Native American cliff dwelling, the semicircular building has floor-to-ceiling glass walls supported by huge treelike timber. It serves home-baked goods, breakfast and lunch. For seclusion, you can't beat renting one of two luxurious rooms in **Kiva Cottage** (r $$$;), also built into the cliff. No TVs, no phones.

The Hogback

East of Calf Creek, between mile markers 78 and 80, Hwy 12 crosses the narrow **Hogback** ridge, with precipitous drop-offs into seemingly bottomless canyons and rolling slickrock desert. There are no guardrails; pull off at designated turnouts to take in the mesmerizing views of undulating stone as far as the eye can see.

Boulder

pop 250 / elevation 6675ft

To get to Boulder from the west, you have to traverse a narrow and winding road across a monocline ridge; to reach it from the east, you cross over 11,317ft-tall Boulder Mountain. No wonder then, that this town received its mail by mule until 1940, and the road wasn't fully paved until 1985. You can still sense the rural history of the place, but today Boulder is home to a diverse collection of down-to-earth people – from Zen Buddhists and artists to farmers and cowboys. Surrounded by forests and the GSENM, Boulder has a more outdoorsy

PIECING TOGETHER THE PAST

More than 260,000 site-excavated shards of pottery lie tucked away on archive shelves in Anasazi State Park Museum (below). The one partially reconstructed jug on display represents a summer's worth of work. But pottery is not all that museum curator, Don Montoya, and his interns are piecing back together. They're puzzling out the story of ancestral peoples. What he would like visitors to know more than anything is that the Native American presence in the area 'persists through time.' They were here at least 11,000 years ago, and they're here still. Montoya himself is of mixed European and Taos Indian origin.

The Coomb's site where the museum is located dates to the 1100s and is hypothesized to be in a transition zone between areas inhabited by Freemont and Ancient Puebloan cultures. But there's still much to learn. 'I've hiked this area for 30 years and I still find ancient sites I've never seen,' says Montoya. As technology develops, so does what we know. A geo-referencing project is underway to map in 3-D where every jar or bowl was located on the site and at what depth. According to Montoya, combined with location, the jug shape, how the pottery was decorated and the composition of the clay helps them differentiate between local and tradeware. And that in turn sheds light on the interaction between peoples, clans and ideologies. Who knows what new theories will emerge.

Interested in visiting some of the many area sites? 'Go with a guide,' says Montoya. Outfitters know where the rock art and ancient granaries are hidden, and they're sensitive to the sites.

feel – and a higher elevation – than Escalante, but far fewer services.

ORIENTATION & INFORMATION

Boulder is 28 miles northeast of Escalante and 60 miles southwest of Capitol Reef National Park. To learn more online, visit www.boulderutah.com. Most of the town's businesses close November through March, when heavy snow sets in. You can get cellphone service outside, and wi-fi inside **Hills & Hollows Country Store** (☎ 435-335-7349; Hwy 12; 9am-7pm, gas 24hr), the only gas station and grocery supply in town. Some organic snacks available.

The **interagency desk** (☎ 435-335-7382; 9am-5pm mid-Mar–mid-Nov) in the Anasazi State Park Museum (below) can answer questions about all surrounding public lands, including Dixie National Forest.

SIGHTS & ACTIVITIES

GSENM's Boulder Mail Trail (p183) and Burr Trail (p177) originate in Boulder.

In the 1950s, thousands of artifacts were excavated from the Coomb's Site that **Anasazi State Park Museum** (☎ 435-335-7308; www.stateparks.utah.gov; Hwy 12; admission $4; 8am-6pm Jun-Aug, 9am-5pm Sep-May) now protects. You can wander parts of the site itself, inhabited from AD 1130 to 1175. But the museum is even more interesting, with its pottery-preservation gallery and excellent exhibits on the Ancestral Puebloan peoples. For more see the boxed text, above.

Head across the slickrock plateau, into Box-Death Hollow Wilderness or up the mountain on horseback, with **Boulder Mountain Trails** (☎ 435-335-7480; www.boulderutah.com/bmr; off Hell's Backbone Rd). Multiday pack trips and cattle drives also available. Lodging and meals at Boulder Mountain Ranch (p190), next door, can be included in packages.

Half-day horseback rides, as well as other outfitter trips (all March through November only), start around $80 per person. Hiking guides can all lead you to rock art and ruins in the area. Recommended outfitters:

Boulder Mountain Fly-fishing (☎ 435-335-7306, 435-231-1823; www.bouldermountainflyfishing.com)

Earth Tours (☎ 435-691-1241; www.earth-tours.com) Interpretive hikes and drives led by a fascinating (and fun) PhD geologist.

Escalante Canyon Outfitters (☎ 435-691-3037, 888-326-4453; www.ecohike.com) Excellent canyon hikes and ancient archaeology treks. More than 20 years in the area.

Red Rock 'n Llamas (☎ 435-616-7421, 877-955-2627; www.redrocknllamas.com) Llama-supported day trips, overnights and drop-camp services (kids love the half-day 'take a llama to lunch' hike). Hiker shuttles and 4WD tours, too.

SLEEPING & EATING

Pole's Place (☎ 435-335-7422, 800-730-7422; www.boulderutah.com/polesplace; r $; Mar-Oct;) Small and simple, this 11-room, mom-and-pop motel is lovingly and immaculately maintained.

Boulder Mountain Ranch (☎ 435-335-7480; http://bouldermountainguestranch.com; off Hell's Backbone Rd; r $, cabins $$;) Wow, what a peaceful 160-acre setting. At the time of writing, new owners were spiffing up the giant log cabin with eight rooms and three out-cabins, but it will always be rustic. The dining room serves chef-cooked meals by arrangement.

our pick **Boulder Mountain Lodge** (☎ 435-335-7460, 800-556-3446; www.boulder-utah.com; cnr Hwy 12 & Burr Trail Rd; r $$-$$$;) High-thread-count sheets, plush terry robes and Aveda bath products: Boulder Mountain Lodge is the ideal place for day hikers who like luxury. Watch the birds flit by on the adjacent 15-acre wildlife sanctuary before dipping in the hot tub or dining at the organically oriented Hell's Backbone Grill (below) on site. Pet fee ($15).

Burr Trail Outpost (☎ 435-335-7565; cnr Hwy 12 & Burr Trail Rd; snacks $; 8am-8pm Mar-Oct;) Equal parts gallery, bookshop and cafe; don't miss the molten chocolate muffins.

Burr Trail Grill (☎ 435-335-7503; cnr Hwy 12 & Burr Trail Rd; sandwiches $, mains $$; lunch & dinner Mar-Oct) Organic vegetable tarts, local-beef burgers and changing specials rival dishes at the more famous restaurant in town. Great desserts and cookies (ginger's our fave).

Hell's Backbone Grill (☎ 435-335-7464; Boulder Mountain Lodge, cnr Hwy 12 & Burr Trail Rd; breakfast $-$$, mains $$$; breakfast & dinner May-Sep, dinner only Mar, Apr & Oct–mid-Nov) Artistic, earthy interpretations of Southwestern cuisine. Menus are seasonal but think chili and piñon-crusted lamb for dinner, and brown rice, organic greens and poached eggs with chipotle aioli for breakfast. Zen Buddhist owners Jen Castle and Blake Spalding not only feed the stomach, they feed the soul, training staff in mindfulness and inviting the whole community to a July 4 ice cream social and talent show.

HIGHWAY 89

The southern portion of Hwy 89 is not as egregiously scenic as Hwy 12, but along it lie Kanab (the region's largest town), dirt access roads to GSENM's southern section and the must-see Paria Canyon-Vermilion Cliffs Wilderness Area.

Kanab

pop 3516 / elevation 4925ft

Western history – both real and reel – unspools at this remote outpost. John Wayne truly did eat, sleep and film here – as did many other movie stars in 'Utah's Little Hollywood' from the 1930s through the 1960s – and for many, that's authentic enough. Much of the town looks like a false-front set, but it's the desert that's the star attraction. Kanab is the biggest town near GSENM and Paria Canyon-Vermillion Cliffs Wilderness Area, plus it sits at a crossroad between other parks. Zion is 44 miles away, Bryce 83 miles, the Grand Canyon's North Rim 81 miles and Glen Canyon 74 miles. Those doing the Grand Circle will find this a very convenient stopping point.

ORIENTATION & INFORMATION

Most businesses lie along Hwy 89, which snakes through the center. South of town, the highway continues east along 300 S, leading to the monument and Big Water. Alternate Hwy 89A follows south along 100 E toward the Grand Canyon.

BLM Kanab field office (☎ 435-644-4600; 318 N 100 East; 7:45am-3:45pm Mon-Fri) Mid-November through mid-March it issues permits for the Paria Canyon-Vermilion Cliffs Wilderness Area (p194).

GSENM Kanab visitor center (☎ 435-644-4680; 745 E Hwy 89; 8am-5pm) Provides interagency info on roads, trails and camping in GSENM and beyond. Check weather conditions here.

Kane County Hospital (☎ 435-644-5811; www.kchosp.net; 355 N Main St) Twenty-four-hour emergency room.

Kane County Office of Tourism (☎ 435-644-5033, 800-733-5263; www.kaneutah.com; 78 S 100 East; 8am-8pm Mon-Fri, 9am-5pm Sat, 9am-1pm Sun Mar-Oct, 8:30am-5pm Mon-Sat, 1-5pm Sun Nov-Feb) Great old Western movie posters and artifacts are on display at this town visitor center. Jackie was a stunt gal in the famous films; ask her about it.

Library (☎ 435-644-2394; 374 N Main St; 10am-5pm Mon & Fri, to 7pm Tue-Thu, to 2pm Sat) Free internet and wi-fi access.

Post office (☎ 435-644-2760; 39 S Main St; 9am-4pm Mon-Fri, 1-4pm Sat)

SIGHTS

If you want a tour of all the Old West movie sites, attend the **Western Legends Roundup** (☎ 800-733-5263; www.westernlegendsroundup.com), which, for five days in late August, celebrates all things cowboy. Johnson Canyon (p179) and Paria Valley (p193) in GSENM were oft-used locations.

Stars stayed at movie-central **Parry Lodge** (☎ 435-644-2601; www.parrylodge.com; 89 E Center St;

KANAB, YOU OUGHTA BE IN PICTURES

The movie industry has known about the rugged wilds around Kanab since early days. In the 1920s, film adaptations of Zane Grey novels were shot here. And in the '40s and '50s, dozens of Westerns were filmed in the area, including those by screen legend John Ford. Movies set locally have included the following:

- *Drums Along the Mohawks* (1939), John Wayne
- *Bandolero!* (1968), James Stewart, Dean Martin, Raquel Welsh
- *Planet of the Apes* (1968), Charlton Heston
- *The Outlaw Josey Wales* (1976), Clint Eastwood
- *John Carter of Mars* (2010), Disney-Pixar

TV shows:

- *The Lone Ranger*
- *Have Gun Will Travel*
- *Gunsmoke*
- *Six Million Dollar Man*
- *Lassie*

movies $2; 8pm Sat Jun-Aug), built in the 1930s. Back then the owner provided horses, cattle and catering for the sets. Look for the nostalgic photos on the lobby walls. Saturday nights in summer, the hotel shows the old movies in a barn out back.

A few of the actual buildings used on Western movie sets, including *The Outlaw Josey Wales,* are collected at **Frontier Movie Town Museum & Trading Post** (435-644-5337; 297 W Center St; admission free; 8am-10pm May-Sep, 10am-5pm Oct-Apr). Along with several other shops in town, it sells all the Western duds and doodads you could care to round up.

Another interesting tourist trap, **Moqui Cave** (435-644-8525; www.moquicave.com; Hwy 89; adult/child under 12 $5/3; 9am-7pm Mon-Sat May-Sep, 10am-4pm Mon-Sat Oct-Apr), 5 miles north of town, is an oddball collection of genuine dinosaur tracks, real cowboy and Indian artifacts, and other flotsam and jetsam that the football-star father of the owner collected in the 1950s – all inside a giant cave.

Travel 0.25 miles further north to visit the no-kill **Best Friends Animal Sanctuary** (435-644-2001; www.bestfriends.org; Hwy 89; tours free; 8:30am-5pm;), with 1700 animals on a 33,000-acre ranch in Angel Canyon. The facility offers 45-minute and 1½-hour tours several times a day (reserve ahead), so you can meet some of bunnies, horses, pigs, dogs, cats and parrots. It also shows a complimentary film. You can stay overnight here in motel-like **cottages** ($$) or on **RV sites** ($), and it is always looking for volunteers. While you're there, look around you: the clifftop rim of the canyon is where the Lone Ranger reared up and shouted 'Hi Ho Silver!' every TV episode.

ACTIVITIES

Half bookstore, half outdoor supply store, **Willow Canyon Outdoor** (435-644-8884; www.willowcanyon.com; 263 S 100 East; 7am-7pm Mar-Nov;) can outfit most of your camping and climbing needs. Plus, it serves a darn good espresso.

Horseback rides (from $60 for two hours) and horse boarding are available by arrangement with **Lit'l Bit Ranch** (435-899-9655; http://litlbitranch.org; 2550 E Hwy 89). The more engine-inclined might opt to rent from **Canyon Country Jeep Rental** (435-644-8250; http://canyoncountryjeep.com; 285 S 100 East), and three- to five-day four-wheeler trips are available from **Anasazi ATV Tours** (435-689-1237, 866-256-7628; www.anasaziatv.com).

The only outfitter that leads guided hike and drive tours into the monument is outside of town, at mile marker 21 on Hwy 89. Explore petroglyph panels, dinosaur tracks, slot canyons and more with **Paria Outpost & Outfitters** (928-691-1047; www.paria.com; Hwy 89);

A GRAND DETOUR

Visiting the **North Rim of the Grand Canyon** is a very accessible day trip, 81 miles south of Kanab on Hwy 89A. This side of the park is higher (at 8200ft) and sees far fewer visitors than the South Rim, and yet the views are as good or better. Note, though, that the North Rim and the services listed below are closed from mid-October through mid-May.

It's 14 miles from the North Rim entrance station to **Bright Angel Point**, where you'll find the **North Rim visitor center** (☎ 928-638-7864; ☼ 8am-6pm mid-May–mid-Oct), the lodge and restaurants. This should be your first destination. An open-air deck overlooks the classic view, and a paved, wheelchair-accessible 0.3-mile trail leads from here to the point itself. The 3-mile round-trip **Transept Trail** skirts the rim from the lodge to the campground. Ask about mule rides.

Day-trippers' next foray should be the 23-mile drive from the lodge to **Cape Royal** (about 40 minutes one way). This route features a handful of incredible turnouts, including a 6-mile round-trip detour to **Point Imperial**, and it ends at what feels like the edge of the Earth. Along the route is a selection of short, easy trails (0.2 to 4 miles round trip) that allow you to stretch your legs without making a big commitment; these include the **Point Imperial Trail**, **Roosevelt Point Trail**, **Cape Final Trail** and **Cape Royal Trail**. Those with more time and energy should hike a section of the **North Kaibab Trail**, the only North Rim trail that descends into the canyon.

Grand Canyon Lodge Dining Room (☎ 928-638-2611; breakfast & lunch $-$$, dinner $$-$$$; ☼ breakfast, lunch & dinner mid-May–mid-Oct) requires reservations at dinner. **Grand Canyon Cook-Out** (☎ 928-638-2611; adult/child $35/22; ☼ 6:15pm mid-May–Sep; ♿) is a chuckwagon-style dinner – beef brisket, roasted chicken, fresh biscuits – with a show. The lodge also has a general store, deli and saloon.

On the way from or to the Grand Canyon, you can detour to **Pipe Spring National Monument** (☎ 928-643-7105; www.nps.gov/pisp; adult/child under 16 $5/free; ☼ 7am-5pm Jun-Aug, 8am-5pm Sep-May). The spring was a vital water supply and seasonal home for Ancestral Puebloan people and their descendents. It later served as an important way station and fortified ranch for Mormon pioneers in the late 19th century. Today the monument sits on the Kaibab Paiute Indian Reservation. Museum exhibits tell the indigenous peoples' and the Mormon story side by side. Outside there's little to suggest Native American inhabitation. The spring itself is covered by Winsor Castle, the Mormon's original ranch; free tours are offered every half-hour. Pipe Spring is 73 miles from the North Rim and 20 miles from Kanab.

Note: Arizona does not observe daylight-saving time, so in summer it's one hour behind Utah time. For a complete destination rundown, pick up a copy of Lonely Planet's *Grand Canyon National Park*.

hiker shuttles and basic lodging are available also.

SLEEPING
Kanab hosts a relative surplus of older, independent motels; not all have been updated. Look for a complete list at www.kaneutah.com.

Hitch-N-Post Campground (☎ 435-644-2142; www.hitchnpostrvpark.com; 196 E 300 South; tent & RV sites $, cabins $; ☼ year-round; ☞ ♿) Folksy Old West antiques decorate the area around the reception at this small and shady campground near the town center. Half the RV sites are taken up by long-term residents. Rustic camping cabins (shared bath, with linens $2) have one queen or two double beds.

Parry Lodge (☎ 435-644-2601; www.parrylodge.com; 89 E Center St; r $-$$; ☒ ☐ ☞ ☒ ♿) The aura of Western movie days gone by is more special than many of the rooms at this rambling old motel. Room name plates indicate who slept where. If quality is your concern, opt for the L-shape double queens, nicely refurbished in cottage decor.

our pick **Quail Park Lodge** (☎ 435-644-8700; www.quailparklodge.com; 125 N 300 West; r $$; ☒ ☐ ☞ ☒ ♿) A colorful retro style pervades throughout this refurbished 1963 motor hotel. Turquoise Schwinn Cruiser bicycles stand near vibrant beach balls bobbing in the pool; yellow clamshell chairs wait outside plush rooms. Mod cons include free phone calls, microwaves, mini-fridges and complimentary gourmet coffee. One dog allowed per room.

Purple Sage Inn (☎ 435-644-5377, 877-644-5377; www.purplesageinn.com; 54 S Main St; r incl breakfast $$-

$$$;) From a cabinet-encased, fold-down bathtub to brass push-button light switches, the antique details here are exquisite. In the 1880s this was a Mormon polygamist's home, then in the 1900s it became a hotel, and Western author Zane Grey stayed here. As a B&B, Zane's namesake room – with its quilt-covered wood bed, sitting room and balcony access – is our favorite.

More good choices:

Kanab RV Corral (435-644-5330; www.xpressweb.com/~rvcorral/; 483 S 100 East; RV sites $; year-round;) Spiffy RV campground surrounded by gardens; superclean facilities.

Bob Bon Inn (435-644-3069, 800-644-5094; www.bobbon.com; 236 N 300 West; r $-$$;) Log cabin–like motel with small tidy rooms and Western spirit; the lobby is plastered with old movie-star photos and autographs.

Aiken's Lodge (435-644-2625, 877-644-2105; www.aikenslodge.com; 79 W Center St; r $-$$;) Family-run motel; nice little pool and laundry.

EATING

Kanab is the only town around the monument with chain restaurants, fast food and more than a handful of options.

Linda Lea's Cafe & Bakery (435-644-8191; 4 E Center St; sandwiches $; 7am-2pm Mon-Fri, 8am-2pm Sat;) Barista coffee served with a side of local gossip. The freshly made lunch sandwiches are better than those for breakfast, with precooked egg.

Houston's Trail's End Restaurant (435-644-2488; 32 E Center St; breakfast $, mains $$; 7am-10pm) The food must be good if locals frequent a place where the waitresses wear six-shooters. Order up chicken-fried steak and gravy for down-home goodness. No alcohol.

our pick **Rocking V Cafe** (435-644-8001; 97 W Center St; mains $$-$$$; dinner) Fresh ingredients star in dishes like hand-cut buffalo tenderloin and chargrilled zucchini with curried quinoa. Local artwork decorating the old brick building is as creative as the food.

Also worth a taste:

Honey's Marketplace (435-644-5877; 260 E 300 S; 7am-10pm) Full grocery store with deli; look for the 1950s truck inside.

Nedra's Too (435-644-2030; 310 S 100 East; breakfast & mains $-$$; 7am-10pm Thu-Tue) A little of everything Mexican or Western: creamy enchiladas, Navajo tacos, charbroiled steaks…

Luo's (435-644-5592; 365 S 100 E; mains $$; lunch & dinner) Surprisingly good Chinese food; great vegetable selection.

Spurs Grill (435-644-8080; 36 N 300 West; breakfast $, mains $$; 7am-10pm) Cheesy buffet food, but there's a full bar.

Coral Pink Sand Dunes State Park

Coral-colored sand is not especially strange in the southern half of GSENM, but seeing it gathered as giant dunes in a 3700-acre **state park** (435-648-2800; Sand Dunes Rd; day use $6; day use dawn-dusk, visitor center 9am-9pm Mar-Oct, to 4pm Nov-Feb) is quite novel. The pinkish hue results from the eroding, red Navajo sandstone in the area. Note that 1200 acres of the park are devoted to off-highway vehicles, so it's not necessarily a peaceful experience unless you're here during quiet hours (10pm to 9am). A 0.5-mile interpretive dune hike does lead to a 265-acre, traffic-free conservation area.

The same winds that shift the dunes can make tent camping unpleasant at the 22-site **campground** (reservations 800-322-3770; http://utahstateparks.reserveamerica.com; campsites $), with toilets and hot showers. Reservations are essential on weekends when off-roaders come to play.

Paria Valley Road & Movie Set

Thirty-three miles east of Kanab, Paria Valley Rd (pronounced pa-*ree*-uh) follows an

TRACKING DOWN DINOS

Experts locating dinosaur tracks in the vast wilderness expanse around the monument is not unheard of, but they are usually prohibitively difficult to reach. Not so for the 185-million-year-old prints found at the **Moccasin Mountain Dinosaur Track Site**, 3 miles south of Coral Pink Sand Dunes State Park (above) on freely accessible BLM land. The last 2.2 miles are deeply sandy, high-clearance 4WD track. Without the appropriate vehicle, you could park and hike the remaining distance. Six different dinosaurs, sized 1ft- to 20ft-long, left their tracks in a slickrock expanse the size of a football field. Pick up a map and directions at the state park. If you see a beehives formation, you've gone too far. For more BLM track sites, see www.blm.gov/ut/st/en/prog/more/cultural/Paleontology.html.

evocative ridge north into the Vermilion Cliffs. The 5-mile dirt track leads to the former location of the **Paria Movie Set** that burned down in 2007. Now interpretive signs near a picnic area depict what the area looked like. A mile further north, on the other side of the river, hike to look for the little that's left of **Pahreah ghost town**. Floods in the 1880s rang the death knell for the 130-strong farming community. Since then, time and fire have taken the buildings and all but the most rudimentary signs of settlement. But the valley is a pretty introduction to GSENM.

Paria Canyon-Vermilion Cliffs Wilderness Area

With miles of weathered, swirling slickrock and slot-canyon systems that can be hiked for days without seeing a soul, it's no wonder that this wilderness area is such a popular destinations for hearty trekkers, canyoneers and photographers. If you've looked at postcards in southern Utah, you've probably seen a picture of the sculptural orange sandstone bowl known as the Wave. But that formation and others are far from easily accessible. This is the remotest of remote Utah lands, straddling the Arizona border, and permits are required for the most sought-after routes.

For general information, visit www.blm.gov. The **Paria contact station** (☎ 435-688-3246; 🕑 8:30am-4:15pm Mar 15-Nov 15), which is 43 miles from Kanab on Hwy 89, is permit-central in season. It also sells topographical maps, offers water and provides advice and updated road and trail conditions. Year-round the rangers at the BLM Kanab field office (p190) can answer questions, but they're only in charge of Paria permits off-season, from November 16 through March 14. Trailheads for routes mentioned below lie along House Rock Valley Rd (4.7 miles west of the contact station), a rugged dirt road, passable in dry weather.

Hikers fight like dogs to get a permit ($7) for **Coyote Buttes North** – the trail-less expanse of slickrock that contains the **Wave**. The nearly magical sight of the slickrock, which appears to be seething and swirling, is well worth the 7-mile, five-hour round-trip hike. Go to www.az.blm.gov/paria to try for the 10 advance permits that are available four months ahead. Otherwise you can hope (usually in vain during spring and fall) for one of the 10 next-day, walk-in permits assigned by lottery. As many as 120 people have lined up for the lottery in May. Directions to the protected site are not divulged until you have a permit. Note that overnight permits are also reserveable for Paria Canyons, four months in advance, but do not include access to Coyote Buttes North and the Wave.

An alternative way to see related slickrock formations is to get a next-day permit ($6) for **Coyote Buttes South**. The permit is in much less demand (and not reserveable online), but 4WD is absolutely required for the deep-sand access roads. Ask rangers for directions.

You don't need a permit, but you do need to pay $6 to hike on other area wilderness trails. Starting from the same trailhead as the Wave, but going the opposite direction, **Wire Pass** (3.4 miles round trip) is a great slot-canyon day hike. The parking lot is 8 miles south along House Rock Valley Rd. You start out descending in a sandy wash and eventually the gorge slots up, narrowing to shoulder-width in places. You'll scramble down a few boulder-choked sections, and under logs jammed 50ft overhead, before reaching a wide alcove with what was likely an ancient granary ledge; look for the petroglyph panel on the far end. Wire Pass dead-ends here at the confluence with **Buckskin Gulch**. Stop there (1.2 miles along) or continue exploring the Buckskin slot canyon as far north or south as you like. Note that at times there may be water in one or both of the canyons.

Another option is a 16-mile backpack starting at the **Buckskin Gulch trailhead** and ending at **White House trailhead**. As noted above, permits are required for camping overnight, and some areas are off-limits. Check with rangers. **White House Campground** (tent sites $), with five primitive walk-in sites, is off the road next to the contact station, at the White House trailhead.

Toadstools

About 1.5 miles east of the Paria contact station on Hwy 89, turn north and follow the dirt road to the rounded rock tops you can see from the highway. The **Toadstools** are red hoodoos that are easily and freely explored on BLM land. To get to the formations is less than a 1-mile hike from the end of the road. Slanting, late-afternoon light is best for catching the shape and depth of the eerie features.

Big Water

About 56 miles from Kanab, this small town with little more than a convenience store is known because of the dinosaur finds (and polygamist residents) in the area. The **Big Water visitor center** (☎ 435-675-3200; 100 Upper Revolution Way; 🕑 9am-6pm Apr-Oct, 8am-5pm Nov-Mar) has great paleontology exhibits, which include a replica of a dig, various bones that have been found in the monument (including the 13ft tail of a duckbill) and a spectacular 9ft-by-45ft mural by expert dinosaur painter Larry Felder. Dinosaur tracks are fairly common in the area; ask here about day hikes.

The south end of **Smoky Mountain Rd** (p180) emerges at Big Water. The nearest town of consequence – Page, Arizona – is 17 miles southeast, and is the access point for Lake Powell and Antelope Canyon.

Capitol Reef National Park

Towering slabs of chocolate-red rock, yellow sandstone arches, giant cream-colored domes and stark gray monoliths jut skyward at Capitol Reef, revealing millions of years of geologic history in an area less than 10% of the Grand Canyon. Native Americans once called this vast landscape of tilted buttes, jumbled rocks and winding canyons the 'Land of the Sleeping Rainbow.'

Capitol Reef harbors fantastic hiking trails, rugged 4WD roads and 1000-year-old Fremont petroglyph panels. At its heart grow the shady orchards of Fruita, a Mormon settlement dating back to the 1870s. Take a break underneath a stand of cottonwood trees sprawled beside the Fremont River, where you'll find swimming holes that will baptize your red-dirt-caked body anew.

The park's centerpiece is Waterpocket Fold, a 100-mile monocline – a buckle in the Earth's crust – that stymied early explorers. They dubbed it a reef, as it blocked their way west like a reef blocks a ship's passage. Capitol Reef is also known for its enormous Navajo sandstone domes, one of which resembles the US Capitol building in Washington, DC... if you've been wandering around the desert long enough to start seeing mirages, that is.

The usual approach to Capitol Reef is to wind over Boulder Mountain on Hwy 12, then turn onto Hwy 24 near tiny Torrey. You'll pass scenic viewpoints, historic sites and hiking trailheads. South of the visitor center, the park's main scenic drive starts near Fruita. Alternatively, the partly paved Burr Trail (p177) is a beautifully scenic back door to Capitol Reef's wonders.

HIGHLIGHTS

- Plucking apples, peaches and cherries in the historic orchards of **Fruita** (p198)
- Peering through binoculars at **ancient Native American petroglyphs** (p200)
- Hiking up red-rock cliffs and over slickrock to stand underneath natural **Hickman Bridge** (p203)
- Scaling the Waterpocket Fold to secret slot canyons and skyscraping lookouts in **Cohab Canyon** (p204)
- Bumping along the backcountry **Cathedral Valley Loop** (p201) to the Temples of the Sun and the Moon

- **Total Area** 378 sq miles
- **Elevation** 5500ft (at Fruita)
- **Average high/low temperature in July** 91°F/62°F

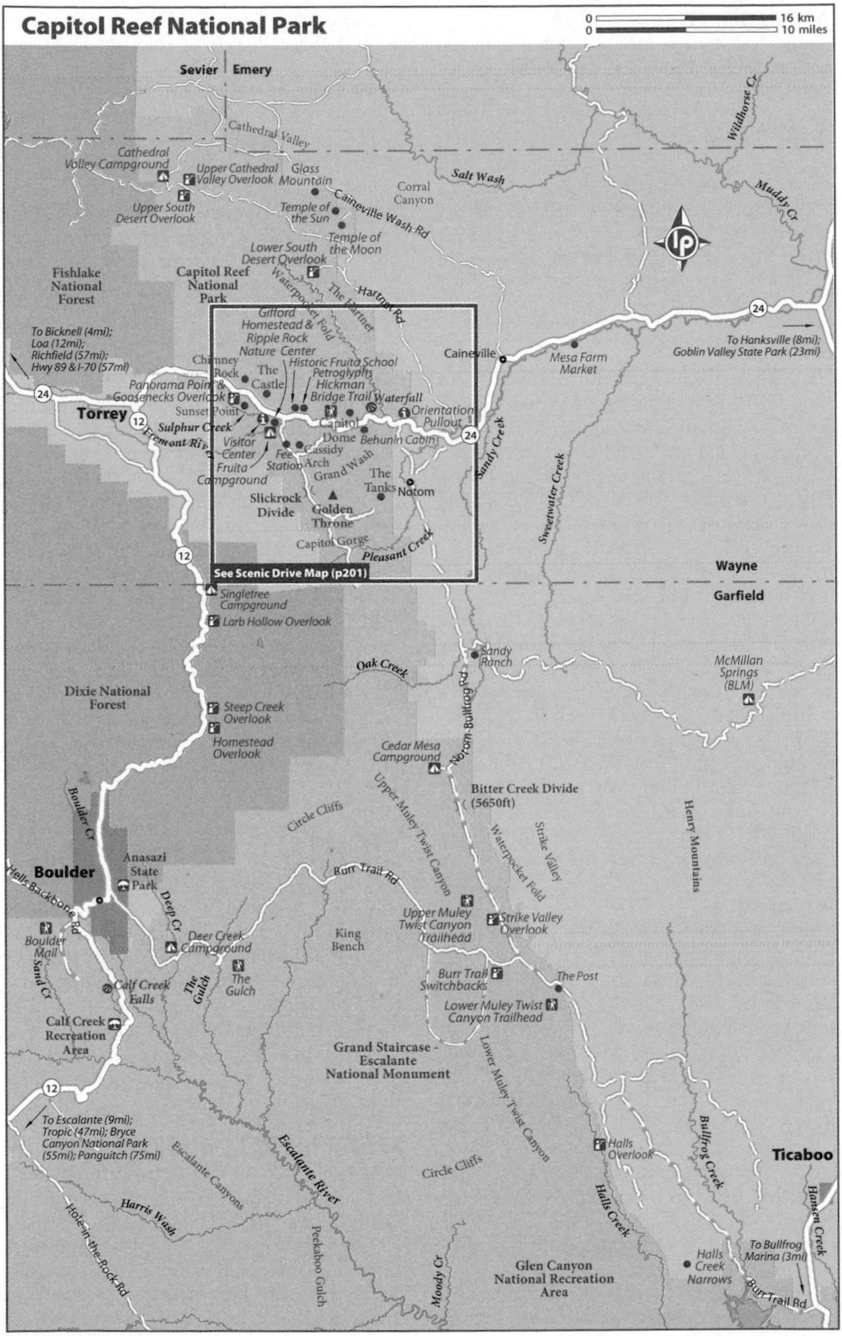
Capitol Reef National Park
0 16 km
0 10 miles
Sevier
Emery
Cathedral Valley
Cathedral Valley Campground
Upper Cathedral Valley Overlook
Glass Mountain
Upper South Desert Overlook
Salt Wash
Corral Canyon
Caineville Wash Rd
Temple of the Sun
Temple of the Moon
Lower South Desert Overlook
Wildhorse Cr
Muddy Cr
Fishlake National Forest
Capitol Reef National Park
Waterpocket Fold
The Hartnet
Hartnet Rd
Gifford Homestead & Ripple Rock Nature Center
To Bicknell (4mi); Loa (12mi); Richfield (57mi); Hwy 89 & I-70 (57mi)
Chimney Rock
The Castle
Historic Fruita School
Petroglyphs
Hickman Bridge Trail
Waterfall
Panorama Point & Goosenecks Overlook
Sunset Point
Orientation Pullout
Caineville
Mesa Farm Market
To Hanksville (8mi); Goblin Valley State Park (23mi)
Torrey
Sulphur Creek
Fremont River
Capitol Dome
Behunin Cabin
Visitor Center
Fruita Campground
Fee Station
Cassidy Arch
Grand Wash
The Tanks
Notom
Sandy Creek
Sweetwater Creek
Slickrock Divide
Golden Throne
Capitol Gorge
Pleasant Creek
See Scenic Drive Map (p201)
Wayne
Garfield
Singletree Campground
Larb Hollow Overlook
Sandy Ranch
Oak Creek
Notom-Bullfrog Rd
McMillan Springs (BLM)
Dixie National Forest
Steep Creek Overlook
Homestead Overlook
Cedar Mesa Campground
Bitter Creek Divide (5650ft)
Upper Muley Twist Canyon
Circle Cliffs
Boulder Cr
Henry Mountains
Strike Valley
Waterpocket Fold
Anasazi State Park
Boulder
Hells Backbone Rd
Burr Trail Rd
Deep Cr
Upper Muley Twist Canyon Trailhead
Strike Valley Overlook
King Bench
Boulder Mail
Deer Creek Campground
Sand Cr
The Gulch
Burr Trail Switchbacks
The Post
Calf Creek Falls
Lower Muley Twist Canyon Trailhead
Calf Creek Recreation Area
Grand Staircase - Escalante National Monument
Lower Muley Twist Canyon
To Escalante (9mi); Tropic (47mi); Bryce Canyon National Park (55mi); Panguitch (75mi)
Escalante Canyons
Escalante River
Circle Cliffs
Halls Overlook
Bullfrog Creek
Ticaboo
Harris Wash
Halls Creek
Hansen Creek
Hole-in-the-Rock Rd
Peekaboo Gulch
Moody Cr
Glen Canyon National Recreation Area
Halls Creek Narrows
To Bullfrog Marina (3mi)
Burr Trail Rd

When You Arrive

Unlike most of southern Utah's national parks, Capitol Reef lacks any entrance stations. Arriving via Hwy 24, the main paved route through the park, you'll turn south at the signed road to the visitor center, where you can pick up information and speak with rangers and volunteers. There's a $5 motorized vehicle fee (or $3 per cyclist) to drive the park's Scenic Drive south of Fruita Campground. Pay at the self-service kiosk and save your receipt, as it's valid for seven days.

Orientation

Hwy 24 cuts through the northern section of this long, thin national park, which stretches north–south along the Waterpocket Fold. South of the visitor center, Capitol Reef's central region is the Fruita Historic District. The park's paved Scenic Drive runs over 7 miles south of Fruita. To the north lies Cathedral Valley and its moonscape of towering monoliths, the least-visited section of the park.

Several unpaved roads access the extreme northern reaches of the park around Cathedral Valley; the easiest route is Caineville Wash Rd, though some stretches require a high-clearance 4WD vehicle. Notom-Bullfrog Rd heads south from Hwy 24, first through private land, then into the park, roughly paralleling Waterpocket Fold. Notom-Bullfrog Rd merges with the Burr Trail (p177), then continues south to Glen Canyon National Recreation Area.

Information

The park is open year-round. Just south of Hwy 24, the **visitor center** (☎ 435-425-3791; www.nps.gov/care; 52 Scenic Drive, Torrey; 🕑 8am-4:30pm Sep-May, to 6pm Jun-Aug) is also the park's headquarters. It's the only source for information in the park. Rangers and volunteer staff offer advice and can help you plan hikes and backcountry trips. The **Capitol Reef Natural History Association** (☎ 435-425-3791; www.capitolreefnha.org) runs the center's bookstore, which stocks topographic maps. Pay phones and recycling bins are available at the visitor center and Fruita Campground. Cell-phone reception is spotty to nonexistent throughout the park.

For all other tourist information and services, the gateway town of Torrey (p210) is about 11 miles west of the visitor center, near the intersection of Hwys 12 and 24.

Park Policies & Regulations

Capitol Reef's hiking, backpacking and backcountry camping regulations include those listed for all of southern Utah's national parks (see p40). For park-specific backcountry information, including permits, see p205. The park's pet policies are also the same as for other parks (see p57). For information on bringing your own horses, see p207.

Getting Around

Capitol Reef has no public transportation system. In summer you can drive most dirt roads, including Notom-Bullfrog Rd and the Burr Trail, in a regular passenger car. In remote regions like Cathedral Valley, you'll likely need a high-clearance 4WD vehicle, although some sections of road may be passable by 2WD vehicles. The closest 24-hour gas stations are outside the park in Torrey (11 miles west) and Hanksville (37 miles east).

Bicycles are allowed on all park roads, whether paved or dirt, but are prohibited on all hiking trails. Cyclists and hikers can arrange drop-off/pick-up shuttle services (from $25) with **Hondoo Rivers & Trails** (☎ 435-425-3519, 800-332-2696; www.hondoo.com; 90 E Main St, Torrey).

SIGHTS

The Hwy 24 driving tour (p199) highlights more of the park's main sights, in addition to what's described below. Stop by the visitor center (p198) to watch a short orientation video that explains some of Capitol Reef 's unique geology (see also p63) and to gawk at a 4ft-by-16ft relief map of the park that was handcrafted using dental instruments!

FRUITA HISTORIC DISTRICT

Offering welcome respite from the menacing red-rock desert, Fruita (*froo*-tuh) is a shady green patch, where mature, shade-giving cottonwoods and fruit-bearing trees line the banks of the Fremont River. The first Mormon homesteaders arrived in 1880, while Fruita's final resident left in

1969. (For more about Capitol Reef's history, see p84.)

The park now maintains the 2700 mostly cherry, apricot, peach, pear and apple trees planted by early settlers, and if you visit between June and October you can eat ripe fruit straight from the trees for free (there's a nominal fee for any fruit taken from an orchard). To learn what's in season, ask at the visitor center or call the **fruit hotline** (☎ 435-425-3791). You're welcome to pick fruit from any unlocked orchard during designated harvest times; just follow the ranger-posted instructions at the gates. Pick only mature fruit and leave the rest to ripen. You may not climb the trees, but ladders and handheld fruit pickers are available. Near the orchards is a restful **picnic area**, where deer roam and you'll hear birdsong in the trees, a rarity in the desert.

Displays at the **Gifford Homestead** (usually 8am-5pm daily Jun-Aug), just over a mile south of the visitor center, reveal the day-to-day world of a typical Mormon settlers' homestead. At the small store you can buy handicrafts and reproductions of 19th-century household items, along with fresh-baked fruit pies, fruit jams and jellies, and homemade ice cream. A short way back up the main road is the old **blacksmith shop**, though it's little more than a shed with period equipment inside (press a button to hear Dewey Gifford, the town's last resident, reminisce about life in Fruita). Nearby is the family-oriented **Ripple Rock Nature Center** (p208).

South of Fruita Campground (p209) the historic district ends, yielding to a trail alongside the Fremont River and the beginning of the park's **Scenic Drive** (p200).

DRIVING

Many routes through the park follow rough dirt roads that are sometimes accessible to standard vehicles, but may require high clearance and/or 4WD. Recent rains and winter snows can render some routes completely impassable. Always check road conditions at the visitor center before heading out.

If you have time for only one backcountry drive, head up the Burr Trail's switchbacks. To reach the Burr Trail, take **Notom-Bullfrog Road**, a so-so dirt road – the prettiest stretch lies south of the Bitter Creek Divide – or better yet, approach the switchbacks along the mostly paved section of the Burr Trail beginning outside Boulder (see p177).

The visitor center sells self-guided-auto-tour brochures ($2) for the Loop-the-Fold and Cathedral Valley Loop (p201). Starting from the visitor center, the 127-mile **Loop-the-Fold** tour offers the most comprehensive overview of Waterpocket Fold. Parts of it follow the Burr Trail, Hwy 12 and Hwy 24, while about half the trip is on dirt roads generally accessible when dry to regular 2WD passenger cars with standard clearance.

TOP FIVE SCENIC VIEWPOINTS

- **Panorama Point** (p199)
- **Sunset Point** (p200)
- **Cohab Canyon trail overlooks** (p204)
- **Temples of the Sun & Moon** (p201)
- **Rim Overlook** (p205)

HIGHWAY 24

Duration 1–4 hours
Distance 22 miles one way
Start Torrey
Finish Orientation Pullout
Nearest Town Torrey (p210)
Summary This easy, winding route gives you a taste of everything that Capitol Reef offers: striking geology, dramatic desert overlooks, ancient Native American petroglyphs, early Western settlers' sites and hiking trails for stretching your legs.

From Torrey, head east into Capitol Reef on Hwy 24. There is no entrance station; driving this route is free. Be sure to stop at turnouts along the way to read interesting geologic interpretive panels. Then pull over at **Chimney Rock**, the towering reddish-brown rock formation 7 miles east of Torrey. If you're in great shape, consider hiking the strenuous 3.5-mile loop for wide-open clifftop views of Capitol Reef.

A half-mile east of Chimney Rock, turn right toward **Panorama Point** and drive 0.7 miles along a graded dirt road to the **Goosenecks Overlook**. An easy 0.1-mile walk from the parking area over rock slabs takes you to this viewpoint above Sulphur Creek, which twists through the canyon in elegant S-curves. Though the observation platform is fenced in, much of the area around it is open – watch your little ones! From the parking area it's an easy 0.3-mile stroll to **Sunset Point**, where the ambient light on the cliffs and domes is best for photographers in the late afternoon.

Another 2.4 miles further east on Hwy 24, you'll arrive at the well-signed turnoff to Capitol Reef's **visitor center** (p198), just north of the **Fruita Historic District** (p198) and the paved **Scenic Drive** (p200). Rising majestically just north of this junction is the snaggle-toothed **Castle**; an interpretive panel details its geologic history.

East of the visitor center, Hwy 24 skirts the Fremont River, the surrounding rock growing paler and more yellow as you approach the park's Navajo sandstone **domes**. Peer through the windows of the **historic Fruita school**, 0.7 miles east of the visitor center, before stopping at the **ancient petroglyphs**, 0.4 miles further east. Created by Fremont Native Americans, these carvings helped convince archaeologists that the Fremont culture was distinct from that of Ancestral Puebloans. The fenced-in boardwalk is wheelchair-accessible. Bring binoculars or a camera with a zoom lens.

Stop at the turnout 0.8 miles east of the petroglyphs for views of **Capitol Dome**, a giant sandstone dome that vaguely resembles the US Capitol. This parking area beside the Fremont River is where you'll find the trailheads for **Hickman Bridge** (p203) and the more strenuous **Rim Overlook & Navajo Knobs** (p204) route. On the south side of Hwy 24 is an alternate trailhead for **Cohab Canyon** (p204), while 2.7 miles further east is the end of the **Grand Wash** (p202).

About 4 miles east of Hickman Bridge, on your right, stop to peer through the window of the one-room 1882 **Behunin Cabin**, once home to a Mormon settler's family of 10. On the north side of the highway, 0.7 miles east of the cabin, you'll pass a **waterfall**. Do *not* swim in it. More accidents (usually compound fractures) occur here than anywhere else in the park. Rocks are slippery, currents strong and the pool at the bottom shallow. At the park's eastern **orientation pullout**, just over 9 miles from the visitor center, are restrooms and an information kiosk. It's on the north side of the intersection with Notom-Bullfrog Rd.

SCENIC DRIVE

Duration 1–4 hours
Distance 9.3 miles one way
Start Scenic Drive fee station, just south of Fruita Campground
Finish Capitol Gorge
Nearest Town Torrey (p210)
Summary This rolling, mostly paved drive along the Waterpocket Fold is like a geology diorama come to life, with arches, hoodoos, canyon narrows and other unique features easily within view, plus day-hiking opportunities, too.

About 1.5 miles south of the visitor center, beyond the point where the tree-shaded oasis of Fruita Campground yields to rocky desert, stop at the self-service fee station and pay $5 to drive the park's Scenic Drive. The following stops in our text correspond to numbered roadside markers, which are fully explained in the park's self-guided driving-tour brochure ($2) and audio CD ($6), which detail the geologic and ecological significance of each stop. For a free printout, visit www.nps.gov/care/planyourvisit/scenicdrive.htm.

Until 1962, when Hwy 24 was rerouted, this drive was part of the main highway through the Capitol Reef region and passed through Capitol Gorge, which flooded following rainstorms. It's a narrow, undulating road with no center stripe. To avoid bottoming out, drive slowly, especially where the road dips into washes. The spur road leading into the Grand Wash and the last stretch of the Scenic Drive into Capitol Gorge are unpaved; don't enter either if rain threatens.

The reddish-brown Moenkopi rock escarpment above the first marker **(stop 1)**, at the self-service fee station, is 225 million years old, while the thin, grayish-green layer of shale just above it is part of the Chinle formation, rich in petrified wood. As you drive south, the road soon opens up to a view of Capitol Reef itself **(stop 2)**, which reveals the park's defining geologic features – sedimentary rock, erosion and buckling along Waterpocket Fold.

If road conditions allow, turn left 1.8 miles south of the fee station and drive a

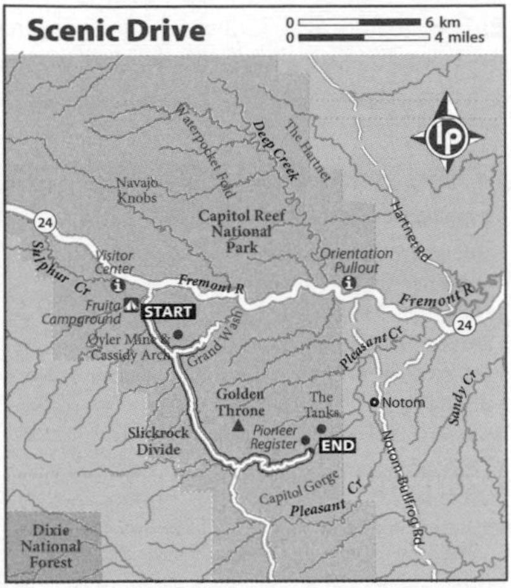

mile up **Grand Wash Rd**. In the hills off to your left **(stop 3)**, look for shaft openings at the abandoned **Oyler Mine**, which dates to 1904 and once mined radioactive uranium for use in 'curative' potions. You can walk to the mine, but for obvious reasons it has been sealed. Pause **(stop 4)** for a view of **Cassidy Arch**, named for outlaw Butch Cassidy, who reportedly hid out here. Look for it high on the cliffs behind you on the left. At the base of sheer walls on the right, look at the cross-bedded **Wingate sandstone**, once the shifting, wind-blown sand dunes of an ancient desert. Where the spur road ends **(stop 5)**, you can walk into the wash and through the **Narrows** (see p202) or tackle the tougher 3.5-mile round-trip trail to Cassidy Arch.

Back on Scenic Drive, continue through the Moenkopi formation **(stop 6)**, layers of red shale that formed when this area was a tidal flat – look for telltale ripples in the rock. About 2 miles further south, you'll reach **Slickrock Divide (stop 7)**, a hill between two major drainages. North of here, runoff drains into Grand Wash, while streams to the south channel into Capitol Gorge. As water travels through these washes, it changes the landscape not by carving rock, but by carrying away rubble. Flash floods move a lot of debris all at once. About 0.5 miles ahead, atop the cliffs you'll notice unusual **hoodoos (stop 8)**, created by fallen boulders of Wingate sandstone that have armored the softer, yellowish-gray rocks of the Shinarump Member of the Chinle Formation below, preventing erosion.

The final 2 miles of the route will knock your socks off, especially the final 0.5 miles as you zigzag through the canyon along a gravel spur road. The right fork leads to **Pleasant Creek** (p208), while turning left takes you into **Capitol Gorge**, its entrance guarded by sheer walls of Wingate sandstone **(stop 9)**. Look for rare desert bighorn sheep scrambling atop the rocky ledges. Soon coming into view on your left is a massive outcrop of pale **Navajo sandstone (stop 10)**, a layer more than 1400ft thick in places. It erodes in sweeping contours and comprises the park's most famous domes, including Capitol Dome. The **Golden Throne** (6489ft) sits about 1000ft above this viewpoint.

The road ends 0.5 miles deep within the gorge **(stop 11)**, one of the few passages through Capitol Reef's defining feature, the Waterpocket Fold. If it's not raining, you can hike from here past **petroglyphs**, the **Pioneer Register**, where early settlers carved their names into the walls, and up to the **Tanks**, which are natural rock cisterns (see p203).

CATHEDRAL VALLEY LOOP

Duration 4–6 hours
Distance 58 miles
Start Caineville Wash Rd, off Hwy 24 near mile-marker 97.8, about 18.5 miles east of the visitor center
Finish Hartnet Rd, at Hwy 24
Nearest Town Torrey (p210)
Summary This bumpy, roughshod backcountry route explores the remote northern area of the park and its alien desert landscapes, pierced by giant sandstone monoliths eroded into fantastic shapes. Avoid it on the hottest summer days.

Though in places this backcountry route requires 4WD and high clearance, you can usually drive a 2WD vehicle at least the first section of **Caineville Wash Rd** from Hwy 24. The turnoff road is marked 490W, but look for a small sign that says 'Cathedral.' At the first fork, stay to the right on Caineville Wash Rd, then stay straight just over 2 miles later. Finally, 15.5 bumpy miles from Hwy 24, turn left onto the dirt spur road leading west out to the striking monoliths, the **Temple of the Sun** and the **Temple of the Moon**. Make time for a quick detour to **Glass Mountain**, a 20ft mound of fused selenite crystals. This short in-and-out trip offers a taste of Cathedral Valley without the headaches of 4WD.

Unless you're driving a high-clearance 4WD vehicle, do *not* attempt the entire 58-mile loop, which continues slowly around past a spur road leading to a **gypsum sinkhole**, the primitive Cathedral Valley Campground (p209), **desert overlooks** and rugged hiking trailheads. The last part of the route follows **Hartnet Rd**, which fords the Fremont River just before rejoining Hwy 24, under 12 miles east of the park's visitor center. With high-clearance 4WD, you may want to do this entire loop counterclockwise, doing the river ford in the morning and arriving at the Temples of the Sun and Moon in the late afternoon, which is best for photography.

HIKING

Capitol Reef has diverse hiking trails, mostly over loose rock; wear hiking boots with ankle support. There's little shade, and it gets very hot in summer. Summer thunderstorms pose a serious risk of flash floods (p285); check weather with rangers at the visitor center before heading out. See p283 and p46 for more hiking safety tips and desert hiking etiquette.

If you're tight on time and want the most variety, stop at Goosenecks Overlook (p199), stroll to Sunset Point (p200), visit Hickman Bridge (p203) and hike Capitol Gorge (p202). An easy walk in the Narrows of the Grand Wash (p202) or the hardy climb to Cohab Canyon (p204) are two rewarding, relatively short shuttle hikes, or follow each of these routes just partway as satisfying out-and-back trips. Three difficult but worthwhile trails not described below lead to **Cassidy Arch** (off the Grand Wash), the **Golden Throne** (off Capitol Gorge) and atop the cliffs near **Chimney Rock** (off Hwy 24, see p199). For definitions of our hike difficulty ratings, see p37.

Among southern Utah's best hiking and backcountry guide services, **Hondoo Rivers & Trails** (☎ 435-425-3519, 800-332-2696; www.hondoo.com; 90 E Main St, Torrey) leads one-day and multiday hikes, including slot canyons and combo camping and horse-packing trips. Also offering half- and full-day guided hikes in Capitol Reef, **Earth Tours** (☎ 435-691-1241; www.earth-tours.com; spring-fall) is run by a PhD in geology who knows how to translate his scientific knowledge into lay terms.

DAY HIKES

GRAND WASH

Duration 45 minutes–1½ hours
Distance 2.25 miles one way
Difficulty Easy
Start/Finish Grand Wash trailhead, at end of 1.3-mile-long dirt spur road off Scenic Drive, 3.3 miles south of visitor center
Nearest Town Torrey (p210)
Transportation Private
Summary Capitol Reef's most dramatic canyon is worth visiting just to walk between the sheer walls of the Narrows. Avoid this hike if rain threatens, as the wash is prone to flash floods.

Start from the parking lot at the end of the Grand Wash spur road. It's an easy stroll up the packed-sand wash from the parking area. Look for seasonal wildflowers such as reddish Indian paintbrush, shrubby white-flowering Apache's plume and stalky, yellow-flowering prince's plume. The canyon's walls inch closer and closer together until, about 1.25 miles from the trailhead, you reach the **Narrows**, where the 80-story canyon is just 15ft wide – a thrilling sight. The canyon walls shrink and spread out again as the flat trail approaches Hwy 24. Return the way you came, or arrange for someone to pick you up on Hwy 24, around 4.6 miles east of the visitor center (look for a trailhead marker on the south side of the highway, where there's a small gravel pull off).

CAPITOL GORGE

Duration 1–2 hours
Distance 2.2 miles
Difficulty Easy–moderate
Start/Finish Capitol Gorge trailhead, at end of 2-mile-long dirt spur road off Scenic Drive, 9 miles south of visitor center
Nearest Town Torrey (p210)
Transportation Private
Summary Leave your car behind for an easy canyon ramble past historic petroglyphs, then scramble up to hidden water pockets. Avoid this flood-prone route if rain threatens.

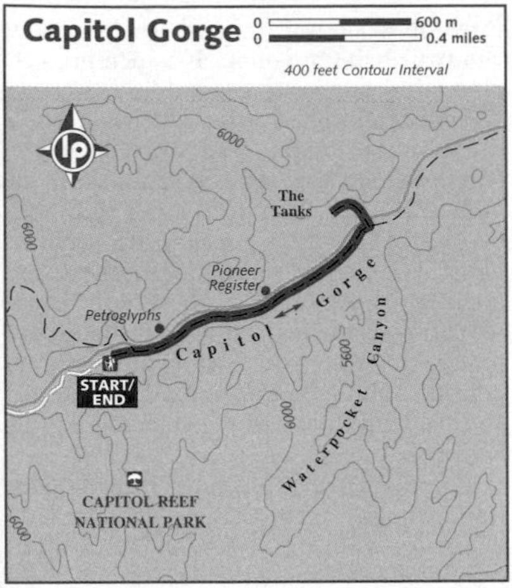

Until a few decades ago, Capitol Gorge was the primary automobile route through the Waterpocket Fold. Pioneers first brought wagons through in the late 19th century, and the route remained in use until 1962. Today the sheer canyon walls are stained with desert varnish (p62), which stands out in dramatic contrast to the rock. Keep your eyes peeled for bighorn sheep, a rare but exciting sight for wildlife-watchers.

About 0.25 miles from the trailhead, you'll reach a vandalized panel of ancient Fremont **petroglyphs**. A quarter-mile further, look up to see the **Pioneer Register**, a collection of carved names and dates that go back to the first pioneer passersby in 1871. Despite more recent graffiti, you can clearly make out many of the historic names and dates. Don't be confused by signatures on the right-hand wall, back closer to the petroglyphs. These date to 1911, when a USGS survey team lowered its leader over the wall to incise the party's names – vandalism by today's standards.

Just over 0.8 miles from the trailhead, bear left and follow signs to the **Tanks**, which lie atop a fairly steep 0.2-mile spur. These giant potholes (p69), or water pockets, hold significant volumes of water much of the year. They were invaluable to early settlers and remain so for animals, so don't drink from or disturb them. When you're rested and ready, head back the way you came – the onward wash trail crosses park boundaries onto private land.

HICKMAN BRIDGE

Duration 1–2 hours
Distance 2 miles
Difficulty Easy–moderate
Start/Finish Hickman Bridge trailhead, off Hwy 24, 1.9 miles east of the visitor center
Nearest Town Torrey (p210)
Transportation Private
Summary If you've only got time for one hike, Capitol Reef's most popular trail is diverse, offering a canyon and desert-wash walk to a natural bridge, plus long sky views and spring wildflowers.

This popular hike is easy enough for anyone from kids to grandparents to enjoy. Since the route is largely exposed, it's best to hike it in the early morning. Cairns mark some of the route, which starts off the same way as the longer, more strenuous hike to the Rim Overlook and Navajo Knobs (p204). Pick up a self-guided Hickman Bridge nature trail brochure at the trailhead, which corresponds to numbered signposts along the route.

Starting from the Fremont River, where kids love to splash around, the trail ascends a red-rock cliff via a few easy switchbacks. As you cross an open area of desert vegetation strewn with volcanic black rocks, the highway vanishes behind giant white sandstone domes. A short spur leads to a tiny **archaeological site** where you can inspect the foundations of Fremont Indian pit houses.

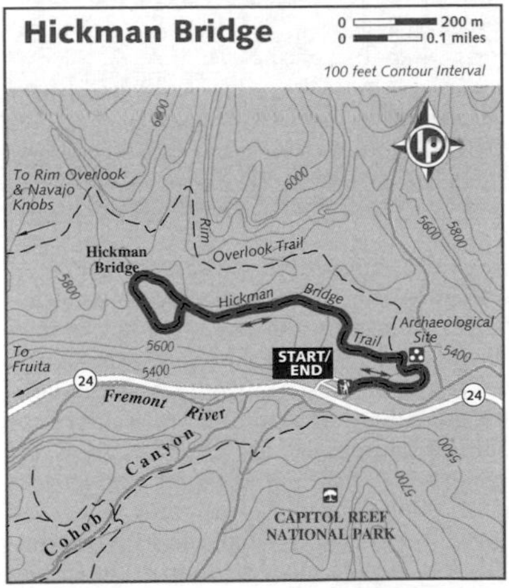

WATER, WATER ALMOST EVERYWHERE

Hidden inside Capitol Reef's towering jumble of rocks and winding canyons are giant natural cisterns that are full of water. These caches are a rare commodity in this arid landscape. John Wesley Powell, the first Western explorer here, found this precious resource and nicknamed the monocline Waterpocket Fold.

During April and May look for scarlet claret cup and pink-flowering prickly pear cacti blooming beside the path.

The trail soon drops into a wash, where you can rest in a shady alcove before ascending over slickrock to **Hickman Bridge**, having gained 400ft in elevation from your start. While this chunky yellow arch can be tricky to spot from afar, the trail loops right beneath it for a marvelous appreciation of its mass. Hike counterclockwise and bear left beyond the arch to keep following the trail's loop. Pause to look over the rim and downriver to Fruita, an oasis of green.

COHAB CANYON

Duration 1–2 hours
Distance 1.7 miles one way
Difficulty Moderate
Start Cohab Canyon trailhead, off Scenic Drive, 1.2 miles south of the visitor center
Finish Hwy 24, 2 miles east of the visitor center
Nearest Town Torrey (p210)
Transportation Private
Summary Often overlooked, this trail deters crowds with a steep climb at the beginning, but exploring a hidden canyon and the views from atop Capitol Reef are worth every sweaty step.

If you're with people whose ability or interest in hiking isn't as great as yours, leave them to laze by the river or tour Fruita's historic sights while you tackle this climb with killer views. Starting across the road from Fruita Campground, just south of the Gifford Homestead (p199), this trail makes a steep 0.25-mile initial ascent atop a rocky cliff. From there it levels out though a desert wash, beside which small slot canyons nestle. You'll pass more striking geologic features on your way through sheltered but windy Cohab Canyon itself, which protects piñon and juniper trees (and lizards!).

About 1.1 miles from the trailhead, a short but steep spur trail veers off left to climb to two **overlooks** of Fruita and the orchards. After about 0.25 miles of switchbacks, this spur trail splits into separate branches heading toward the southern and northern overlooks – visiting both before returning to the main trail adds just over a mile to this hike. This is a good turnaround point if you'd rather do just a 3.2-mile out-and-back hike, instead of a one-way shuttle hike over to Hwy 24.

The main trail continues threading its way through Cohab Canyon. It ascends to a junction with the **Frying Pan Trail**, a moderately difficult route that leads atop an escarpment for panoramic views, including of Cassidy Arch (p201), before dropping into the **Grand Wash** (p202) 4 miles from Cohab Canyon; add another mile if you take the worthwhile side trip to the arch. Otherwise, from the Frying Pan Trail junction, the main trail switchbacks down to Hwy 24, ending almost opposite the Hickman Bridge trailhead, around 2 miles east of the visitor center.

RIM OVERLOOK & NAVAJO KNOBS

Duration 4–6 hours
Distance 9.5 miles
Difficulty Difficult
Start/Finish Hickman Bridge trailhead, off Hwy 24, 1.9 miles east of the visitor center
Nearest Town Torrey (p210)
Transportation Private
Summary This slickrock route to twin bumps of Navajo sandstone perched on the precipitous western edge of Waterpocket Fold yields unsurpassed views. A steep, strenuous climb offers little shade and no water.

Start hiking from the Fremont River along the popular Hickman Bridge Trail (p203), but after 0.3 miles, fork right at the signed junction and you'll leave most of the crowds behind. Follow cairns along much of this dry-wash and slickrock route, which sidles around Capitol Reef's giant white domes. Pause at the well-marked **Hickman Bridge Overlook**, south (left) of the trail. Blending

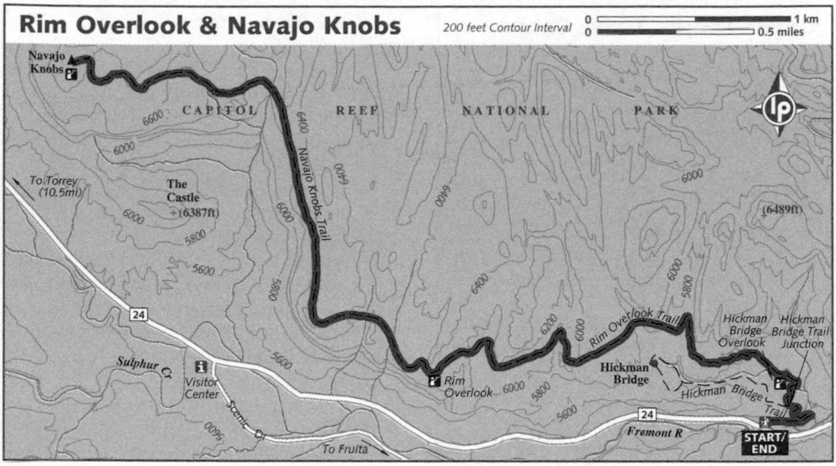

in amid the surrounding rock, this natural bridge is visible across a small canyon at eye level with the overlook.

Onward, the trail zigzags along the edge of a south-facing side canyon, a pattern that repeats for much of the remaining hike. As you continue climbing, you'll wind past the mouths of three more side canyons before reaching the **Rim Overlook**, 2.25 miles from the trailhead. Gorgeous views encompass a profile of the fold and its north end, along with mesas, domes, mountains and Fruita over 1000ft below.

After climbing up and down more sandstone pitches, you'll pass between cliffs (on your right) and a weather tower and find yourself on a broad ledge that faces the Castle, a large, eroded, freestanding chunk of Waterpocket Fold. The trail rambles along this ledge to the northwest edge of a west-facing, W-shaped canyon. Following cairns, you'll climb the west rim of the W and soon spot the **Navajo Knobs** (6980ft), twin bumps that mark the high point on the next promontory. Watch your step as you clamber over loose rock to the double summit, then retrace your steps all the way back to the trailhead.

BACKCOUNTRY HIKES

To experience the vastness of Waterpocket Fold and the ruggedness of the land, there's no better way than backcountry hiking. Capitol Reef gets extremely hot in summer, and dehydration is a serious concern. You'll have to carry in *all* of your water (eg for drinking, for cooking, extra for emergencies) – don't count on finding any water pockets.

Careful planning is essential for any backcountry trip. Be sure to get rangers' advice before setting out on any of these hikes. Pick up a free backcountry permit and check trail conditions at the visitor center. Ground fires are prohibited in the backcountry, so bring a camp stove. There are no established campgrounds in the backcountry. *Never* camp in a wash. Always stay on the trails, don't shortcut switchbacks and avoid stepping on cryptobiotic soil (p74).

In addition to the two backcountry routes described below, ask rangers about the hike to **Halls Creek Narrows**, a 22-mile round-trip requiring a high-clearance (and often 4WD) vehicle just to access the trailhead.

UPPER MULEY TWIST CANYON

Duration 1–2 days
Distance 15 miles
Difficulty Difficult
Start/Finish Upper Muley Twist Canyon trailhead, off Burr Trail
Nearest Town Torrey (p210)
Transportation Private
Summary The upper canyon is less dramatic than the lower (see p207), but offers easier terrain and expansive views atop the fold. You'll pass arches and sculpted sandstone narrows, too.

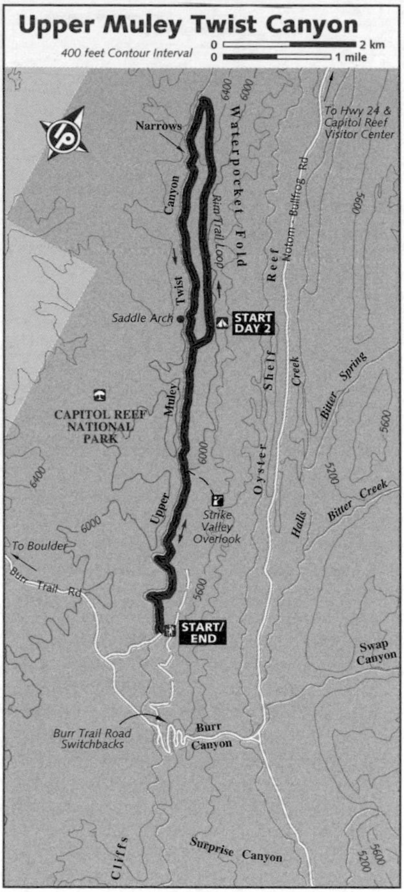

Though you can approach Upper Muley as a long, difficult day hike, it's better to spend two days and enjoy the scenery. Most people camp near the Rim Trail junction, then hike the Rim Trail Loop without a pack. Don't enter this flood-prone canyon if there is *any* chance of rain in the weather forecast.

To reach the trailhead, drive 3 miles west of the intersection with Notom-Bullfrog Rd on the Burr Trail, then turn right onto the signed side road to Strike Valley Overlook. Alternatively, from Boulder follow the mostly paved Burr Trail (p177), driving just over 2 miles on graded dirt to the turnoff above the switchbacks. With a high-clearance 4WD vehicle, you can usually drive the first 3 miles of this hike to the Strike Valley Overlook trailhead.

From the Upper Muley Twist Canyon trailhead, walk along the gravel wash and head generally northwest. The canyon is wide and the wash level for the 3-mile hike to the Strike Valley Overlook trailhead. The 0.5-mile round-trip jaunt to the **overlook** is worth the energy, especially if you set down your pack at the trailhead.

Upper Muley Twist Canyon narrows 0.5 miles past the overlook, as steep red sandstone cliffs to the east (right) turn in toward the wash. About 1.2 miles further you'll see **Saddle Arch**, visible near the rim of the west wall. A sign on the east side of the wash marks the beginning of the Rim Trail Loop. Follow cairns up the canyon's east side, being prepared for some rock scrambling and climbing uphill.

In about 15 or 20 minutes, you'll reach a broad bench capped with juniper trees and **camping** spots. Avoid treading on the crumbly cryptobiotic soil. If you want a view, but don't mind potentially high winds and not having any shade, camp at the saddle where the trail crests the fold. The Rim Trail Loop is slippery when wet, so use caution. From the potential campsites, follow cairns up to the east rim for spectacular views. A sign at the top points back down to the Canyon Route, which you'll be following later. You may find several sandy potential campsites nearby, too.

Follow the ridge north to a high point for views north along the fold to the grand white domes near the visitor center, 35 miles away as the turkey vulture flies. After around 2 miles of roller-coaster ridge hiking, the trail plunges toward Muley Twist Canyon. Several cairned routes lead to the canyon floor, each requiring tricky scrambling. Turn down-canyon (south) and stay high, close to the east wall. After passing some wonderful hat-shaped formations, the trail swings east (left) away from the **Narrows** below. Several deep potholes serve as water-storage tanks.

Beyond the gap in the west wall, the trail returns to the canyon floor. A quarter-mile down-canyon, the cairned trail climbs the east wall again, though in dry periods you may be able to continue along the canyon floor. After about 2 miles you'll pass **Saddle Arch**, high on the west (right) wall, soon after which a sign for the Rim Trail Loop signals the end of your loop. After closing the loop, the high, red canyon walls wax low and golden as you retrace your steps to the Strike Valley Overlook trailhead, 1.7 miles away, and another 3 miles south to the Upper Muley Twist Canyon trailhead.

LOWER MULEY TWIST CANYON

Duration 1–2 days
Distance 15 miles
Difficulty Difficult
Start/Finish Lower Muley Twist Canyon trailhead, off Notom-Bullfrog Rd
Nearest Town Torrey (p210)
Transportation Private
Summary This loop follows the dramatic lower canyon through narrow red walls, then returns through grasslands broken up by colorful hills. The entire region must be relatively dry when you undertake this dangerously flood-prone hike.

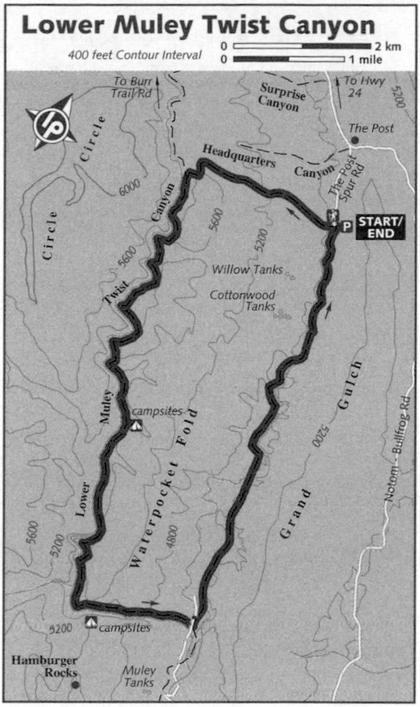

Be sure to check with rangers about current conditions and the weather forecast before heading out. Less than 3 miles south of the Notom-Bullfrog Rd/Burr Trail junction, 35 miles south of Hwy 24, a well-signed road leads right from the Post. The trailhead is at the southwest edge of the parking lot.

The first mile is steep and exposed, with narrow drop-offs and ledges. From the parking area, follow the well-marked trail west up Waterpocket Fold's red, sloping back. After about an hour of steady climbing, the trail hits sand and the canyon's red walls come into view to the northeast. You'll level out and cross a sandy area strewn with vegetation. Leaving the wash, the trail bears south to Lower Muley Twist Canyon, staying high on the canyon's east side, then cutting gently to the canyon floor, about 2 miles from the trailhead.

Sheer red Wingate sandstone walls tower 300ft on both sides. The hike now starts to follow a familiar pattern – from riverbed to high ground and back again – as the canyon twists south. Each alcove seems bigger, deeper and more graceful than the last. After passing two gaps in the west (right) wall, you'll reach a big side canyon to the northeast, home to several good campsites. Back in the main canyon, the trail soon turns from sand to sandstone and continues straight where the main canyon swings west. Mount a sandy plain to more campsites amid sage and junipers.

Eventually you'll reach the canyon's **narrows**, where the 800ft walls are less than 10ft apart at points – narrow enough to 'twist a mule.' Soon afterward the canyon ends where its riverbed flows toward Halls Creek. At this point, cairns mark the return route north to the Post trailhead. The Grand Gulch opens ever wider the further north you hike.

OTHER ACTIVITIES

HORSEBACK RIDING & PACK TRIPS

If you're bringing your own stock, backcountry permits for horse-packing trips are free, but special use regulations apply. Reservations are required at least two weeks in advance to use the **Post corral**, off Notom-Bullfrog Rd. Contact the visitor center for details, permits and reservations.

CAMPGROUNDS IN & AROUND CAPITOL REEF

Campground	Location	Number of sites	Elevation (ft)	Open	Reservations available?
Cathedral Valley	cnr Hartnet & Caineville Wash Rds	6	7000	year-round	no
Cedar Mesa	Notom-Bullfrog Rd	5	5600	year-round	no
Fruita	Scenic Drive	71	545t	year-round	no
Goblin Valley State Park	Goblin Valley Rd	24	5100	year-round	yes
Sandcreek RV Park	Hwy 24	24	6900	Apr-Oct	yes
Singletree	Hwy 12	13	8600	May-Sep	yes
Sunglow	Forest Rd 143	7	7200	May-Oct	no
Thousand Lakes RV Park	Hwy 24	61	6900	Apr-Oct	yes

Drinking Water *Flush Toilets* *Ranger Station Nearby* *Great for Families* *Wheelchair Accessible* *Dogs Allowed* *Grocery Store Nearby*

For guided horseback trips:

Capitol Reef Backcountry Outfitters (☎ 435-425-2010, 866-747-3972; www.ridethereef.com; cnr Hwys 12 & 24, Torrey; 1/2hr ride from $35/60, half-/full-day trip from $120/160) Rides in the national park and on Boulder Mountain.

Hondoo Rivers & Trails (☎ 435-425-3519, 800-332-2696; www.hondoo.com; 90 E Main St, Torrey; 3-day pack trips from $840) Mulitday pack trips include camping or a more expensive inn-to-inn accommodations option.

CYCLING & MOUNTAIN BIKING

The park's mostly paved **Scenic Drive** (p200) satisfies beginners and intermediates, while experienced mountain bikers love **Cathedral Valley** (p201), though it becomes a muddy mess when wet. Check road conditions at the visitor center. You can rent mountain bikes from **Capitol Reef Backcountry Outfitters** (☎ 435-425-2010, 866-747-3972; www.ridethereef.com; cnr Hwys 12 & 24, Torrey; 1-/2-day rental from $38/60).

FOUR-WHEEL DRIVING

4WD roads crisscross Capitol Reef (see p199). To avoid bottoming out your precious Prius, rent an SUV (from $100 per day) at **Thousand Lakes RV Park** (p210) or book a guided 4WD tour with the following:

Capitol Reef Backcountry Outfitters (☎ 435-425-2010, 866-747-3972; www.ridethereef.com; cnr Hwys 12 & 24, Torrey; full-day tours from $120)

Hondoo Rivers & Trails (☎ 435-425-3519, 800-332-2696; www.hondoo.com; 90 E Main St, Torrey; half-/full-day tours from $90/125)

SWIMMING

Only wade in wide, calm sections of a creek or river when there's no threat of a flash flood. Check the weather forecast and ask about current water conditions at the visitor center. Across Hwy 24 from the Chimney Rock parking area, an easy, level trail leads to **Sulphur Creek**. Near the visitor center, you can hike a mile up Sulphur Creek to a large **wading pool** shaded by cottonwoods. You can also wade along **Pleasant Creek** from the end of the park's Scenic Drive.

RANGER PROGRAMS

From May to September, the park offers free public programs, including ranger talks, guided walks and evening shows at Fruita Campground's amphitheater. Check at the visitor center for a current schedule. Families should also stop by the visitor center to pick up a **junior ranger activity guide**. Once kids complete the activities, they can return to the visitor center to receive an official junior ranger badge. The visitor center also loans out free **family activity backpacks** stuffed with games and outdoor activities. In Fruita, visit the **Ripple Rock Nature Center**

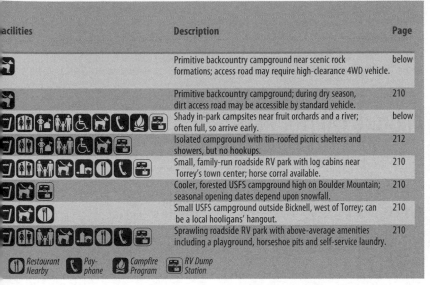

acilities	Description	Page
	Primitive backcountry campground near scenic rock formations; access road may require high-clearance 4WD vehicle.	below
	Primitive backcountry campground; during dry season, dirt access road may be accessible by standard vehicle.	210
	Shady in-park campsites near fruit orchards and a river; often full, so arrive early.	below
	Isolated campground with tin-roofed picnic shelters and showers, but no hookups.	212
	Small, family-run roadside RV park with log cabins near Torrey's town center; horse corral available.	210
	Cooler, forested USFS campground high on Boulder Mountain; seasonal opening dates depend upon snowfall.	210
	Small USFS campground outside Bicknell, west of Torrey; can be a local hooligans' hangout.	210
	Sprawling roadside RV park with above-average amenities including a playground, horseshoe pits and self-service laundry.	210

Restaurant Nearby *Pay-phone* *Campfire Program* *RV Dump Station*

(usually noon-5pm daily late May-Jun, 10am-3pm Tue-Sat Jul-early Sep) for kid-friendly hands-on exhibits and activities.

ROCK CLIMBING

Technical rock climbing is allowed, and you don't need a permit if you're not camping in the backcountry. Though you'll find lots of climbable cracks in the Wingate sandstone, be aware that it can flake unpredictably. Follow clean-climbing guidelines, and take all safety precautions. Climbing is not allowed near rock-art panels, prehistoric structures or natural features like Hickman Bridge, Chimney Rock or the Temples of the Sun and Moon. For details, check in at the visitor center, which sells local climbing guidebooks.

FISHING

You'll find surprisingly good fishing on the rivers and in the mountains around Capitol Reef. For guided trips:

Alpine Adventures (435-425-3660; www.alpineadventuresutah.com; 310 W Main St, Torrey; day/overnight trips from $225/850) Lake fishing and combination horse-pack trips.

Fremont River Guides (435-491-0242; www.flyfishingsouthernutah.com; PO Box 186, Bicknell; half-/full-day trips from $200/300) Go fishing on the Fremont River or Boulder Mountain.

SLEEPING & EATING

There's no lodging or food in the park, except for the park's pick-your-own **fruit orchards** and the baked goods sold at the **Gifford Homestead**, both in the Fruita Historic District (p198). Eleven miles west of the visitor center, Torrey (p210) is the nearest place to sleep and eat.

Camping

our pick **Fruita Campground** (435-425-3791; www.nps.gov/care; Scenic Drive, 1.2 miles south of visitor center; campsites $; year-round;) The park's only developed campground provides water, toilets, picnic tables, grills and an RV dump station, but no showers or campfire rings. The 71 sites are level, and most are shaded by cottonwoods. All sites are first-come, first-served (except for groups), and often fill by early afternoon from spring straight through fall. An RV dump station is open in summer only.

Ask at the visitor center about current road conditions and the weather forecast before heading out to the following remote, primitive and little-visited campgrounds:

Cathedral Valley Campground (435-425-3791; www.nps.gov/care; cnr Hartnet & Caineville Wash Rds, 38 miles from visitor center; tent sites free; year-round)

The drive here requires a high-clearance vehicle and may demand 4WD. Six first-come, first-served campsites have no water, but there are pit toilets, fire grates and picnic tables.

Cedar Mesa Campground (☎ 435-425-3791; www.nps.gov/care; Notom-Bullfrog Rd, 23 miles south of Hwy 24; tent sites free; 🕑 year-round) Five first-come, first-served sites lack water, but have pit toilets, fire grates and picnic tables, as well as great views east along the fold.

AROUND CAPITOL REEF

Torrey (11 miles west of Capitol Reef) and nearby Teasdale and Bicknell together provide the closest lodgings, restaurants and tourist services to the national park.

TORREY

pop 187 / elevation 6830ft

Sitting about 1300ft higher than Capitol Reef, temperatures here are often 10°F cooler. A peaceful town built along a main street (Hwy 24), Torrey's primary money-making biz has shifted from logging and ranching to tourism. The town shuts down during winter, but in summer there's a whiff of counterculture in the air. If you're here during the third weekend in July, don't miss the **Bicknell International Film Festival** (www.thebiff.org), a wacky spoof featuring the most awful B-movies ever made, plus the 'fastest parade in America'. July also has the **Torrey Music Festival** (www.torreymusicfestival.com), a one-day singer-songwriter jam, and traditional **Torrey Apple Days** (www.torreyutah.com), with live music, BBQ, pie-eating contests, a dance, derby and parade held around the July 4 national holiday.

Orientation & Information

The town center is west of the motels and gas stations found at the Hwy 24/12 junction.

Austin's Chuckwagon General Store (☎ 435-425-3288; 12 W Main St; 🕑 7am-10pm Apr-Oct, showers & laundromat till 9pm) Has an ATM, hot showers ($5) and a self-service laundromat.

Capitol Reef Backcountry Outfitters (☎ 435-425-2010, 866-747-3972; cnr Hwys 12 & 24; 🕑 7:30am-7pm May-Oct, 8am-5pm Nov-Apr) Sells outdoor gear, activity guidebooks and topographical maps.

Castle Rock Coffee & Candy (☎ 435-425-2100; cnr Hwys 12 & 24; per hr $3; 🕑 from 7am daily, seasonal hr vary; 💻 📶) Free wi-fi, plus one internet terminal.

Post office (☎ 435-425-3716; 75 W Main St; 🕑 7:30am-1:30pm Mon-Fri, to 11:30am Sat) At the Torrey Trading Post.

Robbers Roost Bookstore (☎ 435-425-3265; 185 W Main St; internet access per min/hr 10c/$5; 🕑 8am-4pm Mon-Sat, 1-4pm Sun May-Oct; 💻 📶) Free wi-fi; sells local-interest books and maps.

Sevier Valley Medical Center (☎ 435-893-4100; 1000 N Main St, Richfield; 🕑 24hr) Closest hospital emergency room, 64 miles west of Torrey via Hwy 24.

Wayne Community Health Center (☎ 435-425-3744; 128 S 300 W, Bicknell; 🕑 9am-5pm Mon-Fri, to 1pm Sat) Nearest non-emergency clinic, about 10 miles west of Torrey via Hwy 24.

Wayne County Travel Council (☎ 435-425-3365, 800-858-7951; www.capitolreef.org; cnr Hwys 12 & 24; 🕑 9am-5pm Sun-Thu, 8am-7pm Fri & Sat Apr-Oct) Well-stocked tourist information office.

Sleeping

CAMPING & CABINS

The area's public and private campgrounds are open seasonally (see the camping chart, p208). Hot showers are available at Sandcreek RV Park (below) or Austin's Chuckwagon General Store (opposite), which also has a laundromat.

Thousand Lakes RV Park (☎ 435-425-3500, 800-355-8995; www.thousandlakesrvpark.com; 1050 W Hwy 24; campsites & cabins $; 🕑 Apr-Oct; 🏊 📶) A mile west of the town center, this roadside campground offers tent and RV sites, basic log cabins and decent facilities, including a heated swimming pool and hot showers. Western-style dinner cookouts often available in peak summer season.

Sandcreek RV Park (☎ 435-425-3577; www.sandcreekrv.com; 540 W Hwy 24; campsites & cabins $; 🕑 Apr-Oct; 🐾) At the west end of town, this friendly spot offers 24 tent and RV sites with hookups, coin-op laundry, picnic tables and fire pits, rustic log cabins with double and bunk beds, hot showers and a horse corral.

Sunglow Campground (☎ 435-836-2800; www.fs.fed.us/r4/fishlake; Forest Rd 143, Bicknell; campsites $) Often windy, this USFS campground tucked back amid red-rock cliffs has seven first-come, first-served tent and RV sites with drinking water, picnic tables and vault toilets. Beware that this can be a locals' drinking hangout at night. Look for the turnoff from Hwy 24, just east of Bicknell.

Singletree Campground (☎ 518-885-3639, 877-444-6777; www.recreation.gov; campsites $) The Fishlake National Forest also runs this basic 13-site tent and RV campground at an elevation of 8600ft on forested Boulder Mountain, 12 miles south of Torrey along Hwy 12. There's drinking water, vault toilets and an RV dump station.

Pine Shadows Cabins (☎ 435-425-3939, 800-708-1223; www.pineshadowcabins.net; 195 W 125 S, Teasdale; cabins $;) Tucked between juniper and piñon pines beneath white cliffs, these freestanding one- or two-bedroom cabins with chalet ceilings and kitchenettes make a great hideaway for families (some allow pets, too).

Also worth a look:

Torrey Trading Post (☎ 435-425-3716; www.torreytradingpost.com; 75 W Main St; cabins $;) Bare-bones but tidy and dirt-cheap cabins with heating and shared bathrooms.

Cowboy Homestead Cabins (☎ 435-425-3414, 888-854-5871; www.cowboyhomesteadcabins.com; Hwy 12; cabins $;) Rustic, pine-paneled roadside cabins with kitchenettes, 3.4 mi les south of Torrey; horse stalls available.

MOTELS & B&BS

Hwys 12 and 24 are speckled with independent and chain motels, most overpriced for the amenities you'll get.

Rim Rock Inn (☎ 435-425-3398, 888-447-4676; www.therimrock.net; 2523 E Hwy 24; r $; Mar-Nov;) Among the red-rock cliffs east of town, this family-owned hilltop place offers basic, standard-issue motel rooms, but with superb sunset views. Pet fee $10.

Sandstone Inn (☎ 435-425-3775, 877-342-6099; www.sandstonecapitolreef.com; 955 E Hwy 24; r $;) Spacious hilltop motel rooms are set back from Torrey's busy highway junction. Soak sore muscles in the glass-enclosed heated swimming pool or Jacuzzi. Pet fee $10.

Austin's Chuckwagon Motel (☎ 435-425-3335, 800-863-3288; www.austinschuckwagonmotel.com; 12 W Main St; d $, cabins $$; Apr-Oct;) Popular with motorcyclists, rustic wooden buildings ring the shady grounds of this motel with two-bedroom roadside cabins. Amenities include satellite TV, a hot tub and the next-door general store (right).

Muley Twist Inn B&B (☎ 435-425-3640, 800-530-1038; www.muleytwistinn.com; 249 W 125 S, Teasdale; r $$; Apr-Oct;) Overlooking the Fremont River, this big wooden farmhouse with a wraparound veranda looks small against the towering sandstone domes that rise behind it. Rooms at the casual, down-to-earth inn are bright and airy. Rates include a full breakfast and afternoon snacks.

OUR PICK **Torrey Schoolhouse B&B** (☎ 435-633-4643; www.torreyschoolhouse.com; 150 N Center St; r $$; ; Apr-Oct) Decked out in dressed-down country elegance, this reborn 1914 schoolhouse harbors rooms that include period fixtures, down comforters, en suite baths and auto-massage recliners. Guests share kitchenettes. Rates include a hot, organic breakfast (vegetarians and vegans OK).

Also worth a look:

Cactus Hill Ranch Motel (☎ 435-425-3578, 800-507-2624; www.cactushillmotel.com; 940 E Birch Creek Rd, off CR 3262; r $; Apr-Oct;) Quiet rooms on a working ranch, 6 miles south of Hwy 24, and 2 miles west of Hwy 12, near Teasdale.

Best Western Capitol Reef (☎ 435-425-3761, 800-780-7234; www.bestwestern.com; 2600 E Hwy 24; r $$;) Best red-rock views and amenities among the chains.

Eating

GROCERIES & SELF-CATERING

A seasonal Saturday-afternoon farmers market kicks off around 4pm at Robbers Roost Bookstore (opposite).

Austin's Chuckwagon General Store (☎ 435-425-3288; 12 W Main St; 7am-10pm Apr-Oct) Next to Austin's Chuckwagon Motel, this convenience store sells camping supplies, sundries, groceries, beer, doughnuts, deli sandwiches and so-so Mexican-American takeout.

Mesa Farm Market (☎ 435-487-9711; Hwy 24, Caineville; usually 7am-7pm Mar-Oct) About 23 miles east of Capitol Reef's visitor center, near mile marker 102. Stop here for straight-from-the-garden organic salads, freshly baked artisan bread and cinnamon rolls, homemade cheeses, homegrown organic coffee and fresh-squeezed juices.

In winter, you'll have to drive 16 miles west of Torrey via Hwy 24 to **Royal's Foodtown** (☎ 435-836-2841; 135 S Main St, Loa; 7am-8pm Mon-Sat, to 7pm in winter) supermarket.

RESTAURANTS

Hwys 24 and 12 are lined with ho-hum, touristy American diners, cafes and Mexican takeout shops for cheap eats.

Slacker's Burger Joint (☎ 435-425-3710; 165 E Main St; mains $; 11am-9pm Mon-Sat, to 8pm Sun Mar-Oct) Order at the takeout window: old-fashioned burgers (beef, chicken, pastrami or veggie), hand-cut fries (the sweet-potato version is delish) and thick milkshakes in a rainbow of cool flavors.

Rim Rock Restaurant (☎ 435-425-3398; 2523 E Hwy 24; mains $$$; 5-10pm Mar-Dec) Every table features a million-dollar view of towering red-rock cliffs. On the straightforward ranch menu, choose from grilled steaks, river trout, meat loaf or pastas. Come before sunset. Full bar.

our pick **Café Diablo** (☎ 435-425-3070; 599 W Main St; mains $$$; 5-10pm Apr-Oct) One of southern Utah's best, Café Diablo serves highly stylized Southwestern food like turkey *chimole*, Mayan tamales or fire-roasted pork tenderloin on a cilantro waffle. For something you definitely won't get back home, try the rattlesnake cakes. There's also a selection of 23 tequilas (drinkers, request a free ride home).

Drinking

Robbers Roost Bookstore (☎ 435-425-3265; 185 W Main St; 8am-4pm Mon-Sat, 1-4pm Sun May-Oct;) Linger over a latte and a scone on comfy couches by the fire at this peaceful cafe-bookstore with bohemian bonhomie.

Castle Rock Coffee & Candy (☎ 435-425-2100; cnr Hwys 12 & 24; from 7am daily, seasonal hr vary;) Convenient whether you're coming or going, this coffeehouse and art gallery roasts Utah brews, bakes its own candy and banana bread, and blends up fruit smoothies.

Rim Rock Patio (☎ 435-425-3398; 2523 E Hwy 24; 5-10pm;) The only place in Torrey where you can just drink beer also serves up pizzas, sandwiches and ice cream. Play darts, horseshoes or disc golf and listen to live bands while your buddies chugalug.

Entertainment

Supporting the local arts scene, **Entrada Institute** (www.entradainstitute.org) hosts Saturday-night events, like cowboy poetry readings and live music jams, at Robbers Roost Bookstore (left) between May and October.

An old-fashioned movie house, Bicknell's **Wayne Theater** (☎ 435-425-3123; www.waynetheater.com; 11 E Main St, Bicknell) shows first-run Hollywood blockbuster movies and hosts a B-movie film festival (p210).

GOBLIN VALLEY STATE PARK

Melted rock formations from a Salvador Dalí fantasy fill the coliseumlike valley in this small, 3654-acre **park** (☎ 435-564-3633; www.stateparks.utah.gov; Goblin Valley Rd; day-use entry per vehicle $7) in the San Rafael Desert. A couple of short canyon hiking trails let you roam around the eroded mushroom-shaped mounds of Entrada sandstone. If you stare at them for a while, they really do look like little goblins. An exposed 24-site **campground** (☎ 801-322-3770, 800-322-3770; http://utahstateparks.reserveamerica.com; tent sites $18) provides covered picnic tables, drinking water, hot showers and an RV dump station. Campsites fill fast most weekends.

From Capitol Reef's visitor center, follow Hwy 24 east for about 38 miles to Hanksville (fill up your gas tank), then north 19.5 miles. Look for a signed turnoff on the west side of the highway, from where a paved road leads 5 miles west, then 7 miles south to the park's entrance station.

Canyonlands National Park

Canyonlands offers an echo of ancient Earth. The sun is strong and rock forms are brute and rugged. It's no surprise that early adventurers were told to put forth wills before proceeding. Today almost anyone can explore it. Roads and rivers make inroads to this high-desert wilderness stretching 527 sq miles with wide-angle views of wonder. Yet it's still an untamed environment. Needles and arches sprout from sandy washes. Under the rim, the Colorado and Green Rivers carve vast serpentine canyons. Mesas and buttes ripple the sky.

If Arches is red-rock 101, Canyonlands requires some homework. Those looking for desert adventure, deep quiet or a longer trip will find ample options. The park is divided into two main districts: Island in the Sky has rim-top panoramas, many short hikes and access to the famed 4WD White Rim Trail; while the Needles is wilder and more remote, ideal for backpacking. But options don't stop with footpaths. Running the rivers or mountain biking the red-dust roads are some of the best ways in to stunning landscapes.

It is possible to day trip with the family and still get plenty out of Canyonlands. For anything more, self-sufficiency is a must. Most areas are completely waterless. Off the paved main access roads, dirt roads are difficult to navigate, many trails are steep and the summer heat can be brutal. It's not hard to understand why, despite its beauty, this is the least visited of all the major Southwestern national parks.

Yet if it's solitude you seek, there's no better alternative.

HIGHLIGHTS

- Gazing at the desert panorama atop **Grand View Point** (p219)
- Putting sweat equity into the **White Rim** (p221), a world-class mountain-bike journey
- Navigating wildflower meadows, curvy slickrock and slot canyons around **Chesler Park** (p224)
- Watching a flaming sun peek through **Mesa Arch** (p218) at sunrise
- Examining ancient artistry in the exquisite rock art of **Horseshoe Canyon** (p227)

■ **Total Area** 527 sq miles	■ **Elevation** 5800ft	■ **Average high/low temperature in July** 118°F/51°F

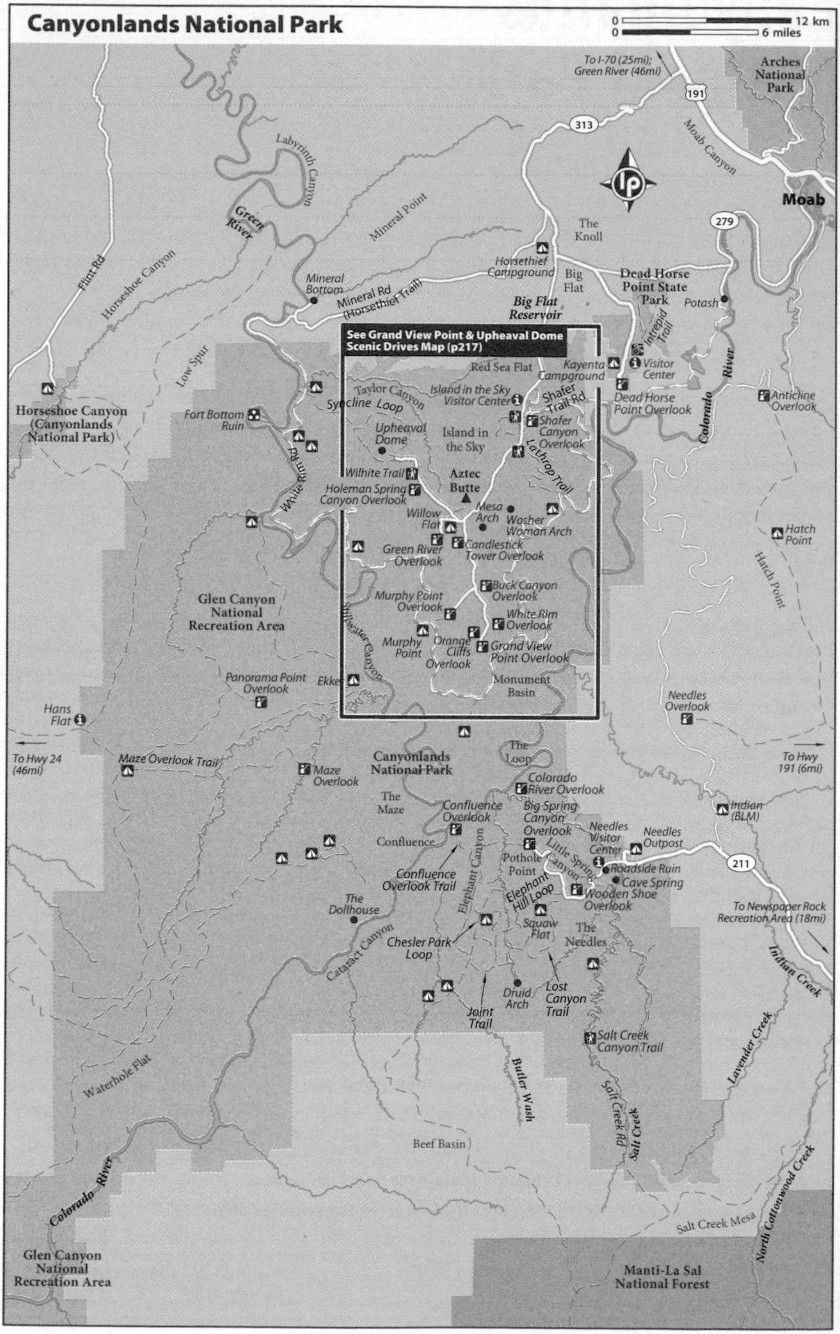

CANYONLANDS NATIONAL PARK

When You Arrive

Canyonlands is open year-round. Admission to the Island in the Sky and the Needles districts, good for seven days, costs $10 per car or $5 per person arriving by motorcycle, bicycle or foot. There is no fee to enter the Maze. Consider purchasing a Local Passport ($25), good for admission to Arches and Canyonlands National Parks and Natural Bridges and Hovenweep National Monuments for a year.

TOP THREE ADVENTURES

- Squeezing through the mile-long crevice known as the Joint Trail (p225)
- Blasting the legendary rapids of Cataract Canyon (p250)
- Greeting days of utter solitude in the rugged wilderness of the Maze (p227)

Orientation

The Colorado and Green Rivers divide the park into three separate and distinct areas – called 'districts' by the National Park Service (NPS) – Island in the Sky, the Needles and the Maze. Island in the Sky and the Needles feature visitor centers, developed campgrounds and paved roads to scenic overlooks, as well as dirt roads and hiking trails. The less-visited Maze and Horseshoe Canyon, an unconnected unit northwest of the Maze, offer only 4WD-accessible dirt roads, hiking trails and primitive campgrounds.

These districts remain separate because the park's river canyons form a Y – the Colorado forms the stem and northeast arm of the Y, while the northwest arm is the Green. Though the districts abut each other, they are inaccessible to one another from within the park – no bridges and few roads mean long drives to see the sights.

No roads cross the park. Instead, well-marked secondary spurs from two major highways access Canyonlands' districts. Hwy 191 runs north–south through Moab near the eastern park boundary. Take Hwy 191 north to reach Island in the Sky or south to reach the Needles. West of the park, Hwy 24 runs north–south through the San Rafael Desert; spur roads connect it to the Maze and Horseshoe Canyon.

Cradled by the two rivers atop the Y, Island in the Sky is the most developed district. To get there from Moab, drive north on Hwy 191 about 40 minutes to Hwy 313; both roads are paved. Southeast of the Colorado, the Needles district lies about 75 miles (90 minutes) from Moab via paved Hwys 191 and 211. The Maze is about 130 miles from Moab, accessible along dirt roads off Hwy 24; take Hwy 191 north to I-70 then west to Hwy 24 south. Horseshoe Canyon also lies off of Hwy 24 via dirt roads.

Information

To start, pick up maps, guidebooks and information at the **Moab information center** (p241). For information only, call or visit the **Canyonlands NPS Headquarters** (☎ 435-719-2313; www.nps.gov/cany; 2282 SW Resource Blvd, Moab; 🕑 8am-4:30pm Mon-Fri). The **Canyonlands Natural History Association** (☎ 435-259-6003, 800-840-8978; www.cnha.org; 3031 S Hwy 191, Moab) helps the NPS run the visitor centers and Moab information center and also serves as a bookseller for the NPS.

The **Island in the Sky visitor center** (☎ 435-259-4712; www.nps.gov/cany/planyourvisit/islandinthesky.htm; Hwy 313; 🕑 9am-4:30pm) features exhibits, an excellent introductory video, books, maps, schedules of ranger-led activities and information on permits and campgrounds.

West of the two rivers, the **Needles visitor center** (☎ 435-259-4711; www.nps.gov/cany/planyourvisit/needles.htm; Hwy 211; 🕑 9am-4:30pm) provides books, maps, the same introductory video, excellent exhibits and information on permits and campgrounds; make it a point to see the 25-sq-ft relief map of the park.

Ranger station **Hans Flat** (☎ 435-259-2652; www.nps.gov/cany/planyourvisit/maze.htm; Hans Flat Rd; 🕑 8am-4:30pm) has books and maps, but no other services. It's three to six hours west of the Maze.

Park Policies & Regulations

Canyonlands follows most of the national park hiking and backcountry use regulations (see p40), with a few exceptions.

On its dirt roads, 4WD vehicles, mountain bikes and street-legal motorbikes are permitted, but not all-terrain vehicles (ATVs). Off-roading is not allowed.

In the backcountry, campfires are allowed only along river corridors; use a fire pan, burn only driftwood or dead, downed tamarisk, and pack out all unburned debris.

Rock climbing is allowed (no permit needed), but only under specific regulations; contact a visitor center for details on restricted areas and permissible climbing hardware.

Dogs are not allowed on hiking trails or in the backcountry – even in a vehicle. For a kennel, see p256.

BACKCOUNTRY PERMITS

Permits are required for all backcountry camping, overnight backpacking, mountain biking, 4WD trips and river trips. These are in addition to the park entrance fee. Backpackers pay $15 per group of up to seven people. Day-use mountain bike or 4WD groups pay $30 for up to three vehicles. River trips cost $30 per group in Cataract Canyon or $20 per group in flat-water areas. Permits are valid for up to 14 consecutive days. Certain backcountry sections of the Needles are open to day use by horses, bikes and 4WD vehicles; permits cost $5 per day per vehicle or per group of up to seven bikes or horses. Horses are allowed on all 4WD trails; contact the park for restrictions on feed and details about day or overnight permits.

You must secure reservations at least two weeks in advance, by fax or mail only, with the **NPS reservations office** (☎ 435-259-4351, fax 435-259-4285; www.nps.gov/cany/planyourvisit/backcountrypermits.htm). NPS operators answer questions from 8am to 12:30pm (sometimes till 4pm) Monday through Friday (phones are often busy; keep trying). To reserve a backpacking, mountain-biking or 4WD trip, contact the NPS no earlier than the second Monday in July for the following calendar year; reservations are particularly recommended for spring and fall. Rafting and day-use reservations are accepted in early January for the same year.

If you don't have a reservation, you can get a permit on a space-available basis the day before or the day of your trip from the visitor center in the district in which your trip begins, though fall and spring are hard to book at the last minute. Though you can call ahead to ask whether permits are available, phone reservations are not accepted.

Getting Around

The easiest way to tour Canyonlands is by car. Traveling between districts takes two to six hours, so plan to visit no more than one per day. Speed limits vary but are generally between 25mph and 40mph. Beware of cattle on the road, particularly in winter and spring. They are frequently the cause of accidents. There are no gas stations within the park. Fuel up in Moab, and carry extra gas in the backcountry.

Many tour operators guide rafting, hiking, biking and 4WD tours in the park (see p248). For shuttle services, see p242.

ISLAND IN THE SKY

You'll comprehend space in new ways atop the appropriately named Island in the Sky, a narrow, 6000ft flat-topped mesa that drops precipitously on all sides, providing some of the longest, most enthralling vistas of any park in southern Utah. The views far into the wilderness are punctuated to the west by the 11,500ft Henry Mountains near Capitol Reef, and to the east by the sky-punching 12,700ft La Sal Mountains, which remain snowcapped in early summer. You can stand beneath a sparkling blue sky and watch multiple thunderstorms, many miles from one another, inundating far-off regions with gunmetal-gray sheets of rain while you debate whether to apply more sunscreen.

Offering paved roads and fine views, this is the park's most easily reached and popular district, welcoming about 260,000 visitors a year. The island is perched atop a sandstone bench called the White Rim, which does form a white border 1200ft below the mesa top. Cliffs below the rim drop another 1500ft into the river canyons.

The small Island in the Sky visitor center (p215) sits atop the mesa about 2 miles beyond the park boundary and entrance station. From the visitor center, the road heads 12 miles south to Grand View Point. About halfway to the point, a paved spur leads northwest 5 miles to Upheaval Dome. A number of overlooks and trails line each road.

Bring water – Island in the Sky lacks any water sources. And if one of those spectacular thunderstorms heads your way, get in your car or seek shelter immediately.

DRIVING

Two main roads cross the mesa top at Island in the Sky, forming a Y. The visitor center and entrance station sit atop the northeast (right) arm of the Y, Grand View Point is at the foot of the Y, and Upheaval Dome caps the northwest (left) arm.

One primary 4WD route, the White Rim Rd (p221), loops around the district about 1000ft below the mesa top.

GRAND VIEW POINT SCENIC DRIVE

Duration 50 minutes
Distance 12 miles
Start Visitor center
Finish Grand View Point
Nearest Town Moab (p239)
Summary A meander down the park's main road (paved), on a mesa top surrounded by cliffs and steep escarpments. Great views shift with every stop. Time it to catch a park ranger presentation at Grand View Point.

About 0.5 miles south of the visitor center, pull off to the left at the **Shafer Canyon Overlook**, where you can peer down 1000ft. Below is Shafer Trail Rd, the steep access route to the 4WD White Rim Rd.

A quarter-mile ahead you'll cross the **Neck** (slow down for great views), where the ridge narrows to 40ft across – eventually this strip will erode away, further isolating the mesa. The road levels out as it crosses **Grays Pasture**, where you might spot a bighorn sheep.

Just past Grays Pasture, take the left turn for **Mesa Arch** (p218). This easy hike is worth every step – especially at sunrise when the arch's underside glows a fiery red. The road to Upheaval Dome (p218) bears right here.

A mile past the arch, pull off on the right to take in the sheer sandstone walls of **Candlestick Tower**. Visible to the southwest is the **Maze** and its many fins and canyons, all capped with white and orange horizontal lines.

Continue 1.5 miles to a turnout for the **Murphy Loop** (p218). From the stunning overlook you'll see more of the Maze and the snaking Green River. The trail forks left just before the overlook.

Back on the road, 0.5 miles further on the left, take the paved walkway to the **Buck Canyon Overlook** for spectacular views of the La Sal Mountains. Another 1.8 miles south is the **White Rim Overlook**, a good picnic spot and starting point for the **White Rim Overlook Trail**, an easy, 1.2-mile round-trip hike.

Grand View Point & Upheaval Dome Scenic Drives

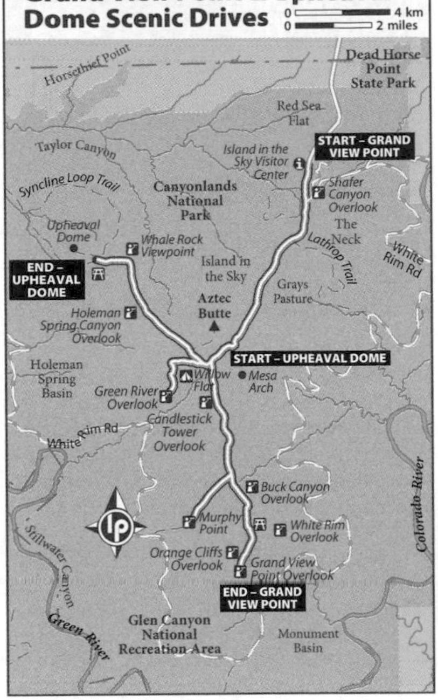

Three-quarters of a mile down the road, just before Grand View Point, the **Orange Cliffs Overlook** offers views west to the Henry Mountains, the last-charted mountain range in the Lower 48. The Orange Cliffs lie southwest, beyond the Maze. Come at sunset when the canyons glow orange in the waning light.

Five hundred feet ahead, the drive ends at **Grand View Point**, with one of the Southwest's most sweeping views, rivaled only by the Grand Canyon and nearby Dead Horse Point (p227). In the foreground to the southeast, Monument Basin contains spires similar to those in the Needles; to see them, look south. To spot the Maze, follow the Green River from the northwest to the Confluence, where it meets the Colorado. West of the Confluence, the Doll House formations mark the edge of the Maze and the head of Cataract Canyon, one of North America's most intense stretches of white water (see p250).

Stand beside the interpretive panel at the overlook and look down at the rock – the south-facing gashes occurred when lightning struck a man here in 2003 (he lived). Off to your right is the **Grand View Point Trail** (p219).

UPHEAVAL DOME SCENIC DRIVE

Duration 30 minutes
Distance 5 miles one way
Start Spur Junction, 6 miles south of visitor center
Finish Upheaval Dome
Nearest Town Moab (p239)
Summary In a few miles, this drive packs in the sights. Visit an ancient granary and peer down on the snaking Green River. Rock scrambling and crater gazing prove a hit with kids.

At the spur junction 6 miles south of the visitor center, turn northwest. A quarter-mile from the junction, turn left and drive to the **Green River Overlook** and **Willow Flat Campground**. Walk to the overlook for views of the Green River, Orange Cliffs and Henry Mountains. The small mesas in the foreground bear the marks of flash-flood erosion.

Large piñon trees around the parking area are 300 to 400 years old, while most of the blackbrush is more than 100 years old. The hardest thing for such desert plants is simply taking root. Nothing is growing on the parking-lot island, nor is anything likely to for another 50 years. Water and cryptobiotic crust (see p74) make all the difference by providing nitrogen and a foothold for plants.

Back on the main road, 0.5 miles further on the right, pull over at the **Aztec Butte Viewpoint and Trail** (p220). Above the parking area is a **granary** built by Ancestral Puebloans.

About 2 miles ahead on the left (past a twisty section of road), you'll reach **Holeman Spring Canyon Overlook**, the only point along this drive that offers long views west across the Green River. A mile further, stop at the **Whale Rock Viewpoint and Trail**. Named for its smooth slickrock hump, Whale Rock lies at the end of an easy, mile-long round-trip hike that gains only 100ft. The path is exposed, so use the handrails.

Three-quarters of a mile ahead, the road ends at the **Upheaval Dome** parking lot and picnic area. To see the dome, stroll the short trail (p219) from the parking area.

HIKING

With the exception of trails that descend to the White Rim, hikes at Island in the Sky are short and moderately easy. For a hike along the mesa top, walk the first mile of the west-trending **Wilhite Trail**, off the road to Upheaval Dome.

For a longer hike, descend 1000ft to the White Rim. The easiest route is the **Murphy Loop**, but it's still an 11.3-mile, five- to seven-hour round trip. The **Gooseberry Trail** (5.4 miles, four to six hours) is for fit hikers only. Check conditions with rangers before long hikes. Where trails are indistinct, walk on rock or in sandy washes to avoid damaging fragile cryptobiotic crusts.

For information about hiking safety, including dehydration, see p283. For definitions of our hike difficulty ratings, see p37.

Easy Hikes

Canyonlands has a rep for serious hiking, but Island in the Sky offers a good selection of short trails with great vistas that are perfect for families. For a workout, do a few in a day.

MESA ARCH

Duration 30 minutes
Distance 0.5 miles one way
Difficulty Easy
Start/Finish Mesa Arch trailhead
Nearest Town Moab (p239)
Transportation Private
Summary This easy trail leads to Canyonlands' most photographed arch, one of the best places to watch the sunrise – though don't expect to be alone.

As you ascend, notice the trailside cryptobiotic soil, riddled with bubbly minicanyon systems. This is among the healthiest soil of its kind in the park.

A moderately easy walk up a gentle rise brings you to the **arch**, an elegant sweep of Navajo sandstone that dramatically frames the La Sal Mountains. A thousand feet below, the basin extends in layers of red, brown, green and tan. Look carefully in the near distance to spot a narrow green strip of the Colorado River. To your left, through the arch, search atop the red spires for Washer Woman Arch (so named for its resemblance to a crouching laundress).

Resist the temptation to climb on the arch. Climbing is prohibited on most features named on USGS maps. Anyway, the sheer drop below will surely give you a case of the butterflies. Scamper up the rocks for a look down on the arch.

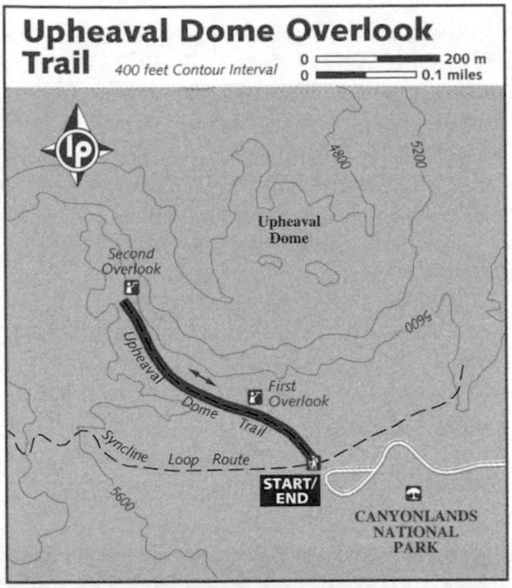

UPHEAVAL DOME OVERLOOK TRAIL

Duration 1–1½ hours
Distance 1.8 miles
Difficulty Easy–moderate
Start/Finish Upheaval Dome parking area
Nearest Town Moab (p239)
Transportation Private
Summary With views of a crater and upheaval canyon, this mysterious destination is debated to be the site of a meteor collision or just a strange geological feature.

This trail leads to overlooks of Upheaval Dome, one of the park's great geologic mysteries. Scientists disagree over how the feature formed – some suggest it's a collapsed salt dome, while others posit it's the site of meteorite strike some 60 million years ago. Looking more like a mound of gray sand, the dome rests in a depression – one doesn't look up to it, but down on it, like a belly button.

It's an easy 0.4 miles to the first overlook. From the parking area, climb to the fork in the trail, bear right and ascend the slickrock to the **viewpoint**. If you find yourself on switchbacks, you've made a wrong turn.

To reach the second **overlook**, return to the fork in the trail and bear left, clambering over slickrock to a final steep descent. Here you'll have a broader panorama of the surrounding landscape. If you're pressed for time, skip the second vantage point. Otherwise, the afternoon light here is magnificent.

GRAND VIEW POINT TRAIL

Duration 1–1½ hours
Distance 2 miles
Difficulty Easy
Start/Finish Grand View Point parking area
Nearest Town Moab (p239)
Transportation Private
Summary Easily earned panoramic views from the cliff's edge to the broad mesa below and wide desert beyond; follow cairns and keep to the rocks.

After marvelling at 100-mile views from the roadside observation area, take this easy stroll to the point itself for a better perspective of the massive mesa underfoot. Review the interpretive panels for interesting background. To the right of the panels, the trail descends stone steps to a fairly level, easy walk along the exposed rim – watch the little ones!

To the south, scan the skies over Junction Butte for the peregrine falcons that nest atop it.

Scramble atop the rocks at trail's end for spectacular views. The Needles' namesake spires rise to the south, while off to the west lie the Henry Mountains (on Capitol Reef's eastern flank) and distant Boulder Mountain (eastern terminus of the Aquarius Plateau and top step of the Grand Staircase). Glance below to spot the chalky sandstone of White Rim and the placid Green River. If storm clouds start to roll in, particularly from the west, quickly return to your car.

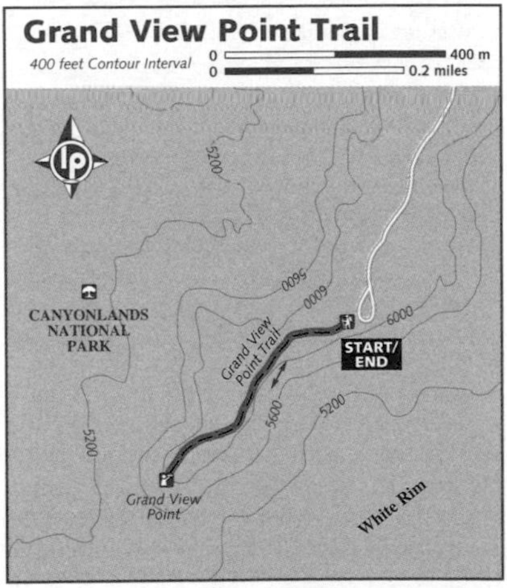

Day Hikes

AZTEC BUTTE TRAIL

Duration 1–1½ hours
Distance 2 miles
Difficulty Moderate
Start/Finish Aztec Butte trailhead
Nearest Town Moab (p239)
Transportation Private
Summary This short ascent of a Navajo sandstone dome yields stellar views; it's a steep hike over slickrock to the top. Check out the ancient granaries.

Be sure to wear rubber-soled shoes or hiking boots for traction. Stay on the trails, as fragile cryptobiotic crust is widespread atop the dome. In summer bring plenty of water and wear a wide-brimmed hat, as the exposed butte offers no shade. In winter the trail may be icy and impassable.

The first half-mile cuts across grassland to the base of the dome. Cairns mark the ascent. The second half-mile is moderately strenuous. The butte levels off at the top, revealing panoramic views and endless sky. Look for the small, ancient **granary**, evidence of an Ancestral Puebloan culture, a likely precursor to modern-day Hopis and Zunis. A small spur trail leads to more ruins. This is the only archaeological site at Island in the Sky.

NECK SPRING

Duration 2½ hours
Distance 6 miles
Difficulty Moderate
Start/Finish Shafer Canyon Overlook parking area
Nearest Town Moab (p239)
Transportation Private
Summary Good for solitude seekers, this stream canyon attracts wildlife and fills with wildflowers in springtime. Look for the remnants of pioneer ranching.

Perhaps because it isn't cliffside, this loop trail attracts fewer hikers. Following the sign in the Shafer Canyon Overlook parking area, it crosses the street and descends Taylor Canyon to Neck and Cabin Springs. The initial trail is an old roadbed built in the 1800s by ranchers to bring livestock to water. Hitching posts, water troughs and pipes are still visible (please leave them in place).

Descending slightly, the trail reaches **Neck Spring**. If you stay quiet here, you may see animals (mule deer, chipmunks and bighorn sheep) approaching for a drink. The moisture makes it an ideal climate for Gamble oak, maidenhair fern and Fremont barberry.

Leaving the alcoves, start to climb to white sand hills before reaching **Cabin Spring**, with a cabin, troughs and corrals near the site. A short, steep ascent climbs over sandstone. Follow the cairns to the mesa top, where the trail crosses the main road and continues 0.5 miles along the rim of Shafer Canyon to the parking lot.

LATHROP CANYON

Duration 2½ hours up to 2 days
Distance 5 miles to rim, 22 miles to Colorado River
Difficulty Moderate
Start/Finish Lathrop Canyon trailhead
Nearest Town Moab (p239)
Transportation Private
Summary An extensive hike into the canyon with stellar views. For an easy stroll, consider an out-and back to the rim. Less trodden than other trails, it's perfect for solitude.

A ranger favorite, Lathrop Canyon is one of the few longer trails in this district. If short on time, hike out to the canyon rim for views of the Colorado River and La Sal Mountains.

Follow the level sandy single-track through the grasslands. It passes over undulating slickrock marked by cairns. Canyon views start here, including a glimpse of a gorgeous bend in the Colorado.

The trail returns to sandy paths and twists along the canyon rim. It then descends steep switchbacks to a boulder-strewn wash that leads to **White Rim Road** (p221). Hikers can follow the spur road down into **Lathrop Canyon**, a descent of 2100ft. Three at-large permits are available for camping below White Rim Rd.

Backcountry Hikes

After a glimpse of the rugged landscape that surrounds Island in the Sky, you may be chomping at the bit to hit the backcountry.

Keep in mind, though, that this is unforgiving wilderness – any hike requires proper advance planning.

Aside from White Rim Rd (see p221), which is mostly a biking route, there's just one major backpacking route in the district: the **Syncline Loop** (8.3 miles, five to seven hours), a primitive route requiring some navigational skills. A side trip to the Green River is 3.5 miles one way. If you're fascinated by Upheaval Dome, or would like a closer look at the Green River, this is a perfect route with lots of places to camp. Since the trail is largely exposed, it gets blazing hot in summer. Rangers consider this a route and not a trail – the difference is that you will have to pay close attention in places to stay on the path. In fact, most park rescues occur along this stretch, primarily because day hikers underestimate the trail, get turned around and/or run out of water. Pay close attention to trail markers. You'll need a permit to stay overnight (see p216).

If you love hiking the mesa top but don't want to stay at Willow Flat Campground, the park issues one permit a day for the Murphy Point campsite. An easy flat hike across grasslands, through juniper stands and over rocks takes you to this solo site with stunning views. Ask a ranger for details.

OTHER ACTIVITIES

For details about **river rafting, kayaking** and **canoeing** the Green and Colorado Rivers, see p249.

Four-Wheel Driving & Mountain Biking

Blazed by uranium prospectors in the early 1950s, primitive **White Rim Road** circles Island in the Sky. It is considered one of the premier multiday mountain-biking routes in the world. Accessible from the visitor center via steep Shafer Trail Rd, the 70-mile route is the top choice for 4WD and mountain-biking trips. It generally takes two to three days to travel the loop in a 4WD vehicle, or three to four days by bike. As the route lacks any water sources, cyclists should team up with a 4WD support vehicle (there are 4WD rentals in Moab) or travel with an outfitter (see p246).

The park service limits the number of motorized vehicles. If you arrive without an overnight permit, call the visitor center about possible cancellations or no-shows. Rangers regularly patrol the route to check permits. Always stay on trails. No ATVs are allowed.

To learn more about the White Rim, pick up *A Naturalist's Guide to the White Rim Trail* by David Williams and Damian Fagon.

Kids' Activities

When you arrive at the park, stop by the visitor center to pick up a **Junior Ranger Activity Guide**. Once kids complete certain activities, they can return to the visitor center to receive a special certificate and badge from a ranger.

Kids particularly like the Whale Rock (p218) and Mesa Arch (p218) trails, both easy walks with big payoffs. Keep an eye on your little ones, especially near overlooks, which are often unfenced.

Ranger Programs

For information about park attractions and insight on its human and geologic history, attend a ranger-led program. April through October, rangers give daily talks at Grand View Point at 10:30am and 11:30am. Talks are given daily at the visitor center at 10:30am and 1:30pm. For additions, check schedules at the visitor center.

SLEEPING

You won't find any rooms or restaurants in the park. For a hot meal and a warm bed, drive to Moab (p239). There is one developed campground at Island in the Sky. If it's full, check the campground at Dead Horse Point State Park (p228) and the Bureau of Land Management (BLM) sites on Hwy 313 (see p255). For a list of campgrounds around the area, see p254.

Willow Flat Campground (☎ 435-719-2313, 435-259-4712; www.nps.gov/cany; sites $; year-round) A quarter-mile from the Green River Overlook, down a mile-long dirt spur from the road to Upheaval Dome, this small, first-come, first-served campground with 12 sites for tents or RVs under 28ft provides limited amenities, including vault toilets, picnic tables and fire grates, but no water. Bring your own firewood. Don't expect shade, as most of the vegetation is low and scrubby. Each site accommodates up to 10 people and two vehicles. The campground fills up nearly every night in spring and fall, so arrive early.

THE NEEDLES

Named for giant spires of orange-and-white sandstone that jut skyward from the desert floor, the Needles offers otherworldly terrain completely distinct from the scenery in Island in the Sky. Despite paved access roads, however, this district receives only half the number of visitors. Why? Perhaps because it's a 90-minute drive from Moab, and once you finally arrive, you have to work harder to appreciate its wonders – in short, you have to get out of the car and walk. But if you expend a little energy, payoffs include peaceful solitude and an opportunity to experience, not just observe, the vast beauty of canyon country.

The Needles visitor center (p215) lies 2.5 miles inside the park boundary and provides drinking water. (If you've already visited Island in the Sky, be sure to bring your entrance receipt to avoid having to pay again.) From the visitor center, the paved road continues almost 7 miles to the Big Spring Canyon Overlook. Parking areas along the way access several sights, including arches, Ancestral Puebloan ruins and pictographs. About 3 miles past the visitor center, a side road leads to Squaw Flat Campground (p226) with year-round water.

GPS has limited reception and is best used in conjunction with a map. Likewise, cell phones rarely have reception here. Credit card–operated pay phones outside the visitor center can be used at any hour.

DRIVING

Be aware that storms wash out roads periodically and any road may be in poor condition. If the weather's been poor, check conditions at the visitor center before heading out.

The following drive can also be done by cyclists; be careful as the shoulder of the road is narrow.

To see the rock spires at Big Spring Canyon Overlook in the best light, visit in the morning – in the afternoon, the sun drops behind them.

BIG SPRING CANYON OVERLOOK

Duration 30 minutes
Distance 6.4 miles
Start visitor center
Finish Big Spring Canyon Overlook
Nearest Town Monticello
Summary Lovely at sunset, this short spurt goes by cool rock formations and slickrock to finish with gaping canyon views. The road is paved and well maintained.

Stop first at the **Roadside Ruin** (0.25 miles from the visitor center) and stroll the easy 0.3-mile loop trail (p222) to this ancient granary.

Unless you're bound for the 0.6-mile Cave Spring Trail (p223), bear right at the fork in the road and pull over at the **Wooden Shoe Overlook**, on your left. Scan the cliffs overhead for the namesake rock formation with a tiny arch at its base.

Pass the turnoff for the campground and continue across the wide, even terrain of **Squaw Flat**. Two miles ahead on the left is a picnic area with shaded tables. The 0.6-mile **Pothole Point Trail** (p223) starts from the small parking lot just west of the picnic area. From here the road curls around the point to the moderately easy 2.4-mile **Slickrock Trail** (p223).

Just past this trailhead, the road dead ends at the **Big Spring Canyon Overlook**. Park along the road and walk out on the rocks for a peek into the shallow canyons. Above the rocks rise 100ft formations that look as though they're made of whitish petrified sand dunes.

HIKING

Open country and strange rock forms make these trails excellent for exploring. However, they are not well marked – always carry a topographical map, as people often get lost. Take notice when a trail crosses a wash – you may be tempted to follow the wash, but look closely for cairns (which usually take you across). Some trails have 50¢ trail brochures at the trailhead.

Easy Hikes

One quick option is the **Roadside Ruin Trail**, a 0.3-mile loop that takes 30 minutes to walk. It starts out across uneven gravel and finishes over slickrock. Look for a remarkably well-preserved Ancestral Puebloan granary tucked into a gap in the slickrock. If you're here in late spring, keep an eye out for blooming yucca.

CAVE SPRING TRAIL

Duration 30–45 minutes
Distance 0.6-mile loop
Difficulty Easy–moderate
Start/Finish Cave Spring trailhead
Nearest Town Monticello
Transportation Private
Summary Kids love this short hike for the cowboy artifacts, ladders and slickrock scampers. There are also prehistoric pictographs to view.

Pungent sagebrush marks this trailhead at the end of a well-maintained, mile-long dirt road. Hikers will first reach an abandoned **cowboy camp** with miscellaneous remnants left by cowboys in the 19th and 20th centuries. The trail continues beneath a protruding rock lip, then through 6ft sagebrush to **Cave Spring**, one of few perennial water sources in the Needles. Look for the rust-colored pictographs painted on these walls more than 1000 years ago.

From Cave Spring you'll climb two ladders up the slickrock for wraparound views of rock formations, steppes and mesas. The trail has awesome views of rock spires and the La Sal Mountains.

After crossing the undulating sandstone, the trail drops into a wash and returns to the trailhead.

POTHOLE POINT TRAIL

Duration 45 minutes
Distance 0.6-mile loop
Difficulty Easy
Start/Finish Pothole Point trailhead
Nearest Town Monticello
Transportation Private
Summary This short loop across slickrock explores the microcosmic ecosystems of potholes. It features views of distant cliffs, mountains and rock formations similar to those along the Slickrock Trail.

The slickrock along this trail features naturally occurring dimples that collect water during rainstorms. To the naked eye, these potholes appear to be nothing more than mud puddles, but closer inspection reveals tiny organisms that must complete their life cycles before the water evaporates. Keep hands and feet out of the potholes, since these organisms are fragile (see p69). Though this is an excellent walk for contemplative souls and the scientifically inclined, it does lack drama, unless the potholes are teeming with life (which isn't always readily visible). Acrophobes, take heart: you won't have to stroll beside any cliffs.

LOCAL VOICES: INSIDE CANYONLANDS

Canyonlands has tons of options for exploring. The more you learn about the desert, the more you can appreciate its subtleties. At night the bats come out and there are kangaroo rats hopping around. We have the largest remaining herd of desert bighorn sheep – around 300, usually spotted in the fall. One of the coolest places in the park is **Horseshoe Canyon** (p227), with four big panels of pictographs, off a 4WD road with shifting sand dunes.

-Sierra Coon, Canyonlands ranger

Day Hikes

The following trail plus the easy hikes listed above total 3.6 miles and are easily doable in a single day. Taken collectively, they offer an overview of the region's human and geologic history. Unfortunately, none is wheelchair accessible. Cairns often mark sections across slickrock.

If you like long day hikes, the Needles also includes easily accessible backcountry treks you can do in a day (see p224).

SLICKROCK TRAIL

Duration 1½–2 hours
Distance 2.4 miles
Difficulty Easy–moderate
Start/Finish Slickrock trailhead
Nearest Town Monticello
Transportation Private
Summary This ridgeline trail is high above the canyons with views below. After ascending gentle switchbacks to slickrock, you'll follow cairns. A semiloop trail, it's tricky to follow in places.

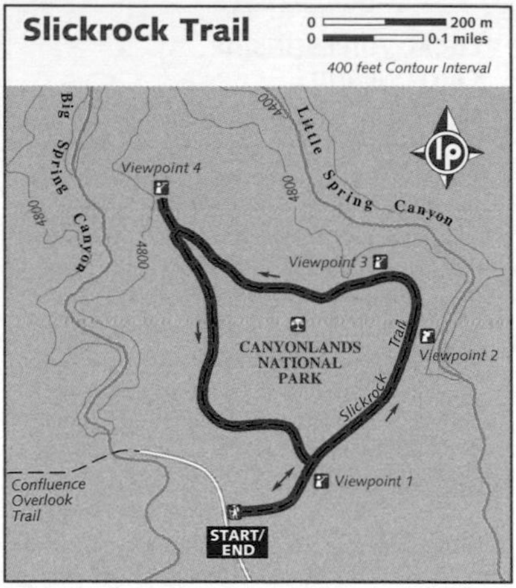

Brochures available at the trailhead describe four main viewpoints, each marked by a numbered signpost. Keep an eye out during your hike – bighorn sheep are occasionally seen here.

If you're short on time, at least visit **Viewpoint 1** for a panorama you simply can't get from the road. Giant red cliffs hang like curtains below high buttes and mesas, the district's namesake needles touch the sky, and the La Sal and Abajo Mountains lord over the whole scene.

Bear right at the 'Begin Loop' signpost to reach **Viewpoint 2**, where hearty vegetation clings to the desert crust and lines the watercourses. Scamper up the rocks for a primo view. At **Viewpoint 3** giant boulders ring Lower Little Spring Canyon, where purple and gray rock layers offer telltale evidence of an ancient shallow sea.

Viewpoint 4 is a high promontory that overlooks Big Spring Canyon, a vast rugged gorge. Watch overhead for birds soaring on thermals. To the north you'll spot Grand View Point at Island in the Sky, perched high atop the red Wingate sandstone cliffs.

On the return path you'll face the needles and spires to the south that define this district. The Abajo Mountains lie beyond.

Backcountry Hikes

The Needles is Canyonlands' top backpacking district, making it hard to get the backcountry permit necessary for an overnight hike. Yet nothing quite compares to sleeping far from the roar of internal-combustion engines. If you can't secure a permit, fret not: strong hikers can do many of the best trails in one day. Day hikers don't need a permit. Backcountry campers should see p216.

In addition to the hike described in this section, consider the **Confluence Overlook Trail**, a moderate four- to six-hour round-trip hike from the Big Spring Canyon trailhead to watch the Green River flow into the Colorado – one or the other may be silty or muddy depending on recent rainfall. Many other hikes connect in a series of loops, some requiring route-finding skills. Among the best are the **Big Spring Canyon** and **Lost Canyon Trails**. For gorgeous scenery, the **Elephant Canyon Trail** to Druid Arch is hard to beat. Rock art along the **Salt Creek Canyon Trail** is highly worth a look. Ask rangers for further options and advice.

If you venture off trail, stay in washes or on slickrock to avoid trampling the fragile cryptobiotic crust.

For information about backcountry and hiking safety, see p283.

BACKCOUNTRY CAMPING

Designated campsites abut most trails; you can request a specific site when applying for your permit. At-large camping is not permitted in side canyons that lack designated sites.

Water is scarce in the backcountry. Ask rangers about potential sources and current availability, but plan to pack in all you'll need.

Human waste must be carried out or buried in a 4in to 6in hole at least 300ft from any water sources; consider using human waste containment bags. Carry out used toilet paper.

CHESLER PARK LOOP & JOINT TRAIL

Duration 1–2 days
Distance 11-mile loop
Difficulty Moderate overnight hike, moderate–difficult day hike
Start/Finish Elephant Hill trailhead
Nearest Town Monticello
Transportation Private
Summary With ample ups and downs, this loop gives great perspective on the Needles. Don't skip the Joint Trail, a narrow section that slips through deep fractures in the rock. A short segment follows a 4WD road.

Among Canyonlands' most popular backcountry treks, these combined routes cross desert grasslands, pass red-and-white-striped pinnacles and thread through tall hairline fractures. Though the trails aren't flat, elevation changes are mild and infrequent. You won't find any water. For most hikers, the *Trails Illustrated Needles District* map ($10) should suffice, but if you're inclined to wander, carry a 7.5-minute USGS map.

Park at the Elephant Hill trailhead, 3 miles from Squaw Flat Campground via a gravel 2WD road. From the parking area, the trail climbs to a bench, then undulates over slickrock toward rock spires. The next section is typically where people make a wrong turn. Cross the wash at the T-junction and follow signs to Chesler Park (*not* Druid Arch), descending 300ft along switchbacks into **Elephant Canyon**. Continue to follow signs along the canyon floor.

The final 0.2 miles to the **Chesler Park Viewpoint** climbs 100ft, topping out on the rocky pass amid spires 2.9 miles from the trailhead. This marks the beginning of the 5-mile **Chesler Park Loop**. Five campsites lie southeast (left) of the junction.

The next morning, leave your backpack at the campsite and explore the claustrophobia-inducing **Joint Trail**, where the fractured rock narrows to 2ft across in places; the trail junction lies to the south, about midway around the Chesler Park Loop. Pause just east of the Joint Trail for stellar views of the towering pinnacles that ring Chesler Park. On the southwest section of the loop, you'll follow a half-mile stretch of a 4WD road. If staying two nights, take the side trip to **Druid Arch**.

OTHER ACTIVITIES

For details about **river rafting**, **kayaking** and **canoeing** the Green and Colorado Rivers, see p249.

Four-Wheel Driving & Mountain Biking

Fifty miles of 4WD and mountain-biking roads crisscross the Needles. Stay on designated routes. Motorists and cyclists must obtain a permit for overnight trips (see p216), but not for day use, with the exception of

Chesler Park Loop & Joint Trail

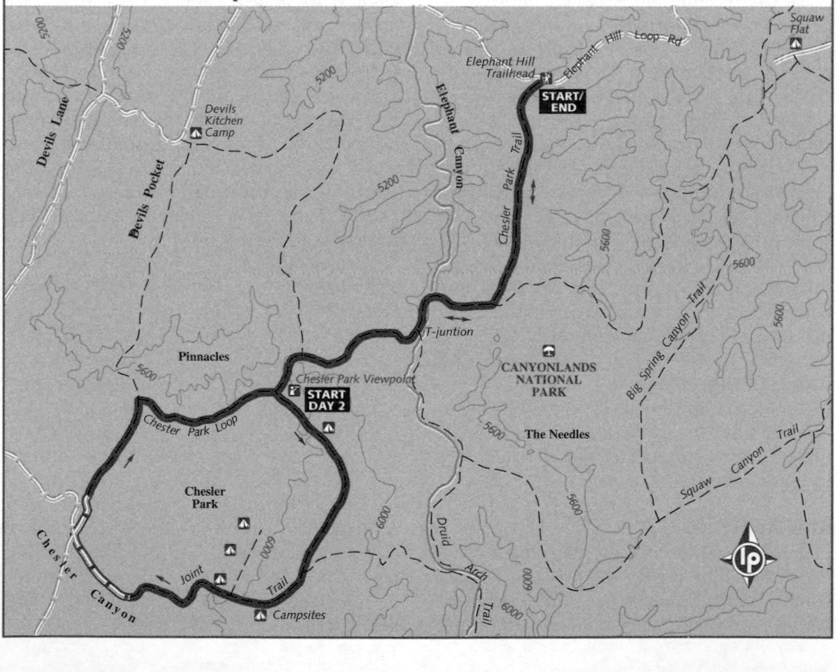

ESSENTIALS

- Cell-phone reception is poor or nil – rely on the credit-card phones at the visitor center (p215)
- For food, showers and laundry, visit Needles Outpost (right)
- For more camping options, check out the BLM website: www.discovermoab.com/campgrounds_blm.htm

Lavender and Horse Canyons, which require a $5 day-use permit fee; book in advance or check at the visitor center for cancellations, no-shows or leftovers.

All 4WD roads in the Needles require high-clearance vehicles (many off-the-lot SUVs do *not* have high clearance; AWD is not sufficient). Know what you're doing before you set out, or risk damaging your vehicle and/or endangering yourself. Towing fees can run to about $1000. If you're renting a 4WD vehicle, check the insurance policy; you might not be covered here. For more information, including 4WD routes and road conditions, check with a ranger when you book your permit. No ATVs are allowed.

Several 4WD and mountain-biking trails – formerly cattle roads – lead into the backcountry. **Elephant Hill** is the most technically challenging route in the district, with steep grades and tight turns. The route to the **Colorado River Overlook** is usually moderate in a vehicle and moderately easy on a mountain bike; check at the visitor center first since all conditions are possible. You will want to park and walk the final, steep 1.5-mile descent to the overlook. Following the district's main drainage, the **Salt Creek Trail** is moderately easy for vehicles, but sand makes it not recommended for bikes.

Ranger Programs

From March through October, rangers lead evening campfire discussions. Check schedules at the visitor center when you arrive in the park.

Kids' Activities

When you arrive at the park, stop by the Needles visitor center to pick up a **Junior Ranger Activity Guide**. Once kids complete certain activities, they can return to the visitor center to receive a special certificate and badge from a ranger. Ask at the visitor center about renting a **Master Explorer Day Pack**, which contains binoculars, a magnifying lens and nature guide. Kids especially like the Cave Spring Trail (p223). To get kids inspired pretrip, check out the free puzzles and coloring pages available online at www.nps.gov/cany/forkids.

SLEEPING

You won't find any rooms in the park. There is one developed front-country campground in the Needles. Just outside the district, there's the private Needles Outpost campground, which sells limited supplies. Drive to Moab (p239) for lodgings and all other services.

Store your food in your car or hang food in a stuff sack in the backcountry – campground ravens and small animals are notorious for getting into everything, including coolers.

Squaw Flat Campground (☎ 435-259-4711; www.nps.gov/cany; sites $; ⏲ year-round) This first-come, first-served campground, 3 miles west of the visitor center, fills up nearly every day, especially in spring and fall (come around 8:45am to snag a site). Unlike the campground at Island in the Sky, this one provides flush toilets and cold running water. It has 26 sites for tents or RVs up to 28ft, and each site includes a picnic table and fire grate, with many in the shade of mature juniper trees. If the campground is full, ask at the visitor center about sites on BLM lands, or stay in Moab. Three group sites can be reserved in advance; call the NPS reservations office (p216).

Needles Outpost (☎ 435-979-4007; www.canyonlandsneedlesoutpost.com; Hwy 211; sites $; ⏲ Apr-Nov) If Squaw Flat is full, this dusty private campground with 20 sites is the closest alternative. Some campers have reported poor service. Campsites sit amid mature juniper trees alongside west-facing rock walls offering morning shade. Hot showers cost $3, or $7 for noncampers. Other amenities include flush toilets, fire rings and an RV dump station. The Outpost also accepts reservations. An on-site store sells limited camping supplies, firewood, groceries, beer, ice, gasoline and propane. The lunch counter and grill (open 8:30am to 4:30pm) serves sandwiches and burgers.

THE MAZE

A 30-sq-mile jumble of high-walled canyons, the Maze is a rare preserve of true wilderness for hardy backcountry veterans. The colorful canyons are rugged, deep and sometimes inaccessible. Many of them look alike, and it's easy to get turned around. The district's name refers to one area within this sector. To visit the Maze, plan on spending at least three days, though a week may be ideal.

As the district lies west of the Confluence, the only way to reach it from Moab is to drive a 133-mile crescent-shaped route to the **Hans Flat ranger station** (☎ 435-259-2652; www.nps.gov/cany/planyourvisit/maze.htm; 8am-4:30pm), accessible by non-4WD vehicles. Take Hwy 191 north from Moab, to I-70 west, to Hwy 24 south. About 25 miles south of I-70, just past the paved turnoff for Goblin Valley State Park (p212), head southeast on the gravel road for 46 miles to Hans Flat. On the way, you'll cross the Glen Canyon National Recreation Area and Orange Cliffs Special Management Unit; if you plan to stop at either one, pick up a permit at Hans Flat.

There is no entrance fee or visitor center, but the ranger station sells books and maps (no food or water). The few roads into the district are very poor and can be closed by rain or snow; bring tire chains if visiting between October and April. You'll need a 4WD vehicle with a short wheelbase and high clearance. If you're inexperienced at four-wheel driving, stay away. You must also be prepared to repair your vehicle and, at times, the road. Those entering the Maze in a vehicle must reserve their backcountry campsite in advance.

If you don't have a 4WD, you can also leave your vehicle behind and hike into the district directly from the ranger station. For more advice and a full list of necessities, contact the ranger station in advance of your trip.

The **Maze Overlook Trail** requires that hikers carry at least a 25ft length of rope to raise and lower packs. Camping is at-large, and you'll find several reliable water sources (ask a ranger for locations). You can drive a 2WD vehicle to the North Point Rd junction, 2.5 miles south of Hans Flat, then hike 15 miles to the Maze Overlook.

HORSESHOE CANYON

A separate unit of Canyonlands, west of the northern reaches of Island in the Sky, the little-known gem of Horseshoe Canyon shelters millennia-old Native American rock art. The centerpiece is the **Great Gallery**, which consists of superb Barrier Canyon–style pictographs that date to between 2000 BC and AD 500. These heroic, life-size figures are nothing short of magnificent. Artifacts recovered in this district date back as far as 9000 BC. Damaging the rock art is a criminal offense. Don't touch or disturb it in any way. Even the oils from your skin can harm the paintings.

The Great Gallery lies at the end of a 6.5-mile round-trip trail that descends 750ft from the main dirt road. Budget for six hours. Rangers lead hikes here on Saturdays and Sundays from April through October; to arrange a group walk, contact the **Hans Flat ranger station** (☎ 435-259-2652; www.nps.gov/cany/planyourvisit/horseshoecanyon.htm; 8am-4:30pm).

You can camp on BLM land at the trailhead, though it's not a campground per se, but a parking lot. There is a single vault toilet, but no water or services. If you don't like primitive camping, Moab is three hours away.

Shifting sand dunes can affect road conditions, so talk to a Canyonlands ranger before going. Take Hwy 191 north from Moab, to I-70 west, to Hwy 24 south. About 25 miles south of I-70, just past the turnoff for Goblin Valley State Park (p212), turn east (left) and follow the graded gravel road 30 miles to the Horseshoe Canyon unit.

AROUND CANYONLANDS

DEAD HORSE POINT STATE PARK

The views at Dead Horse Point pack a wallop, extending 2000ft below to the meandering Colorado River, 12,700ft up to the La Sal Mountains and 100 miles across Canyonlands' stair-step landscape. If you thrive on epic landscapes, you won't regret a side trip here.

The turnoff to Dead Horse is on Hwy 313, just 4 miles north of Island in the Sky

(Moab is 30 miles away). Toward the end of the drive, the road traverses a narrow ridge just 30yd across. Ranchers once herded horses across these narrows – some were forgotten and left to die, hence the park name. A rough footpath skirts the point for views in all directions. To escape the small (but sometimes chatty) crowds, take one of the short hikes that rim the mesa. Visit at dawn or sunset for the best lighting.

The **visitor center** (☎ 435-259-2614; www.stateparks.utah.gov; day-use per car $10; 🕑 8am-6pm summer, to 5pm winter) features exceptionally good exhibits, shows on-demand videos and sells books and maps. Rangers lead walks and talks in summer. The 21-site **Kayenta Campground** (☎ 801-538-7220, 800-322-3770; www.stateparks.utah.gov; sites $; 🕑 year-round) provides limited water, 20-amp RV hookups and a dump station, but not showers. Recently, electrical hookups were added. Reservations are accepted between March and October, though you can often find a site (priced per car, not tent) if you show up early, even in summer. RV drivers should fill up with gas and water before arriving.

Mountain bikers should check out the new **Intrepid Trail**, an excellent 9-mile singletrack on the rim with great views. Rare for the Moab area, it's flat, so good for beginners, but its twists and turns keep riders on their toes. Another advantage – at 6000ft it can be cooler than riding in the bottom of a canyon on a hot day. The plateau is known to be 10°F cooler.

Pets are OK on a leash on all hiking trails but not on the Intrepid Trail for bikes.

NEWSPAPER ROCK RECREATION AREA

If you're fascinated by petroglyphs, Newspaper Rock features a single large sandstone face covered with images chipped out by various Native American groups and pioneers over a 3000-year stretch. It's beside Indian Creek on Hwy 211, about 12 miles west of Hwy 191. For more details contact the **BLM Monticello field office** (☎ 435-587-1500; www.blm.gov/utah/monticello).

Arches National Park

A threshold of thousands of arches leads into this bare, wild landscape, a collage of layered red rock forming windows, fins and spires. Though the 119-square-mile Arches only earned national-park status in 1971, its story started 10,000 years ago with the hunter-gatherers who came here to quarry materials for darts and cutting tools. Later, writer and desert anarchist Edward Abbey penned the American classic *Desert Solitaire* while working here as a park ranger in the late 1950s. Today nearly 1 million visitors make the pilgrimage every year.

With the highest density of rock arches anywhere on Earth, Arches is nothing short of awe-inspiring. Different from other Western parks, it's small and user-friendly, with short trails or roadside stops at the most spectacular sights. For this same reason, its popularity continues to grow, making its once extreme isolation a thing of the past. Now it's a particularly good destination for kids, whose imagination can conjure whole universes in these wiggling rock forms.

The arches range in size from just 3ft across to the 300ft Landscape Arch, one of the largest in the world. Arches are formed over millions of years by erosion; ultimately, the very same forces dissolve them. A visit only captures a nanosecond of geological time in these processes. Since the park is doable in a day, most rush through but it wouldn't hurt to take your time. Sit on a rock. Linger. The scenery is truly mind-blowing.

ARCHES NAT ONAL PARK

HIGHLIGHTS

- Clambering up a curving slickrock slope to **Delicate Arch** (p237)
- Marveling at the precariously poised 3577-ton **Balanced Rock** (p234)
- Peering down at the Colorado River from beneath the sweep of **North Window** (p235)
- Finding solitude down the rugged road to **Klondike Bluffs** (p231)
- Exploring an unmarked maze of giant sandstone fins in the **Fiery Furnace** (p234)

■ **Total Area** 119 sq miles	■ **Elevation** 4085ft (at the visitor center)	■ **Average high/low temperature in July** 100°F/87°F

Arches National Park

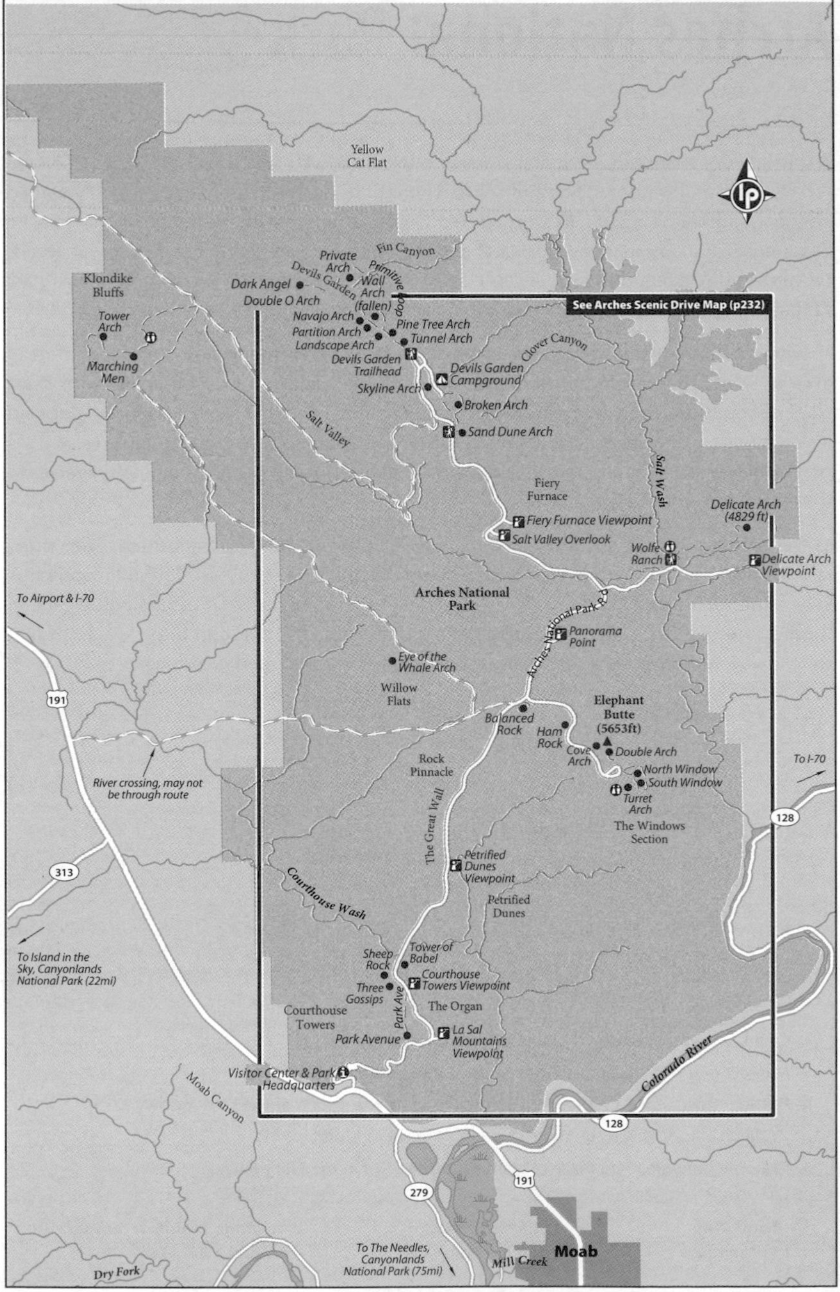
0 4 km
0 2 miles
Yellow Cat Flat
Fin Canyon
Private Arch
Devils Garden
Primitive Loop
Wall Arch (fallen)
Klondike Bluffs
Dark Angel
Double O Arch
Navajo Arch
Partition Arch
Landscape Arch
Pine Tree Arch
Tunnel Arch
Devils Garden Trailhead
Tower Arch
Marching Men
See Arches Scenic Drive Map (p232)
Clover Canyon
Devils Garden Campground
Skyline Arch
Broken Arch
Sand Dune Arch
Salt Valley
Salt Wash
Fiery Furnace
Fiery Furnace Viewpoint
Salt Valley Overlook
Delicate Arch (4829 ft)
Wolfe Ranch
Delicate Arch Viewpoint
Arches National Park
Arches National Park Rd
To Airport & I-70
Panorama Point
Eye of the Whale Arch
Willow Flats
191
Elephant Butte (5653ft)
Balanced Rock
Ham Rock
Cove Arch
Double Arch
North Window
South Window
Turret Arch
The Windows Section
Rock Pinnacle
River crossing, may not be through route
To I-70
128
The Great Wall
Petrified Dunes Viewpoint
Petrified Dunes
313
Courthouse Wash
To Island in the Sky, Canyonlands National Park (22mi)
Sheep Rock
Tower of Babel
Three Gossips
Courthouse Towers Viewpoint
The Organ
Courthouse Towers
Park Ave
Park Avenue
La Sal Mountains Viewpoint
Visitor Center & Park Headquarters
Moab Canyon
Colorado River
128
191
279
To The Needles, Canyonlands National Park (75mi)
Mill Creek
Moab
Dry Fork

When You Arrive

Arches is open year-round. The entrance station lies off Hwy 191, 5 miles northwest of Moab. Admission, good for seven days, is $10 per car or $5 per person arriving by motorcycle, bicycle or on foot. A Local Passport, good for admission to Arches and Canyonlands National Parks and Natural Bridges and Hovenweep National Monuments for a one-year period, costs $25.

Orientation & Information

The park includes 22 miles of paved roads, and most sights lie on or alongside the pavement. Crowds are often unavoidable, and parking areas overflow at peak times (weekends, spring through fall). Every year the park takes new measures to handle the problem. The NPS may eventually institute a shuttle system if visitation increases. For now, to keep drivers from parking in dangerous or sensitive areas, rangers have stepped up ticketing for illegally parked cars.

The best strategy is to arrive at the park by 9am, when crowds are sparse and the temperatures not so bad; or visit in the evening after 7pm. If you can't find a designated parking spot at one place, continue to the next. Also, drive carefully; accidents occur when drivers focus on the scenery, not the road – an easy trap to fall into at Arches.

There are no places in the park to buy prepared food, groceries or supplies. For all services, drive to Moab.

The **visitor center** (☎ 435-719-2299; www.nps.gov/arch; 🕑 8am-4:30pm, longer hr spring-fall) has educational exhibits and a bookstore. Rangers are on hand to answer questions and help you plan your visit; ask about ranger-led activities. You can also pick up your reserved tickets for the Fiery Furnace (p234) guided walk. If you arrive after hours, stop at the parking lot and read the information panels. Potable water faucets are located at the entrance. Stock up on water while you're here; the next water source is 19 miles up the road, at Devils Garden.

For books and maps by mail or online, contact the **Canyonlands Natural History Association** (☎ 435-259-6003, 800-840-8978; www.cnha.org; 3031 S Hwy 191, Moab, UT 84532); the CNHA also staffs the **Moab Information Center** (p241).

There is no wi-fi access in the park. Cell signals are limited; certain providers work better than others. Your best bet on finding a signal is to ascend the nearest hill. In an emergency, dial ☎ 911 or contact a park ranger.

Park Policies & Regulations

Arches' hiking and backcountry-use regulations include those listed for all the parks on p40. If you need to board your pet, refer to p256. Horses aren't allowed in Arches National Park.

Getting Around

Currently the only way to see Arches is by bicycle or private vehicle, on foot or through an organized tour. For information about organized tours, see p242.

SIGHTS

Arches' main sights lie along the park's scenic drive (p232). Visible from the road are towering rock walls and rounded formations, sandstone fins, red-rock arches and windows. Far in the distance, look for the snow-covered La Sal Mountains to the east.

DRIVING

There is one main park road, with two short spurs that lead to more sights. The most popular stops lie closest to the visitor center and park entrance. If you're tight on time, visit the **Windows section**, off the first spur. The more time you have, the further you can go.

The park also includes three unpaved roads. **Salt Valley Road** is generally accessible to 2WD cars (though not when wet). It leaves the main road a mile before Devils Garden and heads 9 miles west to the scenic **Klondike Bluffs**, where the landscape is much like Devils Garden but lacking the crowds. A moderately difficult 3-mile round-trip hike leads to the remote **Tower Arch**. There's no shade there so it can be brutal in summer.

From Klondike Bluffs, an unnamed, 10-mile 4WD dirt road doubles back to the scenic drive at Balanced Rock. This is best done from north to south (the northbound route tackles a steep and sandy climb that may be impassable).

From Balanced Rock, **Willow Flats Road** leads due west about 8 miles to Hwy 191. Formerly the main route into the park, it requires a high-clearance or 4WD vehicle. The road doesn't offer any important features, just distant views and solitude.

Always check with rangers about road conditions before heading out; seasonal closures may apply.

ARCHES SCENIC DRIVE

Duration 2.5 hours
Distance 43 miles, including spurs
Start/Finish Visitor center
Nearest Town Moab (p239)
Summary Hitting all the highlights, this paved drive visits Arches' strange forms and flaming desert landscapes. It's packed with photo ops and short walks to arches and iconic landmarks.

From the visitor center, the steep road ascends Navajo sandstone, once ancient sand dunes. Stop at the **Moab Fault Overlook**. Below, Hwy 191 parallels a fault line through the Moab Canyon. The rock on the opposite side of the highway stands 2600ft higher and is 180 million years older than the side

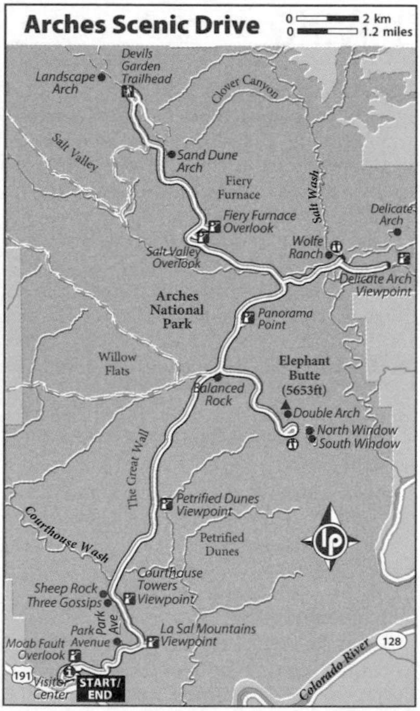

on which you're standing. Interpretive panels explain the geology.

A mile ahead, stop at **Park Avenue**, where you can take a walk (see p235) past a giant rock fin that calls to mind a row of New York City skyscrapers. While tiny scrub oaks to the right of the trailhead look young, they may be as much as 100 years old. The light here is best in the morning. If you've got antsy kids who want to hike, but you don't want to, this is your chance for 30 minutes of quiet time; pick them up 1.4 miles up the road, at the Courthouse Towers Viewpoint.

Half a mile past Park Avenue, stop at the **La Sal Mountains Viewpoint**. This laccolithic mountain range developed underground during volcanic activity, then rose to the surface, fully formed, some 24 million years ago. (The Henry Mountains, near Capitol Reef, formed the same way.) Atop the mesa in the distance you'll catch your first glimpse of arches.

If the scenery looks familiar, many of the driving scenes in the film *Thelma & Louise* were shot in Arches. This stretch is where they locked the cop in the trunk; the final scene was shot at nearby Dead Horse Point.

As you descend toward the **Courthouse Towers Viewpoint**, look left for the **Three Gossips**, towers that resemble three figures sharing a secret. From the viewpoint turnout, look up at the monoliths. These walls were likely once connected by arches since fallen away, particularly at **Sheep Rock**. Just ahead in **Courthouse Wash**, stands of bright-green cottonwood trees offer dramatic proof of how water can transform the parched desert into an oasis.

About 1.5 miles further, on the right, the undulating landscape at **Petrified Dunes** was once a vast sweep of sand dunes. (Technically, the dunes aren't 'petrified,' as they contain no carbon, the determining element in petrification.) As you continue up the road, particularly in spring, notice the increased density of roadside vegetation. The extra bit of runoff from the pavement makes it possible for these plants to survive; a few feet away, they'd shrivel up.

After a 3-mile ascent, you'll arrive at the 3577-ton **Balanced Rock**, which teeters precariously atop a narrow stone pedestal. Pull over and take the 15-minute loop trail (p234), then turn right onto Windows Rd, a 5-mile round-trip spur. You'll find pit toilets beside the parking lot at road's end.

THE BARD OF ARCHES

Edward Abbey (1927–89), one of America's great Western prose writers, worked as a seasonal ranger at Arches National Monument in the 1950s, before it became a national park. In his essay collection *Desert Solitaire: A Season in the Wilderness,* Abbey wrote of his time here and described the simple beauty and subtle power of the vast landscape. In one of his essays, perhaps the book's most famous, he bemoaned what he dubbed 'Industrial Tourism' – exploitation of the natural environment by big business acting in cahoots with government, turning the national monument into a 'Natural Money-Mint.'

At the core of the problem: cars. Abbey severely criticized how the rising auto industry led to paving the wilderness. For Abbey, wilderness was religion, so tourists who never left their cars ('upholstered mechanized wheelchairs') would never transcend the mundane, experience the sanctity of the land and, in so doing, liberate their consciousness.

Ironically, Abbey's evocative descriptions have only brought more visitors to his cherished remote outposts. Nonetheless, his polemic lays out a clear, viable plan for ridding the parks of vehicles, which would free up more room for everyone and leave the parks 'unimpaired for the enjoyment of future generations,' as is the mandate of the National Park Service.

Many of Abbey's predictions have come true – you need only arrive at Arches in high season and get stuck in a line of idling SUVs to know that he was, in his way, a prophet. Leave your summer beach reading in your suitcase and instead pick up a copy of *Desert Solitaire*. Not only will you appreciate the desert in new, unexpected ways, you'll also have something to read in traffic.

Take the easy, short walks to **North** and **South Windows** (p234) and to **Double Arch**. It's hard to grasp the immensity of these gigantic marvels until you're beside them. If you want a long view of the vast surrounding landscape but are short on time, head to North Window and stand right beneath it.

Back on the main road, stop at **Panorama Point**. The 360-degree view includes an overlook of **Salt Valley**, a onetime salt dome that collapsed when water washed away the salt. Interpretive panels explain the geology.

Two-and-a-half miles past the Windows spur, turn right on the signed spur to **Wolfe Ranch** and Delicate Arch. Pull into the first parking lot (which includes pit toilets) and take the short, easy walk to the primitive 1880s cabin, with its juniper-log walls and shale roof. **Salt Wash**, which is wet year-round, runs from the cabin to the Colorado River. If you're lucky, you may spot a river otter. Cross the footbridge for a surprisingly close look at a small petroglyph panel, incised by Ute people sometime after the year 1600 (look but don't touch, as oils from fingers deteriorate the rock). If you're up for a moderately strenuous hike, climb the trail to **Delicate Arch** (p237), the park's premier hike. Otherwise, continue driving to the **Delicate Arch Viewpoint**, 1 mile beyond the Wolfe Ranch turnout.

Two short trails lead to views of the arch, which has also been nicknamed the 'Schoolmarm's Breeches' and the 'Cowboy Chaps.' Follow the crowds to the right for an easy 50yd walk to the lower view, or bear left for a moderately strenuous 0.5-mile hike and 200ft ascent to the better view.

Return to the main road, turn right and drive 3 miles to the **Salt Valley Overlook** for a perspective down to Wolfe Ranch and Salt Valley, then pull off again at the **Fiery Furnace**. A short walk between split-rail fences leads to the overlook, from which you can peer between the giant fins of Entrada sandstone – at sunset they resemble flames in a furnace. Rangers lead daily **guided hikes** of this rocky maze (see p234), but you must purchase advance tickets at the visitor center.

From here the main road skirts past the Fiery Furnace and the **Sand Dune Arch trailhead** (p236) to road's end at the Devils Garden trailhead. Refill your water bottle and picnic before taking the moderately easy walk to **Landscape Arch** (p235), the span of which longer than a football field. Drive out the way you came, omitting the spur roads.

HIKING

Arches is geared more to drivers than hikers, with most of the main sights within a mile or two of paved roads. There are a few exceptions, but you won't find an extensive

ARCHES AND BRIDGES

What's the difference between an arch and a bridge? All are formed by the erosion of sandstone. An arch forms when water freezes and expands in cracks, causing portions of the rock to break away. A bridge forms when a watercourse passes beneath it, eroding the sandstone from below. That said, rivers dry up or change course over time, and it's sometimes difficult to distinguish a bridge from an arch.

system of trails as at other national parks. Still, you can enjoy several hikes that will take you away from the sound of traffic, at least for a few hours.

Backpacking isn't popular at Arches, but if you're bound and determined, you can do so with a backcountry permit, available in person from the visitor center. There are neither designated trails nor campsites. Due to the fragility of cryptobiotic soils, the park discourages backcountry treks. The closest you'll come to an established backcountry route is the **Devils Garden Primitive Loop**.

If you're fit and would like to join a guided hike through the narrow sandstone labyrinth at the **Fiery Furnace**, you must buy tickets (in person only; adult/child $10/5) at the visitor center. You can reserve tickets (in person or at www.recreation.gov) up to seven days in advance. Walks run two to three hours and are offered twice daily (morning and afternoon) April through October.

Accomplished hikers can explore the Fiery Furnace unguided. To do so, you must still pay a fee, watch a video and discuss with rangers how to negotiate this confusing jumble of canyons before they'll grant you a permit. Permits are limited and usually sell out, so go early.

Arches is wildly popular and stays busy through Thanksgiving weekend. One tip is to try sunrise hiking (less popular than sunset).

For definitions of our hike difficulty ratings, see p37.

EASY HIKES

An ideal place for families or those looking more to sightsee than break a sweat, Arches features a number of easy hikes. For a workout, you can do several in a day.

BALANCED ROCK

Duration 15–20 minutes
Distance 0.3-miles
Difficulty Easy
Start/Finish Balanced Rock parking area
Nearest Town Moab (p239)
Transportation Private
Summary The draw is a boulder as big as a naval destroyer, teetering on a spindly pedestal. Loop around the formation to have a good look at the forces of erosion at work.

A 3577-ton boulder atop a leaning pedestal, Balanced Rock shoots from the earth like a fist. The pedestal is made of soft Dewey Bridge mudstone, which erodes faster than the rock above. Eventually, this pedestal will snap, and the boulder will come crashing down.

While you can see the formation clearly from the trailhead, the loop allows you to grasp its actual size (55ft to the top of the pedestal, 128ft to the top of the rock). On the outside of the trail look for narrowleaf yucca, an important desert species that can provide food, soap, needles and rope.

There is wheelchair access to the viewpoint.

THE WINDOWS

Duration 30–60 minutes
Distance 0.6 miles
Difficulty Easy
Start/Finish The Windows trailhead
Nearest Town Moab (p239)
Transportation Private
Summary A gravel loop trail makes an easy climb to three massive arches (North and South Windows and Turret Arch); take the alternative, slightly longer return for a back view of the two windows.

Perhaps the park's most heavily trodden path, this trail leads directly to North and South Windows and offers a terrific view of Turret Arch. Rangers lead interpretive talks here from spring through fall; if you're interested, check the bulletin board at the parking area. The trail forks about 500ft from the lot. Bear right for a close look at **Turret Arch** along a short loop that rejoins the main trail.

The left fork climbs to the **North Window**. Stand beneath this arch for one of the park's best views, taking in red-rock cliffs along the Colorado River and Castle Valley in the distance. Above you is the giant smooth sweep of the mature arch, supported by a base of lumpy Dewey Bridge mudstone. **South Window** sits higher than North Window. Though tempting, keep off the arch (climbing is prohibited on most named features).

Two trails lead back to the parking lot from here: the wide, graded main trail and the narrow primitive trail. The latter heads east and then north, with great views and a brief respite from the crowds. Follow the cairns.

PARK AVENUE

Duration 30–45 minutes
Distance 1 mile one way
Difficulty Easy–moderate
Start Park Avenue trailhead
Finish Courthouse Towers viewpoint
Nearest Town Moab (p239)
Transportation Private
Summary A good intro to Arches beauty; walk between towering sandstone monoliths on Park Avenue, named for the rocks' resemblance to Manhattan skyscrapers.

This hike is a straight shot to the end, all downhill from the trailhead. You can arrange for a shuttle but it's a pleasant enough round trip. You could hike up from the bottom, but views are best on the descent.

From the trailhead, you'll descend to the Dewey Bridge rock layer, also called mudstone for obvious reasons. (A soft rock that erodes faster than layers above it, mudstone forms the pedestal at Balanced Rock.) In places, the primitive trail crosses uneven terrain; follow the cairns. As you near the trail's end, glance ahead to spot the **Tower of Babel**, and left to spy on the **Three Gossips**. From the viewpoint, look for **Baby Arch**, which has just begun to form.

If you want to assess the trail before committing, walk to the second interpretive panel at the end of the paved path; from here, almost the entire route unfurls below. The light is best in the morning.

There is wheelchair access to the viewpoint (a short section).

DAY HIKES

LANDSCAPE ARCH

Duration 30–60 minutes
Distance 2.1 miles
Difficulty Easy–moderate
Start/Finish Devils Garden trailhead
Nearest Town Moab (p239)
Transportation Private
Summary Among the world's longest natural stone spans, Landscape Arch is a spectacular ribbon of rock reached via a moderate gravel trail with spurs of interest.

Landscape Arch lies 0.8 miles along the Devils Garden trail at the northern end of the main park road. Along the trail, don't miss the short spurs (0.5 miles) to Tunnel and Pine Tree Arches. To make it more of a full-day hike, continue to Dark Angel spire or do the entire Devil's Garden Primitive loop. Before setting out, fill up with water at the trailhead parking lot. If you can, try to walk this trail in the morning; it's much more pleasant than in mid-afternoon heat.

From the trailhead, you'll thread through sandstone fins that stand on end like giant wedges. A third of a mile in, bear right at the fork and head downhill to **Tunnel Arch** (on your right) and 45ft **Pine Tree Arch** (on your left). High on a cliff, aptly named Tunnel Arch looks like a subway tube through the Entrada sandstone. In contrast, Pine Tree Arch is meaty, with a bulbous frame around its gaping middle. Look for the gnarled namesake juniper, which juts from the base of the window.

As you approach **Landscape Arch** along the main trail, the terrain opens up, revealing long views to distant ridges (beyond which lie Colorado) and a vast expanse of sky. In the past visitors could hike right beneath the elegant 306ft sweep of desert-varnished sandstone, longer than a football field. But in 1991 a 60ft slab of rock fell from the arch, nearly killing several hikers. When you notice the cracks on the left side of the arch, it's easy to understand why the NPS closed the trail.

From here you can continue on a moderately difficult out-and-back hike to the trail's end at **Dark Angel** spire, adding about

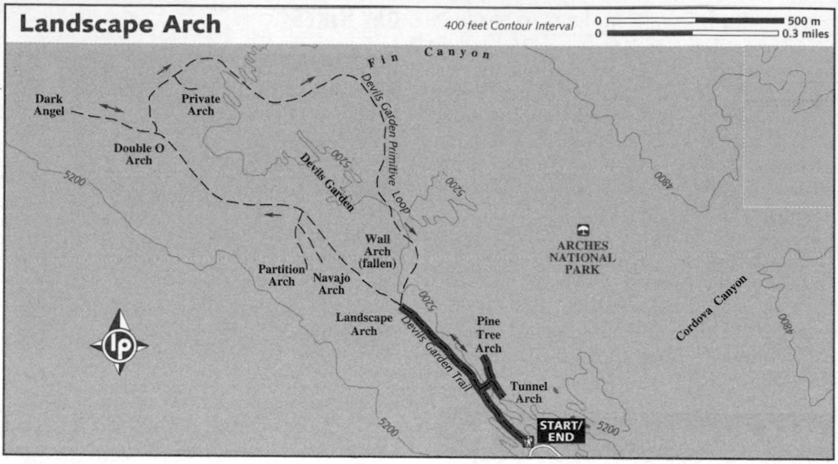

3.4 miles to your journey. You can also add the difficult **Devils Garden Primitive Loop**, an additional stretch of 4.3 miles. Both lead to **Double O Arch**, where you'll negotiate the narrow edge of a sandstone fin with a 20ft drop on either side. (This rocky route is not suitable for little ones.) Pick up a trail guide at the trailhead or ask a ranger for route details.

SAND DUNE & BROKEN ARCHES

Duration 15–30 minutes to Sand Dune Arch, 30–60 minutes to Broken Arch, 2 hours for complete loop
Distance 0.4 miles (Sand Dune Arch), 1.2 miles (Broken Arch), 2 miles (complete loop)
Difficulty Easy–moderate
Start/Finish Sand Dune Arch parking area
Nearest Town Moab (p239)
Transportation Private
Summary A varied walk that leads though rock fins (giving a taste of the Fiery Furnace), cool sand dunes and slickrock; a good place to take the kids.

From the Sand Dune Arch parking area, follow the trail through deep sand between narrow stone walls that are the backmost fins of **Fiery Furnace** – a good teaser if you haven't already hiked the Furnace. In less than 0.25 miles you'll arrive at **Sand Dune Arch**, which looks something like a poodle kissing a polar bear. Resist the temptation to climb or jump off the 8ft arch.

From here you can bear left to return to your car or bear right across open grassland en route to 60ft Broken Arch. At the next fork (the start of the loop trail), grasses give way to piñon pines and junipers along a gentle climb to **Broken Arch**. The treat here is the walk *through* the arch atop a slickrock ledge. Wear rubber-soled shoes or boots, or you may have trouble climbing to the arch.

When you're ready, return to the parking area or continue north to Devils Garden Campground. The route follows cairns over slickrock, passing through stands of

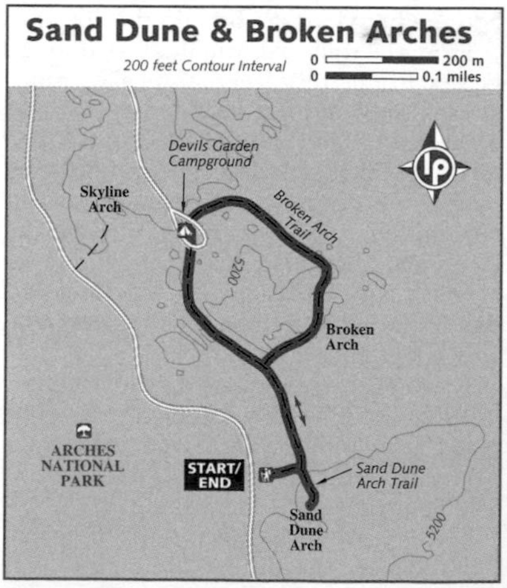

ARCHES WAY BACK WHEN

Curious about life among the rocks in the past? Check out the following:

- The Wolfe family cabin (p233), located near the Delicate Arch trailhead
- Rock art near Delicate Arch trailhead (p237) and lower Courthouse Wash
- The Old Spanish Trail – info at the visitor center (p231)

For a mobile play-by-play, pick up the Arches self-guided driving tour CD at the Arches visitor center.

desert pines. Watch for new arches forming near the trail. If you're staying at the campground, you can join the loop trail there. From the campground spur it's another 0.5 miles back to the start of the loop trail.

This is a good trail for kids, especially the first section, though savvy adult hikers may find it too tame.

DELICATE ARCH

Duration 2–3 hours
Distance 3 miles
Difficulty Moderate–difficult
Start/Finish Wolfe Ranch
Nearest Town Moab (p239)
Transportation Private
Summary A shadelesss ascent to a bowed sandstone arch that Edward Abbey likened to cowboy chaps. Follow rock cairns on slickrock and mind yourself on exposed heights.

The trail to Delicate Arch may seem interminable on the way up, but the rewards are so great that you'll quickly forget the toil – provided you wear rubber-soled shoes or boots and drink a quart of water along the way (there is no shade). You won't be alone – this is the most popular long hike at Arches.

Start out behind **Wolfe Ranch**, where a short spur trail leads to a small **petroglyph panel**. The trail is wheelchair-accessible to the petroglyph panel. The illustrations with horse riders are believed to be authored by nomadic Utes, since they adopted riding only after the arrival of the Spanish.

Past the panel, the trail climbs a series of small switchbacks, soon emerging on a long, steady slickrock slope. (This hill is visible from the trailhead, as are the tiny figures trudging up the slickrock like pilgrims.) Take your time on this stretch, especially on hot days. If you keep a steady pace, plan on making it to the top in 45 minutes.

As you approach the arch, the trail skirts a narrow slickrock ledge that may be daunting for those afraid of heights – yet it's worth pushing on to round the final corner. To your right, a broad sandstone amphitheater opens up below, and **Delicate Arch** crowns its rim, framing the 12,700ft La Sal Mountains in the distance. Circle the rim to the base of the arch, which sits atop a saddle that drops precipitously on either side. (If you bypass the bowl and bear left, it's possible to clamber high atop large flat rocks for a different perspective – and fewer people.)

There is one drawback to this trail. Many people climb up only to take a snapshot before heading back down. Yet one of the great joys of visiting Delicate Arch is to linger beside it and soak in the scene. If you do, however, expect someone with a camera to ask or even holler at you to get out of the way. (Edward Abbey predicted this sort of thing; see p233). To avoid a confrontation (and if you're not afraid of heights), head beneath the arch and drop down the other side of it a few yards, where few people venture, least of all the 'industrial tourists.'

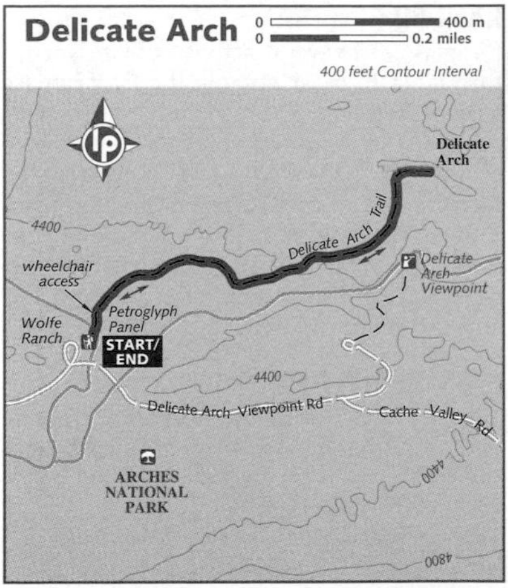

UP THE ANTE

For extra credit, try these challenging hikes (dry conditions only):

- **Tower Arch** (p231; 3.4 miles, three hours) Steep and short from Klondike Bluffs
- **Double O** (p236; 4.2 miles, three hours) A jaunt over sandstone slabs with rocky footing
- **Devils Garden** (p236; 7.2 miles, five hours) A hike and scramble that includes the Double O plus a primitive loop.

OTHER ACTIVITIES

ROCK CLIMBING

Rock climbing is permitted at Arches (though guided canyoneering is no longer allowed), but you are prohibited from climbing on any named features. Most routes require advanced techniques. Currently a permit is not necessary although this may change in the future. Before you set out, ask at the visitor center about current regulations and route closures. Leave dull-colored webbing only when recovery is impossible. Follow established trails or hike in sandy washes or over slickrock to avoid stepping on fragile macrobiotic crusts. White chalk is prohibited; purchase sandstone chalk at climbing shops in Moab. Remember, it's easier to ascend than descend, so always plan your route down, lest you get stuck on a rim.

RANGER PROGRAMS

Rangers lead several activities from spring through fall, most notably the **Fiery Furnace guided hike**, leaving at 9am and 4pm (by reservation) in summer; you can also reserve online (see p234). In addition to evening **campfire talks** at Devils Garden Campground, rangers also hold talks at the Windows Section. Check current schedules on bulletin boards at the visitor center, the campground and the Windows parking area.

KIDS' ACTIVITIES

When you arrive at the park, stop by the visitor center and pick up a **Junior Ranger Activity Guide**. Once kids complete certain activities, they can return to the visitor center to receive a special certificate and badge from a ranger. Kids can also get an **Explorer Pack** on loan with stuff to do throughout the park; Island in the Sky is another drop-off point for the pack.

Arches is very kid-friendly. Distances between sights are short, offering frequent opportunities to hop out of the car and run around (encourage kids to stay on marked trails to avoid crushing the fragile desert soil). Keep an eye out for faces and figures amid the rocks.

SLEEPING

Arches offers one developed campground, but no rooms or restaurants. Drive the 5 miles to Moab for all services.

Devils Garden Campground (☎ 877-444-6777 or 518-885-3639 for reservations; www.reserveusa.com; campsites $; year-round) The park's only camp-ground sits at the end of the main road, 18 miles from the visitor center. It has 52 sites for tents, and some for RVs up to 30ft. Amenities include water, picnic tables, fire grills and flush and pit toilets, but no showers. Though tall piñon pines and junipers provide moderate shade, the camp-ground gets very hot in summer – this is the desert. As you pull into the camp-ground, sites on the right (by the rocks) offer more privacy, while sites on the left boast better views. Two group sites are also available. From March through October, half the sites are available by reservation only; the remaining sites are first-come, first-served. For same-day availability, do not just drive to the campground. Instead, check at the entrance station or visitor center anytime after 7:30am. You can reserve sites online or by phone between four and 240 days in advance. Ask about cancellation and no-show fees before you book, particularly if your travel plans are tentative – you could get stuck with the bill.

For a list of other campgrounds around the area, see p254.

Moab

Shop for groceries till midnight, browse the shelves of indie bookstores, buy a bottle of tequila, chat on your cell phone, sit down for dinner at 9pm and you'll still find several places to grab a beer afterward. All this convenience comes at a price: corporate chain motels line Main St, souvenir shops abound and streetlights and neon signs blot out the night sky. For those coming from the wilderness, the hubbub can be jarring.

Still, there's a distinct sense of fun in the air. Moab bills itself as Utah's recreation capital, and that's why everyone flocks here – to play outdoors. From the hiker to the four-wheeler, recreationists' enthusiasm borders on fetishism.

Now the largest town in southeast Utah, Moab has nearly lost its small-town rural roots, and some residents fear that it's on its way to becoming the next Vail. While the town won't ever become a sprawling suburb (it's surrounded by state and federal lands), it does get overrun with tourists every year, and the impact of their tracks on the fragile desert is a serious concern. People disagree over how the town should evolve. Talk to anyone and you'll quickly learn that Moab's polarized political debates are yet another high-stakes extreme sport.

One thing is certain: people here love the land, even if they don't always agree on how to protect it. If the noise and debates prove too much, remember that you can disappear into the vast desert without a trace in no time flat.

HIGHLIGHTS

- Paddling through the red-rock beauty of the **Colorado River** (p250)
- Treading the roller-coaster rock face of the **Slickrock Bike Trail** (p247)
- Taking in long views of Castle Valley while hiking the eroded sandstone of **Fisher Towers** (p245)
- Climbing to mountain meadows and aspen forests on the **La Sal Mountain Loop Rd** (p243)
- Pedaling and people-watching along the colorful main street of **Moab** (p242)

Population 4800	**Elevation** 4026ft	**Average high/low temperature in July** 100°F/87°F

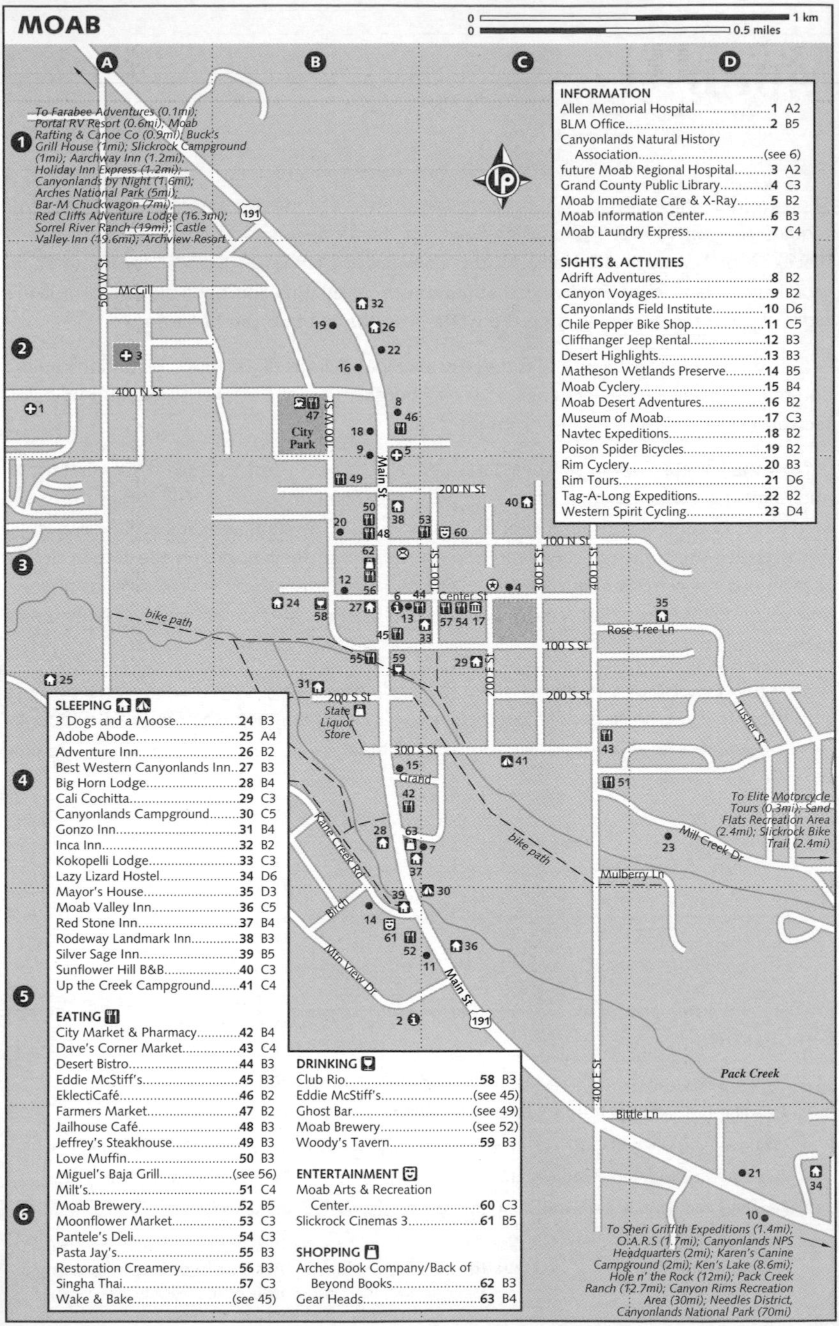

INFORMATION
- Allen Memorial Hospital 1 A2
- BLM Office 2 B5
- Canyonlands Natural History Association .... (see 6)
- future Moab Regional Hospital 3 A2
- Grand County Public Library 4 C3
- Moab Immediate Care & X-Ray 5 B2
- Moab Information Center 6 B3
- Moab Laundry Express 7 C4

SIGHTS & ACTIVITIES
- Adrift Adventures 8 B2
- Canyon Voyages 9 B2
- Canyonlands Field Institute 10 D6
- Chile Pepper Bike Shop 11 C5
- Cliffhanger Jeep Rental 12 B3
- Desert Highlights 13 B3
- Matheson Wetlands Preserve 14 B5
- Moab Cyclery 15 B4
- Moab Desert Adventures 16 B2
- Museum of Moab 17 C3
- Navtec Expeditions 18 B2
- Poison Spider Bicycles 19 B2
- Rim Cyclery 20 B3
- Rim Tours 21 D6
- Tag-A-Long Expeditions 22 B2
- Western Spirit Cycling 23 D4

SLEEPING
- 3 Dogs and a Moose 24 B3
- Adobe Abode 25 A4
- Adventure Inn 26 B2
- Best Western Canyonlands Inn 27 B3
- Big Horn Lodge 28 B4
- Cali Cochitta 29 C3
- Canyonlands Campground 30 C5
- Gonzo Inn 31 B4
- Inca Inn 32 B2
- Kokopelli Lodge 33 C3
- Lazy Lizard Hostel 34 D6
- Mayor's House 35 D3
- Moab Valley Inn 36 C5
- Red Stone Inn 37 B4
- Rodeway Landmark Inn 38 B3
- Silver Sage Inn 39 B5
- Sunflower Hill B&B 40 C3
- Up the Creek Campground 41 C4

EATING
- City Market & Pharmacy 42 B4
- Dave's Corner Market 43 C4
- Desert Bistro 44 B3
- Eddie McStiff's 45 B3
- EklectiCafé 46 B2
- Farmers Market 47 B2
- Jailhouse Café 48 B3
- Jeffrey's Steakhouse 49 B3
- Love Muffin 50 B3
- Miguel's Baja Grill .... (see 56)
- Milt's 51 C4
- Moab Brewery 52 B5
- Moonflower Market 53 C3
- Pantele's Deli 54 C3
- Pasta Jay's 55 B3
- Restoration Creamery 56 B3
- Singha Thai 57 C3
- Wake & Bake .... (see 45)

DRINKING
- Club Rio 58 B3
- Eddie McStiff's .... (see 45)
- Ghost Bar .... (see 49)
- Moab Brewery .... (see 52)
- Woody's Tavern 59 B3

ENTERTAINMENT
- Moab Arts & Recreation Center 60 C3
- Slickrock Cinemas 3 .... 61 B5

SHOPPING
- Arches Book Company/Back of Beyond Books 62 B3
- Gear Heads 63 B4

CROWD CONTROL

Moab becomes a mecca in high season. To make the most of your visit:

- Arrive at first-come campsites at around 8:45am to snag a spot
- Hit the trail early with a picnic breakfast
- For desert solitude, avoid coinciding with big events (like the Jeep Festival) or college spring breaks

History

Tucked beneath high rock walls in a fertile green valley – an important wildlife corridor along the Colorado River – Moab was founded by Mormon ranchers and farmers in the late 1870s after resident Native Americans' repeated failed attempts to get rid of them.

Nothing much changed until the Cold War climate of the 1950s, when the federal government subsidized uranium mining, and Moab's population tripled in three years. In search of 'radioactive gold,' miners bladed a network of primitive roads, laying the groundwork for the region to become a 4WD mecca half a century later. (The miners also left ponds of radioactive tailings, residue from the mineral extraction process.) Though uranium mining bottomed out in the 1980s when the feds quit paying premiums for the stuff, salt and potash mining continue, as does drilling for natural gas in the surrounding area, a contentious issue.

Hollywood loves Moab and has shot hundreds of Westerns here, mostly from the 1950s to the 1970s. But neither the mining boom nor Hollywood has had as much influence on Moab's current character as the humble mountain biker. In the mid-1980s, an influx of fat-tire enthusiasts discovered the challenging and scenic slickrock desert and triggered a massive surge in tourism that continues unabated.

Orientation & Information

Hwy 191 becomes Main St through Moab. Town follows a fairly typical Mormon grid, in which numbered streets radiate from the intersection of Main and Center Sts. Compass points indicate where you are in relation to that hub: thus, 100 E 300 South is one block east and three blocks south of Main and Center. It's easy once you get used to it.

Cell phones work in Moab but not in river canyons. Free newspapers include *Moab Happenings,* geared to visitors, and the iconoclastic *Canyon Country Zephyr.* Tune to Moab Community Radio (89.7 FM and 106.1 FM) for alternative local programming, from folk to funk.

EMERGENCY

Allen Memorial Hospital (☎ 435-259-7191; 719 W 400 North) With emergency room; in service until the new, expanded Moab Regional Hospital is completed.

Moab Immediate Care & X-Ray (☎ 259-5276; 267 N Main St; ⏲ noon-8pm) Nonemergency care.

Police (☎ 435-259-8938; 115 W 200 South)

INTERNET ACCESS

Grand County Public Library (☎ 435-259-1111; www.moablibrary.org; 25 S 100 East; ⏲ 9am-8pm Mon-Fri, to 5pm Sat) Great library resources, wi-fi and free 15-minute internet.

MEDIA

Radio KCYN 97.1 (☎ 435-259-1036) Canyon-country adventure sports report, daily from 7am to 9am.

POST

Post office (☎ 435-259-7427; 50 E 100 North; ⏲ 8am-5pm Mon-Fri, 9am-1pm Sat)

TOURIST INFORMATION

BLM (☎ 435-259-2100; www.blm.gov/utah/moab) Phone and internet assistance only.

Manti-La Sal National Forest Moab ranger station (☎ 435-259-7155; www.fs.fed.us/r4/mantilasal) No walk-in visitors, but provides information online and by phone.

Moab Area Travel Council (☎ 435-259-8825, 800-635-6622; www.discovermoab.com; PO Box 550, Moab, UT 84532; ⏲ 8am-5pm Mon-Fri) Excellent for pretrip planning.

Moab Information Center (cnr Main & Center Sts; ⏲ 8am-8pm) The best source of information in the region, this is one-stop shopping. It's walk-in visitors only, with extensive information on campground availability and permits, weather forecasts, astronomical data and river updates. Select from an outstanding selection of books and

BOOKS, MAPS & GEAR

Moab is the best spot in the region to replenish gear and grab maps or a regional read. For camping items hit **Gear Heads** (☎ 435-259-4327, 888-740-4327; 471 S Main St; 8:30am-10pm, shorter winter hr). Locally owned **Arches Book Company/Back of Beyond Books** (☎ 435-259-5154; www.backofbeyondbooks.com; 89 N Main St; 9am-10pm) carries a comprehensive selection of regional guides, histories, political nonfiction, news and magazines. Staff show regional expertise and are happy to help.

Canyon Voyages (☎ 435-259-6007, 800-733-6007; www.canyonvoyages.com; 211 N Main St) rents camping and backpacking gear, while **Tag-A-Long Expeditions** (☎ 435-259-8946, 800-453-3292; www.tagalong.com; 452 N Main St) rents tents and sleeping bags. Otherwise, many tour outfitters will rent gear only to their trip participants.

maps. The Canyonlands Natural History Association staffs the center in conjunction with the NPS, BLM, Utah State Parks, Grand County and the town.

Getting Around

At Canyonlands Field airport, 16 miles north of town via Hwy 191, **Enterprise Rent-a-Car** (☎ 435-259-8505; N Hwy 191 mile 148; 8am-5pm Mon-Fri, to 2pm Sat) has cars and SUVs.

You'll find several gas and service stations in town. Obey speed limits, or police will ticket you.

Several companies operate shuttle services to Arches, Canyonlands and environs, plus the town of Green River; some will also shuttle your private vehicle to meet you at a trailhead. Contact **Acme Bike Shuttle** (☎ 435-260-2534; www.acmebikeshuttle.com; 702 S Main St), **Coyote Shuttle** (☎ 435-259-8656; 55 W 300 South) or **Roadrunner Shuttle** (☎ 435-259-9402; www.roadrunnershuttle.com; 197 W Center St). Services also go to the airport for around $50 for two passengers.

For town transportation, choose **Moab Pedicab Company** (☎ 435-210-1382; 5-8pm Mon-Fri, weekends), a luxury bike taxi available nightly and on weekends – hail it on the street or call dispatch.

For details on getting to Moab, see the Transportation chapter (p271).

SIGHTS

Primarily a destination for recreationists and visitors to Arches and Canyonlands National Parks, Moab's indoor attractions are minimal.

The **Museum of Moab** (☎ 435-259-7985; www.moabmuseum.org; 118 E Center St; adult/children under 12 $3/free; 10am-6pm Mon-Fri, noon-6pm Sat) preserves and displays regional artifacts and presents exhibits on everything from paleontology and geology to uranium mining and Native American art. If you're interested in learning about the dinosaurs that once thudded around Utah, start here.

Take the self-guided **Moab Area Historic Walking Tour** to see several original buildings and learn some local history. You can pick up the pamphlet at the Museum of Moab or the Moab Information Center.

An unabashed tourist trap, 12 miles south of Moab on Hwy 191, **Hole 'n the Rock** (☎ 435-686-2250; www.moab-utah.com/holeintherock; 11037 S Hwy 191; adult/child $5/3.50; 8:30am-7pm, shorter winter hr) is a 5000-sq-ft cave home carved into sandstone and decorated in knockout 1950s kitsch. Admission covers the 10-minute tour; the petting zoo and gift shop are free.

The nonprofit Living Rivers seeks to decommission the Glen Canyon Dam and reestablish a free-flowing Colorado River through the Grand Canyon. Even if you don't agree, catch the fascinating interpretive displays on the walls of **Restoration Creamery** (p258), which sells delicious ice cream to benefit Living Rivers.

Stop in at **Moab Museum of Film & Western Heritage** (☎ 435-259-2002, 866-812-2002; www.redcliffslodge.com/museum; mile marker 14, Hwy 128; free; 8am-10pm), based at Red Cliffs Adventure Lodge (p257), 15 miles north of town, to see Hollywood memorabilia from films shot locally; there are also historical displays on area ranches.

Organized Tours

Moab hosts hundreds of tour and rental companies; the ones listed under each activity in this chapter are all recommended. For a complete list of tour operators and outfitters, contact the Moab Area Travel Council (p241) or visit the Moab Information Center (p241).

DRIVING

People come from around the world to drive in Utah, using Moab as their hub. From paved desert highways for retirees in RVs to vertical slickrock trails for four-wheeling adrenaline junkies, you'll find scenic drives for every taste.

For details of four-wheel-driving trips, see p251.

COLORADO RIVER SCENIC BYWAY (HIGHWAY 128)

Duration 45 minutes
Distance 31 miles one way
Start Moab
Finish Dewey Bridge
Summary This curvy drive follows the winding Colorado River through gorgeous red-rock country of mesas, rock walls, alfalfa fields and sagebrush. Extend the trip with the La Sal Mountain Loop Rd.

Drive north on Main St/Hwy 191 and turn right (east) onto Hwy 128. The road winds through red-rock canyons along the Colorado River's serpentine course, which is why it is known in the area as 'the river road.' Arches National Park lies on the north side of the river for the first 15 miles.

Six miles from Hwy 191 you'll reach **Big Bend Recreation Site**, where you can picnic by the river.

Eleven miles further, you'll pass the **La Sal Mountain Loop Rd** (right) turnoff and **Castle Rock**, a narrow spire that rises above Castle Valley.

At mile marker 21, the **Fisher Towers** (p245) rise almost as high as the Eiffel Tower (at 900ft, Titan is the tallest).

Ten miles ahead, you'll reach the **Dewey Bridge** site. Built in 1916, it was among the first spans across the Colorado. The bridge was destroyed by accidental fire in 2008 and its future is currently in limbo due to the high cost of reconstruction. Park near the site to watch rafters running downriver.

When ready, return to Moab or double back to the La Sal Mountain Loop Rd. I-70 lies 13 miles north.

LA SAL MOUNTAIN LOOP ROAD

Duration 2½ hours
Distance 67 miles
Start/Finish Moab
Summary This route through Manti-La Sal National Forest runs from the scorching desert into cool green woodlands. Though paved, it's narrow and lacks any guardrails.

When the desert gets too hot to handle, take this route through Manti-La Sal National Forest and let it whisk you to where you can camp, bicycle, hike or sit by a stream and listen as wind ruffles the aspens.

Snow closes the road between November and March. Allow three to four hours off-season.

About 15 miles northeast of Moab, off Hwy 128, the La Sal Mountain Loop Rd (aka Castle Valley Rd) climbs southeast into the national forest, up switchbacks

DETOUR TO MONUMENT VALLEY

From Moab, skirt south on Hwy 191 for stellar desert scenery. Two hours, or 100 miles, south of Moab, the pinprick-sized **Bluff** (www.bluff-utah.org), a historic town surrounded by red rock, makes a good base. From here, motor the rugged hairpin turns of the **Moki Dugway** (30 miles) or visit **Natural Bridges National Monument** (61 miles; ☎ 435-692-1234, ext 16; www.nps.gov/nabr; entry per car $6, per motorcycle, bike or walk-in $3), a white-sandstone canyon with a scenic, paved 9-mile loop perfect for pedaling. But nature's grand slam is **Monument Valley Navajo Tribal Park** (☎ 435-727-5874; www.navajonationparks.org; entry per person $5; 6am-8pm May-Sep, 8am-4:30pm Oct-Apr), where a 17-mile unpaved driving loop circles reddish mesa formations that sprout like earthen giants. A favorite for Hollywood shots, it's in the Navajo Indian Reservation, 47 miles south of Bluff. Camping is $10 per site.

BEST DESERT FESTIVALS

Moab loves a party and throws a pretty good one. For calendars, contact the **Moab Area Travel Council** (☎ 435-259-8825, 800-635-6622; www.discovermoab.com).

- **Skinny Tire Festival** (☎ 435-259-2698; www.skinnytirefestival.com) Road biking; first weekend in March.
- **Jeep Safari** (www.rr4w.com) The week before Easter, more than 2000 4WD vehicles overrun town in the year's biggest event. Register early; trails are assigned.
- **Moonshadows in Moab** (☎ 435-259-2698; www.moonshadowsinmoab.com) Biking by July moonlight.
- **Moab Music Festival** (☎ 435-259-7003; www.moabmusicfest.org) Each September, world-class classical musicians converge on the landscape of the Utah canyonlands region.
- **Rumble in the Red Rocks Motocross** (☎ 435-259-7814; www.racemoab.com) Motocrossers rev up in September.
- **Moab Fat Tire Festival** (☎ 435-260-1182; www.moabfattirefest.com) One of Utah's biggest mountain-biking events with tours, workshops, lessons, competitions and plenty of music in October.
- **Moab Folk Festival** (☎ 435-260-2488; www.moabfolkfestival.com) Folk music and environmental consciousness combined. This November festival is 100% wind powered, venues are easily walkable and recycling's encouraged.

(a problem for large RVs) into the forest. Four miles from the turnoff, look to your left for the spires known as the **Priest and Nuns**, as well as **Castle Rock**. The route winds past junipers and piñon pines, followed by scrub oaks and, finally, alpine slopes of majestic pines, firs and white-barked quaking aspens, the leaves of which turn a brilliant yellow-gold in autumn. Here, high above canyon country, you'll gain a fresh perspective on the vastness of the Colorado Plateau.

At the crest, you can turn left on a dirt spur road and climb 5 miles further to the picnic area and developed campground at **Warner Lake**. For information on hiking and camping, check with national forest rangers (see p241). From the Warner Lake spur junction, the loop road descends to Hwy 191, 8 miles south of Moab.

POTASH ROAD SCENIC BYWAY

Duration 40 minutes
Distance 15 miles one way
Start Cnr Hwys 191 & 279
Finish Shafer Trail Rd
Nearest Town Moab
Summary This very scenic desert drive passes mining remnants into dry country with soaring rock walls and solitude. Petroglyphs, dinosaur tracks and arches are highlights.

Three miles north of Moab, off Hwy 191, the paved Potash Rd (Hwy 279) skirts south along the Colorado River. It's named for a potash extraction plant at road's end, where broad, sky-blue fields look out of place beneath the red-rock cliffs. Just past the turnoff you'll pass a radioactive tailings pond from Moab's uranium-mining days, while mid-route, stunning natural beauty abounds. Such are the region's contradictions.

Highlights: **Wall Street** (for rock climbers); Native American **petroglyph panels** (look for signs); **dinosaur tracks** (bring binoculars for a better look); a 1.5-mile hiking trail to **Corona Arch** (opposite); and **Jug Handle Arch**, 3ft wide but 45ft high. Also find the **Potash Dock** put-in for float trips down the Colorado. Past the potash plant, the road continues as a rough 4WD track into Canyonlands' Island in the Sky district, linking with Shafer Trail Rd.

HURRAH PASS ROAD

Duration 3 hours
Distance 33 miles
Start/Finish Moab
Summary The high Hurrah Pass offers jaw-dropping vistas of the Colorado River, Dead Horse Point and Grand View Point. Drivers can continue on but the road gets rougher and is best for 4WD vehicles; 4WD is mandatory beyond the pass.

This route starts out west along paved Kane Creek Rd, off Hwy 191 in Moab, soon passing **petroglyph sites** and a **rock climbing** area. The pavement yields to gravel as you enter **Kane Springs Canyon**. About 10 miles in you must ford the creek, which, depending on the weather, may be impassible; 4WD is recommended.

After 15 miles you'll reach 4470ft **Hurrah Pass**. The stupendous scenery includes views up to Dead Horse and Grand View Points. South of the pass the road descends toward the Colorado River, with views of the potash plant on the opposite bank (look for the fields of blue). Explore the desert and when ready, double back to Moab or continue south on **Lockhart Basin Rd** toward Canyonlands' Needles district.

From Lockhart Basin Rd the road is much more difficult (4WD is *mandatory*) and often confusing, eventually emerging about 50 miles south on Hwy 211, just east of the Needles. Contact the BLM (p241) for maps and information if you want to do the whole route.

CANYON RIMS RECREATION AREA

Duration 3½ hours one way (including spur)
Distance 54 miles
Start/Finish Hwy 191
Nearest Town Moab
Summary A lovely out-of-the way drive to the Needles and Anticline Overlooks, with great views of the Needles and Hurrah Pass; it's accessible to cars and buses.

The BLM-administered Canyon Rims Recreation Area lies south of Moab, west of Hwy 191 and east of **Canyonlands National Park**. If you've already visited the area's other major overlooks (eg Dead Horse and Grand View Points) and have time, this byway makes a good day trip. It's also a fine detour on the way to or from the Needles. Don't fret if you miss it, however. The area is especially popular with hikers, campers and all-terrain vehicle (ATV) enthusiasts. For more information, contact the BLM or stop by the Moab Information Center (p241).

Turn west off Hwy 191, 32 miles south of Moab. The paved road leads 22 miles west to the **Needles Overlook**, a great panorama of the national park. About two-thirds of the way to the overlook take the spur, where a gravel road stretches 16 miles north to the **Anticline Overlook**, a promontory with awesome views of the Colorado River, Meander Canyon and Hurrah Pass Rd below.

HIKING

Carry plenty of water, and wear insect repellent between spring and early summer to repel aggressive gnats.

For backpacking hikes, Canyonlands National Park is your best bet. Or consider the Canyon Rims Recreation Area (p245), where backpacking trails crisscross the Dark Canyon Primitive Area. For a moderate–difficult rim hike above Moab, try the **Hidden Valley Trail**, which meanders through a pristine hanging valley in the Behind the Rocks Wilderness Study Area. The trailhead is on BLM land at the end of Angel Rock Rd. Plan on taking four to six hours. Following a series of switchbacks, you'll emerge on the level grassy valley for a mellow 2-mile walk. Expect shade in late afternoon.

To take in petroglyphs and two spectacular, rarely visited rock arches, hike the moderately easy **Corona Arch Trail**, the trailhead for which lies 6 miles up Potash Rd (opposite). Follow cairns along the slickrock to **Bowtie** and **Corona Arches**. You may recognize Corona from a well-known photograph in which an airplane is flying through it – this is one *big* arch! The 3-mile walk takes two hours.

The ever-popular, moderately easy **Negro Bill Canyon Trail** is a 2.5-mile walk along a stream where the flow fluctuates based on beaver activity. Scoot down a cool, shaded side canyon to find petroglyphs on the smooth red-rock walls, then continue to the 243ft-wide **Morning Glory Natural Bridge**, which sits at the end of a box canyon. Plan for three to four hours. The trailhead is at a BLM information display 3 miles along Hwy 128, on the right.

The **Fisher Towers Trail** takes you past these towering sandstone monoliths, the tallest of which rises 900ft. The west-facing monoliths get quite hot in the afternoon, so wait for sunset, when rays bathe the rock in color and cast long shadows. (Bring a flashlight; many lingering hikers have ended up stuck on the trail in the dark.) The moderate–difficult 2.2-mile (one-way) trail lies off

Hwy 128, 21 miles northeast of Moab; follow signs.

If you're short on time, take the easy 1-mile round-trip hike along **Moonflower Canyon**, a shaded stroll on mostly level ground that ends at a sandstone bowl beneath hanging gardens. A perennial stream makes this hike a cooler, less dusty alternative. The trailhead lies 1.2 miles from town along Kane Creek Rd. Look for petroglyphs at the parking area.

To escape the summer heat, head up to the **La Sal Mountains** and hike through stands of white-barked aspens and towering ponderosa pines. You'll find numerous developed campgrounds along La Sal Mountain Loop Rd, including the one at Warner Lake. For more info, contact the Manti-La Sal National Forest Moab ranger station (p241).

For guided hikes, **Canyonlands Field Institute** (☎ 435-259-7750, 800-860-5262; www.canyonlandsfieldinst.org; 1320 S Hwy 191) has excellent multiday trips and very affordable half- or full-day excursions with a naturalist. Also check out *Moab Classic Hikes* by Damian Fagan.

BIKING

Moab is the mountain-biking capital of the world, and it's easy to see why. The slickrock surrounding town makes a perfect 'sticky' surface for the knobbly tires of mountain bikes. Challenging trails ascend steep slickrock, wind through woods and travel 4WD roads into the wilds of canyon country.

People come from everywhere to ride the famous Slickrock Bike Trail and other challenging routes like the White Rim Trail in Canyonlands (p221). Considering the high volume of riders, it's important to protect the surrounding desert. Avoid all off-trail riding, and pack out everything you pack in.

The busiest seasons are spring and fall. In summer start riding by 7am at the latest – after that, it's too hot. In winter snow might cover trails, but you can bike the roads.

Several companies provide bicycle shuttles (see p242).

For further reading on mountain biking in Moab, pick up a copy of *Above & Beyond Slickrock* by Todd Campbell. A fun read by a serious biker is *Rider Mel's Mountain Bike Guide to Moab,* which is small enough to carry on a ride. A good resource for more Moab biking trails is www.gomoab.com/moab_mountain_bike_trails.html.

For road-cycling and mountain-biking safety tips, see p286.

Tours & Outfitters

Service can be spotty in Moab but options are plentiful, with some of the best listed below. Also ask locals which companies they prefer. If you still have a hard time choosing, ask what the outfit serves for lunch. Full-day tours (including bike rental) start at around $100.

Rim Tours (☎ 435-259-5223, 800-626-7335; www.rimtours.com; 1233 S Hwy 191) leads half-, one- and multiday trips throughout Moab. It also holds permits for Canyonlands National Park, as does **Kaibab Adventure Outfitters** (☎ 435-259-7423, 800-451-1133; www.moabcyclery.com; 391 S Main St), **Nichols Expeditions** (☎ 435-259-3999, 800-648-8488; www.nicholsexpeditions.com; 497 N Main St) and **Western Spirit Cycling** (☎ 435-259-8732, 800-845-2453; www.westernspirit.com; 478 Mill Creek Dr). If you're a die-hard, ask about trips to the Maze. All four outfits lead trips to other Southwestern destinations, including Zion, Bryce and Grand Canyon National Parks.

Bicycle Rental

If you want to set out on our own, reserve a rental in advance. Full-suspension bikes start at around $30 per day.

The friendly **Rim Cyclery** (☎ 435-259-5333; www.rimcyclery.com; 94 W 100 North), Moab's longest-running bike shop, includes a museum of mountain-bike technology. Also consider **Moab Cyclery** (☎ 435-259-7423, 800-451-1133; www.moabcyclery.com; 391 S Main St), **Poison Spider Bicycles** (☎ 435-259-7882, 800-635-1792; www.poisonspiderbicycles.com; 497 N Main St; 🕒 8am-8pm spring & fall, shorter off-season hr) and **Chile Pepper Bike Shop** (☎ 435-259-4688, 888-677-4688; www.chilebikes.com; 702 S Main St). All provide excellent service and helpful websites for planning your trip. Chile Pepper also makes repairs and serves espresso.

Road biking is also becoming popular; rent a road bike from Poison Spider.

Trails

Many mountain-biking trails follow 4WD routes; yield to vehicles and horses. Inquire at bike shops about conditions before setting out. Stay on trails, out of water potholes and off fragile cryptobiotic soil crusts. For info about Moab area trails, inquire at bike shops or the Moab Information Center (p241).

BAR-M LOOP

Duration 1–2 hours
Distance 7.9 miles
Difficulty Easy–moderate
Start/Finish Bar-M Chuckwagon
Nearest Town Moab
Transportation Shuttle
Summary Ideal for novices or families, this mellow loop trail skirts the edges of Arches National Park. Terrain includes a graded 4WD road and stretches of slickrock.

One of a handful of trails in Moab appropriate for families and novice riders, the Bar-M Loop features a gentle gradient and few technical challenges. If you have a small child, you could even do this trail with the little one on a second seat.

To reach the trailhead, drive 7 miles north of town on Hwy 191, and turn right at the Bar-M Chuckwagon, just south of the Hwy 313 turnoff. Park by the kiosk at the south end of the lot.

From the kiosk you'll follow the original highway south. After 1.2 miles, turn left (the second major left from the trailhead). The route gets a smidgen rougher as it climbs slightly. Follow trailside markers to the beginning of the loop, 2.3 miles from the trailhead. Turn left and continue to bear left as you make your way around the loop.

MOONLIGHT MEADOW TRAIL

Duration 2–4 hours
Distance ±7.5 miles one way, 10 miles round-trip
Difficulty Moderate
Start Trans–La Sal trailhead
Finish cnr Geyser Pass & La Sal Mountain Loop Rds (one way) or Trans–La Sal trailhead
Nearest Town Moab
Transportation Shuttle
Summary When Moab is scorching, head to the La Sal Mountains. Moderate terrain includes aspen forest and mountain meadows with desert views. Up at this altitude, riding is definitely more demanding.

Riders may be attracted to this alpine trail with aspens since it's markedly cooler than the desert trails. You can make it a one-way downhill ride or a round-trip loop. High-altitude riding can be taxing, so take it easy.

For the one-way downhill, leave a vehicle at the junction of Geyser Pass Rd and La Sal Mountain Loop Rd (p243). Drive a second vehicle uphill about 8 miles on gravel to Geyser Pass (10,600ft) and park at the trailhead. Follow signs to Moonlight Meadow. The trail eventually emerges downhill at the junction of Geyser Pass Rd and the Trans–La Sal trailhead; descend the road the remaining 2.5 miles to the shuttle car.

For the loop, park at the Trans–La Sal trailhead, about 2.5 miles up Geyser Pass Rd, and bike up to the pass. From there, take the Moonlight Meadow Trail downhill to emerge at your parked car.

SLICKROCK BIKE TRAIL

Duration 3–4 hours
Distance 12.7 miles (main loop trail 9.6 miles)
Difficulty Very difficult
Start/Finish Sand Flats Recreation Area
Nearest Town Moab
Transportation Shuttle
Summary The premier mountain-biking route, Slickrock is ideal for advanced riders. Terrain includes undulating slickrock and nice desert views – if you have time to look.

First forged as a motorcycle trail, Slickrock can humble good riders. You need to be both in shape and technically savvy. Even the initial 2.2-mile practice loop is difficult and should not be your first attempt at mountain biking. If you do find you're in over your head, hike out – don't ride any further. Typical riding season for the trail is mid-February through November. At the trailhead you'll find vault toilets but not water.

From downtown Moab, follow signs from 400 East to the trailhead at the **Sand Flats Recreation Area** (www.utah.com/playgrounds/sand_flats.htm; car/cyclist entry $5/2). From the parking lot, the trail leads 0.3 miles to the practice loop – turn right here for a good warm-up, or turn left and pedal 0.4 miles to a junction with the main trail.

When you reach the main loop, 2.5 miles from the trailhead, bear left (the gradient

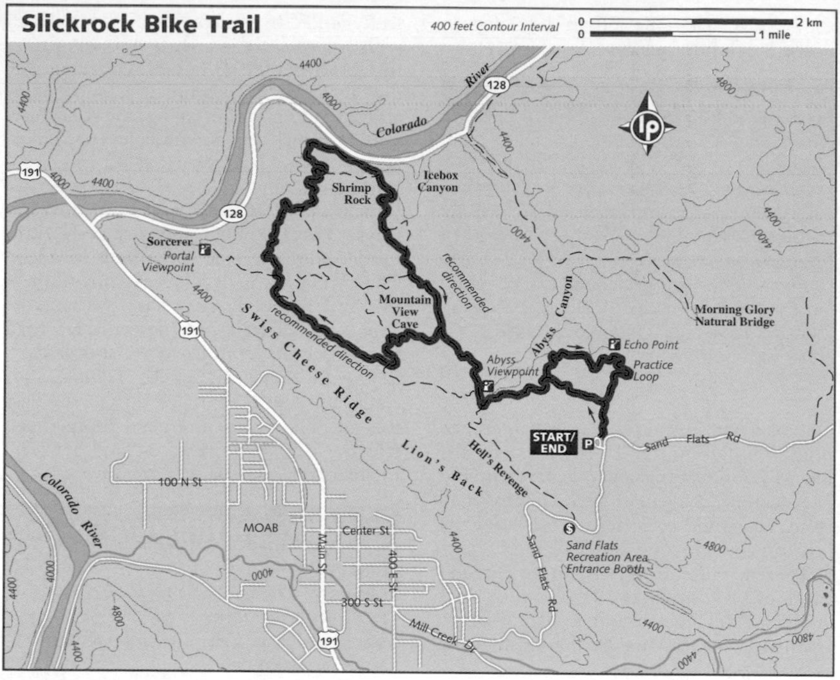

is more difficult if you bear right). Painted white dashes on the rock mark the trail route, while yellow markers indicate caution zones or areas of interest. The trail occasionally crosses sand. Highlights include steep drops, vertical climbs and incredible views of the La Sal Mountains and Arches National Park.

KLONDIKE BLUFFS TRAIL

Duration 3–5 hours
Distance 15.6 miles
Difficulty Moderate
Start/Finish Klondike Bluffs trailhead
Nearest Town Moab
Transportation Private
Summary The perfect intro to slickrock, Klondike Bluffs is ideal for intermediate riders. A 4WD road alternates with slickrock and the terrain drinks in the beauty of Arches National Park.

This trail north of town takes a 4WD road to slickrock marked with painted stripes, dead-ending at Klondike Bluffs in Arches. Cairns and brown marker posts guide the way.

To reach the trailhead, drive north on Hwy 191 for 16 miles to mile marker 142, and turn right on Klondike Bluffs Rd. (If you reach the airport, you've gone too far.)

From the trailhead, follow the 4WD road 2.7 miles northwest, then bear left (a better-maintained road veers right). At mile 3.8 veer right (away from a road leading north up a wash) and follow trail markers up a small canyon toward the white rocks. Once atop the slickrock, look for **dinosaur tracks** off to the left.

At mile 5.2 the ride tops out. Past a big cairn on the hillside, bear right and leave the road to pedal over slickrock. At trail's end, 1.4 miles ahead, park your bike and walk 0.3 miles to the **Klondike Bluffs overlook** for a view east to Devils Garden. When ready, return the way you came.

OTHER ACTIVITIES

Biking is religion in Moab, where most of the population loops around town on two wheels. But there's much more here. One highlight is water – try rafting the Colorado River, or taking a canoe out on flat water on a hot day. Extreme sports are no stranger to Moab either – rock climbing, canyoneering and sky diving all have a number of disciples thrilled to make a convert.

The Nature Conservancy oversees the 890-acre **Matheson Wetlands Preserve** (☎ 435-259-4629; www.nature.org; 934 W Kane Creek Rd; ⏰ dawn-dusk), an important stopover for migrating waterfowl, raptors and shorebirds. Bring binoculars and insect repellent. Guided walks are offered at 8am on Saturdays between March and October.

RIVER RUNNING

More than a dozen outfitters run a variety of float trips on the Colorado and Green Rivers. Though permits limit the number of people on the water, favorite takeout beaches can get pretty crowded, and for good reason: this is fun – *really* fun! Whatever your interest, be it bashing through rapids or studying canyon geology, rafting may well prove the highlight of your vacation.

Rafting season runs April to September; jet-boating season lasts longer. Water levels usually crest in May and June. Most day trips cost $50 to $65, while longer full-day trips start at about $150. Two- to five-day excursions run from about $350 to more than $800 per person. Jet-boat trips cost about $75. Discounts often apply to children accompanying parents. Many companies combine rafting trips with hiking, 4WD or mountain-biking trips.

Do-it-yourselfers can rent canoes, inflatable kayaks or rafts. Rates run $35 a day for canoes and kayaks, and $65 to $130 a day for rafts, depending on size (all come with life jackets and paddles). Advance permits are required for trips within the national parks and certain areas outside them.

While guided half- and full-day trips are often available on short notice, you should book overnight trips well ahead.

Pick up the indispensable *Canyonlands River Guide*, made by Belknap and fully waterproof.

Choosing a Boat

Outfitters ply the rivers in a variety of boats. Resembling a rowboat, an **oar rig** is a rubber raft that a guide rows downriver. Also made of rubber, a **paddle boat** is steered by a guide and paddled by passengers. Not technically a raft, a **motor rig** is a large boat driven by a guide (**jet boats** fall into this category). While this is the quickest way downriver, speed isn't so conducive to slowly soaking up desert landscapes. You can also float in a **kayak**, **inflatable kayak** or **canoe**.

Levels of White Water

Rapids are rated on a scale from one (I) to six (VI), with Class I being still water and Class VI an unnavigable waterfall. Class II rapids are good for novices and families with little kids. Class III are thrilling, while Class IV are borderline scary, depending on your perspective. Class V rapids are technical and dangerous.

Rafting Tours

Outfitters on guided tours take care of everything, from permits to food to setting up camp and shuttling you back to town.

Reputable outfitters include **Canyon Voyages** (☎ 435-259-6007, 800-733-6007; www.canyonvoyages.com; 211 N Main St), **O.A.R.S.** (☎ 435-259-5919, 800-346-6277; www.oars.com; 2540 S Hwy 191), **Sheri Griffith Expeditions** (☎ 435-259-8229, 800-332-2439; www.griffithexp.com; 2231 S Hwy 191) and **Adrift Adventures** (☎ 435-259-8594, 800-874-4483; www.adrift.net; 378 N Main St).

Several bigger outfits are geared to large groups. Try **Tag-A-Long Expeditions** (☎ 435-259-8946, 800-453-3292; www.tagalong.com; 452 N Main St), **Navtec Expeditions** (☎ 435-259-7983, 800-833-1278; www.navtec.com; 321 N Main St) or **Western River Expeditions** (☎ 435-259-7019, 888-622-4097; www.westernriver.com; 1371 N Hwy 191).

For educational trips, **Canyonlands Field Institute** (☎ 435-259-7750, 800-860-5262; www.canyonlands

TOP FIVE WAYS TO SEIZE THE DAY

- Grab a paddle and snake down the lazy Green River by canoe (p251)
- Skip siesta and take a slickrock walk to Corona Arch (p245)
- Mosey Castle Valley's scenic sagebrush flats on horseback (p252)
- Take a leap into the landscape on a skydive (p253)
- Hit the road to find red-rock nirvana in Monument Valley (p243)

fieldinst.org; 1320 S Hwy 191) can't be beaten. If traveling with someone with a physical or mental disability, book with **Splore** (☎ 801-484-4128; www.splore.org), based in Salt Lake City.

For guided canoe excursions, call **Moab Rafting & Canoe Co** (☎ 435-259-7722, 800-753-8216; www.moab-rafting.com; 1371 N Hwy 191), which provides excellent instruction and interpretation.

For guided jet-boat trips, call Adrift Adventures, Navtec or Tag-A-Long.

Rafting Without a Guide

Good outfitters provide complete information to help you plan a self-guided trip. Reserve equipment, secure permits and book shuttles far in advance. Without a permit, you'll be restricted to several mellow stretches of the Colorado and Green Rivers, but if you want to run Class III and IV rapids in Westwater Canyon or enter Canyonlands on either river, you'll need a permit.

Permits may be solicited a year in advance. Check the river permits link on www.discovermoab.com, or contact the **BLM** (☎ 435-259-2100; www.blm.gov/utah/moab) or the **NPS** (☎ 435-259-4351; www.nps.gov/cany/planyourvisit/backcountrypermits.htm) directly. Backcountry permits are issued at the appropriate visitor center. Strict rules govern sanitation and fires, depending on where you raft; confirm regulations with the appropriate agency.

To rent a raft, canoe or kayak, contact **Canyon Voyages** (☎ 435-259-6007, 800-733-6007; www.canyonvoyages.com; 211 N Main St). For canoe rentals, call **Moab Rafting & Canoe Co** (☎ 435-259-7722, 800-753-8216; www.moab-rafting.com; 1371 N Hwy 191).

For shuttles to or from the rivers, call **Roadrunner Shuttle** (☎ 435-259-9402; www.roadrunnershuttle.com; 197 W Center St), **Acme Bike Shuttle** (☎ 435-260-2534; www.acmebikeshuttle.com; 702 S Main St) or **Coyote Shuttle** (☎ 435-259-8656; www.coyoteshuttle.com; 55 W 300 South). Roadrunner offers the best long-distance service. To get back from the Confluence, you must book a jet-boat shuttle in advance; try **Tag-A-Long Expeditions** (☎ 435-259-8946, 800-453-3292; www.tagalong.com; 452 N Main St).

COLORADO RIVER NORTHEAST OF MOAB

Boating the 36 miles of river northeast of Moab from Westwater Canyon to Takeout Beach takes two to five days. This section is divided into three distinct stretches. All fall within the jurisdiction of the BLM. Take Hwy 128 from Moab, which roughly parallels the river, making put-in and takeout a breeze.

If you're seeking serious white water, **Westwater Canyon** is the place. The first canyon along the Colorado in Utah, Westwater boasts Class III and IV rapids through the oldest exposed layer of rock on the planet. Most people make the 17-mile trip in one long day (10 hours) from Moab, though some choose to camp and make it a two-day trip. Most outfitters offer both options. A BLM permit is required.

Like mellow water and just want to float along? **Dewey Bridge to Hittle Bottom** is a 7-mile section of flat water with great scenery and wildlife-watching. One stretch passes through a bird sanctuary. No permit required.

Also known as Fisher Towers, or simply as the Daily, **Hittle Bottom to Takeout Beach** is the most popular stretch of river near Moab, perfect for novices who aren't ready for Westwater. Families can safely bring small children without boring their teens. The Daily offers mostly Class I and II rapids, with one short section of Class III known as White's Rapid (Class IV at high water, when it's not recommended for kids). Camp at riverside BLM campgrounds. No permit is required.

COLORADO RIVER SOUTHWEST MOAB (MEANDER CANYON)

This 48-mile section takes three to five days, starting at Potash Dock and ending at Spanish Bottom. The flat-water trip from Potash Dock (see p244) to the Confluence moves slowly on the wide river. It's a scenic trip, good for mellow souls or novice boaters. You can put in at Moab Dock to lengthen the trip by 15 miles, but since it parallels the highway this section is usually skipped.

A mile and a half north of the Confluence, you'll reach the **Slide**, a moderate rapid that you can portage. In the 4-mile stretch from the Confluence to Spanish Bottom, eddies and whirlpools kick in as you approach Cataract Canyon (*do not* miss the takeout). An NPS permit is required to enter Canyonlands. (For a half-day flat-water paddle, put in at Moab and take out at Gold Bar; for a full day, take out at Potash.)

CATARACT CANYON

The Class V rapids of Cataract Canyon are legendary. Twenty-six rapids churn and roil

THE SCOURGE OF THE COLORADO

As you float down the Colorado, notice the dense stands of wispy-looking trees. Tamarisk, also called salt cedar, is an ornamental tree imported to the US in the 19th century and later planted along the river for erosion control. It has since taken over the banks of the Colorado and is choking the waterway.

A single large tamarisk transpires 300 gallons of water *a day*. Some estimates place the species' combined water consumption as high as one-third of the river's overall flow. If that water were returned to the river, the Colorado might again reach the sea.

The good news? In Death Valley, California, land managers have almost entirely eradicated tamarisk stands, and once-threatened wetlands are rebounding. As you cross the bridge into Moab, and elsewhere along the Colorado, look for charred tree stumps and scorched riverbanks – evidence of the local eradication effort by fire (and herbicides). To learn more, visit Living Rivers at Restoration Creamery (p242).

over this 14-mile stretch where the Colorado squeezes through narrow canyons. Trips down the Cat are extremely technical and dangerous; there's no room for error. Though a jet boat can do it in a day, it is well worth taking your time, camping on beautiful beaches and living the pace of the river.

This 112-mile trip takes from three days to a week, starting at Moab and ending in Hite. The intensity of the rapids fluctuates hugely, depending on snowmelt and drought. Many fail to realize that you have to float on flat water quite a ways to reach the canyon (rafts put in at Potash or Mineral Bottom), and once through the rapids, you'll wind up on flat Lake Powell – though you'll be so high on adrenaline, you probably won't even notice. Peak flow runs mid-May to mid-June. An NPS permit is required; reserve through the NPS.

GREEN RIVER (LABYRINTH & STILLWATER CANYONS)

Discovered by John Wesley Powell during his famed expeditions, this flat-water stretch down the Green is ideal for canoes. You'll pass rock art along the scenic route. Start at Green River State Park and end at Mineral Bottom (68 miles) or Spanish Bottom (124 miles); the trip takes between three and nine days.

Take out at the Confluence or use extreme caution en route to Spanish Bottom, lest you get sucked into Cataract Canyon. An NPS permit is required south of Mineral Bottom.

FOUR-WHEEL DRIVING

In the Cold War era, uranium prospectors forged thousands of primitive paths across the vast deserts surrounding town; today most of these are maintained as 4WD routes. Four-wheelers should always be sensitive to the fragile desert environment and respect other users on the trail by passing at reasonable speeds.

For experienced drivers only, the best-known 4WD road in Moab is **Hell's Revenge**. In the BLM-administered Sand Flats Recreation Area east of town, it follows an 8.2-mile route up and down shockingly steep slickrock. Also for experts, the shared-use **Moab Rim Trail** loops high on the rim rock southwest of town.

Avoid unsigned roads in BLM Wilderness Study Areas, and never drive off road, which could irreparably damage fragile cryptobiotic soil. The consequences are evident all around the area, where tire tracks and grazing cows have trampled the cryptobiotic soil. Without this living crust, the desert sands blow free. Without protection, what only *seems* barren now could turn into a veritable wasteland.

For more details about routes, pick up a pamphlet from the Moab Information Center, ask a tour operator or inquire at a 4WD rental agency. Also consider *Moab Utah Backroads & 4WD Trails* by Charles Wells.

Tours & Rentals

If motoring up a 50-degree slickrock wall sounds like fun, check out the backcountry tours and combination land/river trips. The following provide excellent interpretation.

Adrift Adventures (☎ 435-259-8594, 800-874-4483; www.adrift.net; 378 N Main St) and **Canyon Voyages** (☎ 435-259-6007, 800-733-6007; www.canyonvoyages.com; 211 N Main St) both offer backcountry trips

THE ROCK JOCK

Angela Hawse is a professional climber and guide who runs climbing clinics and guides around Moab and abroad.

Describe the pull of Moab. The Colorado Plateau is geographically and geologically one of the most fascinating and interesting places I've explored in the world. And it's beautiful. The Colorado River has carved through it all, revealing layer upon layer of history, back to beyond the age of the dinosaurs. It's an excellent place to learn to rock climb since the sandstone has tons of friction, making it a very sticky climbing surface.

What are some of your favorite spots? The River Rd and the hikes up Negro Bill Canyon (p245), bouldering at the River Bend and, of course, the spectacular Castle Valley.

How can visitors get away from it all? The openness of the terrain is fantastic for exploring. As soon as you get off the Jeep roads, find a trail and set off across the desert, you are unlikely to see anyone but the lizards and birds.

Any tips? The soil is extremely fragile and very prone to erosion when disturbed. Learn how to recognize it: cryptobiotic soil looks like black, clumpy dirt and is often in patches like a rug. One footprint can kill it.

Angela Hawse is an International Federation of Mountain Guides Associations (IFMGA)–certified guide.

in Chevy Suburbans and lead combination 4WD/rafting tours. **O.A.R.S.** (☎ 435-259-5919, 800-346-6277; www.oars.com; 2540 S Hwy 191) and **Navtec Expeditions** (☎ 435-259-7983, 800-833-1278; www.navtec.com; 321 N Main St) hold permits for Canyonlands National Park and guide single- or multiday combination 4WD/hiking/rafting tours. **Tag-A-Long Expeditions** (☎ 435-259-8946, 800-453-3292; www.tagalong.com; 452 N Main St), Moab's biggest outfitter, leads single- or multiday backcountry 4WD trips into Canyonlands (including the Maze), as well as land/river combinations.

For a 4WD tour, good ol' boy **Dan Mick** (☎ 435-259-4567; www.danmick.com) can get you in the deep backcountry. Drive in his 4WD vehicle or yours. He'll also shuttle hikers.

If you rent a 4WD vehicle, *read the insurance policy* – it may not cover damage from off-road driving and will likely carry a $2500 deductible. Check when you book. Whenever possible, rent a relatively new vehicle. Reputable companies: **Farabee Adventures** (☎ 435-259-7494, 877-970-5337; www.moabjeeprentals.com; 1125 S Hwy 191); **Cliffhanger Jeep Rental** (☎ 435-259-0889; www.moab-utah.com/cliffhanger; 40 W Center St).

You could also rent dirt bikes from **Elite Motorcycle Tours** (☎ 435-259-7621, 888-778-0358; www.elitemotorcycletours.com; 1310 Murphy Lane), which also offers street-legal motorcycles but specializes in off-road tours and rentals.

HORSEBACK RIDING

Rates for horseback riding generally range from $70 for a three-hour ride to $100 for a four-hour outback ride. Kids must be eight years old or older.

Cowboy Adventures (☎ 435-259-7410; cowboyadventures@hotmail.com) leads trips year-round, including half-, full- or multiday trips in the desert and multiday trips to the La Sal Mountains or combined with rafting.

Red Cliffs Adventure Lodge (☎ 435-259-2002, 866-812-2002; www.redcliffslodge.com; mile marker 14, Hwy 128) guides half-day rides (March through November) around Castle Valley, in the red-rock desert north of town.

ROCK CLIMBING & CANYONEERING

Moab offers solid rock climbing. West of town, off Potash Rd, **Wall Street** (Moab's 'El Capitan') gets crowded on weekends and is an excellent spot to meet other climbers. Advanced climbers should check out the BLM-administered **Indian Creek**, off Hwy 211 on the way to Canyonlands' Needles district. Canyoneering expeditions offer chances to rappel into slickrock canyons and hike through cascading water.

For top notch guided rock-climbing or canyoneering trips, call **Moab Desert Adventures** (☎ 435-260-2404, 877-765-6622; www.moabdesertadventures.com; 801 Oak St; guided rock-climbing $110-195). Also try **Desert Highlights** (☎ 435-259-4433, 800-747-1342; www.deserthighlights.com; 50 E Center St; guided canyoneering $80-120), with trips and excellent interpretation to such spots as Arches' Fiery Furnace (p234).

To buy gear, go to **Gear Heads** (☎ 435-259-4327, 888-740-4327; 471 S Main St; 🕑 8:30am-10pm, shorter winter hr). For a guidebook to climbs, we recommend Fred Knapp's *Classic Desert Climbs*.

SKYDIVING & AIR TOURS

Two companies run one-hour air tours out of Canyonlands Field: **Slickrock Air Guides** (☎ 435-259-6216; www.slickrockairguides.com) and **Redtail Aviation** (☎ 435-259-7421; www.moab-utah.com/redtail). Rates start at around $100 per person. Both also operate air shuttles for extended river trips.

Jump out of an airplane or off a cliff with help from **Skydive Moab** (☎ 435-259-5867; www.skydivemoab.com; Canyonlands Field; tandem dive $235).

WINTER ACTIVITIES

From December through February, there's snowfall in the desert parks. Trails may be icy and route finding becomes more difficult. Manti-La Sal National Forest receives tons of light, dry Utah powder, perfect for cross-country skiing. For current information on weather and road conditions and the avalanche risk, call ☎ 435-259-7669 or visit www.avalanche.org.

The La Sals provide a hut-to-hut ski system, which you can access via snowmobile. To reserve a self-guided trip and book the huts, contact **Tag-A-Long Expeditions** (☎ 435-259-8946, 800-453-3292; www.tagalong.com; 452 N Main St). **Rim Cyclery** (☎ 435-259-5333; www.rimcyclery.com; 94 W 100 North) rents ski equipment, while **Gear Heads** (☎ 435-259-4327, 888-740-4327; 471 S Main St; 🕑 8:30am-10pm, shorter winter hr) rents snowshoes and stocks gear.

SLEEPING

Rates listed below are for double occupancy during high season (March through October). Keep in mind that some places close in winter. Listings are given in order of price.

For a small town, Moab offers a lot of lodgings; unfortunately, most are cookie-cutter, yet even those fill during busy holiday weekends and in high season. Book ahead, or at least settle your lodging needs in the morning, pre-excursion.

Cyclists should ask whether a property provides *secure* bike storage (ie only one person holds the key – 'bike storage' isn't the same thing). Most lodgings provide coffeemakers, many include refrigerators and some have microwaves; ask when you book. For current lodgings, check out www.discovermoab.com/hotels.htm.

CAMPING

Make reservations when possible. During busy holiday weekends all of the campgrounds around Moab are full. For more information and options, visit the Moab Information Center (p241) or check the online links at www.moab-utah.com and www.discovermoab.com.

In Town

Up the Creek Campground (☎ 435-260-1888; www.moabupthecreek.com; 210 E 300 South; sites $; 🕑 Mar-Nov) The only tent-only campground, it's perfect for backpackers and attracts a lot of students and foreign travelers. There are 20 walk-in sites in a parklike setting a few blocks from shops and restaurants. Showers are included ($6 for nonguests).

Archview Resort & Campground (☎ 435-259-7854, 800-813-6622; www.moab-utah.com/archview/archview.html; Hwy 191; sites & cabins $; 🕑 Mar-Nov) Near the Hwy 191/313 junction, Archview includes a pool, gas station and grocery store. Be forewarned: it's completely exposed and bakes in summer.

Canyonlands Campground (☎ 435-259-6848, 800-522-6848; www.canyonlandsrv.com; 555 S Main St; sites $; 🕑 year-round;) On the main drag, walkable from downtown, Canyonlands provides 140 sites (many are in shade, with RV hookups), eight air-conditioned camping cabins, showers and a swimming pool.

Slickrock Campground (☎ 435-259-7660, 800-448-8873; www.slickrockcampground.com; 1301 1/2 N Hwy 191; sites $; 🕑 Mar-Nov;) At the north end

ESSENTIALS

For fresh spring water, take Hwy 191 north to Hwy 128 east and continue 100yd to **Matrimony Springs**, on the right; southbound drivers should stop at the **Phillips 66 Station** (cnr Main St & 300 S) spigot. Gear Heads (p242) offers free filtered water.

You can wash your whites at **Moab Laundry Express** (471 S Main St, Desert Plaza; 🕑 24hr;). Up the Creek Campground (p253) has tidy and clean showers, also available at Archview Campground (p253), Canyonlands Campground (p253) or Poison Spider Bicycles (p246).

CAMPGROUNDS IN & AROUND MOAB, CANYONLANDS & ARCHES

Campground	Location	Number of sites	Elevation (ft)	Open	Reservations available?
Arches National Park					
Devils Garden	Arches National Park	52	5200	year-round	yes
Canyonlands National Park					
Needles Outpost	Hwy 211	20	5100	Apr-Nov	yes
Squaw Flat	The Needles	26	5100	year-round	no
Willow Flat	Island in the Sky	12	6000	year-round	no
Moab					
Archview Resort & Campground	Hwy 191	77	4026	Mar-Nov	yes
Canyonlands Campground	Main St	140	4026	year-round	yes
Portal RV Resort	Hwy 191	80	4026	year-round	yes
Slickrock	Hwy 191	200+	4026	Mar-Nov	yes
Up the Creek	E 300 South	20	4026	Mar-Nov	yes
Around Moab					
BLM Campgrounds	Hwy 128	n/a	4000	year-round	groups only
Hatch Point Recreation Area	Canyon Rims	10	5900	year-round	groups only
Horsethief	off Hwy 313	56	5800	year-round	no
Kayenta	Dead Horse	21	6000	year-round	Mar-Oct
Sand Flats Recreation Area	Sand Flats Rd	120	4500	year-round	no
Warner Lake	off La Sal Mountain Loop Rd	20	9500	Apr-Oct	no
Wind Whistle	Canyon Rims Recreation Area	17	6000	year-round	groups only

Drinking Water *Flush Toilets* *Ranger Station Nearby* *Great for Families* *Dogs Allowed* *Grocery Store Nearby* *Restaurant Nearby*

of Moab, a short drive from downtown, this well-maintained campground offers more than 200 shaded sites, RV hookups and a dump station, air-conditioned cabins, a pool, hot tubs and groceries. Tent sites have shade canopy. Showers are available for $3.

Portal RV Resort (☎ 435-259-6108, 800-574-2028; www.portalrvresort.com; 1261 N Hwy 191; sites & cabins $) Also at the north end of town, Portal provides air-conditioned camping cabins and grassy sites for tents or RVs. Full electric hookup is available but expect little shade in summer.

Outside Town

Sand Flats Recreation Area (☎ 435-259-2444; www.discovermoab.com/sandflats.htm; Sand Flats Rd; sites $; year-round) To be the first on the Slickrock Bike Trail in the morning, stay here by the trailhead. Surrounded by undulating sandstone, 120 sites have fire rings and pit toilets but no water. No reservations.

Facilities	Description	Page
	Trailside, with picnic tables and grills but few amenities; extremely popular, book far in advance.	238
	Dusty, private campground outside Needles; hot showers but lagging service.	226
	Popular, exceptionally pretty sites located trailside with some shade and slickrock.	226
	On a dirt road near the Green River Overlook, close to trails; few amenities; popular.	221
	Shadeless but has wi-fi, grills and pool, 10 minutes from downtown.	253
	RV village complete with pool and playground, shade for tents; central.	253
	Upscale RV resort, with pool, wi-fi and grassy tent sites; borders golf course.	254
	Well maintained, with air-conditioned cabins, tent canopy, a pool and hot tubs.	253
	Nice tent-only campground with picnic tables and shade; in center of town.	253
	10 popular campgrounds along Colorado River, buggy if without breeze.	below
	Dirt-road campground with fire rings and pit toilets, by Anticline Overlook.	256
	Mesatop sites that are open but well spaced, attractive; bring water.	256
	Near trails, good sites with picnic tables, fire rings and grills.	228
	Sandstone setting with pit toilets, near Slickrock Bike Trail; bring water.	254
	High-altitude lake sites with picnic tables in national forest.	below
	Dirt road access, scenic and less crowded, with picnic tables and pit toilets.	256

Payphone *Campfire Program* *RV Dump Station*

BLM campgrounds (☎ 435-259-2100; www.blm.gov/utah/moab; Hwy 128; sites $; year-round) The best place to stay to beat the heat (other than in the La Sals) is along the Colorado River. Vegetation and the canyon walls provide shade at these 10 BLM campgrounds along a 28-mile stretch of the river. Each includes fire rings and vault toilets but not water. Only group reservations are accepted. Bring insect repellent. One other great option is Onion Creek campground, located on the opposite side of the river, 13 miles from Fisher Towers.

Warner Lake Campground (☎ 435-587-2041, 888-444-6777; www.fs.fed.us/r4/mantilasal, www.reserveusa.com; off La Sal Mountain Loop Rd; sites $; Apr-Oct) When it's 100°F in Moab, the La Sals may be a balmy 75°F by day and downright chilly at night. Warner Lake Campground sits up high at 9400ft and is one of several developed campgrounds that provides water.

Horsethief Campground (☎ 435-259-2100; www.blm.gov/utah/moab; off Hwy 313; sites $; year-round) If you are headed to Dead Horse Point or Island in the Sky, this attractive campground (see Map p214) is a great option, and cooler than lower-elevation spots. There are 56 sites with picnic tables, vault toilets and grills. Bring water. It's first-come, first-served.

Canyon Rims Recreation Area (☎ 435-259-2100; www.blm.gov/utah/moab; Hwy 191; day/week pass per car $5/10) This oft-overlooked recreation area lies 30 miles south of town, just west of Hwy 191. It's remote but well toward the Needles. Two developed campgrounds have well-spaced sites in desert vegetation. The 17-site Wind Whistle Campground lies off a paved road 8 miles west of Hwy 191, while the 10-site Hatch Point Campground is on the gravel road to the Anticline Overlook, 32 miles south of Moab. When other campgrounds are full, these spots are a good bet, with drinking water (March through October), fire rings and pit toilets. Only group reservations are accepted.

HOTELS

Budget

The cheapest beds in town are at the clean, bare-bones **Silver Sage Inn** (☎ 435-259-4420, 888-774-6622; www.silversageinn.com; 840 S Main St; r $;) and the rough-around-the-edges **Lazy Lizard Hostel** (☎ 435-259-6057; www.lazylizardhostel.com; 1213 S Hwy 191; dm & cabins $;), offering dorms and cabins with flimsy rooms and dated installations. It's behind A-1 Storage; follow the signs.

Inca Inn (☎ 435-259-7621, 866-462-2466; www.incainn.com; 570 N Main St; r $;) The service is good and the 23 utilitarian rooms clean at this one-story mom-and-pop motel.

Kokopelli Lodge (☎ 435-259-7615, 888-530-3134; www.kokopellilodge.com; 72 S 100 East; $;) On-site owners carefully tend this clean, old-fashioned, eight-room motel. Amenities include a hot tub and secure bike storage. Pets are allowed.

Adventure Inn (☎ 435-259-6122, 866-662-2466; www.adventureinnmoab.com; 512 N Main St; r $;) A great indie motel, the Adventure Inn features clean rooms (some with refrigerators) and decent linens, as well as laundry facilities.

Midrange

MOTELS

Big Horn Lodge (☎ 435-259-6171, 800-325-6171; www.moabbighorn.com; 550 S Main St; r $-$$;) The cozy, old-fashioned knotty-pine paneling is at aesthetic odds with the modern floor-to-ceiling black glass windows at this well-maintained two-story motel, but service is great. Pets are allowed.

Red Stone Inn (☎ 435-259-3500, 800-772-1972; www.moabredstone.com; 535 S Main St; r $-$$;) The small pine-paneled rooms here are decorated with rustic wood furniture, lending a cozy feel to their otherwise utilitarian boxiness. Pets are allowed.

Moab Valley Inn (☎ 435-259-4419; www.moabvalleyinn.com; 711 S Main St; r $$;) Kids will love the swimming pool, half-shaded by awnings. Rooms are nondescript but pets are allowed.

Rodeway Landmark Inn (☎ 435-259-6147, 800-441-6147; www.rodewayinn.com; 168 N Main St; r $$;) Kids love the 50ft waterslide at this two-story motel within walking distance of downtown. Rooms are spacious, scrupulously maintained and ever-so-slightly kitschy. Amenities include great bathtubs and a hot tub.

Holiday Inn Express (☎ 435-259-1150, 800-465-4229; www.hiexpress.com/moabut; 1653 Hwy 191 N; r $$;) At the north end of Moab, this boxy prefab motel provides the most comfortable mid- to upper-range rooms in town. It's ideal for business travelers and includes expanded continental breakfast and a hot tub.

Aarchway Inn (☎ 435-259-2599, 800-341-9359; www.aarchwayinn.com; 1551 Hwy 191 N; r $$;) Another boxy prefab, the Aarchway has the best pool in town. Its spacious rooms are spotless, if ho-hum; several accommodate up to six people. Amenities include kitchenettes and gas grills, a fitness room and hot tub.

Best Western Canyonlands Inn (☎ 435-259-2300, 800-528-1234; www.canyonlandsinn.com; 16 S Main St; r $$-$$$;) A fine choice at the crossroads of downtown with spacious rooms, expanded

DOG LODGINGS

Moab's best kennel is **Karen's Canine Campground** (☎ 435-259-7922; 2781 Roberts Dr), where Fido is another one of mom's brood. There's a kiddie pool, shade canopies and a play area. Call ahead.

continental breakfast, a fitness room, hot tub and laundry. Do not confuse it with the Best Western Greenwell Inn across the street.

B&BS

Castle Valley Inn (☎ 435-259-6012; www.castlevalleyinn.com; HC64 Box 2602, Moab, UT 84532; r $$;) For tranquility, it's hard to beat this top option off La Sal Mountain Loop Rd, 15 miles north of Moab. With cozy quilts and handmade Aspen furniture, rooms (in the main house or new bungalows) sit amid orchards of apples, plums and apricots. Bungalows offer full kitchen and grill; there's also an outdoor hot tub. It's ideal for cycling Castle Valley. The welcome is warm and the style says why worry.

our pick **Cali Cochitta** (☎ 435-259-4961, 888-429-8812; www.moabdreaminn.com; 110 S 200 East; r $$;) Charming and central, these adjoining brick cottages offer snug rooms fitted with smart decor. A long wooden table on the patio makes a welcome setting for community breakfasts. You can also take advantage of the porch chairs, hammock or backyard hot tub. The vibe is warm but the innkeepers live off site, leaving you alone to enjoy the house.

Mayor's House (☎ 435-259-6015, 888-791-2345; www.mayorshouse.com; 505 Rose Tree Lane; r $$;) The Brady Bunch would be at home at this prim modern brick house, surrounded by lush lilac bushes. But spacious, quiet and immaculate rooms take the vibe down a notch. A lower-level suite is ideal for families and the hosts are quietly welcoming. Plus, it boasts a hot tub and Moab's largest pool.

Sunflower Hill Bed & Breakfast (☎ 435-259-2974, 800-662-2786; www.sunflowerhill.com; 185 N 300 East; r $$-$$$;) A top-shelf B&B, Sunflower Hill offers rooms in two inviting buildings – a cedar-sided early-20th-century home and a 100-year-old farmhouse amid manicured gardens and cottonwoods. Rooms have an elegant country style, with quilt-piled beds and antiques. The staff are eager to please and the hot tub works magic.

3 Dogs and a Moose (☎ 435-260-1692; www.3dogsandamoosecottages.com; 171 W Center St; r $$-$$$;) Lovely and low-key, these four cottages in central Moab are the ideal base camp for groups and families who want a little socializing in situ. Each house is rented separately. The style, with smart linens, corrugated-tin showers and recycled doors, is playful modern. Even better, you can pick your own tomatoes in the landscaped yard, where there's also hammocks, a grill and hot tub. There's also a bicycle washing area and pets are allowed.

Adobe Abode (☎ 435-259-7716; www.adobeabode-moab.com; 778 W Kane Creek Rd; r $$-$$$;) On the upper outskirts of town, this modern adobe pays homage to pioneer style with a mélange of antlers, bear rugs and antique guns. The grounds are xeriscaped and rooms comfortable.

Top End

Gonzo Inn (☎ 435-259-2515, 800-791-4044; www.gonzoinn.com; 100 W 200 South; r $$-$$$, incl breakfast in high season;) Less an inn than a chain-style motel spruced up with steel accents and sleek cement showers, the Gonzo Inn is friendly but not quite personal. It does cater well to cyclists, with a bicycle wash and repair station as well as a laundry. Rooms have refrigerators and coffee makers. Pets OK.

Pack Creek Ranch (☎ 435-259-5505; www.packcreekranch.com; PO Box 1270, Moab UT 84532; cabins $$$;) This hidden Shangri-la's 11 log cabins are tucked beneath mature cottonwoods and willow trees in the La Sal Mountains, 2000ft above Moab. Most of the individually owned cabins feature wood-burning fireplaces; all have kitchens and gas grills (bring groceries). Ed Abbey is among the artists and writers who have come here for inspiration. Amenities include horseback riding and an indoor hot tub and sauna.

Red Cliffs Adventure Lodge (☎ 435-259-2002, 866-812-2002; www.redcliffslodge.com; mile marker 14, Hwy 128; r $$$;) Dude ranch meets deluxe motel, Red Cliffs has comfortable rooms with vaulted knotty-pine ceilings, kitchenettes with dining tables, and private (though cramped) patios, some overlooking the Colorado River. It's good for families, as some rooms sleep up to six. Also offers horseback riding and a hot tub, an on-site movie museum for Western buffs and wine tasting. Pets allowed and horse boarding is available.

Sorrel River Ranch (☎ 435-259-4642, 877-359-2715; www.sorrelriver.com; mile marker 17, Hwy 128; r $$$;) Southeast Utah's only full-service luxury resort was originally an 1803 homestead. The lodge and log cabins sit on 240 lush riverside acres, with riding areas and alfalfa fields, on the banks of the Colorado. Details strive for rustic perfection, with bedroom fireplaces, handmade log beds, copper-top tables and Jacuzzi tubs. Amenities include an on-site spa (open to the public), fitness facility, salon and hot tub, kitchenettes and horseback riding and there is a gourmet restaurant. Families welcome.

EATING

Moab has a lock on good restaurants in Utah and coffee is actually the genuine article. Restaurant hours fluctuate seasonally; call before you go. To review menus in advance, pick up the free *Moab Menu Guide* from the Moab Information Center (p241).

GROCERY STORES

Moab's main grocery store is **City Market & Pharmacy** (☎ 435-259-5181; 425 S Main St; 🕑 6am-midnight, shorter winter hr). For health food, visit the nonprofit **Moonflower Market** (☎ 435-259-5712; 39 E 100 North; 🕑 9am-8pm Mon-Sat, 10am-3pm Sun). Local hangout **Dave's Corner Market** (☎ 435-259-6999; 401 Mill Creek Dr; 🕑 6am-10pm) has shade-grown espresso. Swanny City Park hosts a **farmers market** (400 N 100 West; 🕑 8-11:30am Sat May-Oct).

BUDGET

Love Muffin (☎ 435-259-6833; 139 N Main St; mains $; 🕑 7:30am-2pm; wi-fi) Love Muffin ensures the espresso is strong and complemented by breakfast burritos, warm quinoa and honey yogurt with granola. Lunch is gourmet salads and panini sandwiches.

Restoration Creamery (☎ 435-259-1063; 21 N Main St; ice cream $; 🕑 1-10pm Mar-Oct) Scoops up homemade ice cream with proceeds benefitting Living Rivers (see p242).

Wake & Bake (McStiffs Plaza, 59 S Main St; mains $; 🕑 breakfast & lunch; wi-fi) The feel is friendly and a little bit groovy, and it's the best spot to grab a breakfast taco or bagel. There are also coffees, gelato and a lunch menu of paninis, pizzas and good old hot dogs.

EklectiCafé (☎ 435-259-6896; 352 N Main St; mains $; 🕑 7:30am-2:30pm Mon-Fri, to 1pm Sat & Sun; wi-fi V) The antidote to omnivore dilemmas, this garden cafe runs a tight ship on an organic mission. Offerings include homemade granola, breakfast burritos, quiche and mammoth salads with homemade dressing. Nobody will mind if you while away the hours at an outdoor table, unless it's rush hour. Dinner is served on summer weekends.

our pick **Milt's** (☎ 435-259-7424; 356 Mill Creek Dr; mains $; 🕑 11am-8pm Mon-Sat) Meet greasy goodness. A triathlete couple bought this classic 1954 burger stand and smartly changed nothing. Heaven is one of their honest burgers, jammed with pickles, fresh lettuce, a side of fresh-cut fries and creamy milkshake. Be patient, the line can get long. It's near the Slickrock Bike Trail.

Pantele's Deli (☎ 435-259-0200; 98 E Center St; mains $; 🕑 11:30am-4pm Mon-Fri, noon-3pm Sat) Doing a brisk business, this authentic Michigan deli makes everything fresh. Salads come in heaping bowls, there are homemade soups, a divine hummus plate and high-piled sandwiches. Even if you're stuffed, it's worth grabbing a homemade cookie to go.

MIDRANGE

The following have full bars, unless noted. Some close in winter.

Singha Thai (☎ 435-259-0039; 574 92 E Center St; dishes $-$$; 🕑 11am-9:30pm Mon-Sat, 5-9pm Sun) Ethnic food is rare as rain in these parts, so locals pile into this authentic Thai cafe for pad thai and organic basil chicken. Service is sleepy and the ambience generic, but if you're hot for spice, it delivers. No bar.

Eddie McStiff's (☎ 435-259-2337; 59 S Main St; dishes $-$$; 🕑 5:30pm-midnight Mon-Fri, 11:30am-midnight Sat & Sun) Moab's biggest restaurant aims to please all with great pizza, steaks, pastas, salads, burgers, sandwiches and consistently good bar food. McStiff's also brews 13 tasty microbrews.

Moab Brewery (☎ 435-259-6333; 686 S Main St; dishes $-$$; 🕑 11:30am-10pm) Serving frosty mugs of house microbrews alongside tacos, stir-fries and salads, this cavernous brewery is a good bet for groups with diverse tastes. It's popular with families with kids.

Jailhouse Café (☎ 435-259-3900; 101 N Main St; dishes $-$$; 🕑 7am-noon) The eggs benedict is hard to beat but breakfast isn't cheap. Sure, it's cute as a button, but if there's a wait (and there usually is), you can do just as well elsewhere.

Pasta Jay's (☎ 435-259-2900; 4 S Main St; mains $-$$; 🕑 11am-9pm Nov-Feb, to 11pm Mar-Oct) With shady outdoor patio seating, Jay's serves heaping portions of garlicky pasta served with hot homemade bread. Lunch specials are a bargain.

Miguel's Baja Grill (☎ 435-259-6546; 51 N Main St; mains $$; 🕑 5-10pm) Dine on Baja fish tacos in the sky-lit breezeway patio with crayon-bright walls. Fajitas, *chiles rellenos* and seafood mains are ample portions. For vegetarians, the portobello salad is excellent. And, yes, it does have margaritas.

Buck's Grill House (☎ 435-259-5201; 1393 N Hwy 191; mains $$; 🕑 5:30-9:30pm; ♿) Big and bustling, upscale contemporary Southwestern specialties, such as duck tamales with adobo and elk stew with horseradish cream, are what Buck's does best (there are veggie options, too). Don't miss the buffalo chorizo and cheese quesadilla. This is white-tablecloth service for down-home food. There's also a kid's menu.

TOP END

Make reservations for the following.

Desert Bistro (☎ 435-259-0756; 92 E Center St; dinner mains $$-$$$; 🕑 5:30-9:30pm) Stylized preparations of wild game are the specialty at this down-to-earth, convivial white-tablecloth restaurant, where everything is made in-house, from freshly baked bread to delicious pastries. Service is warm and attentive, and there is a great wine list.

Jeffrey's Steakhouse (☎ 435-259-3588; www.jeffreyssteakhouse.com; 218 N 100 West; mains $$$; 🕑 5pm-close) Rumored the best steak in town, this elegant newcomer is serious about beef, which comes local, wagyu-style and in generous cuts. There's a good wine list and just-right vegetables include pan-fried zucchini or spinach salad. If the night is too good to end, head upstairs to the Ghost Bar.

River Grill at Sorrel River Ranch (☎ 435-259-4642; mile marker 17, Hwy 128; mains $$$; 🕑 7-9:30am, 11:30am-2pm & 5-9pm) For romance, it's hard to beat the wraparound veranda overlooking red-rock canyons. At this luxury resort, the new American menu changes with seasonal ingredients, but expect delicious seared steaks, succulent rack of lamb and fresh seafood flown in from the coast. Come before sunset.

DRINKING

Moab has a number of bars – or, as they're called in Utah, 'private clubs.' **Woody's Tavern** (☎ 435-259-9392; 221 S Main St) is happening with the 20s crowd. For tequila and a TV sports match, hit the raucous **Club Rio** (☎ 435-259-6666; 100 W Center St). Chug-a-lug pitchers of microbrews at **Eddie McStiff's** (☎ 435-259-2337; 59 S Main St) or the **Moab Brewery** (☎ 435-259-6333; 686 S Main St); both serve good bar food (see opposite).

A grown-up alternative is the new **Ghost Bar** (☎ 435-259-3588; 218 N 100 West; 🕑 7pm-close), a loungy, dime-sized jazz nook serving wine and a full list of cocktails, upstairs at Jeffrey's Steakhouse.

DO WHAT LOCALS DO

- Pedal to Milt's (opposite) for a thick butterscotch milkshake.
- Take a refreshing dip in **Ken's Lake**, located 10 miles from town, off US-191.
- Join the biweekly Weed and Feed: pitching in at a community garden is rewarded with a fantastic organic dinner, sponsored by the **Youth Garden Project** (☎ 435-259-2326; www.youthgardenproject.org).

For more impromptu gatherings and concerts, check Moab's library and cafe message boards.

ENTERTAINMENT

The **Moab Arts & Recreation Center** (☎ 435-259-6272; www.moabcity.state.ut.us/marc; 111 E 100 North) holds everything from yoga classes to special events; call for schedules.

Great for kids and grandparents, **Canyonlands by Night & Day** (☎ 435-259-2628, 800-394-9978; www.canyonlandsbynight.com; 1861 N Hwy 191; adult/child with dinner $65/55; 🕑 nightly spring-fall) runs a two-hour guided sunset boat trip on the Colorado (including a light show on the canyon walls), with an optional barbecue dinner beforehand.

For unapologetic tourist fun, **Bar-M Chuckwagon** (☎ 435-259-2276, 800-214-2085; www.barmchuckwagon.com; Hwy 191; adult/child $27/14), 7 miles north of Moab, starts the evening with a gunfight in the faux Western town, followed by a meaty cowboy dinner and Western music show. Reservations are suggested.

See first-run movies at **Slickrock Cinemas 3** (☎ 435-259-4441; 580 Kane Creek Rd).

Directory

CONTENTS

ACCOMMODATIONS

Only Zion and Bryce Canyon have the luxury of in-park lodges, but all of southern Utah's national parks and monuments have campgrounds. You'll find other kinds of accommodations in gateway towns and cities just outside the parks, especially in St George, Cedar City, Springdale and Moab. Good options also exist in towns along Hwy 12, including Torrey, Boulder, Escalante and Tropic, and Kanab on Hwy 89.

Weekends and big festivals are the busiest times, filling every room. At any time, make reservations if park proximity or a certain standard of quality are important. Most campgrounds, some motels and B&Bs, a few hotels and the Bryce Canyon Lodge all close during the off-peak winter season (roughly November through March). Still, you'll be able to find something open year-round near all of southern Utah's parks, even if off-season choices are limited. Walk-in customers can try politely bargaining about room rates during slow months. Discount cards (p264) may save you money at participating motels and hotels.

In this guide, accommodations listings are ordered by peak-season summer rates, from least expensive to most. The price categories – $ (under $100), $$ ($100 to $150) and $$$ (over $150) – are for rooms with private bathrooms. Unless otherwise stated, room rates do *not* include breakfast or taxes (12.85%). If you're traveling with children, some places advertise that 'kids sleep free' in the same room as their parents, but an extra fee may be charged for a rollaway bed or cot. To find pet-friendly accommodations, see p57.

Where an online computer terminal is available for guests' use, you'll see the inter-

PRACTICALITIES

- Electricital voltage is 110/120V AC, 50/60Hz.
- Newspapers include the *Salt Lake Tribune* (www.sltrib.com), *Las Vegas Review-Journal* (www.lvrj.com) and *Moab Times-Independent* (http://moabtimes.com).
- National Public Radio (NPR) is at the lower end of the FM dial; in rural areas, country-and-western music, conservative talk shows and Christian and Spanish-language programming predominate.
- TV stations include PBS (public broadcasting); and CNN (news), ESPN (sports), HBO (movies) and Weather Channel, all on cable.
- DVDs are coded for region 1 (US and Canada only).
- Distances are in feet, yards and miles; weights are tallied in ounces, pounds and tons. To convert between metric and imperial, see the inside back cover.

net icon (💻); wherever a wireless network is provided, you'll see the wi-fi icon (📶). Either way, internet access may be free or fee-based. The air-con icon (❄) denotes properties where in-room air-conditioning is available (not just fans). The swimming pool icon (🏊) denotes either an indoor or outdoor pool. Look for the child-friendly (👶) and pet-friendly (🐾) icons, too.

Many accommodations in Utah are entirely nonsmoking. Cleaning fees of over $100 may be charged if there's any evidence of someone having smoked in your room.

B&Bs & Inns

Bed-and-breakfasts are usually higher-end accommodations in converted private homes. Hosts tend to be knowledgeable about the local area and can make travel recommendations. People in need of lots of privacy may find B&Bs a bit too intimate.

B&B rates often include a home-cooked breakfast. Minimum stays are common in high season and on weekends. Amenities vary widely, but rooms with TV and telephone are the exception; the cheapest units share bathrooms.

Most B&Bs require advance reservations, though some will accommodate the occasional drop-in guest (always call ahead – don't just show up). Smoking, children and pets are generally prohibited.

Camping & Cabins

Camping in southern Utah can be a lot more than just a cheap way to spend the night under the stars. The nicest sites have you waking up to views of awesome rock formations or under a canopy of pine trees. A few campgrounds are open year-round; most generally open in March, April or May and stay open until the first snowfall, usually between late October and mid-November.

Campgrounds in state and national parks tend to have flush toilets and sometimes hot showers and RV dump stations. Private campgrounds cater more to the RV crowd, with water and electricity hookups and sometimes wi-fi internet access. In national forests (USFS) and Bureau of Land Management (BLM) land, expect more basic campsites with fire pits, picnic benches, vault toilets and possibly no drinking water. USFS and BLM lands may allow free, dispersed roadside camping, although campfires may require a permit.

The most popular campgrounds fill up fast, especially at national and state parks and everywhere in summer. Some accept reservations, while others are strictly first-come, first-served (show up early in the day to claim a site, especially on weekends and holidays). For camping reservations in national parks, national forests and other federal recreation lands (eg BLM), contact the **National Recreation Reservation Service** (☎ 518-885-3639, 877-444-6777; www.recreation.gov). For Utah state park campgrounds, contact **Reserve America** (☎ 518-885-3639, 800-322-3770; reservation fee $8).

Expect to pay more at private campgrounds, especially for RV sites with water and electricity hookups. Some belong to the national networks, such as **Kampgrounds of America** (KOA; ☎ 406-248-7444; www.koa.com), which also rents basic camping cabins, or Good Sam RV Club (p273). Many private camping 'resorts' line Hwy 12 throughout southern Utah, usually offering housekeeping cabins, too.

> **BOOK YOUR STAY ONLINE**
>
> For more accommodation reviews and recommendations by Lonely Planet authors, check out the online booking service at www.lonelyplanet.com/hotels. You'll find the true, insider low-down on the best places to stay. Reviews are thorough and independent. Best of all, you can book online.

Hotels & Motels

Just about every hotel and motel offers air-conditioned, nonsmoking rooms with a TV and phone. Rooms are often priced by the size and number of beds in a room; rates are usually the same for single or double occupancy, with a surcharge for the third or fourth person. 'Suites' may simply be oversized rooms, not necessarily two separate rooms.

There are some great family-run accommodations throughout southern Utah. Chains may be generic, but generally provide the level of quality you would expect. You can make reservations at the chains online or by calling toll-free reservation lines, but to learn about specific amenities and local promotional discounts, call the property directly.

Rates may include breakfast, which may be just stale donuts and wimpy coffee, or an all-you-can-eat breakfast buffet with eggs, biscuits and gravy, cereal, muffins and pastries, fruit, juice, milk and more.

Lodges

Of the national parks described in this guide, only Zion (p122), Bryce Canyon (p165) and the Grand Canyon's North Rim (boxed text, p192) have lodges. Although amenities are limited, their historic rooms and cabins always book up fast; you can make reservations up to 13 months in advance. Check for last-minute availability either online or by calling the lodge directly. You may find that sold-out dates suddenly become available three to five days prior to your intended stay, so it's worth rechecking for availability then, if your plans are flexible.

Ranch Resorts

Luxury resorts and guest ranches (aka 'dude ranches') are often destinations in themselves. Start the day with a round of golf or a horseback ride, then luxuriate with a massage, swimming, hot-tubbing and wine-tasting, or family-friendly programs such as rodeo shows and Western cookouts. You'll find a few ranch resorts scattered outside Zion's East Entrance and around Capitol Reef and Moab.

ACTIVITIES

Hiking is the activity of choice, but it's just one of many pursuits possible in and around southern Utah's parks. Rock climbing and canyoneering are also huge, while horseback trail rides and 4WD roads are popular activities back down closer to earth. Although the parks aren't great for mountain biking, there are miles of fat-tire trails outside Moab, also a jumping-off point for river-rafting and paddling trips. Winter brings snow play, cross-country skiing and snowshoeing to the mountains.

For a full rundown of outdoor activities in and around the parks, see p36. For more family-oriented fun, see p54.

BUSINESS HOURS

Regular business hours are from 9am until 5pm weekdays. In bigger towns, supermarkets may stay open until 8pm or later. In Utah, many restaurants are closed on Sunday; if you find one open, snag a seat and be happy. Unless otherwise noted within reviews, standard opening hours for listings in this guide are as follows.

Banks are usually open 9am to 5pm Monday to Friday; some will also open 9am to 1:30pm Saturday. Post offices are open 8:30am to 4.30pm, and also may be open Saturday morning, usually 9am to noon. Shop hours are 10am to 5:30pm Monday to Saturday and noon to 5pm Sunday; malls stay open later.

At restaurants, breakfast is usually served from 7am to 10am, lunch from 11:30am until 2:30pm and dinner from 5pm to 9pm daily. Some restaurants stay open throughout the day, while others close between meals. Bars are usually open from 5pm to midnight daily.

In summer many businesses, especially in park gateway towns, keep longer hours. In winter most keep shorter hours and a few even close (depending on seasonal demand and the weather, but typically from November through March).

CHILDREN

Traveling with children, especially during summer in southern Utah, means taking it easy. The hot sun, dry climate and occasionally high altitude can quickly turn into sunburn, dehydration and fatigue (for health and safety information, see p279). Break up long car journeys with frequent stops; try not to jam too much activity into the day. For more family travel tips, see p53.

CLIMATE CHARTS

The weather in southern Utah can vary wildly from one park or town to the next, even from one day to the next, especially during the unpredictable shoulder seasons of spring and fall. Then there's the summer heat, which routinely hovers above 90°F. Winter brings snowstorms. Altitude makes a difference in temperature year-round: hikers in Zion Canyon may be sweat-soaked at noon, but campers at Bryce Canyon will shiver in their sleeping bags later that night.

For more advice on seasonal weather patterns and when to visit the parks, see p19.

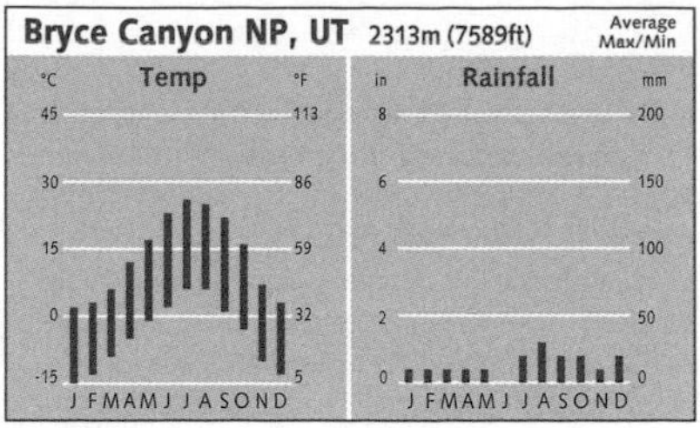

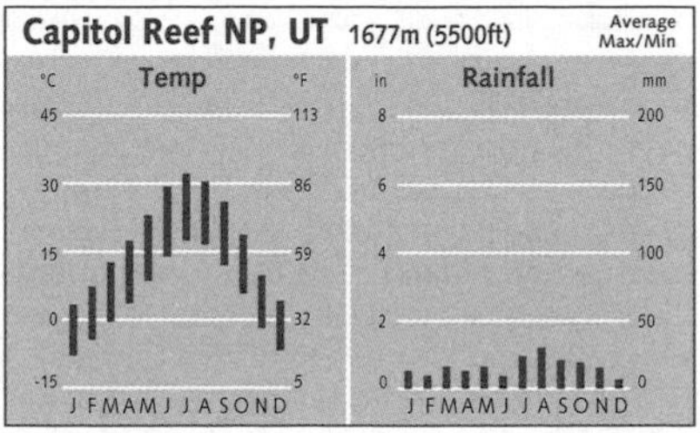

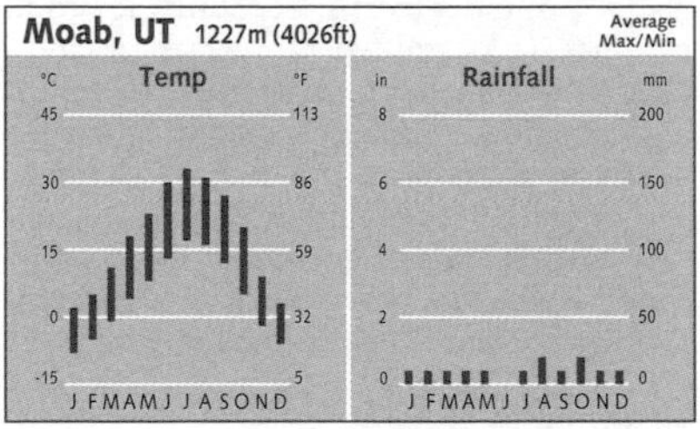

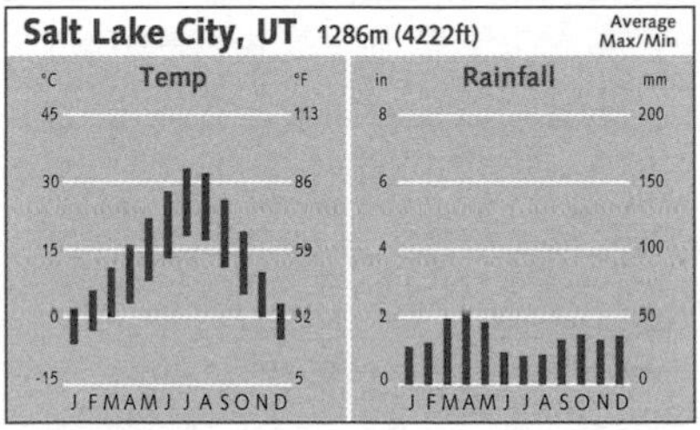

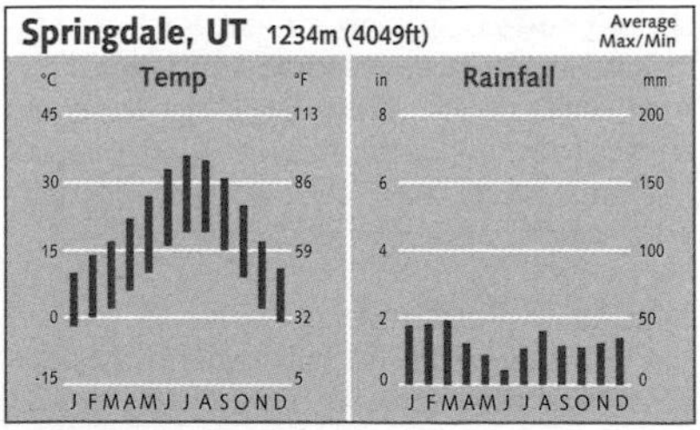

COURSES

Southern Utah's parks offer a range of outdoor-education opportunities, from naturalist-guided hikes and photography walks to extended learning vacations and college-credit courses. Most require advance reservations and tuition fees, although some are freely available for drop-in visitors, such as ranger-led programs (boxed text, p52). For rock-climbing, canyoneering and other outdoor-activity courses, see p36. For kid-oriented classes, including junior ranger programs, see p56. Private photography classes are available in Springdale (boxed text, p93) and Escalante (p186).

Zion Canyon Field Institute

Associated with Zion National Park, the nonprofit **Zion Canyon Field Institute** (☎ 800-635-3959; www.zionpark.org) offers year-round educational field trips, such as archaeology programs and wildlife-watching, as well as volunteer opportunities and photography workshops (eg wildflowers, fall foliage, winter scenes). Guided hikes are led by naturalists, some of whom are park rangers, and they introduce visitors to Zion's unique geology, flora and fauna, and cultural history. Advance sign-up is required. Fees range from $45 to $100 for a one-day experience, $200 to $300 for a multiday workshop.

Contemporary scientists share their discoveries at the field institute's free monthly lecture series, usually held at the Canyon Community Center in Springdale, outside the park. Call or check the website for upcoming special events.

Canyonlands Field Institute

Associated with Canyonlands and Arches National Parks, the nonprofit **Canyonlands Field Institute** (☎ 435-259-7750, 800-860-5262; www.canyonlandsfieldinst.org) offers some field trips and programs to the general public, although it primarily caters to school groups, summer youth camps and corporate retreats.

From mid-April until mid-October (except during late July), the institute offers half-day nature tours of the Moab area, including van transportation and naturalist-guided walks and hikes. Other half-day tours include 'Wet & Wild' creekside walks for families, sunset picnics or rock-art tours of Arches National Park. Advance sign-up is

TIPS FOR TEACHERS

Each of southern Utah's national parks runs field-trip programs specifically for teachers who wish to bring their students to study in the park. For details about education programs and fee waivers, teachers should contact the education coordinator at each individual park after checking out what's available online in the 'For Teachers' section of each park's website (p23).

Some national parks, including Bryce Canyon, now offer virtual (electronic) field trips for classes who can't visit the park in person. Bryce Canyon also offers field seminar programs for educators looking to earn graduate-school course credit in geology and biology; these seminars are usually held in early June. Teachers can also apply for summer employment (p270) or volunteer (p269) in any of southern Utah's national parks.

srequired; fees range from $20 to $85 for a half-day trip.

During summer and fall, the institute also offers multiday camping, horseback riding, river-rafting and 4WD trips, called 'ED Ventures,' designed for families to learn all about astronomy, archaeology, natural and cultural history, and more. These trips cost around $100 to $300 per person per day, all-inclusive.

For groups, private custom tours are available, including tours of Canyonlands and Arches National Parks and the La Sal Mountains outside Moab. Rates for private tours range average $35 to $180 per person, depending on how many people are in your group (the more you have, the cheaper it is). Private river-rafting trips require more advance notice and command higher prices.

The institute also offers professional river-rafting guide and wilderness medicine training courses, as well as a free monthly guest lecture series, usually held at the Moab Information Center, during summer. Call or check the website for upcoming special events.

High Plateaus Institute

Mostly for the academic community, this institute run by the **Bryce Canyon Natural History Association** (☎ 435-834-4784, 888-362-2642; www.brycecanyon.org) provides in-depth studies of Bryce's unique geology, along with a few courses, like photography, that are geared for the general public. Call or check the website for current offerings.

DISCOUNT CARDS

America the Beautiful Park Passes

The **America the Beautiful annual pass** (http://store.usgs.gov/pass; $80) is valid for free admission to all national parks and federal recreation lands for 12 months from when you buy it. Each pass admits four adults and all accompanying children under age 16. Buy the pass online or from any participating federal agency, including at national park entrance stations. Upon entry, be prepared to present your pass along with a photo ID (eg driver's license).

With the **America the Beautiful senior pass** (lifetime fee $10), US citizens and permanent residents 62 or older receive free admission to all national parks and federal recreation lands, plus 50% off select activity fees (eg camping in national parks). The lifetime **America the Beautiful access pass** (free) is for US citizens or permanent residents with a permanent disability; bring documentation if your disability is not readily visible. These discount parks passes must be obtained in person.

Automobile Clubs

Members of the **American Automobile Association** (AAA; ☎ 800-922-8228; www.aaa.com; annual membership from $47) and its foreign affiliates (eg Canada's CAA) qualify for small discounts (usually 10%) on hotels and motels, Amtrak trains, car and RV rentals, chain restaurants and shops, tours and more.

Senior Cards

People over the age of 65 (sometimes 55, 60 or 62) often qualify for the same discounts as students; any ID showing your birth date should suffice as proof of age.

Members of the **American Association of Retired Persons** (AARP; ☎ 800-566-0242; www.aarp.org; annual membership $12.50), for those 50 years of age and older, often get discounts (usually 10%) on hotels, car rentals and more.

Student & Youth Cards

For international and US students, the **Student Advantage Card** (☎ 877-256-4672; www.stu

dentadvantage.com; 1yr membership $23) offers 15% savings on Amtrak train and Greyhound bus fares, plus discounts of 10% to 20% at some motels, hotels, chain stores and airlines.

FESTIVALS & EVENTS

From art and music festivals to county fairs and chili cook-offs, southern Utah has scores of special events. Dates vary from year to year, so check with tourist information offices (p268). For southern Utah's most popular festivals and events, see the boxed text p20. The destination chapters have even more recommendations.

FOOD & DRINK

Meals are often an afterthought on a trip to southern Utah's national parks, but gateway towns do provide a decent variety of options, from basic cafeteria eats to upscale Southwestern cuisine. Zion and Bryce Canyon's park lodges offer filling, but just-OK food; their top-end prices and historical atmosphere make them better for a special occasion than everyday dining. Restaurant reviews in this book are ordered by price range: budget ($; mains less than $10), midrange ($$; mains from $10 to $20) and top end ($$$; $20 or more). Unless otherwise specified, prices listed are usually for dinner – expect lower prices for breakfast and lunch.

Groceries & Self-Catering

Small grocery stores in park gateway towns usually stock only a limited selection of items, such as canned goods, bread, milk, ice and other staples. If you're driving to southern Utah, you may want to stop off in larger towns and cities like St George and Moab to stock up on groceries – it'll cost less than buying supplies in smaller park gateway towns.

To fill up your cooler, ice is sold at almost every convenience store and gas station, but they may run out on hot summer days. In-room refrigerators are not always a standard amenity at motels and hotels, and they're not available inside park lodges. In all of southern Utah's national parks, you'll find picnic areas and campsites with picnic tables; the latter may have fire pits or grates for cooking.

HOLIDAYS

On holiday weekends, especially Memorial Day, Fourth of July and Labor Day in summer, expect the parks to be ridiculously busy, with campgrounds full and all nearby accommodations booked out weeks, if not months, in advance. For more advice on when to visit, see p19.

On the following national holidays, banks, schools and government offices (including post offices) close, and transportation, museums and other services operate on a Sunday schedule. Holidays falling on a weekend are usually observed the following Monday.

New Year's Day January 1
Martin Luther King Jr Day Third Monday in January
Presidents' Day Third Monday in February
Memorial Day Last Monday in May
Independence Day July 4 (aka the Fourth of July)

LIQUOR LAWS

Utah has some of the oddest liquor laws in the country. As with everywhere in the US, you must be aged 21 to drink legally. But that's where the similarities end.

In Utah, grocery stores sell near-beer (which doesn't exceed 3.2% alcohol content) seven days a week. State-run liquor stores and package agencies sell beer, wine and spirits Monday through Saturday (closed Sunday). You'll find licensed liquor stores and package agencies in southern Utah in St George, Hurricane, Cedar City, Kanab, Panguitch and Moab.

Lounges and taverns only serve near-beer. Stronger drinks are served at restaurants with liquor licenses between noon and midnight daily, as well as at 'dining or social clubs' that are open to the general public. At restaurants, servers aren't permitted to offer alcoholic drinks or show you a drink menu unless you specifically ask. When you order a drink, you must also order food, but a snack or appetizer will do. Wherever you're doing your drinking, you can only order one drink for yourself at a time. A pitcher of margaritas? Fuhgeddaboutit.

Alcohol is legally prohibited on Native American reservations and cannot be transported on tribal lands, even if you're just passing through.

Labor Day First Monday in September
Columbus Day Second Monday in October
Veterans' Day November 11
Thanksgiving Day Fourth Thursday in November
Christmas Day December 25

INSURANCE

Getting travel insurance to cover any theft, loss or medical problems you may encounter is highly recommended. Some travel insurance policies do not cover 'risky' activities such as motorcycling, skiing or even trekking, so read the fine print. Make sure the policy covers hospital stays and an emergency flight home.

Paying for your airline ticket or rental car with a credit card may provide limited travel accident insurance. (For information about car insurance costs and requirements, see p273). If you already have private health insurance or a homeowners or renters policy, find out what they will cover and only get supplemental insurance. If you have prepaid a large portion of your vacation, trip cancellation insurance may be a worthwhile expense.

Worldwide travel insurance is available at www.lonelyplanet.com/travel_services. You can buy, extend and claim online at anytime – even if you are already on the road.

INTERNATIONAL VISITORS

All travelers should double-check current visa and passport requirements *before* coming to the USA. For the latest entry requirements and eligibility, consult the Visa section of the US Department of State website (http://travel.state.gov) and the Travel section of the US Customs & Border Protection website (www.cbp.gov). If you're still in doubt, contact the nearest US embassy or consulate in your home country (visit www.usembassy.gov for a complete list).

Entering the Country

Under the US Department of Homeland Security (DHS) registration program, **US-VISIT** (www.dhs.gov/us-visit), almost all visitors (excluding, for now, most Canadian and many Mexican citizens) will be digitally photographed and have their electronic (inkless) fingerprints scanned upon arrival; the process typically takes less than a minute.

Passports

Under the Western Hemisphere Travel Initiative (WHTI), all travelers (including returning US citizens) must have a valid machine-readable (MRP) passport when entering the US by air, land or sea. An MRP has two lines of letters, numbers and <<< at the bottom of the data page.

MRP passports issued or renewed after October 26, 2006 must be e-passports (ie have a digital photo and integrated chip with biometric data). MRP passports issued or renewed between October 26, 2005 and October 25, 2006 must have a digital photo or integrated chip on the data page.

The only exceptions to these MRP requirements are for select US, Canadian and Mexican citizens who are able to present other WHTI-compliant documents (eg pre-approved 'trusted traveler' cards).

For full details, visit www.getyouhome.gov.

Visas

Currently, under the US Visa Waiver Program (VWP), visas are not required for citizens of 36 countries for stays up to 90 days (no extensions) if you have an MRP. If you don't have an MRP, you'll need a visa to enter the USA.

Citizens of VWP countries *must* register with the Electronic System for Travel Authorization (ESTA) online (https://esta.cbp.dhs.gov/) at least 72 hours before their trip begins. Once approved, ESTA registration is valid for up to two years.

Citizens from all other countries need to apply for a visa in their home country. The process costs a nonrefundable $131, involves a personal interview and can take several weeks, so apply as early as possible.

INTERNET ACCESS

This guides uses an internet icon ( ) where there's an online terminal available for use and the wi-fi icon ( ) when wireless internet access is offered, whether free or fee-based. Many hotels, motels and private RV campgrounds have either a public computer terminal or offer wi-fi (sometimes free, or costing $10 or more per day); ask when reserving.

In the national parks, wi-fi hot spots are rare (look for unsecured networks near visitor centers and lodges). Pay-as-you-go self-service internet terminals are rarely

LOST & FOUND

If you lose something in the parks, first retrace your steps to wherever you think you lost it, whether at a campground or a visitor center. On hiking trails and at scenic viewpoints, other visitors may put nonvaluable lost items (such as hats, gloves or jackets) in an obvious place, like on a trailhead sign, where you can easily find them. Failing that, or if your item is obviously valuable (eg wallet, cell phone, car keys, camera), call or ask at the park's visitor center, where most lost-and-found items usually end up. If you leave something behind on a park shuttle, visitor-center staff can also contact the bus company to check if drivers have found your item. Good luck!

available and can also be slow, unreliable and/or expensive.

Nearby towns and cities usually have at least one coffee shop, cybercafe or copy center offering online terminals (typically $5 to $12 per hour) and wi-fi. Some cybercafes may let you upload your photos and/or burn them onto CDs.

Public libraries usually offer internet terminals (though these may have time limits and require advance sign-up or waiting in line) and sometimes wi-fi. Out-of-state residents may be charged a small fee for internet terminal use.

MONEY

For more advice about planning your trip's budget, see p20.

ATMs

ATMs are available 24 hours, seven days at many banks, shopping malls, gas stations and grocery and convenience stores. You may also find them at park bookstores, concessionaire shops and lodges. Expect a surcharge of at least $2 per transaction, on top of any fees applied by your home banking institution. Most ATMs are connected to international networks and offer fairly good exchange rates. Avoid ATMs inside Las Vegas casinos, which tack on exorbitant surcharges and fees of $5 or more per transaction.

Credit Cards

Credit cards are almost universally accepted. In fact, you'll find it next to impossible to rent a car, book a hotel room or order tickets over the phone without one. Visa, MasterCard and American Express are most common.

Most ATMs will dispense cash if you use your credit card, but that can be expensive because, in addition to steep service fees, you'll be charged interest immediately. Ask your credit-card company for details and a four-digit PIN number.

Currency Exchange

If you're arriving from abroad, exchange money at the airport or in the nearest city, for example, at a major bank or currency-exchange office such as American Express. In smaller park gateway towns, exchanging money may be impossible. There are currently no currency-exchange services inside the parks, so make sure you have plenty of US cash and a credit card.

For US dollar exchange rates, see the inside back cover.

Tipping

Tipping is *not* optional. Only withhold tips in cases of outrageously bad service.

Airport & hotel porters $2 per bag, minimum per cart $5
Bartenders 10-15% per round, minimum per drink $1
Hotel maids $2-5 per night, left under the card provided
Restaurant servers 15-20%, unless a gratuity is already charged on the bill
Taxi drivers 10-15%, rounded up to the next dollar

Traveler's Checks

Traveler's checks have pretty much fallen out of use. National park concessionaire businesses (eg lodges, restaurants, shops) will often accept traveler's checks (in US dollars only), but smaller businesses, markets and fast-food chains outside the parks may refuse them.

POST

The **US Postal Service** (USPS; ☎ 800-275-8777; www.usps.com) is inexpensive and reliable. Postcards and standard letters up to 1oz cost 46¢ within the USA, 75¢ to Canada, 79¢ to Mexico and 98¢ to all other countries. Postal rates increase by a few pennies every couple of years.

You won't find any post offices inside the parks, but visitor-center bookstores, concessionaire shops and lodges may sell stamps. Outside the parks, gateway towns usually have at least one post office, while cities have multiple branches.

Convenient post offices for park visitors:

Boulder (☎ 435-826-4314; 325 N 100 East; 🕑 9am-1pm Mon-Fri, to noon Sat)

Bryce Canyon City (☎ 435-676-8853; Ruby's Inn, 1000 S Hwy 63; 🕑 9am-5pm Mon-Sat, 10am-4pm Sun)

Moab (☎ 435-259-7427; 50 E 100 North; 🕑 8am-5pm Mon-Fri, 9am-1pm Sun)

Springdale (☎ 435-772-3950; 625 Zion Park Blvd; 🕑 7:30-11:30am & noon-3pm Mon-Fri, 10am-1pm Sat)

Torrey (☎ 435-425-3716; 75 W Main St; 🕑 7:30am-1:30pm Mon-Fri, to 11:30am Sat)

To find the nearest post office or to double-check opening hours (which are highly subject to change), visit the USPS website or call ☎ 800-275-8777 toll-free.

TELEPHONE

Cell (mobile) phone reception is sketchy at best in southern Utah's national parks, and varies depending on your exact location and service provider. In most park gateway towns, cell-phone reception is usually decent, though again it depends on where you are. Full details are given in the regional chapters of this book.

Please be considerate of other park visitors when using your cell phone. Being woken up by phones ringing in a neighboring campsite, or listening to someone conduct a loud conversation at a scenic viewpoint, can really tarnish the outdoors experience for everyone in the immediate vicinity.

Public payphones are found in southern Utah's national parks at campgrounds, lodges and visitor centers. Local payphone calls cost 50¢ minimum, the cost increasing with the distance and length of call. Increasingly, in-park payphones are not coin-operated and will only accept credit cards or prepaid calling cards. You're usually better off using a prepaid phonecard, typically sold at park bookstores and concessionaire shops and lodges. Be sure to read the fine print for hidden costs, such as activation fees or connection surcharges for making calls from payphones.

For helpful local telephone numbers and dialing codes, see the inside back cover.

TIME

Utah is on Mountain Standard Time (GMT minus seven hours). When it's noon in Salt Lake City, it's 11am in Los Angeles, 3pm in New York, 8pm in London and 5am (the next day) in Sydney.

Daylight Saving Time (DST) starts on the second Sunday in March, when clocks are set one hour ahead, and ends on the first Sunday in November. If you're driving to Utah, beware that the state of Arizona (including Grand Canyon National Park) does not observe DST, but the Navajo Nation does. Confused yet? We thought so.

TOURIST INFORMATION

For national park and monument contact telephone numbers and websites, see p23. National park visitor centers and regional public lands information offices are your best bets for parks travel information once you arrive in southern Utah.

The state's official tourism agency, **Utah Travel Council** (☎ 801-538-1030, 800-200-1160; www.utah.com), offers loads of free information to help plan a vacation, including downloadable travel e-guides and website sections dedicated to national and state parks, outdoor recreation, annual festivals and events, and more. You'll find a **Utah Welcome Center** (☎ 435-673-4542; http://travel.utah.gov; Dixie Convention Center, 1835 Convention Center Dr, off I-15 exit 6; 🕑 8:30am-5:30pm) in St George.

County and other regional travel bureaus are also helpful:

Capitol Reef Country Travel Council (☎ 435-425-3365, 800-858-7951; www.capitolreef.travel) Covers Capitol Reef and Hwy 12.

Cedar City & Brian Head Tourism & Convention Bureau (☎ 435-586-5124, 800-354-4849; www.scenicsouthernutah.com) Covers Cedar City, Brian Head and Hwy 14.

Escalante Chamber of Commerce (☎ 435-826-4810; www.escalante-cc.com) Covers Grand Staircase-Escalante National Monument and Boulder.

Garfield County Office of Tourism (☎ 435-676-1160, 800-444-6689; www.brycecanyoncountry.com) Covers Bryce Canyon and Hwy 12.

Kane County Office of Tourism (☎ 435-644-5033, 800-733-5263; www.kaneutah.com) Covers Kanab and Hwy 89.

Moab Area Travel Council (☎ 435-259-8825, 800-635-6622; www.discovermoab.com) Covers Moab, Canyonlands, Arches and everything north.

Zion Canyon Visitors Bureau (☎ 888-518-7070; www.zionpark.com)

For more local tourist information offices and chambers of commerce, see the destination chapters.

TOURS

Most ranger-guided walking, hiking and shuttle-bus tours of the parks are free; ask at park visitor centers about what's currently being offered. The parks' natural history associations also offer excellent guided tours and field trips (see p263). For local tour operators and outdoor-activity guides, see the destination chapters, as well as those recommended in the Activities chapter (p36).

Region-wide tour operators include:

Adventure Bus (☎ 909-633-7225, 888-737-5263; www.adventurebus.com) Similar to Green Tortoise, but for all ages, offering sleep-aboard bus tours of southern Utah's national parks, departing from Salt Lake City.

Backroads, Inc (☎ 510-527-1555, 800-462-2848; www.backroads.com) Offers walking, hiking, cycling and multisport trips for all ages (including families with children) at Zion, Bryce Canyon and the Grand Canyon's North Rim.

Exploritas (☎ 800-454-5768; www.exploritas.org) Formerly Elderhostel, this nonprofit organization offers learning trips (including bus, walking and hiking tours and group-oriented outdoor activities) for active people over 50.

Green Tortoise (☎ 415-956-7500, 800-867-8647; www.greentortoise.com) Youth-oriented backpacker trips utilize converted sleeping-bunk buses to visit southern Utah's national parks, departing from Las Vegas.

Southern Utah Scenic Tours (☎ 435 867-8690, 435 867-8690; www.utahscenictours.com) Offers Grand Circle tours of the Southwest and southern Utah backroads trips (including the Grand Canyon's North Rim and Monument Valley) by bus, van or SUV, departing from Las Vegas.

TRAVELERS WITH DISABILITIES

The national parks exist for the enjoyment of all, offering opportunities for those in wheelchairs or with hearing, visual or other physical or mental disabilities to experience the wilderness. For information about obtaining a free lifetime 'America the Beautiful' entry pass, see p264. The **National Park Service** (NPS; TTY ☎ 800-877-8339; www.nps.gov/accessibility.htm) publishes *National Parks: Accessible to Everyone*, a free online, downloadable and printable large-type guide with helpful info and details about facilities at specific parks. Also check individual park websites (see p23) or ask at park visitor centers for up-to-date accessibility guides, details of which are often printed in the parks' free newspaper guides.

All of southern Utah's national parks have wheelchair-accessible visitor centers, at least one accessible campsite in their main campground and a few viewpoints and/or trails that are wheelchair-accessible. Some parks also offer ranger programs for the hearing impaired. Service animals (ie guide dogs) may accompany visitors on park shuttles, inside museums and visitor centers, and on hiking trails and in the backcountry (check current regulations to see if permits are required at visitor centers). Ensure your service animal wears its official vest at all times, to avoid any misunderstandings with park rangers or other visitors.

In Zion and Bryce Canyon, park shuttles are wheelchair-accessible and lodges offer ADA-compliant wheelchair-accessible rooms. Accommodations outside the parks are required to have at least one wheelchair-accessible room, though few are fully ADA-compliant. More often, these are ground-floor rooms with wider doorways, less furniture, and handles around the tub and toilet. Always ask exactly what 'accessible' means when making reservations. In this book, the wheelchair icon (♿) highlights sights and activities, accommodations, restaurants and other venues that are especially wheelchair-accessible. Some car-rental agencies offer hand-controlled vehicles and vans with wheelchair lifts at no extra charge, but you must reserve them well in advance.

Access Utah Network (☎ 801-533-4636, 800-333-8824, relay line 711; www.accessut.org) is a state agency that provides accessibility information for all Utah parks and referrals to other helpful organizations. The nonprofit, Salt Lake City–based **Splore** (☎ 801-484-4128; www.splore.org) specializes in providing outdoor activities (eg river rafting, canoeing, rock climbing) for those with special needs.

VOLUNTEERING

There are many opportunities to volunteer in and around southern Utah's parks, from one-day projects to longer-term endeavors. Volunteers can do trail maintenance, pull invasive plants, train to be an interpretive ranger or work with youth organizations.

To find volunteer opportunities, check with the following:

Bureau of Land Management (BLM; www.blm.gov/ut/st/en/res/volunteer.html) Apply online or contact the nearest BLM office.

National Park Service (NPS; www.nps.gov/volunteer) Apply for the Volunteer in Parks (VIP) program and search for opportunities by park name or state online.
Sierra Club (www.sierraclub.org) Day or weekend service projects and volunteer vacations, including for families, focus on conservation (annual membership $25).
Student Conservation Association (SCA; www.thesca.org) Nonprofit organization offers conservation internships that earn academic credit, as well as summer trail-crew work.
Volunteer.gov (www.volunteer.gov) Online searchable database of volunteers for all public lands agencies, including NPS and the US Forest Service (USFS).
Zion Canyon Field Institute (☎ 800-635-3959; www.zionpark.org) Arranges day-long service projects, typically in the Narrows of the Virgin River during summer and fall.

WORK

Nearly everyone who works inside the parks is employed by the National Park Service (NPS), the parks' cooperating nonprofit organizations (p23) or by park concessionaire businesses. Most employment opportunities are low-paying seasonal jobs that are mostly filled by young people, teachers or retirees. Planning ahead is essential, whether you are applying with NPS or park concessionaires – applications for summer jobs are typically due around December.

US citizens can browse for seasonal and permanent jobs with all federal public lands agencies (eg NPS, BLM, USFS) online at **USA Jobs** (www.usajobs.com). Anyone may apply for work with park concessionaires, including **Xanterra** (www.xanterra.com) in **Zion Lodge** (www.zionlodge.com) and **Forever Resorts** (http://foreverresorts.com) at **Bryce Canyon Lodge** (www.brycecanyonforever.com). Seasonal work may be available in larger park gateway communities, such as Springdale and Moab, though most of these jobs are not advertised online; ask around and check local bulletin boards and newspaper classified ads.

If you are not a US citizen, you can't work in the USA without a proper visa. Unless an employer sponsors you (nearly impossible for seasonal work), you will need to apply for a J-1 (international student and youth exchange) work visa. Organizations that can help arrange J-1 visas include:

Bunac (www.bunac.org) For UK citizens.
Council on International Educational Exchange (www.ciee.org)
InterExchange (www.interexchange.org)
International Exchange Programs (IEP) For citizens of Australia (www.iep.org.au) and New Zealand (www.iep.co.nz).
Swap (www.swap.ca) For Canadians.

Transportation

CONTENTS

GETTING THERE & AWAY

To get to southern Utah you can: fly into Salt Lake City (Utah), Las Vegas (Nevada), Denver or Grand Junction (Colorado), then rent a car; or from Salt Lake City fly into regional airports in St George, Cedar City or Moab. Taking an Amtrak train or Greyhound bus is possible but inconvenient, and you'll still need to rent a car or hire a shuttle to reach the national parks.

Flights, tours and rail tickets can be booked online at www.lonelyplanet.com/travel_services.

AIR

Airports

Salt Lake City International Airport (SLC; ☎ 801-575-2400, 800-595-2442; www.slcairport.com), Las Vegas' **McCarran International Airport** (LAS; ☎ 702-261-5211; www.mccarran.com) and **Denver International Airport** (DEN; ☎ 303-342-2000; www.flydenver.com) are all major hubs served by US and international carriers. All of these airports have car-rental-agency desks, taxi and limousine stands, airport shuttle buses and local public-transportation options.

From Salt Lake City, daily flights operated by SkyWest (code share AirTran, Delta and United) arrive at southwestern Utah's **St George municipal airport** (SGU; ☎ 435-673-3451; www.sgcity.org/airport) and at least once daily at **Cedar City regional airport** (CDC; ☎ 435-867-9408; www.cedarcity.org/airport.html). Commuter flights also land at southeastern Utah's **Canyonlands Field** (CNY; ☎ 435-259-4849; www.moabairport.com), 18 miles north of Moab via Hwy 191. Currently, Great Lakes Airlines operates once or twice daily from Denver. For airport shuttle services and local transportation, see the destination chapters.

More frequent commuter flights land at southwestern Colorado's **Grand Junction regional airport** (GJT; ☎ 970-244-9100; www.walkerfield.com), including major US carriers' regional jets from Salt Lake City, Denver, Phoenix (Arizona) and Dallas–Fort Worth (Texas). Grand Junction is about a two-hour drive northeast of Moab, 115 miles away. If you aren't picking up a rental car, reserve ahead with **American Spirit Shuttle** (☎ 970-523-7662; www.americanspiritshuttle.net), offering on-demand airport service. Alternatively, **Grand Valley Transit** (☎ 970-256-7433; www.gvt.mesacounty.us) runs hourly airport buses to/from downtown Grand Junction ($1, 30 minutes).

> **THINGS CHANGE...**
>
> The information in this chapter is particularly vulnerable to change. Check directly with the airline or a travel agent to make sure you understand how a fare (and ticket you may buy) works and be aware of the security requirements for international travel. Shop carefully. The details given in this chapter should be regarded as pointers and are not a substitute for your own careful, up-to-date research.

Airlines

US AIRLINES

Air Tran (airline code FL; ☎ 800-247-8726; www.airtran.com)

Alaska Airlines (airline code AS; ☎ 800-252-7522; www.alaskaair.com)

Allegiant (airline code G4; ☎ 702-505-8888; www.allegiantair.com)

American Airlines (airline code AA; ☎ 800-433-7300; www.aa.com)

Continental Airlines (airline code CO; ☎ 800-523-3273; www.continental.com)

Delta Air Lines (airline code DL; ☎ 800-221-1212; www.delta.com)

ROAD DISTANCES (mi)

	Arches National Park	Bryce Canyon National Park	Capitol Reef National Park	Grand Staircase-Escalante National Monument (Boulder)	Las Vegas	Moab	Salt Lake City	St George	Zion National Park
Arches National Park	---								
Bryce Canyon National Park	275	---							
Capitol Reef National Park	130	125	---						
Grand Staircase-Escalante National Monument (Boulder)	185	80	45	---					
Las Vegas	455	255	360	325	---				
Moab	5	280	145	190	460	---			
Salt Lake City	230	270	225	250	440	235	---		
St George	335	130	245	205	125	335	305	---	
Zion National Park	340	90	200	155	165	345	310	45	---

If you're going backcountry exploring, renting a 4WD vehicle such as a Jeep costs more (from $45 per day). The cheapest places to rent 4WD vehicles are Las Vegas and Salt Lake City, but then you'll be stuck with a higher-priced, fuel-inefficient vehicle for your entire trip. Renting a 4WD locally in southern Utah is more expensive on a daily basis (easily over $100), but may work out cheaper overall if you only need 4WD for a couple of days. For 4WD tips, see p46.

Car-rental rates usually include unlimited mileage, but hefty surcharges apply for additional drivers and one-way rentals. Child or infant safety seats are required by law (reserve when booking), renting from $10/50 per day/week.

Major international car-rental companies:
Alamo (☎ 877-222-9075; www.alamo.com)
Avis (☎ 800-331-1212; www.avis.com)
Budget (☎ 800-527-0700; www.budget.com)
Dollar (☎ 800-800-3665; www.dollar.com)
Enterprise (☎ 800-261-7331; www.enterprise.com)
Fox (☎ 800-225-4369; www.foxrentacar.com)
Hertz (☎ 800-654-3131; www.hertz.com)
National (☎ 877-222-9058; www.nationalcar.com)
Thrifty (☎ 800-847-4389; www.thrifty.com)

Most of these companies have rental desks at Salt Lake City, McCarran (Las Vegas) and Denver international airports and Grand Junction regional airport. In St George and Cedar City, you can rent cars from Avis, Budget, Enterprise or Hertz; reserve ahead for airport pickup. For Moab's Canyonlands Field, make reservations in advance with Enterprise.

MOTORCYCLE

Motorcycle rentals and insurance are not cheap, especially if you have got your eye on a Harley-Davidson. Depending on the model, it costs $100 to $250 per day plus taxes. Rental rates usually include helmets, unlimited miles and liability insurance, but collision insurance (CDW) costs extra. **Eagle Rider** (☎ 888-900-9901; www.eaglerider.com) motorcycle rental outlets include Salt Lake City, Las Vegas and Denver; rent in one city and return in another for a surcharge of $250.

RV

Despite narrow, twisting roads, RVs remain a popular way to travel around southern Utah. Although RVs are cumbersome to navigate and burn fuel at an alarming rate, they solve transportation, accommodation and cooking needs in one fell swoop. Rental rates vary by size, model and mileage; expect to pay at least $100 per day.

Rental agencies include the following:

Canyonlands RV Rentals (☎ 435-229-2746; www.rentrvutah.com; 31 N 700 East, St George; ⏲ 9am-5pm Mon-Sat) Rents trailers and RVs; ask about free pickups from St George's airport.

Cruise America (☎ 800-671-8042; www.cruiseamerica.com) Rents RVs and trailers in Salt Lake City, Las Vegas, Denver and other major gateway cities.

El Monte RV (☎ 562-483-4956, 888-337-2214; www.elmonterv.com) Rents in Salt Lake City, Las Vegas (Henderson), Denver and other major gateway cities.

Road Bear RV (☎ 866-491-9853; www.roadbearrv.com) Rental locations include Las Vegas and Denver, with complimentary airport shuttles available; German spoken.

Road Rules

Drive on the right-hand side of the road. The use of seat belts is required for drivers, front-seat passengers and anyone under age 20. Children under eight years old are required to sit in a car seat or booster, unless they are taller than 57in. Motorcycle helmets are not required for adults over age 18.

Unless otherwise posted, the speed limit is 65mph on freeways (minimum 45mph), 55mph on two-lane undivided highways, 25mph in business and residential districts and 20mph near schools. It's illegal to pass a school bus when its rear red lights are flashing. You may make a right turn on a red light after first coming to a full stop, unless signs say otherwise. U-turn laws vary by city; look for posted signs.

Strict penalties for driving under the influence (DUI) of drugs or alcohol in Utah include steep fines and jail time. Police can give roadside sobriety checks to assess if you've been drinking or using drugs. You'll fail if your blood-alcohol is over the legal limit (0.08%). Refusing to be tested can result in immediate suspension of your driver's license. It's illegal to carry open containers of alcohol inside a vehicle, even when they're empty; store them in the trunk instead.

TRAIN

Amtrak (☎ 800-872-7245; www.amtrak.com) operates a fairly extensive rail system throughout the US. Trains are comfortable, if slow, and are equipped with dining and lounge cars on long-distance routes. Amtrak's daily *California Zephyr* train between the San Francisco Bay Area and Chicago stops at Green River, Utah, over 50 miles northwest of Moab, and Grand Junction, Colorado. In Grand Junction, you can rent a car (p273), but from Green River you'll have to hire a private shuttle to Moab (p242).

TRANSPORTATION

Costs

Fares depend on the day of travel, the type of seating etc. Round-trip fares cost the same as two one-way tickets.

AAA members (p273) can save 10%. Seniors over 62 and students with an International Student Identity Card or Student Advantage Card (p264) receive a 15% discount, while up to two children (aged two to 15) get 50% off when accompanied by an adult. Children under two years old ride free, but only if they don't require their own seat. Check the Amtrak website for special promotions or ask about all available discount fares when making reservations.

TRAIN SERVICES

From	To	Coach Fare	Duration
Chicago, IL	Green River, UT	$129	29hr
Denver, CO	Grand Junction, CO	$46	8hr
Emeryville, CA	Green River, UT	$98	22hr
Reno, NV	Green River, UT	$86	15hr
Salt Lake City, UT	Green River, UT	$32	4½hr
Salt Lake City, UT	Grand Junction, CO	$43	7hr

Reservations

You can buy tickets at Amtrak stations, by phone or online. Reservations can be made up to 11 months prior to departure. During summer and around holidays, trains sell out quickly, so buy tickets as early as possible, especially for sleeping-car accommodations (hefty surcharge applies).

GETTING AROUND

Most people get around the parks the same way they got to southern Utah, either by car, motorcycle or RV. Limited seasonal park shuttles operate in Zion and Bryce Canyons, but these won't get you everywhere you want to go. That said, use these free shuttle services as much as you can, to help cut down on traffic problems and pollution in the parks. Also consider renting a bicycle or bringing your own.

BICYCLE

Zion Canyon, Bryce Canyon and Capitol Reef have scenic drives open to recreational cyclists. Although national park trails are off-limits to bicycles (except for Zion's Pa'rus Trail), bicycles are usually allowed on any paved or dirt park road. Companies offering bike rentals and guided trips are positioned in gateway towns near all of the parks. USFS and BLM recreation areas, such as Grand Staircase-Escalante National Monument, are more mountain-bike friendly (see also p43).

Touring southern Utah by bike is a hardy endeavor and best done with the support of an outfitter or tour operator. The **Adventure Cycling Association** (☎ 406-721-1776, 800-755-2453; www.adventurecycling.org) provides info on cycling routes, sells bicycle maps and arranges tours. Helmets aren't required by Utah law, but they're still a good idea. For more safe biking tips, see p286. For emergency roadside assistance, join the Better World Club (p273).

BUS

There is no bus service to or between southern Utah's national parks. However, both Zion and Bryce Canyon offer free seasonal park shuttles that are handy for seeing the main sights and avoiding traffic headaches.

In Zion, the mandatory park shuttle (p92) runs from early April through late October, when the canyon's main scenic drive is closed to private vehicles. Another free shuttle route connects Zion Canyon with the gateway town of Springdale. Both routes run frequently. Shuttles do not serve Hwy 9 east of Canyon Junction through the Zion–Mt Carmel Tunnel or the park's more remote Kolob Terrace and Kolob Canyons Rds.

In Bryce Canyon, an optional park shuttle (p149) runs from early May through September. Although this free shuttle connects the dots between the park's most popular sightseeing spots, as well as the lodge, visitor center, campground and Ruby's Inn tourist complex just north of the park, it does not travel all the way down the canyon's scenic drive, except on twice-daily guided shuttle-bus tours (free).

CAR, MOTORCYCLE & RV

There are usually no restrictions on travel by private vehicle in the national parks, although Zion Canyon is only accessible to free park shuttle buses (left) from early April to late October. Otherwise, cars and motorcycles are allowed on all public paved and dirt roads inside and outside the parks. Some roads in southern Utah are not appropriate for RVs, however, and a few roads expressly forbid travel by RVs (or sometimes only for models over a certain length). For details, see the individual destination chapters, consult seasonal park newspapers or ask the staff at visitor centers.

Be aware that if you're planning on driving an RV or other oversized vehicle through the Mt Carmel–Zion Tunnel inside Zion National Park, you'll need to pay an escort fee and time your trip during specific hours (see p92). RV dump stations

ARE WE THERE YET?

Judging how long it will take to drive from point A to point B in southern Utah is an art form. Some highways drive like dirt roads, some dirt roads like highways, and slow-moving trucks and RVs can impede your progress for miles uphill. While this book does include driving times, most southern Utah road savvy is only gained through hard-won experience. When in doubt, always plan for it to take longer than you think.

As a rule, if a dirt road is noted as 'good' and passable to passenger cars, you can usually drive an average of 30mph on it, but numerous rough sections and washes will force you to slow to 20mph or even 10mph. On most blacktop roads you can average 55mph, but you'll need to slow to 40mph or 25mph through small towns (unless you like speeding tickets) and sometimes on twisting mountainous sections. Only on the interstates can you be assured of making good time; I-15 and I-70 allow speeds up to 75mph.

and electrical hookups are found at private campgrounds outside the parks. Inside the parks, dump stations may only be available seasonally (if at all) and generator use is usually restricted to certain hours at NPS campgrounds, which may not have pull-through sites and may restrict RV camping to vehicles of a certain length only.

Fuel & Repairs

Always start out with a full tank of gas and extra gallons of drinking water, plus food and blankets in case of emergencies. Gas stations are few and far between in southern Utah. There are no gas stations inside any of the parks, and gas can be expensive in gateway towns. Try to fill up in bigger cities and along interstate highways, where gas is cheaper and stations are often open 24 hours. In smaller towns, look for 24-hour pumps where you can pay by credit card even when there's no one on duty.

For emergency roadside assistance and towing services, join an auto club (p273). In case of any roadside emergencies, keep in mind that cell phones work in most towns and cities, but only in very limited areas of the national parks. Just outside Bryce Canyon, **Ruby's Inn American Car Care Center** (☎ 435-834-5232; 105 S Main St, Bryce Canyon City; 🕒 7am-11pm May-Sep, 8am-6pm Oct-Apr) offers full-service repairs for cars, trucks and RVs, although parts are limited and you may have to wait quite a while for all but the simplest of repairs. It also sells standard auto supplies and decently priced gas, and offers a car wash and 24-hour, AAA-approved towing services. Otherwise, your best bets for faster car repairs and finding auto supplies are in St George and Moab.

Road Conditions

For highway driving conditions, contact the **Utah Department of Transportation** (UDOT; ☎ 511, outside Utah 866-511-8824; www.udot.utah.gov). Every national park provides updates on roads within its boundaries; either visit the park website or call the visitor information numbers (see p23). For road conditions outside the national parks, contact the federal agency in charge of that area – most often it's the BLM or USFS (see the destination chapters for regional-office contact details). For Grand Staircase-Escalante National Monument, call ☎ 435-826-5499.

Overall precipitation is low, but when it does rain, it can wreak havoc. Most common during July and August, short, heavy thunderstorms cause flash floods and turn dirt roads into impassable mud slicks, though they dry quickly. Even the lightest rain can leave desert slickrock and hard clay roads treacherously slippery and too dangerous for any vehicle (including 4WDs) for at least a day or two afterward. Long inured to the desert's unpredictability, the National Weather Service often covers itself by forecasting a 20% to 30% chance of showers, which by itself tells you nothing. Always check with rangers before driving dirt roads, and watch the skies. Never park your vehicle in a desert wash, where it could possibly get swept away by a flash flood.

In winter higher elevations get socked with snow, while lower elevations see freezing rain, occasional snow and nighttime temperatures that can turn blacktop roads icy. High-elevation mountain roads may be closed completely from the first snowfall in late October or early November until the snow melts away, usually by late May or early June.

Road Hazards

Speeding not only poses a danger to humans, but also wildlife. Many animals, including deer and livestock, are hit by motorists every year. Slowing down saves lives, maybe even your own. Not only does plowing into a deer or cow mean a bad ending for the animal, it could also damage or total your car and seriously injure or even kill yourself and your passengers. Smaller animals such as squirrels also regularly dart out onto the road, and most people's natural reaction is to swerve to avoid hitting them. Nothing could be more dangerous. Slow down if you can do so safely, then wince and cross your fingers, and keep driving. Strangely, by driving straight ahead, you'll often avoid hitting these smaller animals, which will dart sideways at the last possible second.

Driving too slow or erratically can be just as much of a hazard in the parks. Maintain a reasonable speed on crowded scenic drives. Do not block traffic by suddenly stopping in the middle of the road to take a photo, or use a roadside pullout without signaling first. All of the rules of the road (see p275) still apply in national parks, although some visitors ignore them. If you're driving an RV or other oversized vehicle, be courteous and don't hog the road – use signposted pullouts to let faster traffic pass.

HITCHHIKING

Hitchhiking is never entirely safe anywhere in the world, and we don't recommend it. That said, hitchhiking is sometimes the only way to get between trailheads after an end-to-end hike, if you don't happen to have two cars to shuttle. The rules for hitchhiking in each national park change every year, so ask at the visitor center before you stick your thumb out. Keep in mind that hitchhiking is usually only allowed at designated roadside pullouts within the parks.

Outside the parks, hitchhiking is illegal in Utah, although it's considered only a minor infraction and police often look the other way. Hitchhiking can still be difficult, since hitchhikers are usually viewed with suspicion by drivers. Traffic in southern Utah can be sparse in rural areas or else heavily tourist-driven, either of which makes your chance of getting a ride less likely. For first-hand reports from the road and advice, search **Digihitch** (www.digihitch.com). You can browse and post ride-sharing ads for free on **Craigslist** (http://stgeorge.craigslist.org).

Health & Safety

CONTENTS

Key to health and safety are good predeparture preparations and common sense while traveling. While the potential problems may seem frightening, few visitors experience anything worse than a skinned knee. Much of this chapter covers worst-case scenarios, which can be avoided or at least dealt with more effectively if you're well prepared.

BEFORE YOU GO

If you're planning on doing any hiking, start getting regular physical exercise a few weeks prior to your trip. When possible, visitors from lower elevations and cooler climes should allow at least a day or two to acclimatize before undertaking any strenuous activity in southern Utah's deserts or at higher mountain elevations.

For information about travel and health insurance, see p266.

MEDICAL CHECKLIST

In addition to any over-the-counter and prescription medications you normally take, consider adding these to your first-aid kit:

- acetaminophen (Tylenol) or aspirin
- adhesive or paper tape
- antibacterial ointment for cuts and abrasions
- antidiarrhea and antinausea drugs
- antifungal cream or powder
- antihistamines (for allergies)
- anti-inflammatories (eg ibuprofen)
- Band-Aids, bandages, gauze swabs and rolls
- calamine lotion, sting-relief spray or aloe vera
- cold and influenza tablets, throat lozenges and nasal decongestant
- cortisone (steroid) cream for allergic rashes
- elasticized support bandage for knees, ankles etc
- eye drops
- insect repellent
- moleskin for blisters
- nonadhesive dressings
- oral rehydration mix
- pocket knife (blades longer than 4in are prohibited in airplane carry-on luggage)
- safety pins
- small pair of scissors
- sterile alcohol wipes
- sunscreen and lip balm
- thermometer (note, mercury thermometers are prohibited by airlines)
- tweezers
- water-purification tablets or iodine

INTERNET RESOURCES

Centers for Disease Control & Prevention (www.cdc.gov) US government agency offers a wealth of information, from travel health precautions to environmental hazards and emergencies.

MD Travel Health (www.mdtravelhealth.com) US vaccination recommendations and updates on infectious disease outbreaks nationwide.

National Park Service Public Health Program (www.nps.gov/public_health) Background information on disease and water issues.

Utah Department of Health (http://health.utah.gov) Local advice about infectious diseases and health precautions.

Wilderness Medicine Institute (www.nols.edu/wmi) Nonprofit organization offers wilderness-medicine training courses; the website's 'Curriculum Updates' section offers real-life case studies, news articles and more.

FURTHER READING

Hikers, climbers, backpackers, paddlers and other off-road explorers may want to stuff one of these excellent first-aid guides into their packs.

- *Backcountry First Aid and Extended Care* by Buck Tilton (2007) Pocket-sized guide is compact and lightweight, but info-packed for situations when medical help is over an hour away.
- *Wilderness 911* by Eric A Weiss (2007) A step-by-step guide to first aid and advanced care in remote areas when you have limited medical supplies.
- *Medicine for the Outdoors* by Paul S Auerbach (2009) Hefty layperson's reference gives explanations of wilderness medical problems and practical treatment options.

IN THE PARKS

While crime is not a particular problem in any of the national parks, you should still lock your car, and place any valuables you don't carry with you in the trunk, especially when you park at less-visited trailheads.

For casual park visitors, staying safe and healthy is usually a matter of hydrating properly, being aware of the weather forecast (eg watch for flash floods) and not goofing around near precarious cliffs and canyon rims. Many emergencies arise when visitors overestimate their own physical abilities or underestimate the power of Mother Nature.

When visiting southern Utah, you'll need to be more self-sufficient and prepared for the unexpected than usual. The desert offers innumerable ways to come to a bad end, and people discover new ways all the time.

MEDICAL ASSISTANCE

In any emergency, dial ☎ 911. Unfortunately, if you're injured in rural areas or inside the parks, calling may not be an option; cell phones often don't work outside the major interstate corridors, and canyon walls block signals. Satellite phones and personal locator beacons (PLBs) are your best options in the backcountry.

Park rangers with medical training can help visitors who get into trouble, free of charge for basic first aid. For more serious ailments, drive to the nearest hospital emergency room or clinic. Search-and-rescue (SAR) and helicopter evacuations are only for truly life-threatening emergencies. Emergency operations are costly and also put the lives of rangers and other staff at risk.

Major hospitals with 24-hour emergency rooms in southern Utah include the following:

Allen Memorial Hospital (☎ 435-259-7191; www.amhmoab.org; 719 W 400 North, Moab) Level-4 trauma center open until construction of new Moab Regional Hospital is finished.

Dixie Regional Medical Center (☎ 435-251-1000; http://intermountainhealthcare.org; 1380 E Medical Center Dr, St George) Level-3 trauma center is among the region's best.

Garfield Memorial Hospital (☎ 435-676-8811; http://intermountainhealthcare.org; 200 N 400 East, Panguitch) Offers air-ambulance life flight services for emergencies beyond its ability to treat.

Kane County Hospital (☎ 435-644-5811; http://kchosp.net; 355 N Main St, Kanab) Closest to the Grand Canyon's North Rim.

Valley View Medical Center (☎ 435-868-5000; http://intermountainhealthcare.org; 1303 N Main St, Cedar City) If you can't make it to St George.

INFECTIOUS DISEASES

Rabies

Rabies is a viral infection of the brain and spinal cord that is almost always fatal. The rabies virus is carried in the saliva of infected animals and is typically transmitted through an animal bite, though contamination of any break in the skin with infected saliva may result in rabies. In the US, most cases of human rabies are related to exposure to bats. But rabies may be contracted from any mammal, including squirrels, raccoons and unvaccinated cats and dogs.

If there is any possibility, however small, that you have been exposed, you should seek preventative treatment, which consists of rabies immune globulin and rabies vaccine and is quite safe. In particular, any contact with a bat should be discussed with health authorities, because bats have small teeth and may not leave obvious bite marks. If you wake up to find a bat in your room, especially if you have small children, rabies prophylaxis may be necessary.

Travelers Diarrhea

AMEBIC DYSENTERY

While a change of water, food or climate may give travelers an aggravating case of the

WATER PURIFICATION

All groundwater in the desert, whether a river, seasonal stream or sandstone seep, should be considered unsafe to drink and treated accordingly.

Giardiasis and *cryptosporidiosis* are common intestinal diseases that stem from drinking untreated water. Symptoms include diarrhea, abdominal cramps, gas, headaches and fatigue. *Giardiasis* can be treated, but there is no effective treatment for *cryptosporidiosis*. Both can last for anywhere from a few weeks or months to several years, though neither is typically life-threatening.

The most reliable way to destroy the offending organisms is to boil water. Water purification tablets and portable water filters (0.5 microns or smaller) are also effective. Drinking water provided at national park visitor centers and campgrounds is reliably safe, unless posted notices indicate otherwise.

runs, serious diarrhea caused by contaminated water can be a problem in the parks, especially in backcountry areas. If diarrhea does occur, fluid replacement is essential. Weak black tea with a little sugar or a soft drink allowed to go flat and diluted 50% with water are good. In cases of severe diarrhea, oral rehydration therapy is necessary to replace lost minerals and salts. Commercially available oral rehydration salts are useful. Gut-paralyzing drugs such as diphenoxylate or loperamide may bring relief from symptoms, but do not actually cure the problem. Stick to a bland diet as you recover.

GIARDIASIS

Symptoms of this parasitic infection of the small intestine may include nausea, bloating, cramps and diarrhea. To protect yourself from giardia, you should avoid drinking directly from lakes, ponds, streams and rivers, which may be contaminated by animal or human feces. The infection can also be transmitted from person to person if proper hand washing is not performed. Giardiasis is easily diagnosed by a stool test and readily treated with antibiotics.

ENVIRONMENTAL HAZARDS

Altitude

The rim at Bryce Canyon ranges in altitude from 8000ft to 9000ft above sea level, while Cedar Breaks rises above 10,000ft. A common complaint at high elevations is altitude sickness, characterized by shortness of breath, fatigue, headaches, dizziness and loss of appetite. You may avoid it by drinking plenty of water and taking a day or two to acclimatize before attempting any long hikes. If symptoms persist, return to a lower elevation.

Bites & Stings

Common-sense approaches to these concerns are the most effective: wear boots when hiking to protect from snakes; wear long sleeves and pants to prevent tick and mosquito bites.

ANIMAL BITES

Do not attempt to pet, handle or feed any wild animal, no matter how cute and cuddly it may look. Most injuries from animals in the parks are directly related to people trying to do just that. For example, squirrels on Zion's Riverside Walk are notoriously aggressive, because so many park visitors have illegally fed them.

Any bite or scratch by a mammal, including bats and squirrels, should be promptly and thoroughly cleansed with large amounts of soap and water, followed by application of an antiseptic such as iodine or alcohol. Local health authorities should be contacted for possible rabies treatment (opposite), whether or not you've already been vaccinated against rabies. It may also be advisable to start an antibiotic, because wounds caused by animal bites and scratches frequently become infected.

MOSQUITOES

When mosquitoes are present, keep yourself covered and apply a good insect repellent, preferably one containing DEET, to exposed skin and clothing. Don't overuse the stuff, though, because neurologic toxicity – though uncommon – has been reported from DEET, especially in children. DEET-containing compounds should not be used at all on kids under the age of two.

Insect repellents containing certain botanical products, eg oil of lemon eucalyptus, can be effective but last only 1½ to two hours. Products based on citronella are not effective.

SNAKES

Despite southern Utah's abundance of venomous snakes, fatalities are rare. Snakebites can usually be prevented by giving the animal space – when you encounter a snake, back away slowly. Most reported snakebites result from people picking up the snake, either out of bravado or mistakenly assuming the animal is dead. If you're bitten by a snake, seek immediate help. Snakebites don't cause instantaneous death, and medical centers usually stock the necessary antivenins. If you're bitten on a limb, a light constricting band above the bite can help. Keep the affected area below the level of the heart, and move as little as possible. What you should *not* do is wrap the limb in a tight tourniquet, slash or suck the wound, put ice on it or take any alcohol or drugs. Simply stay calm and get to a hospital.

SPIDERS & SCORPIONS

There are no particular first-aid techniques for spider or scorpion bites. Some (like tarantula bites) are merely painful, while others (like black widow and scorpion bites) contain venom. Doses are generally too small to kill adult humans, but children face a risk of serious complications. Cool the wound using cold water or ice, and if you're hiking, return immediately; reactions can be delayed for up to 12 hours, and you may want to call **Utah Poison Control** (☎ 800-222-1222) and seek medical help.

TICKS

Always check your skin, hair and clothes for ticks after walking through high brush, grasslands or thickly forested areas. If ticks are found unattached, they can simply be brushed off. If a tick is found attached, carefully grab the tick's head with tweezers, then gently pull upwards – do not twist or force it. (If no tweezers are available, use your fingers, but protect them from contamination with a piece of tissue or paper.) Do not rub oil, alcohol or petroleum jelly on it.

Some ticks carry infectious diseases, such as Lyme disease. If you experience flulike symptoms or notice a circular red rash around the tick bite site during or after your trip, consult a doctor (diagnosis will be easier if you keep the dead tick).

Cold

FROSTBITE

Frostbite refers to the freezing of extremities, such as a nose, fingers or toes. Signs and symptoms of frostbite include whitish or waxy cast to the skin, as well as itching, numbness and pain. If possible, warm the affected areas by immersion in warm (not hot) water only until the skin becomes flushed. Frostbitten body parts should not be rubbed, and any blisters that form should not be broken. Pain and swelling are inevitable. Seek medical treatment immediately.

HYPOTHERMIA

While generally associated with winter hiking at altitude, hypothermia is a real danger in the desert in any season. Even a sudden rain shower or high winds can rapidly lower your body temperature. Symptoms of hypothermia include exhaustion, numbness, shivering, stumbling, slurred speech, dizzy spells, muscle cramps and irrational or even violent behavior.

Hypothermia often strikes people hiking narrow canyons, where they must wade or swim in pools that are frigid even in summer. One such place is Zion's Narrows, where hikers spend most of their time immersed in the Virgin River. Hypothermia is also a danger for campers from fall to spring, when overnight temperatures routinely drop near or below freezing, even in the desert or following mild days in the mountains.

To help avoid hypothermia, don't wear cotton clothes (which dry slowly and provide no insulation when wet). Instead wear woolen clothing or synthetics that retain warmth even when wet. Always carry waterproof layers (p287) and high-energy, easily digestible snacks like chocolate, nuts and dried fruit.

To treat hypothermia, take shelter from bad weather and change into dry, warm clothing. Drink hot liquids (no caffeine or alcohol) and snack on high-calorie food. In advanced stages, carefully put hypothermia sufferers in a warm sleeping bag cocooned inside a wind- and waterproof outer wrapping. Do not rub victims, who must be handled gently.

Heat

DEHYDRATION & HEAT EXHAUSTION

You don't need to do much to become dehydrated in the desert – just stand around. If you do engage in an activity, expect water and salts to leave your body at a vastly accelerated rate.

It's very important to both drink water and eat salty foods when hiking in the desert. The minimum is a gallon of water a day per person, or 16 ounces every hour while active. Though that may sound like a lot, you'll drink that and more if you're active. Keep a few extra gallons of water in the car. Eating is just as important, however, and is the half of the equation many people forget. Always carry high-energy bars, trail mix or something else to munch.

Dehydration (lack of water) or salt deficiency can cause heat exhaustion. Signs and symptoms of heat exhaustion, which occurs when you lose water faster than your body can absorb it, include nausea, vomiting, fatigue, headaches, dizziness, muscle cramps, heavy sweating and/or cool, clammy skin. Treat heat exhaustion by drinking, eating, resting in the shade and cooling the skin with a wet cloth and fanning yourself.

HEATSTROKE

Heatstroke, which can be fatal, occurs when your internal cooling mechanism breaks down and your body temperature rises dangerously. Symptoms include flushed, hot and dry skin (ie sweating has stopped), severe throbbing headaches, hyperventilation and a rapid pulse. Some victims may act uncharacteristically bizarre, display a lack of coordination and eventually go into convulsions. Immediate hospitalization is essential. Meanwhile, move the victim into the shade, remove clothing and cover with a wet cloth or towel, fan vigorously and seek immediate help. Ice packs can be applied to the neck, armpits and groin.

HYPONATREMIA

Hyponatremia (low sodium blood level) occurs when you drink a lot of water but don't eat. The water essentially flushes all nutrients from your body. Symptoms are similar to heat exhaustion (and can become life-threatening if left untreated), including nausea, muscle cramps, headache and vomiting. Treatment is to rest in the shade and eat salty foods until the blood's sodium-level balance is reestablished. Rapidly evacuate if the victim's mental status changes.

> **PREHYDRATION**
>
> Because your body can only absorb about a quart of water per hour, it's beneficial to prehydrate before embarking on a long hike. To get a head start on hydration, drink plenty of water the day and evening before your hike, and avoid diuretics like caffeine and alcohol.

Sunburn

You can sunburn quickly in the desert, sometimes in less than an hour, even on a cloudy day. Apply sunscreen (SPF 30 or higher) religiously every morning, reapply throughout the day, and don't forget the kids. Always wear a hat, preferably one with a wide brim.

SAFE HIKING

Hiking into a desert means taking extra precautions to make sure you return safely. This is true whether you plan to be gone an hour or a week. The desert has a way of compounding simple errors in judgment very quickly, and consequences range from unpleasant to grave.

Respect the sun and heat. *Always* wear sunscreen and a wide-brimmed hat. The rule of thumb is to drink a gallon of water a day; on the hottest days, or on a strenuous hike, this is a minimum, not a maximum. Always carry more water than you think you'll need; if your bag isn't too heavy when you start your hike, it will be too light by the end. If there's any chance you'll be gone more than a few hours, bring a water purifier or purification tablets, as all stream and groundwater needs to be treated. Keep an extra gallon or two of water in your car.

Water is not enough. Bring food too, particularly salty foods. While dehydration can lead to heat exhaustion (left) and heatstroke (left), drinking too much water and not eating enough can lead to hyponatremia (left), an equally debilitating condition. One of the symptoms that severe dehydration and hyponatremia have in common is impaired judgment, which can lead you to make poor choices that will actually worsen your situation.

One little-talked-about risk facing hikers is their own enthusiasm. Respect your limits. Remember that even in the middle of a national park, you're in a remote, wild place. Don't act foolishly by tackling a trail that's above your skill level. Twisting an ankle or breaking a leg is surprisingly easy – many people do, particularly young men. Depending on where you are when you're injured, it could take several hours or even days before a SAR team can find you and get you to a hospital. Needless to say, if no one knows where you are, or what time to expect you back, they won't even come looking.

For 'Leave No Trace' desert hiking tips, see p46. For advice about hiking with dogs, see p57.

GETTING LOST

Getting lost is another danger. Bring a map. For short nature walks and day hikes, national park maps are usually adequate. But route-finding skills never hurt; trails across slickrock usually require following cairns – small piles of rocks. Bring, and know how to use, a compass (see p288), and be familiar with prominent landmarks. If you bring a topographical map, know how to read it. Handheld GPS units can be helpful, but remember that batteries fail and sometimes it's impossible to get a clear satellite signal when you're inside a canyon.

Always stay on the trail; don't take shortcuts. Not only does this help avoid accidents and injuries from steep drop-offs and hidden hazards, but it makes it easier for potential rescuers to find you. If you do get lost, stay calm and stay put, making your location as visible as possible (eg spread out brightly colored clothing or gear in an

COMMON AILMENTS

Plaguing hikers of all ages in southern Utah, the following may not pose problems if you're prepared.

Blisters

To avoid blisters, make sure your walking boots or shoes are well worn in before you hit the trail. Your boots should fit comfortably with enough room to move your toes; boots that are too big or too small will cause blisters. The same goes for socks – be sure they fit properly and are specifically made for hikers; even then, check to make sure that there are no seams across the widest part of your foot. Wearing a thin pair of liner socks under hiking socks also helps stop blisters. Wet and muddy socks can cause blisters, so even on a day walk, pack a spare pair of socks. Keep your toenails clipped but not too short. If you do feel a blister coming on, treat it sooner rather than later by applying a bit of moleskin (or duct tape).

Fatigue

A simple statistic: more injuries happen toward the end of the day than when you're fresh. Although tiredness can simply be a nuisance on an easy walk, it can be life-threatening on narrow exposed ridges or in bad weather. You should never set out on a walk that is beyond your capabilities on the day. If you feel below par, have a day off or hop on a park shuttle. To reduce the risk of accidents, don't push yourself too hard – take rests every hour or two and build in a good half-hour or hour-long lunch break. Toward the end of the day, take down the pace and increase your concentration. Also eat properly throughout the day; nuts, dried fruit and chocolate are all good, energy-giving snack foods.

Knee Strain

Many hikers will feel the burn on long, steep descents, especially in southern Utah's canyon country. Although you can't eliminate strain on knee joints when dropping steeply, you can reduce it by taking shorter steps that leave your legs slightly bent and ensuring that your heel hits the ground before the rest of your foot. Lightweight hiking poles are effective in taking some of the weight off your knees. Compression bandages may also help.

exposed place). Use a signal mirror or whistle to alert other hikers that you need help.

FALLS & JUMPING

Nothing focuses one's attention like the edge of a 2000ft-high crumbling sandstone cliff. The consequences of a fall are self-evident and keep most people from taking unnecessary risks. Yet people fall to their deaths every year in southern Utah. Cliff edges are sheer and trails along them very exposed. Rocks can be loose and slickrock, when wet, is indeed slick. There are no guardrails along the parks' hiking trails; watch your children carefully at all times.

The more pernicious danger is carelessness. Most park rescues involve young men fracturing their legs while having fun leaping off rocks, jumping into shallow, murky pools or falling while bouldering. Some mishaps can be chalked up to youth, but it's also true that one's sense of scale can get thrown out of whack here. In the shadow of that 2000ft-high cliff, a 15ft or 20ft boulder looks like nothing, and a trail with a sheer drop of 50ft isn't scary at all. But these translate into falls of two to four stories, and should be treated with appropriate respect.

FLASH FLOODS

Flash floods are an ever-present danger in the desert. No matter how dry a streambed looks, or how sunny it is overhead, a sudden rainstorm miles away can cause a creek to 'flash' in minutes, sending down a huge surge of rock- and log-filled water that sweeps away everything in its path. Flash floods have killed hikers caught in creeks, dry riverbeds and narrow canyons. Never park or camp in dry washes. Always check the weather report for the entire region before setting out; this is crucial if you're planning on hiking through any slot canyons. Flash floods are more common during the summer 'monsoon' season (roughly, mid-June through mid-September), but they can happen anytime year-round.

Telltale signs of an impending flash flood include sudden changes in water clarity (eg the stream turns muddy), rising water levels and/or floating debris, and a rush of wind, the sound of thunder or a low, rumbling roar. If you notice any of these signs, immediately get to higher ground (even a few feet could save your life). If that's not possible, get behind a rock fin, to break the initial debris-filled wave. Do not run down canyon – you can't beat a flash flood. Instead, wait it out, as water levels usually drop within six to 24 hours.

CROSSING RIVERS & STREAMS

On some backcountry trails, especially popular canyoneering routes, you may have to ford a river or stream swollen with snowmelt that is fast-flowing and cold enough to be a potential risk. Before stepping out from the bank, ease one arm out of the shoulder strap of your pack and unclip the belt buckle and chest compression straps. That way, if you lose your balance and are swept downstream, it will be easier to slip off your pack.

If you're fording alone, plant one of your hiking poles upstream to give you greater stability and help you lean against the current. Walk side-on to the direction of the current so that your body presents less of an obstacle to the rushing water. If you're linking hands with others, grasp at the wrist – this gives a tighter grip than a handhold. Alternatively, cross arms around each others' shoulders or at the waist.

LIGHTNING

If a thunderstorm is brewing, avoid exposed ridges or summits. Never seek shelter under objects that are isolated or higher than their surroundings, such as a lone tree. In open areas where there's no safe shelter, find a dry depression in the ground and take up a crouched-squatting position with your feet together; do not lie on the ground. Keep a layer of metal-free insulation, such as a camping pad, between you and the ground. Avoid contact with metallic objects, including backpack frames or hiking poles.

If you're hiking with a group, spread out, keeping at least 50 feet between each person. If anyone is struck by lightning, immediately begin first-aid measures such as checking their airway, breathing and pulse, and treat any burns. Prolonged rescue breathing may be necessary, due to respiratory arrest. Evacuate and get medical help as quickly as possible.

ROCKFALL

Always be alert to the danger of rockfall, especially after heavy rains. If you accidentally let

DON'T HORSE AROUND!

Day hikers are bound to encounter horses and mules, which always have the right of way. If you're hiking when horseback riders or a mule train approaches, stand quietly on the inner side of the trail, turn your pack away from the animals (lest one bumps your pack and knocks you off balance) and listen for directions from the lead rider.

loose a rock on a trail, loudly warn other hikers below. Bighorn sheep, deer and other large animals sometimes dislodge rocks, another reason to be especially vigilant while hiking.

WILDLIFE

Southern Utah is awash in critters that, if bothered, can inflict a fair bit of pain, including rattlesnakes, scorpions, tarantulas, black widows, wasps and even centipedes. Spiders rarely bite unless harassed, which is also true of rattlesnakes, which like to warm themselves on trails or rock ledges, particularly in late afternoon. Avoid shoving your hand beneath logs and rocks or into piles of wood, and never reach blindly over ledges or beneath boulders. Always shake out your hiking boots before putting them back on. For information about what to do if an animal bites or stings you, see p281.

If you encounter a mountain lion (p65) while hiking, maintain eye contact and do not look away. Wave your arms or hiking poles above your head to make yourself appear larger, and therefore possibly a threat. Gather young children to your side and stick together. Back away slowly, but resist the urge to run, which makes you look like prey. If the lion approaches you, yell loudly, throw rocks and sticks, and fight back by whatever means possible.

Learn to identify poison ivy: round, ivory-colored berries and oaklike leaves that grow in clusters of three. Particularly in moisture-laden canyons, this toxic plant grows in thickets that hikers must inevitably tackle or else circumvent with difficulty. Even dead plants remain covered in urushiol oil, which can cause a severe itchy rash or allergic reaction when touched. If you think you've been exposed, immediately wash the affected area with soap and water. If a rash does appear, apply ice or cool compresses. Over-the-counter medications such as Benadryl may also help reduce inflammation and itchiness. Don't scratch.

RESCUE & EVACUATION

Hikers must take responsibility for their own safety and plan to prevent emergency situations. That said, even the most safety-conscious hiker may have a serious accident requiring urgent medical attention. In case of accidents, self-rescue should be your first consideration, as search-and-rescue operations are very expensive and require emergency personnel to risk their own safety.

If a person in your group is injured or ill and can't move, leave someone with them while others seek help. If there are only two of you, leave the injured person with as much warm clothing, food and water as it's sensible to spare, plus a whistle and flashlight. Mark their position with something conspicuous (eg an orange tent, a large cross made of white stones laid out on the ground).

SAFE BIKING

Newcomers to desert road cycling and mountain biking should pay particular heed to safety. Wear a helmet, carry lots of water and bring high-energy foods. Also pack a map and keep track of your route. Don't start out on rough trails – first get your bearings on easier rides. The vibration from rougher trails can loosen headsets, so be sure to check your fittings.

Expect the best, but prepare for the worst. In addition to extra water and food, carry a windbreaker, a wide-brimmed hat, sunscreen, sunglasses, a patch kit, tools and matches. Avoid riding alone, and always tell someone where you're going. The desert is unforgiving and should never be underestimated.

Road cyclists must adhere to traffic regulations and should use caution along heavily trafficked roads, especially during the busy summer season. On Zion Canyon's Scenic Drive, cyclists must pull over and allow park shuttle buses to pass. Although not required by Utah law, always wear a helmet as well as bright colors to improve your visibility to drivers. Emergency roadside assistance for cyclists is offered by the Better World Club (p273).

Clothing & Equipment

CONTENTS

Arriving in southern Utah outfitted with the proper clothing and equipment will keep you safe and comfortable on a hike and any other outdoor adventures. Much of what you should bring depends on which season you're visiting in and what activities you plan to do. Many visitors are surprised by the region's variable weather, from the extreme desert heat to the high-country cold. We've covered most of the basic equipment and clothing here, along with buying tips and what to look for.

CLOTHING

Modern outdoor garments made from new synthetic fabrics (which are breathable and actively wick moisture away from your skin) are better for hiking than anything made of cotton or wool. The exception to this is if you're hiking out of the canyon in midsummer, when cotton is a godsend. Soak cotton shirts or bandannas with water at every opportunity, and allow the evaporative cooling effect to ease your journey.

Layering

To cope with changing temperatures and exertion, layering your clothing is a good way to regulate your body temperature.

For the upper body, the base layer is typically a T-shirt made of synthetic fabric. The second layer can be a lightweight, breathable long-sleeve shirt for sun protection or a synthetic fleece sweater that will keep you insulated. The outer shell consists of a weatherproof jacket that also protects against strong cold winds.

For the lower body, shorts will probably be most comfortable in midsummer, although some hikers prefer long pants – light, quick-drying fabric (eg nylon) is best. Thermal 'long john' type underwear can't be easily removed, and it is not recommended except when conditions are expected to remain very cold all day. Waterproof overpants are an outer shell for the lower body.

Waterproof Shells

Hikers in southern Utah should always carry a windproof and waterproof rain-jacket and pants that are properly seam-sealed. The jacket should have a hood to keep the rain and wind off your head.

BUYING TIPS

The ideal specifications for jacket and pants are a breathable, waterproof fabric, such as Gore-Tex. For the jacket, look for a hood that's roomy enough to cover headwear but still allows peripheral vision; a spacious map pocket; and a heavy-gauge zip protected by a storm flap. Choose pants with slits for pocket access and long leg zips that pull on and off easily over your boots.

Footwear & Socks

Trail-running or walking shoes are fine over easy terrain, but for more difficult trails and across rocks and scree, the ankle support offered by boots is invaluable. It is vital that your boots are properly worn in before you begin any serious hiking.

Synthetic socks that draw moisture away from your feet are a must. Wearing a thin, lightweight pair of synthetic liner socks underneath regular hiking socks can keep your feet more comfy and prevent blisters.

River sandals are useful when fording waterways or doing water sports (eg rafting, kayaking).

BUYING TIPS

Nonslip soles (such as Vibram) provide the best grip. Hiking boots should have a flexible midsole and an insole that supports the arch and heel. Buy boots in warm conditions or go for a walk before trying them on, so that your feet can swell slightly, as they would on a walk.

Hiking socks should be free of ridged seams in the toes and heels, and should be made from wicking material that draws

NAVIGATION EQUIPMENT

Maps & Compass

Carry a good map of the area you are hiking in (see p22), and know how to read it. Before setting off on your hike, ensure that you understand the contours and the map symbols, plus the main ridge and river systems in the area. Familiarize yourself with the true north–south directions and the general direction in which you are heading. On the trail, try to identify major landmarks (eg mountain peaks) and locate them on your map. This will give you a better grasp of the region's geography.

Buy a compass and learn how to use it. The attraction of magnetic north varies in different parts of the world, so compasses need to be balanced accordingly. Compass manufacturers have divided the world into five zones. Make sure your compass is balanced for your destination zone. There are also 'universal' compasses on the market that can be used anywhere in the world.

How to Use a Compass

This is a very basic introduction to using a compass and will only be of assistance if you are proficient in map reading. For simplicity, it doesn't take magnetic variation into account. Before using a compass we recommend you obtain further instruction.

Reading a Compass

Hold the compass flat in the palm of your hand. Rotate the bezel so the red end of the needle points to the N on the bezel. The bearing is read from the dash under the bezel.

Orienting the Map

To orient the map so that it aligns with the ground, place the compass flat on the map. Rotate the map until the needle is parallel with the map's north–south grid lines and the red end is pointing to north on the map. You can now identify features around you by aligning them with labeled features on the map.

Taking a Bearing from the Map

Draw a line on the map between your starting point and your destination. Place the edge of the compass on this line with the direction-of-travel arrow pointing towards your destination.

moisture away from your feet. If you will be hiking through snow, deep mud or scratchy vegetation, gaiters will protect your legs and help keep your socks dry. The best are made of strong fabric, with a robust zip protected by a flap, and secure easily and snugly around your hiking boots.

EQUIPMENT

Backpacks & Daypacks

For day hikes, a daypack will usually suffice, but for multiday hikes you'll need a backpack.

BUYING TIPS

Daypacks with built-in hydration systems (such as Camelbak) eliminate the hassle of toting unwieldy water bottles.

Backpacks with a relatively large capacity (between 2500 and 5500 cubic inches, or 40L to 90L) are best for overnight hiking in the backcountry.

A backpack that weighs on your shoulders as you hike is not just uncomfortable, it may be doing permanent injury to your back. You should look for backpacks with robust, easily adjustable waist-belts that can comfortably support the entire weight carried, effectively transferring the load from your shoulders onto your hips. Shoulder straps should serve only to steady your backpack.

A good backpack should also be made of strong fabric, and have a lightweight frame. Internal-frame backpacks fit snugly against your back, keeping the weight close to your center of gravity.

Even if the manufacturer claims your pack is waterproof, use heavy-duty liners or a pack cover.

Rotate the bezel until the meridian lines are parallel with the north–south grid lines on the map and the N points to north on the map. Read the bearing from the dash.

Following a Bearing
Rotate the bezel so that the intended bearing is in line with the dash. Place the compass flat in the palm of your hand and rotate the base plate until the red end points to N on the bezel. The direction-of-travel arrow will now point in the direction you need to walk.

Determining Your Bearing
Rotate the bezel so the red end points to the N. Place the compass flat in the palm of your hand and rotate the base plate until the direction of travel arrow points in the direction in which you have been hiking. Read your bearing from the dash.

GPS

Originally developed by the US Department of Defense, the Global Positioning System (GPS) is a network of more than 20 earth-orbiting satellites that continually beam encoded signals back to earth. Small computer-driven devices (GPS receivers) can decode these signals to give users an extremely accurate reading of their location – to within 15m, anywhere on the planet, at any time of day, in most kinds of weather.

The cheapest handheld GPS receivers now cost less than $100 (although these may not have a built-in averaging system that minimizes signal errors). Other important factors to consider when buying a GPS receiver are its weight and battery life.

Remember that a GPS receiver is of little use to hikers unless used with an accurate topographical map. The receiver simply gives your position, which you must then locate on the map.

GPS receivers will only work properly in the open. The signals from a crucial satellite may be blocked (or bounce off rock or water) directly below high cliffs, near large bodies of water or in dense tree cover, and give inaccurate readings. GPS receivers are more vulnerable to breakdowns (including dead batteries) than the humble magnetic compass – a low-tech device that has served navigators faithfully for centuries – so don't rely on them entirely.

Tents

A three-season tent will suffice for most backpacking trips in southern Utah. Ultralight backpackers may opt to ditch the tent and use just the rainfly and footprint (ground tarp).

If you're planning a backcountry trip during winter, then you'll need a four-season tent to keep you sheltered from the snow and harsh windy, wet and freezing conditions.

BUYING TIPS

The floor and the outer shell, or rainfly, should have taped or sealed seams and covered zips to stop leaks. Most hikers find tents of around 4.5lb to 6lb a comfortable carrying weight. Dome- and tunnel-shaped tents handle windy conditions better than flat-sided tents.

Sleeping Bag & Mat

As with tents, three-season sleeping bags will suffice for most campers in southern Utah. Cooler seasons and higher elevations, for example at Bryce Canyon, call for both sleeping bag and a sleeping pad (mat) for insulation from the cold ground.

During the summer lower desert elevations are usually hot enough to forego a sleeping bag altogether; backcountry campers might consider bringing just a sleeping bag liner or a sheet. Some campers soak a sheet in a nearby river for the evaporative cooling effect to ensure a more soothing sleep.

BUYING TIPS

Down fillings are warmer than synthetic for the same weight and bulk but, unlike synthetic fillings, do not retain warmth when wet. Mummy bags are the best shape for

EQUIPMENT CHECKLIST

Backpackers will have a longer list than this, but try to pack light. If you forget something, southern Utah has enough camping supply stores and outdoor outfitters (opposite) to fix you up.

Clothing

- ☐ broad-brimmed sun hat
- ☐ hiking boots, or sturdy trail-running shoes, and spare laces
- ☐ river sandals or flip-flops
- ☐ shorts and lightweight trousers or skirt
- ☐ socks and underwear
- ☐ sweater or fleece
- ☐ thermal underwear
- ☐ T-shirt and long-sleeved shirt with collar
- ☐ warm hat, scarf and gloves
- ☐ waterproof jacket
- ☐ waterproof pants

Equipment

- ☐ backpack with waterproof liner or cover
- ☐ first-aid kit*
- ☐ high-energy food and snacks and one day's emergency food supplies
- ☐ insect repellent
- ☐ map, compass and guidebook
- ☐ map case or clip-seal plastic bags
- ☐ pocket knife
- ☐ sunglasses
- ☐ sunscreen and lip balm
- ☐ survival blanket or bag
- ☐ toilet paper and trowel
- ☐ flashlight or headlamp, spare batteries and bulb
- ☐ watch
- ☐ water containers
- ☐ whistle

Overnight Hikes

- ☐ biodegradable soap
- ☐ cooking, eating and drinking utensils
- ☐ matches and lighter
- ☐ sewing/repair kit
- ☐ sleeping bag and/or liner
- ☐ sleeping pad (and, if inflatable, patch kit)
- ☐ spare cord
- ☐ stove, fuel and lighter/matches
- ☐ tent, pegs, poles and guy lines
- ☐ toiletries
- ☐ towel
- ☐ water-purification filter or tablets

Optional Items

- ☐ altimeter
- ☐ bandanna
- ☐ binoculars
- ☐ camera, film/charger and batteries
- ☐ candle
- ☐ cell phone**
- ☐ emergency distress beacon
- ☐ GPS receiver and spare batteries
- ☐ groundsheet
- ☐ hiking poles
- ☐ mosquito net
- ☐ notebook and pen
- ☐ swimsuit

* See the medical checklist, p279.
** See Telephone, p268.

weight and warmth. The given figure (23°F, for instance) is the coldest temperature at which a person should feel comfortable in the bag (although the ratings are notoriously unreliable).

An inner liner helps keep your sleeping bag clean, as well as adding an insulating layer. Silk liners are lightest, but they also come in cotton or polypropylene.

Self-inflating sleeping mats put an air cushion between you and the ground. More importantly they insulate from the cold. Foam mats are a low-cost but less comfortable alternative.

Stoves & Fuel

The type of fuel you'll use most often will help determine what kind of camp stove is best for you. The following types of fuel can be found in the US, and local outdoor outfitters and camping supply stores can help you choose an appropriate camp stove if you aren't traveling with your own.

Butane, propane and isobutane are clean-burning fuels that come in nonrecyclable canisters and tend to be more expensive. These fuels are best for camping in warmer conditions, as their performance markedly decreases in below-freezing temperatures.

Inexpensive white gas is reliable in all temperatures. It's more volatile than other types of fuel, but overall it's the most efficient and clean-burning type of fuel available in the US.

The most sustainable alternative is renewable denatured alcohol, which burns slowly but also extremely quietly. Lower temperatures mean longer cooking times, so you'll have to carry more fuel with you.

Remember it doesn't matter how lightweight or efficient your stove is if you forget to bring a way to ignite it. Waterproof matches are a smart idea.

BUYING TIPS

Portable fuel stoves fall roughly into three categories: multifuel, methylated spirits (eg denatured alcohol) and butane or propane gas. Multifuel stoves are small, efficient and ideal for places where a reliable fuel supply is difficult to find. However, they tend to be sooty and require frequent maintenance. Stoves running on methylated spirits are slower and less efficient, but are safe, clean and easy to use. Butane and propane gas stoves are clean and reliable, but the gas canisters can be awkward to carry and a potential litter problem.

BUYING & RENTING LOCALLY

If you haven't come prepared with all the equipment you need, it can actually be better to buy locally. That way, you can take advantage of local expertise to choose what works best in the region. Although it can be expensive, renting may be a good way to go if you've never tried an activity before, or if you only need something for a short time, and it's not worth lugging it with you from home.

Southern Utah has plenty of outdoor outfitters and supply shops that rent and sell just about any kind of clothing or equipment you'll need, including sleeping bags, tents, camp stoves and fuel canisters, hiking poles and even cross-country skis in winter. These outfitters are usually found in national park gateway towns, such as Springdale, Moab, Bryce Canyon City, Escalante, Torrey and Kanab, but not inside the parks themselves, where concessionaires sell only limited supplies.

Glossary

4WD – Four-wheel-drive vehicle

AAA – American Automobile Association; usually called 'triple-A'
ATV – all-terrain vehicle

backcountry – anywhere away from roads or other major infrastructure
backpacking – multiday hiking with full camping gear
basalt – hard, dense and very common volcanic rock; solidified lava
BLM – Bureau of Land Management; government agency that controls large areas of public land
butte – prominent hill or mountain standing separate from surrounding ranges

cairn – pile or stack of rocks used to indicate a hiking route or trail junction
caldera – very large crater that has resulted from a volcanic explosion or the collapse of a volcanic cone
cascade – small waterfall
concessionaire – private business allowed to operate inside the parks
conifer – trees or shrubs with evergreen leaves and bearing cones
CR – county road

deciduous – plants, trees and shrubs that shed their leaves
docent – volunteer educator at museums, visitor centers etc
drainage – course of a creek or streamlet
dry suit – waterproof body suit worn for insulation from cold water; see also *wetsuit*

fin – narrow wall of rock, formed by joints and fractures
fire pan – metal sheeting (mandatory in some wilderness areas) to protect the ground from campfires
flash flood – sudden, potentially dangerous surge of muddy, rock- and log-filled water along a creek, river canyon or normally dry *wash*
ford – to cross a river by wading
fork – branch or tributary of a stream or river
FR – forest road
front country – developed park area accessible by road

gap – mountain pass or *saddle*; notch
GPS – Global Positioning System; electronic, satellite-based network that allows for the calculation of position and elevation using a handheld receiver/decoder
graded – leveled (road or trail)
Grand Staircase – series of geological rock layers extending from the Grand Canyon upwards to Bryce Canyon
granite – coarse-grained, often gray, igneous rock formed by the slow cooling of molten rock (magma) deep below the earth
gulch – narrow ravine cut by a river or stream

hoodoo – eroded pillar of rock
hookup – campground site amenity providing RVs with electricity and/or water

igneous – type of rock formed by solidified magma; can be volcanic or plutonic
inlet – (principal) stream flowing into a lake

karst – water-eroded rocky landscape featuring caves, springs and sinkholes
kiva – ceremonial chamber used by ancient and modern Pueblo peoples
KOA – Kampgrounds of America; a private chain of campgrounds with many amenities, popular with RVers

limestone – *sedimentary* rock composed mainly of calcium carbonate
lithification – conversion of loose sediments into solid *sedimentary* rock

mesa – Spanish word for elevated tableland or plateau
metamorphic – *igneous* or *sedimentary* rock that has been transformed by high heat, high pressure and/or mineral-rich fluids
monocline – a 'step-up' fold in geological rock strata

national forest – area of public land administered by the *USFS*
NPS – National Park Service
NRA – National Recreation Area (similar to a *wilderness* area but with some controlled development); also National Rifle Association

obsidian – black, glassy volcanic rock
old-growth – virgin forest more than 200 years old and never altered by humans
outfitter – business supplying guides, equipment and/or transportation for outdoor activities
outlet – stream flowing out of a lake

parkland – any public recreation land or protected *wilderness* area
petroglyph – carved rock lines and figures made by indigenous peoples
pictograph – rock paintings made by indigenous peoples
public land – any federal or state land, especially that administered by the *BLM*, *NPS* or *USFS*
Pueblo – an indigenous culture of the Colorado Plateau

quad – 1:24,000 *USGS* topographic map

RV – recreational vehicle; motor home or camper

saddle – low place in a ridge
sandstone – *sedimentary* rock composed of sand grains
SAR – search and rescue
scree – weathered rock fragments at the foot of a cliff or on a slope
sedimentary – type of rock formed when layers of sediment are compacted and cemented together
sidle – to cut along a slope; contour; see also *traverse*
slickrock – large expanse of exposed rock that has been sculpted and smoothed by erosion
slot canyon – narrow, deep canyon carved by water
snow line – level above which snow remains on the ground throughout the year
spur – usually a small branch of a main trail, or a small ridge that leads up from a valley to a main ridge
switchback – route that follows a zigzag course up or down a steep grade

topo – topographic (contoured) map
trail mix – snack-food mixture of nuts, dried fruit, seeds and/or chocolate; also known as gorp
traverse – to cut along a slope (sometimes also along a ridge); see also *sidle*
travertine – *sedimentary* rock formed by calcium carbonate deposits left by water

USFS – United States Forest Service; manages the system of national forests
USGS – United States Geological Survey; national cartographic organization

vault toilet – a nonflushing toilet without running water

wash – a dry streambed or channel where flooding occurs in the desert
washboard – process by which gravel roads develop a bumpy, car-rattling series of wavy ridges
wet suit – permeable body suit worn for insulation from cold water; see also *dry suit*
wilderness – officially designated primitive area

Behind the Scenes

THIS BOOK

This 2nd edition of *Zion & Bryce Canyon National Parks* was researched and written by Sara Benson, Lisa Dunford and Carolyn McCarthy. The previous edition was written by Jeff Campbell, John A Vlahides and David Lukas. This guidebook was commissioned in Lonely Planet's Oakland office, and produced by the following:
Commissioning Editor Suki Gear
Coordinating Editors Andrew Bain, Charlotte Orr
Coordinating Cartographer Joelene Kowalski
Coordinating Layout Designer Kerrianne Southway
Managing Editors Brigitte Ellemor, Bruce Evans
Senior Editor Helen Christinis
Managing Cartographers Shahara Ahmed, Alison Lyall
Managing Layout Designers Indra Kilfoyle, Celia Wood
Assisting Editors Kate James, Helen Koehne
Cover Research Naomi Parker
Internal Image Research Aude Vauconsant

Thanks to Melanie Dankel, Heather Dickson, James Hardy, David Kemp, Lisa Knights, Raphael Richards, Andrew Smith

THANKS

SARA BENSON

Without the good cheer, indefatigable patience and mad Boy Scout outdoor skills of Michael Connolly Jr, this book would never have gotten done. Coauthors Lisa Dunford and Carolyn McCarthy, your regional expertise and enthusiasm for southern Utah's wild lands made coordinating this book an absolute joy. I'm indebted to my ex-colleagues at Zion National Park, who answered all kinds of questions and provided insider tips for this book. Editor Suki Gear hired me for this book's A-Team and gave me an excuse to return to southern Utah (and Las Vegas, too!). Cartographer Alison Lyall went above and beyond to create a new hiking topo map – thanks! Special thanks to Andrew Bain for his keen editorial eye.

LISA DUNFORD

I met so many kindred spirits on the road. Big thanks go to Trista and Matt Rayner and Greg and Valerie Istock for sharing their canyon with me. To ranger Barb Graves, it was great talking to you – hope we meet soon. Kristy Schmitt, glad I got to share part of your Zion journey. Michelle and Dan Cook, keep taking pictures. And Catherine, I swear I didn't tell anyone about your secret trail. Even more than usual, I also want to thank my coauthors Sara and Carolyn and editor Suki Gear; this has been an incredible book to work on.

THE LONELY PLANET STORY

Fresh from an epic journey across Europe, Asia and Australia in 1972, Tony and Maureen Wheeler sat at their kitchen table stapling together notes. The first Lonely Planet guidebook, *Across Asia on the Cheap,* was born.

Travelers snapped up the guides. Inspired by their success, the Wheelers began publishing books to Southeast Asia, India and beyond. Demand was prodigious, and the Wheelers expanded the business rapidly to keep up. Over the years, Lonely Planet extended its coverage to every country and into the virtual world via lonelyplanet.com and the Thorn Tree message board.

As Lonely Planet became a globally loved brand, Tony and Maureen received several offers for the company. But it wasn't until 2007 that they found a partner whom they trusted to remain true to the company's principles of traveling widely, treading lightly and giving sustainably. In October 2007, BBC Worldwide acquired a 75% share in the company, pledging to uphold Lonely Planet's commitment to independent travel, trustworthy advice and editorial independence.

Today, Lonely Planet has offices in Melbourne, London and Oakland, with over 500 staff members and 300 authors. Tony and Maureen are still actively involved with Lonely Planet. They're traveling more often than ever, and they're devoting their spare time to charitable projects. And the company is still driven by the philosophy of *Across Asia on the Cheap*: 'All you've got to do is decide to go and the hardest part is over. So go!'

CAROLYN MCCARTHY
Sincere thanks goes out to all those who helped me. Utah is truly one of the kindest places in America. In particular, rangers Nancy Holman, Sierra Coon, Dan Ng, Jan Schollard, Meghan Blackwelder and Kevin Poe shared valuable expertise. Many thanks also to Sarah Heffron, David Svenson, Charlie Francisco, Christian Santelices and Angela Hawse. Thanks to Mitch, Ellen, Jocelyn, Bjorn and Cam for good company on the trail. I am grateful for this opportunity to work with dream-team Sam Benson, Lisa Dunford and Suki Gear. Finally, hats off to the in-house editors and cartographers at Lonely Planet who put it all together.

OUR READERS

Many thanks to the travelers who used the last edition and wrote to us with helpful hints, useful advice and interesting anecdotes:

Suzanne Held, Martha Menton, Jenny Sachtjen, David Shadovitz, Ronni Weinberg.

SEND US YOUR FEEDBACK

We love to hear from travelers – your comments keep us on our toes and help make our books better. Our well-traveled team reads every word on what you loved or loathed about this book. Although we cannot reply individually to postal submissions, we always guarantee that your feedback goes straight to the appropriate authors, in time for the next edition. Each person who sends us information is thanked in the next edition, and the most useful submissions are rewarded with a free book.

Visit lonelyplanet.com to submit your updates and suggestions or to ask for help. Our award-winning website also features inspirational travel stories, news and discussions.

Note: We may edit, reproduce and incorporate your comments in Lonely Planet products such as guidebooks, websites and digital products, so let us know if you don't want your comments reproduced or your name acknowledged. For a copy of our privacy policy visit lonelyplanet.com/privacy.

Index

INDEX

D

000 Map pages
000 Photograph pages

000 Map pages
000 Photograph pages

INDEX

INDEX

HIKES

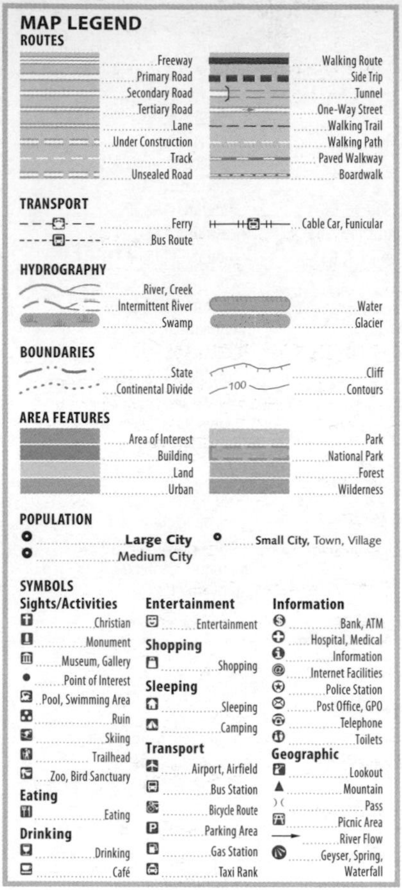
MAP LEGEND
ROUTES
Freeway
Primary Road
Secondary Road
Tertiary Road
Lane
Under Construction
Track
Unsealed Road
Walking Route
Side Trip
Tunnel
One-Way Street
Walking Trail
Walking Path
Paved Walkway
Boardwalk
TRANSPORT
Ferry
Bus Route
Cable Car, Funicular
HYDROGRAPHY
River, Creek
Intermittent River
Swamp
Water
Glacier
BOUNDARIES
State
Continental Divide
Cliff
100
Contours
AREA FEATURES
Area of Interest
Building
Land
Urban
Park
National Park
Forest
Wilderness
POPULATION
Large City
Medium City
Small City, Town, Village
SYMBOLS
Sights/Activities
Christian
Monument
Museum, Gallery
Point of Interest
Pool, Swimming Area
Ruin
Skiing
Trailhead
Zoo, Bird Sanctuary
Eating
Eating
Drinking
Drinking
Café
Entertainment
Entertainment
Shopping
Shopping
Sleeping
Sleeping
Camping
Transport
Airport, Airfield
Bus Station
Bicycle Route
Parking Area
Gas Station
Taxi Rank
Information
Bank, ATM
Hospital, Medical
Information
Internet Facilities
Police Station
Post Office, GPO
Telephone
Toilets
Geographic
Lookout
Mountain
Pass
Picnic Area
River Flow
Geyser, Spring, Waterfall

LONELY PLANET OFFICES

Australia

Head Office
Locked Bag 1, Footscray, Victoria 3011
☎ 03 8379 8000, fax 03 8379 8111

USA

150 Linden St, Oakland, CA 94607
☎ 510 250 6400, toll free 800 275 8555
fax 510 893 8572

UK

2nd fl, 186 City Rd,
London EC1V 2NT
☎ 020 7106 2100, fax 020 7106 2101

Contact

talk2us@lonelyplanet.com
lonelyplanet.com/contact

Published by Lonely Planet Publications Pty Ltd
ABN 36 005 607 983

Cover photographs by Lonely Planet Images: Rainbow over Bryce Canyon, Kevin Levesque (front); North Fork of the Virgin River, Zion National Park, Eddie Brady (back). Many of the images in this guide are available for licensing from Lonely Planet Images: lonelyplanet images.com.

Printed by Hang Tai Printing Company, Hong Kong. Printed in China